Y0-BFK-440

What Are You Doing Here?

To the Barnegat Navy League—
Thank you for all you do for our
military. I hope you enjoy my
stories!

Sheila

SHEILA McNEILL

First Edition

PAGE PUBLISHING, INC.
New York, NY

First originally published by Page Publishing, Inc. 2019

ISBN 978-1-64424-953-6 (Paperback)
ISBN 978-1-64424-956-7 (Hardcover)
ISBN 978-1-64424-954-3 (Digital)

Printed in the United States of America

CONTENTS

FOREWORD

One question has swirled around Sheila McNeill since her involvement with the Navy League began fifty years ago. Sometimes it was overheard from nearby conversations when she walked into a room filled with mostly active duty or retired military personnel. Other times, those questioning why a woman with no prior military experience was in the same room. They took a more direct, sometimes confrontational approach when they asked McNeill, "What are you doing here?"

I first met McNeill in 1994 as a new reporter for the *Florida Times Union*, where an important part of my coverage area was Naval Submarine Base Kings Bay. It took one interview for me to recognize McNeill's knowledge of the submarine force provided me an opportunity to gain better understanding of the issues facing the Navy's ballistic submarine force. I quickly learned McNeill wielded more influence than imagined during our first interview. She convinced US Sen. Sam Nunn, chair of the Armed Service Committee, to be the guest speaker at the Camden Kings Bay Navy League Council in 1994 by sending him a series of short, snappy one-sentence letters. Nunn was among those who recommended her in 1997 to serve on the Defense Advisory Committee on Women in the Services. The three-year appointment took her to installations across the world, where she interacted with many of the military's top leaders.

In 2003, McNeill became the first woman to serve as national president of the US Navy League, where she toured bases across the world as an advocate for sea services. She was the voice who could take positions on issues that military officials were reluctant or unable to comment about with the media. She never, to the best of my knowledge, spoke about an issue that drew the ire of the military. She likely expressed what military officials wish they could have said if they weren't concerned about political fallout.

McNeill helped convince the Navy and DoD to convert the four oldest Ohio-class submarines to carry guided missiles and conduct covert operations along troubled coastal waters across the world. She led the drive to save a Coast Guard Maritime Safety and Security Team based in St. Marys, Georgia.

She continues to be a strong advocate for the military despite her diminished role in the Navy League. When new commanders come to Kings Bay, one of the first people they are told to meet is McNeill because of her knowledge of the issues and her contacts in the community.

The question that has followed McNeill the past half century isn't asked as frequently nowadays because of her long, dedicated service and her interactions with some of the nation's most influential military leaders and elected officials. She can still walk the halls in the Pentagon, Congress, and the Capitol and be recognized by many of those serving.

McNeill's reputation as a staunch advocate for the Navy, Marine Corps, and Coast Guard has answered the question that has followed her the past half century: What are you doing here?

Gordon Jackson

Preface

When I was growing up, succeeding at anything other than being a wife and mother was never a consideration. That was all I originally wanted. I don't know how or why my ambitions changed so much. When Arlie asked me to marry him when I was a senior in high school, I couldn't think of anything better. And after fifty years, I count marrying Arlie as one of my best decisions. Later in 1994, when he was fifty-nine and grappling with some big business decisions and contemplating if he might be ready for retirement, he asked me what else I wanted to accomplish. I told him I had just started! And that was true. My innate and constant desire to achieve in something larger than myself began at an early age and that is why I am including my childhood experiences.

The most frequent question I am asked today is, "How did you get to be the first woman national president of the Navy League?" When I was president and traveling, I would often run into the assumption that I was a career officer's wife and the Navy League must be some kind of family support organization. It always gave me a chance to set them straight—and have a potential member.

A few years out of high school I went to work at Concrete Products, a local industrial plant. It was eventually bought out by another company and a new president; Bob Bledsoe was hired. My job required me to spend a good bit of time in the plant. These visits to the plant required a hard hat. For several months it was difficult trying to please Mr. Bledsoe: he didn't want a woman in management, he didn't want a woman negotiating "his" union contracts, and he didn't want a woman wearing a hard hat. Yes, he really told me that. And after doing all I could to please him he called me in to his office one day and fired me—after seventeen years. That was my first taste of "what are you doing here." I was happy in the job and I would have stayed forever. However, it was not to be. I have learned from that experience and others that there is a benefit that can be learned from negative situations.

I suppose the battle and being fired by Bob gave me a determination I might never have had. A few months later I decided to sue Concrete Products for sex discrimination.

It seems that many of the milestones in my life could begin with "What are you doing here?" My firing and my service as a member of the Defense Advisory Committee on Women in the Services (DACOWITS) and my two years as national president of the Navy League gave me several of "what are you doing here?" moments. The attitude of many of the military members I met with was not that I was a woman but because many wondered, "What did this civilian think she knew about our military issues?" The best example was my focus group meeting with a group of senior enlisted Marines in Germany who all pondered the same question. By the time we left the bases, the troops understood and appreciated our mission.

My personal campaign to get the Navy League national president Jack Fisher to assign me the national responsibilities for legislative affairs took two years. No woman had ever held this position. He finally relented and the experience was exciting and remarkable. No one in the military or congress questioned my presence. We established programs and standards that are still used today. VADM Cutler Dawson, who was then the chief of legislative affairs, told me the Navy League legislative program put the Navy on the front burner on Capitol Hill those three years I was vice president of legislative affairs.

When I made the decision to run for national president of the Navy League, there were those men who really objected to a "skirt" running the Navy League. At the national meeting during interviews with the national nominating committee, I was asked by one of the members at my interview, "What will the service chiefs think of a woman running the Navy League?" My response was, "I haven't been a woman for thirty years. I've been an advocate for the sea services. And the services are beyond that kind of prejudices. The Navy League is the one behind the times. I am friends of all the service chiefs now due to my work on Capitol Hill and none have a problem with my gender."

On a positive note, my progress up the ladder in the Navy League and my tour as national president were some of the best years of my life. Once elected, I never had a bad moment.

After my tenure as national president of the Navy League and after I think, perhaps, I have nothing to prove, I was wrong. I am asked to speak at the annual Thursday night dinner of the Submarine Veterans of WWII in November 2008. I came in at the last minute and sat down at the designated table full of submarine veterans and their wives. I was the last one to sit down. The submarine veteran next to me listens while we visit at the table for a few minutes and then turns to me and says, "What are you doing here? You don't know anything about us. You aren't a submariner. Why should you be speaking to us?" And I thought, *Here we go again.*

At a Navy League convention five years after my presidency, I'm was sitting at a table in front of the podium with two recipients of our public service awards, Keith Post and Don Giles, and heard the current president Dan Branch say, "I would like to recognize all of the past national presidents. Would each of you *gentlemen* stand?"

Arlie began waving his arms to get the president's attention. Kathleen Branch, Dan's wife, called out loudly "Lady, add lady" to her husband to correct him. Dan's mistake in not adding *lady* in his introduction didn't matter a whit to me. I stood along with Morgan Fitch, Jack Spittler, Evan Baker, Jack Kennedy, Bill Kelley, Tim Fanning, and Mike McGrath. Memories rushed to my head about how many times this "lady" wasn't supposed to be there and I kept smiling.

When I thought about it, it was actually humorous and a little surprising that after all that has happened it's still hard for some to grasp, even to me.

These are my stories and people I've met along the way. Anyone who knows me realizes that I always have a story. I hope you continue to read about these events and more and find my answer to "What are you doing here?" and understand my reason for being there.

PART ONE

Anchors Aweigh

Chapter One

The Journey Begins

The US Airways flight leaving Jacksonville, Florida, was scheduled to arrive in Washington, DC, on a chilly afternoon in October 2002. My husband, Arlie, and I were on the way to the most important event of my career. Arlie was there for my support and would be there no matter the outcome.

My mother, Nora, and sister, Debbie, were to join us later in Washington. They were excited about the possibility of me making Navy League history as the first female to hold the office of national president since it was founded.

The Navy League was established in 1902 and received enthusiastic cooperation and funding from President Theodore Roosevelt when he donated a portion of his Nobel Peace Prize money to the Navy League. The Navy League supports the need for strength in American sea power. Having served as the assistant secretary of the Navy and as recipient of both the Nobel Peace Prize and Medal of Honor, he fully understood that superior sea power sustains peace and is a deterrent to war.

The Navy League has grown from these wise roots to become the foremost citizens' organization to serve, support, and stand for all United States sea service—the Navy, Marine Corps, Coast Guard, and US Flag Merchant Marine. During this time, we had a network of more than 275 councils, representing more than seventy-six thousand members around the globe. Navy League members are widely respected by leaders throughout government, industry, and military for their support and patriotic service to our men and women in uniform.

Decade after decade, the Navy League has demonstrated its leadership in advocating superior sea power to safeguard national security, protecting American economic interests and freedom of the seas.

I was dedicated to these principles and somewhat in wonder that I found myself running for the top position in this great organization.

My family was a little more optimistic than me about my prospects of becoming national president of the Navy League. Sure, I was confident but apprehensive and I had a right to be. I was intruding on territory where no woman dared to tread.

I felt like I was about to board the *Titanic* as soon as the plane landed. And my reservations were well founded. I would be facing a nominating committee of eighteen Navy League members representing every region in the world before facing more than three hundred national directors—quite a lot of folks to decide if a woman should run this man-dominated organization. I had no idea what questions the nominating committee was going to ask me, plus the fact there was already a small but vocal group of men vehemently opposed to a female entering a private sanctuary of males. But I knew I could do it.

I had over prepared as Arlie often says I do. Having been national vice president for legislative affairs gave me the perfect training and access. Obtaining that position had also been a battle. No woman had every represented the Navy League on Capitol Hill before I did. During my turnover from the prior vice president of legislative affairs he told me *he* should continue to be the face on Capitol Hill and I could handle the paperwork. This was another of those "what are you doing here?" moments.

The fact that I ran for the presidency in 2001 and had lost was a positive factor. I ran knowing I would lose. It was too early for me and I had to prove I could lose and continue my hard work and dedication to the Navy League without any drama. Although I had been a member of the Navy League since 1966 my leadership positions didn't begin until 1999.

I smiled to myself, leaned back in my seat, and closed my eyes. I would later think about this moment a year later when I was speaking at a WWII Submarine Veterans reunion in Camden County.

In November 2009, I was asked by John Crouse, who was a retired submarine master chief and now manager of the St. Marys Submarine Museum to speak at the annual Submarine Veterans of WWII annual dinner in Camden County, Georgia. This dinner preceded the WWII remembrance ceremony and the tolling of the bells the next morning at Naval Submarine Base Kings Bay.

I was running late that evening and slipped into my seat at the head table at the last minute. I saw a couple of folks I knew but the gentleman sitting next to me I had never seen. The guests at the table had pleasant conversation as dinner began. Arlie, my husband, was seated at the table adjacent to me.

Suddenly a very tall, distinguished retired submarine veteran who was sitting to my left leaned over and said very angrily, "What are you doing here? Why are you speaking to us? What gives you the right to speak to us? You don't understand the submarine force!"

He was so abrupt that I was taken back a little. I debated to myself. How could I let him know how much I respected what he and others had done in WWII in support of our country and the war effort? I thought how could I convey to him during dinner that I had supported the submarine force for many years. How could I convince him in the few minutes that we had during dinner? Instead I answered in a way that I knew would just frustrate him more,

"I'm a member of the Navy League," I said.

"A member of the Navy League, are you? Well, that's just great—that sure makes you qualified," he said sarcastically. I then excused myself, smiling as I stood and walked over to John Crouse, who was standing by the bar overseeing all of the guests and making sure no one needed anything.

"John, this gentleman is not very happy that I'm speaking," I told him. John and I worked together to build the St. Marys Submarine Museum in 1995 and 1996. I was president of the committee to build the museum and John was a very committed volunteer. He was hired as manager of the museum when it opened.

John gave a chuckle and told me he knew the man I was talking about and said, "Don't worry, he'll change his mind." When John introduced me that evening he gave almost as long an introduction as my remarks were. He told of my involvement with the building of the St. Marys Submarine Museum, cochairing the fund-raising with him for the monument celebrating the one hundredth anniversary of the submarine force. Using the sail of the USS Bancroft *(SSBN 643) this monument now greets everyone as they enter Kings Bay Submarine Base. He also talked on my service on the Defense Advisory Committee and my service as national president of the Navy League. He ended by saying, "She knows more people in the Pentagon than almost anyone. You can't walk down the halls without Sheila running into some admiral or general she knows!"*

I gave the "high sign" to John that he had said quite enough. He finished the introduction. I then spoke for about twenty minutes. At the close of my remarks the submarine veterans started rising. All of them were in their late to mid-eighties to nineties. Many required help standing. They didn't stop rising. They continued to applaud, and I then saw him. The unhappy veteran was also standing. I returned to my chair, and he turned toward me, bowed from the waist, and said, "I would have listened as long as you talked. Thank you."

That night, after the dinner, I fell asleep thinking about the comments the submarine veteran had made. After all that has happened I am still getting the "what are you doing here?" attitude. Little did he know at that time that I had been through far stronger storms than this one and I had time to gain enough confidence not to let it bother me.

* * * * *

When Arlie and I arrived in Washington, we checked in the hotel suite and were greeted by several supporters, including Carla Carper, the executive director of the Camden County Chamber of Commerce; Bill Dawson, manager of the Georgia Ports Authority in Brunswick; and Bill Kelley, former national president and his wife, Nancy, who was my first and best supporter when I was trying to decide if I should run. RADM Raymond and June Coutour joined us shortly along with RADM Chuck Beers, former Group Commander at Kings Bay and then an executive with Lockheed Martin.

Many of the national Navy League staff stopped by, some dressed in costume for Halloween. The development director, Veronica Brandon, was Elvira. We enjoyed the fact that they were in disguise and could come and go freely to our suite without anyone knowing. Those that would fight to keep me away from the presidency were in rooms close by.

My suite was made possible by donations from the Camden County, Carla Carper, executive director, and Glynn County communities. Word got out and every few days someone would drop by my office in Camden with a check. It was incredibly humbling. Woody Woodside, executive director of the Brunswick, Glynn County Chamber, got all the liquor furnished and Bill Dawson, manager of the Brunswick Port Authority flew up to tend bar. It was amazing.

Carla Carper kept a full duffel bag with her at all times to replenish the supply of buttons. Arlie, Nancy, Bill, Debbie, Carla, Fred Orton, and a dozen others were giving them out to everyone. Carla later told everyone, "It wasn't a walk in the park. It was grace under fire." The highlight of my life was being with Sheila at her election. This has put Camden County on the map."

Carla was so important to the campaign that week. Her enthusiasm and people skills made a big difference. She is comfortable around everyone and made a great ambassador for Camden County.

During the campaign week my nephew, Larry Youngner Jr., and his fiancée (at that time—now his wife), Kristy, both lieutenant colonels in the United States Air Force at that time were also in town. He had told me they would attend the Navy League board of directors meeting that day. This was the day the entire board was voting for the new national president. The night before, at dinner in a Crystal City restaurant. Larry and Kristy kept seeing individuals at dinner wearing the Sheila button and realized the Sheila they were supporting was his aunt!

The next day my supporters passed out buttons all day and Arlie and I went to the Presidents' Circle meeting. At that time, the national Navy League was building a 214,000-square-foot building occupying an entire block in Arlington, Virginia. This would house the headquarter staff and allow another six floors to be rented out bringing much needed revenues to the Navy League.

On the way, Arlie and I stopped by the building exhibit and made a financial pledge for a naming opportunity for the legislative affairs director's office. It was a great opportunity to support this program. My heart will always be our work to obtain the funding the services need to perform their mission. To have this office named after us was awesome. Chuck Breslauer, my former boss and family friend for many years, and my mother and my sister arrived in Washington that afternoon to help with my campaign.

Later that afternoon, I attended the executive committee meeting and it was as painful as I thought it might be. Tim Fanning, the current national president, had proposed several changes to the bylaws, the most controversial being the removal of the past presidents from the executive committee, a committee composed of the vice presidents, secretary, treasures, the region presidents, a few people appointed by the current president, and the past national presidents. I had a completely different view from Tim and felt that those who had had the ultimate responsibility would be the best advisors. My actions were always to convince a few at a time until I had complete agreement—or as complete as one could get. The past presidents lent a unique perspective. Unlike Tim, I wanted them prodding and asking the tough questions.

Most of the nominating committee also served on the executive committee and would be attending this important executive committee meeting. Frankly, I didn't want to be argumentative that day. As much as you hate to admit it you often must be political. All of those on the nominating committee were a part of the executive committee. I knew that Tim and two or three others would do everything possible to make me look bad. My appearing uninformed or emotional minutes before I appeared before them as a candidate for president would not be wise. The opposition would do everything they could to make the case that I could not lead the Navy League. They knew I was one of the key members opposed to most of these by laws changes. However, I found that most of the past presidents were making the argument and I didn't have to. Of course, President Fanning used that as an opportunity—as did a couple of the steering committee members—that this meeting was consumed by the past presidents and that made their point of trying to get rid of them. The past presidents felt they had to speak up to protect the Navy League. There were many changes that day and they were presented as one package and the debate continued. We were not getting anything accomplished and I suggested we take the recommended changes one at a time. Tim finally said, "We'll take Sheila's suggestion and take them one at a time, but it's going to take a long time!" Thankfully it was accomplished quickly. That fact was obvious to all present and my "silly idea" worked. I had been very vocal leading up to this meeting against Tim's suggestions. And the amendment to remove the past national presidents was defeated.

The "welcome aboard" dinner was immediately after the directors meeting and was held on the ship, the *Odyssey*, a commercial cruise ship that takes short dinner cruises on the Potomac. The Navy League had the entire ship for the evening and there was no way to avoid running into my opponent, John Panneton, as we both campaigned all evening. We were courteous to one another but understood what this event meant. He and Tim had taken the first table as guests entered the ship. John was a retired lieutenant colonel in the US Marines and has a lovely wife, Alice.

During the evening, a young waiter approached me. He asked, "Are you Sheila?" I turned to answer him and I was surprised to see that he had my button on. "Good luck to you, we are all rooting for you. We've been watching you all evening," he commented. "Everyone seems to really like you. I think you will win."

"Thank you so much," I answered. And I truly meant it. I would need a lot of luck. I would be entering a lion's den. With all the comments over the past few months from Tom Benning and Mike Wilson, it had been an uphill battle.

It was amazing what a boost those waiters were! About that time, I realized *all* the waiter staff was wearing my button. Arlie told me later he gave them five dollars to each if they would wear them. This was so unlike Arlie's nature but indicative of the unbelievable support he would give me over the next two years.

That evening turned out to be just wonderful. Many of my supporters were very vocal all evening. Rear Admiral Jerry Ellis and his wife, Rosemary, were both there and Jerry was determined to have conversations with the majority of those present on behalf of my candidacy. Rosemary told me she campaigned for me very hard; however, she laughed and said, "Jerry hasn't stopped campaigning all night." Jerry tried to talk with the Navy League judge advocate, a former Navy JAG in support of my campaign but there was no changing his mind. After I became president, this same attorney was with me at a dinner event I had organized with the secretary of the Navy and top defense companies. He walked over after the dinner and shook my hand and told me I was an excellent president. It was a very nice gesture as he definitely was prejudiced during the election.

Jerry was well qualified to speak about my history in support of the sea services, the Navy, Marine Corps, Coast Guard, and Merchant Marine. He was group commander (a flag level position—*flag* meaning *admiral*, for those not familiar with the military) at Submarine Group 10 at Kings Bay. I held my executive board meetings in his conference room, and he tried to be at all the meetings. He was the military officer who nominated me for service on the Defense Advisory Committee, a committee that reports to the secretary of defense. The committee that gave me the knowledge and confidence to later run for president.

Mother and Debbie and the rest of the "family" were in the back table, so all night I went back to see them and send folks to meet my mother. Many of the tables chanted "She-lah, She-lah" as I passed. I didn't see much of my opponent that evening but there were many who came up to tell me what a small button he had. They told me, "Yours is bigger than John's!" Thanks, Brian and Chris; you're right, bigger is better.

That evening on the *Odyssey* ended with my seventy-eight-year-old mother, Nora, and Rosemary Ellis doing a fast dance on the dance floor. On the bus during our drive back to the hotel, Charo from Puerto Rico started chanting "She-lah" again. Our group included about fifty Navy League members and we sang patriotic songs as we enjoyed the camaraderie and as we marveled over the incredible monuments. Nothing beats the sight of the Lincoln Memorial and the Washington Monument at night. This would climax one of the most momentous evenings of my life.

Chapter Two

Really, a Woman?
Why my election was so difficult

The weeks before the election was stressful. I tossed and turned as thoughts danced in my head trying to sleep. I wondered why these few men were so adamantly opposed to my election. Again, Bob Bledsoe popped into my head: "Sheila, I don't want a woman in the plant. I don't want a woman negotiating the union contract." How could I be safety director when he didn't want a woman wearing a safety hat? How could I convince him that in spite of being a woman I could do it? And now, how could I convince the Navy League that in spite of being a woman, I could run the Navy League?

In fact, the following is a rather crude example but is at the crux of the barriers I faced. One of the officers at Kings Bay for several tours was attending Navy Week in New York back in 2002. The admiral who was the speaker for the evening was without his aide, so my friend Mike Altiser was his "loop" for the evening. The event was at the New York City Yacht Club. Vic Gainer, then president of the New York City Council of the Navy League, begins talking about his campaign against Sheila McNeill who was running for national president of the Navy League.

He said, "We don't want a skirt running the Navy League. Sheila will never win this election. She doesn't even have a penis."

The naval officer, Mike, tells me he answered, "Excuse me, gentlemen. I know Sheila McNeill and she doesn't need one."

Unless you understand the military, you don't know what a major thing this was. An aide does what his admiral wants and needs—he doesn't contradict someone they are meeting with. I'm amazed that Mike spoke up but that man always was a wonderful officer and a gentleman. I laughed and realized how much this illustrated the supportive attitude of all the military officers I had worked with. I never understood Vic or Tim's extreme arrogance and attitude toward me. To explain I have to go back to Sea Air Space (SAS), the Navy League's maritime expo in April 2002. I knew that Vic was against a woman in leadership in the Navy League. He didn't mind women doing the work, but they must stay in the background.

During one of the events, I saw assistant secretary of the Navy Susan Livingston and Admiral Skip Bowman, head of Naval Reactors, and I walked over to say hello. A photographer quickly came over and took our picture.

When I returned to my table where Vic was also sitting, he said sarcastically with a smirk, "I guess that one goes in your book for your campaign for president."

"I hope I can count on your support," I replied, knowing how he felt.

Vic said, "No, you cannot. You will cause irreparable harm to the Navy League and the sea services if you are elected."

I said something inane like, "I'm sorry you feel that way."

Later that evening, I was at a cocktail party talking to Mark Rosen, the Navy League's legal counsel and the senior director for Communications. Mark, Vic, and I found ourselves together at the dinner hour. Vic suggested we go to the hotel restaurant. Thinking that maybe an evening with him might change his mind and at the very least might neutralize him, I agreed to join them for dinner. When we got to the restaurant in the hotel, we had to wait and I walked over to some staff members, Katie, Louise, and Marsha, who were having dinner in the same restaurant.

They said laughing, "You won't believe this. We thought you were having dinner with Vic Gainer."

I smiled and said, "I am."

"How could you do this?" they asked. "After all he has said about you and all the trouble he has made for you?"

"We just can't believe after he has been so nasty you are having dinner with him." I replied. "Maybe I can change his mind."

I watched the ladies give me that "hope you know what you are doing" look!

Mark, Vic, and I had a nice dinner discussing military issues the entire time. At the end of the evening, Vic said, "You know, Sheila, in another century you and I could have been partners. There are a lot of things we agree on. I want you to know it's nothing personal, I'd feel the same way about…" He used the n-word.

Yes, that's what he said—in front of Mark. I was too stunned to reply. But I did make the decision at that moment if I became president he would not serve in any leadership job. That kind of talk just stunned me.

A couple of months later, I attended a Marine Corps, silent parade sponsored by the Navy League. Tim and Vic were in attendance. Vic and I were staying at the Ritz-Carlton in Pentagon City and we stopped by the club room for coffee. Vic said, "Did you see anyone there [at the Marine Corps parade] that looked like you?" I thought to myself, *What is he talking about?* He continued, "Did you see any woman there that wasn't a wife? You should be at home cooking dinner for your husband.

You have no business doing this. You will harm the Navy League. We know the numbers and the nominating committee will never elect you."

I just smiled and said, "I'm sorry you feel that way but I'm still running."

I was just amazed anyone could be so insulting. He then went on to say, "We've got to do something about Tim. He controls everything and doesn't give anyone the opportunity for input… You and I are the only ones who work."

I remember thinking at the time, this man is a total paradox. Ironically, he was Tim's friend and partner in the opposition to my election yet also wanted us to become conspirators. We then talked Navy League for a while. All the time I was being careful not to say anything he could twist and distort.

I knew he was playing both sides and anything I said would be repeated to those that would want to discredit me. I made a pact with myself a long time ago that I would respect the office of the national president even if I could not respect the man and would not say anything negative about him. Later Vic and I walked to our rooms and found we were next door to one other. When we got to my room, he leered and said, "Joking, that's the only way I could take it." If you get an urge in the middle of the night, just scratch on the wall and I'll come over." I just ignored the remark and entered my room. Yes, I was shocked that he would say something like this, but it was in tune with his earlier comments. Perhaps in his strange mind and after all the "sweet talk," he thought he had won me over.

A few weeks before the Navy League winter board of directors meeting, I was visiting San Francisco and I received a call from Bill Kopper, state president of Ohio. He said he had heard that Tim would quit serving on the building committee if I were elected. I told him I didn't know if he would quit or not he'd have to ask Tim for that answer. The idea of the Navy League building, our own building, was originally proposed by Tim. Tim had a background is construction and corporate leasing and his expertise was needed by the Navy League. Bill said this was way out of line and that Tim was blackmailing the Navy League. What I didn't tell Bill was that others had reassured me we would be fine and that most of the time Tim was so difficult in negotiations that he made everyone mad and distrustful.

On another occasion the few weeks before the election, as national vice president of legislative affairs for the Navy League, I attended a legislative affairs reception on Capitol Hill, hosted by the Navy League. Secretary of the Navy, Gordon England, greeted me with, "Sheila, how many more days?" Many of the leadership predicted it would happen. Tim (also in attendance as the national president) and I circled the room but did not meet one other. However, many were coming up to me telling me he was being very negative about me.

He told anyone who would listen, "Sheila is an uneducated woman from South Georgia who owns a card shop. She is not qualified to run the Navy League. If she is elected, I will not serve on her steering committee." (This is the committee is composed of the national vice presidents, secretary, treasurer, and past national presidents.)

I decided it was now or never and pulled Tim aside and asked, "Tim, if I am elected, will you work with me?

He said with a satisfied smirk, "No, and I will not stay on as the past national president. Read your bylaws. Any past president can serve—get Bill Kelley or one of your past president friends to do it." I was stunned. Tim strutted off with a satisfied smile and walked around the room bragging about his conversation on how he told me off. He also repeated his story to a member of the staff as well as a Navy captain who was present and, unknown to Tim, was my ride back to the hotel that night. "I've been cleaning up her shit for a year and a half," he told everyone. This was pretty raw language for our leader, the current national president.

Over the next few days after the Capitol Hill reception, a couple of our corporate sponsors called the Navy League and complained of Tim's comments at the Capitol Hill reception. He had managed to offend two corporate gold sponsors with his negative comments about me.

That evening, Shirley Fages and her husband, VADM Malcolm Fages, both dear friends, were waiting in my room. She had been visiting her daughter, Meredith, in Norfolk and was on the way back to Brussels where Malcolm served as the military representative for the United States at NATO. She had a car and offered to take me to headquarters for the hour I had before I had to leave for the airport. I had a chance to introduce her to everyone and show her the national headquarters. When we got to Tim's office, the lights were out, so I was surprised to find him sitting there with his feet on the desk and a ball cap on.

"Tim, I'd like to introduce you to my friend, Shirley Fages. Shirley, Tim is our national president," I told Shirley. Tim just stared and did not acknowledge either of us in any way. We couldn't believe it—we waited, and finally we just walked away. Later someone explained to Shirley, "He didn't know who you were!" It turned out that during this same time *Seapower* was trying to get an interview with her husband. My point was it didn't matter who she was. Anyone who is introduced to him as he represents the Navy League should be treated with respect. Later, Shirley wrote a letter recounting the events and said to forward or copy as I wished. I'm glad she did because Tim told others I was lying, that we just walked by and never stopped at his office.

On another occasion, Tim said, "Sheila presents herself as an admiral." This accusation was frustrating, hurtful, and potentially dangerous to my reputation. How ridiculous this accusation was! I confronted him one night on the way to the car and he readily admitted this. When I pushed him for an explanation, he referred to an article someone had sent to him from the *Georgia Trend* magazine.

This was a term Senator Max Cleland always used in that article and whenever we met. Also, many of my friends affectionately called me Admiral. The magazine *Georgia Trend* featured me on the cover with the title, Admiral McNeill. It was the July 2001 issue. How exciting that was. I was excited when *Georgia Trend* called me to say they had decided to feature my picture on the cover magazine. The article was a very positive one and I was proud of the honor.

They also had the questions of how many copies of the magazine I wanted. "One hundred and sixty-five," I answered. I laughed and then changed the number to twenty-four. I called Arlie, Mom, and Debbie and everyone else I thought would listen. Debbie was great calling me for a week trying to find it on the website and Arlie is stopping at every bookstore and gift shop between Atlanta and Brunswick trying to get an early copy. He actually found one, bought several, and took a picture of it on the shelf. Of course, I called Shirley Fages, who was to be in DC the following week, and I promised to save her a copy.

To take this very positive article and turn it into a negative showed the lengths others would go to. And that is how I became "Admiral McNeill" to a few of my friends.

Georgia Trend is well read in the political and the business communities in Georgia. They have been very good to me over the years and are responsible for many of my great moments. Their May 2002 issue had an article on "Spotlighting the Big Mules"

They wrote,

> *There's Sheila McNeill of Camden County. Called "Admiral McNeill" (there it is again) by her friends, she is vice president of the Navy League, a national organization of 74,000 members that is dedicated to maintaining U.S. Naval strength. When she goes to Washington, important people take note. Her main influence will be to help keep Camden's Kings Bay Naval Base safe from future government base reduction plans.* After commenting on a few others, he ended with, *"There are other Big Mules you can name. They do not seek publicity. They usually take up causes but are not hard or abrasive. They win people over by thoughtful conversation. They can stand and fight, but usually convince people to their cause with quiet logic. A Big Mule could be the richest man in Macon, or the owner of a small dry goods store in Canton. Mules are the keystones of any community because they place principles above self-interest."* (Neely Young, editor and publisher of *Georgia Trend*)

I wrote to Mr. Young on May 13, 2002:

Dear Mr. Young,

I was quite surprised and truly flattered to find myself included in your May 2002 article on Georgia's "Big Mules." I'm not so sure about the term "Big Mules"—but being a true Georgia girl—and not too far removed from the farm I understand the compliment. Even the biggest mule cannot accomplish very much without guidance and assistance and I am quite fortunate to be surrounded by a very dedicated group of folks in Camden County who like to get things done. Thank you very much for this honor!

Sincerely,
Sheila

Georgia Trend continued to bring good things to my life. In December 2003 after I became president, I had a call from the Navy League's public affairs officer, Ramona Joyce. "I've just had a call from a magazine by the name of *Georgia Trend* and they wanted to know your age," she said. When I asked why she said, "You are being listed as one of the most influential Georgians in the January issue."

* * * * *

About three weeks before the national meeting when the election was to be held, I received a call from a Navy League past president in California who had heard that my nomination package with my letters of recommendation and platform were withheld from the nominating committee. I called Navy League headquarters and when I asked the specific question. "Has the chairman of the nominating committee told you not to send my package to the committee? I have heard that they were ordered to put them in a locked closet at headquarters."

Linda Hoffman answered, "Yes, but we will return them to you in today's mail for next day delivery if you would like for us to." She had not been able to tell me about the incident but was relieved I had found out and was happy to get them out of the locked closet and in the mail to me. I was not at home that evening, but Arlie answered a call from the chairman of the nominating committee and a past national president, Jack Kennedy, who explaining they did not forward my "scrapbook" because the cover of the package stated I was running for president and it was supposed to be senior vice president.

It was accepted procedure with the Navy League that the person elected as senior vice president would take over as president at the next Navy League meeting. A dozen Navy League members had helped me by reviewing the package and none made note of the fact I had said that I was running for president rather than senior vice president. This was a technicality that was changed a few years later to an election to president-elect reflecting the job. I was amazed that some members of the Navy League would go to that length to see that I was not elected. I immediately wrote a letter to the nominating committee telling them my package had been withheld and sent all eighteen the package to their homes. Withholding my election package backfired on those who would do most anything to see that I was not the president because it gave each of the nominating committee an opportunity to study the entire package before they left for the meeting. The package included the recommendations from about one hundred Navy League members along with my array of pictures with military leaders and a detailed platform. It also pointed out just how far those who didn't want to see a woman as president of the Navy League would go.

Chapter Three

The Election and Celebration

We arrived at the lovely suite our friends made possible. Bill and Nancy Kelley and Raymond and June Coutour arrived soon after. Raymond and June bought pizzas for all of us. But we had very little chance to get our bearings *My God, I might win*, I thought

The morning of the election, my region, the South Atlantic Coast Region, had a meeting in our suite. Carla had gone with Suzy Williams to get orange juice and sweet rolls, while we ordered coffee. My appointment was at ten with the nominating committee. Arlie, mother, Debbie, and Chuck came to wait with me outside the door as I waited for the interview. Dick Faharenwald, vice chairman of the nominating committee and a Navy League member from Hawaii, came out and told me it was time for my interview. I was told there were questions to "set me up." As usual, I had overprepared. My experience as national vice president for legislative affairs and my experience with the governance issues of the Navy League gave me the background I needed. I was confident. Someone would surely question my educational background. With just a high school education, I knew this issue would be a negative. There was also the question of a national president who had no prior military experience. All the past national presidents had a military background, most at the flag and general officer level.

There are times when you know you strike out. There are times when you think you hit a home run. I felt good about the interview. I got so enthused when I discussed our support for our sea services. This is especially true discussing the issues on Capitol Hill and how just one person can make a difference. They allowed me to talk at length about our support of the Navy, Marine Corps, Coast Guard, and US Flagged Merchant Marine on Capitol Hill. In order to discuss this, I had to understand the issues. I did. During the interview, someone asked, "What will the service chiefs think of a woman running the Navy League?" This question was from one of the more progressive Navy League members, so I knew it was asked to get the subject out in the open and give me a chance to respond.

My reply was, "I haven't been a woman for thirty years. I've been an advocate for the sea services. And the services are beyond that—the Navy League is the one behind. I am friends of all the service chiefs now due to my work on Capitol Hill, and none of them have a problem with my gender."

I left the interview confident that I had done my best. The nominee from the nominating committee had to be presented and voted on by the entire board of directors. As confident as I felt about my interview, I didn't know if I would be that nominee. We had to have a backup plan. We had to prepare for a nomination from the floor. A rare floor fight was not the best thing, but we felt that may be the only way a woman might win the election. So many unscrupulous acts had gone on we felt there would be no other choice. Earlier that morning I had asked John Thorne to be one of my endorsers. John was the civilian public affairs officer with the Coast Guard. While I could not involve the military, civilian employees were allowed to be involved. He had encouraged me and worked with me from the beginning. He agreed and said he was truly honored. We decided to ask Mike McGrath to second the nomination. Mike and John were to get with Bill Kelley and work out the process.

The committee had adjourned. A decision had been made. We had our legislative affairs meeting that I was running as national vice president. Don Ten Eyck, a member of the committee and also a member of the nominating committee, arrived, but he really didn't give me an indication of the results. He did shake his head one time, but I didn't know if he was greeting me or telling me something. I did have the fleeting thought: *My God, I may have won the nomination.* An indication of my support was demonstrated to me when a Navy League member later said he arrived at my meeting with my opponent's button on and halfway through the meeting he removed it and was a supporter.

I later ran into the chairman of the nominating committee, Jack, on the second-floor lobby next to the escalator. He very abruptly said, "You are the recommended candidate from the nominating committee." Obviously, he was not very happy about it. He didn't extend his hand, but I did and he had to shake it. "Use a little integrity here and don't tell anyone, even your mother, until I advise John Panneton, the other candidate. I'll call you when you can tell it."

We walked upstairs to our suite with about ten family and friends walking with us and people joining us as we walked. They all wanted to know if I had heard anything from the nominating committee. I just smiled and they followed. Despite Jack's instructions not to tell anyone, as soon as we got into the room, I turned to everyone and told them I was the nominee. There was a burst of excitement and cheering. But I added, we can't leave or make a call until we had gotten the okay from Jack Kennedy. We waited. We continued to wait and wait. I never heard from Kennedy again. He never called to tell me it was all right to speak about it. As far as he knew, I continued to wait for a call from him that never came. I'm sure that ignoring protocol to let me know of my nomination gave them great delight.

However, we finally received a call from a Navy League member who said the results of the nominating committee were posted on the bulletin board for everyone to see. As far as the nominating committee chairman knew, I continued staying in my room waiting for his call. Still "maintaining my integrity" as Jack had instructed, we all went down to look *and it was posted*! We took pictures.

Calvin Cobb, an attorney and a former Navy League national president came up and saw the notice and almost got teary. Tim actually shook my hand. It was quite a moment—seeing that notice for the first time, not my shaking hands with Tim, however momentous that was. I was supposed to be at a Sea Cadets meeting, so I went to the meeting to give them word of my nomination. As I waited in the back all the Sea Cadet board of directors began to rise as they applauded. After it got quiet, I said, "I guess you heard."

They laughed and Jim Ward, the chairman, said, "Sheila, I understand you have lots to do now so we'll understand if you cannot stay for the meeting." The steering committee took our official photograph for *Seapower*, the Navy League's official magazine and returned to our room. We then returned downstairs and mingled with other Navy Leaguers.

We later attended the national board of directors' meeting. The board of directors consists of three-hundred-plus directors. Sitting in the audience were representative from every region in the United States, Europe, and Asia. Even as the nominee from the nominating committee, a feat in itself, we expected there would be a nomination from the floor for John Panneton. But if that happened, we had felt we had the majority of the board who would vote for me. Carol Ann Hackley, a national vice president and the only other woman on the steering committee, was seated next to me at the long dais. I sent her a note.

I wrote, "It is so strange to see the 'Sheila' buttons on people I don't know."

She answered, "Yes and so many of them!"

It took all the composure we both had not to sit with big smiles. I had been very uncomfortable with Larry and Kristy having to stay so long, so I sent them a note by a staff member telling them they didn't have to wait through all this. They gave me the high sign that it was okay.

The past presidents had met and written a recommendation that all governance issues and past president elimination issue be turned over to a commission headed by the senior vice president. That would be me! This really annoyed Tim. In fact, he made the comment to others, "She's already running the Navy League and she hasn't been elected yet." The past presidents had met without my knowledge, so I was not aware of the recommendation. Tim was convinced otherwise. On the other hand, maybe it's best he sees me as someone that powerful. What a wonderful endorsement from the board of directors. They not only voted for me but put the governance issues in my hands.

The chairman of the nominating committee made an awkward, stumbling recommendation announcing that I was the nominee from the nominating committee. As soon as my name was announced, all three hundred members began rising. They shouted, stomped, clapped, and whistled. It was the most overwhelming moment of my life. Tim asked over the noise if there were any other nominations—and then he said, "We'll take this as a unanimous proclamation." When it quietened down, he called me up for the swearing in. As I raised my right hand, I repeated as the national judge advocate gave the oath of office:

"I do solemnly swear that during the term of office for national president-elect I shall faithfully serve, to the best of my ability, the interest of our nation, its maritime services and the Navy League." My heart was pounding so hard I could feel the rush of blood in my ears. It would have been most appropriate for me to have thanked everyone.

But Tim Fanning, standing next to the judge advocate as the current national president, whispered to me, "Don't talk, you'll have your chance tonight." That didn't matter to me. I didn't have to say a word. The fact that I had won speaks for itself. He could have his last final word if he wanted to. Again, the audience stood and repeated the stomping, shouting, and whistling. Arlie was sitting next to past national president Al Friedrich, who was one of those whistling through his fingers.

Arlie said to him, "I wish I could do that."

Al said, "I'll just whistle louder."

We had very little time to get ready for the evening. I only had to freshen up. I wore the same suit, but it was still close timing with so many happy folks stopping to congratulate me. It was time for the formal dinner recognizing the new president. We were fifteen minutes late for the reception arriving about 7:15 p.m. and met with a strange situation. My opponent and the president greeting everyone like the hosts of the evening. They did not look in our direction, so we walked into the ballroom. I immediately saw Admiral Vern Clark, chief of naval operations, and his wife, Connie. When I greeted them, I could tell he seemed uncomfortable, apologetic, and somewhat sad when he approached me.

I said, "Admiral Clark, do you know I won?"

He was shocked and said, "I assumed when I saw John with Tim…" Then he gave me a big grin and a hug and said, "I couldn't be happier."

We would become very good friends over the next two years and a special section is written about some of those experiences. We were seated with the admiral and Mrs. Clark at dinner. At one point, I went to the table Mother was sitting at and asked her to come to the head table to meet everyone. I introduced her to Admiral Clark and Connie. When she returned to the table, Jack Kennedy asked her, "Who did you meet?"

"Oh, some admiral friend of Sheila's," she said. She later became quite familiar with the name Vern Clark and was delighted when she could call me and say she saw my friend on television.

The conversation at dinner would take another hour. As we sat that evening, Admiral Clark told me about a new class of ships he was working on. He even drew a sketch of a joint high-speed vessel that was needed. (You will find an interesting coincidence in the story of the USNS *Brunswick*) The Clarks were wonderful. Tim had Rabbi Kloner give the invocation and he prayed for me as president-elect and for the recipients of the SECNAV award. At the podium, Tim thanked him and said, "You promoted Sheila and let the cat out of the bag on the remainder of the evening but thank you, Rabbi." Rabbi Kloner later told me that Tim went over to his table and repeated his frustration with his prayer, which was embarrassing to the rabbi. I loved that man.

When I called him later to ask him to be my chaplain for the national Navy League, continuing his tour for many years, he replied, "Sure I will, Sheila, but are you sure you want a rabbi?"

I replied, "Every Southern Baptist girl needs her rabbi. Of course, I'm sure."

Early in the campaign Rabbi Kloner had apologized to me saying as the Navy League's chaplain he would not be able to campaign for me. I assured him I understood. Later that same day he brought some members over to me and said, "I want you to see the next Navy League national president. She's going to be the best we ever had!" I looked at him questioning this action but smiling as I raised my eyebrow. His responded, "I just can't help myself, Sheila—you are going to change the Navy League and we need that."

When Tim introduced me, I received a second standing ovation. That evening when Tim introduced me, everyone stood again. I was particularly appreciative since this showed the Navy that all were fine with a woman president. I had bouquets of roses presented to me at the podium from Nancy and Bill Kelley and Arlie. When the chief of naval operations, Admiral Clark, spoke from the podium, he said, "Someone told me tonight that Sheila is a woman." He stopped, looked at me, and said, "Well, so she is," Admiral Clark. The room howled. He received a standing ovation when I talked about Admiral Clark and Connie and the impact that had made. Everyone stayed until 2:00 a.m. in the room. We didn't leave the banquet until eleven, having fun with the Clark's, who usually have to depart fairly early. I was thrilled they stayed until eleven. When we got to the suite, we found dozens waiting in the suite and most stayed until late. What an ending to an evening that celebrated and recognized my forty years of service to our men and women in the sea services.

When Arlie and I got to the airport the next day, a Sunday, I called former CNO, Admiral Kelso, and let him know that I had won the election. He was, I believe, a little surprised, but he told me he was grateful for the decision the Navy

League had made. I thought it was interesting when *Navy Times* had news of the election that had the headline:

Woman to Lead League

> *The Navy League will have its first female president next year. Sheila McNeill, of Brunswick, Ga., will assume the post in June. McNeill started out as a member of the Navy League more than 30 years ago, along with her husband, Arlie McNeill, who served four years as a dental technician. Arlie McNeill is a national director emeritus. McNeill was elected senior vice president at the Navy League's board of director's winter meeting Nov. 2 in Arlington, Va. As senior vice president, she succeeds the outgoing president for a two-year term. McNeill most recently served as the Navy League's vice president for legislative affairs, making dozens of trips to Washington, D.C. to lobby Congress on sea-service issues.*
>
> *As president, McNeill said she wants to help cultivate a new generation of leadership for the century-old organization which has 76,000 members. "We have a great opportunity going into the second century to turn up the voice for the sea services," she said. While not a veteran, McNeill sees her work with the Navy League as her contribution. "I've never served in the military, but I feel like this is my service to my country."*

PART TWO

Home Life

Chapter Four

Growing Up

The small town of Brunswick lies just off the Georgia coast on the mainland and is the gateway to the out islands of St. Simons, Jekyll, and Sea Island. Brunswick was founded in 1776 by General James Oglethorpe, commissioned by King Georgia II of England and founded as a debtor's colony. At the outbreak of WWII, the ports of Brunswick became a major port for ship building. They built ninety-nine Liberty ships, which were used to transport troops and supplies. Many of the families that immigrated to Brunswick to work in the yards remained in Brunswick and made it their home.

Located an hour's drive between Jacksonville and Savannah, Brunswick, is the seat for the county of Glynn. Today the Golden Isles stands rich in history dating back to the Spanish, Revolutionary, and Civil Wars. To the east of Glynn County lie miles and miles of golden marshland leading to the Atlantic Ocean. To the west and north lie the boarding counties of Wayne and McIntosh and to the south Camden County, the home of Kings Bay Naval Submarine Base, which would incidentally become a significant part of my life in later years. Kings Bay was constructed in 1976 and was once an army depot. Driving through its highly secure gates one might think Kings Bay was a private resort. Its beautiful woods and marshes might remind one of an environmental reserve complete with protected endangered species. The submarine base is host to six ballistic missiles and two guided missile submarines. The Marine Corps and the Coast Guard also call Kings Bay home.

Summer nights and during high school my best friends were Phyllis Harvey Johns, Joyce McPherson, Josephine Mallard, Alice Joy Hall, and Jeanne Earle Varnadoe. Some of us would park for curb service at the local Shoney's Big Boy, Pig and Whistle, and Twin Oaks Drive-In, the only place for teenagers looking for a good time and just to hang out and eat cheeseburgers, fries, and milkshakes. The three of us all attended Glynn Academy, the second oldest high school in the state of Georgia and one with academic excellence and strict standards with a championship football team. One day just after high school all this changed. And my life would never be the same after I married Arlie McNeill.

* * * * *

I was born Sheila Diane Mobley to Kenneth Lewis Mobley and Nora Lee Walling Mobley in 1943 in Brunswick, Georgia, the oldest of five children. As a baby born in the war years, the first child, and the first grandchild, I understand I was the "toy" of my aunts and uncles and very much loved by my parents. I have faint memories of being a very young child in the modest "war projects" with many friends of my parents living close by. Since I was the oldest of all the children, my mothering instincts came out pretty early. Some would call it my bossing instincts. These still apply today.

Mother was originally from Lodge, South Carolina, and moved to Brunswick because her father could not find work in South Carolina. Daddy moved to Brunswick from Baxley when he was eighteen to work in the booming shipyard industry. Daddy served in the US Army Air Corps during WWII. He joined when I was six months old. He was part of the crews that ferried airplanes overseas for the war effort. Although he never was stationed overseas, he was gone from the family most of the time when I was a baby. When he was drafted, he decided to throw away all his beer bottles. There must have been a hundred. He continued his hoarding of scrap metal, rusty nails, broken utensils, and even old toilets, etc., until he died. He always believed that his treasures would one day bring good money in a garage sale. Mother went to Amarillo, Texas, where Dad was stationed and stayed a couple of months. She went by troop train, and it was very crowded with soldiers. She doesn't remember there being other civilians but the soldiers helped take care of me, changed my diapers, and consoled me when I was less than a year old. This was my first experience with the military.

Mother's side of the family had no alcoholics that we knew of. I once joked, "The women of the family have the good genes." Our grandmother, whom we called Dessie, worked as a waitress at The Oglethorpe Hotel on Newcastle Street in downtown Brunswick. It was the popular place for the Rotary, Kiwanis, and most civic meetings. Mother and her sister, Irene, would work at night and help Dessie. Mother was fourteen years old.

When Mother and her sister, Dorothy, worked at a popular upscale restaurant, the Deck, it was a most prestigious place to eat. Waitresses were required to stay in eye contact and respond immediately. They were known not only for their food but for their service. We were proud to tell everyone our Mom worked at the Deck. The restaurant was located right on the corner of US17 at the entrance to the island causeway and was the most popular seafood restaurant in Glynn county and possible southeast Georgia. It was so exciting when we picked her up. Kenny and I would be waiting in the car and she always had a treat—usually those famous hushpuppies in her pocket. That white uniform always had the wonderful smell of fried shrimp, battered french fries, and hushpuppies. The highlight of mine and Kenny's day was counting her tips. But her job at the Deck gave Daddy a new thing to harass Mother about. She worked in a bar; she must be drinking, he would say. The owner's son had a bet with the bartender about who would get a date with Mother. No one won the bet! She was always and was, until her death on June 9, 2014, above board and loyal to Daddy. However, Daddy never let up on his jealousy of Mother.

My paternal grandparents and my grandfather's mother, Julia Benton Walling, whom we called Mamer, lived in a quaint three-room house next door to them on Norwich Street. We were always curious about her background. Had we pursued her past we may have learned more about her five husbands. We did know that her number three husband was the son of number one husband and two of the five husbands died on their honeymoon. She was quiet and stayed in her rocking chair, smoking a corncob pipe and kept all her thoughts to herself. She was never close to Dessie although Dessie took good care of her. It would sometimes aggravate Dessie that Mamer would come to the back door each night and wait for her to bring out her plate. She would never join them for dinner.

* * * * *

In later years Kenny would refer to Mom and Dad as the Beauty and the Beast. Mom was very beautiful jet-black hair, flowing over her shoulders and deep blue eyes. Dad was equally handsome, and both had the same color blue eyes. We were one of the first in the neighborhood to have a TV. Everyone came to our house to watch *The Ed Sullivan Show*, *Jackie Gleason*, and *What's My Line*. There must have been twenty people at our house every Sunday night. Speaking of high cotton!

Mother was born in 1925 in Lodge, South Carolina, and moved to Brunswick as a two-year-old. Her father, Raymond Walling, was working with the saw mill. His brother, Roebuck, had already moved and brothers, Laurie and Clevie, stayed in South Carolina. Much of the next few years were just getting by and trying to find good employment. They lived on Wolf Street right behind where we would later live at 2800 Norwich. Mother and her parents and siblings lived with her grandmother, Minnie R Demery, always referred to by everyone as Granny Demery.

* * * * *

Mother was in the fourth or fifth grade. It was the middle of the Great Depression. Dessie and Granddaddy would give mother and her sisters, Irene and Dot, a nickel for lunch. They were so hungry they would spend the nickel for food on the way to school and would be hungry all day. She went to Glynn Academy

High School and quit school in the eleventh grade to marry Daddy. She won all the spelling bees and loved school. She was on the girls' basketball team. She was a beautiful girl, but she didn't date much. That may be because she met Ken Mobley when she was so young. She was a freshman when she met Daddy. They were at a wiener roast with other friends at Freda Spell's house. Louise Raulerson, her best friend introduced her to him. Louise was part of the family and years later would go with us on our family vacations. The first night they met, Daddy said he was going to marry her and she didn't stand a chance. At one time, they were in a car and Daddy was standing on a running board and threatened to jump off and kill himself if she didn't marry him. That was the first of many threats over the next fifty years. Mother begged him not to jump. Louise was later heard to say she should have let him jump.

My grandparents on my mother's side, Virgie Demery Walling, lived directly across the street from us. We called her "Dessie" and my grandfather Raymond Alton Walling "Granddaddy." They were very loving souls, gentle folks, and I don't remember Granddaddy ever taking a drink. I had never thought about it until writing this book, but I think I'm more like Dessie than anyone. She was a determined woman and occasionally she'd even have a drink, especially when we were out at a party. Not only that but she was a strong woman, and she loved us all except she loved her son, Alton, more. That was okay. We all loved Alton best.

Dessie's mother I knew well. She was Minnie but was called by all the grandchildren as Grannie Demery. She died after Arlie and I were married. We have a gallery of ancestors on our home office with each of their pictures. Grannie Demery's husband, Edward Elmo Demery, died in 1917; she died in 1967, fifty years later. I wish I had asked her about her husband. Granddaddy was kind, gentle, and easygoing and never had a bad word to say about anyone. Alton is so much like him; Mother only remembers her father saying "damn" one time. And Arlie is like him, such a lovely man to get to live with.

By the end of the Depression, Raymond got a job at Hercules, a local industry. He remained there until his death in 1960 of lung cancer due to asbestos. He had a hard death. He was going to a chiropractor who took an x-ray and told him he couldn't help him he needed to go to a medical doctor. He went to a local doctor and he told him he didn't find anything. He kept saying he was sick and mother found him in the floor one day. He had continued to go to a local doctor who continued to say nothing was wrong with him. The next week, he went to Jacksonville and they diagnosed lung cancer and he was dead within three months. I went with Arlie to the hospital and showed him my engagement ring. He was so happy for us, but all we could all think about is that Granddaddy would not be around to go to the wedding.

Arlie spent a lot of time with Dessie. He said, "I don't know why I went so much but she was fun. She always had a pot of coffee going and always wanted to talk. Sometime many years later Dessie married Tim who was a shrimper and had his own shrimp boat. Tim got along well with the family and took everyone out on his shrimp boat when they asked. He and Dessie had completely different personalities, but they got along well. She helped him begin to save money and having a normal life. Dessie was a pistol who didn't mind giving you her opinion.

As a foot note to this reference to our Demery side of the family in 2014, Brannon Walling, one of my first cousins, sent his DNA to ancestory.com. What an interesting outcome. In November 2014, he called us to come have dinner with our new cousin Vergil Demery and his wife, Angie. A great-grandson of our great-great uncle. an uncle we never even knew we had. Granny Demery, my mother's mother, was born in 1886 and died in 1967 six years after I married Arlie. So I knew her for twenty-four years. Her husband, Edward Elmo Demery was born in 1878 and died in 1917. They had four children, Dessie (my grandmother), Pat, Mary, and Ed. Okay, perhaps based on Uncle Ed's story, Elmo was not his father but his rescuer. It turns out that Elmo was black and as my new cousin, Vergil, put it, he was in Brunswick "passing." For the first time, I saw pictures of Elmo's brothers and sisters—eight of them less than a couple of hundred miles away, and as far as the family knew, they didn't exist. What a terrible thing for he and my great-grandmother, keeping their secret all those years. Or perhaps she didn't know and how terrible for Elmo if that were the case. It is so good that times have changed. I wish I had talked with her about our great-grandfather. Arlie and I have visited Vergil and Angie in their lovely home, and hopefully life will get simpler and we'll have some time to really get to know them.

In the next ten years, Mother would have three more children, Debbie, Ricky, and Brian. Debbie was born in 1951, when I was eight, and I thought we had a new doll to play with. Debbie was a beautiful baldheaded baby who later developed the most gorgeous blond curls, and she was the pet of us all. Granny especially loved Debbie and would urge her to spend as much time as possible with her. Debbie loved to spend the night—we later found that she and Granny would bring bars of chocolate to bed and watch anything Debbie wanted to watch on television. It was a very special relationship. We all loved to visit Granny and her fine country cooking, but there is no doubt that Debbie had the inside track. Arlie loved her like a sister or perhaps a daughter. We took her at about age fourteen or fifteen for her first plane ride. Debbie married Larry Youngner and they had a beautiful daughter Andi.

When Ricky was born, his face was terribly red. It would become even redder when he cried. Granddaddy Walling thought we should throw out a pan and name him the sound it made. He convinced us that's what the Chinese did. Mother held out for the name Ricky. We find it interesting now that she didn't give him a more formal name of Richard. Ricky was always known for his sweet nature. He loved everyone and from an early age he loved his beer. He is the only person I've ever heard of who got a traffic ticket for running a red light while riding his bicycle to work. He had earlier had his license revoked for driving intoxicated. He later married a girl named Chris, and they had a daughter, Shana, whom he loved dearly. After the divorce, he came back to Brunswick and eventually went to work as a firefighter, which he loved. After his first bout with brain cancer, he had to give up this job he loved but came to enjoy a dispatcher position with the fire department. After many ups and downs, he died at fifty-five. His last fifteen years were spent with surgeries, chemo, and radiation. The doctor said when he died that the cancer was gone, but he died from the effects of the treatment! A year or so before his death, he had to stay with mother. Debbie and I were over constantly giving him advice he didn't want. We would put his pills together every week with him looking us over and insisting we were going to kill him by mixing up his pills. We would hear him say many times "No, I don't take those but once a day" and "No, not those in the morning. I'd be sleeping all day" and "Didn't you just do those?"

We had to admit he was better at it then we were, but secretly he got a kick out of badgering us about our ineptness. Right before his death, I was cutting his hair in mother's backyard when I saw a screw in the top of his head. We took him to the surgeon. He got the biggest kick out of me answering the receptionist.

"What is the doctor seeing him for today?" the reception said.

"He has a screw loose," I answered.

"Oh no," she said smiling, immediately taking up for him. "I think he's fine." Ricky, sitting in the wheelchair next to me, smiles sweetly as it looks like I'm making fun of him. "No seriously, he has the top of a screw coming out of a hole in the top of his head." I'm trying my best to explain it as Ricky continues making faces like I'm crazy.

The same thing happened when we get back with the doctor. "So what can I do for you today?" he asked Ricky. Ricky looks at me and nods as if to say, "Go ahead."

I have the same conversation with the doctor and finally said, "Just stand up and look at the top of his head."

"Well, you are right. He does have a loose screw!" he exclaims.

The doctor told us he would be better to leave it since it wasn't hurting him. Putting him under anesthesia and exposing his brain to the elements could cause more problems. As we were leaving and passing some of the young, pretty women in the office, Ricky said, "Let's show them my screw." He had lots of fun with that screw until he died later that year.

I was at the Navy League's Sea Air Space in 2005 when Ricky had to be taken to the hospital by ambulance. Ironically, one of the men who came with the ambulance was a firefighter he worked with. Debbie called me crying. "They say they can't do anything to help Ricky and he is going to be dismissed but he can't walk or get out of bed. We must find a place for him to live. Mother can't take care of him. She can't lift him out of the chair and get him to a bathroom."

Debbie told me not to come home, that she would check out some of the assisted living places in Brunswick. She called me later just sobbing, and she cried the entire time she was touring each of the places. I know because I was on the phone during those times. No one there was his age. She had already talked to the doctor who told her he had to be within six months of dying to go to hospice, and he couldn't say he was. She didn't know what to do. She called in her pastor from St. Mark's, Pastor Tula. She talked to Ricky and he told her he was ok to go to hospice, but he wanted to be able to take his seizure medicine. He also told her he had prayed, and she told Debbie she was comfortable that his soul was with God. I decided to leave the Navy League's Sea Air Space meetings and come home.

Once home, we again called the doctor to try to convince him that we needed hospice. We tried to convince him that they might have a "respite" program to relieve the caregivers for a few days. We had to find a way to take care of him for a couple of weeks for us to make arrangements. The doctor finally said, "I'll ask hospice to see you. If you can convince them, I'll sign the papers."

I then went to Ricky. He was asleep, so I just leaned over him to whisper that I was there.

"Boo!" he said when I got close. Scared the s—— out of me!

"Ricky, we are taking you to hospice. Do you know what that means?"

"Yes, it means I'm dying," he said.

"No, it means you are getting a new doctor. God is going to be your doctor and he will make all the decisions about what happens to you now. They will not continue to give you medication except for pain. Are you okay with that?"

"Yes," he said.

We took him to hospice an hour later. He still had not opened his eyes. He never did. He went into a coma. We could not get him back. We called his daughter, Shana, who lived in Michigan. She was there in just a few hours. She got in bed with him and he died that evening after she arrived. He was waiting for her. He died not six months later but twenty-four hours later. Doctors really don't know when someone's time is near.

I called Emory University and told them Ricky wanted to leave his brain to science. He had suffered with cancer these fifteen years and wanted to help someone. His body was sent to Emory after the funeral.

Brian was the baby. In 1955 when Mom was pregnant with Brian she told dad she wanted to stay home from church on a Wednesday night prayer meeting. He told her she had to go to church anyway. She realized she had begun bleeding but that didn't matter. She could rest after church. When she got home her water broke, and she delivered Brian that night. Ricky and Brian were wonderful together. When Brian got to be about six, they were the same height and did everything together. Brian was always a little quieter than the others. We didn't know what demons he was dealing with as the one left home. Now we all look back and think what hell he must have endured being left at home with Mom for them to deal with it all alone. Brian's biggest recollection of Daddy is that he got off from work at Hercules at 3:30 a.m. every day, and as a young boy of six to seven, he dreaded that time.

Brian never married—although we loved his partner, Chris, whom he was with for fifteen years. He and Chris are still friends to this day. He has a wicked and funny and had a dry sense of humor. He sent the obituary for his dear cat to me:

> *Allie Mobley died today after a brief illness. She was 15. (84 in human years.) She was survived by her father Brian Mobley and brother Pumpkinhead Mobley. Allie was adopted at the Atlanta Humane Society and a lifelong resident of Atlanta living all her life indoors. She was interred in a shallow unmarked grave 15 minutes ago. Active pallbearer was her father Brian and services were watched from the window by her brother Pumpkinhead.*
>
> *RIP Allie*

It showed his compassion even though it was done tongue in cheek.

The addition of our two brothers and sister were the links that bonded us all together. They all turned out to be wonderful loving people My brother, Kenny, worked with me on remembering all those family issues—and helped me write some of the family stories. Kenny died suddenly on July 9, 2016. He fought alcoholism his entire adult life. One of the things Kenny was most proud of was the publishing of his book *Bubba Goes to Alabama.*

Long after my brothers and sister had moved away from my parents, my sister and I convinced Mom she was an intelligent woman and had her own place in the world. She had more to offer than just being a maid and servant to our father. My mom was typical of women in post WWII, and prior, "a woman's place is in the kitchen" was and still is the attitude of some men today. Her business was raising children, washing clothes, cleaning house, and cooking. We didn't want Mother to end up like Granny Mobley, so Debbie, my sister, and I took on a mission to liberate mother. I hired her in one of my gift stores and that and her strength in "defying" Daddy gave her confidence and I think a more content life. She seemed to love getting involved with the public and meeting new people and looked after my business as no other did. I later added her sister, Irene Franklin, and my daughter, Leslie, and we had a wonderful time working in retail.

Later she would travel with my husband and me, and with her longtime friend Louise Raulerson, where she saw for the first time: Paris, New York City, Las Vegas, California, a lovely Alaskan cruise. And all the while, Daddy was setting in his recliner taking his pills, grumbling to himself, wondering what had happened to mother with this independence and who would wait on him. This is in the '70s when many women, like mother, were finding their own identity away from their spouses. Unfortunately, those chauvinistic attitudes toward women are still alive and well today although much rarer, and my election to national president and a lawsuit I would later file for sex discrimination are two of examples of these attitudes.

When Dad was about fifty-two years old, Mother wanted to go to Jacksonville with Louise to visit their girlfriend. Dad threatened if she did, he would quit work and retire. She did and he quit that day. She should have known better than to disobey him. As an added punishment, he made sure he drew a larger retirement by not protecting mother and signing the clause that would cover her with a reduced amount in the event of his death. There was a ten-year period where he was too young to draw social security, and had he died during that time, Mother would have had nothing. On Saturday, August 24, 2002, my sister, Debbie, wrote the following:

> *Daddy, all five of your children have taken a step of faith. Now you hold the power to change their lives—belief or nonbelief—literally in some case the difference in heaven and hell—does prayer really work?—five lives—six, counting Mother—at a cross road in their lives. Which road will you lead them down? As we've said before words are useless. A changed life will speak for a life time. How will you be remembered? THIS is your testimony. I was worried at first about how it would affect everyone if we turn this over to God and nothing happened. I realized I had to have faith and believe myself God is powerful enough. Only thing left is your will to change to let go and ask God to take away the anger or hurt that you have been burdened with. If this hurt and anger are bigger than you, then ASK FOR AND GET HELP. But you know all the scripture, you just have to let it penetrate to your heart instead of your brain. Mother can't fake happiness or keep the trust a secret. She's tried before not to let us know but we do know—its written all over her face. And true happiness and peace will also be written on her face for all us all to see. I believe this is THE most important time in your life and in our lives. The power you hold—to help your children choose love over hate, life over death, good over evil. Choose God.*

He died on July 9, 2005, at eighty-two years old and mother lived on a reduced income until her death nine years later on June 9, 2014. Thankfully, Arlie and I could help them with a new house and better furnishings and the fun trips for Mother.

CHAPTER FIVE

Finding Lasting Love

In the winter of 2011, my husband, Arlie, pulled out a trunk out of the guest room closet. It had been there ever since we moved to our home in 1974 but it was locked, and we had forgotten about it. I came in from work one day and he had the trunk out and had broken the lock. He was dressed in his boxer shorts, a white T-shirt and his black socks. It was so hot, he was perspiring. He could hardly wait for me to come upstairs and in the room. "Just sit down," he said. "I want you to read something out loud to me." Then he gave me a letter he had written to me in 1960, fifty years earlier. I read it out loud and he then produced one that I had written him. He said, "I don't look very sexy right now but I need a hug." He looked very appealing.

We pulled all the letters out. For about five months before we married we wrote each other every day. I put them in date order and read a couple. I was amazed and thought my next few weeks would be caught up with reading these wonderful love letters. But things got busy and I gave a few to my mom to read with the comment that "Don't worry, Mother, they can't be too personal. We were both virgins, and although we loved each other and did our share of making out, there would be nothing embarrassing."

She begged to differ a couple of weeks later. She returned them and suggested that I not share them with anyone else until we had reviewed them. She said, "Sheila these letters are pretty personal. I was a little embarrassed reading them. I wouldn't let anyone else see them until you have read them."

In May, we talked about having our fiftieth wedding anniversary. We didn't want the formal dinners, we didn't want a "hassle" of invites and planning—and we really couldn't afford anything elaborate with the decline in the business at the store. We decided when the time came we'd just go out to dinner somewhere. One day, we were reminiscing about how we met at Twin Oaks. The more we talked about the fun of having friends and family together fifty years after we met at Twin Oaks to celebrate with us it sounded pretty good. We thought there would be obstacles. They didn't stay open at night. But one day I was coming from a chamber meeting on St. Simons Island and decided to stop by Twin Oaks and see if they would have a private party. They were most accommodating and it was decided.

We started making a list. How could we not invite so many of our friends we love dearly who had been such a part of our lives? Friends we have shared so much with. But every name we wrote down expanded the list to five more couples. So we reconsidered. "How about we invite just family and those in the wedding?" I asked Arlie. Arlie wanted to include those he had worked with at the funeral home when we were dating. Believe it or not, there were four still alive and three were still working. And with that, I wanted to invite those I work with now. It was settled.

Our daughter, Leslie, advised us that she, Blaire (our granddaughter-in-law), and our granddaughter, Norah, would do all the planning. And they did! I do, however, wish those girls in the family could cut a straight line. While this has always been the case, I have learned to be less critical and find some amount of humor and love looking at those programs with everything just so but the adhesive pages they had cut out to fit in the book slightly crooked.

It was also decided that Arlie would begin by telling how we met and why we were meeting at Twin Oaks. As he told it (which was correct), he was at the Bijou Theater. I was fourteen at the time and was there with my next-door neighbors, the Meltons. He walked by the aisle on the way to the concession stand. I was bored anyway and was polishing my fingernails. I walked to the lobby, looked at him—he looked back, and we both looked hard and I returned to my seat. I'm thinking *What a nice-looking boy* but not expecting to ever see him again.

We both left with our friends and, later, again, saw each other at Twin Oaks Drive-In. I remember David Bluestein and Archie Davis II from McIntosh County introducing us at the car as we were parked close to each other. McIntosh County is the adjoining county and home of Arlie's friends from North Carolina. I thought he lived in Darien since he was with them. I never dreamed he was a sailor. He knew many Darien teenagers and lived in Darien part of the time. The Parks, family friends, in Darien had lived in Seagrove, North Carolina, Arlie's hometown many years ago. They welcomed him in their home and treated him like a son.

Arlie found out where I went to church and the next Sunday he was there. He continued to come to church for several weeks. I was fourteen and in the church choir. This had nothing to do with my talents as a singer. In fact, I was awful. But daddy was happy when I did anything in the church and it was a chance to make Daddy happy. Arlie's best friend, Tom Hanlon was Catholic, so Arlie dropped him off at the Catholic church and drove down Norwich Street to my church.

I am in church one Sunday morning sitting in the choir and Arlie walks in. I can remember so well, sitting in the choir and choir member and Mom's good friend Freddie Thompson, saying, "Get your lipstick on, that sailor is back!" And Peggy Ann Moore gave me hers! We never had a real date, but we went with other couples and with chaperones and with church groups to various church functions. Who could resist a man with a 1941 Ford Coupe? It was immaculate. The front seat had plenty of room for three—we always had four with us. *And* white floor mats with never a spot on them. We rode around with the car full many times. We were always enamored with each other but there was no real date and certainly no commitment.

The Rainbow Girls was a wonderful organization that should be one of the good memories, but it was not. Mom and Dad were both active. Dad was in the Masons, later becoming the Master of the Lodge, and Mom in the Eastern Star. It only made sense for their oldest child, a girl, to join the Rainbow Girls. A religious organization that would reinforce the good things she had been taught

This was a time in Brunswick when sailors were, well, not trusted with the local girls. But evidently, I was seen talking to Arlie somewhere and I was blackballed because I "dated sailors." It was devastating at the time, and Mother and I never forgot it. The irony was that we didn't date—he only went on church social outings. Years later the adult leader and instigator of my blackball died. I remember how bad that time was. I guess it one of the "miscarriages of justice" that makes us all stronger for other "trials and tribulations." That was a situation where I didn't even get the chance for someone to say, "What are you doing here?" But they surely decided I shouldn't be asked to be there.

(As a big supporter of our military community, I am so glad that the stigma is not present now. It might be in some places, but the opposite is more the case. Our military men and women are the best this country produces, and that is now recognized in our cities and towns across the county.)

Arlie was transferred to Bermuda for a year. We were both dating others by then. I was now the ripe old age of sixteen and fell in love twice before I saw him again. He tells me later, "I didn't fall in love with anyone else."

One day about sixteen months after we had seen each other he showed up at church. I thought about Freddie telling me about the lipstick and my heart started pounding. We started real dating! It's 1960, and he has now upgraded to a 1953 cream-colored Ford. Again, it was immaculate. You just can't say no to a man with a pretty, clean car. We dated for a year. A typical date cost about five dollars. That included gas, movie (unless we went to the drive in and that was only one dollar for as many as you could get in the car), popcorn, coke, and eating hamburger steaks at the Pig & Whistle. The hamburger steak dinner costs one dollar, which includes the meat, baked potato, salad, dessert, and tea. We never talked about marriage but in general what we wanted out of life. And we did a lot of kissing. My family just loved him. I always jokingly said, "My family loves him best and his family loves him best." What's not to love anyway?

Arlie left just a few weeks later. My teachers became a big part of my planning and happiness during the next few months while Arlie was in Nashville, Tennessee.

He was attending John A. Gupton School a Mortuary Science, a part of Vanderbilt University.

I was one of the first to get married and they all talked about playing house and being grown up with a real husband. That's all I wanted anyway. To get married, have children, and be a secretary. We wrote each other every day the year we were separated. Mac was the name I called him the first half of our marriage. These are excerpts from a couple of those letters. So many letters expressed a desire for just one phone call but it was too expensive. We even talked about not saying "I love you" so the operator wouldn't cut us off. Some of the letters the weeks before the wedding were pretty steamy. but were not included.

It's been a wonderful fifty years. We've been blessed with a close-knit family, a beautiful daughter, Leslie, a beautiful and sweet granddaughter, Norah, and a wonderful grandson, Ryan. Ryan had the good sense to find Blaire and they have produced remarkable creations by the name of Rayne. Rayne's birth made mother a great-great-grandmother and us great-grandparents, but we've forgiven them for that.

Since then Norah had a beautiful girl, Kylie.

The day of the fiftieth anniversary party my daughter Leslie and her daughter, Norah, brought the programs that my grandson Ryan's wife, Blaire, had worked on. They had pictures and scrapbooks, music, flowers, and such. We sat down to discuss the agenda. Arlie was going to welcome everyone and was to tell the story "How I met your mother." I would read the "What happened in 1961," the list of those in the wedding and Leslie would finish with thanks to all. Then Norah said, "Mimi, I can do that. I could read what you are reading." I was surprised and had her do it, and she did a remarkable job. At seventeen she was smart enough, but I didn't know she would have what it takes to stand before fifty people and project! She began and continued as master of ceremonies. I ended up just reading those two letters we had picked out that we wrote each other, along with a letter my sister Debbie sent to Arlie (known as Max and Mac at that time).

When Norah looked over the popular songs for 1961, she said, "I have never heard of any of them."

"Of course, you have," I told her.

Then, Leslie and I started singing them as she read the names beginning with "Twist and Shout," "Killing Me Softly," "Great Balls of Fire," "Under the Boardwalk," and many Elvis songs. Norah started joining in—she knew them all! Amazing the great songs we had back then. I often wonder what the legacy will be for the songs of today. Is there any chance they'll be singing those in thirty years? I hope not.

We did the same at the party and by the time we had read and sang the first line of three or four songs everyone at the anniversary party were singing at the top of their lungs. Those '60s songs remain good today. I asked everyone to introduce themselves and tell everyone their connection to us that evening. My first cousin, Eve, was our flower girl and now she is a grandmother. Debbie, my sister, a junior bridesmaid and she too is a grandmother. Alice Joy and Phyllis were two of my bridesmaids and both are great-grandmothers. When Ryan's time came he surprised us with eloquent and endearing remarks and told everyone how blessed we were to have this close-knit family and friends. Leslie read her prepared notes—without standing up due to her phobias. They were poignant, loving, and emotional for us.

These are her words:

> *When I think about luck and love all I have to do is look at my life. Mom and Dad chose to be my parents. I was not expected, I was selected, as my birth announcement said. I cannot imagine who would have adopted me, what kind of life I would have had. All things happen for a reason. They adopted me, loved me and raised me even though that was not an easy task, to say the least. But we will not talk about that. Because they adopted me, I met the people I did which in return gave me a son that has brought nothing but love to my life. When everything was going wrong, I had this precious life depending on me to love him and take care of him. Then later in life I had a mother's true joy, a daughter who has opened my eyes in ways I cannot describe! This also made Mom and Dad proud grandparents. Mom and Grandma came to Texas when Ryan was born and came into my hospital room with the big fake black rimmed glasses with the big noses and said, "Does he look like our side of the family?" When little Norah was born, Mom stayed in the room the entire time. Ask her that story sometimes. She held Norah before I did, and when Grandma Nora found out I had named her after her and Mom (Norah Diann) she squealed, "I never have liked my name until now!" When I look at my family and realize I could have missed all of this if Mom and Dad had a second thought and not gone through the adoption.*
>
> *I am truly blessed and thank God, every day for bringing these two people together in life because without them I would not be the woman I am today. I have my Mother's sense of business, and her courage to stand up for what I believe, my Dad's smile and his caring heart and love for animals, my grandmother's ability to cook and how to be a grandma myself, and my granddaddy's temper. I am all of these people wrapped in one which is the making for one hell of a woman. I think you so much for loving me and choosing me to be yours and standing by me no matter what the cost, for being beside me through all the illnesses and surgeries. You are both my strength.*

Oh, and without me you would not be great-grandparents, right? You forgive Ryan I am sure because what a precious miracle we have in little Rayne. And bless Blaire for putting up with all our madness.

Leslie

I'm glad we expanded our dinner for two for this lovely gathering.

CHAPTER SIX

A Chance to Lead in the Navy League Major changes in my life and how did I ever get in retail

I started working for Concrete Products in 1967. I loved that job. However, when the new president came in around 1980 he didn't want a woman doing my job. That story and my lawsuit are in a separate account.

I never thought any good would come of this horrible situation, but it did get me to Camden County and began another life supporting our sea services in a much bigger way. My girlfriend, Miriam Tollison, talked me into retail. I don't know why I did it. I hate shopping. I'm in and out as quick as I can if I must buy something, but when you've had the rug pulled out from under you, your mind doesn't think properly. Every minute you are desperate to find out what you are going to do with your life. Miriam and I opened a small kiosk in the Brunswick Mall. A major fire destroyed the mall and our store. Another location was in the Glynn Place Mall, another in the Emmeline and Hesse Marina, and one day I decided to look at Camden County.

It was 1984 and the Navy had come to town just six years earlier, in 1978. Everything seemed to be bustling. I wanted a Hallmark store but when I called Hallmark headquarters I couldn't get anyone to talk with me. So when I met with Mike Akel, the landlord at Kings Bay Village Shopping Center, I added to my lease that I was the only one who could open a Hallmark store in that center. A few years later within a week or so, various people stopped by the store telling the staff that they were considering locating at the shopping center. One of them said they were thinking about adding a Hallmark store to the center. I called Mike and reminded him of the addition to my lease. He had forgotten but immediately gave me the name of the gentleman from Hallmark that he was working with. When I called the gentleman from Hallmark, he was reticent about discussing a store with me. He told me he had retailers in Jacksonville and Brunswick who were already interested. I told him about my lease and I suggested he call the landlord. The next day he called. "Mrs. McNeill, where would you like to meet? We can meet in Atlanta, Brunswick or St. Marys."

I replied, "St. Marys would be more convenient and we can meet at my store."

A couple of weeks later, the day came and Arlie decided he would join me and visit some Navy League members in Camden. Arlie was one of the group that started the Navy League in Camden County. When the Hallmark representative came into my store they went immediately to Arlie. Arlie is such a great guy. He can talk to anyone and it never dawned on him that they thought he was the owner. They talked at length, and finally the Hallmark representative said, "Arlie, where would you like to go to sit down and discuss this?"

"Oh, I don't have anything to do with Sheila's business, you'll have to ask her."

And *then* they turned to me. Talk about a "what are you doing here?" moment!

I became a fixture in Camden County and made many friends. Many things happened over those twenty-eight years. One was getting involved with Navy League. Although I'd been a Navy Leaguer since 1966, Camden is where I really got involved. When Arlie and I were members of the Glynn County council, it was in early sixties and women did not have leadership roles.

I attended a Camden Kings Bay Council meeting. Dr. Bew, a local anesthesiologist, was president. At my first meeting, I noticed that women were taking a part in the meeting. That was a surprise to me since that was not the case in the Brunswick council. I started attending meetings and one night the program was Dr. Bew's own home movies of his vacation in the Bahamas. I was surprised and asked him if he had a program chairman. He answered, "No, why do you think I'm showing my home movies?" I asked him if I could be his program chairman. He was delighted. I never stopped after that. I had done the same thing for the Brunswick–Golden Isles Council, but everything was through Arlie. He even had me introduce the speakers. He was always supportive!

I reached out to high-level speakers. After all, this was the Naval Submarine Base Kings Bay! And over the next few years we had secretary of the Navy, John Dalton, chief of naval operations, Mike Boorda, Senator Sam Nunn, and others.

After Arlie's tour as council president he was appointed state president. He had one of the first state meetings in 1991 and used the facilities at Kings Bay for the meeting. The theme for this event was "Lessons learned from the Persian Gulf." Captain John Nuremberger, the commanding officer of Kings Bay, was the keynote speaker as was his counterparts, Captain Dean M. Hendrickson, commander of Carrier Air Wing 17 on the USS *Saratoga*, and Colonel Paul J. Kern, commander of the Fifth Battalion, Thirty-Second Armor, Twenty-Fourth Mechanized Infantry Division of Fort Stewart—and to top it off, Rear Admiral W. Ted Leland, chief of the Office of Law Enforcement and Defense Operations for the Coast Guard. (Paul and I would meet again at Kings Bay when he accompanied Secretary of Defense Perry as a Lt. General.)

1993: Bill Kelley, national president of the Navy League, spoke to NL in Camden January 1993. His wife, Nancy, came with him. More of that in the stories portion.

1994: I was elected as president of the council. In a first and an indication of the wonderful relationship with our military Captain Chuck Ellis, former commanding officer of NSB Kings Bay, was my vice president and Judy Ellis, his wife, was treasurer. Sherry Schlosser as secretary and Jim Wells as judge advocate rounded out the team.

Arlie became state president, then region president, and I followed in his footsteps with every job. We joked during that time that we were the only state and region president sleeping together. We were a good team. We don't know of an instance where both husband and wife reported to one another. This first was once reported in an article in *Seapower* magazine. I urged Arlie to run for national office when he completed his region position, but he was not interested. He encouraged me to do so.

We made some remarkable friends that included RADM Arleigh and Bonnie Campbell. Although they were in Charleston, as were RADM Stan and Ellie Bump, they were in Camden often and we visited them in their quarters (homes) many times. During that time—the mid to late '80s, early '90s—there were about seven or eight commanding officers we were close to. We remain friends with most of them today. We put together a trip to Brunswick and St. Simons for all the captains. We were able to get rooms comp'd at the new hotel at the Glynn Place Mall and toured Brunswick and the islands over that weekend. What a great time we had.

Rosemary Ellis enlisted me for the local Navy Ball Committee while RADM Ellis started the Navy League off with a bang as the guest speaker in January.

On January 29, 1994, the USS *Tennessee* (SSBN734) and its crew were honored with the US Atlantic Fleet Ballistic Missile Submarine Outstanding Performance Award for 1993. RADM Ellis and I presented the award. It was a real honor for me to participate in the program. Community involvement had been an attribute of the Tennessee crew. Since adopting St. Marys Elementary in 1990, more than 2,600 volunteer hours had been logged at the school. The school was recognized in 1992 as a National Blue Ribbons School of Excellence.

The *Southeast Georgian* covered the event and said,

> *Sheila McNeill, Kings Bay Camden Navy League president said the fleet ballistic missile submarines assigned to Kings Bay are the best in the nation. To be selected as the best of these very best is quite an accomplishment. On behalf of the National President Evan Baker, The Navy League councils of Groton, Connecticut*

and Charleston. S.C., and as president of the Camden Kings Bay Council, I am deeply honored to participate in the presentation of the 1993 U.S. Atlanta fleet Ballistic Missile Submarine Outstanding Performance Award to the USS Tennessee.

The USS *Tennessee*, the first Trident II submarine to arrive at Kings Bay, has achieved honors for the efforts of both the blue and gold crews. Captain Hahnfeldt, blue crew commanding officer and Captain George Jurand, gold crew commanding officer spoke on behalf of the crews.

Also in February was Senator Nunn's visit to our Navy League at Kings Bay. The entire story is under Nunn in the stories section.

It was time to say goodbye to the submarine tender USS *Canopus*. Congressman Jack Kingston was the principal speaker. Captain C. J. Ihrig, departing commanding officer, said, "The crew of *Canopus* is the very definition and benchmark of submarine support. The leadership of the submarine force uses this crew as the yardstick in measuring a successful submarine tender. Never have I served with such a group of hard workers and talented, expert professionals more dedicated in ensuring readiness of tended submarines as well as the readiness and success of their own ship."

RADM Ellis said submarine tenders are not the most glamorous or exciting ships in the Navy, but they have been an integral and essential component of the strategic submarine force from the beginning. For almost twenty-nine years now, USS *Canopus* has been a most important member of our strategic deterrent team. *Canopus* has not only supported Squadron 16 in a most outstanding matter but also has provided superb services to submarines of other squadrons including fast attacks and both the Sturgeon and Los Angeles class.

US congressman Jack Kingston was on hand to recognize the accomplishments of USS *Canopus* and its crew. "We spend a lot of time in Congress worrying about the Base Realignment Committee and a lot of time defending people and places that need to stay open," he said. "In this unsafe world of ours we want to be ready at a moment's notice."

Just a week later, Canopus honored Captain Jack Mead, executive officer, who was retiring after thirty-five years. Jack was a Georgia native and he and his wife, Vickie, decided to stay in the area when Jack retired. Vicki, a registered nurse, had worked both in Camden and Nassau Counties. "I feel like I've come home after all the years I was away from Georgia," he said. "I'm very comfortable here and I want to be a member of this community. There's no place I'd rather live." See their story and our friendship in the stories section.

Arlie and I were invited to fly to Norfolk and sail on the USS *Canopus* (submarine tender/repair ship) for their last voyage to Kings Bay. It was an extraordinary opportunity. He and the executive officer, CDR Mike Mair, couldn't have treated us better. We've told the story for years. We were at sea for a couple of days. The second night we had a beach party on the deck. It was a good morale booster for the crew. For the record, they not only would not put us in the same cabin, but they made sure we were on separate decks and I was told not to visit his cabin.

We received a return letter from Captain Ron Glover:

Dear Sheila and Arlie,

What great cruisers! Thanks for making CANOPUS' final voyage a more enjoyable adventure. The two of you added a lot of success of the Norfolk to Kings Bay trip. Thanks for the book "In Praise of Sailors" I especially like the last poem in the book page 288. "Sea-Fever." It kind of explains how I felt as when we brought CANOPUS to her moor for the last time; maybe my last time at sea… "I must go down to the seas again…"

Thank you,
Ron

Ron and Charlotte continued to be our friends, although we live too far apart to see each other. I do run into Ron at the airport frequently, and that is always a treat.

The British submarine HMS *Vanguard*—the very first to come to Kings Bay—arrived in April. We began the great mission of having fun with the British crew. We were pleased that RADM Ellis embraced the Navy League and offered them the chance to cohost this event. I received a letter from commanding officer Captain D. J. Russell, that shows "just a little" of the fun time we had.

Dear Sheila

On behalf of my officers and crew I would like to thank the Navy League for providing such a warm and earnest welcome right at the start of VANGUARD's first visit to King's Bay. For many of my people it was also their first visit outside Britain and the friendly Georgia welcome was greatly appreciated.

The speeches, both at the reception and after dinner, gave a clear indication of the depth, sincerity and warmth of the welcome extended to us. It was also apparent that your own role in making all of this happen cannot be overstated, evidently you devote a great deal of effort and time to this Navy League and I for one am most grateful. I should add that Tony Hewitt managed to retain his cap for the remainder of the visit and still claims he does not know how it found its way into the ladies' restroom! Once again very many thanks for your efforts on our behalf, I am only sorry that our visit was so short. Perhaps the Starboard Crew, who will be here for much longer, will make up for that.

Yours sincerely,
Daniel Russell

May brought us to the Sailor/Marine of the Year banquet. The guest speaker was a change from our usual speakers and a real boost to the program. We had BMC (SW) Joseph Wilson, the 1993 top sea sailor of the Atlantic Fleet as speaker.

That same month we were invited on board the USS *Tennessee* SSBN (734) with commanding officer Captain George Jurand. The ship had an "Honorary Submarine Qualification Card." The first four of the sixteen items for qualification were as follows:

1. Don an EAB.
2. Count the number of cylinders on the diesel engine.
3. Find the ship's position at the quartermaster's stand.
4. Look out the *Periscope.*

As you discovered, the answer you would have the applicable crew member sign the form. What a great way to get our citizens involved in a very complex submarine and her sailors. And how do they stand that cold all the time! Captain Jurand presented me with a picture of the USS *Tennessee* that remains on the wall in my office over twenty years later.

In June, we had as speaker Dr. Harold P. Smith, assistant secretary of Defense for Atomic Energy. Dr. Smith reports to the president on atomic energy issues and serves as a liaison in nuclear dismantlement negotiations.

He told the council, "I've been given a portfolio to reduce nuclear weapons during the next sixteen years of democratic rule. If we do our job correctly no one will notice. But if we fail, no one will forget. The threat of Armageddon has disappeared, but the chance of a nuclear shot from anger is much higher than during the Cold War." He said that the government is assisting the former Soviet Union by providing economic aid and federal employees in an attempt to prevent nuclear and chemical weapons from falling into the wrong hands.

He sent me a letter a week later. In that letter, he said, "This was my first interaction with the Navy League and I am impressed. The support you give to the Navy, both locally and on the national level, is outstanding. I know it means a great deal to the men and women of the Navy. And it is very important for a political appointee to see such marvelous support for our operating forces. Please extend my thanks to your members. I hope we will meet again soon—perhaps a visit to Washington is in order!"

Later in June, we had a ceremony for the departure of Squadron 16 from Kings Bay. Rear Admiral Tom Robertson, commander of Submarine Group 6 climbed aboard USS *Mariano G. Vallejo* just before the vessel pulled away from the pier and made its last voyage down the channel. The squadron was established in WWII and was decommissioned after the war. It was later reactivated and arrived at Kings Bay in 1979. RADM Ellis said the aging submarines are being decommissioned because the modern Tridents can fulfill the duties of the strategic deterrence program and meeting the changing needs of national defense. Captain John T. Byrd, commander of the deactivating squadron, expressed gratitude for the continuing hospitality shown by the local community. "I extend a hearty thanks to the community of great neighbors here in Camden County who welcomed my predecessors here back in 1979—and who have kept their arms open to every new arrival in order to make this a choice duty for all of our servicemen and their families."

Our July speaker was the very senior (in rank only, not age) Vice Admiral George W. Emory, commander of the US Atlanta Fleet Submarine Force. Vice Admiral Emory spoke on the war on drugs and said in the Caribbean the submarine force fast attacks are very much involved on a day-to-day basis in counter drug operations. He reported that between 25% and 33% of the drugs that would otherwise flow into this country are intercepted every year because of this relatively small task force, which consists of seven ships and a bunch of aircraft. The submarine contributes to this by being a covert collector of intelligence information, which is passed on to allow our Coast Guard forces, Air Force, and Navy force to intercept and apprehend illegal drugs. More and more frequently we are being asked to support special operating forces. In the Atlantic, the sub force continues to police the areas despite the end of the Cold War. He told the audience that he knows there is no intent for Russians to attack the US today; he does not worry about intent.

"Intent can change tomorrow, next year or five years from now," he said. "My responsibility is to make sure the ten years from now we still have a submarine force that can take on the best possible adversary in the world and win."

The chief of naval operations (CNO) is coming! CNO Admiral Mike Boorda is scheduled to arrive on September 8—and he did. He was the first CNO that I had speak at Kings Bay and it was nerve racking. Some of my funniest and saddest occasions were about Mike Boorda. You will read the happy and the sad in the stories section.

The Camden Kings Bay Council was named meritorious Council. Selection as a meritorious council is based on the degree to which a competing council meets the established criteria which are membership and retention, community education activities, legislative education/public affairs activities, maritime services' support, and recruiting assistant activities. This award is presented to only twenty-five councils or 5 percent of the total Navy League councils worldwide. I was proud to pick up our award in San Diego at the following meeting.

* * * * *

1995: Rear Admiral Michael Bowman had a barge outing on May 26, 1995. He and his wife, Sally, were joined by Captain Gary Williams and his wife, Linda, retired Captain Chuck Ellis and his wife, Judy (Chuck was then president of the local Navy League Council), Bryant and Ashley Black, and Arlie and me. What a lovely evening.

Commanding Officer Gary Williams had the only ceremony for area veterans in the V-E tribute. Victory in Europe commemorates the anniversary of Germany's surrender in Europe ending a grueling chapter in World War II.

Captain Mark Keven, commanding officer of Trident Training Facility at Kings Bay, gave a big open house with the note "Since you 'own' the place, this is mostly for your employees, if they so desire." Arlie and I bid for a "Las Vegas" party at TTF for his fiftieth birthday back in 1986. This was a rare opportunity and would have only happened in the '70s and '80s.

In June 1995, I was Georgia State President, the first woman in Georgia to hold a state position and our local Navy League council was named one of the meritorious councils in the world.

Things were hopping at Kings Bay as we welcomed the HMS *Victorious*, a new British submarine. We had an awesome reception for the Brits—they are such fun—and don't you love the names of those British submarines: *Vanguard*, *Victorious*, *Vigilant*, and *Vengeance*!

The USS *Maine* (SSBN 741) arrived at Kings Bay with Captain Gary Gradisnik on Saturday, August 9, 1995. I was grateful to chief of staff, Captain N. A. Marks, for asking me to be a part of the small group of area business and civic leaders to greet the ship. We began at the wardroom for Submarine Group 10 and traveled by van to the pier to greet the ship.

Commanding officer of the USS *Tennessee* (SSBN 734) was Captain Don Hahnfeldt. He wrote the book *The Heart that Beats in the Shark of Steel.*

We watched the last submarine from Squadron 16 depart with RADM Tom Robertson topside. RADM Jerry Ellis turned to us and said, "If that doesn't bring a tear to your eye, you ain't no friend of mine!"

Jim Wells, who preceded me in many of my community chairman jobs, asked if I would be the "roastee" at a fund-raiser for the local Rotary Club. In August, Captain Jack Mead, USN (R), was president of the local council and Captain Tim Giardina, commanding officer of the USS *Kentucky* (SSBN 737), hosted the Navy League tour. (Look for their full story in the stories section.)

The local Navy League council worked with the base that year and we had a partnership for the Navy ball. This was one of those "out of the box" things that RADM Jerry Ellis would do.

On October 14, 1995, the clubs of Kings Bay were transformed to create the atmosphere of the '40s. Vice Admiral Joseph Moorer (retired) was the principal speaker. VADM Moorer retired in 1980, following his tour as commander in chief, US Naval Forces, Europe. During World War II, Moorer served aboard USS *Columbus* participated in operations in the Philippines, Borneo, and Okinawa. It was the gala event of the year. We had a professional trio of beautiful women who gave a tribute to the Andrew Sisters, complete with uniforms and hairdo! They were incredible. We had a canteen with news clips from WWII, walls with posters, artifacts and displays from the era. It was a night of nostalgia and fun for everyone. The clubs of Kings Bay were bursting at the seams with 260 in attendance.

I wrote the guest column in the *Southeast Georgian* on October 3, 1995, that follows:

Camden, Navy have cohesive relationship.

> *There is a feeling of pride and a deep sense of patriotism when you hear a mention of World War II and its veterans. It brings back the memories of a past era that also brought us "Rosie the Riveter," the music of Glenn Miller, the voices of "Axis Sally," Tokyo Rose, Franklin D Roosevelt, and Winston Churchill, the hunting refrains of "Lili Marlene," and the staccato war-reporting of Edward R. Murrow. More importantly, however, it was a period that brought us a mixture of sadness and happiness, heroism and sacrifice; international infamy as well as man's unkindness and brutality and his willingness to fight to overcome them. For those of you old enough to have participated in World War II either in uniform or on the home front, I need not elaborate. For those of us too young, there remains a fascination with these important times and much to learn from them—and much for which to be thankful.*

I was thrilled on June 7, 1995, to receive an honorary lifetime membership in the Kings Bay Submarine Officers' Wives Club. What a surprise and no one could know the pleasure it gave me. It was presented by Charlotte Glover, president of the SOWC. Her husband, Ron, was commanding officer of the USS *Canopus*. Admiral Hank Chiles, commander of US Strategic Command, visited the base. This was the year he invited me to bring about thirty Navy supporters to Strategic Command. See the memories of Adm. Hank Chiles in the stories section.

In August 1995, when I was working on building the submarine museum, RADM Jerry Ellis, commanding office of Submarine Group 10 in Kings Bay called me. He wanted to nominate me for a Defense Advisory Committee under Secretary of Defense, Perry, and later, Secretary William Cohen. "Are you interested in serving on this committee?" RADM Ellis asked.

I responded, "Yes, I am. It sounds like a wonderful opportunity."

"The only problem is that you need letters of recommendation—more than just from the one who is nominating you. And you have to get them all within ten days," he told me.

I wrote to ten people hoping that I would get back three. All ten came in time. That complete story is in RADM Ellis's section.

RADM Al Konetzni spoke to the Sailor/Marine of the Year banquet. Hugh Mayberry relieved Evan Baker as national president of the Navy League.

1996: I received the appointment from the Defense Department. I had been selected for the Defense Advisory Committee on Women in the Services (DACOWITS). My first meeting was in April—just a couple of weeks after the St. Marys Submarine Museum's commissioning. From 1996 to 1998, I was consumed by the work of DACOWITS. As I look back at it, I'm amazed I was able to do anything else! It was busy but it was most rewarding. Judy Marsh, my secretary, left me that year. She was a remarkable woman and I hated to see her go, but her family was ready to move back up north. I hired Amanda Gross who would help me through those DACOWITS years!

Major General Thomas L. Wilkerson spoke at our March 1996 meeting of the Navy League, at the requests of old friends Jim Kiss and Charlie Smith starting with a reception at Jim's home. I had known Tom Wilkerson for several years. He was one of the best speakers I had heard. "The United States has succeeded in created a military that is the best that the nation has to offer," he told those present that evening. "So when talks of spending cuts come, don't talk about equipment," he said, "Talk about people and how much this country gains from these highly qualified people. All the people in the military will be better leaders in society after they are discharged. They will be disciplined, reliable, and morally upright. We must never forget that defense requires eternal vigilance." He ended with "The Navy League is a powerful force for good in our society."

1997: We continued the history of wonderful, informative speakers. January, we had Commander Dean Spratlin, one of President George H. W. Bush's rescuers. By this time, I am vice chair of DACOWITS and super busy with a good bit of traveling.

Rear Admiral Beers, commander of Submarine Group 10, spoke in February and his long history with the McNeills is also in the stories section.

Major General Ron Smith, who introduced me to Brigadier General Scott and hosted the most colorful DACOWITS visit that I made, also spoke.

Admiral Paul Reason was the speaker in May when we had our Sailor/Marine of the Year banquet. I never got to know Admiral Reason well but he was most gracious when we saw each other.

Our submarine tour for the Navy League that year was on the USS *Nebraska* (SSBN 739). The commanding officer was Captain Mel Williams who had a very distinguished career retiring as a vice admiral many years later. It was a pleasure to follow Captain Williams's career and he *always* remembered his tour at Kings Bay and the people he met here with great affection. He introduced me to many senior leaders in DC.

In August, Captain Jack Mead, USN (R), was president of the local council, and Captain Tim Giardina, commanding officer of the USS *Kentucky* (SSBN 737), hosted the Navy League tour. (Look for their full story in the stories section.)

Most of the year is covered in individual stories, but I must mention the USS *Louisiana* (SSBN 743). She arrived in great style. A long line of "food trailers" with "official" Louisiana specialties made for a wonderful reception. The commissioning was held on September 6, 1997. RADM Chuck Beers was the group commander and Jack Mead was the local council president. The ceremony was held at the drydock, which is a specular building. Look for Jack Meads story.

I was honored to speak at the World War II Shipyard workers event in Brunswick (see story).

The British ship HMS *Vigilant* came to Kings Bay in October and the commanding officer was speaker at the Navy League. Jack Mead and RADM Chuck Beers welcomed commanding officer John Tottenham to the Navy League. He gave a rousing speech. This was his second visit to Kings Bay but his first as commanding officer.

While all of this was going on, I was at the St. Marys Submarine Museum daily. This month was when the check came from Jack Schiff. The check that enabled us to open on the date we had planned. The check that made the difference.

Arlie was going to national Navy League meetings with our friend Hugh Mayberry, who would later be elected as national president of the Navy League. Arlie and Hugh would hang out with one of the senior women in the Navy League, Edith Callahan. She was a very professional and very no nonsense and climbed up the Navy League ladder to be one of the best leaders we had.

1998: My last year on DACOWITS and busier than ever.

One of the highlights of the year was the visit from Jack Schiff. The *Florida Times Union* had the headline "The Angel of St. Marys." This story is found in my 'stories' section.

In February 1998, the community has a fly-in to talk with legislators about major cutbacks.[1] Two of the submarines at Kings Bay are to be transferred to Bangor, Washington, our sister base. I believe, unlike most communities, we didn't go to

---

1 We have continued to have our Washington Fly Ins every year.

complain about the loss or to ask the legislators to try to reverse the decision. We wanted to know if there were other missions to help offset the loss. I have always believed and tried to instill that belief to others in the community that if the decision is in the best interest of the country—not a political or a budget decision—that I would not fight it. There were two significant times in my career that it was political/budget driven and we did fight both of those times: The Coast Guard budget in 2011 and the SSGN in 1996–2003.

Lynn Hudson of the *Tribune & Georgian* reports,

Camden delegation promotes Kings Bay
Camden County is going to Capitol Hill

A delegation representing Camden's business, military, education and government segments will travel to Washington, D.C. on February 10 and 11 for two days of meetings with national elected officials. The trip is being organized by the Military Community Council (MCC), a committee of the Camden Kings Bay Chamber of Commerce. MCC Chairperson, Sheila McNeill said the trip is an opportunity to promote Kings Bay Naval Submarine Base on a national level.

"This trip is about educating the Congress on the facilities and the capabilities at Kings Bay," McNeill said. "We're going to tell our story," The group has appointments with U.S. Senators Paul Coverdell and Max Cleland of Georgia as well as U.S. Rep Jack Kingston. McNeill said the group also would like to meet with military leaders at the Pentagon if their schedule permits. Chamber administrator Carla Carper said the trip signals an aggressive approach to promoting Kings Bay. "I think we've realized it's time to take a very active stand on our Navy base." She said. Carper said the group is hoping to continue educating legislators about Kings Bay before decisions are made about the future distribution of submarines and other Navy forces.

"Bangor (Wash) and Norfolk (VA) have been lobbying for years," she said. "We realized that shows there is concern and unity here," Mrs. McNeill added. "I think it's super." McNeill said the trip remains open to everyone in the community. Travel arrangements are being coordinated through the chamber office. In preparation for the visit, McNeill and others are soliciting input from a variety of groups. She plans to talk with union leaders at the base and other groups attached to the military before making the trip. The next MCC meeting also will focus on topics that will be discussed during the trip. The MCC meets on a quarterly basis with the next meeting

scheduled for Feb 2 at noon at the Clubs of Kings Bay. The meeting is open to the public. McNeill said she also is seeking input from anyone in the community She said suggested topics can be submitted to her in writing at Sheila's Hallmark in the Kings Bay Village Shopping Center.

In February, I introduced the United States Army Field Band from Washington, DC, who was performing at the Brunswick High Gym. Also in February, our new Senator, Max Cleland visited Kings Bay.

In March, I co-chaired a reception for General John M. Shalikashvili, USA (ret.), then chairman of the joint chiefs of staff for Woody Woodside of the Brunswick Golden Isles Chamber of Commerce.

In April, Congressman Jack Kingston brought in US representative Ralph Regula of Ohio, who was chairman of the congressional subcommittee that approves funding for the National Park Service. One of the projects was the purchase of two tracts of land on the island currently being held by the Nature Conservancy. They planned to sell it to the park service. I was invited to speak to the Exchange Club of Brunswick on military issues.

In May, Arlie and I traveled to Groton for RADM Malcolm Fages's change of command. He was to assume command from RADM John B. Padgett III. More on this in Malcolm and Shirley's stories.

I started serving on the advisory board of the Camden Center, the junior college in Brunswick, Camden Coastal Georgia Community College Campus with offices in Camden County. A decision was made to build a college in Camden County. The *Tribune & Georgian* ran the following editorial on June 26, 1998.

MEETING THE NEED—in our opinion

Camden Center of Coastal Georgia Community College has a solid plan in place to meet the growing educational needs of the community. What the center is lacking right now, though, is the financial backing from the community that will allow it to act on the plan. The Camden Center is planning to build a $17 million facility in Kingsland if the state Board of Regents and state legislature approves funding for the construction. In order to remain in the competitive race for college construction projects, school supporters are raising $100,000 for an endowment that must be in place before additional state funds ae allocated for the facility.

In effect, the endowment represents the community's commitment and support of the post-secondary facility. The establishment of a permanent college facility that can offer expanded academic,

> *technical and professional courses offer residents an opportunity to gain valuable knowledge, and businesses will benefit by having a better trained workforce. The Camden Center will be a vital part of Camden's future—but it needs our financial support in the present to ensure the facility is capable of growing to its fullest potential.*
>
> We were two of thousands who donated toward the college. Trish McMillan, former public affairs officer for Naval Submarine Base Kings Bay was the Director of the college during that time. She and I worked on a Wall of Honor to be located at the new college and Arlie helped with auctions! Trish and I remained friends and can see each other today and connect like it is yesterday. I don't know how we get so busy. Dr. Dorothy Lord was a new president and did so much for the college.

We celebrated the twentieth anniversary of Kings Bay on June 26 and we were able to convince Senator Max Cleland to be our speaker. He was incredible.

The week of June 30, the St. Marys Submarine Museum received a sixty-thousand-dollar grant from the state. The funds would help purchase control panels, mannequins, and many other badly needed items.

In July, we had a great party at the quarters of RADM Joe Henry who was group commander at the time. He had a farewell party for Captain Jim Alley, commanding officer of Kings Bay. Although I have not seen Jim since he left Kings Bay, Joe and I have had many opportunities to keep in touch. I spot him in a room and head to him to get caught up!

Captain Randy Zeller invited me to be the guest speaker at the 1998 Trident Refit Facility, Apprentice Graduation Ceremony on July 10. Captain Zeller was instrumental in much of my education on the facility. Over his tour, we spent many hours making sure I understood the mission and processes of the facility. Some of those initiatives that he began are still being used.

One of my biggest honor was speaking at the retirement of Command Master Chief Royal Weaver on August 7, 1998. He was in the Navy from 1974 to 1998. That story is told in my stories section.

On September 22, Captain Mike McKinnon, relieved captain T. M. (Tim) Giardina as commanding officer of USS *Kentucky*.

In October, I was asked to speak to veterans who were assigned to the USS *Cory*. It was an incredible evening. I believe it was my first time to speak to veterans and I was relieved by the reception I received. It was a poignant evening. And that month I was relieved as co-chair of the Military Community Council by Jack Gross.

I spoke to the seniors at our church, Norwich Street Baptist Church. There were about 40 percent, including my mother. As I remember, I talked too long. My mother couldn't believe I knew all "that stuff."

Arlie auctioned at the fund-raiser for the St. Marys Submarine Museum and new Commanding Officer of the base Captain Frank Stagl and his wife, Mary, were in attendance. We asked Frank to talk a little about the museum and he did a wonderful job.

The National Capitol Council of the Navy League has an annual cruise on the Potomac. Joan Jones, the executive director and moving force behind so many projects of the National Capitol Council, invited me to join them. In the middle of all this, my retail store sponsored a luncheon for couples married 50 years or longer. What a nice day.

I closed out my three years on DACOWITS in December.

1999: I don't know where I got this from, but it started my scrapbook for 1999.

Prayer for today: *Dear Lord, so far today, I've done all right. I haven't gossiped, haven't lost my temper, haven't been greedy, grumpy, nasty, selfish, or overindulgent. I'm very thankful for that. But in a few minutes, God, I'm going to get out of bed. And from that moment on, I'm probably going to need a lot more help!*

At our first Navy League meeting of the year, national president of the Navy League Hugh Mayberry spoke and swore in our new council president, Frank Frasca, who relieved Mike Flenniken. I am now the Navy League region president for Georgia, South Carolina, and North Carolina.

On January 16, I had the opportunity to meet John Amos, who played on *Good Times* television show for years, at the Rev. Martin Luther King Jr. Memorial banquet celebration in Camden County. This was a wonderful way to first meet him. I saw him at several events in DC in later years when was on the television series *The West Wing*. He played the role of chairman of the joint chiefs of staff. He and John Thorne, Public Affairs for the US Coast Guard, were good friends. I tried to talk him into getting the writers of *The West Wing* to add in a line as he was going to the car. "I have to leave now, I'm on the way to a Navy League meeting." He jokingly asked if I wanted a part—I could play myself as national president.

I answered, "No, why don't you get Gwyneth Paltrow to play me." That got a big laugh from him.

Arlie and I attended the Coastal Georgia Community College Foundation where David Eisenhower and Julie Nixon Eisenhower lectured to a sold-out crowd.

My friends will never believe this, but it's true, I cooked a Southern dinner for a diverse group of individuals in late March. Captain Randy and Debbie Zeller, commanding officer of Trident Refit Facility; RADM Joe Henry; Federal Law Enforcement Center (FLETC) director Charlie Rinkovich and his wife, Sara; Colonel Uli and Sandy Keller; and Major General Jim Rylie and his wife, Linda, from Ft. Stewart were all guests for the evening. What a wonderful, relaxed evening. Imagine the conversation with this diverse group. While we are friends with the current director of FLETC, Connie Patrick, and her husband, John, I've stopped cooking!

Captain Ike Puzon, USN (retired), and now the military advisor for Senator Cleland, visited Kings Bay. Ike was commanding officer of NAS Atlanta when I conducted a DACOWITS visit. We have been friends since then.

I left on April 26 for a Defense Advisory Committee on Women in the Services annual meeting.

Captain Zeller hosted the television crew from *This Old House* at Trident Refit Facility. He had his picture with the crew. He took that picture and superimposed my face on his uniformed "self." That picture is still hanging on my wall.

Military Appreciation Day was on May 22 at the Kings Bay Village Shopping Center. We had the Navy Band, the Camden County High School jazz and percussion ensembles, and demonstrations by Navy League Sea Cadets and Naval Corps students from both Camden County High School and Brunswick High School perform. Military vehicles and equipment as well as six-foot-long model of the fleet ballistic missile submarine SS *Georgia* (SSBN 729) were on display. Buses with tour guides gave windshield tours of Kings Bay Naval Submarine Base including waterfront areas.

Base security personnel were available to photograph and fingerprint children as part of the Ident-A-Kid program and McGruff, the Crime Dog, was also present. There were military working dog demonstrations and base fire department equipment on display as well as military recruiters available to answer questions from those considering joining the Armed Forces. I headed the planning committee.

I began with "Like most people, when we have something great, we often take it for granted. We would not want the personnel—military and civilian—assigned to Naval Submarine Base Kings Bay to feel that they are taken for granted. That is why we at the Kings Bay Village would like to take this opportunity to give our own positive recognition to all the personnel at the base and say thank you for making Camden County a better place to live." Letters of appreciation from our congressional delegation were read. Kingsland mayor Kenneth Smith told the audience, "Kings Bay has had a tremendous impact on this county, on the country and the world. We wish and hope that you'll stay here many more years." Ann Proctor, superintendent elect of the Camden County School System, told base officials that the system was recommending five Kings Bay Sailors—Lt. Rosario D. McWhorter, Chief Petty Officer Mark Wojeik and Petty Officer First Class Randolph M. Argote, Scott Seddon, and Sam Shanks received the Military Outstanding Volunteer Service Medal.

Those honored by the base itself as the outstanding personnel last year were also recognized during Saturday's event. Sailor of the Year, Shore Command, Petty Officer First Class Paula A. Creel; Sailor of the Year, Sea Command, Petty Officer First Class Anthony Jared; Marine of the Year Cpl. Lawrence D. Bryant; submarine base (subase) Supervisor Civilian of the Year, Alice Hurley; and Subbase Civilian of the Year Jacqueline A. Williams received American flags that had been flown over the capitol in their honor. The tributes and expressions of gratitude were received by base commander Capt. Frank Stagl, who said, during the course of his naval career, he'd "never witnessed such a sincere display of appreciation. There's no home port where the Navy and the community have a closer bond."

Also on hand was RADM Joseph Henry, commander of Submarine Group 10, who encouraged audience members to tell promising young people about careers with the Navy and the Marines. "There's no better place to have, or begin, a career," he said. "God bless Kings Bay," said Henry in conclusion. "God bless this community and God bless the US Navy."

Thanks to Amelia Hart of the *Tribune & Georgian* staff for covering this event.

In July, we left for the Navy League convention in Chicago. I had decided again to run for national vice president. I was so anxious about the interview.

This quest is fraught with mixed feelings. I believe I have a little chance. I've got enough ego to know I'm the best candidate but whether I can convey this without appearing arrogant or self-centered is the question—there is also politics. Thank goodness that the Kelleys and Contours are very supportive. They and Arlie started grilling me in preparation for the nominating committee. I gave them the six to eight minutes I planned to give, and they interrupted me every minute or so with comments. At the end, I told them the nominating committee would be a breeze after the workout with them. Bill turned to Raymond and asked, "How long has it been since we've had a candidate this qualified?" They both answered, "Never." These two men that I admire more than almost anyone I know and to have them say this was pretty incredible. I needed that positive energy.

For the nominating committee meeting I prepared myself by wearing my "power suit," removing part of my jewelry, painting my fingernails a clear color (I don't want a red-fingered girl scaring those guys off), preparing a binder with every bit of information I could ever need, and practicing my presentation. I had hoped Bill or Raymond could speak on my behalf, but three weeks before, I had received a letter saying there would be no personal recommendations—only letters. I did not call my colleagues and ask them to write letters of support, but Dick Knight received a request asking for letters for one of my opponents. Dick told me he had not responded but offered to write a letter on my behalf. He asked, "Why haven't you asked me to write a letter for you?"

"I am not comfortable putting you or anyone else on the spot," I told him.

He wrote the best letter and asked that the state presidents do the same. They told me of their support. Also, running for national vice president was Herb Jordan and Ron Weeks.

In the nominating committee, I was told I had ten minutes. I could use all that ten minutes in talking or could let them ask me questions. I asked them to first let me tell them why I thought I should be vice president and would then answer any questions. I talked for a while and asked how much time I had used (six minutes), so

I talked for another one minute or so and asked for questions. I was so relieved when the first question was "How did you get on DACOWITS?"

This gave me a chance to tell them about the letters of recommendations I received for that committee and drop Jerry's name. "You will remember RADM Ellis—we had a reception at his quarters at Ford Island at the Hawaii convention." I also told them that listening to the concerns of our military men and women for the past three years had been the best experience of my life and I wanted to do something with that newfound knowledge.

The second question was "How do you feel about women on submarines and integrated training?"

I was prepared for women on submarines since I had been vocal about my concerns, but I didn't expect the question. I emphasized that it was not the point that women could do the job; it was the fact that the quality of life for our submarines is already diminished and to further diminish the already cramped living spaces would be a disadvantage to all the crew.

I was disappointed when I heard the chairman say, "Thank you, Mrs. McNeill," and I had to leave. He said I was in twenty minutes—double the time I was supposed to have.

I was in the Maritime Policy Committee meeting when Roz Ellis of Detroit sent me a note: "I expect you to be the first woman president of the Navy League! We'll break the 'good ole boys' syndrome." I received the word. I was being nominated for national vice president. Arlie and I were thrilled. RADM Malcolm Fages sent me an e-mail: "I'm not worthy to be talking to you… I snivel in your presence." Mal, always good for a laugh!

Congressman Jack Kingston announced my election at the annual chamber dinner. He commented on our visits to Washington and how effective they were. He told everyone "the heart of your community is just beginning to bloom." He made the same announcement to a group of veterans on Jekyll Island.

One of the very senior Navy League members was Seymour Knee. He was not at the meeting due to knee surgery. I gave him a call. Seymour could be very cynical so I didn't know what to expect. I just knew that Arlie and I sat with him toward the front of the auditorium and he had always seemed interested. He was just getting home from the surgery, and he told me he was thrilled! So much for that older generation of the Navy League being opposed to a woman. Most of my best supporters were that older class of Navy Leaguers. Go figure!

On September 10, 1999, RADM Joseph G. Henry was relieved by RADM Richard P. Terpstra. There was almost a half-page spread in the local paper:

> *Bill Weisensee said "Rear Adm. Henry is an exceptionally fine leader. I knew him before—when he was CO (commanding officer) of USS Kentucky, and I was CO of Trident Refit Facility." He has*

a wealth of knowledge and has a knack for being able to communicate with everybody military and civilian alike. Sheila McNeill of Brunswick, who is one of the vice presidents of the Navy League of the United States has been working with Henry since he came to Kings Bay. "I have had the pleasure of working with Rear Adm. Henry both as chairman of the Friends of Kings Bay and in my work with the Navy League," she said. He has recognized the support that Kings Bay enjoys with the community and has been invaluable to me in his straight-forward approach that effect the Navy community. Rear Adm. Terpstra comes to Kings Bay from an assignment as Chief of Naval Operations Fellow at the Strategic Studies Group in Newport, R.I. "I have met Rear Adm. Terpstra, and we have already discussed our excellent Navy community relations," Mrs. McNeill said.

When RADM Henry left, he sent me a wonderful letter:

7 SEPT 1999
Dear Sheila,

Just a short note to thank you. While I know your many efforts have been in support of Kings Bay in general, I want to express my personal gratitude for all the support and assistance you have given me personally during the last two years. It is a great benefit to the Group Commander to know that there is someone out there in the community that understands the Navy and has both the Navy's and the community's best interest at heart.

Sheila, it has been wonderful working with you and Arlie, both professionally and socially. I look forward to our continued association.

Sincerely,
Joe

It doesn't get any better than that! Thank you, Joe!

I ran again for national vice president and was elected! A woman was rare. There were ten Navy League national vice presidents who are elected for one year. I had to thank my campaign managers and biggest encouragers and coaches Nancy and Bill Kelley and Raymond and June Contour.

Poor President Jack Fisher. He appreciated my enthusiasm and my work ethic. He just didn't know what to do with this woman who wanted to do so much. So he gave me vice president for strategic planning and development. Back then I had only heard of the term "fund-raising" and seriously didn't know what was expected. I had no background in this and really no interest. I had never worked on a strategic plan—especially for an organization with more than sixty-eight thousand members. But I went to work. I learned a lot from the professional staff and it turned out to be good training. I opened a couple of meetings with something like "I really don't know how to do this" or "I'm not familiar with this." Karen Coltrane, development director at Navy League headquarters, pulled me aside and said, "Never say that in a meeting. We'll get a plan and you will be up to speed but never let them think you don't know what's going on. You are going to be great at this job, you are the expert, I'm going to make you one!" She sent me the following letter dated November 23, 1999:

Dear Sheila,

Please forgive my delay in writing to thank you and Arlie for dinner and for your hospitality throughout the Kansas City meetings. It was great to spend time with you. Your enthusiasm and positive approach are a real inspiration, especially as we try to work through some of the issues involved with creating a development program that makes sense for the entire Navy League.

Your support of the effort to attempt to align the organization's charitable programs has meant a great deal to me. If we are successful in overcoming the objections on December 7, I believe the best aspect of this arrangement for me will be the opportunity to work more closely with you. I was delighted that Ed Campbell called for your nomination to the Foundation Board as a full member regardless of the outcome of the agreement. Best decision made in Kansas City as far as I'm concerned! Sheila, I suspect you might be feeling a bit frustrated regarding the pace of change, but I hope you will not. Your leadership on this initiative has the promise of truly giving birth to a development program for the Navy League, where only disjointed fund-raising efforts have existed before. I marvel at the foresight Jack Fisher showed in tasking you with this vital transformation… among the other organization-changing responsibilities he placed on your capable shoulders. Again, many thanks for dinner and everything else. Please express my gratitude to Arlie and my best wishes to you both for a wonderful Thanksgiving. I look forward to seeing you on December 7.

Sincerely,
Karen S. Coltrane

And she was right. I faked it until I did get pretty good at both jobs. What an absolute professional she was. Karen later left the Navy League and Veronica Brandon came in. How lucky could I be—she, too, was awesome. Later, when I was president, Susan Fallon continued the high level of professionalism needed for this position. The day I was given my new job, we had our formal dinner that evening for all attendees of the convention. Seated next to me was a man I had not remembered ever meeting. He introduced himself as Peter Kent. After we talked a while I asked him what he did. "I travel across the country and give seminars and work with large companies and corporations on strategic planning."

My jaw dropped. Now I knew why fate put me at that table. (I think God is a little too busy to deal with seating.) "Do you know what job I was given today with my duties as national vice president?"

"No, I don't," he answered.

"Strategic planning," I answered.

"Really? I'll be happy to help." And help he did. We produced the first (I believe) strategic plan in the Navy League.

The *Georgia Times Union* had this article:

Navy League taps VP Appointee stunned by announcement
By Gordon Jackson—Times Union staff writer

August 6, 1999

Sheila McNeill, one of Southeast Georgia's most powerful voices in military affairs, has been elected national vice president of the Navy League. The league is a civilian organization that supports maritime services such as the Navy, Coast Guard, Marines and U.S. Flag Merchant Marine through advocacy and public education. There are more than 68,000 members serving in almost 300 Navy League councils throughout the world. McNeill was named national vice president at the annual convention in Chicago on July 24. She is the fourth woman to serve as vice president in the organization's 98-year history. "I could not believe it," McNeill said of her appointment. "I felt completely stunned by it."

U.S. Senator Max Cleland, D-Ga., who serves on the Senate's armed services committee, said he has known McNeill 20 years and she has a reputation as one of the most knowledgeable people on military affairs in the nation. "Nobody has worked harder in America or more selflessly on behalf of the men and women serving our country, particularly, the United States Navy." Cleland said, "I've always told commanders at Kings Bay (Naval Submarine Base) they are second in command to her. Rear Admiral Joseph Henry commanding officer of Submarine Group 10 at Kings Bay, praised McNeill's dedication to the Navy. "She really has a feel for what our armed forces are like today and I think that's sort of unique for someone in her position in the Navy League," Henry said. McNeill, 56, was the first woman president in the Navy League in Georgia and also served as president of the leagues Camden Kings Bay Council and the regional league. Most recently, she served a three-year stint on the Defense Advisory Committee on Women in the Services. McNeill said those experiences probably helped her earn the new appointment. "It puts me in the position to talk to a lot of people," McNeill said. Besides educating public and government officials about the importance of maintaining a strong Navy, McNeill said an important goal for her is to get more young people and minorities to join the organization. Former national Navy League president Hugh Mayberry predicted McNeill would help the organization attract new and younger members.

This article was featured on the poster at the DACOWITS San Diego conference in October 1999. Captain Barbara Brehm came through. More about that conference in my special.

On August 13, I spoke to the Rotary Club of Camden County. In September, I also represented the Navy League at the Navy League Batchelder Awards at the Navy Supply School in Athens, Georgia. The official party was Captain Ben Mathieu, SC, USN; RADM Keith W Lippert, SC, USN; and VADM Henry C. Griffin III, USN. Details are in the stories section.

2000: On January 27, 2000, I attended the State of the Union address by President Bill Clinton. That experience is told in my stories collection. You must read this one!

Lots of great stuff going on, and on February 25, I introduced Peter Maas to a large audience at the Cloister Plantation at Sea Island. Maas was the author of *The Terrible Hours: The Man behind the Greatest Submarine Rescue in History* for the Table of Contents Dinner. The coolest thing: RADM Terpstra and Sue and Rear Admiral Malcolm Fages and Shirley were present. On RADM Terpstra's behalf, I am including the letter from Barbara Spouse Chair of the library's Table of Contents Benefit Dinner:

Dear Sheila, you were a big help in so many ways that I don't know where to begin to thank you. First, thank you for making all the arrangements for Peter Maas and family to tour the Sub Base (from me to RADM Terpstra: Thank YOU) which didn't work out but what required a lot of your time I know.

All of the sailors and submarine caps that the Pilot Club of Brunswick used on their table and podium decorations added a nice touch for Peter Maas' presentation of The Terrible Hours. Thank you for procuring all those items. And you were the best person in the world to introduce Peter Maas and what a masterful job you did! Thank you very much. I could tell you spent some time working on that introduction, and people were spellbound listening to you. I appreciate your bringing the Admirals to the Dinner. Rear Admiral Terpstra looks like he just graduated from Annapolis. What a youthful Rear Admiral. I meant to ask them to stand but in my anxiousness to get on to Peter Maas I didn't. It sounds as though a lot of pictures were taken of them. I'll get them to you when I pick them up. It was a distinct pleasure to get to work with you and I look forward to some other event where our paths may cross.

Again, many thanks for making our Table of Content Benefit Dinner so successful.

Warmest regards,
Barbara C. Sprouse, Chair, Table of Contents Benefit Dinner
Friends of the Brunswick—Glynn Regional Library

At the same time, I am chairman of the Personnel Committee at our church. In January Arlie and I and the personnel committee hosted the pastor David Stokes and his wife Felecia and the staff. We really had a wonderful time. Everything was very formal. We were all in black pants, white shirts and black bowties. The flowers, table settings and food were topnotch. Amazing how much fun you can have doing something for someone else.

Captain Jo Dee Jacobs, an old friend from DACOWITS gets orders to Guam as COMNAVMARIANAS.

We had an opportunity to have Brian and Susan Piedfort over. Brian was the Flag Sec at Group 10 for several years and always seemed to bail me out when I needed it.

I was given the same responsibilities—development and strategic planning. "Again? Strategic planning? Development?" I asked Jack. "Why can't I have legislative affairs?"

"Maybe next year," he told me. He could not see a woman in that job. He was adamant.

"That was what you told me last year," I whined.

Then Jack actually discussed with me how a particular vice president might be as vice president for legislative affairs. I couldn't believe he was asking my opinion and still denying me the job. It was very frustrating. You couldn't get angry with

Jack. He was such a gentleman and he really didn't know what to think of me. And I enjoyed these two years. I would be particularly glad when I became president and realized how important this knowledge was. Karen was right!

Around that time, I was asked to serve on both Senator Paul Coverdell and Senator Zell Miller's military advisory committees. This was the closest I got to legislative affairs the first two years. I was honored and pleased to be asked to serve. At the same time, I'm busy back in Georgia. In December 2000, I rode with Woody Woodside to Atlanta for the swearing in of the Georgia Military Affairs Coordinating Committee. The committee was created during Zell Miller's administration and has been very productive.

Woody and I had arrived at the hotel and had a few minutes with Major General Bill Bland, Georgia's adjutant general, before going to lunch. We were joined by Congressman Bob Barr and Senator Max Cleland. When Max first saw us, he said, "Where two or three are gathered in the name of the military there you will find Sheila McNeill." We had a nice swearing in and I left the next morning for DC.

That evening Shirley Fages picked me up at Dulles and had arranged dinner with Jerry and Rosemary Ellis and Chuck Beers—what a nice treat. They are such good friends. We had a lively discussion and one of the topics was if the admiral at Kings Bay should hold a meeting for the community about the upcoming loss of the two submarines. One thought was "they've already been told—what was the purpose?"

Rosemary said, "The admiral is 'the source' at Kings Bay and the community would never really let it sink in until they had heard it from him." Go, Rosemary!

We talked about the show the evening before when Malcom was on C-SPAN for four hours. It was the one hundredth anniversary of the submarine force and he was interviewed that night. I didn't see it because the hotel didn't cover C-SPAN.

Later we had a meeting with Major General Corwin, Office of Legislative Affairs for the Marine Corps at his office in the Pentagon. I got a little lost going to his office and I passed Malcolm's office—it was fun to stop by and see everyone. It was a great meeting with General Corwin and his staff. Back to headquarters and on the way in the door Pat Holmgaard mentioned she had heard my name on C-SPAN. I couldn't imagine why and thought she might have made a mistake. I went back to Pat and she told me that Adm. Chiles had mentioned me and Arlie as great supporters of the Navy and the Submarine Force! I could not believe it. And what an opportunity to give Malcolm an even harder time.

One evening during my second year as vice president I was at dinner with Jack and his wife, Kit. "What about Sheila, Jack? She has asked you for this for two years for legislative affairs. So why not Sheila?"

He replied, "First Sam [not his name] and the next year Sheila can do it." That would be four years waiting for the job I wanted. I guess Kit went to work on him because when I was elected the third year, the first thing he told me is that he wanted me to handle legislative affairs. I was vice president for legislative affairs for three years for a total of five years as vice president. And then I ran for president with Arlie's encouragement. Jack Fisher seems to have made a decision of some kind. Katie says he is trying to do all he can for me to be elected for president. I talked with him about what I had heard about the US Coast Guard's recapitalization. He agreed with me and suggested I contact John Thorn and RADM Pat Stillman and get the ball rolling on Deepwater. Deepwater would become a big part of my next two years.

It was during this time that I was working on saving the four submarines that were going to be destroyed. Read the story about our lobbying efforts on the SSGN in the stories section. That April we again went to Washington for our fly-in group. This year's trip was made with the knowledge that the US Navy plans call for two Trident submarines to be transferred from Kings Bay to Naval Submarine Base, Bangor, Washington. This was the third trip to DC carrying the SSGN banner but losing these two submarines was a big deal and had big economic impact. Over the years, I have told our congressional members. "If it is in the best interest of our country we will not fight it. But if it is a political decision or a decision based on budget then we will fight it and expect our legislators to fight it just as strongly." This was personally a test for me. This could have a terrible effect on my integrity and my lifetime of work. This *was* that instance.

This was known as the "pivot to the Pacific" and Navy leadership determined that we needed more boats in the Pacific. I write this, in November 2016, and those boats are still in the Pacific—ten boats while we have eight on the East Coast. We didn't fight that decision—based on the country's needs. We gave the sailors a good-bye party and we wished them well. That makes it hard when it has such an economic impact on our community and our small businesses. I was one of those businesses. But I'm proud of that philosophy and the fact that our entire delegation continues to take that stand. We met with RADM Malcolm Fages, head of Submarine Warfare at the Pentagon, and asked if there might be other mission or if there were plans for any fast attack submarines to be relocated at Kings Bay. He told us that there're was almost no chance that any fast attack submarines would be homeported at Kings Bay. Carla Carper, our executive director of the Chamber responded, "That news will not discourage community leaders from reminding congressional and military officials of the support of the base and its personnel and to keep Camden in mind when basing decision arise. We will never stop asking to be reviewed for additional responsibilities for the base," she said.

I was quoted with Carla in the paper on SSGN: "Sheila McNeill a vice president of the US Navy League and a local businesswoman said our news about the possible conversion of four Tridents which are slated to be decommissioned, to carry conventional weapons and special operation forces was more positive. Everyone seems to be looking at this, and even the Secretary of Defense William Cohen has been saying it's a good program."

As vice president of development and strategic planning, I attended the annual Sea Air Space. The secretary of the Navy, Richard Danzig, was present, and it was the first opportunity I had to have a conversation with him.

In May, Senator Coverdell's Military Advisory Committee met at Fort McPherson and Fort Gillem. The commanding officer, Colonel William D. Clingempeel, was most gracious with his time. We had informative briefs on the installation, on US Forces Command and on US Army Reserve Command.

In June 2000 I sent a letter to the editor entitled as follows:

TAX MONEY SHOULD NOT BE USED TO MODIFY SUBMARINES FOR WOMEN

I had a nice letter from Steve Pietropaoli. At that time, he was Captain Pietropaoli with the Office of the Chairman. He would have no idea what I would ask of him a few years later. The steering committee for 2000–2001 were as follows:

Carter Conlin, Corporate Affairs
Robert White, Sea Services Liaison
Melvin Burkhart, National Treasurer
Bruce Smith, Youth Programs
Tim Fanning, Finance
Donald Steel, Strategic Planning
Jerome Rapkin, Corporate Secretary
Bill Evanzia, Community Education
Paul Baldridge, Marketing and Membership
Jack Fisher, President
Ward Shanahan, Judge Advocate
John Panneton, Region Training
Sheila McNeill, Development and Legislative Affairs

Past presidents at the July 2000 meeting:

Evan Baker, Jack Spittler, Morgan Fitch, Jack Fisher, Calvin Cobb, Jack Kennedy, and Bill Kelly

At that same meeting, I was presented the U.S. Coast Guard Meritorious Public Service Award by Rear Admiral Ralph Utley.

The Citation read, "The Commandant of the United States Coast Guard takes great pleasure in presenting the Coast Guard Meritorious Public Service Award to Sheila M. McNeill in recognition of her service to the Nation and her strong support of the United States Coast Guard while serving in several Navy League leadership positions, most recently as National Vice President. With a sincere objectivity, combined with compassion and incredible energy, Ms. McNeill has been effective in relating to the highest echelons of the military services as well as the most junior enlisted families. Service chiefs know her well and appreciate her private counsel; and junior members open up to her, expressing concerns about quality of life issues and the needs of their females. Likewise, when asked to serve with other national organizations—while serving on the board of DACOWITS, for example—Ms. McNeill has been exceptionally effective as she visited numerous military bases and, with a common-sense intelligence and keen insight, listed and observed, and then provided suggestions to the commanding officers who, more often than not, gratefully incorporated her ideas to the betterment of the entire command. As one Admiral put it, 'Sheila McNeill simply has changed the we do things.' Ms. McNeill also made her mark on the Coast Guard. She has been sensitive and responsive to the critical needs of our service and of the individual men and women who serve. Ms. McNeill's leadership, dedication and outstanding support of the Coast Guard, as well as her deep devotion to the nation's Sea Services and the Navy League organization are most heartily commended and in keeping with the highest traditions of the United States Coast Guard."

And finally, President Jack Fisher finally gave me the assignment for legislative affairs—I was happy!

June 23, 2000, was a memorable day for me. I was asked by Captain Frank Stagle to speak at his change of command where he would be relieved by Captain Walt Yourstone. It was held at the Bancroft Memorial at the entrance to Naval Submarine Base Kings Bay. Walking down that red carpet with all those people, that big black sub and those sailor whites was an honor I will never forget. Details are included in Captain Stagle's stories section.

In October, some of my old DACOWITS friends came for the weekend. Lori Hunter, Elizabeth Bilby, and Ginger Simpson. What a wonderful time. Arlie escorted us everywhere in the funeral home limo.

Also in October, Admiral Skip Bowman spoke to our Navy League—I was pleased to introduce him and present him with the "famous" throw featuring an SSBN submarine.

At the winter meeting, I ran for national president against Tim Fanning. I knew I would not win. I knew I had to run, then lose and come back again before *they* would take a woman seriously. Of course, I would have liked to have won, but I'm so pleased today that I did not. I needed that next two years in legislative affairs. I'm grateful for the time I devoted to this critical program. I also needed those next two years of grooming. And maybe I needed that experience so that I could handle most anything after that.

The best letter of recommendation that I received was from Jeffrey Readinger, a former director of legislative affairs at the Navy League. I was surprised to hear from him and that he was so supportive of my presidency. He was a wonder to work with.

And to close out the year 2000, I continued to serve on the governor's Military Affairs Coordinating Committee. Governor Roy Barnes appointed me on November 21 to continue to serve. This committee was established under Governor Zell Miller.

Former commander of Submarines Forces Atlantic Fleet, Vice Admiral Dan Cooper, and his wife, Betty, stopped by my office on December 28 and left me this note:

> *Sheila, Betty and I were in town for the New Year and I stopped by to see if you really worked. Guess you don't.*
>
> *—Dan Cooper*

Every time I see him I think of it. And what a fun message to find on my desk!

2001: The year stated with a region meeting in Charleston onboard the USS *Yorktown*. There must have been twenty-five attendees. It gets harder and harder to enlist folks to give that kind of time and loyalty.

And I continue my quest on the SSGN.

On February 14, I did an interview with the *LA Times* on the USS *Greenville* accident. It amounted to a small quote: "Sheila McNeill, who runs a greeting card shop in Kings Bay, Georgia has taken two trips aboard submarines. 'I learned how professional our submarine sailors are, how young they are, and all the difficult things they do. Everyone I know who has done one of these cruises has come back more patriotic, more energized and a great recruiter for the Navy.'" The reporter added, "For the submarine community, such praise comes at a crucial time."

Since I now have the responsibilities for legislative affairs, Shannon Graves, the legislative staffer, and I spent a lot of time together! I was honored to speak at the 2001 New Flag Seminar. Rear Admiral Jerry Talbot was director of the Navy staff and had responsibilities for this conference. The dinner at the Cloister in February for the USS *Kentucky* is in the stories section.

Naval Submarine Base Kings Bay held a flag conference and branched out into the community. We had one of the events at Orange Hall. How nice to see so many of the friends I usually must travel to see. I spoke at the Savannah Navy League council on the conversion of the four ballistic missile submarines. Back home to reality. Arlie and I had a great time at a party at our home. I was chairman of the personnel committee of our church. The committee wanted to thank the staff and we decided a formal dinner with the committee dressed in white shirts and black bowties waiting on them hand and foot. It was a wonderful evening.

In March, I joined our local community for the annual fly-in, continuing our advocacy for the SSGN. As I was waiting at the Rayburn building I ran into some former Army Rangers and started talking with them. They were on Capitol Hill to protest the Army's decision that every soldier would wear the Rangers' black beret as a new symbol of unity and excellence. I agreed with the soldiers and it turned out that interview was on Tom Brochaw's show the next morning with me saying the Rangers should be able to keep their trademark black berets. The next night at the Capitol Hill reception was when I met General Shinseki, chief of staff United States Army. I was hoping he didn't make the connection. He is such a gentleman that he would not have said anything if he had. Major Brian Moore, who had been a fellow in Congressman Jack Kingston's office, introduced us.

Note: The entire story of the quest for the conversion of the SSBNs to SSGNs is in the stories section.

* * * * *

In May, the Hill, listed as the *Capitol Newspaper*, had the caption "**Top defense and aerospace lobbyists in D.C.**" on their front page, with pictures. The three listed are Robin L. Beard, president of government relations, Raytheon Company; Brian D. Dailey, corporate vice president, Washington operations, Lockheed; Martin and Sheila M. McNeill, national vice president for legislative affairs, Navy League of the United States.

We received word that Malcolm Fages was nominated for his third star. More about that in the Fages stories.

Also in May, Sr. Chief Brian Piedfort retired. Some of us got together and put a huge block in the local paper with

Congratulations Sr. Chief Brian Piedfort
1981–2001
Thank you for your service to your country and the submarine community
Fair winds and following seas from your grateful Friends

Boy, I miss him!

* * * * *

I attended the War College current strategy forum in June. Also in June, I had a call from one of my favorite people, Tony Cobb. He was retiring, and he wanted me to speak. It was to be a simple ceremony—and a casual one, with a cook out thrown in—and it was in just a few days! Of course, I wanted to be there. Later I received an e-mail from his commanding officer on the USS *Pennsylvania*.

June 10th, 2001
Dear Sheila,

Thank you for contributing to Chief Cobb's retirement ceremony this past Thursday, especially as it came on such short notice. I think we were all surprised at the last-minute request to add official pomp and circumstance to the original plan for a crew picnic. Your personal comments about Chief Cobb's contribution to the Submarine Museum and your insight into the challenges ahead for the submarine force certainly added a lot to the ceremony. Please let me know if I can be of help in "spreading the word" about our submarines and missions to area organizations.

Bon voyage a Bruxelles
CDR Ken Perry, CO Pennsylvania Gold

It was a wonderful opportunity to tell everyone how essential Tony was to the building of the St. Marys Submarine Museum and how much we appreciated his service to our great country.

At the June 2001, Navy League convention, I was presented the secretary of the Navy Superior Pubic Service Award by RADM Richard J. Naughton, commander of the Naval Strike and Warfare Center. It was so rewarding to receive a medal for the work thats you've wanted to do for years. It read,

For her superior role in developing a keen knowledge of maritime issues and constantly utilizing that knowledge to promote the Sea Services, particularly the United States Navy, from 1995 to 2001. As an excellent spokesperson, for the Navy, her community, and the Navy League, she has tremendously enhanced public awareness and increased support for Navy programs. Mrs. McNeill has consistently demonstrated successful, results-oriented leadership, which has greatly benefited the Department of the Navy, is most deserving of the Navy Superior Public Service Award.

Signed by Secretary of the Navy Gordon England
June 20, 2001

The next month I was on the cover of the *Georgia Trend* magazine with an article on my work on the SSGN. That full story is found in the *Georgia Trend* portion. I do believe that I learned to let people know how much you appreciate them from all the e-mails, cards, and letters I received on the award and the magazine cover. I try to do the same thing. I keep a book with every name and date to remind myself how good it is for friends and colleges to recognize your work. It makes me feel good every time I write someone. A letter from Captain Walt Yourstone, commanding officer of Kings Bay was a thrill.

> *Dear Ms. Sheila, I read in the Tribune & Georgian that you were awarded the Superior Public Service Award. I can appreciate why you were the candidate of choice and applaud you for this noteworthy achievement. You are truly making a difference in your efforts for the American people. On behalf of the men and women at the Naval Submarine Base Kings Bay, please accept my heartfelt congratulations for a job well done and best of wishes for continued success. Walter H, Yourstone.*

This was a red-letter year when the papers run a front-page story:

Bush moves to convert 2 Trident subs

This was also the year that Horst Schulze with the Ritz-Carlton hotels spoke to our chamber and when we both became friends. That is covered in the stories section.

On June 27, the Navy League sponsored a Navy, Marine Corps, and Coast Guard liaison officers' reception. Congress was out and what a great time to sponsor this. We must have had six hundred to eight hundred come through over the two hours. Congressman Ed Sherock was president of the 2001 freshman class and was a great help with this 107th Congress. He was a retired Navy captain and was tireless in his support of the Sea Services. I look at the pictures today and it is the who's who of the military. Admiral Jim Loy was there as Commandant of the Coast Guard with then Captain Bob Papp, military liaison for the Coast Guard who would later become commandant.

Lt. General McKissock was there and I enjoyed meeting his representative, Sanford Bishop, and his wife. General McKissock was at Moody Air Force Base in Albany in Congressman Bishop's District. And Rear Admiral Jay Cohen was there representing the Navy.

Congressman Ed Sherock left Congress and was replaced by Congressman Ander Crenshaw. The Fourth District of Florida has been very blessed with knowing and working with both men.

I had a great time speaking to the new flag office spouse orientation. Vice Admiral Pat Tracey asked me to speak, and I would do most anything Pat Tracey wanted. She was an incredible officer as director of the Navy staff and we worked together on several projects.

Rear Admiral Mal Fages spoke to the Navy ball that year. Shirley always makes for a better party. RADM Gerry Talbot and Captain Tim Lindstrom posed for a picture and Shirley was most fetching in her cowboy hat taken from the USS *Wyoming* decorations!

Arlie and I hosted some of the USS *Ohio* SSBN (729) Gold crew for Thanksgiving. Commanding officer of the *Ohio*, Captain McIlvaine, sent such a nice letter and closed with the following:

> *(I suppose it should come as no surprise to me that someone in your position would be thinking of Sailors during the holidays, and I particularly appreciate your attention and thoughtfulness." We had a wonderful time. Eight of the crew that couldn't get to their home arrived at ours around 11:00. After lunch, I urged them all to go upstairs and call home. They then watched TV, napped, drank beer (maybe not in that order) and stayed for dinner. It was a wonderful day.*

Note: Neither of us had any idea we would be working together when he commanded the USS *Georgia* and I would speak at his change of command. Look for him in the stories section.

2002: I traveled to San Diego to speak at their council meeting at the invitation of Ray Roth the council president who was relieved by Jack Clark. Some of those who were at the dinner remained friends for years. The retired rear admiral and his wife, Peggy, were there as well as Fred Orton, who would help my campaign when I ran for president a few months later. Jim and Jewell Bonner are two of the most dedicated Navy League members we have so it was always great to get caught up on their latest project. Jim Bras, a dedicated Navy Leaguer and who knew all the Marine Corps brass, would be steadfastly devoted to our legislative program for many years. Peter Kent and his wife, Joan, were in attendance. He was my strategic planning guru and he continued to help with the Navy Leagues strategic plan. They brought with them Marilyn Crist who held her own in the Pacific Northwest. It was like the Hall of Fame for Navy League members.

On the way to San Diego I ran into Captain Jo Dee Jacobs. She had just retired from the Navy and was now the chief executive officer for Girl Scouts of San Diego. I worked with Jo Dee when I was on DACOWITS and had a ton of respect for her. Over the years there have been remarkable changes. Jo Dee knew what it was like early on. A great article appeared on January 19, 1998, in the *Sun* when she was deputy operations for the Naval Academy that led with: "**A slow voyage to equality Gender: The Navy has done much to narrow the gap between the sexes, but much still needs to be accomplished to reach parity.**"

I traveled to Atlanta at the request of council president Don Giles. Don told me he called many of the members he had not heard from to invite them to the meeting. He was surprised with one of the calls when the man answered, "Sheila is my sister." He had called my brother, Brian, encouraging him to support my visit.

At the winter meeting, I had shared the story of our community's annual trip to DC. "The Camden leadership now travels to DC every year to share their concerns on both military and civilian issues." I reported to our national Legislative Affairs Committee. Allan Groh of Texas was intrigued with our program and after several telephone calls and e-mails the Texas fly-in came about. Allan and his wife and Nick and Anna Ricco with their daughter made appointments with Congressman Sam Johnson, Congressman Pete Sessions, Congresswoman Kay Granger, and MLAs for Senator Kay Bailey Hutchinson and Senator Gramm. I told them I would meet them for this very first fly-in. In February 2002, we met. On a Monday evening, we all had dinner at the Army Navy Club and "rehearsed." They were familiar with the local bases, so we could still get through it but next time they should prepare the one-page summary on each issue I told them. The plan was that they cover local and I would cover national issues. One of them would tell the legislator they were being given a membership in the Navy League and would then pin the Navy League pin on their lapel. I warned them that sometimes the legislator (I'm sure in their attempt to make the constituent feel at home) would take all the time talking about issues that they wanted to support instead of what we might want to support, and most people would leave thinking what a hospitable man/woman they were. So we had to control the meeting, or we would not have discussed our issues.

Our first meeting was with Congressman Pete Sessions. They presented the local issues. I began with the Navy. The senator talked about his work with spousal abuse, then about kids and "fumes," both drugs and "perfume," meaning girl issues. I reached over and put my wrist in front of his nose (as if to let him smell my perfume, which he did), and as he smiled and smelled, I said, "Now, Congressman, about the Marine Corps." He laughed uproariously. I don't think I've ever used that tactic before or since then. He scooted his chair close and gave me his undivided attention. In fact, we only planned to be there fifteen minutes and we were there for thirty minutes. He had many questions, most of which I could answer, and I asked him to call OLA for briefings on those issues he wanted more information on. We could get any information he needed to him. He followed us outside suggesting a picture with each of us the with Capitol in the background. What a wonderful visit.

We then went to Congressman Sam Johnson who was very nice but busy as the locals presented their issues. He took a phone call; his staff came in for something and I knew we didn't have his attention and I also knew he couldn't help it. When my time came, I started with thanks to him for his service and for his sacrifice to our country. He was a POW in Vietnam—his hands had been injured. I told him we didn't have anything new for him that he didn't already know—our only point is that he has constituents who have the same passion as he does for our military and I'd just take a couple of minutes to prove that. Suddenly he stopped, pulled his chair over in front of mine put his hands on his knees, and said, "I'm sure you have a lot you can teach me, let me hear." He then gave us his undivided attention. What a classy man.

In planning for our community fly-in, I made the usual plans to have briefers from each of the services brief our group. Rear Admiral Paul Sullivan was at Navy headquarters at the Pentagon and sent me an e-mail.

> *Sheila, great to hear from you. Thanks for all your help with getting 4 SSGNs in the budget. The Georgia Hill delegation clearly helped. This is the day that the CNO has an all Flag Conference in Orlando (13 March) so both Bruce Engelhardt (my Deputy) and I will be out of town. My trusty EA, CAPT Joe Mulloy, will be more than happy to pitch hit and represent me.) Joe as you know is a wonderful submariner who will shortly depart for Guam to be the CASS—15 Squadron Commander. He knows our programs and issues as well as anyone. If you agree, I want him to be our presenter. Do you want slides or words only? Look forward to hearing from you. Paul*

The plane was an hour late as I arrive in DC. I went straight to Navy League headquarters. Jeremy Miller our legislative affairs director, and I went to lunch and I went over the eighteen items I had for him. He was prepared and had a copy of the budget and the funds used so far. Then we went by metro to the Pentagon to meet with the General Counsel of the Navy at 1400. He was very impressive. He had briefing papers at his conference table but first he had a lot of questions for me. He wanted to know how I got started in this job! He seemed very interested and totally relaxed and certainly not in a hurry. I sort of directed him toward the briefings and shared his convictions. He said he would give us any of the papers he would be briefing later when they could be released. There was a hearing on Capitol Hill coming up and it would finally have some good news about encroachment. We believe he had another meeting at 1430, but he motioned to his secretary that he did not want to be interrupted. I won't go into the brief; I can't. But I was very impressed and pleased to see the Navy-Marine Corps take this stand. He said he would join the Navy League "if it gave him a chance to vote for me for president." I asked how he knew I was running but he was vague. It was a very productive meeting—a meeting that years later would be valuable information.

I was already in DC on March 11. Our Camden DC fly-in was scheduled for March 12–15, 2002. I called Celso Gonzales and asked if he wanted to go ahead to the luncheon as I'd had a call from Carla Carper, our chamber executive director that the plane was late. We arrived and minutes after a staffer dropped by from

Congressman Linder's office—she left with a promise to return with two more staffers. Senator Johnny Isakson and Congressman Sanford Bishop came in and went through the buffet.

I had an opportunity to talk submarines, SSGN, shipbuilding, encroachment, and other issues with them. Congressman Linder came in just as everyone was arriving from Camden and I interrupted everyone to give him a chance to talk. Earlier he asked me if I would refresh and update him on the issue. It was nice to hear him use that update as part of his remarks. Congressman Jack Kingston then arrived and it was chaos as everyone shook hands and he had everyone begin going through the lines for lunch. Then Congressman Saxby Chambliss from Albany (who later became our Georgia senator) walks in, so I got up and introduced him to everyone and asked him if he wanted to speak. I realized even more now how fortunate we were to have so many legislators make the effort to come to our luncheon and hear more about the SSGN. The fully story of the SSGNs if found in the stories section.

He was very charming, gracious and knew his stuff. When Jack thanked him, Representative Chambliss said, "Sheila, you know Parker Green and General Smith? They wanted me to say hello to you." I love those guys—they always make sure anyone from this area that they meet with that might know me they send regards. Saxby would later be our US Senator. We then went to see Senator Zell Miller. I purposely didn't sit at the conference table giving those who have not had an opportunity to "sit within the power." Everyone finished their briefings, and all did super—concise and with no hesitations. I was proud of them all! Then Jim Wells said, "Sheila McNeill would now like to say a few words."

Senator Miller said with a smile, "I would be disappointed if Sheila didn't share a few words."

I talked him into a couple of minutes about the National meeting with OLAs and our two-pager on top issues. I reviewed a few of them and told him I would give Stephen Kay, his military legislative assistant (MLA), a copy.

Miller said he knew he was a new comer in Washington, but in time he had been there our group gave the best briefings of any group he had. He thanked us for the conciseness and the preparedness and then said, "Sheila, could I get a copy of that two-pager?"

"I'll give Stephen Kay a copy, sir."

"Yeah, but knowing him he'll give it to me in a few days as his work, so you'd better give me a copy." Of course, he was kidding, and Stephen and I laughed. You know how good you are when your boss is comfortable giving you a hard time like that! Stephen would work with me years later when he went to work for Hurt Norton after Zell retired.

The next day we went to see Senator Cleland. It was the first time we were not meeting in his office. He was in a committee meeting but met us briefly. He had had a hard day. He joined us for dinner that evening.

We went to the Pentagon the next morning. Captain Joe Malloy, deputy to RADM Paul Sullivan, stayed during our three briefs and then presented his brief on submarine issues. When we got to the SSGN and talked about the time frame (five years), I questioned the long time. He said you have to refuel which takes two years then convert. I said I thought it could be done simultaneously. Captain Malloy laughed and said, "You are right, Sheila."

"Is it purely financial?" I asked.

"A year and a half ago we would have given this conversation a 5% chance of happening, then with Sheila's work with the Georgia delegation, Norm Dicks from Washington state, the events of the world and the effort toward transformation it has been approved. The first four boat built were each a little different as they strived to improve so that presents somewhat of a design problem. There are different designs for each submarine to be converted," Captain Malloy explained to the group.

Carla asked the captain if there were any new missions that were coming up that might consider Kings Bay as a location. He discussed some of upcoming new ships and technologies. Steve Berry, chairman of the County Commission, came up to me at the end of the brief and said, "Looks like you have your next project." I kept in touch with him until his retirement as a vice admiral. He always had the answer at his fingertips and became the guru of the Navy budget.

As Steve and David Moffit predicted, I had several calls on my cell phone when we left the Pentagon. Two from Andy Vanlandingham, MLA, from Senator Cleland's office saying the Senator would be able to join us that night for dinner and would like to bring Nancy. Jeremy from his office had also called. I called him back about how pleased we were.

That evening at dinner, David Moffitt, president of Coastal Bank in Camden County, pulled me aside. "Sheila, we have a note with you at the bank." My heart jumped as I wondered if there was a problem. He continued, "We would like to change that rate to one-half of 1 percent. You are doing so much to benefit Camden County we would like to do this to help you just a little."

I was so shocked I couldn't speak. I excused myself and went to the ladies' room. I stood in from of the mirror grinning like an idiot as tears streamed down my face. I couldn't stop, so I just stood watching the strange combination of smiles and tears. Finally, I was able to go back and give David a grateful hug and my thanks in recognizing my work. Later in the evening Bob Noble, executive director of the Joint Development Authority (JDA), said, "I understand some bankers have been talking with you, the JDA would like to help too. I think we can get two thousand to three thousand dollars from the board for your travels. In these years this was the first time that anyone every recognized that my work had value and needed financial support. It was a wonderful feeling."

That month, John Crouse, director of St. Marys Submarine Museum received a letter from Ben Bastura:

> *Hi John, I am receiving all the Kings Bay base newspapers. Thanks for having them sent here. I am doing very well and am very busy with the museum. Please find an article of interest. It's a copy but do what you want to with it. Please pass my love to Sheila McNeill. Your friend always, Ben Bastura.*

Do you want to know who Ben Bastura is? Read the story about the St. Marys Submarine Museum.

The Atlanta Navy League council arranged a ceremony to meet with Governor Roy Barnes of Georgia. We invited the commanding officer of the base Captain John Nuremberger to join us. That uniform looks great in the picture. I brought up the *Georgia Trend* magazine. Governor Barnes then told us of how honored he was to be on the cover. He said, "I don't think we have a copy here or I would give you an autographed copy."

I answered, "That's okay I brought the one of me on the cover and thought I'd autograph it for you." It was worth seeing his face, and he gave a big belly laugh. I'm so glad he took it that way.

I had a great time as national vice president for legislative affairs. I found these notes that confirm the following:

> *I caught a cab from the hotel to the Rayburn Building on Capitol Hill for the OLA reception, getting there early with my duties as national vice president—legislative affairs. The crowd kept multiplying, It was a huge success. I have never had discussions with so many of the joint staff and to VIPS. Marcia Smith from Navy League headquarters was pitching in as photographer. She was adamant that I would have my picture made with every VIP there! I would be talking with someone else and she would quietly come up, place her hand on my arm and say, "Excuse me, we need Ms. McNeill for a photo." What a hoot!*
>
> *I ended up taking a picture of her with the senior enlisted of both the Coast Guard and the Marine Corps senior enlisted and she took one of me with them. Sergeant Major of the Marine Corps Alford McMichael and Master Chief Petty Officer of the Coast Guard Vince Patton were both very generous with their time and allowed me to take a picture of Marcia with them. As I was taking the picture, her husband came in and couldn't figure out* ***what*** *was going on. She made pictures of me talking with General Shinseki,*

Chief of Staff Army, General Ryan, Chief of Staff Air Force, Admiral Jim Loy, Commandant Coast Guard, Admiral Bill Fallon Vice Chief of Naval Operations and many others.

Major Brian Moore, whom I had worked with in Jack Kingston's office, was there and approached me with "Could I introduce you to some of my generals?" How nice of him, and he did! When we finally go to the Army Chief of Staff, he introduced me as his mentor when he was a fellow on Capitol Hill and I spent my time telling how beautifully Major Moore adapted to all of the Navy issues he had to deal with. I also had a chance to tell General Shinseki what we were doing all day for support of the conversion of the four boats. I talked about the special operations forces and what an asset that would be to have the Army special operations forces located at Naval Submarine Base Kings Bay. We laughed and agreed that would not be a bad place for them to be located.[2]

The Army budget included $13 million for the conversion.

Later, Marcia would share with the office staff how I talked to the chief of staff of the Army and bragged about one of his men.

I also saw Lt. General Gary McKissock and we felt like old friends. When he was commanding general at Marine Corps Logistic Base in Albany, Georgia, I made a DACOWITS visit to his base. It was a great visit and he was a respected and effective commanding office. I was surprised when he introduced me to folks every time he saw me over the years. He would say, "This is the woman who scared the shit out of me when she came to my base." That Marine must be 6'5" and nothing would scare him which makes the comment even funnier.

We arrived on Thursday afternoon and were pleased with the nice suite. Carla, Bill and Nancy Kelly, and Raymond and June Coutour arrived soon after. Raymond and June bought pizzas for us all. We had very little chance to get our bearings. Veronica Brandon whom I worked with as development vice president came dressed as Elvira since it was Halloween. No one recognized her. Friday, we passed out buttons all day. Arlie and I stopped by the building exhibit and made a commitment for a naming opportunity for the Legislative Affairs Office. My heart will always be with legislative affairs and to have the office bear the name of the McNeills was awesome. Mother and Debbie arrived that afternoon.

I went before the nominating committee. These are the points I planned to cover depending on the time:

- Married to Arlie forty-one years—one daughter, two grandchildren.

---

2 The Army funded the first $13 million of the conversion.

- Followed Arlie in every position—great team.
- In this case, you get two for one—Arlie will be an asset.
- The first twenty years we were married we vacationed up and down the eastern coast, and everywhere we could find a Coast Guard unit, Arlie would be stopping by to shake hands and see if they needed anything. He continues to serve on the Coast Guard committee and loves meeting folks. You couldn't find a more dedicated Navy Leaguer.
- For the first twenty years of my career:

  - Industrial relations manager—safety director
  - Union contract negotiator
  - Training with W. R. Grace in Cambridge
  - Additional management training courses

The former president of Construction Products Division of W. R. Grace and Co. has come to our meeting from Florida—he is a member but he has come primarily to support me and to answer any questions anyone might have about my abilities.

I now have a five-thousand-square-foot Hallmark store.

- ❖ I employ fifteen employees.
- ❖ My manger has been with me for eighteen years.
- ❖ Two employees have been with me for fifteen years, one for eight years and one for ten.
- ❖ Four Navy spouses have worked with me.
- ❖ During Valentine's, we have a customer a minute for eleven hours.

The business affords me a full-time manager to run the business and a full-time secretory to keep up with Navy League and other volunteer work.

I think it went well. The best question was a "soft" question I think was meant to get the subject on the table and addressed: "How would the service chiefs react to having a woman president?"

"I know the service chiefs and it doesn't matter to them. I am not a woman in their eyes. I am an advocate for the sea services. They are so beyond being concerned about women in leadership. They do have women admirals."

I then went back and chaired the Legislative Affairs Committee with Chuck Beers. One of the members of the nominating committee came in. He nodded to me but I didn't know if it was a nod about the election or a nod of hello. He gave no indication. *Oh my! I might win*, I thought and prayed. I then received a call from the nominating committee chairman, Jack Kennedy. He told me, "You have won the nomination from the nominating committee but please have some integrity here…

Don't tell anyone until I've had a chance to tell John Panneton." As I was listening to Jack, my supporters started gathering around me. I didn't say anything. I just walked to our room with everyone walking behind me. The crowd kept gathering.

As I closed the door, I told them. But I added, "We cannot tell anyone until he has called John. We should hear any minute. We waited. And we waited. About forty-five minutes passed and someone suggested we go to the check in area and see if the notice was posted. We did and it was posted. It was open information now. I never received that call from Jack giving me the okay to share the news.

We didn't have long before the reception that evening to recognize the new president-elect—known as the senior vice president's dinner. We arrived just a little late and saw Tim Fanning and my opponent John Panneton at the door welcoming everyone. It certainly sent a strange message but I didn't care! When Admiral Vern Clark and his wife, Connie, arrived, he greeted me with a sympathetic smile and a big hug. "I won, you know," I told him.

He was stunned. "But, I thought…"

"Yes, I know but I won!"

Admiral Clark's remarks began with "Someone told me that Sheila was a woman." He looked at me and said, "Well, so she is." His remarks are in my stories about him. Connie, Vern's wife, gave Arlie tips for his new title the First Gentleman. I had a chance to speak to the audience:

> *President Fanning and fellow Navy League members, I want to thank each of you for choosing me to be your next Senior Vice President. It is an honor and privilege to be able to further my services to the Navy League in this capacity. These are trying times for our country—for our Services—and for our Navy League. I recognize the major responsibility that has been passed on to me and I look forward to the challenge.*
>
> *During the next six months, I will work very hard to support President Fanning and the current Navy Leagues mission. I intend to utilize the learning period to the fullest extent possible, knowing the important and challenging job that lies ahead. The process of 'campaigning' for this position has been very rewarding. I now know that I have a great number of friends throughout the Navy League's regions and that I will have their full support in my endeavors toward making the Navy League everything that its members want it to be.*
>
> *We are all working together toward the same end and by pulling together and by pulling in unison there is no telling how far we can go. I have always believed in people being allowed to use their imagination—in innovation—in cooperation—in teamwork. I intend to continue working with you—and for you—in this manner*

and to always maintain a strong focus on the primary mission of the Navy League to support our Sea Services.

When I arrived at the airport the next day, a Sunday, I called former chief of naval operations, Frank Kelso, and let him know I had won. He was, I believe, a little surprised but grateful for the decision the Navy League made.

At the time, I was elected as president-elect, the Navy League was in the middle of construction of a new building. It would occupy an entire city block with five stories and 214,000 square feet. Tim Fanning, former national president, was instrumental in making this happen.

When I was elected, I put together a team of about a dozen experts across the country. They paid their own way—some from as far away as California—to attend the meeting with the contractors for the building, each bringing their own expertise. I wrote to them, "Our new building has certainly taken a lot longer than we expected and they have run into unexpected obstacles—we've spent a lot of money that wasn't planned and there are some areas of concern but until you actually get in there, read the contracts, and are briefed on the issues you won't know the full story. It needs a complete relook—where we are and where we're going."

I've learned a long time ago that you can't be an expert on all things. And you should enlist the best and the smartest people in that field. I have talked to Jack Anderson, a benefactor of the Navy League, as you all know, and a smart builder. He has had a contractor's license in California since 1965. As busy as he is, he has agreed to serve on this Ad Hoc committee to look at where we stand and how we best take the building project forward. I'm talking with others making sure all are comfortable.

Reasonable minds will differ on philosophy of whether a general contractor or a development company handles certain issues. I don't propose to change the good work that Tim has done just for the sake of change. However, all that I do will be open for scrutiny and will enlist the advice of these experts. I know that Tim has said he will have nothing to do with the Navy League if I am elected. I want to assure you we will be fine. There are three or four staffers who have been to all the meetings—our executive director, our office manager, our director of finances, and our attorney.

I believe my background in a manufacturing plant, union negotiations, my work with contracts in every part of my job, my ability to work with people, and my history with enlisting the right experts when they are needed will keep us in the right direction. I enlisted experts across the country, brought in the contractors to brief the group. They had an opportunity to question everyone.

* * * * *

2003: I was invited to speak at the Honolulu Navy League's annual meeting and election of officers on January 27. This press release invitation was sent out by Pauline Worsham, Navy League Communications Committee chair.

> *The Honolulu Council of the Navy League of the United States features Governor Linda Lingle and the Navy League's President-elect Sheila McNeill at the Jan. 27 Annual Meeting.*
>
> *Governor Linda Lingle and Sheila McNeill, Senior Vice President and President-elect of the Navy League of the United States will be guest speakers at the League's Honolulu Council annual meeting on Monday January 27 from 6:30–9:00 in the Coral Ballroom of the Hilton Hawaiian Village. The Honolulu Boy's Choir will perform.*
>
> *The event will feature two firsts—Hawaii's first woman governor, the Honorable Linda Lingle, and the U.S. Navy League's first woman president-elect, Sheila McNeill. In addition to Governor Lingle and President-elect McNeill, other distinguished guests include Flag Officers of the Pacific Command, Navy League Board of Directors, Sailor of the Year Lt. Micajah T. McLendon, USN and other dignitaries. Navy League members and guests are encouraged to attend and participate in the annual election of officers.*
>
> *McNeill, the first woman to be elected in this position in the 100-year history of the organization will deliver the keynote address about the importance of community support of the sea services. A life member, she has been a Navy League member for 36 years, a National Director for the U.S. Naval Sea Cadet Corps and a Trustee for the League's National Scholarship Foundation.*
>
> *"We are honored to welcome President-elect McNeill as our annual meeting's keynote speaker. She will be a great ambassador for the U.S. Navy League as well as the upcoming Navy League's National Convention being held here in Hawaii from June 18–22, 2003, stated Richard Faharenwald, Honolulu Council President-elect, the President's Personal Representative and Chairman of the 2003 National Convention. The site of the convention will be the Hilton Hawaiian Village.*
>
> *One of the 330 Navy League Councils worldwide, the Honolulu Council serves as an educational liaison between the civilian community and our military sea services which include the Navy, Coast Guard and Marine Corps. The Council is actively involved in providing special recognition for outstanding sea service personnel as well as sponsoring and supporting Naval Sea Cadet Units and family*

assistance to sea service families. A non-profit, tax-exempt organization, the League relies solely on its members for support and funds.

Mark Rosen sent me an e-mail with the following article that was picked up and sent out by uscg.mil:

Navy League's first female president visiting Hawaii
By William Cole
Advertiser, Military Writer, Honolulu Advisor

Sheila McNeill recalls Chief of Naval Operations Adm. Vern Clark saying, "You know, someone tonight told me Sheila's a woman." "He turned and looked at me over his shoulder, and he smiled and turned back, and said, 'Well, so she is,'" McNeill said with a laugh. Clark's joke was made at the dinner in November celebrating McNeill's election as president of the 77,000-member Navy League of the United States. She is the first woman president of the Navy League in its 101-year history.

"I've been an advocate of the sea services—and that's the way they (big wigs at the Pentagon and Capitol Hill) see me," said McNeill, who is in town for tonight's annual meeting of the league's Honolulu Council. The Brunswick, Ga., resident also was never in the Navy or one of the other services—unlike her predecessors. McNeill and Gov. Linda Lingle are the guest speakers at tonight's meeting at the Hilton Hawaiian Village's Coral Ballroom.

Honolulu's Harold Estes, who was in the Navy from 1934 to 1955, and a Navy leaguer since 1964, has every confidence in the civilian organization's new skipper. "She is going to be the renaissance of the Navy League nationally," said Estes, a former national vice president. "She is a smart, smart lady and will do a magnificent job." The Honolulu Council, with 3,500 members, is the biggest of 330 councils worldwide. The national league was founded in 1902 with help from President Theodore Roosevelt—a former assistant secretary of the Navy—who gave part of his Nobel Peace Prize earnings to finance the support organization for the Navy, Marines, Coast Guard and Merchant Marine. The group recognizes outstanding sea services personnel, serves as a civilian liaison to the military, supports ship commissionings, lobbies Congress, and generally does whatever it can to help the services.

"I've 'grown up' a product of the Navy League in that I've been taken care of by the Navy League (at assignments) around the world,"

said Adm. Walter Doran, commander of Pacific Fleet. "I have tremendous respect, admiration and gratitude for what the Navy League has done for the United States Navy. "Although McNeill was never in the Navy, she has been a Navy leaguer for 36 years. She initially got involved in the organization through her husband, Arlie, who was in the Navy, and is a national director emeritus. "I've never been in the military, and I feel like this is my service to my country—to support those who are. At 59, I'm too old to join the Navy, so why not," McNeill said. McNeill served on the Defense Advisory Committee on Women in the Services under defense secretaries William Perry and William Cohen. As senior vice president, McNeill has been involved with legislative affairs—making 40 trips to Washington D.C. in two years' time. League support for the Navy includes raising millions of dollars every year for ship commissioning receptions for sailors.

The tab can be anywhere from $50,000 to close to a $1 million for aircraft carriers, such as that planned in May for the USS Ronald Reagan in Norfolk, Va., McNeill said. New Honolulu Council President Richard Faharenwald, who will be installed tonight, said the council has a food bank for enlisted personnel trying to make ends meet, donates to Navy and Marine Corps Moral, Welfare and Recreation programs, and recognizes the Pacific Fleet sailor of the year. "The emphasis really is on the recognition of what young people are doing in the services," Faharenwald said.

Hawaii, meanwhile, has its own woman executive with the Navy League of the United States. P. Pasha Baker is league president for the state. McNeill will be installed at the Navy League national convention at the Hilton Hawaiian Village June 18 to 22. McNeill said Navy brass often rely on the league when they stop in towns across the country.

"When either (the Chief of Naval Operations or Secretary of the Navy) goes into a community, they call ahead to get the Navy League to set up something the day before, and they speak at a Navy League meeting," she said. Estes said the Navy League could do more. "Some councils "need to be kicked in the butt and need to be led to do things—and she is going to be a leader," Estes said. "I called her when she was a candidate and urged her to be sure that she shook the tree real good should she be elected."

McNeill, who owns a Hallmark store in St. Marys, Ga., has moved up through the league ranks from council president to regional president, state president and then national vice president. Past Navy League leadership has included retired flag officers, Estes said.

> *McNeill estimates 15 percent of the league's leadership is now female. As the first woman president, and one without military service, McNeill acknowledges it's a big change at the top. But, she said, "I know the services. I've worked with the service chiefs over the years, and I know that they are very comfortable with me taking the leadership role, so I think that was significant." McNeill said maintaining membership is one of her key challenges.*
>
> *The league also lobbied for the Coast Guard's $17 billion Deepwater ship and aircraft replacement project, and supports Clark's call for a 375-ship Navy. "(We're) just staying focused on our goals—the goals of educating Congress and American people on the need for a strong defense, and supporting our military men and women," McNeill said. "Everything I do will have a focus on that mission."*

It was pretty cool to receive a message from the commander of the Pacific Fleet.

In January, Arlie and I attended the Nuclear Power School Graduation in Charleston, South Carolina, where acting secretary of the Navy, H. T. Johnson, spoke. My cousin Clyde Harrison Jr. was one of the graduates so that made it even more special.

There were many changes going on. I attended the farewell ceremony in honor of the secretary of the Navy and Mrs. England at the Washington Navy Yard on January 23 and a change of watch ceremony where Secretary Norman U. Mineta, Department of Transportation, was relieved by Secretary Thomas J. Ridge, Department of Homeland Security, on February 25, 2003.

In February, I was in Norfolk and Savannah for meetings and spending a lot of time in preparation for the national president responsibilities. On February 6, Arlie and I attended the South Atlantic Coast region meeting in Savannah. Back in Brunswick, I spoke at the Blue Star memorial dedication at the Marshes of Glynn Overlook Park on Highway 17 in Brunswick. My back was so bad, Arlie had to help me out of the car. I'm hoping this isn't going to plague me the entire tour as Navy League president. I squeezed in a Camden fly-in meeting with Congressman Kingston and Senators Cleland and Miller. I traveled with Jim Wells, Deborah Haas (mayor of St. Marys), Tilden and Arlen Norris, and Walt Natzic to the new Navy League building and gave them a tour. I then joined the Maryland delegation—David Sesman, Richard Holland, Rex Kilbourn, Jim Coleman, Jerry Rapkin, and Jim Offutt in their fly-in. We called on Senator Paul Sarbanes and Reps. Ben Cardin and Roscoe Bartlett along with staffers from Senator Barbara Mikulski and Representative Wayne Gilchrest, Steny Hoyer and Dutch Ruppersberger, and Jeremy Miller (Navy League, director of legislative affairs) spearheaded the effort and wrote a nice column in the Navy Leaguer.

While in DC, I met with Rick Barnard, editor of *Seapower*. I loved working with him. He seemed open to all my ideas and over the next two years he took these ideas and language for president's message and turned them into jewels. I would attend a meeting or sometimes just have conversations with senior leadership that turned into a major president's message. One of the suggestions I made was to give each article a sentence or two about the content and lead with that summary along with the title. This was help for those who might only scan the story or not be interested enough to read it at all. Pulling out the meat of the story in a couple of sentences, readers might learn a little about a subject they didn't think would be of interest and might even lead to them reading the entire article. He not only liked it but said he would begin during the next issue.

After meeting with Rick, I went to dinner with some of my submarine friends and their wives. I was really pumped about the meeting with our *Seapower* editor. As I talked the guys—Malcolm, Charlie, Jay—all looked at each other, smirking as I talked. They then gave me a lesson. They explained when they each assumed command of a submarine the crew listened intently. The officers and crew not only accepted their suggestions but were ready to implement them as soon as they could. Every card game they played with *anyone* they won. They were magnificent, they were brilliant, they were invincible. And then orders came. Suddenly, they stopped winning at cards games. The more senior of the crew offered more alternatives. To translate, they told me the editor didn't necessarily like my suggestions for the magazine they just went along with me until they could think of a way around it. I proved to them this was not true in the case of the editor, Barnard, and to further prove to them thirteen years later that feature is still a part of *Seapower*.

I spent a good bit of time with Howard Siegel, director of finance, who reviewed and reviewed the annual budget and the accounting process. Linda, Katie, and I were a constant. There was so much to be done.

The new acting secretary of the Navy, H. T. Johnson, came to Naval Submarine Base Kings Bay and Rear Admiral Jerry Talbot invited me to attend the dinner held the evening of March 10. Secretary Johnson is a gracious, outgoing gentleman, and we would grow close over the next two years. Captain Kevin Wensing, his public affairs officer and my good friend was with him for the visit. Also, accompanying SECNAV was Captain William Toti and Colonel John Kruz. Kevin later sent me the great pictures made that evening.

The base leadership was on hand that night—commanding officers and spouses from all commands: Cohoons, Drennans, Haskins, Lindstroms, Hendricksons, Balzers, and Davis. It was great to have a formal grown up meeting with all the spouses present!

March 19 was the first day of demolition of our old Navy League building in Arlington, Virginia. They let me "drive" one of the wrecking balls and knock the first wall down. There was a fun picture of Charlie Robinson, Tim Fanning, Joe Sacks, and me. The groundbreaking ceremony was on April 14.

I met for the first time with Admiral Vern Clark at his office in the Pentagon on March 20. As I was traveling to his office, I wondered if it might be canceled. This was the first day of the invasion of Iraq. The invasion lasted until May 1 and signaled the start of the Iraq War called Operation Iraqi Freedom. We met and cemented a relationship that would serve the Navy League well over the next two years.

LCDR Tom Prusinowski, one of the best public affairs officers ever was at Trident Refit Facility before he left for the aircraft carrier Theodore Roosevelt. They were in the midst of this invasion according to CNN. We were e-mailing around that time. I received an e-mail from Tom suggesting we look to the east and say, "Kick some ass, TR."

In March 2003, Linda Hoffman sent me a note. I had received an e-mail though my president of the Navy League e-mail wishing me well and thanking me for my participation in an event. It was signed "with love." Linda wrote me back, "I don't recall any correspondence, e-mail, voice mail, etc. that the word love in it anywhere until this."

The March 31 *Islander* newspaper had the following headline:

U.S. Secret Service Director speaks at Chamber lunch.

> *Connie Patrick, the first woman to hold the position as Director of the Federal Law Enforcement Training Center introduced the former Director of FLETC Ralph Basham. Basham was appointed to the Services' top job on January 23 after spending a year as Chief of Staff of the newly created "Transportation Security Administration (TSA). The TSA, along with its parent agency the Department of Homeland Security, was created in the wake of the September 11, 2001 terrorist attack on the U.S.*

I was pleased to attend that luncheon with Connie and John, two people I very much admire.

The theme of the Navy League's 2003 Sea Air Space Expo on April 14–17 was "America's best." This expo had the best media coverage in years. Security had to be exceptionally tight with the recent US led coalition victory over Iraq which also was an additional incentive to attend. Many of our principal speakers had played major roles in the planning for and conduct of the war. In addition, more of the ships, aircraft, sensors, and electronics/avionics systems featured in the SAS exhibits were now truly "combat proven" and for that reason was of even great interest not only to the media but also to the budget decision makers from DoD and Capitol Hill who toured the exhibit reported Tim Fanning, national president. As usual there were many military leaders in attendance. Joining us for lunch was H. T. Johnson (acting secretary of the Navy), Admiral Skip Bowman, and Assistant Secretary Aviles. For lunch the next day was chairman of the Joint Chiefs General Richard Myers and Vice Admiral James Metzger, Assistant to the Chairman. Admiral Vern Clark joined us on the third day with Vice Admiral Tom Barrett, Assistant Commandant of the US Coast Guard. Retired Vice Admiral Herberger, a leader in the Navy League was one of the honored guests.

In April, the *Tribune & Georgian* reports, "A longtime respected local business woman and community leader recently received one of the most significant and highest honors from Rotary International and the Rotary Club of Camden County. Trish McMillan, former Public Affairs Officer for Naval Submarine Base Kings Bay was the past president of the club and the one who made the nomination. McMillian said, "The Paul Harris award is very significant to Rotarians, and the club thought it would be appropriate to award this to Sheila even though she is not a member of the organization."

During that time, the Camden Kings Bay Council welcomed Rear Admiral Steven Maas, who spoke to our council. We really had a good time with Steve and his wife, Barbara, and would connect many times over the next few years.

What a wonderful day when Royce Hall got word that he would be receiving his Air Medals he earned for his service to the nation in WWII. He and his wife, Faye, are old friends and it was an honor to work with Congressman Jack Kingston to make this happen. The award ceremony for M. Royce Hall, chief aviation ordnanceman, was held on May 12, 2003. The program listed his naval war service:

Enlisted USN, November 29, 1940, Savannah, Georgia
Sworn in December 30, 1940, Macon, Georgia
Recruit training and Aviation Ordnance School, Norfolk, Virginia
Ground School Gunnery and Norden Bomb, sight instructor, NAS Pensacola
Leading aircrewman and TBM turret gunner, VC-8, May 1943–November 1944
Major battles, WWII (1044)
Marianas campaign, Philippine invasion, and the battle of Leyte Gulf.
Fleet Service Squadron 5, CASU 25, NAS Oceana, Virginia, 1946.
Separated from naval service, January 21, 1947
Enlisted US naval reserve, July 20, 1950–July 20, 1954

Awards

three Distinguished Flying Crosses
thirteen Air Medals
Presidential Unit Citation
American Combat Action Ribbon

American Defense Service Medal with Fleet Clasp
Assistant Pacific Campaign Medal with three Bronze Stars
Philippine Presidential Unit Citation
Honorable Service Lapel Button

My thanks to Congressman Jack Kingston whose great staff fought long to ensure that Royce's medals were awarded to him. Royce is a very humble man. He never expected to get recognition other than to get his medals so his family would have them. This is not just an ordinary man. "He needs to be recognized even if he doesn't see himself as a hero," I told those present.

On May 13, 2003, the *Florida Times Union* ran an article on St. Marys Airport called a "Security Risk for Kings Bay." The first of many articles over the next fifteen years.

Also on May 28, the newspapers were full of the long-awaited news. St. Marys chosen for patrol unit. The Maritime Safety and Security Team 91108 would be coming to Kings Bay. We had been working with Commandant Thad Allen for months so this was with great pride and relief that the decision was made—more on that unit in the stories section. In the same papers were the Navy's decision to send the USS *Georgia* and the USS *Florida* to Kings Bay:

> *Kingston said the "unofficial" Navy plans are to station the Florida at Kings Bay after the conversion is completed in 2006. The Georgia will arrive at Kings Bay the following year, he said. Nearly $1.6 billion to fund the conversion of the Trident submarines has been authorized by the House and will be funded after the bill clears the appropriations committee, Kingston said. Sheila McNeill, national president-elect for the Navy League said many people have been lobbying for the Georgia and Florida to be home-ported at Kings Bay since the Navy announced the boats would be stripped of their nuclear Trident missiles and converted to carry Tomahawk missiles. The boats, each with the firepower of an entire battle group will be an important tool in the war against terrorist, supporters say. Each submarine will also carry 60 special Forces troops who can be deployed in coastal areas without the boat surfacing.*
>
> *McNeill said the announcement has great public relations value. "We've ask for this constantly," she said. "We felt there would be a certain advantage for everyone with the two boats being right here (in Georgia)."*

June 16–22 was the Navy League National Convention, Honolulu, Hawaii. It is official! I was sworn in at the conference in Hawaii. As a special treat, Jim Nabors of the *Andy Griffith Show* sang the national anthem. The vice presidents elected to serve with me and the assignments I gave to each of them:

- Edwin R. Carter—finance
- Carter B. Conlin—region president, liaison
- Carol Ann Hackley—special advisor, public relations
- Randy Hollstein—legislative affairs
- Glen Hubert—information technology
- Bill Kelley—chairman, National Advisory Council
- Richard Kennedy—national treasurer
- Harold Learson—Sea Cadets and your programs
- Dick Macke—sea service liaison
- Mike McGrath—membership
- Brad Nemeth—development
- John Panneton—public education
- Gene Proctor—corporate secretary
- Bob Ravitz—corporate affairs
- Peter Kent—special advisor, strategic planning

There were several committee that reported direct to the president. Those wonderful staff members assigned to oversee were as follows:

- Awards Committee—Katie Doud
- Bylaws Committee—Linda Hoffman
- Communications Board—Rick Barnard
- Convention Committee—Pat Holmgaard
- Nominating Committee—Linda Hoffman/Katie Doud
- Property Development Committee—Charlie Robinson/Joe Sacks
- Proxy Committee—Katie Doud
- Resolutions Committee—Rich Loganzino

Linda Hoffman and Katie Doud literally had my back during those two years. As a real blessing while writing this book I depended on Katie's work on my schedule that she began in January—about five months before I assumed the duties of national president. At the end of those two years, they presented not one, but two handsome scrapbooks starting with my schedule with letters and cards I had received during those two years. It had not dawned on me that during the years I received copies of all the correspondence and they kept the original to make this book!

Our first night in Honolulu was our traditional pizza. June and Raymond Coutour were the hosts with Bill and Nancy making up the usual six. On June 20–25, 2003, I had my official installation in Honolulu. Rear Admiral Barry McCullough, commander of Navy Region Hawaii, was my official escort for a visit to the USS *Arizona*. I was given a Certificate of Flag Presentation:

> *Mrs. Sheila M. McNeill: On the beginning of her service as the first woman president of the Navy League of the United States In its 100-year History, of Citizens in Support of the Sea Services In tribute to the American fighting men killed during the attack on Pearl Harbor, the national ensign flies continuously from a flagpole mounted to the battleship USS Arizona (BB39). During hours of darkness, the flag is illuminated. The battleship resting in 38 feet of water, is no longer in commission. It was stricken from the active list in 1942. Special permission was granted by the Secretary of the Navy to fly the United States Flag over the ship in memory of the brave men killed during the attack on the morning of December 7, 1941. The United States Flag accompanying this certificate was raised and lowered from this same flagpole on 19 June 2003 @ 1340.*
>
> *Signed and authenticated this date: 24 June 2003*
>
> *Signed*
>
> | | |
> |---|---|
> | *Douglas A. Lentz* | *Bernard J. McCullough III* |
> | *National Park Service* | *Commander* |
> | *Superintendent* | *Navy Region. Hawaii* |

RADM McCullough made quite an imposing figure with his tall frame and that white uniform. Visitors to the Memorial saw this group of people coming and with one movement of his hand they pulled aside as the flag was raised. He surprised me, and I'm sure the visitors were too, when he asked me to say a few words. It was an overwhelming moment. I'm not sure what I said. It was over in a few minutes, but it is an event that will never be forgotten.

Its official! The Navy League sent a press release:

> ***The Navy League of the United States Elects Sheila M. McNeill as National President, First Female President in League's 100-Year History***
>
> *Arlington, Va. Sheila M. McNeill of Brunswick. Georgia was sworn in as the new national president of the Navy League of the United States (NLUS) during the League's annual convention in Honolulu June 21, 2003. McNeill is the first woman to be elected to this position in the 100-year history of the organization. McNeill, a life member of the Navy League who joined in 1966, has served*

in a variety of leadership positions. Most recently she served as a national vice president responsible for the organization's legislative affairs activities. She also served as a national director for the U.S. Naval Sea Cadet Corps and has been a trustee for the Navy League's National Scholarship Foundation. McNeill has a long history of active involvement in the Navy League at the grass roots level including serving as President of the Camden-Kings Bay Council, Georgia State President and Region President of the South Atlantic Coast Region. McNeill also served as a member of the executive committee for DACOWITS, an influential advisory committee to the secretary of defense and other DoD officials. During her three-year DACOWITS tour McNeill visited 48 U.S. naval and military installations throughout the world.

In her home state of Georgia, McNeill serves as a member of the Governor's statewide Military Affairs Coordinating Committee. McNeill was commissioning president of the St. Mary Submarine Museum and Charter Chairman of the Military Community Council. She continues to serve in both organizations. She is also a member of the Advisory Board of the Coastal Georgia Community College and has been on the Board of Directors of the Chamber of Commerce in Glynn and Camden Counties.

McNeill commented: "I am truly honored to lead an organization whose mission is to support the young men and women of our nation's sea services. As the national president, I will continue to focus the organization on educating our citizens and elected officials on the need for strong sea services. I will work to develop future leaders who will move the Navy League through its next century of service while preserving the organization's rich traditions and contributions over the past 100 years." McNeill has received numerous awards including the Secretary of the Navy's Superior Public Service and Meritorious Public Service Medals, the United State Coast Guard's Distinguished Public Service and Meritorious Public Service Medals, and various community service medals.

McNeill is married to Arlie McNeill, a Navy veteran and long-time Navy League member and national director emeritus. They have one daughter, Leslie, and two grandchildren.

The Honolulu Council, host for the national conventions, sent out a press release announcing my visit to the Arizona Memorial as the first official act on Monday, June 23, 2003. Coverage of the election was in various papers—even in *Navy Times*! The picture of the steering committee was different with the bright color clothes instead of the usual black suits. We had two principal speakers at the convention: Admiral Walt Doran, commander, US Pacific Fleet; and Admiral Thomas B. Fargo, commander, US Pacific Command, and a submariner. In writing this book, I constantly researched friends and associates to make sure I had the right titles and dates. Admiral Fargo had a particularly interesting addition. It turned out that he was the inspirations for the character in *Hunt for Red October*. "He was incredibly confident… he was this guy you would follow into hell," Alec Baldwin said of Admiral Fargo. I would see Admiral Walt Doran a year or so later when I made my trip to our Asian councils. At this meeting, I was presented the Distinguished Public Service Medal from the United States Coast Guard by my friend Rear Admiral Kevin J. Eldridge, assistant commandant for governmental and public affairs.

Distinguished Public Service Award

> *The Commandant of the United States Coast Guard takes great pleasure in presenting the Distinguished Public Service Award to Mrs. Sheila McNeill for her outstanding contribution to the Coast Guard from January 2001 to May 2003. As National Vice President of Legislative Affairs for the Navy League of the United States, Mrs. McNeill was instrumental in advancing the Coast Guard's legislative agenda in the 107th and 108th Congress. Mrs. McNeill was extremely effective with the U.S. Department of Transportation and Congress during one of the most fundamentally significant legislative periods in Coast Guard history. During this period, Congress debated and enacted the Homeland Security Act, which affected the historic transfer of the Coast Guard to the Department of Homeland Security, the Maritime Transportation Security Act, one of the most sweeping maritime security legislative packages in the Nation's history and the first Coast Guard Authorization Act in nearly half a decade. Mrs. McNeill and her legislative affairs team orchestrated numerous Navy League hosted events with members of Congress, which provided forums for the comprehensive airing of Coast Guard Issues during the political process. Of particular note was her team's showcasing of the need for major Coast Guard acquisition through the Integrated Deepwater Systems project. Their efforts were key to promoting and securing Congress' 800 million Deepwater appropriation in Fiscal years 2002 and 2004 the largest acquisition project in the Coast Guard's and Department of Transportation's history. Mrs. McNeill's thoughtfulness, integrity and unwavering dedication resulted in substantial improvement in the efficiency and effectiveness of the Coast Guard in its service to the nation. Her exceptional*

> *professionalism and sense of duty are most heartily commended and are in keeping with the highest tradition of the United States Coast Guard and public service.*

June and Raymond and Bill and Nancy celebrated with me and Arlie with our traditional pizza dinner from room service.

Back home the efforts to save the four SSBN is won but now where will they go?

CAMDEN WANTS MORE SUBS

This was the headlines in the *Tribune & Georgian.*

It began, "Sheila McNeill, national Navy League president and a Camden County business owner, hopes that two refitted submarines—with their crews and families—will be sent to Naval Submarine Base Kings Bay." Here she stands on a decommissioned submarine at the base."

The Navy had not released which, if any, SSGNs would come to Kings Bay but we had made our voices known that we wanted the USS *Georgia* and the USS *Florida*, knowing they would be the second and fourth subs to be converted. I kept reminding everyone that having the USS *Georgia* and USS *Florida* here instead of the old USS *Ohio* and USS *Michigan* will delay Camden County receiving the boast by about two years. They were adamant! See the SSGN story for the rest!

I received an interesting invitation to speak at the annual Daughters of the American Revolution meeting in DC. They had adopted the aircraft carrier USS *John C. Stennis* (CVN 74) over the past year. I believe Steve P. had been working with his PAO friends to make the adoption and this ceremony happen. It began with a presentation of the NSDAR Founders Medal for Patriotism given to singer Pat Boone. Who have a wonderful musical presentation. They had two speakers for the evening. They were coauthors of *Endgame: The Blueprint for Victory in the War on Terror*—Lieutenant General Thomas G. McInerney, USAF (ret.), and Major General Paul E. Valley, USA (ret.). I knew Tom, we had been at many of the same events, but I had not met Paul. Steve Pietropaoli was working with the USS *Stennis* for the proper message. Captain David H. Buss, the commanding officer of the *Stennis*, sent me these words to share: "The support rendered to the crew of USS *John C. Stennis* by the Daughters of the American Revolution over the past year has been absolutely fantastic. DAR donations have ranged from Maglite flashlights for each crew member to work out mats for all in the crew. The Daughters have had the most positive impact on both our Quality of Life and Quality of Service board. My personal thanks go out to the entire DDAR organization for its remarkable support to our men and women in uniform around the globe, but most particularly here in *John C. Stennis*."

We were all seated on stage. I believe I was between Pat Boone and Tom McInerney. The full program was close to four hours. About midway through I couldn't wait any longer and stood up to slip behind the curtains and find a woman's bathroom ("head" seems inappropriate for this formal occasion.) I was stopped before I could turn back the curtain and was told that no one can leave once the doors have closed. Oh my, this was not good. Even had I known, I'm not sure with it this cold that I could sit there for four hours without a break. I was wondering what to do when the same young woman came back for me. She told me I had been approved to leave for a short break! I came back to many awards bring presented to DAR:

- DAR Americanism Meal, Eduardo Aquirre, director, US Bureau of Citizenship and Immigrations Services
- NSDAR Motion Picture, Radio and Television Award to Ric Burns, documentary filmmaker
- DAR Medal of Honor: Major General Patrick H. Brady, US Army (ret.), chairman, Citizens Flag Alliance, commissioner of American Battle Monuments Commission

There must have been six hundred in the audience. It was a most impressive evening.

July 23, 2003

I received a nice handwritten note from Jack Spittler, a past national president. To have someone of his era gave me accolades was most appreciated.

> *Sheila, please accept my apology for the tardiness of my correspondence. Please accept my heartfelt offer to assist you in every way possible. Also, I thought your position paper to the National Directors 19 June 2003 was excellent; sorry I couldn't have been in headquarters to express my support personally. Also, wanted to mention the Hallmark Beanie Bear with the N.L. legislative message. It got us a new member—we now have 125 and going strong. Coast Guard Admiral Bob Duncan was our speaker last night—100 attended—a good message of courage. Our best to Arlie. Jack*

The Navy League had voted to approve building a five story 214,043 square foot building in the busy Arlington, Virginia, area. We already owned much of the property and bought the remainder. The magnitude of this project is the amount of the loan: $38,864,000. The Navy League would occupy twenty thousand square feet in the property as its headquarters and lease the remaining space to other tenants. I established an advisory committee to review all contracts and contractors and this article was in the *Navy Leaguer.*

McNeill: "Productive Session" on New Navy League Building

Members of the Navy League's Ad Hoc Building Advisory Committee gathered at NLUS headquarters at the end of July to view the progress achieved to date on the new Navy League National Headquarters Building and discuss the work remaining to be done. "It was a very productive session," said National President Sheila M. McNeill, "and was enhanced considerably by the professional, legal, financial, and property management expertise of numerous members of this committee." John R. Anderson IV, a past national president and a former national treasurer, has agreed to serve as the new chairman of the Navy League's Property Development Committee McNeill said. Photo shows McNeill, Anderson and others of the Ad Hoc Committee being briefed by James G. Davis, Barry Perkins and Dave Purdy of the James G. Davis Construction Company principal contractor for the building project.

The twenty-fifth anniversary of Kings Bay was held on Thursday, July 24, 2003.

The headlines of the *Florida Times Union* was "***Camden wants more subs***—*Area needs to fill lost jobs.*" The article was on our effort to work with our legislators for the conversion of the four Trident submarines to guided-missile subs and to have two of them sent to Kings Bay. It was a huge article and would help as we were coming down to the finish line.

The headlines of the *Florida Times Union*:

Sub Base Surfaces to Milestone: Navy Celebrates Kings Bay's 25th
Influence Is Indelible in Community
Gordon Jackson, Times Union staff writer

KINGS BAY NAVAL SUBMARINE BASE—A quarter-century ago, St. Marys was nicknamed Mayberry by the Sea for its sleepy, small-town atmosphere. Then 37 new residents moved to town. Their names are forgotten by most of those living in the city in 1978. Few would disagree, however, with the significance of the role those first arrivals played at what had been an unused Army ocean terminal until the Navy acquired the site and called it Naval Submarine Support Base Kings Bay.

It wasn't until a year later that local residents realized nearly every aspect of their town and the rest of Camden County would change forever, when the Navy announced the base would be the home to 10 nuclear-powered Trident submarines planned for construction. After 25 years at the 16,000-acre site, the Navy believes it's time to commemorate the silver anniversary at what is now known as Kings Bay Naval Submarine Base, and the strong relationship the 5,400 Sailors and Marines, along with 3,500 civilian workers, have with the surrounding communities. Most civilians won't be able to participate in the main celebration on base tomorrow because of increased security, but Navy and public officials agree the base's 25th anniversary is a significant milestone in local history.

"The 25th anniversary is testimony to the fact the Navy is part of the community," said Capt. John E. Cohoon Jr., commanding officer at Kings Bay. "Our sailors, Marines and civilian workforce not only live and work here, but also take an active role in the community." Gov. Sonny Perdue has declared tomorrow as Naval Submarine Base Kings Bay Day. He described the base as playing an "instrumental role in ending the Cold War and the charge it still keeps by defending our freedoms from the very real threats we face today." "As governor, I recognize the positive impact Naval Submarine Base Kings Bay has had with the local community," Perdue said. "Some are Georgians by birth, some by choice, some by the order of Uncle Sam, but all are part of the Georgia family. I hope our state's hospitality and beautiful coastline makes them feel at home while they carry out their important mission."

SYMBIOTIC RELATIONSHIP

The Navy's arrival did much more than triple the county's population from about 13,000 in 1978 to nearly 50,000 residents today, making it one of the state's fastest growing counties in Georgia during that time. The school district has more than doubled the number of schools; dozens of new roads have been built and many existing ones have been widened; new subdivisions have been constructed; and nearly every government service has been expanded to accommodate the new growth. Navy officials described the $1.3 billion base as the largest peacetime construction program in its history.

National Navy League President Sheila McNeill calls Kings Bay one of the Navy's "premier" bases. "Not only have they preserved the integrity of the cities, but they preserved the environment," McNeill said. "I continue to see former sailors at Kings Bay who call it one of their best tours of duty because of the relationship with the community."

Camden County Sheriff Bill Smith said his office had 19 employees in 1978. There are now an estimated 120 employees working at the Sheriff's Office. Despite the population explosion, Smith said his deputies have had very few problems associated with the sailors and civilian workers at Kings Bay. "Before the Navy came, this was a very small, friendly community," Smith said. "Now it's not so small, but it's still very friendly. Law enforcement has become more complicated, but at the same time more professional. Camden County was then, and still is, a great place to call home."

Edwin Davis, assistant superintendent of Camden County schools, said the school district has added six elementary schools, built two large middle schools and has the eighth-largest high school, population wise, in the state since the Navy arrived. The growth has been dramatic, but manageable because of the close cooperation with the Navy, David said.

"Certainly, it's been for the good," Davis said. "Everything, we have to say is tremendously positive." Nearly 60 percent of the student currently enrolled were born outside the state and many of the teachers and navy spouses who have brought many new ideas, teaching techniques, and experience with them, David said.

It's been a great recruiting opportunity for us." Davis said. "We get exposure from their experience." St. Marys Mayor Deborah Hase attributed the well-planned growth in the city since the Navy's arrival as "fabulous." "It's been great for the economy," Hase said. "it's been great for the community. They're part of us, we're part of them."

The base's future

The $1.3 billion construction of the facilities at Kings Bay lasted nearly 11 years and was designed with convenience in mind for the sailors living on base. The barracks, galley, gymnasium and other support services on the upper base were built within 15 minutes walking distance of each other. The base also had a mandate to protect the environment including nearly 4,000 acres of protected wetlands. Cohoon said a year-long environmental study was conducted before construction began to protect environmentally sensitive areas on base. Foraging areas were established for endangered wood storks and least terns, and propeller guards were installed on small boats to protect manatees. I think Kings Bay's legacy won't necessarily be our mission but our local community involvement and what we

> *did to protect and maintain the delicate ecosystem here for future generations," Cohoon said. The base's mission, however, will continue as the nation's main deterrent to nuclear war said U.S. Rep. Jack Kingston, R-Ga.*
>
> *"It is one of our most important strategic bases on the eastern seaboard and has brought momentous benefits to Coastal and Southeast Georgia, Kinston said. "Two of the ten Trident submarines originally ported at Kings Bay were relocated to Bangor, Wash., last year and the base could lose more submariners if treaties with other nations reduce the nation's nuclear weapons stockpile in coming years," McNeill said. But future growth on base is a very distinct possibility because of the facilities, location and surround community, McNeill said. Plans are underway for four of the oldest Tridents to be stripped of their nuclear missiles and refitted to carry tomahawk missiles and special forces troops with the ability to respond to any military crisis in a coastal area of the world. The first converted submarine could arrive at Kings Bay within the next two to three years. "I think there will be some changes," McNeill said. I see in the future a fast attack squadron and perhaps adding another service unit on base. I think they will all be good changes." Rear Adm. Jerry Talbot, commanding officer of Submarine Group 10, said Kings Bay has always delivered the finest support and lived up to its mission," Talbot said. "I extend a hearty congratulation to the men and women of the submarine base on 25 years of superb support and service to our nation."*

The *Washington Times* picked up on my President's message of July 2003, "Rebalance Security and Environmental Needs," as did *Forbes* magazine. G. Gordon Liddy also covered these encroachment issues on his talk show.

Military Animals

> *The president of the Navy League of the United States has warned every member of Congress this week that "critical defense development and training programs are being delayed or curtailed as our nation approaches a turn point in the war on terrorism."*
>
> *And the problem is?*
>
> *"The Navy and Marine Corps are besieged by overzealous environmentalists that have employed vaguely written regulations to delay or cancel key weapon development programs, severely reduce the size of usable military-training areas and diminish the opportunities for realistic training," the league's president Sheila McNeill,*

tells Congress. She cites, for starters, a six-year delay of deployment of an advanced sonar system because of unproved assertions that it would damage marine mammal populations. (the system would improve substantially the Navy's ability to detect quiet, diesel-electric submarines deployed by North Korea and Iran.) In addition, only a mile of the 17-mile beach at Camp Pendleton, California is available to practice amphibious landings while the U.S. Fish and Wildlife Service wants to designate an additional 56 percent of the camp off limits to military training, labeling it critical wildlife habitat. Same story for 65% of the Marine Corps Air Station Miramar in California. It gets worse. Uncle Sam's green soldiers proposed in October to designate large tracts of military property on Guam off limits to protect such endangered species as the Mariana fruit bat and the Micronesian kingfisher, even though neither of the species lives on military land on Guam.

Last year Navy Adm. Walter F Doran, commander of the Pacific Fleet, said there is a "grievous imbalance between our national security," warning that "In this time of war; vital navy training is being delayed, curtailed and cancelled. The leagues president calls the Navy and Marines "excellent" environmental stewards, noting that 130 full-time natural resources specialists protect about 185 threatened and endangered species on military bases.

I received a letter from Admiral Clark written July 30, 2003:

Dear Sheila, Just a quick note regarding a recent article in the Washington Times on your efforts to inform Congress on some of our training challenges. You're off to a great start. I so appreciate what you and the Navy League do for our sea services. Your efforts make a difference. Thank you for your service. Vern

We sent my president's message and talking points: Environmental Stewardship to every member of Congress. Rear Admiral Gary Roughead, OLA, sent thanks for the supporting this training challenge and other support.

On July 29, 2004, with my fellow Georgia Military Affairs Coordinating Committee, I attended a supper at the Governor's Mansion in Atlanta.

On August 5, I attended the Coast Guard Birthday. Lyford Norton sent the nicest note:

Sheila, Thanks so much for coming up to celebrate the Coast Guard Birthday with us. Officially it means the world to me/us to have the national president support our functions. Personally, I'm always glad to have you grace us with your warm and engaging personality.

Continued success v/r Lynford

You got to love that guy!

* * * * *

I recognized the Golden Isles Council led by Colonel Franklin A. Hart, USMC (ret.), immediate past president of the council and Hubert Lang, III current president for being one of the top councils in the world—only ten of these are awarded to the 330 councils in the world.

Arlie and I attended the commissioning of the *USS Ronald Reagan* (CVN 76). The story is covered in my stories section.

Robert Hamilton, one of my favorite newsmen, sent a note from the *Day* in Connecticut: "Thanks so much for your time. It was really a great interview and I can see how you would be picked—you bring so much energy to the job. It tires me just watching! Good luck and God Bless. Bob."

This was his article:

McNeill Working to Breathe New Life Into Navy League
Published July 10. 2003 12:01AM | Updated December 22. 2009 2:27PM
Robert A. Hamilton Day Staff Writer, Navy/Defense/Electric Boat

Groton—*Sheila McNeill brought the fervor of an old-fashioned Christian revival meeting to Wednesday's session of the local chapter of the Navy League of the United States, exhorting members to back programs to boost membership and improve the organization's finances. The newly elected McNeill, the first woman president in the 100-year history of the Navy League, urged the 50 members present to get the chapter's 300 other members to attend meetings and to attract new people to the League, a civilian organization dedicated to supporting the men and women of the sea services. One visitor from Omaha, Neb., asked what she could do in a Midwestern area where there is no local chapter. "You could start one," McNeill answered. "Would you give me your address and let me send you some information? All you have to do is put together 25 people for a council and I'll be glad to come out and charter it."*

After the meeting, many predicted McNeill will do much to invigorate a group that has been shrinking, down about 3,000 members to 74,000 nationally in the last three years. McNeill wants the League to be able to organize its local chapters into national movements.

"We have some very influential members at the local level, but we haven't even begun to tap that grassroots potential," McNeill said. "I want them to get more involved." Her husband, Arlie McNeill, a former regional president of the Navy League, will be the first male to sponsor the "Ladies Tea" at League meetings. He has thrown himself into the role and plans to use his skills as an amateur auctioneer to raise money for the League-sponsored Sea Cadets. McNeill joined the Navy League in 1967 in Brunswick, Ga., with her husband, a former petty officer in the dental corps, and for 20 years volunteered to support his duties. At the time, she said, women did not hold leadership positions in the League. Then, in the late 1980s, at a meeting of the Kings Bay, Ga., chapter, the local president was showing home movies of his vacation in the Bahamas. She asked him if the group had a program chairman; he answered that if it did, he wouldn't have to be showing home movies.

"One of the premier bases in the world, and we're showing home movies?" she said. "I became the program chairman." In the early 1990s, she served as state president in Georgia while her husband was president of the South Atlantic Coast Region, the first husband-wife team at that level of leadership. She joked that it was the only time in 40 years of marriage that he was the boss—and she soon took over his job.

From 1996 to 1998, she served on the Defense Advisory Committee on Women in the Services, or DACOWITS, and traveled to 45 bases in three years. Meeting in small groups with almost 3,000 members of the military, she heard about the need for more resources and better care for families. "They weren't talking about gender issues, they were talking about flying hours, and getting the parts, they needed to keep their planes in the air," McNeill said. So, in 1999 she sought and won the League posts of vice president for strategic planning and, a year later, vice president for legislative affairs. As the liaison to lawmakers, she wrangled a five-fold increase in the budget for the office, and made 42 trips to Washington, D.C., in 24 months at her own expense. She ran into some resistance with her suggestion of monthly two-page briefings about the legislative priorities of the sea services—the Navy, the Marine Corps, the Coast Guard and the Merchant Marine.

"I wanted something that would be timely, and something that would still be short enough for people to read—everyone is busy today," McNeill said. The result has been so successful that it is now printed in Seapower, the organization's monthly magazine. The pace she set was grueling, but the result was much greater visibility for the League on Capitol Hill and a newfound respect among lawmakers. Although she's only been in the president's job a matter of days, she has embarked on a new fund-raising campaign, asking for $100 from each member, instead of the $1,000 to $5,000 requests that have been made in the past.

"If 10 percent of our members give $100, my operating budget problems would be over," McNeill said. McNeill wants to engage the general public more about the need for strong sea services. Targeting the League's efforts at admirals does nothing because they already believe, and targeting lawmakers is only effective if they know their constituents are behind the message, she said. She envisions a database of contacts around the country so that highly targeted campaigns can be launched at a moment's notice to ensure a positive vote on a key shipbuilding bill or action that would improve the quality of life for sailors' families. "We're a big country, and we're a maritime nation, and our economic survival depends on free and open sea lanes," McNeill said. "I don't know what the answers are, but I do know I don't mind asking the questions."

Note: The author of this article and my friend, Robert (Bob) Hamilton, died at age fifty-seven, He was then the Electric Boat Spokesman and former *Day* reporter who was the first US reporter embedded on a combat submarine during a wartime patrol since World War II died in July 2014. He is very much missed by everyone.

On September 15, RADM Denny Moynihan, public affairs officer for the chief of naval operations, Vern Clark working with CHINFO RADM Terry L. McCreary, made arrangement for me to take media training. Denny was very generous in his time and counsel during this learning period of mine. This media training was the same training that new flag officers took. I met with the man, CDR John Kirby. It was a full day. I was interviewed and challenged with everything I said. They had me standing at a podium in a room just like a press room in the Pentagon with about eight "reporters" throwing questions at me. They had me relaxed at a table and simulated a radio talk show.

Midday when I took a head break and was returning I got "confronted" in the hallway with another six or so "reporters" with huge television size cameras, asking questions as if I were a politician in the middle of a scandal! Finally, I was told that since I was here and available, they had a local TV reporter who wanted to talk with me about the Navy League, my new role as the first woman president of the Navy League and the process of media training that I had to complete. We went outside the office where the TV's trucks and a huge camera with the reporter waiting. I was asked one question after another. Several were unusual and aimed at giving me the "opportunity" to really make things bad for the Navy League and our relationship with the Navy.

I passed the test and will be eternally grateful for Denny and John for providing this training. And speaking of John Kirby, he has had a remarkable career. He retired as a two-star admiral after serving as press secretary under Admiral Mike Mullen, chairman of the joint chiefs. He later became assistant secretary of state for communications. In 2013, he came with secretary of defense, Chuck Hagel, to Kings Bay on a visit, and I had a chance to talk with him and again, to thank him for all the training. RADM Joe Tofalo surprised me by bringing me up to the stage to meet Secretary Hagel and Hagel presented his coin.

During that time, we hired Richard L. Wright to write the one-hundred-year history of the Navy League of the United States. The introduction of the book was written by Morgan L. Fitch, a former national president of the Navy League, and the founder of the Naval Sea Cadets, with a foreword by Senator John W. Warner, from Virginia and chairman of the US Senate Armed Services Committee.

On August 3, the American Maritime Congress's *Washington Letter* had headlines about a recent president's message:

> ***New Navy League President: SeaPower Key to Economic Prosperity, National Security***
>
> *Sheila M. McNeill, the newly elected President of the Navy League of the United States, underscored the need for strong sea services, including a viable United States Merchant Marine, to further the economic and national security interest of the Nation, in an inaugural message to more the 74,000 Navy League members published in the July 2003 issue of Seapower magazine. The future will be challenging, with the Nation's global war on terrorism requiring 'sustained vigilance" of U.S. sea services, McNeill said. Citing the service of the U.S. Armed Forces during military operations that led to the liberation of Iraq, the new Navy League President urged the redoubling of efforts to support the military through strong sea services in the years ahead.*
>
> *"American sea power is the key to our economic prosperity and security," McNeill said in her inaugural message. "There is a crit-*

> *ical and increasing need today for strong sea services that defend our interest and protect our borders, our friends, and our allies. In the aftermath of the conflict in Iraq, our sea services are being revitalized, Our Coast Guard is expanding to take on new missions to defend our homeland. Our U.S. flag Merchant Marine remains a key element of our lift capabilities, which requires continues support." McNeill who was recently elected to a two-year term pledged to continue to inform the U.S. Congress, the media and the public on the needs and accomplishments of the U.S. Armed Forces, and to work closely with sea service leaders "to develop a forward-looking agenda." We are well poised for the challenges ahead," McNeill said. But "more remains to be done. The United States and its friends and allies face new dangers of unknown magnitude. Now more than ever, the nation's armed forces require our help."*

On August 5, I attended a Coast Guard concert and reception at the US Navy Memorial Heritage Center in DC. On August 9–10, Veronica and I went to Santa Barbara and San Diego with Navy League meetings and visits with possible donors. On the eighteenth, a trip to the Pentagon for lunch with acting secretary of the Navy, Hansford Johnson.

I began this day with a breakfast with Gloria Cataneo Tosi, president, American Maritime Congress; and VADM James Perkins, USN (ret.), senior advisor, and ended the day with the vice chief of naval operations, Admiral Mike Mullen, at a National Capitol Council–sponsored event and concert.

The next morning was breakfast with Cynthia Brown, president, American Shipbuilding Association. This is to give readers an idea of the pace of most days! Wonderful days but nevertheless busy days.

On August 22, I had breakfast with Admiral Vern Clark, chief of naval operations; VADM Kirkland H. Donald, commander, Submarine Group 8; RADM Gerald L. Talbot, commander, Submarine Group 10; and master chief petty officer of the Navy (MCPON), Terry D. Scott. It was very gracious of the CNO to arrange this time with my submarine friends! He also had made arrangements for me to receive a Pentagon pass for my many visits to the Pentagon during those two years. Randy Hollstein who had taken over my vice president of legislative affairs and I met regularly during this time.

I had a short meeting and photo session with Lt. Holly Harrison, USCG. First woman in the Coast Guard to receive a Bronze Star.

On September 8, I left for the casting of the bow-stern section for the USS *New York* utilizing steel from the World Trade Center at Amile Foundry and Machine in Amile, LA. That full story is listed in the stories section.

September took a full page in my scheduling record with visits with CHINFO RADM Terry L. McCreary, and attending meetings with the Reserve Officers Association, the American Sea Power Forum with the shipbuilding association on Capitol Hill, a reception at the German Embassy, and a reception on Capitol Hill when the commandant of the US Coast Guard, Admiral Tom Collins, presented the Ellsworth P. Betholf Award to Chairman/Senator Frank A. LoBiondo.

There were also many meetings with committees for the building, strategic planning, legislative affairs, steering, and budget. The steering committee, which consists of the vice presidents, corporate secretary, and treasurer, all met on September 20. Our meeting was at a hotel close to Navy League headquarters. The weather had been bad for a couple of days. Flights were not canceled on any of the flights scheduled at the steering committee members but the next day Hurricane Isabel arrived. According to Wikipedia, it was the costliest, deadliest, and strongest hurricane in the 2003 Atlantic hurricane season. Staff could not join us but we had a great meeting and made several major decisions.

On September 23, 2003, I received an e-mail from the acting assistant secretary of defense for public affairs, Lawrence DiRita inviting me to a meeting at the Pentagon with Secretary Donald Rumsfeld.

> *Secretary Donald Rumsfeld would like to invite you to attend a special meeting Thursday, October 2, in his private conference room at the Pentagon. Also, present will be General Richard B. Myers, Chairman of the Joint Chiefs of Staff. The briefing with the Secretary and other senior USG officials will start promptly at 9:30 am on October 2. Instructions concerning transportation logistics will follow via email or phone by close of business Monday, September 29, 2003. Please R.S.V.P. to Brent Kruger We hope you are able to participate.*

It was an interesting meeting. I think everyone came away with a new sense of responsibility on what we should do to enhance our support of the military. After the meeting, I had lunch with the VCNO Admiral Mike Mullen at his office in the Pentagon. He urged me to let him know when I needed to meet with anyone and he would have them come to my office in Arlington. Of course, I never did that, but it is an indication of the support I received during those two years. Admiral Mullen's story is included in the stories section of the book.

I then met with RADM Barry M. Costello (chief of legislative affairs) and Captain Scott Gray and on to the frocking ceremony for RADM John G. Cotton, chief of naval reserves. That evening, I had dinner with RADM Michael Tracy and his wife. He was then director of Submarine Warfare Division that I continue to believe is one of the hardest jobs in the Navy. The next morning was breakfast with Ed Connitt, General Dynamics.

A few days later, I received an invitation from the Department of Defense to fly to Iraq for a tour and briefing. I quickly accepted the invite. I was ready to go, although Arlie was not as keen about me going as I was. The date was set and I was to fly to DC to catch a plane that would take the group to Iraq. Shortly before time to leave, the trip was canceled. The hotel we were booked to stay in had been bombed and was destroyed.

While planning for the next national meeting in San Diego, many other meetings were held at headquarters. I finished up the week attending the Coast Guard Ball at the Hyatt Regency in Crystal City. Returning home on October 5 in time for the commissioning of the Coast Guard Maritime Safety and Security Team 91108 on October 6. This significant event for Camden County is found in the stories section.

Back to DC, on the eighth for a black-tie Association of the US Army (AUSA) reception at the New Washington Convention Center, a meeting with the brokers, with the builder concerning change orders ending with a Hail and Farewell reception for RADM McKinney and RADM Pierce Johnson hosted by the Navy Memorial Foundation.

Meetings with the Chairman of International Midway Memorial Foundation began the day on the September 10, 2003. Veronica Brandon, our development executive, brought in senior representatives of the Education Finance Resources Corporation and the Education Initiatives for the Catherine B. Reynolds Foundation.

The black-tie Navy ball was held the next evening on September 11 at Crystal Gateway Marriott.

I attended the Submarine Force Command master chief's meeting and returned for the dinner with VADM Patricia Tracy, director of the Navy staff. I worked with VADM Tracy on several initiatives those two years. I left DC the next day for New York where I visited the Merchant Marine Academy for two days. I received briefings, hosted a coffee reception, and had lunch with the Regiment of Midshipmen. There was a formal parade in my honor where I said a few words. It was an incredibly moving and impressive experience.

Back to DC for a conference with Morgan Fitch and others on the staff to work on our history book. Morgan provided a huge donation to make this possible and was adamant about making it a history of the Navy League and not the Navy. The support we give to each of the four services should be covered.

On October 25, Arlie joined me and we had dinner with Admiral Vern Clark and his wife, Connie, at Tingy House. That story is in the stories section.

Finally, on the twenty-sixth, a day to catch up in the office. On the twenty-seventh, Randy Hollstein and I made a call on Admiral Loy.

We had dinner on the twenty-seventh with VADM Barrett, USCG, and his wife, Sheila, at the vice commandant's quarters in Bethesda.

I was pleased to be able to meet with General Michael W. Hagee, USMC commandant, at his office in the Pentagon on the twenty-eighth.

October 30–November 2 was our winter meeting at the Crystal Gateway Marriott in DC.

On the thirtieth, we presented the Thompson Award to Senator Daniel Inouye at the Rayburn House Office Building. It was an incredible event with all three service chiefs and the secretary of the Navy attending. The huge room was packed!

November brought a meeting with Maersk Line Ltd. that included a very impressive briefing. I was back to Camden County and Kings Bay in time to attend the annual Submarine Veterans of World War II memorial on October 7.

This was also the time during which I did the thing that would be most responsible for my success during the next year and a half. I hired RADM Steve Pietropaoli, former special assistant to the chairman of the joint chiefs of staff and as chief of information for the Navy (CHINFO). The press release was on November 6, 2003. That story is under Pietropaoli.

Back in DC on October 10 for the Special Topic Breakfast with John J. Young Jr., assistant secretary of the Navy for research, development, and acquisition, and then a wreath-laying ceremony in honor of the 228th birthday of the USMC at the Marine Corps War Memorial in Arlington.

On the eleventh, our new executive director (Steve Pietropaoli) and I attended a breakfast at the White House and a Veterans Day wreath-laying ceremony at Arlington National Cemetery. Another day to catch up in the office before attended Senator Zell Miller's book signing for *A National Party No More: The Conscience of a Conservative Democrat.* I then had dinner with David Janes, national chairman, Employer Support of the Guard and Reserve.

In December, the Recruiter of the Year luncheon hosted by the National Capitol Council was held at the conference center at the Navy yard with the annual SECNAV cruise on the Sequoia Presidential Yacht Group. There were too many meetings to cover the two days, but I enjoyed the CACI Ritz-Carlton party hosted by my friend Jack London, as well as the holiday reception hosted by RADM Jan Gaudio. I got to know Jan and his wife when they were stationed in Jacksonville, Florida.

My old friend, Captain Ike Puzon, USN (R), Naval Reserve Association, and RADM Steve Keith, executive director, met on the fifth.

After a staff holiday party and attending RADM Richard Porterfield and Mrs. Porterfield's black-tie event at the Army Navy County Club on the fifth, Arlie joined me and we attended the Army Navy Game on the secretary of the Navy's bus. It was a cold day and had been snowing. I sat down right behind Secretary England and Admiral Clark. The bench was full of snow. They brushed it off and sat down, so I gave up on the thought that we might have something to sit on! I'm wearing the warmest Georgia clothing I had, but it was still cold. We all had a megaphone, so that was my salvation. I put it on the ground and put one foot on it to keep it dry and placed one foot on another. While it was the coldest I had been, it was also one of the greatest of events.

I was home from December 17 until January 5. Three of only four weeks I did not travel.

2004 with flashbacks from 2003

In January, I was asked to be the speaker for the Camden Kings Bay council and was asked to install the new officers of the council.

I wrote a column for the Navy League on my activities for the first six months In January:

> *It has been a very busy six months for me since becoming your National President. I have been traveling extensively and am reminded everywhere I go how truly wonderful and selfless Navy Leaguers are through countless stories from service members all around the country. Here's a sampling of what I've been up to these last few months.*
>
> *Since June, I've met with Sailors, Marines, Coast Guardsmen and Merchant Mariners, sea service leaders, elected officials and many of you, my fellow Navy Leaguers.*
>
> *In June, my husband Arlie and I were honored to start my tour by laying a wreath at the USS Arizona Memorial. While still in Hawaii, I had an opportunity to meet with leaders from the military bases there and learn more about how we can best serve their needs, discussing such issues as encroachment.*
>
> *In July, we visited the Coast Guard Academy, attended the commissioning of the USS Ronald Reagan where I had an opportunity to meet with many Sailors and attending elected officials. At the end of July, I met with the building committee. Members briefed me on the progress of the new building project. Our Navy League experts in construction, banking, law and leasing commended all the work done to date on the project and consider it to be an excellent investment in our future. In other news, former Navy League President Morgan Fitch agreed to chair the history book committee.*
>
> *In August, I met with Cindy Brown, president of the American Shipbuilding Association to discuss our partnership with the Sea Power Ambassador Program. Also in August, I had an opportunity to travel to the west coast and visit the Santa Barbara and San Diego councils.*
>
> *In September, the steering committee met for the Strategic Planning Retreat. Despite being hammered by Hurricane Isabel,*

the committee and headquarters staff produced a long-term strategic outline. I attended the National Capitol Council's annual Secretary of the Navy cruise where Council President Mack Gaston gave me an opportunity to talk about our goals. Also, Arlie and I toured the Merchant Marine Academy.

In October, I attended several events celebrating our Navy's Birthday. At the end of the month we kicked off the Winter Meeting with a congressional reception on Capitol Hill attended by Secretary of the Navy Gordon England, Admiral Vern Clark, chief of Naval Operations, General Michael Hagee, commandant of the Marine Corps and Commandant of the Coast Guard Admiral Thomas Collins as well as several members of Congress. I attended service briefings presented to our Maritime Policy and Resolutions Committee. The Winter Meeting also marked Stephen Pietropaoli's start as our new executive director after retiring as the Navy's chief of information. His leadership will be a tremendous asset to our organization. (the great story of how I convinced him to come is found in the stories section).

In November Stephen and I were invited to the White House where we attended a Veterans Day ceremony. I had the pleasure of meeting President George W. Bush and took the opportunity to share with him the Navy League's connection with President Roosevelt and some background on our organization.

We kicked off December with a win against Army in Philadelphia where Arlie and I attended the Army/Navy football game with the Secretary of the Navy, Gordon England and the Chief of Naval Operations Admiral Vern Clark.

With my six-month mark already reached, I'm convinced that long term planning is essential to our growth. We must also keep our main goals in the forefront of everything we do as Navy leaguers. Sea power is the key to our economic prosperity and the security of our nation. Our pursuit of these goals begins at our grass roots and continues through the state, regional and national levels. We need to continue to educate the media, the public and the Congress about the needs and accomplishments of our military forces.

I will continue to work relentlessly with our leaders in the sea services and the Navy League to keep our organization moving at flank speed. And in my future travels, I will also continue to spread the word on all the wonderful things our councils do across the globe. If you would like me to speak in your region or at an event, contact Katie Doud at headquarters.

Beginning this month, I will concentrate on visiting more councils. Your input is very important to me. What all of you do fills me with great pride. Happy New Year. Sheila M. McNeil

2004: As a result of the briefings I had received and much research from the staff my January message was just a little different. It was on encroachment issues:

Maintain Balance with MMPA
January 2004

Dear Members of Congress:

In its first session, the 108th Congress made some great strides to rebalance our national security requirements with the important need to protect our environment. Members of Congress demonstrated great moral courage as they ignored special interest groups that favored the status quo: Interpretations of environmental laws that had curtailed the sea services' opportunities for realistic training and delayed the deployment of vital defense technology. That is indicative of the wisdom and leadership our nation needs to win the war on terror.

As the current session gets under way, you have an opportunity to build on that achievement. The Marine Mammal Protection Act (MMPA) is expected to come up for reauthorization early in the session. This vital law, passed by Congress in 1972 and amended several times since, protects marine mammals. Its principal purpose was to stop the inadvertent killing of hundreds of thousands of dolphins in the tuna nets of Pacific fishing fleets. We support the goals of the MMPA and the efforts of environmentalists to ensure that the world's marine mammals continue to flourish.

In last year's National Defense Authorization Act, Congress amended the MMPA because its vague wording of key provisions affecting military readiness activities left the law open to almost any interpretation. The "harassment" of marine mammals was defined as any act that had the "potential to disturb" behavior such as breathing, feeding or migration. Even environmentalists complained that this vague definition placed all involved in an impossible situation. William T. Holgrath, assistant administrator for fisheries of the National Marine Fisheries Service, told a congressional committee las May that, "the definition is overly broad and does not provide a clear enough threshold for what activities do or do not constitute harassment." This lack of clarity had a damaging effect on

> *our military services, causing training exercises at night and in shallow waters to be canceled, or conducted under unrealistic conditions during the day or in deep water to ensure that marine mammals were not "harassed."*
>
> *Also, the deployment of a vital submarine detection system was delayed for years because special interest groups mistakenly claimed its sound emissions posed a risk to marine life. The Surveillance Towed-Array Sensor System, Low Frequency Active, or SURTASS LFA, is a centerpiece of the Navy's quest to guard against quiet diesel-electric boats of the type deployed by potential adversaries such as North Korea and Iran. Improving that performance is a top Navy priority.*

Related information is found under Rear Admiral Gary Roughead's section.

The *Washington Times* quoted parts of this column.

The prior month, the American Maritime Congress carried—in its entirety—our December message that began: "A strong U.S. Merchant Marine and a high skilled cadre of U.S. citizens, mariners are vital to the economic and national security interest of the United States." We are getting the word out.

January started out busy with Steve Pietropaoli and I meeting with John Douglas, Aerospace Industries Association, then with retired RADM Mack Gaston with the National Capitol Council on the 2004 Sea Air Space Expo coming up. USMC General Robert (Bob) Magnus spoke at our Special Topic Breakfast. General Magnus was the Deputy Commandant for Programs and Resources. I would later ask him to speak at a very special ceremony at Kings Bay.

I was in DC from January 5–8, where Steve and I met with John Douglas with the Aerospace Industries Association.

To give the reader an idea of the enormity and reach of the Navy League's Sea Air Space (SAS) I've included the pace of the next few days and the range of folks we met with on SAS. We called on Captain Joel Whitehead, government affairs, and Lynford Morton, public affairs, at Coast Guard Headquarters. Adm. Skip Bowman, USN director, Naval Nuclear Propulsion, and then VADM Dave Brewer, USN commander, Military Sealift Command, at their offices at the Navy yard. The next day we were at the Pentagon meeting with a host of senior military. The list is in order of the meetings:

- RADM Michael Tracy, director of Submarine Warfare
- BGEN Mary Ann Krusa-Dossin, director of PAO USMC
- RADM Mark Edwards, director of Surface Warfare
- GENERAL Michael Hagee, USMC commandant
- RADM Terry McCreary, CHINFO
- VADM Pat Tracey, director of Navy staff

And the following day: Admiral Thomas Collins, USCG commandant, and RADM Patrick Stillman, USCG Program executive officer, Integrated Deepwater System. It takes the support of these leaders and more.

I was the speaker at the National Capitol Council dinner on January 8 at the Alpine Restaurant in Arlington, Virginia. I was honored to speak to the council. Since this council is in DC, the membership is composed of very strong former military as well as strong leaders from business and industry.

I returned home for a trip to Atlanta on January 12, where Governor Georgia "Sonny" E. Perdue hosted a reception for the Governor's Military Affairs Coordinating Committee at the governor's mansion.

The January 2004 *Georgia Trend* has the list of "100 Most Influential Georgians." I made the list and that story is in the stories section. The list was full of wonderful people—some I knew well, like Senators Zell Miller and Johnny Isakson and Congressman Jack Kingston, and many others I had worked with or known. Just my name was the shocker!

Arlie and I made a trip to California, for the US Coast Guard Cutter Stratton Commissioning and a visit with Jeanne and Bill Sharkey—that story is found in the stories section.

On January 13, we had a meeting of Friends of Kings Bay for a luncheon for community leaders to meet with our new flag officer RADM J. B. Cassias. He would relieve RADM Talbot on the sixteenth. Gerry had taken over the command just three months before the September 11, 2001, terrorist attacks. Besides dealing with his responsibility of the maintenance and patrols of the SSBN submarines he helped to develop a new security system that would better protect the base and its assets from terrorist's attacks. During his tenure, he prepared two of the submarines to transfer to Bangor Washington.

He's probably had more challenges than anyone at Kings Bay. He is incredible.

On January 30, I spoke to the Chicago Council where I was introduced by Rear Admiral Ann Rondeau, who served as commander of the Naval Service Training Command and the Navy Region Midwest, leading all the Navy's accession training activities. She was a wonderful host. Also, attending the dinner was Rear Admiral Dirk Debbink and his wife, Terry. RDML Debbink was commander of Naval Reserve Readiness Command Midwest, providing support for the Tall Ships Challenge programs that year in Chicago.

I was guest of honor at the Recruit graduation on January 30, special guests Amando Fitz and Casey Atwood of NASCAR Fame were attending, and I stood with them as each of the graduating cadets came by, and we shook hands with each of them.

Ann and I hit it off and would see each other from time to time but never had the opportunity to spend much time together. While all this travel is going on, Peter

Kent continues to work on an outline for our strategic plan. He sent me a first draft but told me, "If you don't like it, we hate it!" You've got to love that attitude.

Back in DC, on February 3–4 with more SAS calls:

- VADM Stanley Szenborski, principal deputy director, Program Analysis and Evaluation
- ADMIRAL Mike Mullen, vice chief, Naval Operations
- VADM Charles Moore, deputy, Naval Operations for Fleet Readiness and Logistics
- VADM John Cotton, USN, chief, Naval Reserves
- VADM Gary Roughead, commander, Second Fleet
- CAPTAIN Dan Cloyd, chief of staff
- VADM Kirkland Donald, commander, Submarine Forces Atlantic

On February 4, the Armed Service Liaison Office to the US House of Representatives had a welcome-back congressional reception at the Cannon Caucus Room. It was well attended and gave me a chance to talk to lots of legislators. And in February, Arlie and I drove to the Treasure Cove Council at Vero Beach, where I spoke to the council. They went to a great effort to make it special—there was even a towel swan and white rose petals on the bed.

There was a huge crowd for the dinner that evening. I brought them up to date on all things Navy League

I returned to attend the Military Officers Association of American (MOAA) on St. Simons Island and introduce Vice Admiral Norb Ryan, the national executive director. We had known each other when he was in the Navy so it was it was an easy lift. And later in the month, February 19–20, where Maryellen Baldwin, executive director of the Hampton Roads Navy League, council made the arrangements and joined us for the meetings:

- Adm. William J. Fallon, commander, US Fleet Forces Command
- RDML Steve Turcotte, commander, mid-Atlantic
- RADM Terrance Etnyre, commander, Surface Force Atlantic
- RADM Sally Brice O'Hara, commander, Fifth District, USCG
- Lt Gen. Robert Wagner, US Army, deputy commander, US Joint Forces Command
- Major General Thomas "Tango" E. Moore, deputy commander, USMC Marine Force Atlantic

If all these names don't convince you of the heavy lifting it takes to produce a successful Sea Air Space, nothing will! We are getting word from the CNO's and commandant's office that the flag breakfast to review the SAS schedule is filling up!

The evening of the twentieth, I spoke at the black tie annual meeting of the Hampton Roads Navy League Council dinner at the Marriott Norfolk Waterside Hotel. I spoke too long at this event. I kept seeing people in the audience that had had such an impact on the Navy League I kept adding to my remarks. I was embarrassed that for many this might have been the only time I had an opportunity to reach out to them. Hopefully, I didn't blow it. Two days later, I am on the way to the Mexico/Caribbean region meeting in Acapulco, leaving there for the St. Louis, Missouri, council meeting the next day.

Note: Some heard of the places I went and talked about the fun and the opportunity to see so much of the country. If they had only looked at my schedule it would have shown a lot of airports and hotel rooms.

On February 28, I was in St. Louis to speak to their council. It was an extraordinary meeting. My good friend Jim Erlinger sent me an e-mail after the meeting. Just to set the stage for this, Jim admits that his wife says he only gets up every morning to "stir the pot." He is a jewel for the Navy League and really works to not show his "tender side." He did with this e-mail:

> *Sheila, I know that this should be a handwritten note, but hopefully you'll think like a Congressman and think that email's the way to go—anyway this is all you're going to get. You did good. I think you charmed the majority of our guests! (Sheila's note: see what I mean—doesn't it beg the question—what was the response from the others!) It was great giving our Region members a chance to meet their President one on one. Hope you think the trip was worthwhile. And the book you received was a substitute. The one you were supposed to receive on St. Louis Then and Now was misplaced and we'll mail it to you. And again, thanks Jim Erlinger*

The day was jaw-dropping.

Mel Burkart was the moderator and Pat Traub introduced me. The deputy mayor of St. Louis presented a large proclamation proclaiming Sheila McNeill Day in St. Louis. (I was so pleased and have this proclamation hanging on the wall in my office today.) Rear Admiral Christopher Ames from US Transportation Command was in attendance as was Rear Admiral Dan Koppel, USNR, the commander, Naval Air Forces Reserve. I was seated with Lieutenant General Gary Hughey, USMC, the deputy commander, US Transportation Command at Scott Air Force Base, Illinois, and his wife, Heidi. We meet so many people in the Navy League it's hard sometimes to remember how we know someone—or if, in fact, we really do know them. That is the way I felt about Lt. Gen Hughey. I hated to say, "You look familiar to me, have we met?" So we just had a nice conversation at the table.

One of the women seated at the table brought up the fact that General Hughey was retiring soon and she asked him, "What are you most proud of during your career?" I loved the question and wondered why I haven't heard anyone ever ask it. He hesitated a few minutes in thought. "A woman on a committee came to me when I was stationed in Okinawa. We talked about the needs of our Marines and I suggested that our service members overseas should be receiving WIC. (The Special Supplemental Nutrition Program for Women, Infants, and Children (WIC) is a federal assistance program of the Food and Nutrition Service.) And we got it! That is what I'm most proud of." He stopped, and he looked at me. By now I'm smiling because I remember where I know him from… Okinawa when we talked about WIC! "You were the one! You were the one I talked with and you took it back to Washington!" What a great day that was for our DACOWITS team!

On March 8, my daughter's birthday, I'm back in DC for lunch with William Schubert, administrator for the Maritime Administration followed by a Sealift briefing on current operation Iraq Freedom at the Maritime Administration. I had lunch at the pentagon with secretary of the Navy, Gordon England; National Endowment for Humanities, Bruce Cole; and Captain Kevin Wensing. While in the Pentagon I called on Vice Admiral Tim Keating, director, joint staff, and VADM Gordon Holder, director for logistics, joint staff with Al Bernard about their support of SAS.

Bob Ravitz, our vice president for corporate memberships, was in from New York and met with Steve Pietropaoli, Rick Barnard, Rich Logazino, and Sheila Hallas on the corporate gold profiles in *Seapower*. That evening, Secretary England and I hosted dinner for our corporate gold sponsors. It was both productive and fun.

It seems when I am with the secretary, it ensures a good time as he begins to tease me about one thing or the other. It sets a mood with everyone and they are comfortable with talking about real issues with him. I was pleased when, after the meeting one of the attendees took me aside to shake my hand and congratulate me on my tour. He was not previously happy with my election so this meant a lot to me.

Maintaining the financial security to perform our mission is not easy. Several vice presidents expressed a desire to meet and discuss ways to enhance current sources of revenue and develop alternative sources for the Navy League. This would involve staff responsible for revenue generation as well as the leadership. We had a Navy League Revenue Summit in August 2004. This was one of the ideas of our national executive director, Steve Pietropaoli. The committee was equally divided by our Navy League leadership and our senior staff. Many ideas came from this and well as a commitment from all to add more thrust to our efforts. Steve asked a colleague of his, RADM Craig Quigley, to moderate. Craig was a former chief of information for the Navy known as CHINFO and a valued supporter of the Navy League.

VCNO Michael Mullen was most gracious to host the SAS flag breakfast. There was the best turnout ever!

I was in the Pentagon on the tenth to meet with CDR Jim Rendon, USCG, who was the congressional fellow for speaker of the House Representative, Dennis Hastert, who was very gracious and offered a photo op. Jim treated me to a very nice lunch at the Congressional Dining Room. A first for me, and I had to concentrate not to gawk at the number of representatives I'd have liked to pull aside to talk about our sea services!

And while on Capitol Hill, I visited Congressman Jack Kingston's office to talk to his chief of staff, Bill Johnson. That evening the Marine Corps Reserve Association had a congressional reception in honor of Senator Zell B. Miller. In between meetings, we worked on Sea Air Space and Development.

I'm back in DC from the thirteenth to the seventeenth for office calls and *then* enjoyed dinner with RADM. Thomas L. Wilkerson, US naval institute and publisher, *Proceedings* and *Naval History* magazines.

Our special topic breakfast the next morning featured VADM James "Cutler" C. Dawson, deputy chief of Naval Operations for Resources, Requirements, and Assessment. Cutler was head of the Office of Legislative Affairs when I first took over the responsibilities. I worked with VADM Dawson, Costello and Roughead. What an opportunity! At a reception one evening, Cutler told a group of people we were talking to, "Sheila, has put the Navy on the front burner on Capitol Hill." One of my nicest compliments and one I reminded myself of when things were tough!

A nice evening with David Oliver, COO of EADS, North America with Diane Murphy Vice president of communications for EADS, Steve Pietropaoli and Rich Barnard joining us, so the evening was rich with conversation. I did find out that David was the brother to Tim Oliver, who headed the Submarine League. I also knew David when he was a flag officer in the Navy. It made for a very interesting evening.

On March 19 and 20, Arlie joined me for the New England meeting and workshop. I was so pleased to have Rear Admiral Vivien Crea attend the dinner that evening. She was the newest resident of the Coast Guard's Hospital Point Lighthouse as the commander, First Coast Guard District, overseeing all Coast Guard operations in the northeastern United States.

We stayed with Bill and Nancy Kelley, so we could catch up them along with RADM Ray Coutour and his wife, June. We also learned about the region and had a tour of the USS *Constitution* with the executive director, Burt Logan, and region president, Ivan Samuels. Since snow isn't found anywhere close to where I live, June Coutour and I threw snowballs. Back in Washington, I met up with my newest old friend, Dr. Phil Dur, Northrop Grumman, whom I had met at the USS *New York* ceremony. We went to the Army Navy Club in DC—that is always a treat. We discussed shipbuilding and many other issues with Phil and we became good friends over the two years.

We had a legislative issues breakfast for our corporate members. My old friend from OLA, Vice Admiral Cutler Dawson, was the speaker.

I had lunch with William Schubert, maritime administrator. It's always good to surprise some folks with the amount of support they are getting from the Navy League. He was pleased to hear of our great efforts on behalf of our merchant mariners.

The next day I had lunch at the Pentagon with secretary of the Navy, Gordon England, Captain Kevin Wensing, and their guest, Bruce Cole, president of the National Endowment for Humanities. What a nice lunch and it was so far from what my lunch conversations have been about for the past few years.

The following day was the 2004 Lone Sailor Dinner at the Ritz-Carlton so that made it easy! I just had to walk downstairs—no metro, no cab. Master of ceremonies for the event was Ernest Borgnine! He was so gracious to everyone. Ben Bradlee, vice president at large of the *Washington Post*, and Adm. Stanfield Turner, USN (ret.), director of the CIA from 1977 to 1981, were both honored at the dinner and presented with Lone Sailor awards. It was quite an evening.

On March 24, RADM and Mrs. Jerry Talbot invited me to their home at the Naval Observatory. Malcolm and Shirley had lived there in the past, so I was aware of the tight security. The Vice President of the United States lives in the same gated area so it's fun to see if he might take a nightly walk. I had a great time that evening.

The next day, I joined the Camden Fly-In Group for breakfast with Congressman Jack Kingston and, later, Senator Saxby Chambliss and Senator Zell Miller. We traveled to the Pentagon where we met with RADM Mike Tracey, N97 and SECNAV H. T. Johnson. While the group left late afternoon for Camden County, I attended an event at the Navy Memorial.

There was a lot of talk about BRAC—Base Realignment and Closure, during that time. The plans to implement it were set. I knew as Navy League members, we could not get involved with trying to "save our base/installation." Nothing like that can be done in the name of the Navy League. I drafted a letter to approximately sixty-six thousand members covering the "rules." I met with Secretary Johnson on April 2 at his office in the Pentagon. While I knew that my old friend, Captain Walt Yourstone, worked for the secretary, I was surprised to see him when I walked in. I shared the letter with the secretary and his comment was "You are a mean, mean woman, Sheila."

I laughed and said, "I know, sir, but sometimes it takes mean."

He loved the letter and I later sent it out to the sixty-six thousand or so members. Secretary Johnson wrote the most beautiful letters. Some of those can be found in the stories section.

On April 3, we had the steering committee meeting, our top leadership come in for meetings at headquarters. I was proud of all of them for the work they were doing for the Navy League. Sea Air Space was April 3–7 and that was full of sixteen-hour days, giving it everything you have. It was during SAS that the Japanese delegation asked me to join them for a special ceremony at a location in Ashburn, Virginia, Hee

S. Park, Korean Sea Power League, and Joongsup Chung were the primary organizers of the event. They created a contract that would be signed by Park and me as national president.

We had always used the Capitol Steps for the entertainment at the banquet. They are a wonderful talented group and I'd pay good money to see them anytime. However, much of what they do is political parody. The year before, I had sat with the service chiefs and from their point of view it was just awkward. No one said anything to me, but I was uncomfortable hearing it from what I considered their point of view.

I had earlier seen an incredibly performance of Stephen Lang in "Beyond Glory." This is a stunning one-man show about Medal of Honor recipients adapted from a book by the same name. Stephen Lang was Stonewall Jackson in the Warner Brothers film *Gods and Generals.* Lang also won the coveted Helen Hayes Award for his outstanding performance as Colonel Jessep in *A Few Good Men* at the Kennedy Center. It was an hour show—compelling and riveting account of three of the wars of the twentieth century and is powerful. It forced an audience to consider from an intimate perspective what enables a person to rise "above and beyond the call of duty." I made the change and I presented "Beyond Glory" at the next Sea Air Space meeting. I think it was a good decision.

This Sea Air Space was the first time that the New Safety Awards were unveiled. Secretary England and I presented the first awards to Commander Kari Thomas and Lt. Commander Ray Swanson of Carrier Airborne Early Warning Squadron 117, with the Admiral Vern Clark Unit Safety Award and Keri May, the James L. Jones Individual Safety Award on behalf of Master Sgt. Robert Schechinger, Third Marine Division, and Barbara Wright, a safety and occupational health specialist from Jacksonville, Florida.

It was good to be able to spend a little time escorting Admiral William (Bill) J. Fallon (a.k.a. Susan's dad) as Chairman Al J. Bernard escorted him through the exhibit halls. There was such a wonderful gathering of military officers and the pictures that year in *Seapower* showed the great time we were having. Some people might call those introductions at SAS mistakes, and yes, they were. But they also gave everyone a big laugh and put all in a great attitude for the event. You'll find them mixed in with the stories.

Two of my friends from Camden County attended the expo that year, Charlie Smith Jr. and Jim Kiss. I was pleased that they were so impressed with the vast size and attendance. I invited them to stop by the reception before the banquet and had fun introducing them to the VIPs. It's always good to have folks from back home see how you spend your time in DC!

After Sea Air Space, Stephen and I received an e-mail from Rear Admiral Quigley, USN (retired), and former chief of information for the Navy.

Fine show, folks. Bigger crowds, more senior crowds, better seminars and panels. A marked improvement over last year. Good on you and thanks for all the hard work! Craig R. Quigley

And a very nice note from CNO Clark:

Dear Sheila Thanks for allowing Connie and I to be a part of this year's wonderful Sea Air Space Exposition. It was inspiring to spend the day among a group of people so committed to the Sea Services.

I'm truly thankful to you for the support the Navy League is providing for the Navy. In very short order you have put your thumbprint on the Navy League and the results have been dramatic.

Hope to see you soon. Until then, Godspeed Sincerely, Vern

And then in answer to my update on Sea Air Space:

27 May 2004

Dear Sheila, Thank you for your note on the Sea-Air-Space (SAS) Exposition and your trip to New Jersey. It was a pleasure as always to share our common goals with so many of our supportive citizens.

Like you, I felt there was great synergy between SAS and the All Flag Officer Training Symposium. As with everything in the Navy League, SAS just seems to be getting bigger and better every year. I believe, under your leadership our uniformed civilian partnership has grown even stronger. I would also like to say thanks for the personalized edition of "Almanac of Seapower 2004. It's a super reference that I will be glad to keep here. Hope to see you at the Sunset Fiest. Sincerely, Vern

The news clips were the best. It is amazing what can happen when your executive director is a former chief of information for the United States Navy!

The Atlanta Metropolitan Council had a nice dinner on April 13 at Petite Auberge Restaurant and I was asked to speak. He and Al Mota did a great job, and Danny picked me up in a limo!

VADM Malcolm Fages retired on April 16, and I was one of his "side boys." This was a first for me and a real honor. Details of my friendship with Malcolm and Shirley are found in the stories section.

I then flew to New Jersey for the region meeting. The gentlemen were so gracious when they picked me up from the airport. They were old-school Jerseyites, if there is such a word. All of them were trying to carry my luggage. We went to a remote area for the luncheon. As I looked at them, their accents, and for some reason, this location I felt like I was on an episode of *The Sopranos*. About that time, they started telling me about one of the episodes of *The Sopranos* that was filmed at this location! They all knew what I was thinking and we all laughed, relaxed, and had a great meeting.

I was back in Glynn County in time to attend a Jacksonville Council luncheon with secretary of the Navy, Gordon England, and Congressman Ander Crenshaw.

The YWCA annual Tribute to Women was the same week. I was recognized as an outstanding female leader in the community. Keith Caudell and Dr. Lana S. Skelton were Honorary Chairs and Gail Rose and Cynthia Whittenburg were co-chairs. The speaker for the event was Barbara Dooley, First Lady of UGA Athletics.

Two days later, I was back on the road for the Great Lakes Region meeting. We had a reception and dinner with area VIPs at Greek Town on March 23. Right after the meeting, someone suggested we step outside for a great cigar that he had brought. So we did. As I'm standing on this crowded sidewalk with all these nice men smoking that cigar I again was aware of the wonder of finding myself with them at that moment as their national president and being so included—perhaps embraced by them. Breakfast was at the Detroit Athletic Club, but I decided not to try to break any barriers in the men's locker room.

I gave a couple of speeches during that time and was looking forward to hearing Captain Johnny "Turk" L. Green, USN, commanding officer of the USS *Theodore Roosevelt*, who spoke on the twenty-fourth—a very engaging speech. That afternoon, we had sessions on regional, area, and council Navy Leagues finishing up with a reception/dinner that evening at the Whitney Restaurant. The last day, Roz Ellis had convinced me to speak at the Mariner's Church of Detroit for Navy League Sunday. This was a first and I didn't know what to expect but several past national presidents had spoken at the event. At the end, they gave me a standing ovation. I was very surprised but delighted. The pastor's wife told me that this was the first standing ovation in the church's history. Not bad for a Southern girl! I was thrilled—as much for Roz as for me since she went out on a limb to ask me to speak.

I was back in DC in time to attend a welcome at the Coast Guard Maritime Safety and Security Team (MSST) unit for commanding officers for the next five MSST units throughout the United States.

Mac McClelland, the Navy League's president's personal representative, United Arab Emirates, came to my office at headquarters for a visit. He had recently had an interesting op-ed in the *Wall Street Journal*.

Another event on Capitol Hill where "A Day in the Life of the Sea Services" reception was hosted by the Navy League. The reception featured an exhibit of photographs from the book *A Day in the Life of the United States Armed Forces*. The photographs from the worldwide project were captured over a single twenty-four-hour period in October 2002, when 125 award-winning civilian and military photographers fanned out across the globe to capture an ordinary day in the lives of the men and women who protect America's freedom. The reception exhibit focused on the men and women of the nation's sea services—the Navy, Marine Corps, and Coast Guard—in remote outposts and strategic bases; on Carrier decks and Trident submarines, in helos and small boats patrolling our borders, going about daily routines and saying "goodbye." Project editors and photographers were on hand to describe their experience and participate in a book signing. Boeing, the project underwriter, had generously agreed to provide books for three hundred reception attendees. What a night it was, all sponsored by the Navy League.

Our Camden fly-in for 2004 also included a tour of the Navy League's new building and lunch with the national president (that would be me, so not so exciting for the Camden group).

Our European region visit was from May 5 to 29. Those days are in my stories section.

Returning from Europe, we had a week at home to change out suitcases, spend some time in my business, visit the family, and go out again for our national convention in San Diego.

We arrived a couple of days early, so I could make calls on several senior military. RADM Jose "Joe" Betancourt was commander, Navy Region Southwest, and was wonderful! We really hit it off and that made for a great convention. He managed to attend almost every function.

The convention was from June 9 to 11. Roger Hedgecock interviewed RADM Jose Betancourt, and me on his radio talk show. It was all done on the pier with a couple hundred of our Navy Leaguers close by. That was fun. The *Navy Compass*, San Diego's only authorized Navy newspaper had a picture of us being interviewed with Hedgecock about the Sea Power festivities. Those big ear phones with the attached microphone made me look so cool! Almost like I knew what I was doing!

My mother (Nora), my sister (Debbie), my brother (Brian), and of course Arlie were all at the convention. They took advantage of the nice trips the Navy League had sponsored. We had dinner at the home of Vice Admiral and Mrs. Timothy LaFleur—quarters D the famous Navy residents of Admiral John S. McCain and Vice Admiral "Red" Ramage. Tim and his wife were awesome. I gave them pictures from mutual friends in Spain. What a wonderful evening they gave us. We had a special letter from The White House for the convention program.

During the convention, I presented Carol Ann Hackley the President's Award for the following reasons:

- She is a consummate professional.

- As a PhD and a public affairs professor, she is recognized nationally for her work.
- She has served on the steering committee since 2001.
- She is responsible for the one hundredth anniversary celebration plans.
- She is responsible for the groundbreaking ceremony planning.
- She gave one week of her time to work the press room at SAS with 105 national media attending.
- She has consistently surpassed every goal given to her.

I must admit as the first woman president I did *not* want to give the president's message to a woman. But doing the right thing won over and I did give it to Carol Ann Hackley.

The 2004 Navy League national meeting was held in San Diego. Peter Kent was convention chair. Rabbi Kloner was the national chaplain. The opening ceremony was the Men of Valor. We had thirteen Medal of Honor recipients. It was incredibly moving. Presenting the Coast Guard Awards was Rear Admiral Kevin J. Eldridge, USCG, deputy commander, Pacific area commander, Eleventh Coast Guard District. Presenting the Secretary of the Navy public service awards was Admiral William J. Fallon, US Fleet Forces Command, and as president, I was the master of ceremonies. Also on hand to assist in the awards was Congressman Ed Schrock, Congresswoman Susan Davis, and Captain Scott Gray, Office of Legislative Affairs.

Receiving the Navy awards were the following:

James and Jewell Bonner
Campbell J. McCarthy
Jackson Stevens

Receiving the Coast Guard awards were the following:

Robert L. Castle
Arlie McNeill
Albert D. Grantham

JOSN Cynthia R. Smith
Navy Compass

San Diego—ships and service members of the four United States sea services were joined together on our pier for the first time in San Diego June 9-10. Members of the Navy League of the United States welcomed the public to "Sea Power at the Broadway Pier." The event was part of the Navy League's 2004 National Convention and was sponsored by Science Applications International Corporation (SAIC). Sea Power at the Broadway Pier gave visitors a chance to tour Navy frigate USS Jarrett (FFG 33), Coast Guard High Endurance Cutter Munro, the Star of India, which represented the U.S. Flag Merchant Marine and a Marine Corps 1 MEF (1st Marine Expeditionary Force) display. Additional military exhibits and demonstrations included Navy SEALS, a 6,000-gallon dive tank, a RHIB (Rigid Hull Inflatable Boat), a parachute team, a K-9 unit and a Coast Guard search and rescue operation.

"It's an honor to show the public what we do every day. This event gives the public hands-on experience that will show them what the sea service are all about," said Marine Cpl. Anthony Weave, a member of the 1 MEF's 1st Light Armored Reconnaissance Battalion.

"One important way the Navy League of the United States has helped support the members of the U.S. sea services and their families for over 100 years is by educating local citizens," said Jim Bedinger, president of the San Diego Council of the Navy League. "As the host council for this year's National Navy League Convention, we are very pleased to offer the people of San Diego this unique opportunity to see and learn how the sea services differ and how they use their distinctive talents and assets to work as a team." SAIC also exhibited technologies at the pier that support the maritime community.

"This was a great opportunity for us to salute the Navy League as well as the men and women of the sea services and their families," said Ben Haddad, SAIC senior vice president for communications. "The employee owners of SAIC are proud of the wide-ranging support they provide for the sea services, and we're especially proud to be able to show our respect for them here in San Diego, where SAIC was founded and has its headquarters. Sponsoring this event for our community has been a real honor." After Sea Power at the Broadway Pier opened to the public June 9, with an opening gathering, the public was allowed to experience free ship tours of USS_Jarrett, stationed in San Diego, and Munro from Alameda, Calif. Visitors were also welcomed aboard Star of India for a small tour fee.

"The Navy League was very excited to be able to bring all four sea services on one pier. We enjoy the chance to support and recognize our military members. Sea Power gives us a chance to show the general public what our service members do every day," said Cathy Sang, the public affairs representative for Navy League. Amy Muszynski, from Phoenix, was excited to have the chance to experience all the different sea services and see how the operate. Muszynski's five-year-

old son Alex also enjoyed touring the ships. "It was really cool. I got to see a big tank and go on the ships. I had a lot of fun," Alex explained.

Debbie, Arlie, Mother, and Brian went to Mexico while I was working the events. Mother bought a quart of vanilla flavoring only to have to leave it in San Diego—I think it was about three dollars!

It was tradition that the past national presidents have a dinner one of the free evenings. I was really trying to maintain a balanced budget and to make that issue to my colleges the appetizers consisted of their choice of a variety of bags of potato chips. We had more fun with the potato chips, then we would ever have with a nice appetizer. There is a great picture with every president and their spouse eating a bag of chips.

And for the finest part of the event, we had thirteen Men of Valor at the opening ceremonies. They all wore their medals. RADM Raymond Coutour, USN (ret.), Cole Hackley, and Clair Harter were all inducted in the Hall of Fame, it is a rare thing to see this many Medal of Honor recipients.

Bill Sharkey sent me a copy of his newsletter the *Sea Chant.*

NAVY LEAGUE HAS A TERRIFIC NATIONAL LEADER

(Of course, I would make sure this one got in.)

Jeanne and I, along with Lorraine Hughey, attended the Navy League's national meeting held in San Diego June 9-13. It was very worthwhile with action by committees, workshops, great speakers, a sea service panel with flag and general officers of the Navy, Coast Guard and Marine Corps and awards to Coast Guard and Merchant committees held meeting on ships in San Diego waterfront which made it up close and person.

National President Sheila McNeill is an outstanding leader whose only shortcoming is that she can only serve two years, something which many of us regret with only one more year to go. She is personable, very business-oriented, very "up" on the latest details of what's happening with or sea services, their goals, needs for our help and she has a vision of what we, as Navy Leaguers, can achieve to assist. Her soft pleasant persona (Georgia) belies a leader who has her goals and knows how to achieve them. She is very popular with Pentagon leaders and "on the Hill" in Washington, D.C. which is vital. The Navy League is becoming a first of reference for sea serves leadership looking for assistance on issues of importance to them with Congress o or others. We are being recognized more and more for the expertise and professionalism demonstrated by officers and committee chairs who take their job seriously, Expressions by the top military leaders are effusive.

With best wishes to all, Bill

Then Captain Joel Whitehead took the time to send a letter after the convention recognizing Arlie's support of the Coast Guard.

Sheila, What a successful Navy League Convention you hosted in San Diego! It was a great turnout and one of the most productive meetings I've attended. Martha and I really enjoyed the Convention.

I especially appreciate the opportunity to attend and make a presentation at the Coast Guard Affairs and Legislative Committees. Al Grantham and Greg Hansen again hosted very informative sessions. Randy Holstein, John Thorne and I have already met and cooked up several new ideas for the coming year.

Finally, while it's always a pleasure to see the stand-out leaders of the Navy League recognized, it was personally gratifying to recognize Arlie for his genuine and long-standing support of the Coast Guard over the years. The Navy League and the Sea Services are in good hands with your strong and focused leadership. Joel

On the fifteenth, I'm back in Norfolk for the Joint Force Exercise (CJTFEX) 04-2. What an incredible experience. My first arrested landing! See Admiral Roughead's stories for the details!

And then back to DC, where I attended RADM James Carmichael, USCG, retirement ceremony, at the Ft. McNair Officer's Club. I was so interested in his remarks that they created one of my president's messages. The next few days, I was in my office with back to back meetings.

I had briefings from Jered Industries from Rick Edger, a presentation to the Daughters of the American Revolution (DAR) on their adoption of the USS *Stennis* a military of the year event and meetings with Bill Kopper followed by a building site tour with Jim Davis our builder with Steve.

I'm in Georgia on the twelfth and thirteenth to attend a governor's meeting with the Georgia military installation support groups.

Back to Norfolk for a change of command. My friend Vice Admiral James Hull retired on July 16 and was relieved by Vice Admiral Vivien S. Crea. I attended that ceremony in Norfolk. There was a great article on Jim that told of his portrait that would hang in a hallway of the Coast Guard's Atlanta Area command alongside those of his predecessors. "Yet even among this distinguished group he will forever stand out," the article said. He's the only one wearing camouflage utilities for his official portrait. It's an appropriate uniform for a man known as a bona fide operator. Jim retired with thirty-nine years of service and as one of the services last two remaining admirals with Vietnam combat experience. Vice Admiral Thomas Barrett, assistant commandant, retiring on July 23, was the other. Jim went on to serve the Navy League as chairman of the Coast Guard Committee and as a member of the Maritime Policy Committee. He also was a valued partner in my preparation of the papers to take to Congress on the restoration of the three hundred million dollars years later.

I'm at headquarters from July 20 to 25, working with Steve, Howard, Linda, and Susan Fallon on upcoming revenue summit. I had a very important phone call from chief of staff of the Coast Guard, Thad Allen, USCG. He made sure I was sitting down and announced, "Yes, the USCG would be moving into our new building occupying part of the fifth floor!" That was incredibly good news.

The evening of July 22, I had a dinner cruise on the Sequoia Presidential Yacht with amputees from the wars in Iraq and Afghanistan. Ramona Joyce, public affairs officer, joined me. It was a night I'll never forget. I met James. These were seriously wounded young men. I hit it off with one of the nice looking young men who had just had artificial hands attached to his arms. We were both sitting on the couch with a bowl full of shrimp to be peeled and eaten. I was challenging him with the peeling of the shrimp. Darned if he didn't manage to peel and eat them. I put my coin down on the coffee table and challenged him with "You can have this coin if you can pick it up." As soon as I said it, I was horrified with myself! But immediately he started working on it, and in only a few seconds, he had figured out how to pick it up. We got the best laugh out of that. I told him I just knew he wouldn't be getting that coin. James asked me to help him stay in the Marine Corps. He is an incredible young man—and really good looking! I told his story to everyone who would listen. Later his picture was on the front page of *Navy Times* as a new instructor!

I sent a letter to Gary Silversmith, president of Sequoia Presidential Yacht Group, thanking him for letting me be a part of this outing.

> *Dear Mr. Silversmith: Words cannot adequately capture what an inspiration it was to spend time with those superb American servicemen aboard SEQUOIA. The indelible spirit of your Soldiers and Marines who have given so much for their country is beyond my comprehension, and is something that every American should have an opportunity to experience. Thank you for inviting me to participate in this special cruise, and for your continued support for the men and women of our armed forces. If there is ever anything the Navy League can do to help, don't hesitate to call. I am pleased you are now a member of our organization.*
>
> *Sheila*

Returning from this gut-wrenching event, I met with Steve, Jim Hoffman, Rich, and Don Sacarob on my upcoming European Council. Then met with Morgan Fitch and the history book committee. Answered a call from secretary of the Navy, H. T. Johnson, and left for a retirement ceremony of VADM Thomas Barrett USCG, vice commandant, US Coast Guard, who was being relieved by Vice Admiral Terry Cross, whom I met in California this year. The ceremony was held at Ft. McNair. Tom and Sheila Barrett were a wonderful couple who made it a point to be at as many of our events as they could.

Wrapping up the day, I had dinner with Senator Max Cleland and his special lady, Nancy Ross, at the Ritz-Carlton in Pentagon City. Ritz-Carlton became my home during those two years. Horst Schulze, who created the Ritz, urged me to stay there because it was so convenient to the Pentagon and other places I needed to go. He then had the rate adjusted to what I was paying at the small hotel in Arlington. They always upgraded me to concierge's status, so I became friends with everyone. Breakfast, lunch, and a light dinner was served on the concierge's floor. It always made it easier if I wanted someone to stop by from the Pentagon. It was a metro stop away! I believe Ritz-Carlton was one of the blessings that contributed to the Navy League's success during those two years I received my white robe on my fiftieth visit. They treated me like family. I stop by years later just to say hello to those who were there in 2003–2005. It is just like going back home. Read more about Horst in the stories section.

From July 26 to Aug 1, I was back in Brunswick.

On August 4–8, Arlie and I traveled to Canada to meet with the Navy League of Canada. We arrived on Wednesday, August 4, and were greeted by Tim Porter and Doug Thomas who transported us to the Lord Elgin Hotel. There was a pre–welcome dinner reception at Friday's Roast Beef House and later dinner in the McFarland Room. Distinguished guests included the following:

The Honorable Fred and Gwyneth Miffing, National Honorary Chair, Navy League of Canada.

Rear Admiral (R) Tim and Mrs. Sharon Porter, National President, Navy League of Canada

Captain John and Mrs. McClain, US Navy Attaché to Canada

Colonel Robert and Mrs. Perron, Director of Cadets

Mr. and Mrs. Rod Skotty, Vice President of Government Relations, Lockheed Martin

Mr. and Mrs. Gary Payne, National Vice President of Communications, Navy League of Canada; Senior Project Manager Aurora Update, General Dynamics

Mr. and Mrs. Jim Cummings, National Vice-President of Dund Development, Navy League of Canada/CEO Captions

I spoke that evening at dinner. The next day we opened the papers to see headline news of Rear Admiral and Mrs. Jay Cohen's visit to Canada the week before. I later mailed the paper to them. What a small world. The following day, I received a Navy League briefing by Douglas Thomas, national executive director, followed by Colonel Perron, who gave a briefing on the cadet program. Briefs were received from the Canadian Navy and tours of the Parliament with a few hours to see the country.

After attending the change of command for the commanding officer Naval Submarine Base Kings Bay where Captain John Calhoun was relieved by Captain Mike McKinnon, I returned to DC that afternoon. That evening, I had dinner with Bill Kopper, Bob Bishop, Bob Ravitz, and Howard Siegel at Harry's Tap Room. It was good to have all the principals I needed to discuss our finance, membership, and corporate member issues, with final preparations for the 2005 Revenue Summit Meeting at the Boeing Building, Rosslyn on August 23. The next day, I'm back home with three conference calls and ending with a conference call with all region presidents on legislative affairs efforts. I had to be back in Brunswick for the Awards Ceremony for Royce Hall, Dawson Humanitarian Award on the twenty-fifth at the Elks Club

Arlie and I traveled to Panama City, Florida for the Commissioning of the USS *Momsen* (DDG 92) and reception.

The keel laying of the USS *New York* with sponsor Mrs. Dotty England was an incredible event and has its own story in the stories section.

Back to Glynn County where Congressman Jack Kingston was speaking to our Navy League council.

I left for DC on Tuesday, September 14—the week of budgeting and steering committee meetings. Three weeks prior, I had received a call from Patrick Moore in Georgia, Governor Sonny Purdue's office. He said that Parker Green (Moody Air Force Base area) had always handled the issue of getting all branches of the military to visit with the governor at the Pentagon. It was pretty easy for Parker as he was friends with the chairman of the Joint Chiefs, and the chairman put out the word to everyone, they told me. He is an incredible advocate for the Air Force.

This year I was asked to arrange for the Navy and Marine Corps to meet with him. I was a little stressed by this. One, and foremost because I felt like I was asking for a "favor" and I had not done anything like a favor in my presidency. Yes, I saw it was important for the governor to meet our senior military and leadership but making it happen is not always easy.

I asked Steve's help and he suggested I go through the Navy's Public Affairs Office (PAO). Within days he had the assistant secretary of the Navy for installations and environment and the vice chief of Naval Operations. Although Steve said the Navy PAO would take care of the Marine Corps and the commandant of the Marine Corps, Steve can simplify a difficult issue. As it turned out, we had a very casual, informative meeting and lunch and the governor was very pleased. Back to the office with meetings with Susan Fallon and Carolyn Jarvis on development, a Sea Air Space meeting, and a meeting with Randy Hollstein for briefing on foreign shipbuilding, at Maersk Shipbuilding. That evening was the SECNAV barge cruise. It is recounted in Secretary England's stories.

September 17 was full of meetings ending in a reception with the secretary of the Navy, chief of Naval Operations, and command master chief reception hosted by RADM Porterfield and Mrs. Decker at the State Department.

The next few days were committee meetings and conference calls including a brief from the Navy League Building LLC. I had been preparing for my upcoming visit to Chile for the International Federation of Navy League.

I was at the Pentagon having lunch with VADM John Cotton and had office calls with Scott Gray, Office of Legislative Affairs, in RADM Barry Costello's office, a call on Adm. "Black" Nathman, vice chief of Naval Operations, then Brigadier General John F. Kelley, USMC, Legislative Affairs. Admiral Clark set me up with Dr. Greg Perett, with the State Department who was the foreign policy advisor to the chief of Naval Operations before my Chile trip and Denny Moynihan walked me over. I finished my day with Admiral Clark.

During this time, I am working with Randy Hollstein and Jeremy Miller on the regional plan for legislative affairs. We created the position of vice president of legislative affairs for the councils and region. There was training created for these new experts with regular monthly meetings. We continued with the one-page front and back for top issues of the sea services.

Admiral Nathman and his wife were on the cruise with the secretary of the Navy a few nights before and we discussed several issues. I told him I would be at the Pentagon in a few days and would drop off some information. He indicated there was something in his office he wanted to share. While setting up the appointments, Katie Doud told me, "I cannot get you in to see Admiral Nathman. His scheduler said his calendar is too packed."

I picked up my cell phone and called him. "Hey, I've found out you are too busy to meet. How about we meet outside the head down the hall and exchange information." Of course, I presented it like it was some clandestine issue. He laughed and said they would get back with me.

A few minutes later Katie came to my office. "Did you talk with anyone from Admiral Nathman's office? They just called and wanted to know when you wanted to see him." I really would have been okay to deliver the papers I wanted him to read—in that clandestine meeting I had planned in my head—but how nice of him and his staff. When I got there, he started showing me his "toys." He was a real NASCAR fan and had lots of cool stuff, but I wanted to cover the issues I was questioning. I told him if I looked at his toys he would have to give me equal time. He did and I outed him when his staff looked in the office to see if we were ready to close our meeting.

On the evening of September 22, the National Capitol Council presented an award to Congressman Bill Young from Florida, who was chairman of the Appropriations Committee. RADM Mack Gaston, USN (ret.), and president of the National Capitol Council hosted the event. Each of the service chiefs spoke at the event, as well as the chairman of the Joint Chiefs.

I was in Savannah at the Hilton Head Council as guest speaker where they had arranged an interview with a television station. Dale Lewey and others at this council spearheaded my gift of a huge pig with the inscription "Male Chauvinist Pigs for Sheila." I will always be indebted for their support and for that super gauntlet they provided when I walked in the room during my election week. They all stood at the ends of each line of chairs and presented "side boy" for my walk to the podium. See more of this story in Secretary England's stories.

The *Island Packet*'s Sunday, September 26, 2004, had the following article:

NAVY LEAGUE LEADER VISITS ISLAND COUNCIL

BY SHEENA FOSTER

BLUFFTON—When deciding what sort of gift to give Sheila McNeill for speaking at a local event, members of the Navy League of the United States Hilton Head Council considered her past. McNeill made history, and caused considerable flak, when she became the first woman chosen as president of the male-dominated league. So rather than pretend the controversy never happened her hosts at the Friday evening event at the Moss Creek clubhouse decided to recognize it openly.

At stage left, a tall black box with a golden eagle emblem on its front masterfully hid the surprise—a pig in chef's clothing holding a gavel stood inside a glass encasement, its base was emblazoned with the acronym M.C.P.F. S. The letters stood for Male Chauvinist Pigs for Sheila. "It's a labor of love to be here." Said McNeill, who visited the council during its quarterly dinner meeting. The pit stop came during a flurry of traveling for McNeill who visit the Pentagon earlier this week and will leave for Chile soon. "I've traveled 45 of my first 52 week in office," she said. Her 15-minute address highlighted her progress at president, the importance of naval sea power and updates on Capitol Hill initiatives. The Navy League currently has 75,000 members, with Hilton Head Island being one of its 350 councils worldwide. McNeill called the organization "strong and well" and said she was, "Amazed looking at what councils are doing all over the country."

She said an official building is under construction in Arlington, Va. A five-story 214,000 square foot structure that will 'ensure the Navy League stays in existence for another 100 years. McNeill referenced a column she wrote for Seapower magazine, a monthly publication from the Navy League, titled "Navy League Needs 'grass roots' to flourish in years ahead." In the column, she called for increased support from councils nationwide in legislative affairs. "Each of the president's messages are a call to action," she said. She also talked about the Deep-Water Project, which focuses on the "recapitalization of the Coast Guard" and calls for "increased power" considering terror threats against the United States. "They work with less Coasties than the entire New York Police Department. If we ever needed a voice to alert American on the dangers affecting us it is now." McNeill, a member of the Navy League since 1966, became its president in June 2003. She is known for being both the first woman and first non-veteran to lead the organization. After her speech, McNeill pondered what she may do when her two-year term atop the Navy League ends. "I'd like to go to the beach and read a good book.," she said.

I'm back in Atlanta for another Governor's Military Affairs Committee meeting before the next trip to DC. On October 1, I joined RADM Jan Gaudio, USN commander, Naval District Washington, on his barge cruise. What a great evening. That, also, is covered in the stories section.

I flew back into Jacksonville where I enjoyed four days in my business and with my family. I left on the fourteenth for a Twin Lakes Council visit that included "tea time" with local business leaders, local command spouses and Mrs. Pawlenty, wife of the governor of Minnesota, Tim Pawlenty. A council breakfast began the next day with a mediate event, a tour of the Reserve Center and speaking that night to the region Navy League.

Congressman Ed Schrock, who was president of Republican House freshman class and was seated on the House Armed Services Committee, was a great asset to me and the Navy League during his three terms in Congress. I was sad to see him retire.

Events in DC prevented me from stopping by home. The US Navy Memorial Foundation honored Ernest Borgnine, who was sponsored by the Hallmark Channel. Mr. Borgnine was for Navy and we enjoyed swapping stories. I continued with Navy League work for a few days and then was able to be back home for a few days but then went back to DC for appointments. While in DC, RADM Sally Brice O'Hara, who was then in charge of the Coast Guard District, arranged for me to visit the station and take a ride in one of the boats. The Coasties made me feel like I was in charge as I whizzed down the waterway. I knew Sally pretty well then, but we became great friends over the next few years.

On October 28, I spoke to the New Flag Spouse Conference. Steve Pietropaoli came with me and made sure I had all the info I needed. Back to the office for an official tour of the Navy League building construction site. Everything is on schedule.

Stephen and I made an office call to RADM Dale Gabel who was the Navy League rep in the area. That evening, October 2, 2004, Arlie joined me for the US Coast Guard birthday ball where I was presented the Spirit of Hope Award. That evening is in the stories section. Arlie returned home. I went to Vina del Mar, Chile for the FIDALMAR, the International Federation of Navy Leagues.

Shortly after that my president's message, "A Second Century of Service" was posted on our website in Italian, Korean, Japanese, and Spanish.

October 2004: The issue with the American Shipbuilding Association was one of my toughest issue while I was president. I am grateful that Steve was the executive director. I was excited about the program and pleased to be able to join them in our efforts to promote shipbuilding. And many months of discussion we established a method for ASA to send support for shipbuilding to our membership.

We were concerned with the language used in the messages that were going out. I tried to call ASA many times to discuss this. Our executive director, Stephen Pietropaoli, also called and left messages. His quotes in the article present our position. The messages were critical of Navy leadership. We have always been able to differ in our maritime policy and would in many instances quote numbers that were more than what the sea services were asking for. It was always done in a respectful manner. But these messages were troubling. They were being distributed to our membership without our approval.

As much as we tried to contact ASA, we never received a return call. We had no option but to discontinue our agreement.

Defense Daily on 20 October 2004

By Lorenzo Cortes

The Navy League said yesterday that it had withdrawn support of the American Shipbuilding Association's (ASA) Sea Power Ambassador program citing a difference in tactical approaches.

"We shared many goals with ASA and will continue to work with them on issues of mutual concerns," Navy League National President Sheila McNeill said in a statement. "But we have at times found their approach to issues too narrow and their tactic too divisive." ASA say its Sea Power Ambassador program's goal is "to educate the American public and elected officials on the need to rebuild the fleet of the U.S. Navy and Coast Guard to meet America's security

requirements in the 21st Century." The main impetus for the program is ASA's view that the size of the fleet is in jeopardy and that the Navy will continue to cut shipbuilding numbers in future budgets. ASA has spearheaded reports on this issue showing the shipbuilding decline in FY. '06 and encouraged congressional leaders to voice concerns to top defense officials like Secretary of Defense Donald Rumsfeld.

The Navy League's decision to shut down its support of the Sea Power Ambassador Program stems in part from actions that occurred last February, when the program launched criticisms of naval leadership that the Navy League considered "heavy handed." Stephen Pietropaoli, the Navy League's Executive Director, told Defense Daily yesterday. He also noted that Navy League did support increased shipbuilding but also believe it has a broader view of supporting sea power in general.

ASA President Cynthia Brown told Defense Daily yesterday that she was taken "off Guard" by the announcement because the Ambassador program does not receive financial support from the Navy League. She did acknowledge that some Navy League members participated in the Ambassador program, but that there was no formal agreement between the two organizations. An observer noted the tension between ASA and the Navy has been building for months, ASA has been aggressive about boosting the number of ships in the Navy's budget. The Navy has argued that the number of ships, while important, matters less than the capabilities they will have in the future.

This is really between ASA and the Navy," the observer said. "Navy League apparently wants to stay on the sidelines. By withdrawing its support, it accomplishes that." A Navy Official welcomes the move. "It's obvious that the Navy League realizes that a strong naval force is a combination of not only the ship count but also the capability of those platforms and our Navy people." The official said. "They understand that our Navy people are the true strength of our force."

And Chris Cavas ran an article in *Defense News*:

U.S. Navy Support Group Spar over Public Message

Two of the largest organizations concerned with spreading the word about supporting the U.S. Navy aren't talking to each other. The

Navy League of the United States and the American Shipbuilding Association (ASA) are in a squabble over the Sea Power Ambassadors program, which talks to the public and elected officials about the importance of building and maintaining a strong force. The Navy League which says ASA is unfairly criticizing the services leaders in the zeal to lobby for more ships, is leaving what is called a "partnership" with the lobbying group "due to differences over the tactics to be used in advocating for the maintenance of a strong maritime force in America."

Trouble is, said ASA President Cynthia Brown, no such arrangement exists with the booster organization. "There never has been a partnership with the Navy League," she said. October 21, two days after the Navy League announced its withdrawal of support for the program. "There's never been anything to withdraw from." Although Brown declined to further discuss the issues, Steve Pietropaoli, a retired admiral who serves as the Navy League's National Executive Director, insisted a partnership was formed last year with ASA to promote the Sea Power Ambassador program. The Navy League brought the credibility," Pietropaoli said, "of an outside organization that doesn't benefit directly from shipbuilding." Although each organization supports shipbuilding, they represent different groups. About 67,000 civilians are members of the Navy League, while ASA represents the interests of six major shipyards and more than 60 companies in the U.S. shipbuilding industry.

"We share many goals with ASA and will continue to work with them on issues of mutual concern, "Sheila McNeill, Navy League national president, said in a statement, "but we have at times found their approach to issues too narrow and their tactics too division." Pietropaoli said problems with ASA's tactics began in February "after ASA pushed an uncoordinated release to our membership that attacked the president's shipbuilding budget. "Since then, he said, in an email "we've been trying to get ASA and company to play by the rules of our partnership, which include the Navy League having a vote on content pushed to members or posted on the website. They've blown us off."

The last straw for the league appears to have been a September posting on ASA's Sea Power Ambassador Website headlined, "Sen. Trent Lott calls Navy Leadership "weak" on shipbuilding and criticized Navy leaders over reports that only four ships will be order in fiscal 2006. "I don't think anybody in the membership believe (Marine Corps Commandant) Gen. Michael Hagee or Adm. Vern

> *Clark (chief of Naval Operations or (Navy Secretary) Gordon England are weak." Pietropaoli said. "I think the senator has a right to say that, but I don't think we should lead with that." ASA's focus on building ships is too narrow, he said. "Seapower is a lot more than shipbuilding," he said. "Attacking the (Navy) leadership for doing what they must to balance operations, readiness and recapitalization is not the most effective method of advocacy."*

Steve and I spent a couple of weeks contacting many of those companies. There was no backlash to the Navy League. I believe the Navy League made the right decision.

October 14–16, 2004: At the request of LCDR Keith Lawson, Commanding Officer of the Twin Cities Squadron and his wife, Gwen, I made a trip to the Twin Cities Council. Barbara Jacobs-Smith was the committee chair for the National Sea Cadets Council in Twin Cities—one of the best organized and most supportive Sea Cadets' teams. I met and spoke with the cadets. They were most impressive. That evening I spoke at the Navy Ball. It was special to see these same young men as the color guard that evening. And as I told them later, they were flawless. I was honored to present the Navy League Youth Medal to Twin Cities Council selection of the year PO1 James Jacobs-Smith.

The month finished out with the National Capitol Council's famous and exciting Dinner Cruise aboard the *Odyssey*.

The winter meeting was in DC, November 4–7. That time included reports from all vice presidents, treasure and corporate secretary with pre-meetings with each of them. It was going well thanks to everyone's hard work.

In DC, on November 9, I attended the premiere of *Last Letters Home*, about the war in Iraq. Special guests were Bill Couturier Producer of the film and Senator John McCain.

I was in town on December 8 to attend the Congressional Coast Guard Caucus and hear a briefing on the USCG's Helicopter Interdiction Tactical Squadron (HITRON).

And on Friday, December 10, we had our Navy League Holiday party at the Army Navy Country Club. What an opportunity for Steve and me to have some fun time with staff and to let them all know what a great job they were doing.

I was pleased to be able to wrangle Vice Admiral Tom Barrett and his wife, Sheila, for dinner at the Ritz before his retirement. He will surely be missed.

We finished with a Corporate Breakfast with Frank Libutti, undersecretary for information, analysis, and infrastructure, Office of the Secretary of Defense, at the Ritz-Carlton. I had met General Libutti on one of my DACOWITS visits overseas. He was a very impressive man both as a senior officer and a defense undersecretary.

We met with Mrs. Connie Clark and Mrs. Doreen Scott, wife of MCPON, Steve, Susan Fallon, and David Tuma on a memorial for Navy spouses. I loved the idea and hoped to be able to make it happen. I didn't. In my now seven decades, I have never committed to a project that I didn't complete. This is the exception. Somehow the days got away from me and I failed to make this happen. To this day I still have such regret.

The next day, November 11, 2004, was Veterans Day and this time Arlie joined me at the White House. There was a reception and then a receiving line for the president.

As we were talking with the president, Arlie felt so comfortable he put his arms around President Bush. I tried to give him the "evil eye" but noticed the Secret Service were comfortable with it, so I didn't jerk him away.

We then went to the wreath laying at Arlington National Cemetery. It is always a poignant event and we had excellent seats, so we had no problem seeing the ceremony. I was surprised to run into Representative John P. Yates, a state representative from Georgia, who is chairman of the military and veterans' committee. I also ran into Pete Wheeler, who was famous in Georgia as the commissioner, Georgia Department of Veterans Services, and had served as chairman of the National Veterans Day Committee since 1954. He was such a gracious gentleman and was pleased to see a fellow Georgian at the White House. He later sent me a "Certification of Appreciation" from the Department of Veterans Service. We talked with John Thorn and Admirals Loy and Tom Collins. John looked spiffy in his hat! It was good to see General Colin Powell again. And it was just cool to sit in a comfortable chair at the White House and watch all those faces that you see on television walking around!

I was home for the weekend and returned to the office with an assortment of good meetings. I met with the New Zealand council with Steve, Jim Hoffman, Don Sacarob and Bill Waylett on how we could better support this council. Catching up on correspondence and meeting with Katie and Linda which I tried to do as often as I could and attending a National Capitol Council event at the Alpine Restaurant with Admiral Vern Clark speaking after attending the Betholf Award presentation on the Hill sponsored by the Coast Guard. Admiral Tom Collins presented the award.

On November 8, I went with Steve to a retirement/awards ceremony for Captain Dale Lumme on Capitol Hill. Dale had just completed a tour as director, Navy House Liaison, and was most savvy on legislative issues.

I was running a little close, but the ceremony had not started, and I slipped in and sat on the back row. Rear Admiral Barry Costello was running the show. Seven—yes, seven—members of Congress were at the ceremony waiting to speak about Dale. I remember two of them: Congressmen Ike Skelton and Duncan Hunter. They all spoke eloquently on their respect for Dale. At the end and before closing out the program, Rear Admiral (later to be Vice Admiral) Costello walked to the back of the room and took my hand and led me to the podium to speak! That was quite a surprise and to this day, I can't remember what I said. But there was so much good you could say about Dale's tour; it was easy!

Back in Georgia, RADM Cassias hosted a holiday party on December 2, Arlie and I attended this and the Navy League/Marine Corps Toys for Tots on December 5, and then to St. Simons Island the same day for Toys for Tots with the MOAA group.

December 8 and 9 were full of meetings in DC with a Congressional Coast Guard Caucus briefing at the Cannon Building and then to the Pentagon to meet with Admiral Nathman.

Not to miss a party, I attended the National Capitol Council Party that evening.

To bring it back to business, we met with the bankers and those responsible for leasing the building on the ninth with a break for lunch with Rear Admiral Slavonic, USNR, spokesman for Coalition Provisional Authority and a good friend of Steve's, who joined us for lunch. It was fun watching them interact and "make up" stories about the other when it was easier. Back to the hotel to freshen up for dinner but squeezed in a meeting at the Ritz with RADM Cotton, US Navy Reserve and then dinner with my buddy Captain Kevin Wensing and his wife, Hartley. The next morning, we went to Coast Guard headquarters to discuss Sea Air Space with Commandant Admiral Tom Collins and then a Deepwater update with RADM Pat Stillman accompanied by Sharon Gurke, chairman of Sea Air Space that year, and John Thorn, public affairs, and rescuer of Sheila, when she needed it.

I finished the year with a USO holiday party, a holiday reception at Missouri House in Norfolk and a dozen telephone conference calls as everyone was busy with their families. It's *Christmas*!

In the May timeframe, one of our wonderful supporters, Jack Schiff's company Cincinnati Financial Company was appointed to the Fortune 500. I gave him a call. And told him of the Navy League's pleasure. As a shareholder, we knew this was a testament to the company's outstanding leadership and management. I told him I also appreciated the very gracious welcome he had extended to our national treasurer, Bob Bishop, at the annual shareholders meeting the month before. (I wanted to be there myself but was visiting our Navy League councils in Asia.) I also expressed to him the Navy League's appreciation for the ongoing support of the Schiff Foundations. It went a long way in supporting our mission and service to our men and women in uniform. Jack, always so modest and unassuming, gave me a different take. "Sheila, being on that list is not always easy. You are added to many lists—it's easier to be number 501!"

The *Seafarers* covered my column in *Seapower* in December 2004:

Reassess Ready Reserve Force. Navy League President Praises Ready Reserve Force

Sheila M. McNeill, national president of the Navy League of the United States, offered strong support for the Ready Reserve Force (RRF) in a recent editorial. Writing in the Navy League's monthly magazine, SEAPOWER, McNeill described the RRF as "a major element of our successes in recent conflicts." She also suggested that the RRF "could have a broader role as a multipurpose national asset able to serve additional agencies with a variety of missions." Created in 1976, the RRF is a key element of U.S. strategic sealift, according to the U.S. Maritime Administration. The 59-vessel fleet "is specifically structured to transport Army and Marine Corps unit equipment and initial resupply for forces deploying anywhere in the world during the critical period before adequate numbers of commercially available ships can be marshaled," the agency noted. In her column, McNeill said the RRF "is the nation's premier sealift readiness program... The successful operation of the RRF is a joint effort by government agencies and industry. The program is managed by the Maritime Administration to fulfill the requirements of the U.S. Transportation Command.

The ships are operated by commercial companies and crewed by civilian merchant mariners. When activated, they fall under the operational control of the Military Sealift Command (MSC). "That complex structure is no barrier to success for the RRF ships, which met or exceeded most operational goals during Iraqi Freedom," McNeill continued. "The RRF in 2004 has met its goal of 100 percent on-time activation, for example, and exceeded the goal that 95 percent of ships be fully capable while working for the MSC. The RRF's achievement: 99 percent."

She pointed out that the program is funded by the Navy and therefore faces "tremendous competition for Navy funds. That makes a multi-agency assessment more vital. The RRF was created long before 9/11 as a Defense Department resource. It comprises highly capable ships worth billions of dollars. They could be used in a variety of innovative ways to improve the security of the United States during a terrorist alert, an actual attack or in the event of a natural disaster. For example, the Department of Homeland Security might utilize some as medical platforms for triage or emergency care should there be another attack or disaster on the scale of 9/11." As an example, McNeill pointed out that the RRF includes 10 crane ships "with unique capabilities." They could be used to augment Homeland Security efforts "to search suspect ships at sea or in a remote anchorage having no shoreside facilities. A crane ship and companion barge car-

rier could come alongside, offload some containers and move others, facilitating a rapid and effective search of the huge container ships that ply the world's oceans."

She concluded, "The feasibility of this approach should be carefully assessed by the Maritime Administration and the departments of Defense and Homeland Security before the RRF is diminished further and its valuable assets are lost to the nation." The Navy League is the self-described "only civilian organization dedicated to supporting the sea services—the U.S. Navy, U.S. Marine Corps, U.S. Coast Guard and U.S.-Flag Merchant Marine."

McNeill is the first woman to serve as president of the organization, which was founded in 1902. She was elected in 2003 and has been a member since 1966. Her official bio notes that she has served "at every leadership level including president of the Camden-Kings Bay Council, Georgia state president and region president for the South Atlantic Coast Region. Most recently, McNeill served as a national vice president responsible for the organization's legislative affairs activities. While serving in that position, she aggressively sought support on Capitol Hill and made educating congressional members about the sea services her top priority.

I was in Norfolk on January 4–7 to finalize attendance at Sea Air Space. Mary Ellen and I met with the following:

- COX Communications
- RADM Starling, Commander, Naval Air Force, US Atlantic Fleet
- VADM Fitzgerald, Commander, Second Fleet
- VADM Munns, Commander, Submarine Force, US Atlantic Fleet
- RADM Sally Brice O'Hara, Commander, Fifth Coast Guard District
- RADM Archtizel, Commander, Operation Test and Evaluation Force
- ADM. William Fallon, Commander, US Fleet Forces

I attended the Hampton Roads Council event where I installed the new officers. From January 13 to 15, I was in Atlanta for meetings with the council and the governor's committee. From January 16 to 21, I traveled to the Northwest Councils to visit Everett, Seattle, Lake Washington County for their fourth anniversary dinner, Bremerton Council Installation of Offices. More details about these visits in the stories section.

From January 20 to 22, I was in Houston at the Lone Star Region Meeting, Weston Galleria Hotel. And back to DC from January 24 to 28. I met with RADM Barry Costello, chief of legislative affairs for the Navy, and RADM Ann Rondeau, commander Naval Personnel Development Command and special assistant to the chief of Naval Operations for Task Force Excel.

On the twenty-fifth, Susan and I got caught up on development issue while Rick Barnard and I discussed Sea Power Magazine. I had a wonderful dinner with Admiral Tom Barrett and his wife, Sheila. The next day, back to the Pentagon for a meeting with Lt. General Jan C. Huly, USMC, deputy commandant for plans, policies, and operations. Steve, Pat Holmgaard, Sharon Gurke, and Al Bernard met to sign the SAS contract.

Megan Cheek and Carol Hackley created a wonderful public affairs tool with a "Talk in a Box." Megan reviewed the final draft with me. Later, I was attending a Safety Award Committee meeting.

On the twenty-eighth, I'm back at the Pentagon for a visit with RADM Terry L. McCreary, chief of information (CHINFO) at the Pentagon. I've worked with so many CHINFOs during the years and they have always made my life easier! And they all manage to impress.

In February, I'm back home for a couple of days but participate in a conference call with Tom Dwyer, Steve, Jeremy Miller, and Bill Waylett on our grassroots initiative. Bill has continued to do a great job with training our Navy League. And then, you guessed it, more calls for Sea Air Space and back to the Pentagon! It is a short metro ride and the pass that makes these awesome number of trips much easier. And it's amazing how Katie always makes them work smoothly. We called on the following:

- VADM Gerald L. Hoewing, Chief of Naval Personnel
- VADM Lewis Crenshaw, Deputy, CNO for Resources, Requirements, and Assessments
- RADM Joseph A. Walsh, Submarine Warfare Division
- RADM Mark J. Edwards, Director, Surface Warfare Division
- RADM Thomas J. Kilcline, Director, Air Warfare Division

We returned to the office for a conference call with all region presidents and dinner that evening with our vice president for corporate affairs, Bob Ravitz. The corporate breakfast the next morning was at the Ritz and featured The Honorable Dionel M. Aviles, undersecretary of the Navy.

I went to Capitol Hill where the sea services chiefs were testifying. RADM Barry Costello saved me a seat right behind the table where the chiefs sat. It was important to me to hear firsthand what they were saying so I could ensure that we were supporting those issues. During my last meeting with Admiral Vern Clark, he gave me a folder with 8×10 pictures of each of them testifying and my fuzzy face right behind them. I love those pictures. After the hearing, I went outside and one of the officers from the Office of Legislative Affairs caught me. Right behind me, Senator Hillary Clinton was coming down the stairs. He asked, "Have you met Senator Clinton?"

"No, I haven't but I would like to," I answered We waited as she walked our way and he introduced me emphasizing that I was the first woman president of the Navy League.

She said, "Well, I was wondering who you were. You are always at the hearings and seated behind the service chiefs." Interesting that she noticed and remembered.

Back to the office for a farewell party for Jeremy Miller our legislative affairs genius. I'll miss him. He and Veronica were the two that I worked most with. A few months earlier, they came over to the Ritz Charlton after work to review some of the issues we were working on. At one point, I saw his hand cover hers. "What's going on?" I asked. It turned out they had been dating and they later married!

When I arrived back to the hotel that night, I had a gift-wrapped package in my room. I had not realized it but this was the fiftieth night I had stayed at the Ritz-Carlton. Remember now, I had a special rate that was the same at the small hotel close to Navy League headquarters. Andrea Vargas, guest relations manager, left a nice note. She had been wonderful to work with during the past year. I received a nice warm robe with the Ritz-Carlton insignia.

And then to the Navy yard for a SAS call with Admiral Kirkland Donald, director, Naval Nuclear Propulsion. Read more about Admiral Donald in the stories section. *Seafarers Log* picked up my February president's Message. Their headline was "***Navy League President Praises Ready Reserve Force.***"

I talked with Mr. Michael Fagin who worked with the Bob Hope Award. I then sent a letter to Mrs. Delores Hope sharing with her the great honor and experience of receiving the Bob Hope Spirit of Hope Award.

Lunch with VADM John Cotton at the Pentagon. John shared with me many of the issues with the reserve force. We discussed the Navy League and the mutual benefit of the Navy League with our reserve force. The active duty cannot be members of the Navy League. Our advocacy efforts preclude them from being members, but they are, of course, very supportive. He told me he would be sending out a letter to his reserve forces encouraging them to get involved with the Navy League. This was a big deal and I will always be grateful to him for reaching out to his force.

This is the e-mail to his entire reserve force:

28 February 2005
Navy Reservists,

The Active and Reserve Components of the United States Navy continues to be more integrated each and every day while successfully prosecuting the Global War on Terror. Working alongside our superb Sailors in every community where they live, work and often drill, is an organization that is also dedicated to making our Navy as strong as it can be. For more than 100 years the Navy League of the United States has provided support to the men and women who wear the cloth of our great Nation, and their families. 70,000 members across the country and around the world. From hosting ship visit to recognition awards for the troops, the Navy League is there to those who serve. At the national level, the Navy League is a powerful advocate on Capitol Hill in support of the platforms, weapons and training the Sea Services needs to prevail in the Global War on Terror, protect the Homeland and meet our many and varied national security commitments. Many Reservists have found that joining the Navy League enhances their professional contacts within the Sea Services. Navy League Councils work closely with local commands to sponsor presentations by flag/general officers and military commanders. These events are often valuable educational and networking opportunities.

Please consider supporting those who are supporting YOU and your shipmates by becoming a member of the Navy League. You can choose to become active in one of their local councils and help them to attract the next generation of great Americans who will continue to defend our freedoms. Let the people who are tireless advocates on your behalf know that we appreciate their efforts by joining their team. Together we can make a difference for our Sea Services, our Sailors their employers and their families.

J. G. Cotton
Vice Admiral, U.S. Navy, Chief of Naval Reserve

The next morning was the Navy-Marine Corps caucus on Capitol Hill.

Arlie joined me in Connecticut for the USS *Jimmy Carter* Commissioning on February 19. There was a VIP Platform briefing at eleven and the reception after the commissioning.

It was an amazing commissioning and the audience was a 'who's who' in the submarine world. It is always such a pleasure to see old friends. The Carters were most gracious to everyone. Former first lady Rosalynn Carter was the sponsor of the ship. This was the third and last of the Sea Wolf class.

I'm back at headquarter on the twenty-first and the next day went back to the Pentagon. Admiral Clark had suggested I meet with his political advisor before I left for my trip to Asia. I met with his advisor and then Admiral Clark and I reviewed my trip. This was my last visit at his office before his retirement. His photographer was there and made several pictures that I treasure.

The flag breakfast was February 25 with Vice Admiral Nathman, Steve Pietropaoli and me speaking; it was a light hearted fun event. I look at the pictures and see so many laughing faces but what was so funny, I don't remember—and maybe it's best I don't. I left after the breakfast and joined Arlie and Vice Admiral Al Herberger to travel to Las Vegas for the Maritime Trade Department of the AFL-CIO annual executive board meeting. That full story is Undersecretary Mineta and Secretary Pang's story.

For a rare treat, we all attended the Cirque Du Soleil. It was incredible. We traveled from Las Vegas to Salt Lake City for a council event and choral recital at the Mormon Tabernacle Church. The church was packed, and yet somehow, the local council got them to recognize the national president of the Navy League!

Our Camden fly-in was March 7–11, with dinner on the ninth at the Caucus Room and ending with our briefing at the Pentagon.

I was in Denver from March 16 to 18 for the Rocky Mountain Region meeting with Dan and Kathleen Branch, who were most gracious. Dan would later become national president of the Navy League. We met with not only the Navy League council, but also with the Sea Cadet unit that they sponsored. We had a working session with their executive committee and later dinner for the entire council.

Returning on the nineteenth for the steering committee meeting before SAS occurred on March 22–24.

The theme that year was **Ensuring Global Access**. My message in the program:

> *Welcome to the Navy League's 2005 Sea Air Space Exposition. As the foremost national organization representing all of our nation's great sea services, the theme of "Ensuring Global Access" providing a venue for America's inventive defense companies to exhibit innovative goods and services designed to advance America's military capabilities. During these times of heightened awareness and security, more and more Americans understand the need for maintaining a strong military force to protect the freedoms that our forefathers fought so hard to establish. A productive and effective partnership between the defense industry and the military customer is a vital part of keeping our forces prepared and strong.*
>
> *For more than 100 years, the Navy League has faithfully demonstrated its commitment to building and sustaining American sea power. In 2005, we find ourselves in a unique position, caused by the continuing war on terrorism and operations in Iraq, and Afghanistan, to truly rally behind all of the brave men and women who wear the cloth of the nation, including the maritime services—the Navy, Marine Corps, Coast Guard, and U.S. flag Merchant*

Marine. Our deployed service members are on the minds of Americans coast to coast.

The Sea Air Space Exposition is the forum that unites our sea service leaders, our corporate partners in the defense industry and the Navy League to accomplish the needs of a growing national security agenda. We appreciate your attendance and hope that you will continue to join us in strong support of America's sea services: their program… their missions… but most of all their people

Sheila M. McNeill
National President
Navy League of the United States.

Susan Gurke was the chairman that year. She did an awesome job. I was very humbled by her introduction at the banquet:

Tonight, I am honored to introduce the most dynamic National President that Navy League has ever experienced. Not only does this president serve with distinction, but she is unique in the fact that she is the first female to hold the office since the organization's inception in 1902. For the past two years, I have worked closely with Sheila McNeill and it is no secret that she has taken her role as National President seriously. I am sure many of you have gotten to know Sheila on a personal level. She is no stranger around Washington or the world for that matter. Sheila volunteers her time and energy to fully support the advancements of the sea services. She has attempted, and if I am correct, has almost achieved her goal of visiting every Navy League council in the world and there are over 265 (note: that was just Navy League lore but a nice story). In fact, Mrs. McNeill heads to the Pacific next month for a tour of councils including California, Japan, Korea, Singapore, Guam and Hawaii. During her presidency, I don't think she has spent more than a few nights back at her hometown of Kings Bay, Georgia. In fact, I got a call from the ladies that work at the store Sheila owns in Kings Bay who were wondering if they should file a missing person's report. It is no secret that everyone who meets Sheila is impressed by her honesty and her ability to be a straight shooter. So, it is with admiration and gratitude that I introduce to you tonight, the national president of the Navy League, Sheila McNeill.

We had about twenty speakers that year—which is in line with other Sea Air Space Expos. I look back over these names and they bring back fond memories: Secretary of the Navy, Gordon England, chairman of the Joint Chiefs; General Richard B. Myers, chief of Naval Operations; Admiral Vern Clark and Vice Admiral Terry Cross, vice commandant of the Coast Guard; and RADM Jay M. Cohen, chief of Naval Research.

Speaking also was Lt. General James N. Mattis, USMC, commanding general, Marine Corps Combat Development Command, who would later be President Donald Trump's pick for secretary of defense.

One seminar entitled "Ship Building and the Industrial Base" had the speakers the Honorable Allison Stiller, deputy assistant secretary of the Navy for shipbuilding; Michael Petters, president, Northrup Grumman Newport News sector; and Robert Work with the Center for Strategic and Budgetary Assessment. Several other seminars had the same level of speakers. It was an impressive list.

We presented the 2005 Fleet Admiral Chester W. Nimitz Award to Fred Mossally, president, Lockheed Martin, Maritime Systems & Sensors. Our entertainment at the Banquet was celebrated actor Stephen Lang in "Beyond Glory." My introduction:

> *Under the combined auspices of the Department of Defense and the National Endowment for the Arts, Mr. Lang is about to embark on an international tour of U.S. military bases. "Beyond Glory" will open at Pearl Harbor on April 22nd, and will go on to play for our servicemen and women in Japan, Guam, Korea, the Persian Gulf, Italy, Germany, and God knows where else.*

Our visits paid off—we had a huge number of flag and general officers

Romana Joyce, a former public affairs director of the Navy League, who is now with the American Legion, sent me their current magazine with Cpl. Eddie Wright on the cover. "You met him (and fed him shrimp) on our little three-hour tour aboard the USS Sequoia last July." I was so proud to see that he was still in the Marine Corps.

On the twenty-fifth, I had an Asian briefing with Katie Johnson, Coast Guard director for international affairs, and then with VADM Cross vice commandant and John Thorne. At lunch, we met with Mr. James Link, president of the Coast Guard Foundation, along with Susan Fallon and John Thorne.

On April 2, Arlie auctioned at the Dolphin Scholarship Auction at Kings Bay. We left April 3 for the visit to San Diego; Japan (Tokyo and Sasebo), Korea, Singapore, Guam, and Hawaii and speaking at the Defense Technology 2005 and the Korean Naval Academy. The DE fence Technology conference is attended by chiefs of Navy and senior naval officers from several Southeast Asia countries. I am indebted to Paul Chung, Jack Miller, and most especially to Katie Doud for working so hard to make this trip successful.

When we returned on May 3, we took a couple of days off to get acclimated at home and with work sessions with Linda Hoffman and Katie Doud. Then Linda came to our home for several days to get caught up our work. That was a wonderful treat for me—not to have to be the one traveling. I was back at headquarters on the twelfth for a corporate gold dinner with Admiral Vern Clark, CNO, and our corporate gold companies at the Tower Club in Tysons Corner.

On the thirteenth, I met with Megan Cheek on issues from the Singapore Council. That evening, I went to the Marine Corps evening parade hosted by General William "Spider" Nyland, USMC, assistant commandant of the Marine Corps, and Mrs. Nyland in honor of the undersecretary of the Navy, the Honorable Dionel Aviles with a reception preceding the parade.

The May 14 edition of the *Brunswick News* covered the recent news that the BRAC committee had the New London-Groton base on the list:

NEXT UP: Get subs

By Amy Horton Carter

America's "submarine capital" has declared war on a proposal to close its base and redirect up to half of its submarines and thousands of military personnel and civilians to Naval Submarine Base Kings Bay.

The base in New London-Groton, Conn., was one of the more than 150 military installations targeted for closure in the United States and its territories by the U.S. Department of Defense in its 2005 Base Realignment and Closure report. The report recommends that New London's fleet of 16 Virginia-class attack submarines and varied support functions be divided between naval installations in Kings Bay and Norfolk, Va. The report recommends that Kings Bay serve as the new home for the Navy's submarine school which serves as basic training for all submarines. Connecticut officials vowed Friday they would not give up their 90-year-old base without a fight. "I am shocked at the Pentagon decision (Friday) to target the sub base here in New London for closure," said U.S. Senator Joseph Lieberman, D-Conn., in a prepared statement, "We pledge to fight tooth and nail to overturn this decision." Connecticut's congressional delegation and community leaders in New London-Groton were successful in removing the base from a prior BRAC list in 1993, but the numbers are running against the base this time. "There's a 20 percent chance we can reverse this." Said Rep Rob Simmons, R-Conn., during a press conference in New London Friday. "I will be very honest, it will be an uphill climb."

The fight begins Tuesday when the nine-member BRAC commission holds the first of several months' worth of hearings to discuss recommendations and methodology for military base realignment and closure. The independent commission is charged with reviewing the Defense Department's report, visit each base recommended for closure and hearing from each community potentially affected by closure and realignment. By Sept. 8, the commission must have its own list of recommendations or bases to realign or close ready for President Bush, who has until Sept 23 to either accept or reject the list in its entirely. If he accepts the list, it goes to the Congress, which as 45 legislative days to reject the list in its entirety before it becomes binding. It will be harder for targeted communities to make a successful case against closure or realignment because the BRAC is so lean, said Shella McNeill, a Brunswick resident who is serving the final weeks of a two-year term as national president of the navy League of the United States, a civilian support and advocacy group.

The Defense Department went into the current BRAC holding the results of a 1998 study that counted 24% of domestic military infrastructure as excess. The BRAC recommendations released Friday address less than 5% of the 3,700 military installations in the U.S. and its territories. "That shows you they've been really careful in keeping the numbers as low as you can." McNeill said by phone from the Navy League's office in Washington, D.C. Should Connecticut somehow prevail, though, McNeill said Kings Bay and Camden County can feel good that the Pentagon thought enough of the installation and community to advocate for their growth. If they do prevail in some ways I think that just the acknowledgement that Kings Bay is poised and ready and can accommodate more missions and more people is good news for us because they've made that statement that they would prefer to put people and mission at Kings Bay" she said. Kings Bay will have no hearings to come unless the commission recommends that an alternative installation be selected to receive the missions and personnel the Pentagon proposes to put in Camden County.

"They're going to listen to the losers first." Said U.S. Rep Jack Kingston, R-1. Kingston said Georgia officials are preparing to launch their own fight to save four installations targeted for closure within its own borders—Fort Gillem and Fort McPherson, two U.S.

Army command centers located in Atlanta area, as well as Naval Air Station Atlanta and The Navy Supply Corps School in Athens.

That battle will have no effect on the installations that stand to benefit from BRAC, he said. Although the Pentagon set a timeline of six years for achieving the recommendations on the BRAC list, the transition of equipment and personnel between New London-Groton and Kings Bay could be complete with a matter of months," McNeill said (note: where did that come from?) Defense Secretary Donald H. Rumsfeld said the initial list better positions U.S. forces to fight 21st century threats and will save the nation about $50 billion over the next 20 years. The cost to New London alone would be 8,460 jobs and an estimated 13,000 military personnel and civilians, including families. Kings Bay, which currently employs 8,061 active duty and civilian personnel and contractors, stands to gain 3,365 jobs. That may translate into as many as 5,050 people, counting family members who accompany military and civilian personnel who transfer from Connecticut to Georgia.

Every night for the next week were front page stories about this decision by the BRAC committee. Captain Walt Yourstone, US Navy retired, and a former commanding officer of Kings Bay took the lead on the BRAC issue for Camden County.

The June 5 edition of the *Georgia Times Union* had the following heading:

OFFENSIVE CAMPAIGN
Many feel push to save Connecticut base disparages Camden

We took a weeks' vacation and during that time had a productive grassroots sponsor meeting.

I was pleased to have the book *Defending Freedom* come out during the last few months of my presidency. That story is in Steve Pietropaoli's story. The cover page has the following:

The Navy League of the United States is pleased to publish this tribute to America's heroic Sailors and Marines in partnership with the Navy-Marine Corps Relief Society. Both organizations are entering their second century of service in support of our Navy and Marine Corps personnel and their families.

Secretary of the Navy, Gordon England, did the foreword.

The book jacket told of the Navy-Marine Relief Society and the Navy League. The last section was:

About Military Photographers

Historically, Navy photography work root in 1914, when the Navy's first "official" photographer Walter L. Richardson, a cook aboard the battleship USS Mississippi, documented the training and aircraft tests being conducted at a naval station, later to be known as the Cradle of Naval Aviation in Pensacola, Florida.

In the early 1900's photographers used 4 x 5 press cameras, and worked out of crude, make-shift photo labs set up in storage rooms and closets. Now 21st century military photographers are respected professionals armed with advanced digital camera systems and laptops. They are deployed throughout the world, assigned to combat camera teams, ships at sea, aircraft squadrons, and combat teams, ships at sea, aircraft squadrons, and combat units on the ground. Today's photography "visual information" requires no film and is often acquired, captioned, released, and transmitted within minutes of an event. This book serves to showcase the extraordinary dedication and capability of the U.S. military, with particular attention to the Navy and Marine Corps team. These ordinary but highly motivated highly trained men and women defend our democracy, while freeing the people of Iraq from the misery and tyranny suffered at the hands of the Saddam Hussein regime.

Each image presented in this book displays the very best photojournalist captured by military photographers; journalists, and service members who placed themselves in harm's way in an effort to fully document the events leading up to and then through the first days of Operation Iraqi Freedom.

Christopher J. Madden	*T. L. McCreary*
Director Naval Visual News Service	*Rear Admiral U.S. Navy*
Navy Office of Information	*Chief of Information*

As Navy League president, my name was on many documents of other's work. That is especially true of this book. Steve Pietropaoli was the force and the talent working with CHINFO for this wonderful capture of history. While Charles S. Abbott, US Navy (ret.), and I were list as editors, all the work from the Navy League was done by Steve.

I received letters and e-mails from many during that time expressing their thanks for my service. Gordon Peterson, former senior editor for *Seapower* working for the editor James (Jim) D. Hessman sent a copy of *Naval Forces* magazine containing his article repeating my recent editorial call for a properly sized Navy. He had also written a guest editorial for *Wings of Gold* making the same points. "It was the best of time. It was the worst of times! On the one hand, we are blessed with a Navy of unrivaled talent, leadership and technical ability," he told me.

"On the other hand, the Navy's need to advance to the next generation of warship design is in danger of foundering owning to the administration's budget dilemma."

He continued, "My work with Pat Stillman and the Coast Guard as my 'day job' continues to be enriching and rewarding on many levels. He is an inspiring leader, and it is a privilege to be able to serve with him at the Deepwater Program."

Gordon sent me the article entitled "Putting the Cart before the Horse," where he quoted a part of my president's message.

We traveled to Norfolk for my last meeting as national president from June 1–5, 2005. Mother, my daughter (Leslie), my brother (Brian), my sister (Debbie), and our friend Lynn Warwick all attended that last convention. The first evening we attended a dinner hosted by RADM Stephen A. Turcotte, commander, Navy Region Mid-Atlantic.

VADM Ed Giambastini was the speaker at the banquet, a.k.a. my "retirement event." I was so pleased when he said he could make it. I've known Ed since he was a captain and have depended on his advice and support for years. More on the admiral in the stories section.

That evening, Admiral Tom Collins presented me with the following proclamation. In the past that is the time that, if they are presenting a Distinguished Service Medal, it would be done but the Coast Guard awarded that medal in 2004. I am grateful that the commandant wanted to recognize my tour as president:

PROCLAMATION OF THE UNITED STATES COAST GUARD

WHEREAS, Sheila M. McNeill has dedicated nearly 40 years of service to the Coast Guard as a member and an extraordinary leader of the Navy League of the United States, the only civilian organization focused on supporting the sea services; and

WHEREAS, in her role as National President of the Navy League since 2003, Ms. McNeill has led the Navy League's 70,000 members in their efforts to educate American citizens and elected officials about the importance of sea power. While effectively engaging the high echelons of military leadership—including the nation's

Commander in Chief—as well as listening and responding to the concern of the most junior enlisted personnel;

WHEREAS, in her previous position as National Vice President of Legislative Affairs Ms. McNeill was instrumental in advancing the Coast Guard's legislative agenda in the 107th and 108th Congress, one of the most fundamentally significant legislative periods in Coast Guard History, a period in which Congress debated and enacted the Department of Homeland Security; the Maritime Transportation Security Act, the most sweeping maritime security legislation in the Nation's history; and the for Coast Guard Authorization Act in nearly half a decade; and

WHEREAS, during this historic period Ms. McNeill and her legislative affairs team orchestrated numerous Navy League-hosted events with members of Congress, providing essential forums for the comprehensive airing of Coast Guard issues in the political process, and

WHEREAS, Ms. McNeill and her team's efforts helped promote the largest major acquisition in the Coast Guard's history, the Integrated Deepwater Systems project, a landmark project valued at $17 billion that will upgrade the Service's fleet of ships, aircraft and C4ISR systems, and

WHEREAS, she consistently demonstrates outstanding ingenuity in seeking way to support the Coast Guard including during her presidency when she developed the groundbreaking Legislative Affairs Grassroots Project that has increased involvement by Navy League Regions, Area and Councils in legislative affairs activities, and

WHEREAS, during every mission she undertakes on behalf of the Coast Guard, Ms. McNeill always epitomizes professionalism and integrity balanced by compassion and great enthusiasm.

NOW THEREFORE, I ADMIRAL THOMAS COLLINS, Commandant of the U.S. Coast Guard, by the power vested in me, do hereby declare and proclaim Ms. Sheila M. McNeill an official partner with the U.S. Coast Guard, bestowing our debt and gratitude to an outstanding citizen who stands among the strongest supporters in the Nation's oldest maritime service.

IN WITNESS, WHEREOF, I have hereunto set my hand this fourth day of June, in the year of our Lord two thousand five.

THOMAS H. COLLINS, Admiral U.S.
Coast Guard, Commandant

With my family there and the staff, that was like family—Linda, Katie, and others; it was a poignant and unforgettable few days. The last night after the reception, in my suite Arlie had sang "My Way" to me a few weeks before and that evening as we reminisced about the year he sang the same to Linda. We were such a great team during those years, and it was a partnership that will never be equaled. There were many times that Linda and Katie gave me wise advice, and I always knew they had my back. They gave me such confidence as I traveled the world. I always knew they were there and they would make things right.

I also used it as an opportunity to thank so many Navy Leaguers who went beyond what was expected and helped me support the sea services for two years. I found a glass paperweight in the shape of a star and called everyone up individually. When I presented a star to Paul Chung, president of the Korea Council, he turned to the crowd, and with both arms high in the air, he declared, "She made me, King!" I loved that guy. His generosity and support of our military is found in the overseas travel story.

During those two years, there was always the guilt about being away so much—even as much as Arlie tried to eliminate those thoughts. After the convention, Leslie wrote me a note:

Mom, I thought after tonight I would be glad to have you all to ourselves but after watching you and the people who admire you, you are where you are supposed to be. You need to move on to better, bigger fights for our country. We will always be here for you and we know you love us. Reach for the stars, Mom until you reach your own galaxy. You are the greatest, "My hero" Love, Leslie

And this letter from Beverly and Evan Baker one of our past national presidents:

June 10, 2005
Dear Sheila and Arlie,

Congratulations on a great job these past two year!! You both did a wonderful job and it was obvious to all of us. Certainly, your swan song convention was done with great class and the response from the attendees was well deserved. Thank you for hosting the Past President's dinner. We were sorry to miss last year's dinner, but we thoroughly enjoyed this one. The silver tray is displayed proudly in our foyer for those few folks who still understand the protocol of leaving cards. Also, it looks really great! Of course, dinner blew out our Weight Watchers' point for the day, but who cares? It was a gourmet delight and we savored every bite.

Welcome to the limited little club of past nation presidents! We really do try to be a positive influence in spite of coming across as a deterrent too many times. Hope you both can have a restful and relaxing summer. You certainly rate it. Thanks, again for a great dinner.

Fond regards,
Beverly and Evan (Baker)

And this one from John Reu, past national president:

Dear Sheila and Arlie:

As we welcome you to the coterie of the has-beens, Madame Immediate Past President and outgoing First Husband. I do want to send you a quick note to thank you for your hospitality at the dinner; for the tray (a most useful size) and for the cans of nuts—even though they cost me ten dollars. You have been a gracious "First Couple" and you, Sheila have done a tremendous job. While I did a number of things I think were most significant for NLUS including the building, fund-raising, TAOSP, etc. even I did not achieve the TREMENDOUS interaction and rapport which you have had with the Senior Commanders of the Sea Services. Again, thank you for all your hospitality in Norfolk, and for the various kindnesses over the past years.

John M. Rau

From two former national presidents at the end of my tour—these sentiments meant a great deal to me. I am officially in the "boys' club of past presidents."

And a special letter from our senior director of development Susan Fallon with thanks for joining the Presidents' Circle. I'm pleased to have had someone of her professionalism on the staff of the Navy League.

Chuck Beers sent me a message that is so nice I can't even include it!

A wonderful e-mail from Elizabeth Brogan, president and editor of Sierra Wave Council:

We had a grand time and came home energized! Today was a council board meeting and the room was full. Reports were spontaneous, to the point and inspiring! The room was alive with volunteerism. You'd have thought they had all been to Norfolk. So, I guess you laid a glow on me, lady, My regards to your talented husband. Wow, he could charm money out of a stone! The auction was a kick.

Thank you, a great deal,
Betty

At the end of my tour, RADM Mark Kenny, commander, Submarine Group 10, gave a reception to welcome me home at group headquarters. Everyone was there from commanding officers to community leadership. I will always be indebted to Mark for giving me such a welcome home. That story is told in the Kenny section.

CHINFO Clips had this farewell article from *Florida Times Union* on June 26, 2005, by Gordon Jackson:

She serves those at sea without serving at sea June–Dec 2005.

Another wonderful welcome home was done by Coastal Bank. They had a large (6 × 11) ad using the picture from *Georgia Trend* with the submarine in the background:

Sheila McNeill
Mission Accomplished

And this message:

The Coastal Bank of Georgia and Synovus Financial Corp, salute Brunswick resident Sheila McNeill as she concludes two years of exemplary service to our nation's sea services as President of the Navy League of the United States. Sheila's term as President—the first woman to hold the office in the League's 103-year history—is the latest accomplishment in her life of devotion to service in this community and beyond. We congratulate Sheila on her nearly forty years of leadership positions and service in the Navy League, including those at the helm of this 76,000-member national organization. She set a course of energetic leadership and deep commitment to the men and women of the sea services, and we are honored to recognize her.

Congratulations, Sheila! Mission accomplished!
The Coastal Bank of Georgia

During the two years I was national president I visited these councils:

Atlanta Council (GA)
Barcelona Council
Bremerton Council (WA)
Camden County Council (Ga)
Chicago Council (IL)
Commodore Perry Council (CA)
Detroit Women's Council (MI)
Eastern Connecticut Council
European Region (Naples)
Everett Council (WA)
Florida Region Meeting
French Riviera-Monaco, Provence Council
Golden Isles Council (GA) 2 times
Great Lakes Council (Detroit)
Hampton Roads Council 4 times
Hawaii State Meeting
Hilo Council (Hawaii)
Hilton Head Council (S.C.)
Honolulu Council (HI)
Jacksonville Council (FL)
Kings Bay Council (GA)
Kona Council (HI)
Korea Council
Lake Washington Council (WA)
Madrid Spain Council
Mexico/Caribbean Region Meeting
Monterrey Peninsula Council (CA)
National Capitol Council (D.C.) 8 times!
New England Region (Boston)
New Jersey Area (Atlantic City)
North East Florida Region
Pacific Central Region (CA)
Palma Council (Spain)
Panama City Council (Fla)
Rocky Mountain Region (Denver)
Salt Lake City Council (UT)
San Diego Council (CA)
Santa Barbara Council (CA)
Sasebo Council (Japan)
Seattle Council (WA)
Singapore Council
South Atlantic Coast Region (Savannah)
Southern Region (Pensacola)
St. Louis Council (MO)
Stockton Council (CA)
Treasure Coast Council (FL)
Twin Lakes Council (MN)

There are some things I will miss: Like talking to the captain of the flight to Denver. He was standing next to me at the counter when the delay was announced. We began talking. I said to him, "You must be former military—you couldn't be this nice if you'd always done this," I said with a smile.

"Yes, a Marine." I gave him my coin, an application for the Navy League and we talked a few minutes as I told him about the event we were attending.

Later, after the plane took off he announced, "We have a special welcome to Sheila McNeill and good luck on that fancy dinner tonight."

At 6:00 p.m. when the pilot announced we'd picked up speed and would arrive at 6:45 p.m. rather than 7:00 p.m. I turned to Arlie and jokingly said, "He's doing that because of our dinner, and at that exact time, the pilot came by over the speaker, "We'll get you there as fast as we can, Sheila."

Like talking to the Chinese group next to us and finding out they are originally from Beijing, China, now live in Denver and have been on a mission trip to Panama! Christian Chinese missionaries leaving home in Denver to minister to Panamanians.

Like such acknowledge from senior military: Meeting with R&D active duty and the captain told me later that night at a banquet that his staff was amazed and said, "How does that woman know so much?"

He answered, "She is the national president of the Navy League." I think a good part of my success is simply asking questions when I don't understand. Sometimes you hate to admit it.

And some things I won't miss: The downside of meeting so many people in such a short time is keeping them straight. Did I meet them in the States? Did I meet them overseas? Was it during DACOWITS? Was it during a Navy League meeting or perhaps it was someone I went to school with!

It never ends. There was one instance when I was on a plane somewhere in the Midwest and we were deplaning—all standing in the aisle ready to depart when I saw a gentleman I had met on some of my travels. I knew he was in the Navy League, but I couldn't come up with his name.

I turned around and stuck my hand out and said, "Hi, I'm Sheila McNeill with the Navy League. I know we met somewhere before and that you are in the Navy League I just can't remember where."

He answered, "John Stossel, ABC…" And then he gave me a big smile.

Another time, I was leaving the USS George H. W. Bush commissioning and turned around and saw a young man, his wife and three children—a very nice-looking family and I did the same thing. "Hi, I'm Sheila McNeill with the Navy League. I know we've met before." He smiled and shook my hand and said, "Neil Bush." He was the President's brother! No wonder he looked familiar. He and his brother looked a lot alike. There were several of these instances over the years but none as well-known as Neil Bush and John Stossel.

* * * * *

Admiral Vern Clark turned over the command of the Navy to Admiral Michael G. Mullen on Friday, July 22, 2005, at the United States Naval Academy. It was a wonderful poignant event. And it is so nice I already knew the incoming CNO!

It was a wonderful two years as Navy League national president. I could not have done it without Linda Trump and Katie Doud. *Every* trip I made, *every* speech I made, *every* person I visited with, *every* letter I wrote, everything I did was done with the help and assistance of these two professional women.

On Wednesday, August 10, 2005, Vice Admiral and Mrs. Charles Mumms, commander, Submarine Forces hosted a reception in honor of the Honorable Jimmy Carter and Mrs. Carter at the Clubs of Kings Bay.

James Nix of the *Tribune & Georgian*:

CARTER PAYS A VISIT TO KINGS BAY

It seemed like any other submarine arrival at Naval Submarine Base Kings Bay August 12. Two tugboats sailed alongside the sub as it appeared in the harbor. The crew stood out on the boat's hull and watched as the boat pulled into the pier. But the USS Jimmy Carter's arrival at Kings Bay was no routine sub docking. This boat was carrying its famed namesake on board. Former President Jimmy Carter waved from the boat's sail as friends, family and Navy personnel watched from shore. It was the first sub ride since he left the Navy in 1953. Carter and his wife Rosalynn took an overnight trip on the newly-commissioned nuclear submarine. The Seawolf-class attack submarine will eventually sail to a West Coast homeport. "I don't think I've ever received any honor, even including being the governor (of Georgia) and president, that has been more appreciated than having this ship named after me, "Carter said. He said he feels the boat is one of the finest submarines in the Navy, it has extraordinary capabilities and it will be beneficial in today's world. When asked how he felt about his name being attached to a weapon of mass destruction, Carter, a Nobel Peace Prize winner, said perception is a misunderstanding of his life and the deterrent nature of a submarine. "A submarine's purpose is not to fight, but is to be so capable of destruction that it will deter any enemy," Carter said. The trip also marked Carter's first tour of Kings Bay. The former President was in office when the Navy opened the base in Camden County in 1978. Prior to his stint as president, a decision was made to move American submarines docked in Spain back to the U.S. When Carter entered the White House, the Navy had five optional locations for a new submarine base. Carter said he had no influence, despite the fact that he was commander in chief of the military at the time, over the opening of Kings Bay in his home state. He said Kings Bay stood on its own merits. "We just made sure no politics interfered with the choice of the best qualified base" Carter said.

When he was running for governor, Carter said he visited Camden County when it was mostly swamp land and has since watched it grow with a lot of interest. He is very gratified with what has happened at Kings Bay and said he was surprised at all the services it had to offer the Navy. However, Carter's time in the Navy was spent in Groton, Conn., and he said he has "mixed emotions"

> *about the Pentagon's recommendation to close Naval Submarine Base, New London and move submarines to Kings Bay.*

A couple of weeks later August 25, 2005, the *Georgia Times Union* had the headlines:

BRAC REJECTS KINGS BAY PLAN
CARTER DRAWS FIRE FOR GROTON SUPPORT

> *Three months ago, Kings Bay was poised for its biggest expansion since it was established in 1978. Those plans are now on hold—perhaps permanently. Congressman Jack Kingston described the debate to keep New London open as "the most emotional issue facing this commission." "The heavy lobbying from everyone from top congressional leaders to former Navy admirals to former President Jimmy Carter had a big effect," Kingston said… Before the vote, several commission members cited Carter's letter last week urging them to keep New London open as a factor in their decision.*
>
> Retired Navy Captain Walt Yourstone who had my position with The Camden Partnership said the commission's decision was "a vote for New England, not against Kings Bay."

The following week, I had a call from Coast Guard headquarters asking if I would be the sponsor for the newest USCG ship, *Sea Horse*. Of course, I was thrilled, and that story can be found in my stories section.

On September 17, 2005, I spoke at the Daughters of the American Revolution celebrating Constitution Week. I enjoyed sharing with them the strong welcome we received at our overseas councils.

Back to DC, on September 30, to attend the annual secretary of the Navy cruise on the *Odyssey*. I was honored to speak on November 11, at the Veterans Day Service for Hospice of the Golden Isles sharing the program with Colonel Thomas W. Fuller.

Cheers! At the Navy Air Force game, the young man I interviewed and recommended for the Naval Academy, Joey Bullen, made a field goal for the Naval Academy to beat Air Force. "The former soccer star and standout kicker at Glynn Academy played the role of hero for the Midshipmen, kicking a game-winning 46-yard field goal with just 0.4 seconds left in regulation to send Navy to a remarkable come from—behind 27–24 victory over rival Air Force," reported the *Brunswick News*.

The Golden Isles Council asked me to install officers at their December meeting. Bob Morrison was installed as president, Doug Dees as vice president, Linda Kay Lang as secretary, and Jerry Rhyne as treasurer. The judge advocate was Gene Caldwell and immediate past president was Hubert W. Lang III.

Arlie and Nick Hart joined Hubert and Hugh Mayberry as national directors.

The July 2007 edition of *Seapower* magazine had a special message entitled "Adios" by Richard C. Barnard, editor in chief. Rick thanked the presidents he had work with and gave a special thanks to Stephen Pietropaoli, the Navy League's executive director and *Seapower*'s associate publisher who ran interference with our critics and contributed ideas that led to some of our more insightful articles during my tenure. He also introduced Amy Wittman as the new editor in chief of *Seapower*. She had been deputy managing editor of *Defense News* with responsibility for the weekly newspaper's international coverage, and held other editorial posts comprising more than two decades.

Rick, thank you for all you did for me as national president.

It's 2017, and I've finally finished the book. So much happened after 2005, but I must stop!

The large events are covered in the individual stories.

I went to work for The Camden Partnership as the military liaison for the community and have enjoyed continuing my work supporting the Navy, Marine Corps, and Coast Guard.

I've added some responsibilities with the Submarine Industrial Base Council (SIBC). This and the Naval Submarine League annual meetings give me the education with the briefs from the program managers.

My board of directors are professional successful individuals who not only realize the economic impact of Naval Submarine Base Kings Bay but are all also patriots. They also give me great latitude in my work. We've had some impressive speakers since The Camden Partnership was created.

- Congressman Jack Kingston
- Brigadier General Phil Browning, executive director, Georgia Military Affairs Coordinating Committee
- ADM Michael Mullen, Chief of Naval Operations
- August 17, 2007, General Bob Magnus, assistant commandant, US Marine Corps; speaker the next day for the dedication of the Dunham Barracks (found in the stories section)
- August 31, 2007, Governor Sonny Perdue
- Admiral Thad Allen, commandant, Coast Guard
- Admiral Bob Papp, commandant, Coast Guard
- Admiral Jon Greenert, chief of Naval Operations

We continue to have great officers at Kings Bay and that makes support so much easier.

The national leadership since my term as national president includes many that I met and became close to many of them:

For the Coast Guard, Commandants Owen Siler, Jim Loy, Tom Collins, Thad Allen, Bob Papp and then one I didn't know before his tour, but impressive nevertheless, Admiral Paul Zucunft and his wife, Fran. My friends Vivien Crea and Sally Brice O'Hare both received their third stars!

And for the Navy CNOs—Frank Kelso, Mike Boorda, Michael Mullen, Gary Roughead, John Greenert, John Richardson—all extraordinary men who each added to my career.

Rear Admiral Frank Drennan included me in the dinner when secretary of the Navy, Donald Winter, and his wife came. That was a significant event for me.

Senators Mack Mattingly, Paul Coverdale, Max Cleland, Zell Miller, Johnny Isakson, Saxby Chambliss, and David Perdue.

Congressman Lindsay Thomas, Jack Kingston, and later Buddy Carter.

So many great staffers, but no story was as good as Kathryn Murph (Chambliss) and Jared Downs (Isakson) getting married on November 29, 2008. I attended their wedding. They now have two little girls.

Attending the swearing in ceremony for three of our friends, Tony Harrison, Bert Guy, and Alex Atwood who became judges and my young friend James Tuten's retirement ceremony as judge.

The submarine museum has thrived under the leadership of Keith Post, who replaced John Crouse when he died.

Both the USS *Florida* and the USS *Georgia*, the converted SSGNs, came to Kings Bay—the *Florida* in 2006 and the *Georgia* in 2008. I was chairman of the return to service for the USS *Georgia* and that event can be found in my stories section.

One of the commanding officers of the Florida came back to Kings Bay as commanding officer of Submarine Group 10, RADM Randy Crites and his wife, Cheryl. It was nice to have one of our own back to lead. And lead he did! And speaking of going on to bigger things, two of our group commanders have made Vice Admiral: Joe Tofalo and Chas Richards.

We have been blessed by the leadership at Kings Bay and several of those are found in the stories section. The chamber continues the fly-ins that we started with the SSGN campaign nineteenth and now we've added the state for annual visits for state issues and national issues concerning Kings Bay. The Camden Kings Bay Council of the Navy League is still flourishing.

The Camden Partnership has been very rewarding. That awful time in 2017 was endured due to the amazing support of our three mayors (thank you, John Morrissey, Kenneth Smith, and Steve Parrot), the St. Marys and Kingsland City Council (thank you, Jim), and the board of directors.

CLOSING

I never served in the military. However, the almost fifty years of serving the men and women who wear the cloth of our nation, I hope, somehow makes up for that.

PART THREE

My Stories

CHAPTER SEVEN

An Introduction to the Short Stories

The following short stories are my stories. Those I met and had such fun with. Those moments that show a completely different side of some of the people I might otherwise have just seen in the news. The precious friendships I've made—military, government, and civilian.

Anyone who knows me knows that I always have a story. Neely Young, editor and publisher of *Georgia Trend* magazine did a story on "Spotlighting the Big Mules." He said some great things about each of us in the article, but I think what made me the proudest was his last paragraph: "A Big Mule could be the richest man in Macon, or the owner of a small dry goods store in Canton. "Mules" are the keystones of any community because they place principle above self-interest."

I hope you continue to read about the Big Mules and events that have impacted my life and find my answer to "What are you doing here?" to understand my reason for being here.

They are also stories that my friends have heard over and over again. To them I say, "Skip the ones you know!"

A TALE OF TWO *GEORGIAS*

Michael Jordon's documentary on *A Tale of Two Georgias* was about the CSS *Georgia*, a Confederate ironclad warship, and the USS *Georgia*, a newly relaunched guided-missile submarine.

Michael interviewed me on April 16, 2008. As it turned out, the women of Georgia during the Civil War, raised the funding for the CSS *Georgia* and now a woman is spearheading the battle for the SSGNs and the ceremony to welcome the USS *Georgia*'s return-to-service ceremony.

There were three premieres—July 24 in Savannah, Georgia; September 12 in Brunswick, Georgia, at the Ritz Theater; and finally, October 12 in St. Marys, Georgia.

FILM EXAMINES TWO GEORGIAS, ON LAND AND SEA
By Ellen Robinson

Two ships named Georgia from different eras have the efforts of Southern belles to thank for their existence, according to independent film maker Michael Jordan, creator and producer of "A Tale of Two Georgias." The documentary film features a slice of life view aboard the USS Georgia and compares the modern submarine re-commissioning to the first ship named Georgia from the Civil War era.

The film will be shown at the St. Marys Howard Gilman Memorial Park at dusk on Thursday evening. For those who miss the show in the park, there will be another opportunity to view it when it airs on NBC WTLV channel 12 at noon on Sunday, November 23. In his documentary, Jordan feature's interviews and footage shot hundreds of feet beneath the surface of the Atlantic aboard the USS Georgia as well as videos of archaeologists toiling on the wreckage of the CSS Georgia in the Savanah River and historical photographs of the vessel in its prime.

Jordan says there are more similarities in the two ships than first meets the eyes. In this documentary, he tells the story of the commonalities the CSS Georgia and the state's namesake nuclear submarine share. He explains how the efforts and sacrifices of Georgia's women during the Civil War built the first Georgian ship, and it was the efforts of modern day Georgia women that saved the USS Georgia from the submarine graveyard.

"The women of Georgia held fun-raisers and donated their jewelry to help build the CSS Georgia to run the cotton through the blockages." Jordan said. "And it was Sheila McNeill who was the first champion in saving the USS Georgia from being scrapped."

The film highlights how the women and other civilians helped support the state and nation by organizing the grassroots efforts during times of peril. Both Keith Post and I were interviewed for the film.

Jordan features Camden County's lobbying efforts to make the SSGN a reality—a platform that has been referred to the official Chinese news agency as a 'warehouse of explosives, a devil of deter-

rence." McNeill said. "I invite everyone to take 30 minutes out of the day to hear our story, talk to our sailors and meet other friends at the waterfront on Thursday night.

I was so appreciative of Captain Michael Brown and Captain Brian McIlvaine, the two commanding officers of the USS *Georgia* for not only having their crew there but for taking the time to join us—Captain McIlvaine in Brunswick and Captain Brown in Camden County.

I sent a letter to Bob Carlisle of the Brunswick Golden Isles Council who chaired the event at the Ritz Theater in Brunswick.

Dear Bob and the members of the debut committee: Bravo Zulu! Once again you and your council have exceeded all expectations. What a wonderful debut for "The Tale of Two Georgias" at the historic Ritz Theater. I arrived at the very beginning of the reception and your team was organized and ready for action. I was surprised at the number of people who were already there, mingling at your membership table, looking at your scrapbooks and awards and enjoying refreshments. Those I talked with were very interested in the opportunity to learn more about the history and the USS GEORGIA. It felt like a premier! Captain McIlvaine and his crew who attended were very impressed.

I understand the video sales went well and we also enlisted some new members. What an opportunity for the general public to see what the Navy League is all about. Arlie estimated that 8-% of the audience were non-Navy Leaguers. You are fulfilling your mission to educate the public. Thank you.

It is obvious why you continue to be one of the outstanding councils in the world. Sheila

One message Jordan emphasizes in this film is the important role regular citizens can have in supporting the US Navy. "I believe we have a lot more in common with those in our history than we realize," Jordan said.

Jordan lives in Savannah and specializes in military documentaries.

ADOPTION OF UNITED STATES COAST GUARD STATION BRUNSWICK

One of the many things that Colonel Nick Hart, USMC (retired), president of the Golden Isles Council, Navy League of the United States, did was to have the Golden Isles Council of the Navy League adopt the US Coast Guard Station Brunswick.

Nick and I had a meeting later when I became national president of the Navy League when I encouraged him to "make me proud" and he did just that. For many years, the council was one of the top ten in the nation.

The adoption of the local Coast Guard station was one of the first of many accomplishments during that time. We had always had a great relationship with the officer in charge and BMCS Michael Kitchens was no exception. The adoption ceremony was held on August 25, 2001, and RADM James S. Carmichael (Jay), commander, Seventh Coast Guard District, was the speaker. I introduced him that day. Nick began with opening remarks and William (Bill) B. Dawson read the proclamation.

A little information that was in the program:

> *In September 1995 Station St. Simons was decommissioned after 60 years of service, moved to Brunswick and renamed. In March 2002, a new 10,000 sq. ft. multi-mission station was started with completion in 2003. Coast Guard Station Brunswick is a coastal search and rescue station co-located with the Georgia Department of Natural Resources on Plantation Creed near the entrance to the Port of Brunswick. The men and women at Station Brunswick are responsible for performing many missions including Search and Rescue, Enforcement of Laws and Treaties, Recreational Boating Safety, Marine Environmental Protection and Enforcement of Safety and Security Zones.*

The following coverage was in the *Harbor Sound*, September 11, 2001, edition:

> ***LOCAL NAVY LEAGUE ADOPTS COAST GUARD STATION***
>
> *By Jim Dryden*
>
> *A long-standing goal to adopt the local Coast Guard Station was realized recently when the Brunswick-Golden Isles Council of the U.S. Navy League formally adopted U.S. Coast Guard Station Brunswick. It was noted during a 'military style' ceremony that the adoption will make the Council members to become better acquainted with station's crew and mission while making their work better known to the community as well. Coast Guard Station Brunswick and its predecessor Coast Guard Station St. Simons, have served this community since 1935. Today it is composed of 25 men and women ranging in ages from 18-45.*

According to Council President Nick Hart the most formalized relationship represents a commitment on the part of both the Coast Guard and the Navy League to acquire a better understand of what the Coast Guard does. A 31-foot Utility Boat and a 21-foot Rigid Hull Inflatable Boat that are maintained by the station will permit orientation cruises for the Navy League and others to provide opportunities to see how the Coast Guard actually operates. The stations mission includes law enforcement, search and rescue, and environmental protection. Each year they conduct more than 500 law enforcement boarding's and respond to more than 200 search and rescue cases.

Guest Speaker for the ceremony was Rear Admiral James S. Carmichael, commander of the Seventh Coast Guard District, which includes South Carolina, Georgia, Florida and the Caribbean.

RADM Carmichael later went to DC to serve as Department of Homeland Security Ridge's military assistant. When I was national president, I attended Rear Admiral Jay Carmichael's retirement and his remarks inspired one of my president's messages.

SUPERIOR COURT JUDGE ANTHONY A. ALAIMO

Judge Alaimo was the judge at my lawsuit with Concrete Products Inc. I had known and admired him and had many occasions to talk with him over the years, especially after my trial. Just months after the trial, Arlie and I were at the Cloister on Sea Island where we ran into him. He asked me to dance. As we were dancing, the former president who had fired me, walked in the room. I pointed him out to Judge Alaimo. He smiled, kept dancing, and told me, "Sheila, I suggested to him that he should settle when we first met with the lawyers." When I became national president of the Navy League, he called to congratulate me.

I was honored to participate in a reception and book signing for his biographical book *The Sicilian Judge* on September 11, 2009. I said a few words and introduced the military, retired and active who were present. Excerpts from the article on the release of his book included:

Book reveals many chapters in life of Anthony Alaimo
By Susan Respess, Tribune & Georgian *staff*

Prosecutors and defense attorneys who've been on the opposite side of federal judge Anthony A. Alaimo's bench know fear—fear of missteps, an oversight, a lame argument. If they're guilty, that legendary baleful glare from Alaimo, 89, will rivet on them. Alaimo's reputation as a stern taskmaster extends throughout his 37-year tenure in Brunswick in the U.S. District Court's Southern District of Georgia, first as a judge, then chief judge and now senior judge. Alaimo's idea of a work-week is six and a half days, the half day is on Sundays, after church—and not a minute should be wasted. And the venerable judge makes no apology to the fumbling lawyers. But few know about Alaimo's early years as a member of an impoverished Italian Immigrant family settling in 1922 in New York. Nor did they know he was one of the daring American flyboys who assisted Allied prisoners of war in the German camp, Stalag Lufr 3, as they dug tunnels dramatized in the movie "The Great Escape."

Those adventures and more of Alaimo's life are told in "The Sicilian Judge—Anthony Alaimo, as American Hero," by Vincent Coppola, an Atlanta author and journalist. Alaimo will be autographing the book during a reception for him from 10:00 AM to noon on Friday, at the College of Coast Georgia's Camden Center. "The sheer audacity he had in the war, all those attempts to escape," said Sheila McNeill, a St. Marys gift shop owner who's been a friend of Alaimo for many years. "He's always quick not to talk about himself. I had no idea he'd done those things escaping and getting through all those enemy checkpoints where we would be scared to death."

McNeill a Brunswick resident is also head of The Camden Partnership, a group in Camden County that promotes and lobbies for the military and the county and she's a past national president of the Navy League of the United States. She's helping with the book signing and reception and encouraging active-duty military and veterans to attend. She can well understand the judge's demeanor in the courtroom. He was the resident judge during her successful sex discrimination case involving a Brunswick company years ago. "He's a no-nonsense person and he makes decision based on doing the right thing." McNeill said. "I can't picture him ever telling a joke. Lawyers respect him, but they are scared of him, too. They know they aren't going to be able to pull the wool over his eyes."

Charlie Smith, a St. Marys attorney, said it's clear that Alaimo is in charge of his courtroom. "He's just very forceful, a very strong presence," said Smith, who recalled Alaimo presiding over condemnation cases involving Cumberland Island and the National Park Service. Smith said he'd rather try a case before the Georgia Supreme Court than go before Alaimo. "In one case I tried, the other attorney messed up and it was brutal." Smith said. "Judge Alaimo came out of his seat. He would get you in front of the bench and he'd start that loud whispering you could hear all over the courtroom. You wished you could be somewhere else." McNeill said there are rumors of a movie about Alaimo. The script could focus on his civil-rights and voting-rights efforts, drug and corruption cases or his early day.

Alaimo had worked his way through college in Ohio as a barber and took a few law courses before dropping out to work in a foundry. When the Japanese bombed Pearl Harbor, he joined the Army Air Corps the next day and headed to pilot training...

Just months before his death, I called his office and asked if he had time for a visit, he did. I enjoyed my time with him. We reminisced and talked about the world, my travels, and anything else that came to mind. The last time we talked was when I sat with him at the Veterans Day Memorial on St. Simons Island. I was pleased that he wanted me to sit down and catch up.

The following is an article that appeared in the *Florida Times Union* when he died.

Judge Anthony A. Alaimo dies at 89

The former POW treated all with dignity, but was nobody's fool behind the bench.

BRUNSWICK—Senior U.S. District Judge Anthony A. "Tony" Alaimo, a World War II prisoner of war who overhauled woeful prison conditions in Georgia, died Wednesday morning. He was 89. "He was the conscience of the community... Judge Alaimo lived an amazing life, and what an inspiration he was for so many," said Brunswick attorney James Bishop Sr., whom Alaimo hired out of law school in 1967. He was revered in Glynn County, but state lawmakers and prison officials rallied public outrage against the reforms Judge Alaimo ushered through beginning in the 1970s, in trying lawsuits filed by inmates.

"Judge Alaimo was my hero," said lawyer Douglas Alexander, who as a Georgia Legal Services lawyer worked on a federal suit over conditions at the state prison at Reidsville and others in county jails." Having been a prisoner of war, he certainly knew what it was like to be a prisoner," Alexander said.

He was taken prisoner by the Germans during World War II, when his B-26 bomber was shot down and crashed at sea. He was the only survivor. Although he didn't hesitate to send the guilty to prison,

"He'd tell the prison-keeper to do it right," Alexander said. When the reforms were complete, the Georgia Department of Corrections named a prison courtroom for him. "You have been the heart and soul and conscience of prison reform in this country," then-Corrections Commissioner Wayne Garner told Alaimo at the 1997 dedication.

Bishop said Judge Alaimo became like a surrogate father to him and spent Christmas with him and his family. He appeared fine then, but fell ill Sunday evening and was admitted to the hospital. He passed away peacefully about mid-morning Wednesday of congestive heart failure, he said. Jeanne Alaimo, Judge Alaimo's wife of 62 years, died in January. Those who knew the couple described them as "soulmates." "He's at peace, and he's with her. Theirs was a true love story, and he missed her a lot," Bishop said. The couple are survived by a son, Phillip of Savannah, two grandchildren and one great-grandson.

***A sacred trust:** Although most naturalizations are done administratively, Alaimo still conducted the ceremonies for those who wanted them. It was the only time Alaimo didn't maintain strict order as mothers held crying babies and the families of soon-to-be Americans chattered. Alaimo would personally greet each new citizen and once told the Times-Union that in his mother's prayers she thanked God for bringing her family to America. "Becoming an American citizen deserves the solemnity of the court," he said. U.S. Rep. Jack Kingston, R-Ga., described Judge Alaimo as an inspiration. "Judge Alaimo lived the true American dream from the humble, hard-working beginnings in an immigrant family to being appointed federal judge by the president of the United States," Kingston said.*

In 1979, Alaimo swore in Donnie Dixon to practice in the federal courts. Dixon tried many cases before Alaimo as the U.S. attorney in the 1990s and as a private attorney since then. "We've lost a preeminent jurist and a good friend… He was tireless in the pursuit of justice," Dixon said.

***Always prepared:** Two Jacksonville judges on the 11th Circuit Court of Appeals in Atlanta remembered Alaimo fondly. Judge Gerald B. Tjoflat and Alaimo became fast friends shortly after Alaimo was confirmed. "He could handle tough cases because there was no way in the world someone could blindside him," Tjoflat said.*

In the 1980s, a Jacksonville cardiologist determined Alaimo needed five heart bypasses. Saying he had a tennis match the next day, a court picnic a day later and a major sentencing in Waycross on the third day, Alaimo was getting dressed to leave the hospital when

Tjoflat walked in and stopped him. Tjoflat borrowed two decks of cards at the nurse's station and played gin rummy with Alaimo until midnight to make sure he stayed for his surgery. Judge Susan Black said Alaimo had a unique mixture of toughness and kindness. "He was one tough, tough guy, but he couldn't have been nicer to me when I came on the federal bench," Black said.

Friend and mentor Chief: *Superior Court Judge Amanda Williams called his death a loss to the legal justice community Williams, who met Judge Alaimo when she was a trial lawyer, said they had become close friends. "He used to frighten me to death," she said of appearing before him. "He ran a tight ship."*

Vernon Martin, the retired head of the Coastal Georgia Regional Development Center, is another who called the judge a second father, a mentor and a close friend. As chairman of the Glynn County Commission in 1969, Alaimo founded what was then the Coastal Georgia Area Planning and Development Commission and brought the then 26-year-old Martin from Oklahoma to run it. Martin said he always came away from meetings astonished at Judge Alaimo's ease in resolving the most complicated issues. "Every time I spoke with him I left saying, 'Why didn't I think of that?'" Martin said. Still shaken a few hours after being with Alaimo during his last hours, Martin said Judge Alaimo had served his county, his country and Georgia. "I got a chance to tell him I loved him and what he meant to me," Martin said.

'A true Southern gentleman': *Those outside the government and legal community also mourned his passing. The Alaimos had been regular diners at Bennie's Red Barn and the 4th of May Cafe, both on St. Simons Island, where the servers remembered them fondly. "He was very sweet, a true Southern gentleman," said Landon Moorhead, who waited on the couple at the Red Barn, where a table is named in his honor, and then at the 4th of May.*

A memorial service for Judge Alaimo will be at 11 a.m. Jan. 8 at St. Simons Presbyterian Church with the Rev. Bob Brearley officiating. The family has asked that contributions be made to the College of Coastal Georgia Foundation, Bishop said. Bishop choked back tears as he described the title that best described Judge Alaimo: "Friend. He was my friend, and I am going to miss him a lot."

Times-Union writers Gordon Jackson and Paul Pinkham contributed to this report. Terry Dickson, Florida Times Union

He was a war hero—his actions were covered in the Harvard Law Review shortly after his death.

> *On March 29, 1929, Anthony A. Alaimo was born near Termini on the island of Sicily. His family immigrated to the United States when he was two years old. The Alaimo family was naturalized as United States citizens in 1928. Alaimo grew up in Jamestown, New York, and graduated from high school there in 1937. After high school, he attended Ohio Northern University at Ada, Ohio, and graduated in 1940.*
>
> *A fiercely patriotic Italian-American, Alaimo volunteered for active duty and was commissioned as a second lieutenant in the U.S. Army Air Force. He qualified and served as a B-26 bomber pilot, assigned to the 8th Air Force stationed in England. During a low-level attack against German positions in which all eleven American planes were lost, Alaimo's plane was hit by flack and ditched in the North Sea. Seriously wounded, he was the only member of his crew of six to survive. He was picked up by a patrol boat and taken into German captivity. During his imprisonment, Alaimo participated with fellow Americans in preparing the tunnel through which "The Great Escape" (from the movie title) took place. Prior to that escape, Alaimo was transferred to another stalag. After two unsuccessful escape attempts, for which he could have been shot, and two stints in solitary confinement, he finally did escape in February 1945. Blending in with and aided by forced laborers from France, Alaimo was able to eventually cross the Italian border and receive sanctuary from a sympathetic family in Milan. Alaimo has revealed in later years that during his hiding in Milan, he boldly, and perhaps foolishly, persuaded his host family to let him attend an opera performance, The Barber of Seville. Remarkably, he found himself seated at the performance next to a German SS colonel.*
>
> *Thereafter, Alaimo crossed the Italian frontier into Switzerland. Once he convinced them that he was indeed an American Army officer and not an Italian refugee, he was transported to liberated France, and then flown back to the United States. After a short period of leave, he resumed training with a bomber unit for deployment to the Pacific.*

Judge Alaimo extended an offer for me to attend a naturalization ceremony in his courtroom. I am so glad that I did. There is nothing that would make you any more patriotic than seeing the pleasure and pride that those immigrants felt. Tony talked to those who were fulfilling a dream of becoming a citizen of the United

States. As they recited the Pledge of Allegiance and the oath, I wished that everyone could have the experience of attending and welcoming these brand-new Americans. Judge Alaimo was bigger than life and left a legacy that will be remembered. I am pleased and honored to have known Judge Anthony Alaimo.

ADMIRAL THAD ALLEN

COMMANDANT, UNITED STATES COAST GUARD

I first met Admiral Allen when I was national vice president for legislative affairs for the Navy League. He was assistant commandant of the Coast Guard during the time they were recapitalizing the Coast Guard fleet. I was very interested in learning all I could to support this effort. Arlie and I always enjoying talking with him and his wife, Pam. We worked together on the transfer of some of the Coast Guard in the Washington area to our new office building. He called me one day and said, "Sheila, are you sitting down?" I was, and he told me the Coast Guard would be moving into our new building. That was wonderful news.

He was the brains behind the Maritime Safety and Security Teams (MSST). He also set up and named the Maritime Force Protection Unit—however, he was not happy with the acronym MFPU (MIFF-PUE). It was not the acronym he would have liked but he did well with the Deployable Operations Group, or DOG! I went to Thad, when they were setting up all of the MSSTs, and told him what a supportive community we had in Camden County. "We love our sailors and we will love our Coasties too!" I told him. I believe that unit is very happy in Camden and the location has worked for everyone.

In 2007, I was on the board of directors for The Camden Partnership working with Mike McKinnon, who was president. I was pleased that when I contacted Admiral Allen, he was able to arrange a visit to Camden County and speak at our Community that Cares event.

He arrived the morning of October 27, 2007, in Jacksonville with ground transportation to Kings Bay arriving at the conference center at 9:20 a.m. Commanders Joe Raymond and Doug Stark and Keith Post and I met him at the entrance with about ten additional Coast Guard greeters. Accompanying Admiral Allen was his aide, LCDR Jo Cousins, Captains Gene Gray and Sandy Stosz, LCDR Tony Russell, and from *Navy Times*, Amy McCoullough as well as his security team.

There were two large billboards with his picture and "Welcome Admiral Thad Allen." We also had all the marquees in town with the same message. We had the cities and county designate the day as Admiral Thad Allen Day. The conference center was packed. The story was headline news with the local *Tribune & Georgian*.

Community brunch honors Allen

> *The leader of America's oldest continuous seagoing service, Adm. Thad Allen will be honored by The Camden Partnership, the Camden-Kings Bay Navy League of the U.S. and other community groups at the Fourth Annual "A Community That Cares" brunch. Allen, a member of the Council on Foreign Relations with master's degrees from MIT and George Washington University will be honored at the clubs of Kings Bay at the Naval Submarine Base on October 27 from 9:30–11:00.*

And after the event, the *Florida Times Union* story on Admiral Allen was on the front page:

Coast Guard Commandant visit
By Gordon Jackson

> *St. Marys—Adm. Thad Allen, commandant of the Coast Guard has faced difficult tasks during his 37 years of service. After the Sept. 11 terrorist attacks Allen directed the East Coast response efforts for the Coast Guard. He was director of the team that oversaw his agency's transition from the Department of Transportation to the Department of Homeland Security. And, after federal officials were harshly criticized for the response to Hurricane Katrina, Allen was placed in charge of search, rescue and recovery efforts.*
>
> *Allen told an audience at Kings Bay Naval Submarine Base on Monday that his biggest challenge may be revamping the Coast Guard, which had received minimal funding for years. Allen told his audience of elected officials, military and Navy League members he recently retired the oldest vessel in the Coast Guard—a 62-year old cutter. It's replacement—a 60-year-old cutter now the oldest vessel in the department. "There is much left to do in the Coast Guard," he said. "We have cutters that are eligible for Social Security."*
>
> *Besides replacing the aging fleet of vessels and modernizing technology, Allen said the Coast Guard is creating a single operational command that will coordinate all operations worldwide. This would give the Coast Guard the ability to effectively respond to natural disasters or threats to national security. The Coast Guard is also offering more specialized training for counter-terrorism missions, port security, law enforcement and response to hazardous material accidents and oil spills. The department is currently developing what*

> *Allen described as a "virtual bubble" to protect major ports in the nation.*
>
> *All port operations throughout the region, including Kings Bay and military installations in the Jacksonville area, will ultimately have a single command center, Allen said. That center is under construction. Allen also toured Kings Bay and met with base officials.*

After the event Captain Wes Stevens, commanding officer of Kings Bay accompanied Admiral Allen on a tour of the base finishing up with Strategic Weapons Facility Atlantic. Captain Stevens and I were with the group, but before we knew it, they had scooped Thad off to the classified area. It happened so quickly, I didn't have a chance to say goodbye but Thad called me after the tour. "Where did you disappear to? I was talking to you and you weren't there!" That was one of those calls that really makes you smile!

They were all on the way back to Jacksonville airport by 4:15 p.m. They had a full day, but I'm sure every day is a full day when you are commandant. President of The Camden Partnership Mike McKinnon sent Admiral Allen a very nice letter:

> *Dear Admiral Allen, I sincerely want to thank you for taking the time from your busy schedule to be with us today. Our community and military leadership were fortunate that you made a promise to Sheila McNeill several years ago, to come visit when you commanded the 7th USCG District! We're even more fortunate you keep your promises!" Our hope is that you sensed only a fraction of how proud and honored we are to have our military and their families live in this wonderful, supporting community. As you well know an installation, its military commands and the surrounding communities aren't separate entities. Our development, growth and potential for success are closely linked. Your willingness to participate in "Admiral Thad Allen Day" and the events that supported your visit here today, will provide immeasurable returns and has already positively impacted The Camden Partnership's and Camden-Kings Bay Council of the Navy League's efforts to strengthen our military and community partnerships.*
>
> *History shows us that change is not only tough, but it is inevitable. You garnish so much respect for your accomplishments in leading your Coast Guard through historical and monumental changes since 9/11, even prior to your appointment as the Commandant of the Coast Guard. Our community is now experiencing monumental change and the challenges quality growth brings. We needed to hear your message today. It will help provide the fuel to fire our collabo-*

rative efforts to make this community not only a better place for our military to serve, live and play, but by doing so, will enhance the quality of life and service we all enjoy, military and civilian alike.

We, "The Community that Cares," thank you for your service to our great nation. We thank you for the sacrifices you make in exercising the tremendous accountability and responsibility your position encompasses. We are further grateful for the integrity and manner in which you exercise that responsibly. When they "stick that fork in you" and tell you, "You're done" around 2011, you will be able to be justifiably proud that you made an immense difference in the lives we all enjoy. We truly wish you God's speed in the remainder of your time as Commandant.

Again, it truly was our honor and privilege to have you participate in our 4th annual "Community That Cares" event. Thank you again for coming.

Sincerely, Mike
Mike McKinnon
CAPT, USN (Ret)
President, The Camden Partnership, Inc.

Camden County came very close to losing the Coast Guard's Maritime Safety and Security Team 91108 (MSST) based in St. Marys. It was through the advocacy and support of local residents that the partnership was able to educate legislators about the importance of Coast Guard funding. Approximately eighty-five members of the Maritime Safety and Security Team continue to call Camden home. (See full story on the MSST 91108.)

In 2009, Keith Post and I were invited to a meeting at the MSST. They would be presenting awards to the Coasties and an admiral was coming to present them. We attended, and it was a very nice ceremony. However, at the end of the meeting Rear Admiral Dean Lee made the announcement that this MSST would be decommissioned. We were stunned. I don't believe the local commanding officer, Commander Doug Stark, knew before this. We waited until the meeting with the crew was over and we asked RADM Lee for a few minutes. There was no further explanation—only that the unit would be decommissioned.

I flew to DC and met with Admiral Allen. I found out that not only was the Coast Guard and the nation losing our MSST—they were decommissioning four others, along with a net reduction of 1,112 full-time military positions, and decommissioning three sorely needed cutters. All based on budget. (See my story on the Coast Guard budget.)

In April 2010, I received the following letter:

> *Dear Sheila, Thank you for your staunch advocacy of the United States Coast Guard. I truly appreciate your strong support of Coast Guard men and women especially during these challenging economic times when the demand for our services, across all mission areas, is increasing.*
>
> *In reading your letter to the President, dated 12 March 2010, it was clear that you understand the unique value the Coast Guard provides to the nation every day. Our multi-mission nature allows us to be the tremendous force multiplier for our sister services and strong partners for entities within the public and private sectors. I always tell people that we are a "whole of government" organization built to protect, defend, save, and mitigate risk throughout the maritime domain. Your letter captures that sentiment.*
>
> *On behalf of all of our Guardians, thank you for helping tell our story and influencing the opinions of our eternal stakeholders.*
>
> *Semper Paratus! Thad*
> *T. W. Allen, Admiral, U.S. Coast Guard*

Thad and the US Coast Guard had a huge role in recovery efforts for Hurricanes Katrina and Rita in the Gulf Coast region (September 2005–January 2006). On September 9, he was named deputy in charge of overseeing New Orleans relief efforts.

I attended Admiral Allen's change of command on May 25, 2010. He was being relieved by Admiral Robert J. Papp. Admiral Allen told me he was leaving within twenty-four hours to serve as the Unified Command for Deepwater Horizon in the Gulf of Mexico. As far as I know, he is the first commandant to continue to serve after his change of command. He stayed in the Unified Command position for another three or four months. I read that in 2010, President Obama said in a statement that he was "profoundly grateful to Allen for his service after the spill," when he called on him to lead a response team of Coast Guardsmen, National Guard, cleanup workers, and other state and federal agency officials in the Gulf of Mexico in the wake of the Deepwater Horizon explosion.

"At a time when he could have enjoyed a well-deserved retirement from the United States Coast Guard, Admiral Allen stepped up to the plate and served his country when his skills and experience were urgently needed. This unprecedented response effort simply could not have succeeded without Admiral Allen at the helm and the nation owes him a debt of gratitude."

The only other service chief that I know of was General James Jones who was relieved as commandant of the Marine Corps to take command as Supreme Allied

Commande Europe. Every time Thad and I run into each other in DC we are happy to have a few moments to catch up.

AMERICA'S STRENGTH

A NAVY LEAGUE CAMPAIGN

I was pleased to be appointed to chair the America's Strength campaign. Sara Fuentes, director of legislative affairs for the Navy League, asked me to stop by the Navy League while I was in DC. As soon as I got to her office, she said, "Let's go."

"Where are we going?"

"I'll tell you when we get there," she says as she picks up her coat and heads out of the office, assuming I'll follow her.

And I did, and while I followed, I asked, "What's this about?"

"Just wait," is all she told me.

We rode the metro, got off, and went to a large office building, where we met with Greg McCarthy. He had the most provocative posters around the room—all supporting the program America's Strength.

He and Sara discussed the program, what their goals were, and what they wanted to accomplish. I loved it! I loved it all! I'm such a believer in "telling it like it is." I think the best way to educate our public is to quit the double talk and tell them in clear ways what needs to be done. This program did just that. Samples of the posters were as follows:

Good news for Somali pirates... our Navy is stretched too thin.
When the next victims call for help... would you mind if we put them on hold?
There's no pause in the action here... why so slow with the funding?
As the Chinese and Russian Navies grow... can we afford to let ours shrink?

When they finished the briefing, Greg asked if I would be chairman. That was quite a surprise. Ever since I was VP for legislative affairs and created the grassroots program that we continue to use today, I am blessed to have many of the chairs and committee members to continue to ask me to join them and listen to their plans. But I am of the past, and asking me to head such a large campaign was a surprise. I thought about it. I thought long and hard. I thought about thirty seconds and said yes. Sara told me later that she was shocked when he asked. She had recommended me and Greg agreed to interview me but no discussion was made to make the decision that day. I guess we were all excited about this project. I accepted the position as chairman of America's Strength program and remained chairman from 2015 to 2016.

I was pleased that our very first press conference coincided with Camden County's annual DC fly-in and the community was able to attend. Attending were James Coughlin, Celso Gonzales, Dr. Will Hardin, Joel Hanner, Louise Mitchell, Mayor John Morrissey, Shannon Nettles, Keith Post, Dave Reilly, Stephen Sainz, and Charlie Smith Jr.

We had several events on Capitol Hill. This is the agenda for one of them:

> 11/15/15: On behalf of the Navy League of the United States and our distinguished speakers: Welcome!
>
> Thank you for joining us today. I am Sheila McNeill. I am the Chair of the America's Strength campaign and the moderator for today's event. Today's event marks the release of an important study by the Center for Strategic and Budgetary Assessments (CSBA) commissioned by the Navy League America's Strength Campaign.
>
> The report "*Deploying Beyond Their Means: The U.S. Navy and Marine Corps at a Tipping Point*" examines the strain on the Navy-Marine Corps team created by a mismatch between supply and demand in today's fleet and analyzes how the Navy has increased deployments to address this gap over the last 15 years. This report is an important part of the grassroots America's Strength campaign efforts to illustrate and reinforce the many ways in which the Navy-Marine Corps team is currently overextended and underfunded. While today's report focuses on ships, it is important to remember that the health of the Department of the Navy must be measured in more than just the number of ships. The health of the Department of the Navy must be measured in the readiness and availability of many capabilities, ships, aircraft, weapons, equipment and, most importantly, personnel. This event is a significant opportunity to state once again that while we understand the political and fiscal realities of Washington today, our leaders in Congress and the administration must recognize the realities of the world and the strain they are putting on the Navy-Marine Corps team. We had a horrible reminder just last week of how unsafe the world is, and that our allies will need us to stand with them. On a daily basis, members of the Navy-Marine Corps team are patrolling the oceans of the world to protect free trade and counter the threats presented by rogue nations and terrorists. As you will hear, unfortunately, the success of these missions is masking the need for the increased financial support that would allow the Navy and Marine Corps

to be as successful in the future as they have been in the past. The combination of increased daily operations and having to respond to crisis after crisis, combined with underfunding and delayed maintenance, acquisitions and modernization, is crippling the Navy and the Marine Corps. We cannot allow this erosion of capabilities to continue.

Without a significant investment by Congress and the administration in the future of Navy and Marine Corps capabilities, we are placing our national defense, our leadership in the world, the strength of our nation's economy and the health of the global economy at great risk. Let's get to our speakers and the report:

Introductions

Representative Randy Forbes (R-VA-04)

Our first speaker is the Chairman of the Sea Power and Projection Subcommittee and co-chair of the Navy-Marine Corps Caucus—Congressman Randy Forbes...

Representative Joe Courtney (D-CT-02)

Next, I would like to welcome the ranking member of Sea Power & Projection Subcommittee and co-chair of the Congressional Shipbuilding Caucus—Congressman Joe Courtney...

Rear Admiral Sinclair Harris

I am very honored to introduce Rear Admiral Sinclair M. Harris. Admiral Harris recently retired after 34 distinguished years of service in the U.S. Navy. Most recently, Admiral Harris served as the vice director for operations on the Joint Chiefs of Staff. It is a great privilege to have him here today. Admiral Harris...

Commander Bryan Clark, USN (Ret.)

Our final and arguably most important speaker is one of the authors of the study we are releasing today.

Bryan Clark is a senior fellow from the Center for Strategic and Budgetary Assessments (CSBA) and a Navy veteran. Bryan supported former Chief of Naval Operations Admiral Jonathan Greenert where he served as his Special Assistant and Director of his Commander's Action Group. Mr. Bryan Clark...

Thank you to all our speakers. We would now like to open the floor for any questions from the audience.

The *Seapower* Almanac for 2016 had Sara's story about America's Strength.

In 2015, the Navy League launched the America's Strength campaign, a grass-roots effort to increase the Department of the Navy's budget by fiscal year 2017. There has been a series of Capitol Hill events to highlight the current level of stress on the Navy and Marine Corps and raise awareness of the importance of the Navy-Marine Corps team to the nation as defense, economy, and leadership in the world. Op-eds and advertising are another component of the campaign, and the committee appreciates Navy Leaguers who have submitted op-eds and advertising are another component of the campaign, and the committee appreciates Navy Leaguers who have submitted pieces for publication.

Legislative affairs also has provided promotional material for Navy League council events around the county. The campaign has managed to escalate several important stories to the mainstream media, including coverage of the possibility of Marines riding in allied ships in USA. Today. The Navy League commissioned a study with the Center for Budgetary Analysis on the topic that was released in November.

The year ahead: The Legislative Affairs Committee, chaired by Bras and Giles includes past national president Sheila McNeill as Legislative Affairs Advisory Board chairman. The committee always is looking for more Navy League members to get involved.

It was an incredible opportunity to support our sea services. Thank you, Sara.

APPRECIATING OUR SUBMARINE FORCE

ABOARD USS RHODE ISLAND SSBN 740

In October 1997, I received a letter from Don Myers, a pharmacist who had a tour in the Navy as a corpsman and was now serving in the Coast Guard Auxiliary. He had just had the opportunity to go underway on the USS *Rhode Island* an SSBN stationed at Naval Submarine Base Kings Bay. I had been asked to submit names. His reaction is representative of the thoughts of many civilians I've worked with on tours for our fine SSBN force. The effort to bring civilians on board changes from year to year. Most of the time this is controlled by mission and the absence of the number of submarine needed for the mission. Don's letter speaks for those who have had this unique opportunity:

Dear Sheila,

I just want to thank you for allowing me the opportunity to participate in a life-time experience aboard the USS RHODE ISLAND (SSBN 740). It was awesome to say the least and I thoroughly enjoyed every minute of it. I now have a new outlook about our nuclear submarines and those dedicated submariners aboard. They are a fine bunch of guys. The camaraderie was evident and I enjoyed mixing with the crew. I slept only two hours as I can sleep most any time but had only a brief period to live the life at work of a nuclear submarine and I wanted to take advantage of every bit of time available.

We disembarked to a sea tractor off shore. Sheila, as the sub left us going out to sea, I had a moment of reflection over my conversations with members of the crew wishing them a Great Halloween, a Contented Thanksgiving, a Merry Christmas, and a Happy New Year for they would be at sea, underway with no 'port of call' all this time and then some… God bless them all.

Again, thank you, Most Sincerely, Don Myers FC
Cc: Lt CDR Robert Raine
CDR Joseph Lodmell

ARLIE MCNEILL SCHOLARSHIP

I received a phone call from Dolphin Scholarship headquarters. Arlie had been awarded a named scholarship in his honor. He has been auctioning for The Submarine Officers Wives Club auction for over twenty-five years and has raised well over a million dollars. Carol Ann Traub, the spouse of Captain Bill Traub, commanding officer of the USS *Florida*, was one of the senior spouses on the auction committee. She wondered why they could not have a scholarship in Arlie's name. And she researched it. And she called them. She made it happen and we will be forever indebted to her, the SOWC, and to the Dolphin Scholarship board of directors.

PRESS RELEASE: Dolphin Scholarship Foundation
FOR IMMEDIATE RELEASE: June 30, 2009
ARLIE MCNEILL HONORED WITH ENDOWED SCHOLARSHIP

The Submarine Officers Wives Club of Kings Bay Submarine Base appreciates Arlie McNeill. They have appreciated him for over twenty-five years. Arlie, a resident of Glynn County and a staunch supporter of the Kings Bay submarine community has been the resident auctioneer for every one of their scholarship auctions. The Kings Bay gold and silver auctions support scholarships for children of submariners and at the same time have a fun evening.

In fact, the spouse club was so happy with Arlie's work that they recommended him to other submarine spouse clubs. As officers were transferred, word traveled about Arlie's abilities and he offered his services to other clubs around the country. After auctioning well over a million dollars' worth of items at Norfolk, Charleston, Bangor and Kings Bay, and the Kings Bay Officers Wives Club (KBOWC), which sponsors the annual auctions in Kings Bay, made a decision. That decision was something Arlie will never forget. The submarine spouses have pledged to raise eighty thousand dollars over the next four years to endow a "forever" scholarship in Arlie's name. This year, the KBOWC donated thirty thousand dollars to Dolphin Scholarship Foundation as the first installment for the Arlie McNeill Scholarship, which will be administered by Dolphin Scholarship Foundation. Arlie said, "It is exciting to have a scholarship in my name. To think that well after I have died that there will be a scholarship given in my name is humbling. It is a wonderful honor and I look forward to many more auctions."

Chuck Beers, DSF president, said, "This is a very fitting tribute to a man who has contributed so much to the Dolphin Scholarship Foundation over the years! We are very proud to carry his example and name forward for future submariners and their families."

DSF currently awards 137 annual scholarships of $3,400 to each Dolphin Scholar, who may potentially receive a total of $13,600 for up to eight semesters of undergraduate study. DSF has awarded almost eight million dollars to over one thousand students attending universities and colleges throughout the United States.

Auctioning isn't a new talent of Arlie's. In fact, he has been auctioning for the past fifty-five years. A native of North Carolina, he learned auctioning in high school and at R. J. Reynolds's Tobacco Company auctions. Citizens of Camden, Glynn, and McIntosh Counties have seen him in action. He was the auctioneer for the Darien Blessing of the Fleet for over thirty-five years. He has traveled across the country to auction for the Hospice for Children. Local charities and chambers in all three counties know his trademark, "Going once, going twice," and have benefited from his rapid-fire auctioneering. He has worked with over fifty organizations over the past fifty-plus years using his talent of auctioneering. Arlie has never charged for his services as an auctioneer.

McNeill is a long-time member of the Navy League of the United States, and they too have benefited from his talents. He now serves as national director emeritus. Arlie's wife, Sheila, is also a strong Navy supporter. A past national president of Navy League, Sheila, now serves on the DSF board of directors.

The Dolphin Scholarship Foundation (DSF) was established in 1960 with the first scholarship of $350. Funds were raised primarily through the tireless efforts of officers' wives' organizations throughout the United States. As the cost of college educations skyrocket, so did the need for the foundation to assist children of the Submarine Force Today. DSF receives individual, corporate, memorial, and combined federal campaign donations, as well as continued strong support from the submarine community. All donations go directly to support the scholarships. Interest and dividends from the DSF trust fund supplement these contributions for scholarships and operating expenses. Friends and supporters of Arlie may make a donation in his name by mailing a check to Dolphin Scholarship Foundation, 4966 Euclid Road, Suite 109, Virginia Beach, VA 23462.

The *Periscope* ran an article and pictures RADM Tim and Missy Giardina, RADM Barry and Elizabeth Bruner at their change of command as well as Dawn Carlisle, Vice Admiral Jay and Mimi Donnelly, Kelly Huls, Suzanne McAllister, and Sheila and Arlie McNeill

SUB OFFICERS WIVES NAME SCHOLARSHIP FOR AUCTIONEER
Arlie McNeill has helped raise funds for Dolphin Scholarship
From Commander Submarine Group 10 Public Affairs included

The Dolphin Scholarship Foundation was established in 1960. The foundation award scholarship to the children and stepchildren of submarine sailors and is primarily supported by submarine officers' wives' clubs across the United States. Currently, DSF awards 1,237 annual scholarships and has awarded almost eight million dollars to more than one thousand students attending universities and colleges through the country.

The silver/gold Dolphin auction is an important fund-raiser for the foundation and is held on every submarine base. "After this year's auction, we realized we had made over twenty-five thousand dollars," said Carol Ann Traub, a board member of the Kings Bay SOWC. "I called Dolphin Scholarship because I remembered a couple of years ago that you name a scholarship if you raised over twenty-five thousand dollars.

"The DSF confirmed this but said the scholarship would only be named for one year. I asked how could we make it an endowed scholarship, and the director told me that between our auction and Dolphin Store we would have to make an eighty-thousand-dollar commitment within a four-year period.

"I went back to the Silver/Gold Auction Committee and the Kings Bay SOWC and shared the news. Without hesitation, everyone agreed that no one is more deserving of having a scholarship named after him than Arlie McNeill."

The Kings Bay auctions provide the Navy and its supporters provide the Navy and its supporter an opportunity to support the scholarship while having a fun evening. McNeill's style and personality are considered a great contribution to the auctions success. As officers and their wives have transferred from Kings Bay, word traveled about McNeill's abilities, and he was recommended to auction at other submarines bases.

McNeill has volunteered to auction more than a million dollars work of items at Norfolk, Charleston, Bangor, and Kings Bay in support of DSF. "It is exciting to have a scholarship in my name," McNeill said. "To think that well after I have died that there will be a scholarship given in my name is humbling. It is a wonderful honor, and I look forward to many more auctions." McNeill, a North Carolina native, learned auctioning in high school and has been the auctioneer for the Darien Blessing of the Fleet for more than twenty-four years.

He also travels across the country to auction for more than fifty other charitable organizations.

And from the *Darien News* by Sandy Pharr:

ARLIE McNEILL "humbled by a scholarship in his name"

It's an honor that is usually reserved for those who have already passed on. But even though Arlie McNeill is alive and well and bid calling from shore to shore, he has had an endowment scholarship established in his name. Over the course of 55 years, this auctioneer extraordinaire has raised thousands of dollars volunteering his auction chant skills for charitable organizations and churches, as well as for the Darien-McIntosh County Chamber of Commerce's Blessing of the Fleet.

But what landed McNeill this latest reward for his efforts is the fact that he has raised more than a million dollars for the Dolphin Scholarship Foundation, which awarded 137 scholarships to the children of the submarine sailors throughout the United States every year. "To say that is was a pleasant surprise is an understatement. It is humbling to have a scholarship in my name," said McNeill. "But, it is overwhelming to know it will go on forever, even after I'm dead and gone."

The president of the Dolphin Scholarship Foundation contends that the honor has been a long time coming. "This is a very fitting tribute to a man who has contributed so much to the Dolphin Scholarship Foundation over the years," said Chuck Beers. "We are very proud to carry his example and name forward for future submariners and their families." McNeill trained under an established auctioneer during his high school years in North Carolina. He honed his skills at R.J. Reynolds Tobacco

Company auctions. The auctioneering he's found most rewarding has been with the Hospice for Children.

And he's had a lot of fun auctioneering with Darien's Blessing of the Fleet over the last 35 years. Even though there is no Blessing auction any longer, the Darien-McIntosh County Chamber of Commerce still holds an annual auction that wouldn't be the same without McNeill's familiar, "going, once, going twice," Chamber President Wally Orrel appreciates his personality and style. "Arlie McNeill is a good fellow and an outstanding auctioneer who has done a lot for McIntosh County." said Orrel, noting that he has never charged for his services as an auctioneer. "He is a man you can always count on."

McNeill serves as national director emeritus of the Navy League of the United States. His wife, Sheila, is past national president of the Navy League and now serves on the board of directors of the Dolphin Scholarship Foundation, which was established in 1960. Since then, it has awarded almost $8 million to more than 1,000 students attending colleges and universities throughout the nation. Mrs. McNeill thinks there is nobody that is any more worthy of the honor of having a scholarship named after them than her husband.

"Arlie has been donating his auctioneering talents for more than 50 years," she said. "I think that's pretty remarkable."

ATLANTA NAVY WEEK

OCTOBER 13, 2010

Director of Strategic Planning and Communications, Submarine Warfare Division, Rear Admiral Michael J. Yurina, Commanding Officer, USS *Georgia* (SSGN729), Captain Mike Cockey, and Command Master Chief Richard Rose met with Georgia governor, Sonny Perdue. The meeting was to celebrate the Navy's 235th birthday which falls during Atlanta Navy Week 2010.

This is one of nineteen Navy weeks planned across America in 2010

Navy Weeks show Americans the investment they have made in their Navy and increase awareness in cities that do not have a significant Navy presence The Office of Navy Community Outreach reached out to us to arrange a visit to the Capitol with our Navy. Colonel Bill Cain, US Army retired and now serving as Executive

Director of the Georgia Military Affairs Coordinating Committee opened the ceremony at the Capitol, after escorting the Navy leadership to the Governor's office. He then introduced me and I gave the welcome:

Welcome everyone to Navy Week Atlanta. Dozens of similar events are held every year across the county to bring the Navy to all Americans. While Atlanta is a long way from the ocean, logistics are all that separate us. Governor Perdue is a staunch supporter of our Military and has made that support a part of his commitment as Governor. The citizens of this country receive a significant return on America's investment in a Navy that is fast, flexible, global and powerful. And we have one of the best examples of that power in the state of Georgia with our ballistic missile submarines—the SSBNs and the SSGNs.

Every branch of our military has a footprint in Georgia. The Navy, Marine Corps, Coast Guard, Army and Air Force all have installations in Georgia. We also are represented by a professional group of recruiters and reservists. In fact, reservists can be found filling key positions in our military all over the world. Our state has a reputation as being one of the most supportive, military friendly states in the county and we owe much to Governor Perdue and his staunch support The governor went underway with the USS FLORIDA an SSGN and was the honorary chairman of USS GEORGIA's RETURN TO SERVICE.

Making this occasion even more special is the fact that we are celebrating the 235th birthday of the US Navy. As we celebrate this birthday take a moment to remember those currently on watch around the world and those who made the ultimate sacrifice. Helping us celebrating this birthday—we will have Chef Denny, head chef of the Georgian Room and Chef Schultz, pastry chef both with the Cloister at Sea Island who have baked a birthday cake especially for this event. They have with them one of the Navy CS apprentices, PO Joe Marina, who is learning the fine art of cooking from a 5-star rated hotel. At the end of this program we'll ask the Governor to join Captain Cockey and Admiral Uri for a cake cutting for our Navy birthday. COB (Chief of the Boat) Rose, we'll also celebrate your birthday and your 32 years with the Navy—so join us please.

It was a pleasure to have been a part of this great event. I told the audience I was impressed with our Navy Office of Community Outreach and especially in Lt. Tom

Peske, a Navy reservist who works full-time for the Army and who has done most of his work from hundreds of miles away with the help of many folks.

We recognized the many individuals and organizations who helped to ensure Navy Week Atlanta would be a great success in celebrating our Naval heritage: Mary Lou Austin of the USO; Ed Brownlee with Turner Broadcasting; Evan Kellner with the Georgia Aquarium; Diane Ritter with Navy for Moms; Frank Campbell and Don Giles of the Navy League; Captain Moore; Navy Reserve Center Commanding the Navy Recruiting District, CDR Bill Garran; former Blue Angels pilot, Donnie Cochran now with COKE; Capt. Michael Cockey, commanding officer of the USS *Georgia* chief of the boat Richard Rose, the officers and crew of the USS *Georgia*; the local Recruiting District and Reserve Center; the Blue Angels; the Navy Band Pride; the Navy Divers; and Bill Cain with the governor's Military Affairs Committee.

And everyone involved with the Navy Office of Community Outreach.

I will now introduce Rear Admiral Michael Yurina.

Earlier I talked about the incredible responsibilities, our reserve forces have undertaken in the past few years.

In introducing Admiral Yurina, I told everyone that Admiral Yurina is the best example of that. He has served at sea and on shore for our submarine force. His reserve assignments have been with submarine squadrons, for our Supreme Allied Commander, Atlantic, and at the National Defense University. He has served in command at five reserve units. Following a tour as reserve chief of staff, Submarine Force, he served as vice commander, Submarine Force, from August 2008 to September 2009. He is now the director of Strategic Planning and Communications, Submarine Warfare Division. Complimenting his uniformed military service, he joined the Naval Sea Systems Command and served from 1986 to 2003. Rear Admiral Yurina is currently with the Transportation Security Agency.

He almost had a Georgia connection during his early days. While he grew up in Florida, he has been quoted as saying he had to move to Georgia to get an education and he was accepted at the University of Georgia. We almost had him, but in a moment of youthful indiscretion, he accepted an appointment at the Naval Academy instead. UGA's loss has certainly been our gain. "Please help me welcome, RADM Michael J. Yurina."

After Rear Admiral Yurina's remarks we had a cake cutting with Governor Sonny Perdue and everyone enjoyed mingling with those who had come to the Capitol that morning not knowing they would be meeting some of our country's finest.

Rear Admiral Yurina and I presented Governor Perdue the certificate proclaiming Atlanta Navy Week 2010. It was a wonderful opportunity to walk with these sailors around the Capitol and see everyone shaking their hands and trying to talk with each of them. What a great Navy Day!

BACHELDER AWARDS AT ATHENS, GEORGIA

This article appeared in the *Navy Supply Corps Newsletter* in the November/December 1999 issue:

> ***Batchelder Awards Ceremony Held at NSCS***
>
> *The VADM Robert E. Batchelder Awards ceremony was held on board the Navy Supply Corps School. VADM Henry C. Griffin, III, Commander Naval Surface Force, U.S. Atlantic Fleet was the guest of honor and guest speaker. Ms. Sheila McNeill, National Vice President, U.S. Navy League, spoke at the ceremony and presented the awards to the recipients. RADM Keith W. Lippert SC, USN Chief of Supply Corps, attended the ceremony and spoke at the Batchelder Dinner the night prior to the event.*
>
> *The VADM Robert F. Batchelder Award program was established by the Navy League in 1983 in memory of Vice Admiral Robert F. Batchelder, SC, USN. Administered by the Chief of Supply Corps, and sponsored by the Navy League of the United States, "the award is intended to enhance operational readiness by public and official recognition of the Supply Corps officer or officers who make exceptional contributions to supply readiness." This is the 16th annual award. VADM Batchelder (1895-1973) served on active duty from 1917 through 1957. During his career, he served aboard six different ships and provided unparalleled support during both World Wars. He graduated from the Harvard Business School in 1926 and retired as a vice admiral in 1957 after serving as Inspector General at the Bureau of Supplies and Accounts (now the Naval Supply Systems Command. Recipients of the award that day included LCDR Andrew Wickard, SC, USN, LT Sonya Ebright, SC, USN, LT Lawton Johnson, SC, USN, Lt Juanito Buckley, SC, USN and LT Jeffrey Tribiano SC, USNR*

It was a wonderful day and I was honored to be a part of it. Over the next few years, I ran into VADM Griffin and RADM Lippert many times—and always with pleasure!

CAPTAIN EDWARD "NED" L. BEACH, USN

US NAVY LEAGUE'S 2000 ALFRED THAYER MAHAN AWARD FOR LITERARY ACHIEVEMENT

After hanging around submariners for forty years, there is no way I wasn't impressed with the name Ned Beach. Ned is a World War II Medal of Honor recipient and a well-known author. One of his most famous books was *Run Silent, Run Deep*. Considered the Holy Grail by most submariners, and one book, I made sure to read. Now I had the opportunity to have dinner with him. This experience is best told by the following story in *Seapower* magazine the next month:

FISHER PRESENTS 2000 MAHAN AWARD TO CAPTAIN NED BEACH

> *"Thank you for all that you have done for the Navy, the Navy League and the nation." With those words, National President John R. Fisher presented Capt. Edward L. "Ned" Beach, USN (Ret.) with the Navy League's 2000 Alfred Thayer Mahan Award for Literary Achievement. In his remarks, Fisher praised Beach for serving as "an articulate advocate of the sea power principles articulated by Mahan," and called him a "superb leader, teacher, mentor, and outstanding naval officer... Your achievements during a remarkable naval and literary career that started in the 1930s and continues to the present day are without precedent in the modern era."*
>
> *Beach, a 1939 graduate of the U.S. Naval Academy, first earned fame as a submariner during World War II. During that conflict, he was decorated with the Navy Cross, two Siler Stars, and two Bronze Star medals for heroism. During the 1950s while served as naval aide to President Eisenhower, he wrote "Run Silent, Run Deep," a popular portrayal of submarine combat operations during the war with Japan that later was made into a popular feature movie. He was called to Washington to serve as naval aide to General Omar Bradley, USA, the first chairman of the Joint Chiefs of Staff in August 1951. Before his retirement in 1966, Beach also commanded the nuclear-powered submarine USS Triton during her historic submerged circumnavigation of the world in 1960. Beach has authored 13 books during his literary career, continuing a tradition begun by his father Capt. Edward L. Beach, Sr. The U.S. Naval Institute's headquarters building on the grounds of the U.S. Naval Academy in Annapolis, Md. is named Beach Hall in his honor.*

During his acceptance remarks following Fisher's presentation, Beach—who has been described as "the preeminent US naval writer of the post-WWII era"—modestly noted that "writing is what I am, and what I am about." He said that it was a "tremendous honor" to receive the award. "I don't know how to express myself," he said, "except to say thank you ever so much." There is a wonderful photo taken with Jack Fisher, Ned and his wife, Ingrid, and me. One that I treasure greatly.

But that isn't all the story. Navy League headquarters had tried to work out a time for Capt. Beach to receive his award at a Navy League meeting but that became impossible with his schedule, so they planned to present it at dinner one evening. Jack called me and, knowing I would be in town, asked if I wanted to join he and Kit (Mrs. Fisher) and Ned and Ingrid Beach for dinner.

What a thrill! The day came, and I worked on legislative affairs issues all morning. Later in the day, I passed by Jack's office and he looked upset. I went in and asked what was wrong. It took him a few minutes and he told me, "My son has been killed. He is a fireman in Alaska and there was a fire." He just couldn't say anymore. What do you say when you hear something so devastating?

"You have to cancel the dinner tonight. They will understand—we can do this later," I told him. "We can't get a flight out until tomorrow. I'm going to have the dinner. Kit and I will meet you at the hotel." Nothing I said would change his mind and this might help them get through the night, I thought.

"Please don't mention it to Ned and Mary," he told me.

That night was incredible—I don't know how they did it. Joining us for dinner were the editor of *Seapower* magazine, Jim Hessman and his wife, Mary, and Gordy Peterson, senior editor of *Seapower*, and his wife, Diane. I knew them so well it was like having dinner with family, but it was quite a prestigious group.

I enjoyed hearing Ned's stories—Jack had placed me right across from him. I knew it was going to be a relaxed evening when his wife wanted a taste of my soup and Ned finished it. He talked about what he was doing when Pearl Harbor was attacked: at a dance with a girl and thought the alarm was in error. He also discussed his trip around the world on a submarine in sixty-five days—just a few less days than Jules Vern. He became a little emotional several times as he discussed the past. On one patrol, he told us about a young sailor, who lived in Guam, and as they passed, they let him look at his home through a periscope. Later, when they got home, a member of the crew said, "Captain, we wish there was some way we could get him back to his home. He hasn't been home in a couple of years." Captain Beach wrote TWA and told him the sailor's story and they sent a ticket!

It was a fun evening with lots of sea stories. With every word that was said I thought about Jack and Kit's son and what they were going through. The award was presented at dinner that evening and the picture that appeared in *Seapower* was made right outside the restaurant. It was an unforgettable evening.

In March 2000, I attended the funeral of Captain George L. Street III, where Ned did the eulogy for his former commanding officer. At that time, RADM Mal Fages told me he would be the senior officer in attendance and would present the flag. He invited me to go with them. I was deeply honored to be there. Mal presented the flag to his family. I am grateful to Malcolm and Shirley for giving me this opportunity. The account of Captain Street's Medal of Honor was covered in the *New York Times* as follows:

The New York Times by Richard Goldstein, March 5, 2000

Capt. George L. Street III, who won the Medal of Honor in World War II for directing a daring submarine attack that destroyed three Japanese ships off the coast of Korea, died Feb. 26, 2000 at a nursing home in Andover, Mass. He was 86. Serving as the skipper of the submarine Tirante, Street, then a lieutenant commander brought his boat into the Japanese anchorage off Quelpart Island, a high, rocky spot containing an air base, in the early hours of April 14, 1945. The waters, about 100 miles south of Korea, were heavily mined and the Japanese had radar-equipped patrol vessels off the island in addition to five shore-based radar stations.

But Street was determined to find Japanese ships and sink them. He approached the harbor on the surface at night, gun crews at their stations. If the submarine was detected, it would have to shoot its way out of trouble because the waters were too shallow for it to dive. At 4 a.m., the Tirante fired torpedoes at a large ammunition ship. "A tremendous, beautiful explosion," Street would write in his report. "A great mushroom of white blinding flame shot 2,000 feet into the air. Not a sound was heard for a moment, but then a tremendous roar flattened our ears against our heads. The jackpot, and no mistake!" The explosions lighted up the harbor.

"In the glare of the fire, Tirante stood out in her light camouflage, like a snowman in a coal pit," Commander Street would report. "But, more important, silhouetted against the flame were two escort vessels, both instantly obvious as fine new frigates of the Mikura class. Steadied to pick off the two frigates." The Tirante did just that, using two torpedoes to blow up one of the frigates and destroying the other one with one torpedo. Street then took the Tirante out of the harbor at full speed and dived, eluding depth charges from a pursuing patrol. While the Tirante had been approaching the Japanese-held harbor, it had received word over its radio of the death of President Franklin D. Roosevelt and the ascension to the presidency of Harry

S. Truman. A few hours after the Tirante completed its mission, it sent a message to the Pacific submarine command reading: "Three for Franklin... Sank ammunition ship two escorts."

Street received the Medal of Honor from Truman at the White House on Oct. 6, 1945, and was a recipient of the Navy Cross. He was decorated a second time by Truman in December1947, receiving a gold star in lieu of a second Silver Star for his actions in World War II. George Levick Street III, a native of Richmond, Va., graduated from the U.S. Naval Academy in 1937. He took part in war patrols on the submarine Gar before assuming command of the Tirante. After World War II, he held a variety of administrative and seagoing posts before retiring from the Navy in 1966 as a captain. He is survived by his wife, Mary, of Andover; a son, George L. Street IV of Portland, Maine; a daughter, Kris Terry of Kingsport, Tenn.; a sister, Melinda Ogilvy of Old Greenwich, Conn.; and four grandchildren.

Street's executive officer on the Tirante was Capt. Edward L. Beach, also a recipient of the Navy Cross, whose best-selling novel "Run Silent, Run Deep" (Holt, Rinehart & Winston, 1955) drew on his experiences aboard the Tirante and other World War II submarines. Endicott Peabody, a future governor of Massachusetts, was a lieutenant on the Tirante.

Despite all his individual honors, Street was exceedingly proud of a collective award, the Presidential Unit Citation, which went to the Tirante for its overall combat record. As Street put it, "I really treasure that more than the Medal of Honor because every man was there with us."

REAR ADMIRAL CHUCK BEERS AND SUSAN

SUBMARINE GROUP 10 COMMANDER 1995–1997

RDML Chuck Beers is one of three military officers who were most instrumental in my life. He relieved RDML Jerry Ellis in November 1995. We had a funny start to our friendship. I came into my Hallmark store one day and the ladies who work for me told me a very nice man had come in the night before. He wanted a balloon to welcome his wife from a trip. They told me they couldn't get the nozzle opened and he offered to help. They talked for a few minutes and, finding he was new in town, asked his name. I laughed when they told me it was Chuck Beers and I said, "Do you realize he was the new admiral and group commander that I have not met yet?" They did not but commented on what a nice man he was.

Arlie and I became fast friends with Chuck and Susan. Chuck and I agreed on so many issues—in fact, I never found an issue we didn't agree on. There were so many milestones and events that happened during his tour. We worked wonderfully together. We thought a lot alike and we developed a shorthand for corresponding by fax. Yes, fax. Internet was to come to me later! I would have a message for RDML Beers and would slip it into the fax machine, signing it "S," and he would return with the signature "C." We formed Friends of Kings Bay to have a forum for business owners and leaders to sit down regularly and discuss military/community issues.

During his tenure, he established a relationship with Sea Island to allow the culinary specialist to train with the chefs at the Cloister hotel on Sea Island, Georgia. (There is another story included elsewhere.)

The first part of his tour was the commissioning of the St. Marys Submarine Museum. This came just weeks after he arrived. It was a pretty big deal for our community and RADM Gene Fluckey, WWII hero and Medal of Honor recipient, was the keynote speaker. Several years later, the main building that houses the commanding officer of the base and the commander of Submarine Group 10, was later named Fluckey Hall in his honor. Chuck was on the program as a speaker. I never caught it until minutes before we went to the stage and he was listed as RDML Chuck Beers, retired. He did ask me if I knew something he didn't but he was a great sport about it. I'll write about RADM Fluckey and the St. Marys Submarine Museum in another story!

The one hundredth anniversary of the Submarine Force was coming up. As it turned out, Chuck managed to obtain the USS *George Bancroft* SSBN 643 sail. He thought it would make an excellent exhibit in front of the base. Of course, that would take funding, so he told me to get to work. I worked with John Crouse the manager of the St. Marys Submarine Museum who helped me with the campaign. I wrote every senior officer previously stationed at Kings Bay, that I had maintained contact with. We raised enough funds and a tremendous ceremony was held. I hope you will read my memories on the *USS Bancroft* Memorial ceremony.

I had been appointed to DACOWITS. Since we were directed to visit military installation in CONUS I thought it was a good idea to make my first visit a visit to Kings Bay. I talked to Chuck about this. He later told me—and anyone who listened. "A visit from a DACOWITS member as they are learning the ropes is like having a dental student give you a root canal." The visit was approved, and I arrived at the base. I briefed Chuck as the group commander and Captain Jim Alley who was commanding officer of Naval Submarine Base Kings Bay. As I met with the groups of sailors and marines divided by rank and gender, I heard from several sailors about an issue of sexual harassment in one of the commands. This was pretty stunning to me. I called DC DACOWITS headquarters and talked with our director, Captain Barbara Brehm, about the next step. She reminded me that it was not our responsibility to make recommendations or try to rectify the issues. It was simply to let leadership know of our findings. The next morning, I met with the admiral and captain and briefed them on my meetings.

"I would like for you to take another day and have more sailors attend another focus group from that particular command," Chuck told me. I agreed and returned to him that afternoon even more convinced there was an issue.

Chuck's response was like a training manual on how to handle sensitive issues. He immediately brought in the whistleblowers to his command and started an in-depth investigation of the command by calling in the Navy's inspector general. He actually thanked me. His thought was if there was this problem with this commanding officer with sexual harassment, there were likely other issues at the command, and he was right. The commanding officer was relieved most likely averting more issues in the future. Chuck wrote a letter that was to go to every new sailor at Kings Bay that standards would be maintained and that there would be no sexual harassment or discrimination of any kind. However, he still refers to the visit as getting a root canal from a dental student!

It was during his tour that I sent an invitation to Secretary of Defense Bill Perry to speak at a Navy League meeting. My reports on DACOWITS were sent to Secretary Perry. I still laugh when I think of their arrival. The secretary's Executive Assistant General was Paul Kern, whom I had met when he was at Ft. Stewart. He told me of a small change in the schedule. I said to Chuck, "Secretary Perry has to be back in DC for a meeting, so we have to leave in fifty-five minutes." Chuck told him I was in charge and to discuss it with me! An admiral is an important rank but for an admiral to tell a secretary of defense to move it on, wrap it up, or cut it short was not something that would bode well for his career. I, on the other hand, could "boss" him around all day. My reflections on this visit and Secretary Perry have a chapter all their own.

I was surprised one day when Chuck called me for lunch and asked me about putting together a group of the Camden Leadership to meet and make sure they were up to date on what was happening at Kings Bay and in the recent BRAC (base realignment and closure commission) announcements. He offered to have them all for lunch the following week. I contacted about a dozen of the local leadership making sure we had a cross section of the community. The following week, we met and Rear Admiral Beers briefed us on BRAC and everything submarine. We decided to put together a formal group and named it Friends of Kings Bay—I suggested that each company contribute one thousand dollars—and everyone agreed and Friends of Kings Bay became a reality. Friends of Kings Bay eventually developed into The Camden Partnership.

We all gained a lot of knowledge during the next few years, learning that a good thing is not always the best thing. The base had received word that the Child Care Center was being doubled and funds for that building were approved (good) but learned that while the new construction was paid for no funds for the operation were approved (bad). I learned to find out more about each issue. It was time for the change of command." Two of my favorite Group ten staff were in charge of the event: Lt. Diego Hernandez, who was Chuck's flag lieutenant, who later commanded the USS *Wyoming* (SSBN 742) and YNCS Brian Piedfort, his flag writer.

Chuck's wife, Susan, has a wonderful talent. I see it every year with her Christmas cards, but the evening of their Hail and Farewell, she outdid herself:

SUSAN'S WORDS AT HER FAREWELL

I know that it is important to say
What you did at KBSOWC mean to me today

When two years ago in Kings Bay we arrived
Could I have envisioned leaving, making me cry?
Little did I know what wonder abounded
And with what true friends I would be surrounded.

From bike rides to the marshes, and star/moon jackets
From fashion shows to fitness classes
Walks on the beach and Book Club buddies
Navy League meetings and swimming with "guppies"

Snakes, armadillo, deer and painted buntings
Kept me enchanted and always hunting.
Even entertaining, and daycare dealings
Could make little dent in my positive feelings

The planning meetings and Auction workshops
Uncovered such talent—you blew my socks off
I wish you the best—Keep having fun
Enjoy each other (and send me some sun)

I know you'll welcome Patty as you welcomed me
I'll miss you lots and remember you with glee!
Where ever we land, across the miles,
A visit from you will always bring smiles.

I'm filled with deep thankfulness, and as we part
I take each of you with me in my heart

With much love,
Susan

This is what leadership is all about. It should be included in the package of every spouse/family coming into a new location!

* * * * *

When I became vice president of legislative affairs, my first thought was to call Chuck and see if he could help me. I asked him to be my national chairman—we had had many conversations about the Navy League's advocacy programs and I had been trying to get our national president to give me the duties for legislative affairs and he had finally done just that. I told Chuck if he would take national chairman and didn't have the time I would do all the work.

He said, "No, I'll take the job and I'll work with you." And that's what we did for the next three years. Years later, our programs were still referred to as the time our legislative program took off.

Of course, when I ran for national president, Chuck was one of my best supporters. He was at the meeting, wearing that "Sheila for President" button and telling stories!

The most significant issue from Chuck that affected my life was his briefing to me about the conversion of the SSBNs at Kings Bay and Bangor. He told me it was a revolutionary plan to save the four submarines that were about to be destroyed. They could take these submarines, remove the D5 Trident with its nuclear weapons, replace them with convention Tomahawk weapons, and add a platform for special operations forces. With the stealth quality of submarines, they could travel to any country, remain silent and let diplomacy takes it course and if that didn't work these new SSGNs (guided missile rather that strategic missile) would have the equivalent fire power of some entire battle group. (More of that story later.)

He had been 'silenced' by his seniors on the issue. It was not an issue that the rest of the Navy had planned to pursue, but many in the submarine force saw the value and were very eager to save the SSBNs and convert them to SSGNs. (In fact, a couple of years later when I took our community group to DC we were told by a senior officer that "there was no way in hell this was going to happen.") Chuck was passionate about the value to our national defense. He actually discussed this issue on a Jacksonville news program and was told to not discuss it again. But he told me, "There was no reason you can't carry that ball." The conversion of those four boats would occupy much of my time and money over the next eight years. When I heard about it, I just wanted more and more information. A way to save over eighty years of submarine life and at the same time have such a unique ship. I immediately went to Senator Cleland and Coverdale and Congressman Jack Kingston and found Jack on the floor of the house voting on a bill. Look for the rest of the story.

In March 2005, a couple of months before my tour as Navy League president was up, he sent me the following e-mail:

Sheila,

My wife says I give you too much "grief" about too much... Just to set the record straight, I am in awe of what you have done with the Navy League these past two years. The entire complexion and feeling and mission of the NL have changed due to your single-handed effort, energy and leadership. It has been my extreme pleasure to know you and to watch it happen. You are a "one in a trillion" kind of leader and mentor... Good luck and have fun in your last months of office. You have set the bar way high for the follow-on presidents.

All my best and with utmost respect
Chuck

That is what is known as a friend.

Chuck asked me to serve on the Dolphin Scholarship Foundation board of directors. Meetings were in Norfolk where the Beers lived, and they opened their home to me every year for a visit or two. Susan always keeps me grounded and listens to my laments. She has her hobbies and interests and is an interesting woman to talk with. We always enjoy our conversations when we have a chance to sit down and relax. She is a cool lady who has been wonderful to me and Arlie. Sometimes, when I'm in town, she'll decide to go to a ceramics class or have dinner with someone while Chuck and I go to military events. Chuck is gracious about chauffeuring me around and never complains (well, almost never and then sometimes he does it just to be irritating), so the added benefit of being a board member was being able to stay with them and catch up on our lives.

ADMIRAL MIKE BOORDA

CHIEF OF NAVAL OPERATIONS

"You are his son, aren't you?" I asked the man who bears a remarkable resemblance to my friend, Admiral Mike Boorda.

I was on an airplane landing in DC. We had landed, and passengers were lined up to depart the plane. As I was waiting, I turned to the back of the plane and saw him. I didn't have to raise my voice—he saw me. He saw my look. He knew that look of recognition. He must get it a lot. He was the spitting image of his father.

He answered with a nod, "I am."

I told him, "I loved your father."

He answered, "Yes, I did too."

Nothing more was said, and I hurried down the corridor rushing to get to yet another meeting. He caught up with me and thanked me for remembering his dad.

I first met Admiral Boorda when he was chief of Naval Operations. In 1994, when I was council president of the Camden Kings Bay Council, I had asked him to come speak to our council. You just never know who you might be able to bring to the base as a speaker. We'd had pretty good luck in the past and I had heard so much about him that I had been relentless in my desire to have him come speak. His office gave us a date—September 9, 1994. He was coming!

A pre-reception was held at the group admiral's quarters, Rear Admiral Jerry Ellis. It was his wife, Rosemary's birthday and only fitting that the CNO should visit! We had a very nice reception with our Navy League officers and leadership from the base. When it became time to leave for the Navy League meeting, Arlie drove our Lincoln Town Car and Admiral Boorda and I rode in the back.

As we drove down the highway on the way to the clubs, it was evident that security was doing their job. There were Marines and Sailors along the route with weapons ready. Canine units added to the scene as did all the red lights that had been turned to caution to allow a steady drive from the admiral's quarters to the officer's club. A modest man, who was very charming, Boorda turned to me and said, "Sheila, don't you think this is a little ridiculous?"

I answered, "Yes I know, sir, but they do it for me every time I come on base." That really tickled him, and he laughed out loud. In fact, we both got a kick out of it. I don't know what made me say it but it sure broke the ice for us.

As we arrived at the club for the dinner, doors were opened and salutes were received, he turned to me and said, "You know, I'm going to have to travel with you more often. They do treat you well."

He talked to me about his son. He was in the Navy, and Mike was so proud of him. He understood the situation he had with a father as a senior admiral in the Navy and then as chief of Naval Operations. He knew it was not easy on his son. His son really didn't want any special treatment—he just wanted to serve. One day, he arrived at a new assignment—a Navy ship and wrote his father and told him, "I really like this ship. I'm having a good tour—they don't even know we're related."

Mike says on that same day that he received his son's letter he also received a letter from the ship's commanding officer saying, "Your son is doing well." He said one day, years from now, he would share both letters with his son. I hope he was able to do that.

I received a couple of notes from him over the next two years and my respect continued to grow. He remembered my involvement with the St. Marys Submarine Museum and later wrote me when the Master Chief of the Navy (MCPON), John Hagan visited the museum. That began a personal relationship that ended on the day of his death two years later.

The following year, I find myself at a very posh reception in Washington. By this time, I had been appointed to the Defense Advisory Committee on Women in the Services (DACOWITS). It was my first official function and I believe it is the only time I really felt little overwhelmed. The best way I can think to describe the feelings: awkward and being inadequate, almost like an "out of place" feeling.

As I'm standing with members that I haven't had a chance to get acquainted with, and feeling more nervous than I should have been, I hear a hush coming over the room. The chief of Naval Operations, Admiral Michael Boorda, had just entered the room. A few nudged me and let me know who he was. As we watched, he looked around the room, saw me, and headed in my direction. "Sheila, I need to give you a call. I expect I may have to go back to Kings Bay." He stayed only a minute gave me a hug and continued visiting in the room.

Someone asked me, "Does the CNO ask you when he comes to Kings Bay?'

"No," I answered, "he is just a nice, special guy, who is trying to make me look important." He did just that and I never forgot his kindness.

He was the first man in Navy history to advance from seaman recruit to chief of Naval Operations. He served the Navy for over forty years.

I was busy with yet another big event at Kings Bay. The highest official I had ever hosted had just left. Secretary of defense, William Perry, my ultimate boss on DACOWITS had spoken that day. Perry has a whole chapter in my life and I think you will enjoy reading about this day. But for now…

The secretary departs on his black hawk helicopter, accompanied by a second helicopter, rushing to get back to DC for a meeting with President Clinton. I stood at the helo pad with Rear Admiral Chuck Beers to see him off, then returned to my office. Jack Mead, a former Navy captain and now active in the Navy League, comes to my Hallmark store looking stricken. He tells me, "Someone has shot Admiral Boorda."

"Oh no, that can't be true. There must be some mistake," I answered. As I wondered how to find out if this awful rumor might indeed be true, I remembered something. As I toured the White House a few months earlier, I was fascinated with the situation room. The age of those who had the responsibility of listening to the current news, then deciding what was important enough to share with the president, looked to be in their midtwenties. I wondered about the incredible responsibility placed on such a young group. We walked around a while and met some of the staff and I saw the phone. For some reason, the number stuck with me.

That day it came in handy. I dialed the number I had remembered for the White House situation room.

"White House," they answered.

"I have heard that Admiral Mike Boorda has been shot, can you tell me if this is true?" I asked.

"Who is this?"

"This is Sheila McNeill and I'm in St. Marys, Georgia"

"Ma'am, could you tell me again who you are?"

I repeated, "I'm Sheila McNeill from St. Marys, Georgia."

In a few minutes, the staffer was back on the phone. "Ma'am, I can confirm that he has been shot but I cannot give you any details." We were just sorrowful. That day I received many calls of disbelieve and sadness. Mike had gone to his residence in the Navy yard during his lunch hour, went to the backyard, and shot himself.

Navy's top officer dies of gunshot, apparently self-inflicted
Letter left behind offers clues

May 16, 1996
Web posted at: 10:10 p.m. EDT

WASHINGTON (CNN)—The nation's top Navy officer Adm. Jeremy Michal Boorda, died Thursday from an apparently self-inflicted gunshot wound hours after learning Newsweek magazine was raising questions about the legitimacy of some of his combat medals.

CNN has learned from Pentagon sources that Boorda wrote two letters before he died, one to his family and one addressed to sailors. Sources said that in the typewritten note to the sailors, Boorda explained that he took his life because of the questions raised about his wearing of "V" for valor medals on his combat ribbon from Vietnam.

Navy officials had not yet decided whether to release the letters. A U.S. Navy official who met with Boorda in the hours preceding his death said Boorda was "obviously concerned" about a scheduled meeting Thursday with two Newsweek reporters pursuing the story.

The 57-year-old chief of Naval Operations was rushed to D.C. General Hospital after he was found outside his quarters at the Washington Navy Yard, the Navy said. An emergency room physician said Boorda arrived with a gunshot wound to the chest. Five minutes later, at 2:30 p.m. EDT, he was pronounced dead. According to Newsweek editor Maynard Parker, the news magazine was working on a story that called into question two medals Boorda received during the Vietnam war.

According to Navy sources, the magazine claimed to have uncovered evidence that Boorda had for more than 20 years inappropriately displayed "V" for valor on the medals. According to a source who has seen Boorda's note to the sailors, Boorda wrote that he wore the Vs because he thought he rated them.

Boorda told the sailors how much he thought of them, and said that some people will not think he did the right thing, the source said. He ended the letter with a reference to "critics in the media" who have been "hard on the Navy," saying "I have given you more to write about," the source said.

The "V" for valor on such awards is reserved for acts "involving direct participation in combat operations," according to military code. The Navy released documents late Thursday which indicate that Boorda was not authorized to wear a combat "V: decoration.

Rear Adm. Kendell Pease, who was with Boorda a little over an hour before the shooting, said that when he told Boorda, at about 12:30 p.m., what the subject of the interview was, the admiral abruptly announced he was going home for lunch instead of eating the meal that had been brought to his office.

"Admiral Boorda was obviously concerned," said Pease, the Navy's top public affairs officer. He said that Boorda had asked him how they should handle the Newsweek questions, then without waiting for a reply had answered his own question: "We'll just tell him the truth."

The Navy would not say if Boorda's wound was self-inflicted, and Navy Secretary John Dalton said Washington, D.C., police were investigating Boorda's death. Earlier, a Pentagon source told CNN that Boorda's death was "definitely a suicide." According to sources familiar with the investigation, a .38 caliber pistol was used in the shooting. The gun belonged to his son-in-law, sources said.

President Clinton expressed his grief at Boorda's sudden and violent death. Opening a briefing to announce a new U.S. policy on land mines, the president asked for a moment of silence in honor of Boorda. He bowed his head, prayed silently, then whispered, "Amen." Earlier, during a discussion with business leaders, Clinton, who appointed Boorda to his position in 1994, was handed a note from an aide informing him of the shooting. After reading the note, the president's shoulders slumped and he grimaced. He continued the discussion for 20 minutes, without mentioning Boorda. On returning to the White House, he headed for an Oval Office meeting with several somber aides.

Dalton praised Boorda as "a sailor's sailor," and after a pause said, "He will be missed." The Navy secretary said he met with Boorda on Wednesday and found him in "great spirits." Boorda, whose name was Jeremy, preferred to be called Mike. Born in South Bend, Indiana, Boorda was married to Bettie May Moran and had four children. He received a bachelor's degree in political science from the University of Rhode Island in 1971 and postgraduate degrees from the Naval War College in 1971 and 1983. He was commissioned as an ensign in the U.S. Navy in 1962 and advanced through the ranks to admiral in 1984. A top NATO commander, Boorda was in charge of American naval forces in Europe and commander in chief of allied forces in southern Europe before being chosen for the Navy's top job.

CNN Correspondent Jamie McIntyre contributed to this report:

Later reports gave information on his suicide note he left on May 16, 1996 to his sailors:

"What I am about to do is not very smart, but it is right for me. You see, I have asked you to do the right thing, to care for and take care of each other and to stand up for what is good and correct. All of these things require honor courage and commitment... our core values.

"I am about to be accused of wearing combat devices on two ribbons I earned during sea tours in Viet Nam. It turns out I didn't really rate them. When I found out I was wrong, I immediately took them off, but it was really too late. I don't expect any reporters to believe I could make an honest mistake and you may or may not believe it yourselves. That is up to you and isn't all that important now anyway. I've made it not matter in the big scheme of things because I love our Navy so much, and you who are the heart and soul of our Navy that I couldn't bear to bring dishonor to you.

"If you care to do so, you can do something for me. That is take care of each other. Be honorable. Do what is right. Forgive when it makes sense, punish when you must, but always work to make the latter unnecessary by working to help people be all they really can be. My idea of one-on-one leadership really will work if you let it and honestly apply it. We have great leaders, and I know you'll succeed.

"Finally, for those who want to tear our Navy down, I guess I've given them plenty to write about for a while. But I will soon be forgotten. You, our great Navy people will live on. I am proud of you. I am proud to have led you if only for a short time. I wish I had done it better.

The next few days were just awful. No one could get over it. Everyone was affected then and to this day. My secretary at the time, Judy Marsh, wrote a letter to the editor of the Florida Times Union. It read in part:

> *"If the recent suicide death of Admiral Jeremy Boorda is to have any meaning, I hope it will be to give pause to those members of the new media who have chosen as their self-appointed mission in life, to discover and expose the sins of any who have achieved a larger-than-usual portion of "fame and fortune... In the case of Admiral Boorda we have a man who had worked hard all his life, serving his country in many capacities. He was a family man, loved by all who knew him. He was still using his influence and rank in any way possible to improve the lives of the men and women who served under him. Was it really worth destroying a man of this caliber... please, all of you out there who have decided that the public "needs to know" every fault and foible of our leaders, leave us a few heroes, will you?!"*

The Navy League had a special tribute to Mike in their June 1996 issue. They reported that Boorda was always best known for his empathy with people, particularly enlisted personnel and their families. He worked for them constantly and did everything within his power to make life better for them. He tried to make life in the Navy fun again, and exciting and he largely succeed in those ambitious goals.

It was fitting that his closing remarks in a April 24th address at a Naval Institute seminar at the Naval Academy was about people:

> *"My vision for the Navy for the rest of my time is continuous improvements. I'm going to leave it better than when I found it and... I'm going to do it because we have a lot of wonderful people in the Navy... I know nothing is as good as I think it is and nothing as bad as it seems, but... every one of us who could sit down with five or ten sailors out in the real world where the job is getting done would be able to say, "I am so proud."*

I, too, am proud. I am proud to have been a friend of Admiral Jeremy Michael Boorda.

CAPTAIN MICHAEL BROWN AND KATHY

COMMANDING OFFICER USS GEORGIA (SSGN 729) (GOLD)

I received an e-mail from Mike on 8/18/2009

> *Sheila, I will owe you forever for the things that you have done for my sailors and the sailors of Kings Bay!!*

Could you not love a man who would send that e-mail? I was so impressed with the letter that Mike sent to the Georgia Gold wives. He made a real effort to keep them informed. Kathy was always reaching out to spouses who needed to talk or a family that needed help, so I'm sure some of this understanding came from his conversations with Kathy.

He was the speaker at our Navy League meeting:

Navy League Honors USS GEORGIA 3/19/2010
From Commander Submarne Group 10 Public Affairs

KINGS BAY, GA (NNS)—The Camden-Kings Bay Council of the Navy League honored USS GEORGIA (SSGN 729) (G) during a dinner at Naval Submarine Base Kings Bay, Ga. March 11.

Georgia is on a 12-month deployment and the two crews have alternated manning the submarine for approximately three-month periods since the boat departed its homeport in July 2009.

The Gold crew was deployed throughout the holiday season and was called to duty for an additional month, extending their first deployment period to four months. The local council of the Navy League staunch supporters of their namesake submarine, wanted to recognize the Gold crew Sailors for bringing the submarine to life since its return to service as a guided missile submarine. "Many of those (Navy League members) present had worked on the return to service, so they were very interested in the changed and varied mission of the boat," said Sheila McNeill, former national president of the Navy League. Capt. Mike Brown, Georgia commanding officer, served as guest speaker. He discussed the importance of the guided missile submarine mission, Georgia's deployment, voyage repair periods in Diego Garcia and homeport training periods.

Brown highlighted some of the boat's achievements—every crew member completed the tour as a qualified submariner, 15 Sailors advanced to the next rank during the deployment, and the Georgia received the Submarine Squadron 16 Battle Efficiency Award. "No ship has undergone such a tremendous transformation in such a short time period. Being awarded the Battle Efficiency Award is a true testimonial to the hard work and professionalism of both crews and the love and support of our families." Brown said.

"The USS Georgia team, which includes both the Blue and Gold crews and our family members, has been working diligently for the last few years to bring our SSGN to life," said Brown. "After

> *numerous months of shipyard conversion, tactical modernization, and crew training, the USS Georgia, manned by two of the best crews in the Submarine Force, is deployed to the other side of the world executing the military policy of our president and his combatant commanders."*
>
> *Keith Post, Camden-Kings Bay Council Navy League president, was appreciative of Georgia Gold recognizing the contributions the Navy League makes in the local area. "Our support for the USS Georgia return to service was acknowledged, as were our efforts at pushing the SSGN program to fruition. This demonstrates how important community involvement is," said Post.*
>
> *Georgia Godl will be deployed during the annual Sea Services Sailor of the Year banquet this spring. The Navy League recognizes Georgia Gold's Sailor of the Year Machinist's Mte. 1st Class (SS) Roger Gahn, and thank him for his hard work and contributions to the submarine."*

My visit to the USS *Georgia* for an underway is told in a separate story. The next day, Captain Brown presented the following:

Honorary Submariner Certificate:

This is to certify that Sheila McNeill Having boarded and been indoctrinated into the Mysteries of a submerged warship; Having been immersed into the culture, doctrine, and Camaraderie unique to a submarine crew;

Having both dined and slept far beneath the waves; and

Having demonstrated knowledge of both the hardships

endured and thrills enjoyed by the men who call themselves submariners,

I hereby certify the above-named FRIEND OF GEORGIA

as an HONORARY SUBMARINER

Given this 22nd day of DEC 2008 On Board USS GEORGIA (SSGN 729) (GOLD)

MICHAEL W. BROWN, Captain, U.S. Navy, Commanding Officer

That trip is covered in the Underway on the USS *Georgia*. He and his command master chief, Gary Aston, came to Brunswick to speak to a group and mesmerized the audience. We need more Michael Browns and Gary Astons. Gary has retired and now works at Trident Training Facility. His wife, Cheryl, is dedicated to Navy League and does wonderful things for our sea service members. Mike is still working for the Navy.

We loved spending time with Kathy and Mike. The party they had for their crew in Jacksonville showed the respect the officers and crew had for each other. We had a wonderful time. They now live on the West Coast—they should look out—we'll be there to visit one day!

REAR ADMIRAL BARRY BRUNER AND ELIZABETH

COMMANDER, SUBMARINE GROUP 10

We would have loved them anyway. But to have Rear Admiral Bruner as our "long-awaited admiral" at Kings Bay would have made him special even if he had not been!

The *Tribune & Georgian* had front page coverage in May 2009:

KINGS BAY GAINS FULL-TIME ADMIRAL

By Susan Respress

> *A flag officer is being reestablished at Kings Bay Naval Submarine Base, a move that Camden County leaders anticipate will improved submarine operations and readiness and enhance the base's position for growth.*
>
> *The Navy announced yesterday that Rear Adm. Select Barry L. Bruner, a former commander of the USS Florida, will be Commander of Submarine Group 10 at Kings Bay. Bruner is serving as director of the operations division in the Navy budget office in Washington, D.C. Bruner will relieve Rear Adm. Timothy Giardina who is based on the west coast and commands Group 10 at Kings Bay and Group 9 at Bangor, Washington. "Rear Adm. Giardina and his wife, Missy, have done a wonderful job these past two year as our admiral and first lady but were not able to devote the time to Kings Bay that they would have liked to," said Sheila McNeill, a St. Marys business owner and a member of the governor's task force on military issues. "I'm pleased that he will no longer have to travel the 3,000-mile commute and that the group commander will now be a part of this community," McNeill said. "The assignment of a flag officer to Kings Bay is significant. I hope the funding comes through for the staff support that he will need. Rebecca Rebarich, public affairs officer for Group Ten, said she had no more details on the announcement or when Bruner will take command.*
>
> *McNeill, members of the Camden County Chamber of Commerce and members of The Camden Partnership have been advocating for a return to flag rank at Kings Bay. The move, planned*

by the Navy also was endorsed in a Secretary of Defense Task Force on DoD Nuclear Weapons Management report in January. The report supported a flag officer and full staff for each Trident submarine homeport and also recommended that the Trident Training Facility at Kings Bay be brought back up to full staff, which had been trimmed by half in budget reductions.

In a report presented to military and elected officials in Washington in April, as part of an annual chamber of commerce fly-in to promote Camden County, McNeill noted that Kings Bay is underutilized and recommended adding attack submarine and other missions to the base. Kings Bay's sister base in Bangor, Washington has eight ballistic-missile and two guided-missile submarines as well as three attack submarines. Kings Bay has two guided-missile subs and six ballistic-missile subs.

"Bruner certainly brings to the command a significant career in various submarine jobs," McNeill said. "So he has punched the right tickets. The USS Florida gold crew under his command from 1998 to 2001 was named the top SSBN (ballistic missile submarine) in the Pacific Fleet for two years and the top SSBN in the entire fleet for 2000. I don't know if he'll actually pin on his star before he comes, and that certainly doesn't matter. Perhaps we'll be able to witness that at the change of command.

Bruner's command responsibilities at Kings Bay will include Submarine Squadrons 16 and 20, which had been combined and then split into separate commands in March. His career includes commanding Submarine Squadron 7 at Pearl Harbor and chief of staff for the commander of Carrier Strike Group 5 and Task Group 70 and 75 in Yokosuka, Japan.

It was wonderful to have a chance to meet his wife, Beth, and children, Kristin and Michael, at the reception. It was quite a heady audience with Admirals Donnelly, Konetzni, Alexander, Voekler, and Robertson in attendance as well as Captains Stevens, Schmeiser, and Guffey.

I sent an e-mail to the Bruners that week:

Welcome Admiral and Mrs. Bruner,

We cannot tell you how excited we are to have you here!! Your arrival has been the talk for months. Our own admiral and first lady again!! Beth, I know we sometimes take advantage of the 2 for 1 plan but we'll try not to ask too much of you right away. Admiral, that doesn't include you—we'll be pursuing you immediately and expecting all sorts of answers! Please know how much we love the military in Camden County and how anxious we are to help you in any way we can We hope that your tour in Camden County will bring you much happiness and satisfaction.

Everyone in Camden County

He and Beth hosted a social for the Navy League in their quarters in August 2009. Yes, it was good to have our admiral back. God bless him for recognizing the value of the Navy League and bringing in the commanding officers to meet and get to know these loyal supporters.

I am sure that Barry sent word to DC and Norfolk about me receiving the Emory Dawson Humanitarian Award. He was there. They wouldn't have known of it had he not told them. I received very nice congratulatory letters from the chief of Naval Operations, Admiral Gary Roughead, and commander of the Submarine Force, Vice Admiral Jay Donnelly.

In February 2010, Barry was one of the speakers at The Camden Partnership's Kings Bay Camden County Forum along with commanding officer of the base, Captain Wes Stevens, and Steve Howard, Camden County administrator. The forums were created by the partnership to broaden the connection between the military and county residents. He was quoted in the local paper:

Despite talk of deemphasizing and reducing nuclear weapons, Bruner said he doesn't think the Trident fleet at Kings Bay will be affected any time soon. Ballistic missile submarines are thought to be more valuable today than they ever have been, Bruner said. Part of the nation's strategic deterrence is composed of a triad of missile launchers from submarine, group sites and bombers. Bruner said the Trident submarine is the most survivable of the three platforms. "There's been nothing said that we would back off the number of SSBNs."

In June 2010, Admiral Bruner, Beth, and I traveled to Sea Island. The Cloister wanted to discuss the possibility of Kings Bay's culinary specialists to have some time with the chefs at the Cloister. Executive chef Cliff Denny hosted lunch for us all. Being the "ever vigilant" military officer, he would not have what was suggested (a very special treat) but instead went with the less expensive hamburger. We had lunch at the Lodge and toured the beach club.

The chef was discussing Sea Island history and hesitated, trying to remember the exact circumstance. As a native of Brunswick and a fan of the Joneses and Sea

Island, I spoke up and finished his story. He commented, "She knows more about my job than I do."

At which time Barry said, "Welcome to my world."

I still laugh when I think of that conversation. He and Arlie had a special relationship. I think that Barry thought of Arlie as a father figure—perhaps he said that at one point, but I know that Arlie was always especially pleased to spend time with Barry.

One of mine and Keith Post's favorite stories is about the night we had dinner with Beth. He was due back that night from DC, but we didn't expect to see him. However, he called from the airport, and Beth suggested his aide drop him off at the restaurant. He joined us and we had a lovely evening.

On the way back, Keith was driving my car and Beth and Barry were in the back. We went in the back gate, which is close to their quarters. We were stopped by security. They were doing a check and wanted to see my registration and Keith's license. He managed the license okay, but as much as I rampaged through the glove compartment, I couldn't find the current registration. I kept looking back at the admiral, hoping he would put in a good word for us. Why hasn't the guard at least spoken to the admiral? I finally gave him the registration—it was still the wrong one. Finally, with no help from the admiral, we find the right registration and are allowed to travel on with the security guard never having seen who was in the back seat. "Why didn't you help! Why didn't you at least say hello?" I asked the admiral in disbelief.

"Your back window won't work! I've been pushing it and pushing it."

I guess you had to have been there to appreciate it. We have laughed and enjoyed that incident many times.

When Barry and Beth were close to leaving, they had a dinner party at their home for Keith, Brad, Hunt and Alyce Thornhill, and Arlie and me. He gave us each a huge knife in a beautiful case. We couldn't let that go. I asked them all to come to my office where I had gauze and tape and we put it all over our faces, arms, and anywhere we could. We sent that picture to them with our thanks.

Barry was transferred to N97 (submarine division) at the Pentagon. When the chamber fly-in made their next trip to DC, Beth and Barry had us all over for grilled hamburgers with all the trimmings. There must have been twenty of us. The picture was framed in their home. They probably did that right before we arrived! One of the pleasures of working on sea services support for over forty years is that you know you will most likely see folks again. I was delighted to again see Axel Spens, who was working for the admiral and about ready to transfer once again.

Arlie and I attended Barry's retirement at the Pentagon a few years later. To get Arlie to travel with me to DC, it had to be a special event! There are no better folks than the Bruners.

CAMDEN KINGS BAY COUNCIL NAVY LEAGUE

Arlie and Hugh Mayberry were in the group that traveled to St. Marys to talk with local leaders about starting a Navy League Council. Our first Navy League meeting was on the USS *Simon Lake* with Capt. J. D. Williams, Squadron 16 commander. J. D. later was promoted to rear admiral. It was always a pleasure to run into him in DC. We met at Antoinette's first year, and then met at the fire station on base. We eventually ended up at NSB King's Bay's conference center for most meetings

The original board was composed of Kyle Lewis, Flem Hall, Preston Connor, and Carl Shepherd. The presidents were as follows:

Carl Shepherd	1980
Kyle Lewis	1981
Ron Rewis	1982
Denny Reasoner	1983–1984
Dick Currier, Captain	1985–1986
Rowland Eskridge	1987
Billy Frank Woods	1988
David F. Bew, PhD	1989–1990
Roy Kincaid	1991
Jim Wells	1992
Sheila McNeill	1993–1994
Tilden Norris	1995–1996
Jack Mead	1997
Mike Flenniken	1998
Frank Frasca	1999
Norman Mims	2000–2001 Charles Gilman 2002
Walt Natzic	2003–2005
Dave Reilly	2005–2007
Keith F. Post	2007–2010
Dave Reilly	2011
Hunt Thornhill	2012
Dave Burch	2013
Hunt Thornhill	2014–2016
Sam Colville	2017

When I was president, the following individuals served with me:

President-Elect Tilden Norris
Vice President Chuck Ellis
Secretary Sherry Schlosser

Treasurer Judy Ellis
JAG Jim Steele
Chaplin Billy Frank Woods
Chairpersons:
Gerry O'Donoghue for Sea Cadets
Jack Mead for NJROTC and Sea Cadets
Wiley King for membership
Bobby Paulk for member relations
Joan Boeck for door prizes
Rowland and Dottie Eskridge for reservations
Trish McMillan for public affairs
Sheila McNeill for programs
Rosemary Ellis and Audrey Cole for facilities
Cheryl O'Donoghue for the newsletter

I am indebted to each of them for their help in making my first official leadership job in the Navy League successful. The council continues to receive high awards from national and that includes the recent outstanding award received in 2017.

ADMIRAL HANK CHILES AND KATIE

SUBMARINE FORCES ATLANTIC FLEET COMMANDER, STRATEGIC COMMAND

Admiral Hank Chiles is a giant in a field of wonderful leaders. In the summer of 1993, Admiral Chiles spoke to the Navy League. At the time, he was Submarine Force Atlantic Fleet, which means he was in charge of all US submarines in the world. I was a little anxious about the attendance. At a recent chamber meeting we had to table everything due to lack of a quorum. There were so many of our community on vacations. I shouldn't have been concerned. The place was packed. In 1996, when I was working on the building St. Marys Submarine Museum, Admiral Chiles sent a note of encouragement:

> *Sheila, your phone call meant a lot and we're delighted to hear that the museum has received such a wonderful donation. Well done! We all know who to thank for creating the enthusiasm for the project. Will look out for a periscope. All the best, Hank*

In July 1996, Admiral Chiles spoke to the Camden Kings Bay Council. Rosemary and Rear Admiral Ellis were the host of a wonderful dinner at their home.

As state president of the Navy League, Admiral Chiles gave me the opportunity to invite leadership in the community, the state, and the region, including Navy League leadership, to tour Strategic Command under the US Strategic Command's Civilian Distinguished Visitors program. Those who attended included Arlie, Howard Jones, Sea Island Company, Bill Pickard, Ken Tollison, local businessmen, Hugh Mayberry (national president of the Navy League), Rosemary Ellis, Compass, Woody Woodside (executive director of the Brunswick Golden Isles Chamber of Commerce), Chuck Breslauer, W. R. Grace & Company, and other Navy League leaders. We departed on October 11, 1995, from Glynco Jetport right outside of Brunswick at 0730 and we arrived at Whiteman AFB at 0915. Brig. Gen. Marcotte gave us a mission brief on the 509th Wing. We then visited the B2 where we had a photo op. After lunch at the Officer's Club we departed for Offutt Air Force Base at 1330. We arrived at Offutt a couple of hours later where we received a welcome from Admiral Chiles, and his staff briefed on "Global Challenges and Intelligence." That evening, Admiral Chiles hosted a wonderful dinner where we enjoyed music from the STRATCOM band. He introduced the band and remembered the names of every band member!

This article appeared in the *Seapower* magazine in February 1996.

Navy Leaguers Tour Whiteman, Offutt AFBs

Fifteen Georgia Navy Leaguers and one from South Carolina had the opportunity recently to observe strategic warfare operations at Whiteman AFB, MO., home of the 509th Bomb Wing and the B-2 bomber and at Offutt AFB outside of Omaha Nebraska headquarters of the U.S. Strategic Command (STRATCOM).

What is believed to be the first large scale visit by Navy Leaguers to STRATCOM and its subordinate facility was arranged by Sheila McNeill, Georgia state president, and her husband, Arlie, South Atlantic Coast Region president. The program was coordinated with the staff of the commander in chief of the Strategic Command, Adm. Henry G. Chiles, Jr. who became well-known to Georgia Navy Leaguers during his tour of duty as commander, Submarine Force, Atlantic Fleet prior to his becoming CICSTRATCOM.

In February 1994. During his SUBLANT tour Chiles had administrative responsibility for the Navy's fleet of strategic ballistic missile submarines based at Kings Bay, Ga. Close to Brunswick, Ga starting point on 11 October of the Navy Leaguers tour. The group, accompanied by National President Hugh H. Mayberry, first toured one of the most modern Air Force bases during it' s three-hour stopover at Whiteman; there, the visiting Navy Leaguers were briefed on the capabilities of the B-2 stealth bomber and were able to see it both on the ground and in flight. In time, all 20 of the B-2s that have been authorized and funded to date will be assigned to the 509th Bomber Wing; seven have been completed and are under its operation control now.

The tour group then proceeded to Offutt AFB, a former cavalry post in the late 19th century that became the home of the Strategic Air Command (SAC) in the 1940s and is now a virtual city of 35,000 that sprawls for miles across the Nebraska plains. In 1992, control of all strategic forces became the responsibility of the newly formed Strategic Command, first commanded by an Air Force General. At Offutt, the Navy Leaguers had an excellent opportunity to learn about the organization of STRATCOM, its role in national security, its leaders and staff, and the present and future capabilities of its forces. A command briefing was followed by an intelligence briefing, a tour of the command's underground operations center and a reception and dinner hosted by Chiles. The next day began with breakfast with the command's most senior Navy and Air Force enlisted personnel and a question and answer session with Chiles. It continued with a tour of one of the four National Airborne Operations Centers, converted Boeing 747s that can serve as command posts for the national command authority in times of crisis. One of the four aircraft is based at Offutt, the other three are based elsewhere in the United States.

Then came a tour of STRATCOM's own airborne command post, its "Looking Glass" aircraft, a converted KC-135 tanker—which also can function as a command and control center during times of crisis. Finally, the group visited the quarters, now occupied by Admiral and Mrs. Chiles, which had been the residence of Army officers more than 100 years earlier. One of its best-known occupants in the post-WWII era was General Curtis LeMay, the former commander of SAC who resided there for nine years.

From beginning to end," Sheila McNeill said, "the trip was a unique learning opportunity that was enhanced by the efficiency, organization, and courtesy of our hosts at both bases.

It was a wonderful opportunity to gain insight in the nation's ability to wage strategic warfare and our country's efforts to maintain peace. Our plane for the return flight was delayed and Hank and Katie were very gracious in allowing us all to 'hang out' at their house for a couple of hours. The group could not believe the hospitality and the charm of the Chiles. They were also impressed by the fact that Hank knew so many of their names. No one could believe that a four-star admiral with all the issues he dealt with could take the time to remember each of their names. There was a card from Hank in our room when we checked in that included the following:

> *WHEN YOU RETURN HOME ON THURSDAY AFTERNOON, YOU WILL DO SO WITH A BETTER UNDERSTANDING OF THE IMPORTANT ROLE THAT STRATEGIC DETERRENCE PLAYS IN OUR NATION'S DEFENSE. OUR PEOPLE AND THE SYSTEMS THEY OPERATE ARE THE BEST IN THE WORLD.*

Yes, we all did—it was an incredible opportunity and that message inspired us all. On the flight back, they let me make some announcements over the intercom and pretend to be the flight attendant!

It was the one hundredth anniversary of the submarine force in 2000 and Hank was the national chairman. Public TV had a series about submarines. I was at Malcolm and Shirley Fages home at a dinner party. We made sure we finished dinner in time to hear the interview with Admiral Chiles. I had been teasing Malcolm because he didn't mention me in his interview on the same subject, same station. It was a joke! None of us could believe it when Hank said, "Sheila and Arlie McNeill are great supporters of the Navy and the submarine force." I gave Malcolm a really hard time when we heard that! What a thrill to both Arlie and to me.

When we were building the USS *Bancroft* Sail Exhibit in front of Naval Submarine Base Kings Bay in recognition of the one hundredth anniversary of the submarine force, Admiral Chiles was the national chairman. He wrote this note to me and Arlie, which I shared with the group:

> *Dear Arlie and Sheila,*
>
> *Hope ya'll have had a wonderful Christmas and that this year 2000 has gotten off to a rousing, enjoyable start.*
>
> *Thanks for your insight in early December, Sheila, that's very much appreciated. You all have done a terrific job in bringing the Bancroft exhibit together. It'll be interesting to see if DACOWITS will have any input with SECDEF/SECNAV on the women in submarine issue.*
>
> *Hope you saw the sub sailors in the Rose Parade. We're rolling! Enclosed is a small check for the Bancroft exhibit. Holler if we can help. God bless in 2000! Katy and Hank*
>
> *Hank sent me an email August 6th, 2001 when the Georgia Trend cover and article came out.*
>
> *Sheila, loved the magazine cover and article in Georgia Trend. Great comments and appreciate your involvement in keeping folks*

focused on the base and force. I really see the SSGN as the best way to keep the numbers up at Kings Bay. This administration seems more responsive and if we move away from the START agreement it would be more affordable. Keep on charging and holler when you and Arlie are up this way. 57 years old!!!!!!! How did you let 'em put something like that in such a good article? Getting ready for another academic year here at the Naval Academy. Fun! Katy sends hugs,*

Hank

After retirement, Admiral Chiles taught ethics at the Naval Academy. He is an amazing man and we remain good friends.

ADMIRAL VERN CLARK AND CONNIE

CHIEF OF NAVAL OPERATIONS

"Admiral Clark?" I asked hesitantly.

"Now, Sheila, who did you expect to answer my phone?" answered Admiral Vern Clark, chief of Naval Operations.

"Sir, it's like calling heaven and getting God. You just don't expect it to happen."

I then explained, that I only wanted a minute of his time. It was the first Sunday after my election and I was writing my very first president's message for *Seapower*. I wanted to use the term "those who wear the cloth of our nation" in my first message. It was a term coined by Admiral Clark, but I explained to him that I didn't want to refer to him or the Navy in my first message. The Navy League supports all of the sea services—the Navy, Marine Corps, Coast Guard, and the US Merchant Marine—so I wanted to be all inclusive in my first message to members and supporters.

"Rummy uses it all the time," Admiral Clark jokingly retorted.

"Of course, you can use it." I thanked him and was about to hang up.

Admiral Clark asked, "Are you in a hurry? Do you have time to talk?"

I answered, "Since it's Sunday, and Father's Day, I know you must be busy with family and I don't want to interfere with that."

He answered, "Right now, I have time and I'd like to talk with you."

We talked about the year ahead and how the Navy League could best support the Navy. We talked specifics, we talked in general. He urged me to call him every time I made a speech. He encouraged me to meet with him often and he would keep me updated on issues I might be questioned on. That began a relationship that will forever endure and ensured I would have the knowledge I needed to support the Navy.

I met the Clarks on a Saturday night at the annual Kings Bay Submarine Ball held on Jekyll Island in April 2000. At that time, Admiral Clark was commander in chief, US Atlantic Fleet. Rear Admiral Rich Terpstra was the group commander. We knew that Admiral Vern Clark was a contender for CNO.

When we arrived, the first person I saw was Melody Somers, protocol officer for Kings Bay and she was with RADM Terpstra's aide. They both look troubled. In fact, so many of them had such a troubled look that I was actually afraid that something had happened to one of the sailors. My mind is very active and I wondered if someone had been hurt or killed that day. I asked, "What's wrong?" They hesitated and I pushed. "Something terrible has happened, tell me." To learn the rest of that story, read Rear Admiral Rich Terpstra's story.

I was surprised when Admiral Clark said, "Sheila, it's good to finally meet you. I've heard a lot of good things about you." That made me speechless. He was in the surface community, so while I had heard of him—after all, he was a four-star admiral—I had never met him. I'm sure that Rich Terpstra filled them in before we were introduced. The military is great about that. I suppose it comes from those short tours and the fact that everyone must be up to speed in short time and ready to command and improve in two years. You must have good turnover and support. You also learn how to make friends easy… and part of the turnover is a good description of the community leaders and who can be depended on and relied upon.

At dinner, we are told that Admiral Clark had just received word that he would be the next chief of Naval Operations. *Wow!* What news! And how fortunate we were to be a part of that night.

Over the next few years I saw a lot of the Clarks. As vice president of legislative affairs, I saw him at many Capitol Hill, Navy League, and Navy Memorial events. When I ran for president in 2000, I would not involve him in any way and I think he always appreciated that.

I've talked about the night of my election and the Clark's attendance. What I didn't cover, was his speech that night in November 2003. He was the guest speaker that evening. When he got up to speak he said in that very distinct voice that I loved to hear: "Someone told me tonight that Sheila's a woman." He turned and looked at me with a tip of the head and said, "Well, so she is." And that was his attitude for the next two years. Well, maybe not so true. I know he heard of some of the difficulty I had during the campaign, and I believe he was determined to help me take the Navy League where it should be.

My mother was present that evening and I took her over to meet the Clarks. They told me at her table when they asked about the introduction and asked her if she knew who he was she replied, "Oh, some admiral friend of Sheila's." Mother was very pleased over the next two years when she could tell me she saw Admiral Clark on television!

Shortly after my installation in June in Hawaii, I had a call from Admiral Clark. When I answered the phone, a man with a deep voice said, "Sheila, this is Vern, do you have a few minutes?"

"I know who you are and you are not funny. You guys have to stop doing this." I thought he was Bill Dawson from Brunswick being funny because of my new job.

"No, seriously, it's Vern." This time there was no question—I did recognize the voice and it was Vern!

"Oh my, sir, I am so sorry. So many of my friends, even military friends, have called saying they were the CNO, the president, and any number of celebrities. I thought it was another friend teasing me."

We talked for a good while. He told me how important it was that we keep in touch—that I knew the Navy message. He asked me to call him every time I was about to travel so he could bring me up to date. Of course, I ended up traveling some of forty-six out of fifty-two weeks the next two years so I didn't take him up on every trip. He did give me his private numbers and urged me to stay in touch and we discussed an office call in the new future. My story on the Clarks began with the use of one of those numbers!

A few months after I became president, the Clarks invited us to dinner at Tingy house. It took weeks to work it out. With his commitments and mine it wasn't easy, but it was something we really wanted to do. Dinner at the CNO's quarters at the Navy yard was a really big deal. The fact that we loved the Clarks was just icing on the cake.

We arrived that night with the house aglow and shining with lights and candles. It was beautiful, and our reception was akin to that of visiting royalty. There was just the four of us and a chief petty officer who played the guitar beautifully. He was excellent, and this was a first for us to have someone serenade us while having a wonderful dinner. After dinner, we began talking. Arlie and Connie have a real love for gospel music, and they talked about their passion about the same groups. She was so easy to talk to and so approachable to everyone—no matter what their title or rank was. Everyone loved Connie Clark.

We talked about our travels. They had just come home from a trip to Western Pacific. I know they were exhausted, but they never indicated they were. I reminded them that I would need a cab soon and asked about when I should call. Vern sort of tossed me off and said we'll worry about that later, I was fascinated by the schedule of the military officer who had the responsibilities of an entire Navy. One who had meetings with President Bush and Secretary Rumsfeld on a regular basis. I could have sat there all night, but I was concerned we were going to wear out our welcome. I asked where the phone was located so I could call a taxi. He brushed me off again and I asked if one of the CSs (culinary specialists) could call for me. At that time, he said, 'Sheila, everyone has gone home. I'm going to take you back to the hotel."

There was no arguing with that. I didn't want to go and evidently, he and Connie were not interested in us leaving, so we talked some more. It was the most unforgettable evening. We exchanged confidences and told all our stories to each other that night. Connie then said, "Vern, it's midnight. You have to let Sheila go home. And I have got to get to bed!" I remembered they had just returned from the Western Pacific two nights before. So we agreed the night had to end. Vern went out back to get the car, and Connie, Arlie, and I waited at the front of the house.

When we got in, I asked, "How long has it been since you've driven?

"Years," he replied and took off.

As we are sitting in the back seat—me sitting up a little so I could advise him and do a little back seat driving to help this man, who had not driven in a year, to navigate—I had to think to myself, *I'll never forget this evening. Who* would find themselves driving through beautiful DC at midnight with the chief of Naval Operations chauffeuring you. What an evening. We made it safely and we still consider it one of the best nights in our lives.

April 22, 2004
Dear Admiral and Connie,

I know what an effort it must have been to participate in our Sea Air Space Exposition after your busy week at the flag conference. However, it was truly appreciated by the Navy League.

My Navy League duties took me to New Jersey this past weekend where three gentlemen picked me up at the airport. As frequently happens, the conversation turned to the CNO, and I want to pass on a great compliment. One was telling the other about your remarks in November at the Navy League winter meeting. He said, "there must have been 600 at the banquet and Admiral Clark walked around the room talking to everyone. When we left every single one of us felt like they had met Vern Clark."

That is the way the attendees felt at SAS. I am indebted to you for your generous support. Your decision to schedule the flag conference at the time nearly doubled our flag attendance at the Banquet. Additionally, Admirals Balisle, Cohen, Dawson, Keating, Massenburg, Moore, and Nathman gave outstanding presentations at our SAS seminars. I have been so pleased with the many positive remarks I have received about the seminars and SAS in general.

Thank you both for your visible support of the Navy League and me personally. You make my work so much easier. Connie, you are such an asset to the Navy and to our country. How you manage to always be so gracious when, so many want your time is amazing.

I'm approaching the halfway mark of my term. Steve and I will begin my second year with roll-outs of our education and public affairs initiatives. We'll be calling your staff for an appointment to brief you on these programs. Arlie joins me in warm regards to both of you.

Sheila

I probably introduced him six to eight times over the next two years. RADM Steve Petropolis was particularly good at writing—as you would expect from a former chief of information for the Navy. The only problem is Steve liked to live on the edge. He rarely gave me an introduction ahead of time. Sea Air Space was the worse. I probably had a dozen introductions and changes constantly, so I learned to roll with it. As Steve said, "Don't you want a current introduction? Things change quickly around here." And then he would give me that smile.

On November 23, 2004, Vern sent the following letter:

Dear Sheila

Thank you for the opportunity to speak at the Navy League's annual Winter Dinner this past Saturday. It was fantastic to spend the evening with our most staunch advocates.

In your October 18 letter to Secretary Rumsfeld, you wrote of the Navy League responding to his call for "getting the word out on all the progress being made very day in Iraq." I want to personally thank you and the League for all you have done to support our Navy men and women who serve in Iraq and around the world. I am especially grateful to the League councils that have recognized Sailors returning home from deployed operations, many in support of the Global War on Terrorism. Your persuasive advocacy for the U.S. Navy in foreign nations continues to strengthen our partnerships with friends and allies and contributes to the maritime dominance that will lead to victory over terrorism.

On behalf of those whom the Navy League has served for more than 100 years, please accept my deepest appreciation for your continuing support of our Navy men and women.

Sincerely,
Vern

Admiral Clark was speaking two of three times during my last Sea Air Space in April 2005.

I started reading the introduction. It was good. It was smooth. I loved the words as I read them. I turned the page. There was nothing there. Had I been speaking off the cuff or reading my own words or thoughts I would not have had a problem winging it. With Steve's very eloquent words I stopped. I had no ad-lib. I had no words. "Screw it," I said. "Please help me welcome the chief of Naval Operations, Admiral Vern Clark."

The room erupted, and Vern took the microphone with a big smile and no comment. The introduction the next day went smoothly and Vern said, "Well, Sheila, you made it all the way through that."

Someone sent me a copy of his remarks that evening and I want to share them.

> *I want to say a little about Sheila before I go on. Sheila and I are marching toward dates of finality here this summer and as I understand it this will take place in June down in Norfolk. And Sheila, I so appreciate you talking about my association with the Navy League. This relationship is very important to me. What I want to say about you, is you have done a magnificent job as the national president of the United States Navy League. I shouldn't say, "have done." You are doing. And it's important the role of a leader obviously is very important. I remember I was there the night that the election took place. And this was, I shared with other audiences before, that it was an evening when I headed for the event I didn't know exactly what was going to happen because both parties that were running for office are very close friends of mine. And the best of all things is going to happen because John Panneton is going to take her place. And John's a great friend. But Sheila, we're just so impressed with the leadership role that you have—and the way that you have played your leadership role. And you have really set the bar high. And John, all I'd say to you is... a big set of shoes to fill. Figuratively, not literally. John, we have every expectation that you're going to build upon what Sheila has done and that's what we do in our country. And we congratulate you on the future that's ahead of you but to both of you and to Sheila especially, as you move toward the closing months of this time of service to the sea services, please know how much those of us in uniform appreciate what this institution is about and most especially what you have done in leading this great institution. Thank you very, very much.*

This was reported in *Seapower* at that same Sea Air Space:

> *Speaking at the exposition for the fifth time during his tenure as CNO, Clark thanked the Navy League and national president Sheila M. McNeill for their continuing support. "Our Sailors, and for that matter our Marines, Airman, Soldiers and Coast Guard are watching the way Americans are responding to their labors representing this country in the far corners of this earth," he said. "Your message is unequivocal. Your message has sent them a clear indication that you support and believe in the sons and daughters of America."*

He was such an eloquent speaker. Arlie just loved to hear him talk. He was fascinated that he could leave the podium, walk around, and capture the audience. He remains one of the best speakers I've ever heard.

Note: The Navy League was honoring Adm. Gary Roughead (see his story) at a Navy League meeting in DC in 2012. Adm. Vern Clark and former SECNAV Gordon England were there to honor him. They both took me aside and Vern said, "Do you know we both gave you complete access when you were president? We told our staffs when you called they were to try to take the appointment at the time you wanted to meet even if it meant adjusting the schedule?"

"No, I had no idea. Come to think of it I never had a problem getting in to see either of you but I didn't call often."

"We know you were busy traveling," one of them replied.

"Yes, we know and that is the reason our schedulers knew to arrange our schedule, whenever possible, to work with you when you wanted to meet," they told me.

Darn, I wish I'd have known that then, but they sure made my tour as national president so much easier.

UNITED STATES SENATOR MAX CLELAND

The DC plane kept dropping and then picking up altitude. I was exhausted and sleeping during the extreme turbulence. The man sitting next to me, wrapped up his coat and put it on my shoulder to brace my head. That made me almost wake up, but the plane seemed to be rocking me to sleep.

Finally, he said, "Listen lady, this plane could crash any minute and we could all be dead. I think you should be awake for that." That woke me up! We talked for the rest of the flight as the plane continued to dip and dive. The year was 1972 and he was Georgia state senator Max Cleland. He was on the way to Sea Island to speak. We really connected that evening—once I realized we were circling the airport for the fourth or fifth time and were about to have to land at another airport due to the weather I started to take notice. At the airport, my husband and daughter were told, "They can't see anything in this weather. We are going to have it circle one more time, and if they can't land, they will go to South Carolina." We landed safely, and I introduced Max to my husband, Arlie, and daughter, Leslie. We offered to take him to Sea Island, which he accepted, so we could finish our conversation. That began a friendship that would last a lifetime.

We kept in touch as he progressed in his political career. When Senator Sam Nunn retired, Max ran for the job in 1996 and won. Here he was, a United States senator—against all odds. He was injured in Vietnam in 1968. His story is told in his first book *Strong at the Broken Places.*

It reads,

> *I called to the pilot that I was getting out. He nodded and held the ship steady. I jumped to the ground, ran in a crouch until I got clear of the spinning helicopter blades, turned around and watched the chopper lift. Then I saw the grenade. It was where the chopper had lifted off. It must be mine, I thought. Grenades had fallen off my web gear before. Shifting the M-16 to my left hand and holding it behind me, I bent down to pick up the grenade. A blinding explosion threw me backwards.*
>
> *The blast jammed my eyeballs back into my skull, temporarily blinding me, pinning my cheeks and jaw muscles to the bones of my face. My ears rang with a deafening reverberation as if I were standing in an echo chamber. Memory of the firecracker exploding in my hand as a child flashed before me. When my eyes cleared, I looked at my right hand. It was gone. Nothing but a splintered white bone protruded from my shredded elbow. It was speckled with fragments of bloody flesh. Nausea flooded me. I lay where the blast had flung me for a moment, fighting for breath. I found myself slumped on the ground.*
>
> *Then I tried to stand but couldn't. I looked down. My right leg and knee were gone. My left leg was a soggy mass of bloody flesh mixed with green fatigue cloth. The combat boot dangled awkwardly, like the smashed legs on the dead soldier after the rocket attack.*
>
> *What was left of me? I reached with my left hand to feel my head. My steel helmet—now gone—had apparently protected it. My flak jacket had shielded my chest and groin from shrapnel. Intense pain throbbed my body with each heartbeat.*

A few years after we met Max, a gentleman approached Arlie on St. Simons on Memorial Day. "Aren't you a friend of Senator Cleland?" he asked.

"Yes, my wife and I are good friends," Arlie answered.

"I was a chaplain in Vietnam and was called in to give last rites for Lt. Cleland. I didn't think he would last the night. The next day I went back and asked about him. They said they thought he was going to make it. I never saw him again."

We were thrilled to be invited to his swearing in ceremony in DC on January 7, 1997. The ceremony was held in the Dirksen Senate Office building and everyone had lunch afterward. It was a very special day for all of us to be able to share it with Max.

Obviously, as a veteran, Max was very knowledgeable and supportive of the military. In fact, I was with him on St. Simons at a democratic fund-raiser in his early years in the US Senate, when one of the women present approached us. "Well, Sheila, I'm so pleased to learn you are a Democrat. None of us knew what your affiliation was." I hesitated. Because of my work with the military, I had always tried to be neutral. I wanted to be able to talk to those on both sides of the aisle when it came to military issues. Max quickly responded, "Sheila is not a Democrat, she is not a Republican. As long as I support the military, she will support me." What a class act he was!

On June 26, 1998, Max was the keynote speaker for the twentieth anniversary of Naval Submarine Base Kings Bay. I was frequently in his office. Later, when I became national vice president for legislative affairs and I used his office for a rest stop. I could stop by, take my shoes off, lie on the couch for fifteen minutes, and was ready to go again.

In June 1997, at the request of Dr. Dorothy Lord, president of the Coastal College of Georgia, I asked him to speak at a commencement of the current graduating class. He agreed, and Arlie and I picked him up in my black Lincoln with flags on each side of the fender. He did a tremendous job. But as usual, everyone wants to talk with him. We had to push him to wrap it up, so we could get him to the airport. He hadn't had a chance to eat and was really looking forward to fried shrimp. So I called Spanky's, a local restaurant famous for their fried shrimp. When we drove up they brought it out very quickly. Max thanked them for being so kind. The young man, Jeff Maloy, son of my oldest and dearest friend Lynn Warwick, said, "Oh, you are welcome! We'd do that for Mrs. McNeill anytime." That got a big laugh from everyone.

The November 1998 *George* magazine featured a story on Max. He looked quite handsome and distinguished!

Another visit was to speak at Naval Submarine Base Kings Bay at our Camden Kings Bay Navy League Council. He was accompanied by Captain Barry Costello. They landed in Jacksonville and drove to the base. I was waiting for them at the base hotel, Navy Gateway Inn and Suites. The rest of that story is told in Rear Admiral Costello's stories.

We had dinner in DC many times. I remember almost every time as we were riding in the cab I would take his hand and massage it as we talked. I can't remember how I started, but he told me one of the hardest things was not being able to do was to massage one hand with another. He was amazing and funny and frustrating at times. Once I had a call from his staff wanting to know when I was coming to go out to dinner. He was being ornery and needed to relax. The next week, I called him and told him I was taking him to dinner at the Ritz. Due to my friendship with Horst Shultzy, original owner of the Ritz-Carlton, I was able to stay at the Ritz for the same amount I was paying for a hotel close to the Navy League headquarters.

"Hey, when do you have a free night next week? I want to take you to the Ritz."

"I don't want to go to the Ritz—I want to go somewhere for a grilled cheese sandwich."

"Well, you can get that at the Ritz."

He grumbled but met me there. I spoke to the chef earlier and told him what Max wanted. When we settled down the chef came over and described the combination of cheeses and all the ingredients he had planned for that grilled cheese sandwich.

"I want an American cheese sandwich grilled."

"I'd like to have your special grilled cheese," I told the chef.

He was grumpy, and I called him on it. He came back at me—with the first curse words I'd heard from him.

"Are we having our first argument?" I asked.

At that point, he laughed and became "good" Max again.

Many times, we went to a local diner, one of those shaped liked the old diners and read the paper, ate and had little conversation. Just both of us chilling out and enjoying the company.

One day I stopped by and Max looked devastated. I went into his office and sat down.

"What's wrong, you look terrible."

"I just found out the grenade that hit me was not mine. It was one of the others who jumped with me that day. I always thought it was mine and I was responsible." The man had come by his office that day—I think knowing it was not his made it a little easier to bear.

Another of the times we were meeting for dinner Max called.

"Would you mind if someone comes with us tonight?"

"Of course not, who is it?"

"JR."

"J. R. Miller from Brunswick?"

"No, J. R. Ewing from *Dallas*."

"Well, it should be interesting," I replied.

The cab stopped for me and we went to his hotel and picked up Larry Hagman. We went to one of my favorite places in DC, the Capitol Grill. The restaurant was packed but they had a table for us. People kept coming up to meet Max and didn't pay much attention to who he was with. I ordered my usual scotch and knew that Max did not drink any alcoholic beverages, but Larry, too, declined.

I asked, "Am I the only one drinking?"

Larry answered, "You know I can't drink anymore."

"No, how would I know that?"

"You don't know about my kidney transplant, I had liver cancer?" As I shook my head, he started laughing. "It is nice to know not everyone reads the tabloids." We talked about his health, his short time in the Air Force, his mother, Mary Martin—a famous Broadway star—and his good friends Carroll O'Connor (*All in the Family*) and Burgess Meredith. He was going hunting with one of them the following week. But most of all, we talked about submarines. He was fascinated.

Max kept introducing us and we just kept eating and talking as people kept interrupting him. Larry leaned over and said, "They really don't give a shit who we are. They only want to meet and talk with Max." *Dallas* was the number one show on television, and DC didn't care. Larry seemed to really enjoy the privacy.

In 2000, Max was working to pass a greatly expanded GI Bill. His office called me about an interview with a reporter from associated press. I know how much Max supported our veterans and we always agreed on these issues. In fact, the article coving this issue in the *Macon Telegraph* and other papers had this quote:

> *"The military wants the time and resources to do their jobs, and they want their families taken care of," said Sheila McNeill, national vice president of the Navy League. "I think this would send a message to our military families that would be very positive."*

Camden County started their DC fly-ins in 1996—the first year Max took office following Sam's retirement. When we got to his office, he would always call me Admiral and make sure I had the place next to him. Years later, others picked that up. I always considered it a term of endearment, but a few others made it an issue.

Lobbying for the SSGN is covered in another chapter, but Senator Cleland was a big part of that. It was not an easy issue—funding was limited. "Big" Navy wanted to see the future destroyer known as the DDX—Max and I with many others were lobbying to fund the SSGN. We were at a Capitol Hill reception and Admiral Clark was across the room. Max told me he wanted to meet him. As others were talking to Max, I went over to Admiral Clark and asked him if he'd come over to meet the Senator. When we approached him, Max said, "Sir, I want you to know that as soon as Sheila briefed me on SSGN, I started working on it."

Admiral Clark smiled at me and responded, "We appreciate that." Max had a striking article in the new *George* magazine in November 1998.

In June 2000, Max was interviewed by the *Macon Telegraph* about the Senate vote to greatly expand the GI Bill:

> *"Washington—to expand the Montgomery GI Bill as a retention tool, the Senate Thursday approved a measure allowing military personnel to transfer unused educational stipends to spouses and children. The amendment proposed by Sen. Max Cleland, D-Ga, is an attempt to keep key workers who might otherwise be tempted to leave the armed services for high-paying jobs. The House rejected a similar proposal last year, but Cleland believes he might have the votes this time. "We've increased pay, increased retirement benefits, but we need to use the GI Bill as a retention tool." Cleland said. "What is happening now is that the military is basically married, so when these careerists get to that eight—to 10-year mark, they don't need the benefits anymore. We need to recruit a soldier but retain a family." He must have steered them my way. I told them, "The military wants the time and resources to do their jobs, and they want their families taken care of," said Sheila McNeill, national vice president of the Navy League. "I think this would send a message to our military families that would be very positive."*

When I was on the cover of Georgia Trend Max sent me a lovely note:

> *Dear "Admiral McNeill," The title suits you wonderfully! What a fantastic article in the July Georgia Trend. I am so proud of you and our friendship. Godspeed, Most respectfully, Max*

By the way—he should like my nickname—he started it!

COAST GUARD COMMUNITY—AMERICA'S FIRST

Commandant Admiral Robert J. Papp's Visit: March 16, 2012
America's First Coast Guard Community Application Submitted: August 14, 2012
Designation Approved: January 2014
Event—Celebrating the Designation with RADM Poulin: April 25, 2014
Event—Community Picnic: May 21, 2014
Department of Transportation Celebration: October 26, 2015

We were designated the first Coast Guard Community in the Nation.

When I was traveling as president of the Navy League, I was impressed by the cities who had the designation as a Coast Guard City. We now have Coast Guard in Camden County, so I wanted to apply… but Coast Guard City? How could we with three towns have such a designation? We were a community. I talked with Admiral Papp and warned him that I was going to apply for Coast Guard Community. He told me there was not such a designation.

The application is extensive. It took weeks to put everything together. The application is first approved (or denied) by Coast Guard headquarters then it goes to Congress to every committee who has oversight over the Coast Guard. Completing the application took months. The package was completed and mailed on August 13, 2012:

Community Relations Division, Coast Guard Public Affairs
Office of the Commandant (CG-09223)
United States Coast Guard Headquarters
Ms. Deborah Claiborne

Dear Ms. Claiborne

St. Marys, Kingsland, Woodbine and in fact all of Camden County are asking for your consideration to be designated as a "Coast Guard Community." Adm. Robert Papp was the speaker for The Camden Partnership and Camden Kings Bay Navy League Council's Community that Cares Luncheon. We advised him of our wishes and received encouragement to apply. You will find in the package letters from the following individuals:

- *Mayor of St. Marys, William T. DeLoughy*
- *Mayor of Kingsland, Kenneth Smith*
- *Mayor of Woodbine, Steve Parrott*
- *Board of Commissioners Chairman, David L. Rainer*
- *President of the Camden County Chamber of Commerce, Christine Daniel*
- *Director of Brenau University, Robert L. North, Sr., Ed.D.*
- *Executive Director of United Way of Camden County, Christi Gallagher*
- *Superintendent of Schools, William C. Hardin, Ed. D*
- *South Atlantic Coast Region President, Navy League, David J. Reilly*
- *Georgia Area President, Navy League, Keith F. Post*
- *Camden Kings Bay Council President, Hunt Thornhill*

You will find that we are a community that loves our Coast Guard. I have made copies of various events where the Coast Guard was featured, supported in their efforts, and partnered with us to the get their message out. These include:

- *The Maritime Safety and Security Team 91108 was commissioned on October 6, 2003 after fierce advocacy from the community to bring the unit to Camden. Several local individuals were part of the program.*
- *The Maritime Force Protection Unit was welcomed in 2007 as a result of new regulations in the protection of our Trident submarines*
- *The commissioning of the USCGC Sea Dog was in July 2009 with tremendous community involvement. Even to the extent of involving a famous cartoonist, Jack Davis, to create a picture of the Georgia Bull Dog on the ship.*
- *The commissioning of the USCGC Sea Dragon in January 2008*
- *Each year the Camden Kings Bay Council hosts our top Coasties, Sailors and Marines at a banquet that rivals the Academy Awards.*
- *Because of our wonderful relationship with the Coast Guard leadership we have been honored to be present at various unit awards. We always feel honored as civilians to be a part of these events at the units.*
- *Every retirement and change of command finds locals proud to be in attendance*
- *The Coast Guard birthday is always supported by the Navy League and the community*
- *The Camden Partnership, The Navy League, Rotary, Kiwanis have all featured Coast Guard speakers*
- *The Camden Partnership has hosted two of the Coast Guard Commandants for a community wide event involving all cities, all civic clubs and individual citizens for A Community That Cares.*
- *The Camden Kings Bay Council of the Navy League adopted the MSST in January 2012 although this kind of support had been evident from the beginning.*
- *Visitors coming to the area will see a poster with the letters EDICCIMAD which stands for Every Day In Camden*

County is Military Appreciation Day. This is not a slogan it's a way of life!

- *The Chamber sponsors a military member at every month's Business After Hours*
- *The Chamber sponsors an annual D.C. FLY IN and Atlanta FLY IN and The Camden Partnership prepares and briefs Coast Guard Issues.*
- *When the community learned that the Coast Guard budget was being reduced by $300 Million that would eliminate the MSST 91108 we went to work. We sent letters to POTUS, Secretary of Homeland Security, congressional chairs and others. The state and the county did a resolution asking for the restoration. Our congressional delegation wrote letters—in a time when "earmarks" were a political negative but they were convinced that these were not "earmarks." I visited 206 congressional offices and briefed all but 15 as well as all congressional committees that had oversight over the Coast Guard. Our MSST 91108 was never mentioned. We lobbied for the Coast Guard and the entire loss. That budget was restored, and we like to think we had a part. The Coast Guard was foremost in everyone's thoughts and actions for months.*

I have also included a Memorandum from CDR Steve Love, Subject: Solicitation for American Legion Spirit of Service Award on D.C.2 Tyler Arrowood. While this outstanding sailor's dedication is his alone and is extraordinary I'd like to point out that this community embraces our Coast Guard men and women—in our churches, in our school activities and in our civic clubs. We are the winners with the support the community receives but I believe that this meshing of the community with our military results in a better quality of life for both the service member and the community. By embracing them early on their families are a part of our families and our desire to always make this a better community. CDR Steve Love and LCDR Matt Baer have joined the prior Commanding Officers as integral parts of our community.

This is just a sampling of our support. I hope this, and the attached articles convince you of the fact that WE ARE A COAST GUARD COMMUNITY already. However, receiving this formal designation will be tangible evidence of the longstanding and endur-

ing relationships which have already been forged and which will continue to grow in the years ahead.

Respectfully,
Sheila M. McNeill President, The Camden Partnership
Former National President Navy League of the United States

I wrote a column for the *Tribune & Georgian*:

Seeking recognition as a "Coast Guard Community"

Recently we celebrated the 10th anniversary of the Maritime Safety and Security Team in Camden County. It was a wonderful tribute to our Coast Guard.

It wasn't that long ago that seeing the Coast Guard uniform in our community was a rarity. With the creation of the MSST and shortly thereafter the establishment of the Maritime Force Protection Unit (MFPU) at Kings Bay, the Coast Guard has had a strong presence and tremendous impact on our community. MFPU Kings Bay became operational in July 2007. Along with MFPU Bangor, the two MFPU's were conceived to support the Coast Guard's mission of protecting our strategic submarines entering and leaving their respective bases. They are single mission units fully funded by the Navy.

One of the reasons for the assignment of this escort duty is because the Navy or, for that matter, the civilian contractors do not have law enforcement capabilities. Federal statue gives the Coast Guard the authority to prosecute violators of federal laws and make arrests if necessary. The Coast Guard historically has enforced U.S. maritime law, dating to the late 1700s when the Revenue Cutter Service enforced tariff and trade rules. As the only federal military service to reside outside the Defense Department, it is not restricted to conduct law enforcement operations by the Posse Comitatus Act. This act prohibits the Army and Air Force from engaging directly in law enforcement. (The Navy and Marine Corps comply with this act by Defense Department directive.) As a personal observation, the addition of the MFPU adds a safety factor also. I'm sure boaters and fishermen are excited about seeing one of these huge beautiful ships as they leave for sea and the Coast Guard's law enforcement ensures that they move quickly to avoid any obstruction. Thus, the MFPU team is a team of vigilant guardians who provide this fleet security, deterrence by presence, protection by escort, defense by force, and terrorism prevention through strategic partnerships.

Vice Admiral Brian Peterman, then Commander of the Coast Guard's Atlantic Area and one of the keynote speakers said at the commissioning ceremony, "this is a unit ready for initial operations. This is a new and unique mission. It's a great day for the Coast Guard." Preparations for this unit included 10,000 training hours for the Coast Guard personnel assigned to MFPU. Many of you remember the commissioning of the two 87' Coast Guard cutters, SEA DRAGON and SEA DOG. Keith Post was commissioning chairman for both of these cutters and did an incredible job. The unit also has six 33' Special Purpose Craft—Law Enforcement vessels and six 64' Special Purpose Craft—Screening vessels, all new platforms in support of this great mission.

CDR Stephen Love and his Executive Officer, LCDR Tom Evans, have continued the tradition of involvement in this great community. They are familiar faces at many of our Navy League meetings and other events. CDR Love and his team of approximately 150 personnel recently received the prestigious Kimball Award for readiness and standardization excellence. The Maritime Safety and Security Team Kings Bay (MSST 91108) was the first Coast Guard unit in Camden County and has a completely different mission and, in fact, has an entirely different chain of command. They, too, were a new mission for the Coast Guard when they came to Camden County in 2003.

The Maritime Safety and Security Teams were established to bolster the Coast Guard's ability to protect this country's shores from any threats and to respond to specific episodic events requiring an increased security posture for a limited duration. They are capable of deploying personnel and equipment on short notice via air or ground. MSST 91108 also exercises security contingency plans in major ports and augment Coast Guard and Captain of the Port capabilities in Georgia and Florida.

Our unit in St. Marys has the designation of 91108. The 911 is for the day the World Trade Center and the Pentagon were attacked by terrorist and 08 is the 8th unit commissioned. The Coast Guard evacuated over 2,000 people that day in New York and the Maritime Safety and Security Teams were created as a result of that horrific terrorist attack. When we heard of this new mission being formed we let it be known that Camden County wanted a MSST in our community. We were thrilled when we received the call that

MSST 91108 would be located in St. Marys, we were thrilled when the announcement came out that brought to our community a great group of 85 professionally trained men and women.

LCDR Matt Baer is Commanding Officer of this unit and his Executive Office is LCDR Ron Nokamota. They, too have become a part of the community participating in our parades and school's adoptions and familiar faces at our meetings. As a rare fact, the MSST is also a recipient of the Kimball Award—a two-time award recipient and very impressive for a unit to excel at Coast Guard small boat operations, readiness and standardization when primarily used as a deployable force.

On February 2, 2010, we had quite a shock when we were told that this unit would be decommissioned. Keith Post and I were invited to sit in on an announcement from an admiral from headquarters. It was a stunning announcement. MSST 91108 was being decommissioned. I quickly went to D.C. to find out why this was happening. We found that the Coast Guard in response to a budget reduction for FY11 stated they would decommission five of the 12 Maritime Safety and Security teams. Teams that were established after the 9/11 terrorist attacks in response to heightened security levels.

The current threat assessment is a constant concern. This was the wrong time to be reducing five of these anti-terror units. The number of MSSTs should remain at 12 we said. And that was not all. 1112 full time Coast Guard positions would be eliminated, the Coast Guard's operating expenses would be reduced, and three cutters would be decommissioned without replacement. The budget would be reduced by approximately $300 Million.

We went to work writing everyone from President Obama, the Secretary of Homeland Security, our legislators and everyone in between. Our State House and Senate as well as all our cities and count's entire bodies voted in proclamations in support of the entire Coast Guard Budget—not just our MSST 91108. I went to Washington and called on every committee that had oversight over the Coast Guard and 210 congressional offices. I found that there is a deep respect for our Coast Guard. 205 of the 210 sat down with us when they were told that we were there to talk about the United States Coast Guard. We told them what was happening. We also told them that in addition to the operational and support capability that would suffer, the reduction in Coast Guard positions were a mistake. These military positions offer the best return on investment in personnel that this country has. Our military personnel are, by definition, on duty 24 hours a day 7 days a week. This is how they can rapidly respond to national and man-made disasters. These are jobs that matter. We requested the same level of service of the Coast Guard be maintained in the 2011 budget, and that there be a true augmentation of funds and no reapportionment of the already scarce funds be made. The future of our Coast Guard and the security of our nation depend on it.

With our help and many others, the entire Coast Guard budget was reinstated. I don't expect that to be our last fight. We recognize the value of the Coast Guard but as we know these are difficult budget times.

Camden County has had a decade with hundreds of our Coast Guardsmen and women and their families who have lived in our community, taken their children to our schools, attended our churches and have made such an impact in our community. These men and women bring a spirit of professionalism, pride and community involvement that enriches our lives.

When I was National President of the Navy League I was always impressed by those cities that were designated as "Coast Guard Cities." They stood out in their support of the Coast Guard and as a Coast Guard fan I thought it would be wonderful to have that kind of recognition. In 2012 after Commandant, Adm. Robert Papp's visit to speak at our Community that Cares event, I realized that now we are one of those Coast Guard Communities! We have shown and continue to show unprecedented support to our Coast Guard units. So, we applied for this designation. It was not easy. There has never been a Coast Guard Community—the designation only covers a city. But with our three supporting cities we couldn't have that! So, we have this additional hurdle to overcome. The paperwork involved is intensive—everything had to be documented.

After several months, the application was finished and sent to the Coast Guard. First, it has to have approval from the Coast Guard itself. Then it must go through the congressional committees who have oversight over the Coast Guard for approval.

We passed the first hurdle. A letter from Admiral Papp, said, "In accordance with Public Law 105-383, Section 409, my letters to the committees start a 90-day congressional notification period. If there is no objection from Congress, it will be my pleasure to sign a proclamation designating Camden County as "A Coast Guard Community"

We wait with anticipation for that final approval from Congress.
February, 2014… WE MADE IT!
County honored by Coast Guard

The Camden Partnership
By Sheila McNeill

The county of Camden and its cities, St. Marys, Kingsland and Woodbine, have received word that they have been approved for the designation as a Coast Guard Community. The designation, endorsed by Congressional committees which have oversight over the Coast Guard and approved by Coast Guard headquarters, Washington, D.C., is made to recognize the outstanding support the community provides to the Coast Guard, its personnel and their families. Camden County and its cities now join 15 other cities throughout the nation to be designated, but Camden the first to be designated a "community."

The Coast Guard plays a critical role in the safety and well-being of Camden County's residents with almost 300 Coast Guard personnel located throughout the community. The two units in Camden County are the Maritime Force Protection Unit, a vital element in the protection of the Navy assets on board Naval Submarine Base Kings Bay, and the Maritime Safety and Security Team 91108. MSSTs were established after the 9/11 terrorist attacks in response to heightening security levels and now operate throughout the country. To support its Coast Guard members and their families, The Coast Guard Community of Camden County coordinates community recognition events, and programs. The community, with the lead of The Camden Partnership, advocated for the commissioning of Maritime Safety and Security Team 91108.

When the community learned of the Coast Guards' budget reduction, it joined forces to work together with leaders to lobby on its behalf to restore its budget. The Camden Partnership made visit to 210 congressional offices in support of restoring the Coast Guard budget.

Every year, the local Navy League honors the Coast Guard Sailor of the Year and works with the Coast Guard units in recognizing the Coast Guard birthday. The Chamber of Commerce sponsors a military member of the month. We applied for this designation 16 months ago, after Commandant Adm. Bob Papp spoke to our community. We are just thrilled that we have been approved and that the designation is for the community and not just one of the cities. We will continue to advocate for the national needs of this service which does so much to protect our homeland.

A special community feature unlike any other designated city is a motto seen throughout the county on posters with the letters EDICCIMAD, which stands for Every Day in Camden County is Military Appreciation Day. This is not a slogan it's a way of life!

The public will be invited to celebrate this prestigious honor at a luncheon on April 25th, as well as a picnic on Saturday, May 17th, at the St Marys Waterfront. There will be additional information forthcoming about these two events.

HON. JACK KINGSTON OF GEORGIA IN THE HOUSE OF REPRESENTATIVES

Mr. Speaker, I rise today to honor Camden County, GA in light of their recent designation as a Coast Guard Community. Camden is the first county in the nation to be given this distinguished distinction, as it normally only goes to cities. Camden, however, is such a great supporter of the Coast Guard, its personnel, its families and its mission that the award was given to the county as a whole.

Camden County is incredible rich in history. Founded on February 5, 1777, it is one of the oldest counties in Georgia. It was named for Charles Pratt, Earl of Camden, who was an Englishman in favor of the American Independence. Modern day Camden County includes the cities of St. Marys, Woodbine, and Kingsland and is home to the Naval Submarine Base Kings Bay. Kings Bay is the Atlantic Fleet's home port for U.S. Navy's ballistic missile nuclear submarines, the Ohio-class. It is also home to Cumberland Island National Seashore, a National Wilderness Area.

With this honor, Camden County and its cities join 15 other cities to earn this designation, but Camden is the only one to be labeled a Community. The designation was supported by the congressional committees that oversee the Coast Guard and the Coast Guard headquarters in Washington, D.C. The Coast Guard plays a major role in insuring the safety and security of Camden County and The Georgia Coast. Two teams are stationed in Camden County: the Maritime Force Protection Union, which protects assets at Kings Bay, and the Maritime Safety and Security Team 91108, which was established following the 9/11 attacks.

This honor would not have been possible without the strong support of many groups in Camden county. The Camden Partnership which was created to support Navy, Marine Corps and Coast Guard members in Camden, made visits to 210 congressional offices to support restoring the Coast Guard budget when the group faced budget cuts. The Coast Guard Community of Camden organizes events and programs in support of Coast Guard members and families. The local Navy League awards its Coast Guard Sailor of the Year, and the Chamber of Commerce supports a military member of the month.

Camden County is a proud community and a model for the nation. I consider myself fortunate to represent such an incredible group of people, and I am thankful for the hard work and tireless dedication they display for the men and women who protect us.

Jack Kingston GA-1

FOR IMMEDIATE RELEASE
February 11, 2014
Contact: Sheila McNeill
The Camden Partnership

Camden County and Its Cities Designated a "Coast Guard Community"

The county of Camden and its cities—St. Marys, Kingsland, and Woodbine, Georgia—have received word that they have been approved for the designation as a "Coast Guard Community." The designation, endorsed by congressional committees who have oversight over the Coast Guard and the approval by Coast Guard headquarters, Washington, DC, is made to recognize the outstanding support the community provides to the Coast Guard its personnel and their families. Camden County and its cities now join fifteen other cities throughout the nation to be designated but is the first to be designated a "community."

The Coast Guard plays a critical role in the safety and wellbeing of Camden County's residents with almost three hundred Coast Guard personnel located throughout the community. The two units in Camden County are the Maritime Force Protection Unit (MFPU), vital elements in the protection of the US Navy assets located aboard Naval Submarine Base Kings Bay and the Maritime Safety and Security Team 91108 (MSST) which were established after the 9/11 terrorist attacks in response to heightened security levels and operate throughout the country.

To support its Coast Guard military and their families, the Coast Guard Community of Camden County, coordinates community recognition events, and programs. The community with the lead of The Camden Partnership advocated for the commissioning of Maritime Safety and Security Team 91108. With the lead of the Navy League, they were responsible for the commissioning of the USCGC *Sea Dog* and *Sea Dragon*. When the community learned of the Coast Guard's budget reduction, it joined forces to work together with leaders to lobby on its behalf to restore its budget. The Camden Partnership made visit to 210 congressional offices in support of restoring the Coast Guard budget. Every year the local Navy League honors the Coast Guard Sailor of the Year and works with the Coast Guard units in recognizing the Coast Guard birthday. And the Chamber of Commerce sponsors a military member of the month.

"We applied for this designation sixteen months ago after Commandant Admiral Bob Papp spoke to our community. We are just thrilled that we have been approved and that the designation is for the community and not just one of the cities. We will continue to advocate for the national needs of this service that does so much to protect our homeland," said Sheila McNeill, The Camden Partnership President and past national president of the Navy League of the U. S. A. special community feature unlike any other designated city is a motto seen throughout the county on posters with the letters EDICCIMAD, which stands for Every Day in Camden County is Military Appreciation Day. This is not a slogan it's a way of life!

The public will be invited to celebrate this prestigious honor at a luncheon on April 25 as well as a picnic on Saturday, May 17, at the St. Marys Waterfront. There will be additional information about these two events.

The Coast Guard Community luncheon was held on April 25, 2014, at Naval Submarine Base Kings Bay with Rear Admiral Steven D. Poulin, judge advocate general and chief counsel of the US Coast Guard, who called Camden County's application "a comprehensive and compelling application."

"Camden County is a community that truly cares," said Poulin, who said that Steve Love and Matt Baer "gave strong endorsements." The latter have his "unequivocal" support to Camden County's application to become a Coast Guard Community.

"By seeking the designation, you are honoring us who serve in the Coast Guard. Thank you for appreciating what we do in protecting our nations."

He presented the following proclamation:

Proclamation of the
United States Coast Guard
(USCG SEAL)

WHEREAS, the people of Camden County, Georgia, share a special and unique history with the United States Coast Guard and have provided a home for the Coast Guard since 2003, when Maritime Safety and Security Team 91108 was commissioned; and

WHEREAS, the Coast Guard presence in the county has grown and evolved, with the cultivation of a mutually supportive and beneficial relationship between local Coast Guard units and the people of Camden County; and

WHEREAS, local leaders and the community voiced support for Coast Guard units in the area when budget cuts threatened MSST 91108's future; and

WHEREAS, the local chapter of the Navy League of the United States sponsored the commissioning of the Coast Guard Cutter SEA DOG in July 2009 and Coast Guard Cutter SEA DRAGON in January 2008 and adopted the MSST in 2012; and

WHEREAS, The Camden Partnership, civic clubs and individual citizens have hosted two Coast Guard Commandants and honored servicemembers at a community-wide event titled "A Community That Cares"; and

WHEREAS, the Camden County Chamber of Commerce sponsors a military member every month at the "Business After Hours' event; and

WHEREAS, the friendliness and hospitality of the people of Camden County are reflected in the multitude of special events throughout the year and services from local businesses for Coast Guard members and their families to honor their contributions to the nation;

NOW, THEREFORE, I, ROBERT J. PAPP, Jr., Commandant of the United States Coast Guard, in accordance with Public Law 105-383 enacted by the United States Congress and signed by the President on November 13, 1998, do hereby take great pleasure in proclaiming that Camden County, Georgia, is to be known officially as "A Coast Guard Community."

IN WITNESS WHEREOF, I have hereunto set my hand this twenty third day of January, in the year of our Lord two thousand fourteen.

Robert J. Papp, Jr.
Admiral, U.S. Coast Guard Commandant

The governor of Georgia, Nathan Deal, sent a proclamation.

****

> We were pleased that Vice Admiral Bill French, Commander of Naval Installations Command, and his wife Monika were at the base that day and attending this ceremony. I do believe he was impressed by our new designation.

It was such a joy to see photos of our celebration on the Coast Guard's website with this heading:

DATE: April 28, 2014 10:57:28 AM EDT

Celebration held to recognize Camden County's designation as nation's first Coast Guard Community

Community Picnic in the Park—May 21, 2014

The community picnic was incredible. We had several hundred in attendance at the St. Marys waterfront park. It was a beautiful day and our community offered food and booths for entertainment for the children. We had free BBQ sliders and picnic fixings, along with free entertainment provided by the Navy Band. Kings Bay Division Navy League Cadets were in the serving line with ice-cold sweet tea.

As part of the celebration, attendees had the opportunity to interact with our local Coast Guard units and learn about their various weapons and gear, which were onsite for viewing. Their K-9 Explosive Detection Teams were also onsite as well as several response boats. We must have had fifty volunteers mostly under the direction of Tonya Rosado.

There was just one more thing to do. We wanted to have the Department of Transportation (DOT) place signs with our new designation on I-95 as you drive into Georgia. I quickly called Ann Purcell our representative for the DOT. In just a few weeks I was working with the graphic folks on the exact signage.

We arranged a celebration once we had a date on the signs. They agreed to put in two signs and we discussed the location. We especially wanted one as you enter Georgia so Exit 1 was a must—the other was to be at Exit 6, a busy exit that includes the high school, college, and the Center for Industry and Trade. The date for the ceremony was set at October 26, 2015.

I ran into Vice Admiral Chuck Michel at an event in DC and told him of our plans to have a ceremony for the celebration of the Department of Transportation signs with our new designation. I asked if he might come and was thrilled when he said yes!

Camden's Coast Guard signs are coming! We sent this press release:

Wednesday, October 14, 2014

AMERICA'S FIRST COAST GUARD COMMUNITY' SIGNAGE IS UNVEILED

The public is invited to a ceremony to the Unveil Georgia Department of Transportation (GDOT) signage designating Camden County Georgia as 'America's First Coast Guard Community.'

On October 26th, 2015, community leaders, Georgia Department of Transportation representatives and The Camden Partnership will come together with Coast Guard VIPs to unveil Interstate 95 signage for America's First Coast Guard Community Designation. The signs will be placed along the ramps of Exit 6 and Exit 1 on Interstate 95.

In January 2014, Camden County was officially designated as the nation's first Coast Guard Community. The Coast Guard Cities program allows the Coast Guard to formally recognize those cities which have made special efforts to acknowledge the professional work of the Coast Guard men and women assigned to their area and have made Coast Guardsmen and their families feel at home in their home away from home. While 15 other cities have been designated by Congress as Coast Guard cities, Camden County, Georgia is the first county in the nation to be named a 'Coast Guard Community.' "It was an extensive, arduous project. We began preparing the package in early 2012. Letters were written from each city and the county and many organizations. A timeline of the community's support of the USCG was documented. We sent the package off in August 2012. The first response is that we applied for a Coast Guard Community designation and that was not a program. After a few more months—in January 2014 we received the word. The program would accept both Coast Guard City and Coast Guard Community! "That was a wonderful day," explained Sheila McNeill. "We owe Ann Purcell our thanks for working with us to have approved the DOT signs which will be at Exit One and Exit Six."

Camden County comprises Kingsland, GA, St Marys, GA and Woodbine, GA and is home to Coast Guard Maritime Force Protection Unit at Kings Bay and Coast Guard Maritime Safety and Security Team in Camden County. The event will be held at 11:00 AM at the Kingsland Welcome Center located off I-95 at Exit 3, 1190 Boone Avenue in Kingsland. Dignitaries attending include VADM Charles Michel, Vice Commandant of the USCG and Ann Purcell, Department of Transportation Board Member representing the 1st district. In case of rain, the ceremony will be moved indoors to the OF Edwards Center for Industry & Commerce Building at 531 North Lee Street in Downtown Kingsland.

Vice Commandant joins Camden Partnership, GDOT for unveiling
By Lt. Cmdr. Joel Carse
Executive Officer, Maritime Force Protection Unit Kings Bay

On Oct. 26, local community leaders, Georgia Department of Transportation representatives and The Camden Partnership will come together with Coast Guard VIPs to unveil Interstate-95 signage for America's First Coast Guard Community Designation. The signs will be placed along the ramps of Exit 6 and Exit 1 on I-95. The event will be at 11 a.m. at the Kingsland Welcome Center, located off I-95 at Exit 3, 1190 Boone Ave. in Kingsland. Dignitaries attending include Vice Commandant of the USCG Vice Adm. Charles Michel and Ann Purcell, Georgia Department of Transportation Board member representing the 1st District. In case of rain, the ceremony will be moved indoors to the OF Edwards Center for Industry & Commerce Building at 531 North Lee St. in downtown Kingsland.

Camden County comprises Kingsland, St. Marys and Woodbine. It is home to more than 200 Coast Guard members from Coast Guard Maritime Force Protection Unit at Kings Bay and Coast Guard Maritime Safety and Security Team in St. Marys.

In January 2014, Camden County was officially designated as the nation's first Coast Guard Community. The Coast Guard Cities program allows the Coast Guard to formally recognize those cities which have made special efforts to acknowledge the professional work of the Coast Guard men and women assigned to their area and have made Coast Guardsmen and their families feel at home in their home away from home. While 15 cities nationwide have been designated by Congress as Coast Guard cities, Camden County is the first county in the nation to be named a Coast Guard Community.

The huge crowd in the at the Kingsland Welcome Center agreed! The following articles covers it well—we love seeing the nation's first.

Camden County honored by unique designation
America's First Coast Guard Community
By PA 2 Anthony Soto
Coast Guard Public Affairs

Community leaders officially designated Camden County as the nation's first Coast Guard community during a ceremony held in Kingsland. Many towns, municipalities, and cities across the country have been designated as official Coast Guard cities. However, Camden County is the first all-encompassing Coast Guard community. Members from the Coast Guard Cutter Sea Dog and Cutter Sea Dragon, along with members from Coast Guard Maritime Force Protection Unit, Kings Bay, and Maritime Safety and Security Team, Kings Bay, joined community leaders, Georgia Department of Transportation representatives and The Camden Partnership for the official ceremony.

Joining them were Vice Adm. Charles Michel, Vice Commandant of the Coast Guard and Ann Purcell, Georgia DOT board member representing the first district. "The single greatest enabler of success for our families is the community around them, and a great community is why the Coast Guard is here in Camden County—enjoying a truly amazing level of unusual and sustained support," said Vice Adm. Charles D. Michel, vice commandant of the U.S. Coast Guard.

The highlight of the ceremony was the unveiling of two interstate signs, displaying the county's new designation. These signs will be placed along Interstate 95 exits going through the area. "We appreciate DOT for providing the opportunity to showcase our Coast Guard in Camden County," said Sheila McNeill, president of The Camden Partnership. "Not only are we the first Coast Guard community in America, but we will be the best."

The purpose of the Coast Guard city program is to recognize communities who support the Coast Guard across the nation. A city, municipality, or county earns the distinction of being named a Coast Guard city by making special efforts to acknowledge the professional work of the Coast Guard men and women assigned to its area. Coast Guard cities regularly reach out to Coast Guard personnel and their families and make them feel "at home, at their home away from

> *home." The city's efforts illustrate a longstanding and enduring relationship, with an emphasis on considerations the community has made, for the members of the Coast Guard family.*

I couldn't have said it better!

REAR ADMIRAL JAY COHEN AND HIS WIFE NANCY

CHIEF OF NAVAL RESEARCH: UNDERSECRETARY OF HOMELAND SECURITY FOR SCIENCE AND TECHNOLOGY

I remember the first time I met Jay Cohen. It was at the new members breakfast on Capitol Hill in the 2001 timeframe. At that time, he was the chief of Naval Research and had served as Deputy chief of Navy Legislative Affairs, so he appreciated the work that went into pulling off an event like this. It was our first attempt in the years I had been involved in legislative affairs. To have a dozen of the new members of congress and the chiefs of the sea services briefing them was a big deal. We had Admiral Clark, from the Navy, Admiral Loy, from the Coast Guard and Captain Bob Papp, who would later become commandant, were in attendance. To have this opportunity for education for our sea services, the first week of their political career is important. I see Congressman Daryll Issa on television all the time, and I always think of the fact that the Navy League helped with his training his first week on Capitol Hill.

After I spoke, RADM Cohen came up to me with such praise, referring to my "smooth delivery with my Southern honey voice." He went on and I loved every minute of it. And then Chuck Beers, my chairman of legislative affairs at the time, came up and said, "Sheila, he is so full of shit. Don't believe a word he says."

They both laughed as I replied, "You two must be good friends."

They were and from that day, so were we.

RADM Cohen was in his fifth year in the office of Navy Research. After his retirement, he was quickly appointed by President George Bush to serve as undersecretary for science and technology for Homeland Security.

During his tour with Homeland Security, Arlie and I visited Canada on an official Navy League visit. When we looked at the local paper, RADM Cohen was all over it—large picture and long article. I saved that paper and sent it to him. He was in the papers a lot during that time, and I loved reading about what he was doing.

Keith Post, president of the Camden Kings Bay Navy League, invited the commanding officer of USCGC *Sea Dragon*, LTJG Kara Van Echo, to have lunch with him at Ops restaurant in St. Marys. He invited me to join them.

At lunch, he told me he had asked Jay to speak to the council and he was excited as he told us about it. He referred to him as Vice Admiral. "No, it's Rear Admiral," I said.

"I'm supposed to believe you instead of the Congressional Record? I don't think they would make this kind of mistake."

"But I know him and his wife, Nancy, well. He would not want you to introduce him with the wrong rank. Anyway, he is now undersecretary of Homeland Security, so it doesn't matter."

Keith still believed the congressional record instead of the knowledge of a close friend. I finally said, "After lunch, we'll find out."

Keith and I spent the lunch hour regaling the captain with all my Coast Guard stories. Keith said, "She is a friend of your boss."

"Commander Reagan?" she asked.

"No, the commandant," he answered. He was really feeding her with stories and his observations while I corrected him—only a couple of times since he had heard my stories so often. We let her know just who Secretary Cohen was, but I didn't say any more about what I planned to do.

After lunch, they took me back to my office, and I told them to come in while I made a call. The phone was answered promptly by Secretary Cohen. "Jay, this is Sheila. I have a question for you and you are on speakerphone."

"Hello, dahling, how are you?"

"I don't have time to talk right now, but I want to confirm something before you come to Kings Bay. Did you retire as a rear admiral or a vice admiral?"

"You know the answer to that my dear, I retired as a rear admiral."

"Thanks, Jay, see you at the end of the month."

No story that I ever told had more of a reaction than this story. Keith has told it often. How did I get the number? And what a sensitive question to ask! And *he* actually answered the phone. I'll owe Jay for this moment forever! You've got to love a man who has reached such heights and still has no ego.

He spoke to The Camden Partnership and the Navy League on March 13, 2008. He was also gracious enough to meet with a small community group and allowed us to ask questions about new Navy technologies and what might be a good mix for the community and for the base.

Almost any military event I attended, Jay and his wife, Nancy, were there. They are never too busy to talk with me. They are one of the couples in the Ptomaine Club, so I was able to see them every few months. Eight or so couples got together each month for dinner. They rotated responsibilities, but each host had to find an inexpensive (cheap) restaurant with great food. The Ptomaine Club got its name from the likelihood of everyone receiving the named poison at every place they ate. I know that's true. I joined them for a couple of those dinners.

As with a few other of those wonderful friends, I am reminded of something I read: "People might not always remember what someone said but they will always remember how they made you feel." The Cohens always made me feel good.

ADMIRAL TOM COLLINS

COMMANDANT OF THE UNITED STATES COAST GUARD

There is a little irony here. What made this first call even more interesting is that I had been agonizing about whether to call the Coast Guard to see if I could meet and talk with the incoming commandant, Admiral Tom Collins. Jack Fisher urged me to get to work supporting the Coast Guard in their recapitalization program. But some of the seasoned Navy League staff thought it might be a little too soon. We didn't want to "impose" on the Coast Guard. It was doubly sweet when, at the request of John Thorne and RADM Pat Stillman at Coast Guard headquarters, I had a meeting with Admiral Collins. That meeting was in February 2002. I was vice president of legislative affairs and had worked with RADM Stillman and RADM Eldridge as well as Adm. Papp on the recapitalization of the Coast Guard fleet. We were supposed to meet for fifteen minutes but the meeting turned in 30 minutes. With my brand-new job with legislative affairs and a big part of my advocacy was on the United States Coast Guard we needed that time.

Tom assured that during his tour that I had everything I needed for the Navy League to support the Coast Guard. He sent me the following letter on March 31, 2005:

> *Dear Sheila, I have always appreciated your incredible support of the Coast Guard in your role as national President of the Navy League. But, I must say, your tribute in March's edition of "SEAPOWER" to the men and women of the Coast Guard, and to me personally, is a terrific morale booster. I am humbled by your acknowledgement and appreciation and your appreciative of your recognition of our strategic role in the protection of the maritime domain.*
>
> *Congratulations on this year's successful Sea-Air-Space Exposition. The conference was a terrific collaboration between industry and the government in finding solutions to maintain the delicate balance between safety and security and the uninterrupted flow of commerce and military assets. Thank you for bringing all these partners together and for the wonderful reception and dinner*

Wednesday night. I appreciate all the great effort it takes to make such an evening come off so well.

The men and women of the Coast Guard understand and deliver selfless service. As you know, I share your high opinion of these wonderfully dedicated public servants. Your efforts on their behalf are greatly appreciated. Thank you for all that you do. Sincerely,

Tom C.
T. H. COLLINS
Admiral, U.S. Coast Guard

My support of the Coast Guard caused quite a stir at one of the Sea Air Space banquets, when I introduced General Mike Hagee as Commandant of the Coast Guard. I was looking at Admiral Collins table prior to opening the evening and it appeared that his table was set back a little from the first row and I was disturbed. I think I made a bigger issue in my head than it was, and I know Admiral Collins would not worry about such minor details. I stopped by Admiral Collins table as I left the podium and apologized for the mix-up. Thank goodness, he was laughing, and he said he loved it!

Admiral Collins nominated me for the Bob Hope Award. That was a wonderful evening. The event was the Coast Guard Birthday Ball in 2004. I was seated with Fran Townsend, Homeland Security's Condoleezza Rice. She had transferred to the Department of Homeland Security with emphasis on the Coast Guard and was frequently on the morning talk shows. I was amazed when she said, "I've heard of your work for the Coast Guard and was looking forward to meeting you."

I will always be indebted to Admiral Collins for this award—the awards committee installed this monument on a wall in the Pentagon. One day, I'm going to take my grandchildren to see their grandmother's name on this wall thanks to Tom Collins. When I turned over the presidency, Admiral Collins presented a proclamation that hangs on my wall that gives me almost as much pride as the Bob Hope Award. That proclamation is shown, in its entirety in the body of the book. Thank you, Tom, for everything. Tom was relieved by Admiral Thad Allen. His picture was on the cover of *Military Officer* in July 2003 as he led the Coast Guard in its new homeland security role.

In December 2004, I received a letter from Admiral Collins:

I am overwhelmed by the generosity of the Cleveland Council of the Navy League in their support of (omitted). The outpouring of concern and funds which your wonderful members provided the (this) family is extraordinary in itself, but will foster even greater return in appreciation from the men and women of the Coast Guard as we share this story. Such selfless deeds like those of the Cleveland Council and the Cuyahoga County Veterans Service Commission encourage our young people to continue to make sacrifices in service to their country. Please pass along to the Cleveland Council my deep appreciation. Thank you for your leadership in promoting such generosity, care and compassion by your members for all the sea services.

Note: The council president of the Cleveland Council was Bill Keller. The council learned of a young Coast Guard family who had overwhelming medical bills for their new baby. He sent a letter out to the council and received enough to pay for the needs of that new baby.

My last event as President was the meeting in Norfolk in June 2005.

I sent Admiral Collins this letter:

Dear Admiral Collins, I cannot adequately thank you for being our principal speaker for our annual Awards Luncheon during the Navy League's National Convention in Norfolk, Virginia. It is one of the best events we sponsor. Your remarks were excellent—they were very forthright and most appropriate at this important event. And, of course, I appreciate your generous comments about me!

As I leave the presidency of the Navy League, I also want you to know how much I appreciate the friendship Arlie and I have with you and Nancy and the tremendous access you have made available to me. I knew when I needed you, I could pick up the phone. I think this resulted in greater support of the Coast Guard and a better Navy League. Thank you for the awesome recognition I have received as a direct result of your efforts—the Spirit of Hope Award, the Distinguished Service Medal, and the proclamation. I can't thank you enough.

I will forever be a partner with you and a strong advocate for our Coast Guard. I am pleased to have the opportunity to sponsor the USCGC Sea Horse. It is an honor I do not take lightly. I'll miss traveling all over the US and overseas and meeting your Coast Guard men and women at work. I'll miss the brainstorming sessions on how we can better support Deepwater. Please know that I am available should you ever need me. Sincerely, Sheila

I am grateful for Tom Collins.

**See USCGC *Sea Horse*.

VICE ADMIRAL MICHAEL CONNOR

COMMANDER SUBMARINE FORCES

I was just a little intimidated when I first met Vice Admiral Connor. I had not met him until he was at the Pentagon as director of Submarine Warfare—a two-star billet. The Camden County community met with him when we had our DC fly-in. He was promoted from that position to SUBLANT—commanding all US submarines.

In September 2012, when VADM Connor assumed command of the submarine force I was at his change of command. I wrote him a few days later, inviting him to come to Camden and meet with the community. It took some doing but finally working with his aide, Lt. Commander Tom Flaherty, we set it up. We reserved a room at Borrell Creek and invited our community leadership to have dinner with the admiral. I copied the Kings Bay's group commander Rear Admiral Joe Tofalo and base commanding officer Captain Harvey Guffey of our plans. We had an amazing turn out. Looking back on the list, we had everyone we needed there with elected officials and Navy League and community leaders.

VADM Connor discussed the new paper he and Rear Admiral James Caldwell signed four days before as Commanders Task Force 134 and 144 respectively that went to each member of the SSBN force: There were seven points with the summary:

The Continuing Legacy

> *As we have since 1960, the SSBN Force will continue to adapt to new threats and challenges. However, nothing will change the fact that a properly operated submarine is the stealthiest war fighting platform in the world. With nearly four thousand deterrent patrols conducted, SSBN Sailors have consistently and safety prevented major power war. In the tradition of the Silent Service, we will do little to bring public attention or fanfare to your continuing accomplishments. However, we do want to remind you and thank you for your critical work. We challenge each of you to continue the tradition of superior maintenance, training and operation of our nuclear enterprise in support of our national objectives.*

I sent an e-mail to each of the twenty-two who attended the dinner:

Hello everyone,

Thank you so much for attending the dinner with VADM Connor. I thought it was a wonderful venue for a thoughtful dis-

cussion on our submarine force. VADM Connor was most impressive and it turned out to be a very informative evening. If you will remember, he referred to a letter he and RADM Caldwell sent to the fleet. He asked me to send each of you a copy of that letter and it is attached.

* * * * *

He spoke at the Camden Kings Bay Navy League when he was SUBLANT and I introduced him. I shared with everyone one of his early positions was that as a flag secretary. This was my introduction:

We are pleased tonight to have as our guest the top dog of the submarine force, Admiral Mike Connor. Admiral Connor is responsible for the submarines and tenders at:

BANGOR
DIEGO GARCIA
GROTON, CT
GUAM
KINGS BAY
NORFOLK
PORTSMOUTH
SAN DIEGO

Every submarine in the fleet at home, in the shipyard and deployed. His background make him the right man for the job at the right time. He has served on every class of submarines—including the first commanding officer of the first Seawolf. He has served as a group commander in Yokosuka, Japan. He served at the Naval Operational Intelligence Center, the Joint Staff, on the staff of an assistant secretary of the Navy, as assistant deputy chief of Naval operations, on the Navy staff and in one of the hardest and most intense jobs (I am told that this is true by some of the former admirals who had that job) and that is as Director of Submarine Warfare—responsible for the submarine budget and as the senior submariner in D.C. Those of you who have gone to Washington with us know this position as the one we always met with at our Fly Ins.

In my opinion VADM Connor's best start was as Flag Sec to a former Commander of the submarine force. There is great benefit in sitting at the high-power meetings in the early stages of your career, right Lt. Bullock?

He assumed his current duties as Commander, Submarine Forces in September 2012. This is the second time Admiral Connor has met with folks from our community. Sir, you did so well last time we moved you up to the big time. Thanks for being here tonight. Please help me welcome, Vice Admiral Mike Connor.

The *Periscope*, Kings Bay's paper, had an article in the June 13, 2014 paper, "Navy eyes plans for enlisted females on subs."

Task Force Set up Comprehensive Plan Due by January 2014
By Defense Media Activity—Navy

Commander, Naval Submarine Forces in Norfolk established a flag officer-led task force in May to focus on effectively integrating enlisted women Sailors on board multiple submarine platforms. Vice Adm. Michael Connor stood up the task force to officially look at best Integration practices for SSBNs, SSGNs and Virginia-class SSNs.

Commander of Submarine Group Two Rear Adm. Kenneth Perry is leading the task force. The group is charged with developing a comprehensive process used to successfully integrate female officers by including feasibility studies, potential courses of action and candidates' timelines.

Pending the results, a detailed implementation plan will be presented to the Chief of Naval Operations by March 2015. Female officers have been successfully integrated on board OHIO-Class SSBNs and SSGNs and will be integrated onboard VIRGINIA-class SSNs in fiscal year 2015.

The Navy is working with industry to design the Ohio replacement SSBN to support both officers and enlisted mixed-gender crews. Then-commander of Submarine Group 10, Rear Adm. Barry Bruner, announced the Department of the Navy's plan to allow women to serve on submarines, during a press conference at Naval Submarine Base Kings Bay, April 20th, 2010. With the Ohio-class ballistic submarine USS Alaska (SSBN 732) providing the backdrop Bruner formally announced the Navy's policy change to various regional and local electronic and print outlets on the submarine base's waterfront.

On Dec. 5th, 2012, Lt. J.G. Marquette Leveque, a native of Fort Collins, Colo., assigned to the Gold Crew of USS Wyoming

> *(SSBN 742), became one of the first female unrestricted line officers to quality in submarines receiving her submarine Dolphins during a ceremony at NSB Kings Bay.*

Two weeks from this publication I had dinner with RADM Ken Perry and pummeled him with questions.

James Coughlin and I were attending a Strategic Deterrent Coalition meeting in Missouri when VADM Connor walked in. With the room full of Air Force, I felt like I was seeing a member of my family. We had time to talk and catch up that evening. He pulled up a chair and we never left the table… until we had to.

He is a quiet, deliberate, nice-looking man with a rather sardonic look. However, as usual, some of those times when you think you can read someone, you find out how wrong you can be. I'm sure the man I saw is the same man that most active duty submarines meet at work every day. The world the submarines live in is full of intrigue, secrecy, and intelligence. That interpretation of the look I saw with Mike has now changed to that of a friend I always like to see.

One evening after Mike's retirement I was talking with him at a Naval Submarine League reception. The McKinnons and the Kevans and I were having a nightcap and I asked him to join us. (Mark was commanding officer of Trident Training Facility and when he retired he stayed in the community). I told him he could scare me more than most anyone. I can be a smart ass at times, so I used to be very careful with him. I learned though, that a little twerk of the mouth from Mike Connor was him responding hilariously. He told me his wife says he is the man with no expression and his daughter's boyfriends were scared of him.

That was it! All the years I tried to figure him out and he really did think I was funny!

*See TRIAD.

VICE ADMIRAL BARRY COSTELLO

COMMANDER, THIRD FLEET
CHIEF OF LEGISLATIVE AFFAIRS

My introduction to Rear Admiral Costello is still one of my favorite stories. On June 26, 1998, He accompanied Senator Max Cleland to Naval Submarine Base Kings Bay to speak at a Navy League meeting. At that time, he was a captain working in the Navy Office of Legislative Affairs.

They arrived early, flying in from DC to the Jacksonville airport. We had reserved a large suite for him, so we sat down to talk until time for the Navy League meeting. It was almost time and Max reached for his coat. It wasn't there—he had left it on the plane. There was no time to go back to the plane and return in time for the meeting. I called the local Belk store. He was wearing nice gray pinstriped trousers—it would have been nice if it had been black or navy, but gray pinstriped? How could we find a match! I described the pants and gave the size to the manager at Belk. He checked and seemed to have a jacket that he thought would work. I got up to leave, but Captain Costello insisted that he go and Max and I enjoy the time. The jacket was a perfect match. Later, Rear Admiral Costello would laugh about this and thank me for saving his job.

That man has a lot of class. He later became chief of legislative affairs with his last tour as commander, Third Fleet. Barry has been Barry for so long, I was just a little taken aback when I read his bio while writing this story—very impressive, especially this part: "Additionally, his leadership of CTF-55 during Operation Iraqi Freedom was acknowledged by the United Kingdom with the Honorary Award of Commander of the Most Excellent Order of the British Empire (CBE)." Amazing!

After his trip to escort Senator Cleland to Kings Bay, we became good friends. One of the times I took our community for a fly-in to DC, I asked if he would have one of his staff brief us on current Navy issues. He not only briefed us but joined us for lunch.

I attended the retirement ceremony for Dale Lummey, who had worked in legislative affairs. Dale would later serve for a time as the executive director of the Navy League. It was close to the starting time, so I slipped in and sat down at the last row of chairs. It was a very nice ceremony with several high-level speakers including legislators. Imagine my surprise when Barry introduces me and asks if I would like to say a word. I should have said, "No, I don't do well with impromptu remarks," but I didn't. I'm not sure what I said but I should have known to expect anything with the admiral! Even when he was serving as Third Fleet, I would call him when I needed him. There were a couple of testy issues I had as national president and Barry was always a phone call away.

When he retired as commander of the US Third Fleet in 2007, he sent the following letter:

> *Dear Sheila, I wanted to drop you a note of thanks for all you support while I have commanded the THIRD fleet. It has been the honor of a lifetime to lead these great Sailors, and now it is time to start another chapter as I transition to a new career. I will miss being a part of this professional team, but take solace that I will turn over the reins on 4 May to a great officer—Sam Locklear. I intend to have a low-key event—so this note is my way of saying thanks. I look forward to staying in touch as we move forward,*
>
> *All the best, Barry*

He was my favorite person to run into at the annual Navy War College's Current Strategy Forum in Newport, Rhode Island. I enjoyed these forums and the connections you could make—but even more when I was with Barry.

We found a way to work the room that was very effective. One of us would give the other a few minutes with someone, then join them and take them away. It was the perfect way to get around to all of your friends. Barry, like me, loved to see old friends and if we didn't work at it we would be with the same ones all evening. We created the perfect social process. We could cover a room with three hundred to four hundred in an evening's reception. We must have talked to one hundred people each. Later, the War College would be replaced by Sea Air Space as our chance to catch up.

After one of these War College receptions, he told me to come with him. Yes, no question, just come with me. We got in his car and he drove to a home about fifteen minutes away. By then it's about 10:00 p.m., and I was whining and complaining that we could not show up at someone's house at 10:00 p.m. without calling them. Not so. We did. And they opened the door. And we had a nice visit. It turned out that he was one of Barry's classmates from Holy Cross and his wife. They were lifelong friends who would have been disappointed had we passed by without saying hello. That was Barry's story and he is sticking with it!

I would not have opened that door.

UNITED STATES SENATOR PAUL COVERDALE

On February 23, 1996, Senator Coverdell spoke to our Navy League Council. I had the privilege of introducing him. Never will something like this happen again, but we had a speaker for the meeting that had to cancel at the last minute. Why not reach for the top? And I did. I called Senator Paul Coverdell and asked him to be our replacement for the night. What a privilege. In order to accommodate his schedule, we met an hour earlier. I had already met with him on SSGN. Looking back on his remarks, I realize just how important his message was.

Senator Coverdell cosponsored and helped win passage of the historic Line Item Veto. He was the sponsor to the Balanced Budget Amendment. That night, he said the battle to balance the federal budget is pivotal to the nation. "Within a decade, by the year 2006 or before—100% of the U.S. Treasury will be consumed by just five federal programs," he said.

"Government spending will be focused on Social Security, Medicare, Medicaid, federal retirement and interest on the national debt. Other programs, such as national defense, will be placed in jeopardy unless other measures are taken," Coverdale said. (Had everyone only listened.)

I was honored to serve on his Military Advisory Council and to visit military installations in Georgia on his behalf. I will always be grateful to Paul for his support on the SSGN. When I briefed him, he really got it. He was a captain in the Army and served in Okinawa, Japan, remaining in the reserves for years. He recognized the importance SSGNs could be to the seal and other special forces unit in their mission. I believe he influenced many members of congress.

He always praised our Chamber fly-ins—even passing on to the chief of Naval Operations, Admiral Mike Boorda the community knowledge of submarines and their strong support. He told me he also told other districts to call me on how we prepared and presented Camden County issues on Capitol Hill.

Paul had returned to Georgia from Washington for a weekend of speaking engagements and service to his constituents and died in Atlanta on July 19, 2000, of a brain aneurysm. Arlie and I attended the dedication of the new federal learning center at Federal Law Enforcement Training Center at Glynco. President George H. W. Bush was one of the speakers.

Others on the agenda were Congressman Jack H. Kingston and Governor Roy Barnes. Secretary of the Treasury Paul H. O'Neill introduced President Bush, who gave the key remarks. Also speaking was the Honorable Zell Miller, former governor, who was appointed to finish Paul's turn in the US Senate.

The following was in the *Times Union* on August 11, 2001:

ELDER BUSH PRAISES COVERDELL'S SERVICE

Brunswick dedicates federal learning center
By Terry Dickson, Times-Union staff writer

Former President George Herbert Walker Bush joined U.S. Senator Zell Miller, Governor Roy Barns and U.S. Rep. Jack Kington yesterday in praising the late Sen. Paul D. Coverdell at the dedication of a new federal learning center to Coverdell's memory. It is fitting Bush told the crowd of about 700 at the Federal Law Enforcement Training Center, that the new Paul D. Coverdell Learning Center should be named after a man who was dedicated to education and law enforcement. The invitation-only event was held in an air-conditioned gymnasium rather than outside the new $16.1 million academic complex. Congress passed a law mandating that the 135,000-sq. ft. center be named after Coverdell, who died in office last year.

"People in Georgia don't have to be reminded of what a wonderful public servant he was," Bush said. "He truly believed public service was a noble calling." He praised Coverdell for his non-partisanship and his effectiveness in getting things done. Coverdell also spoke in a quiet, earnest manner and people listened, Bush said. Kingston said Coverdell was a politician in a positive sense of the word because he listened and learned. He said that Coverdell, who

was never seen without a white shirt and tie, was not old-fashioned but was timely "like a pinstriped suit." Kingston recalled his last conversation with Coverdell in which the senator encouraged him to "always do what's right and what's best."

Although they belong to the opposition party, Democrats Miller and Barnes remembered Coverdell as a longtime friend in the Georgia Senate before he won the U.S. Senate seat in 1992 and was re-elected in 1998. Miller praised Coverdell for his honesty, integrity and dogged persistence. Miller, whom Barnes appointed to succeed Coverdell, said he sits at the same desk Coverdell used in Washington. "I remain honored and humbled to succeed this good and great man," he said.

Treasury Secretary Paul H. O'Neill introduced Bush and said he has had a long and warm association with the family. He said he distinguishes the George Bushes by the order in which they held the nation's highest office. "The elder Bush is Bush 41 and the current president is Bush 43, he said. The former president had the same praise for Miller and his bipartisan ways. "We Bushes, 41 and 43 have great respect (for Miller). God, I wish he were Republican," Bush said as he pretended to have made the remark accidentally. He said he had suffered an identity crisis, that although he had been president of the U.S., beginning in 1991 and 1993 people began referring to him a Barbara Bush's husband.

"Now it's even worse. I'm being referred to as the president's dad or Jeb's dad," he said. "I'm not called by my name. I was called George Bush, President George Bush for many years. Now, it's 41, get out of the picture.

At the end of the ceremony, Coverdell's widow, Nancy joined Bush and FLETC Director W. Ralph Basham on the stage to watch the televised unveiling of a sign naming the building after Coverdell. The center will be one of the primary training areas for 74 federal law enforcement organizations.

In February 2005, the Legislative Office Building, across the street from the state capitol building in Atlanta, was named after Senator Paul Coverdell.

When I was chairman of the USS *Georgia* Return to Service event, Nancy Coverdell graciously agreed to serve on our advisory board joining every living legislator and governor past and present who also agreed to serve.

VICE ADMIRAL VIVIEN CREA

UNITED STATES COAST GUARD CUTTER *SEA HORSE*

In February 2005, I received a call with a follow up letter from the commandant of the Coast Guard, Admiral Tom Collins:

> *Dear Sheila, please accept my invitation for you and Mr. McNeill to participate in the commissioning ceremony of the Coast Guard's newest cutter, Coast Guard Cutter SEA HORSE will be commissioned in the fall of 2005 in Portsmouth, Virginia. I invite you to be the ship's sponsor and keynote speaker at the commissioning ceremony.*
>
> *CGC SEA HORSE is the 61st Coastal Patrol Boat in the Marine Protection class, built by Bollinger Shipyards, Inc. The primary missions of SEA HORSE will include search and rescue and the enforcement of laws and treaties, including homeland security and port safety. SEA HORSE's additional missions will include migrant interdiction and recreational boating safety.*
>
> *I hope that your schedule will permit participation in this time-honored maritime tradition. If you accept, my Congressional Affairs Liaison, LCDR Bryan Durr, will work closely with your staff to assist in what promises to be a memorable event.*
>
> *Sincerely,*
> *Tom C.*
> *THOMAS H. COLLINS*
> *Admiral, U.S. Coast Guard*

I was so humbled by the honor. A few months later the officer in charge was named and he sent the following letter:

> *July 29, 2003*
> *Dear Mrs. McNeill,*
>
> *Thank you for accepting the crew's invitation to serve as sponsor for United States Coast Guard Cutter SEA HORSE. I am writing to provide you with background information on the cutter and your role as sponsor. This is a very exciting time for the crew, and we hope that you will find your role as sponsor rewarding.*

SEA HORSE is the sixty-first vessel of the Marine Protector Class built by Bollinger Shipyard in Lockport, Louisiana. It is the newest cutter of its class to be stationed in the Fifth Coast Guard District. SEA HORSE arrived in her homeport of Portsmouth on 6 July 2005 and will be placed In Service Active on September 7, 2005 at the High Street Landing, Portsmouth, Virginia. Vice-Admiral Vivien Crea will be the presiding official.

SEA HORSE is on the cutting edge of technology and employs many systems still relatively new to the Coast Guard. These advances allow the small crew of ten to more efficiently perform our primary missions of Law Enforcement, Search and Rescue, Homeland Defense and Environmental Protection. Advances include a computer navigation system built to international standards, which allow the ship to be safely piloted by a single person. Another major change is the addition of a stern launched small boat. This allows the small boat to be launched and recovered with a single person on deck compared to previous class of cutter, which required six people to do the same job.

The role of a vessel's sponsor is unique to military ships and normally is filled by a prominent civilian woman with ties to the service. You will be an advocate of the ship and through her, of other ships and crews of similar size, and your association with SEA HORSE will continue until the day she is retired from active service. You will be part of the official party during our September 7th ceremony and will be given time to speak to the crew and audience. You will also be received gifts from the crew and the ship's builders.

Please feel free to contact me directly if you have any questions or if there is anything that I can do for you. We would be honored if you could pay us an informal visit before the official commissioning so we may get to know each other. You are welcome aboard SEA HORSE at any time. Thank you again for accepting our invitation to be SEA HORSEs sponsor. I look forward to meeting you and showing you our beautiful new ship

Sincerely
Mark J. Rieger, Master Chief Boatswains Mate

Arlie and I made plans and I started looking for a gift for the crew. It was an exciting time. The evening before the ceremony, the Hampton Roads council of the Navy League sponsored a reception. I had been searching for the right gift for the crew, and when I saw the John Perry seahorse, I knew I had the right gift. I was so pleased when I heard that Vice Admiral Vivien Crea would be giving the principal remarks.

Vivien and I had met years before. She was an up and coming one star when I was national president in 2001. She later was deputy commandant of the US Coast Guard. She came to Brunswick when the US Coast Guard Cutter *Eagle* made a port visit. Working with the local Navy League council, Arlie and I were both involved in the visit. Vivien's aide and I had talked several times before their visit. When they arrived and checked in the local hotel, he called me. He had forgotten his dress shoes and would need them the next day for the ceremony. I kidded him because I had tried to get him to let me show them around a little and now we would have the opportunity. Admiral Crea was going to be tied up with a conference call. Arlie and I arrived at the hotel, and to my surprise, he told me the admiral wanted to join us. We were delighted. We had a relaxing walk in the village at St. Simons Island. He bought the book *Beloved Invader* by Eugenia Price for Vivien, and she bought him a tie. I tried talking her into making a surprise visit to the Coast Guard Station Brunswick but she was attuned to the protocol, so this wasn't happening. We did drive to the station and I went in to confirm the time of the evening's event. They were ready for her visit just in case!

IN SERVICE CEREMONY FOR SEA HORSE—
SEPTEMBER 7, 2005, a beautiful day in Portsmouth:
Official Party Arrives
Introduction of the District Commander
Welcoming remarks
Rear Admiral Larry Hereth, USCG Commander, Fifth Coast Guard District
Invocation Captain Robert Marshall, Chaplain, United States Navy
Ship Commissioning Rear Admiral Larry Hereth, USCG
The National Anthem & Colors
Reading of Orders & Assumption of Command
Master Chief Boatswain's Mate Mark J. Rieger, USCG
Setting the Watch & Crewing the Ship
Breaking the Admiral Flag & Rendering Honors
Keynote Speaker Vice Admiral Vivien Crea, USCG
Shipbuilder's Remarks
Bollinger Shipyards, Inc.
Ship's Sponsor Remarks Mrs. Sheila M. McNeill
Officer in Chare Remarks Master Chief Boatswain's Mate Mark J. Rieger, USCG
Official Party Departs

Special thanks to the Navy League of Hampton Roads for their support of this event.

CGC Sea Horse Commission Ceremony September 7, 2005
Remarks by VADM Crea

Thank you, Commander (LCDR Richard Condit). Congressman Pickett, Mayor Holley, Senator Miller, Mr. Smythers, Admiral Ecker, Admiral Venzke, Admiral Johnson, Admiral Donohue, Admiral Ellis, Admiral Beers, General Quinlan, Members of the Portsmouth City Council, Sheila and Arlie McNeill, all of our distinguished guests, friends, family and crew of the Coast Guard's newest Cutter—SEA HORSE.

We are so lucky to be here today, a beautiful day here in Portsmouth, and a GREAT day when the Coast Guard adds another much-needed asset to our cutter inventory!

Today, our attention is keenly focused on the nation's response to the unparalleled devastation in Louisiana, Mississippi and Alabama left by Hurricane Katrina. At times like this, the men and women of the United State Coast Guard—along with ALL of our partners—act to save lives, protect the environment and restore the maritime commerce that is so vital to our economy. This is clearly the largest American disaster response in our nation's history, and we are pushing the limits of imagination to get the job done. We are amidst the greatest all-hands evolution of all times, and time is running out to find and save everyone in peril. There is still much to bring EVERYONE involved in the response. We in the Coast Guard, indeed all of the armed forces, can be very proud of our contributions. We are doing what we all joined to do—we are protecting our citizens, our way of life and our nation.

There was a terrific editorial in the Virginian-Pilot last Friday when national attention was focused on the unfolding plight of New Orleans and our Gulf Coast. I'd like to share a bit of it with you, because I think it captures what your countrymen think of our Coast Guard. The title is "Angels in Orange Give Help and Hope."

While this excerpt evokes images of heroic rescue swimmers dangling from hoist cables, the editorial and accolades apply to all of our Coast Guard men and women who are working so hard... those operating small boats in the flood zones, those loading supplies on cutters and aircraft, those working behind the scenes to restore Coast Guard infrastructure and the many, many other deep in the supply chains providing resources, talent and oversight for our people and our efforts. We could not be as successful without our many partners, including those from DHS, DOD, all echelons of government, and industry. Internally, we could not do what we're doing without our entire workforce: our active duty members, our reserves who we have called up to lead important missions in the affected areas, our civilians, and last—but not least—our all volunteer Auxiliary members who are working so hard on the front lines and behind the scenes.

I am so happy to welcome the SEA HORSE to active duty. The SEA HORSE is the latest of these terrific coastal patrol boats to come on line. These boats are absolutely essential additions to the Coast Guard's inventory—highly capable, fast, and maneuverable, with wonderful concepts like the stern notch for fast, safe small boat launch and recovery. As some of you know, the Coast Guard was only supposed to get 50 of these boats—but after the tragedy of 9/11, when we desperately sought ways to rapidly increase capacity for the security of our homeland, one of the best investments was to buy more of these great boats. The SEA HORSE is number 60, and five more will follow. We couldn't be happier to add them to our lineup—to help in homeland security, search and rescue, law enforcement and everything else we do.

I have mentioned our vital partnerships, which are crucial to our successes. I'm sorry that one of our long-time partners, Dick Bollinger, couldn't be here to share in the celebration as we bring another of his highly capable boats into the fleet. I am, however happy to say that our reports are that he and his family weathered the storm and that Bollinger's Shipyard is still building Coast Guard Cutters

Today as we put our newest Coast Patrol Boat in service, we are honored that its sponsor is a true friend and ardent supporter of the Coast Guard, Ms. Sheila McNeill. Sheila, I'm absolutely delighted that you and Arlie are here today to share in this event and that you will be watching over the SEA HORSE. We couldn't ask for a better friend and ally.

For those of you who DON'T know Sheila, let me brag a little about this lifelong friend of the Coast Guard who has been a very important leader and member of the Navy League of the United States since 1966. Until most recently, she was the Navy League's National President—during a time of historic significance to the Coast Guard. Among other things, Sheila played a key role in pro-

viding pivotal support of national legislation and true reinvention of our government.

Not to mention the fact that she was the first-ever woman to hold the Navy League's position of National President! Last October, Sheila received the 2004 U.S. Armed Forces Spirit of Hope Award, which is presented to outstanding entertainers and other distinguished individuals whose patriotism and service to the troops reflects that of Bob Hope. Bob Hope was designated the first honorary veteran of the U.S. Armed Forces for his decades of entertaining troops, both in peacetime and in combat zones. As our Commandant, Admiral Thomas Collins, noted at the presentation of the award:

"Sheila McNeill has been one of the Coast Guard's most consistent supporters. Her influence is felt throughout the coast Guard at all levels, from adopting local units and taking on the quality of life issues for our sailors to providing trusted counsel to our senior leaders." Sheila, thank you for your unqualified support of the Naval Services, and especially the Coast Guard. You are a wonderful leader, and friend to us all.

Master Chief, congratulations on your command of this remarkable Coast Guard Unit. I couldn't be happier with your assignment as its first Officer in Charge. With your experience, exceptional talents, determination, and personal leadership, I'm sure that SEA HORSE will achieve great things under your command. I know how proud you are of your crew. As I look at them, I can see why you are so eager to show what they can do. With your leadership and experience, I know this small crew of enthusiastic mariner is off to do exception things. I had the pleasure of meeting your crew last night, and I am very impressed with their devotion to duty and pride in THEIR new boat! SEA HORSE will be called upon to do many things. To be quick and agile in her response to save lives, protect our ports, waterways and coast and our beloved United States of America. I know you will answer the call. Welcome to the Fifth Coast Guard District. Semper Paratus!

God Bless America… and the United States Coast Guard!

I've tried to stay in touch with each of the officers in charge, as well as sending seahorse ornaments at Christmas although the last two years have been trying.

There is a story in May 2012 about one of my annual visits to the USCGC *Sea Horse* when my friend Dana Richardson, chairman of the Dolphin Scholarship Board, where I serve as a member of the board of directors. She rescued me when Chuck Beers couldn't take me to the Cutter and Dana offered to do so. (See that story under John and Dana Richardson.) The officer in charge of the *Sea Horse* was Stephen B. Atchley, BMCM. I learned a lot that day from the questions Dana asked and the conversation she had with Stephen.

When Vivien retired, this was the message Commandant Allen left on the Coast Guard website:

Commandant Thad Allen Farewell Wingman:

> *It was a bittersweet moment today as VADM Vivien Crea was relieved by VADM Dave Pekoske. We said goodbye to an iconic figure who thorough her personal and professional achievements led and inspired not only multiple generations of Coast Guard men and women, but the entire nation. It is difficult to describe the value of her service. In addition to her expansive duties as Vice Commandant, she also served as our Agency Acquisition Executive and guided the restructuring and turnaround of our Acquisition Program.*
>
> *As the first female vice service chief in the history of the Nation, she also represented me at high level meetings and was the first woman to sit in the Service Chief's chair in the Tank (the room where the Joint Chiefs of Staff meet). Despite the enormous contributions she made as the Vice commandant, it has been her tireless day-to-day support for me, the Coast Guard, and the Department of Homeland Security that has been truly noteworthy. She has been a confident, counselor, collaborator, mentor and most of all, a friend. She taught us all how to achieve success through quiet competence, firm commitment and extraordinary patience, and by example. We will miss her and we wish her and husband Ron all the best in the future.*

I miss seeing her too and I am honored to have known her.

COMMAND MASTER CHIEF JOHN CROUSE

John was a true Navy chief. He loved to tell stories, he was hard working and he was courteous. He and I worked together on many projects—The St. Marys Submarine Museum and the Bancroft Memorial were the main ones.

I was about to turn in, when I saw John still in the dining room with about eight to ten WWII sub vets. It was the annual World War II event and I was staying at the local hotel. John called me over and told me they were "shooting the bull." At first, they hardly looked at me and then John brought up the SSGN. He loved to do that. He liked to see these guys wonder who this woman was and why she was there, and he would bring me into conversations to get the reaction. When he mentioned SSGN, one of the nice gentlemen began explaining to me what the SSGN was. John said something like, "Sheila is working on that. Tell them what you are doing."

I told him of my work on the conversation from SSBN to SSGN. We talked about the effect of SALT II on conversion, what subs might be transferred to Kings Bay and the impact these boats would have on national security. Eventually, every man was in the conversation and I stayed about a half hour. John told me the next day after I left there was complete silence. They all looked at each other and finally someone said, "Who was that woman?" Another of those "What are you doing here?" moments.

In early September 2010, I had an argument with John Crouse. He was about to leave for the Submarine Veterans convention and I took that as an opportunity to remind him, once again, that he should write instructions, if something happened to him. He had recently been in the hospital and I was reminding him that none of us knew what the future held for us, but I wanted him to make sure that the 'stuff' in his head was on paper somewhere. John knew I loved him—even when I was giving him a hard time. And he always "protected me." He bragged on me like I was his big sister. He agreed that he would get it all down. He died on that trip. To this day, I don't know if he wrote down all the instructions at that time or if he already had them and wanted to make me crazy.

It was devastating. We received the following notice: "We're here at US SUBMARINE VETERANS, INC Convention, where it was announced that John had passed. There was silence in the Banquet Room of 7-800 shipmates and wives who were told the news. We will all remember him and his dedication to the history of US submarine warfare. Sailor… rest your Oars." In John's final requests he asked that I give his eulogy. I was honored. Hawaii was his favorite duty station.

Jill Helton, publisher for the *Tribune & Georgian* wrote a heart wrenching tribute to John: "I can still see him now in his usual attire of cargo shorts, scruff beard, and Hawaiian shirt, gripping a beer at his usual seat at Seagles. He never drank too much and wasn't one to sit around and gossip. But he would always lend an ear to anyone who needed one. He was a friend to many and the relationships he fostered led to many veterans donating their prized possessions to the museum. They knew John and the museum board of directors would take good care of them."

I asked my friend and employee who is Hawaiian, Wenda Munez, to dance to the Hawaiian music. John requested she danced in his will. Her interpretative and beautiful hula was sweet and heartbreaking.

At John's request, I gave the eulogy.

John Raymond Crouse

February 7, 19552–September 4, 2010

John Raymond Crouse was 58 when he died. He was a native of Royal Oak, Michigan and graduated from Kimball High School in 1970. He was an Eagle Scout and later joined the U.S. Navy Submarine Force.

He is survived by his mother Rosemary Crouse, His brother Steve and his family, Sister, Nancy Savickas and her family, aunts, uncles, cousins and friends. He served on the USS Flasher SSN-61, USS Puffer SSN-652 and USS Buffalo, SSN-714. He was stationed in Hawaii for 13 years. As he stated in some of his final papers he left for us, "I was a WESTPAC Sailor—A fast attack Master Chief Petty Officer submariner, USN Retired—that's not a rank but a way of life." He was transferred to the USS Canopus AS-32 at Kings Bay where he served his last active duty tour.

John received 2 Navy Commendation Medals and 4 Navy Achievement Medals. The crews he served with received 7 Battle E Awards, numerous letters of appreciation and Citations and in his words: a very fulfilling adventure to save a great history. Although he said his best award was being the son of R.E. and Rosemary Crouse, his greatest regret was that his Dad never saw him as a Chief Petty Officer because he died shortly after he was selected. He said this was the saddest part of his life.

Nancy, remember that time just before your wedding that he almost missed. He said he wish he could tell you why but do you remember when the Russians shot down the Korean Airliner? There was the submarine looking for the planes boxes while the Russians were topside picking up the pieces. He had his own Rickover story that he shared with us:

Place:

Idaho Fall, Idaho, M Division Student, Reactor Operator Trainee. This is his story:

John: Full Scram the Reactor.

Full Scram the Reactor, aye.

Sir Reactor is Full Scrammed.

You didn't want me to do what? Oh. Well. I completed the drill, was commended by the RO as being one of the best RO trainee he has had. However, Full Scrams were limited by Rickover to two a year. I did one. They had to call Rickover within 5 minutes telling him of their goof up of not briefing me about the part "simulate."

After retirement from the Navy John worked for a local military subcontractor. When plans were made to build a submarine museum he was at the first meeting. John left a very organized detail of what he wanted done after his departure for eternal patrol—at the same time remarking that he hoped the liberty ports in heaven are just as good!" He said a while ago his mom asked him to put together his plans for his estate if something happened to him. "Thank you, mom, for making me do this," he wrote. He had already asked his good buddy, Royal Weaver, USN, retired to be his executor. Royal being a submarine master chief would know how to do it right. We all want a good friend like that when our time comes.

John said that he wanted me to give the remarks today because I taught him how to run a business, she taught me how to become a civilian, and that we worked together on the museum more than anyone else and lastly, because "She, being a lady, can't use nasty words to describe me. Also, we enjoyed talking to and listening to each other.

Now back to John's assertion that "I" taught him how to be a civilian. Let me give a slight disclaimer on that—I was not successful in the proper dress code. He was all things Hawaiian after those years in Hawaii and proper dress to him were flip flops and shorts. He just might put long pants on at a formal event or between January and March but only after a lot of coercion or begging.

I was president of the committee to build the Submarine Museum with John as Manager. Tony Cobb, John and I were inseparable. John and I were also Co-Chairman of the committee to raise funding for USS Bancroft memorial to recognize the 100th anniversary of the submarine force. So, we've spent a lot of time together in the past 14 years. Part of the written instructions John left were to his family and friends and I'd like to share those with you. These are John's words:

"Well if you are reading this it looks like I've completed my last transfer of duty. 'Eternal Patrol' is a submarine term used by subvets who have departed on their last, eternal, patrol. First, I wish to say I've had a hell of a good time getting here. 18 Years in Michigan, with family and friends. Mom and Dad (My Dad is now deceased) thanks for giving me so much. Kind of missed the 4 seasons of the year in Michigan, but do not miss the snow. Sometimes I still act like a kid, which I think is why I had so much fun in the Navy. 22 years in the Navy, with 13 in Hawaii. There they sent me to sea; with stops in Hong Kong, Philippines, Korea, Australia, Thailand and let's not

forget Guam. Then there was the Arabian Sea that we now hear so much about. Duty stations don't get any better than Hawaii. Also visited some Russian ports, but they didn't invite us in.

John then talks about the pig roasts, the scuba diving, deep sea fishing (he hooked one 14' Marlin and landed 4 others) and the hospitality of so many families in Hawaii. They each taught him a little about how to become Hawaiian. There were more stories but as John said," sons aren't supposed to tell their Moms that stuff"

Other stories he knew but never told were his experiences on the long deployments—he completed many six months long deployments to the Western Pacific. Those included Japan, Korea. Guam, Australia and parts of the world he said he couldn't talk about. He spent great bit of time in Idaho, California, upstate New York State, and finally St. Marys his final home. John said, "For 22 years in the Navy I tried to figure out where I wanted to leave the Navy at. I figured out it was going to be a small town, somewhere USA, just like the one's up in northern Michigan. St. Marys fit the small-town ideas. If you can handle the summer heat and gnats, then everything else is nice. The people with Southern hospitality made me feel at home here, even though I was once a Damn Yankee He lamented the death of his fishing buddy Jim and with that loss the loss of Jim's boat. As he said although the fish are a little smaller here, the fishing buddies are great. But that's the life of a sailor, especially a West Pack Pearl Harbor Fast Attack submarine sailor. It isn't a TOUR it's a way of life.

John wanted to make sure we told Tracy, Cindy, Dave, Jerry, Kings Bay Subvets, his old shipmates and about 1,000 WWII subvets that he had the greatest experience to get to know and work with. And to say Aloha to his friends at Seagal's Saloon and Island Lounge. He wanted to thank Maury Stewart for the long hours she expended to raise the money that kept us going for 3-4 years. I would like to recognize his friends and honorary pallbearers his brother, Ken Crouse, CMC USN ® and president of the submarine museum, Doug Cooper, CMC USN ® Royal Weaver, Jimmy Schubert, Command Master Chief Kings Bay Subase, Command Master Chief, Andy Crider (GROUP CMC), and Gordon Jackson our local Times Union reporter and from his hometown in Michigan.

John spent most Thanksgivings at my home with my large family. He so much enjoyed Wenda Munoz, my beautiful Hawaiian employee's spiritual Hula. You will be able to see that hula during this service. He left all his Hawaiian music to Wenda and we thought this tribute to him would be fitting. Arlie talked about his sense of humor and his unique voice. You always knew when John was telling a sea story. He spoke with authority about the service of our WWII veterans. He spoke of his work at memorial events. He was never interested in being "out front" with a lot of praise—he was more of a background type of guy to insure success of the WWII Subvets reunions at Kings Bay. His pleasure came from that success.

Two years ago, he asked me to speak at the Friday or Saturday night event of the subvets. One of the gentlemen was unhappy that it wasn't a submariner speaking and he let me know this. John was aware of his displeasure and in his effort to uplift me in their eyes he took more time to introduce me than I took in my remarks—he always protected me. He was my champion.

He touched many other hearts. I looked at his Face book page after news of his death came out. I want to share with you some of those remarks:

- *Those of us who knew him best will always remember him as a dear friend with a zest for life and a great sense of humor. He filled our hearts and now we're left with a hole. We thank him for preserving history for future generations and this same history will keep him alive forever.*
- *he has left a legacy that will remain for a long, long time. Many have received blessings from his work and a shining example of membership in the Dolphin Brotherhood.*
- *We are all grief stricken with the death of John Crouse. He leaves this earth with our gratitude.*
- *Peace be with you, rest your oars, Shipmate.*
- *He was a shipmate and one of the best submariners I knew—I'm on Oahu right now thinking of old times of BBQs and diving. May his rest be at least as good as those days. God Bless him.*
- *My heart is heavy with sadness right now.*
- *Rest in Peace John. You were the most awesome boss I have ever had. The museum will never be the same without you.*

"John was helpful in my research" so many told me.

John's greatest love was his work with our museum and with the WWII Subvets. The patrol report project was one he spent countless hours on. One day when we have all the patrol reports for WWII finished we will have John and his vision to thank for this history. John has helped to instill that love in all those folks who have served on the board of directors since the museum's opening.

There were special instructions for us for his final arrangements. No flowers except maybe a Hawaiian lei and donations to the museum in lei of flowers. No suit and tie for me, he wrote. He also told us, "There are several photos of lady friends in the master bedroom that I will miss, if they can be buried with me that would be nice." He requested a military funeral at sea on an SSGN or SSN but added that this will take time to set up, even a couple months. But, he wrote, "that's okay—I'm not in a hurry." On behalf of the St. Marys Submarine Museum BOD: To you submariners here today you have our gratitude, our attention and our prayers. We aspire to be associated with each of you and the legacy you bring. We understand that association brings an obligation. It brings an obligation of devotion to your history.

And John, you have our love and gratitude. From the Board of Directors of the Submarine Museum and the officers and crews at Kings Bay Submarine Base: thank you for your service. Rest in Peace. You stand relieved for the last time. We have the watch.

THE TIMES UNION

Byline: GORDON JACKSON

ST. MARYS—Hundreds gathered Friday to pay tribute to John Crouse, a retired Navy master chief who died of a heart attack Sept. 4 while promoting the St. Marys Submarine Museum at a national Navy veterans' convention in Cincinnati.

Mourners, many dressed in Hawaiian shirts and leis, gathered at Our Lady Star of the Sea Catholic Church to pay tribute to the only manager the St. Marys Submarine Museum has had since its creation in 1995. Crouse, who was seldom seen wearing long pants or button-down shirts, specified in his will that he wanted everyone to wear Hawaiian garb. The 58-year-old Michigan native and lifelong bachelor was described as the driving force behind the museum and a passionate supporter of an annual submarine veteran's convention held at Kings Bay Naval Submarine Base.

Former national Navy League president Sheila McNeill chronicled his Navy career, which included tours of duty on three submarines and 13 years in Hawaii. The audience laughed as she described Crouse's claim that she taught him to be a civilian. "He was all things Hawaiian after those years in Hawaii and proper dress to him was flip-flops and shorts," she said. "He just might put long pants on at a formal event or between January and March, but only after a lot of coercion or begging." McNeill praised Crouse's admiration of World War II submarine veterans. "You always knew when he was telling a sea story," she said. "He spoke with authority about the service of our WWII veterans." McNeill's voice cracked with emotion after reading tributes to Crouse from retired admirals, veterans and those still serving in the Navy. "Rest in peace," she said. "You stand relieved for the last time. We have the watch."

After the service, many gathered at the museum Crouse helped establish in downtown St. Marys. We miss John.

DEFENSE ADVISORY COMMITTEE ON WOMEN IN THE SERVICES

(DACOWITS)

Nominations for the DACOWITS can be from any of the military services, Congress and the White House. I received nominations from the Navy, Army, Senate, and State. I was told, it was more than any in the past but I'm not sure they knew for sure. They were probably just making me feel good. When you serve as a member you have the protocol rating of a three-star Vice Admiral or Lt. General depending on the service.

I was appointed to DACOWITS in March 1996. The following year, 1997, I served as vice chair and director of installations—reading and analyzing all reports from all members, ranking top issues, selecting of issues for agenda for the committee, and preparing the report for the secretary of defense. During my three-year tour, I accomplished the following:

- I visited over fifty installations in the US and overseas—Pacific Command, European Theater, Atlantic and Central Command bases over three years. I devoted 40% of my time to this committee.
- I gave briefs at meetings that included the service chiefs and many representatives of the Defense Department.
- I was asked by the Senate Armed Services Committee to serve on the committee on Gender Integrated Training—which carried a three-star salary—and declined due to my commitment to DACOWITS. Probably not one of my best decisions.

All my DACOWITS experience has given me training and experiences that will serve me well with the Navy League. One visit was to Naval Air Station Atlanta with

Captain Ike Puzon, who later became the military advisor to my friend Senator Max Cleland. I believe it gave me an insight in the concerns of both our military members and our military leaders. The experience in protocol would be a valuable tool for the Navy League.

My appointment to DACOWITS was made possible by RADM Jerry Ellis when he was group commander at Kings Bay. We had three days to request and then receive recommendation for the committee. I had to have at least three for the package to the Defense Department. I received nine of ten in the three-day limit we had. They were as follows:

General Edwin Burba Jr., US Army, Retired
Admiral H. G. Chiles Jr., Commander in Chief, US Strategic Command
RADM A. H. Konetzni Jr., US Navy
RADM W. G. Ellis, Commander Submarine Group 10
National President of the Navy League of the United States, Hugh Mayberry
Sam Nunn, United States Senator
Charlie Smith Jr., Georgia State Representative
W. J. Weisensee, Executive Director of the Camden Kings Bay Area Chamber of Commerce
M. H. (Woody) Woodside, Executive Director of the Brunswick Chamber of Commerce

As an example, I have included the letter from General Burba. He wrote,

Selection Committee
Defense Advisory Committee on Women in the Services (DACOWITS)

As current Chairman of the Governor's Military Affairs Coordination Committee (GMACC) for the state of Georgia, I am proud to have the opportunity to join with Rear Admiral W. G Ellis, USN, in recommending Mrs. Sheila M. McNeill for membership on the Defense Advisory Committee on Women In the Services.

During my last assignment as Commander-in-Chief, Forces Command (1989-93), I acquired a firsthand appreciation of the crucial operational impact that the Committee's recommendations have with respect to the optimum utilization of women in the Armed Forces. Clearly, an organization with such awesome responsibility needs talented and dedicated members to be successful. In my view, Mrs. McNeill is just such an individual.

For over thirty years, Sheila McNeill has consistently demonstrated successful, results-oriented leadership in an impressive variety of endeavors in both public and private sectors at local and state

levels. The attached record speaks eloquently for itself and, while little is to be gained by a complete recapitulation, it is worth noting that Sheila's unique ability to articulate military requirements was recently recognized by being elected as the first female president of the Georgia State Navy League of the U.S. As a member of the Military Affairs Coordination Committee, Mrs. McNeill has earned a reputation as one who can be routinely relied upon to do sensitive issues. Among our committee members, I consider her in the top three of over forty highly successful businessmen/women, past and present state legislators, mayors, appointed officials and senior military officers to include active and retired flag officers. All these individuals were selected by the governor for their competence, integrity, leadership and interest in the Armed Services. Sheila McNeill is one of the most impressive leaders and thinkers I know. She would make a magnificent addition to DACOWITS. I am privileged to recommend her without reservations.

Edwin H. Burba, Jr.
General (R) USA, Chairman, MACC

General Burba was a most unassuming man, especially for someone who reached the levels of a four-star general. He was one of the best chairman we had and I hated to see him leave a few years later, but his work with the Army continued. Senior DoD officials later told me these recommendations were considered, not just a recommendation but as four major nominations: from the Army (Burba), the Senate (Nunn), the Navy (Childes, Ellis and Konetzni), and the civilian community leadership (Woodside and Weisensee).

There were about forty members of the committee—all well respected in their communities with many of them PhDs. They came from every facet of life and many had no prior experience working with the military. Our professional staff were active duty. RADM Ronnie Froman was head of Manpower and Personnel for the Joint Staff and was a great asset.

April 1996: The first year of DACOWITS was a learning curve. The first meeting was a real climb. In order to address the many diverse issues that affect service men and women members are broken into three separate subcommittees:

- **Quality of life:** for both men and women in the services; issues that contribute directly to the morale of the forces as well as enhance the state of readiness
- **Forces development:** for the effective utilization of women as well as considering issues concerning standards, accessions, assignments, deploy-

ments, performance evaluations, training opportunities, specialty limitations, promotions, leadership development, and career counseling

- **Equality management subcommittee:** a main focus on issues relating to the negative behaviors in the workplace that adversely affect the full utilization of women

We met twice a year and corresponded frequently. At the meetings, we would divide by subcommittee. At the end of the committee meetings we would all meet as one group and each of the sub committees would bring issues for vote by the entire committee.

Imagine my surprise when the recommendations from the Forces Development Committee was (1) to add females to the submarine force and (2) to commend Admiral Kelso for his support of women in the Navy. Both as one recommendation. The meeting was full of members of the committee, active duty support staff, past members, DOD officials, and press. I was as nervous as I've ever been but stood up and asked, "Why are these two recommendations as one? I admire Admiral Kelso and appreciate that we are recognizing him for his support of women in the Navy. However, I do not support the wide recommendation of women on submarines, so I think we should vote on them separately. Now I know how Congress feels," I added. This was an issue so important and yet two-thirds of the committee were not privy to the background that came with this recommendation.

Obviously, this was a change in protocol. I knew I was jeopardizing my relationship with my committee members—it was an awful situation. The committee adjourned for the Forces Development Committee to meet again and come back with a recommendation. I found out that most of those making the recommendation had never been on a submarine. The two recommendations were split and the tribute to Admiral Kelso was voted on, and the recommendation on women on submarines was postponed until the next meeting. I met with many on the committee and suggested that members take a trip and tour a submarine. While the strategic missile submarines were larger and could better accommodate mixed genders, the fast attacks were smaller.

That evening was my first ever OSD dinner and it was very formal. There was hardly a smile from anyone, including those at my table. In fact, when they played the four service songs, there was not a peep from the audience—no cheers, no applause, not a murmur. I was seated with assistant secretary of defense, Frank Rush, and assistant secretary of defense for Force Management Policy, Fred Pang. Secretary Pang later became a great mentor for me (see his story in the memoirs) but that time they were both just intimidating. *However,* after a while I made some teasing comment and they responded and I relaxed a little. Before the evening was over, I knew I had two new friends!

The following year, I was asked to serve on the executive committee as vice chairman and director of installation: to read and track issues and to prepare the report for the secretary of defense. It included working with all members of the committee to help train the members on the visits and oversee the process. Each of the forty or so members located across the country were to conduct at least two visits in their geographic areas. I was honored by their confidence in me.

It was a great three years that considerably picked up speed with this new job. My local responsibilities included Georgia military installations ships homeported at Jacksonville, and when the Secretary expanded our visits to include training bases, I visited the Coast Guard training at Cape May

As the director of installations, I gave a report at each event including the formal dinner. My only part at the beginning was to handle introductions including the introduction of new members. It was a small part but received many comments. The PAO seemed downright surprised. She said, "You'd think you'd done it a million times."

"I have," I replied.

During that year, we had a special guest—Her Royal Highness Aisha Bint Al Hussein, who is the daughter of King Hussain of Jordan. There was quite a buzz and protocol was giving briefs to everyone. However, I was speaking that evening and trying to get ready for introductions, etc., so I didn't listen as well as I should to the protocol briefings. After all, I had plenty of time to get up to speed on Her Royal Highness, but right then I had to put together my remarks. Imagine my surprise when I was seated next to Princess Aisha. I didn't know what to do, so I decided that honesty was the best thing.

"Princess Aisha, when we received the briefings, I failed to listen properly because I was preparing for this dinner. Would you tell me how you prefer to be called?"

"Please, Sheila, call me Colonel."

I don't think that was in the protocol brief, but Colonel she was. Before the remarks started, I decided to go to the ladies' room. I turned to the colonel and asked her if she wanted to join me. She looked a little startled, then a little determined and said yes in a very positive way. We got up and walked across the huge ballroom. I had not noticed it before, but there were Jordanian guards stationed around the room with obvious weaponry. By the time we got to the ladies' room, there were several guards joining us. They started to open the door when she stopped them and said, "Mrs. McNeill and I will be fine." They checked the bathrooms and stood back for us to enter. I can't imagine having that kind of security all the time. I spent a lot of time with her over the next few years. We went out with the committee a couple of times, but she visited each committee, as I did as the visit coordinator. At one event, HRH and I were on a panel on the dais. Arlie had accompanied me that year, to observe what was taking up so much of my life. When I have to carry a purse, and

I've carried the same small purse for years, and that night I had left it with Arlie to hold on his lap. As I looked out over the room, I saw the colonel's bodyguards all moving closer to Arlie. There were several and it was obvious. I wrote the colonel a note: "Your bodyguards are worried about my purse in Arlie's lap." She smiled and called someone over and said, "Tell them it's Sheila's husband, and it's her purse." I watched as they slowly backed off.

I always admired her posture and her composure. She would sit for hours with that straight back and never squirming or looking uncomfortable. When I asked her about it, she said they were trained from early childhood to sit straight and remain quiet for ceremonies, etc. I found myself copying that posture and found over the years found out that that ramrod straight back really helped your back thus enduring long meetings. In some of our off moments, the Colonel told me about her approaching her father with an idea. She told him she wanted to create a women's army in Jordan. He finally relented, and she proudly told me that some of those women soldiers were now some of the best and they were the official guards for the palace. Colonel Aisha later became a brigadier general of Jordan's Royal Jordanian Armed Forces.

At the middle of the second year, I was asked to be vice chairman and also retain the job as installation visit coordinator. The best way to explain the job is to share the turnover paper I left for my replacement Candice Young-Richey when I completed my tour:

Memorandum to Candace Young—Richey

December 5, 1998

Congratulations! You are beginning one of the most rewarding jobs of the committee. You are also beginning one of the most demanding. You'll have a great time!

I've enclosed in your packet copies of the 1998 installation reports, the spreadsheet on the visit reports received before last week, every letter I have sent as installation visit coordinator and a copy of every compass report both six-month and annual, both training reports and the two overseas reports.

The following are suggestions and words of wisdom that may help you:

- *Always remember—only the issues that come up in focus groups are issues we deal with. For instance, where did violence against women ever get to the issue? I cannot find any references in the installation visits.*

- *You should make an example by making more than your share of visits and submitting timely reports. meetings—you've already shown your willingness for this.*
- *Feedback and "warm fuzzies" make a difference.*
- *Review for change my form letter and reminders on visits.*
- *Remember our members are probably the busiest individuals in the country.*
- *Write a note of thanks when the report is received—this is a hard one!*
- *Give feedback to the office within three days of getting a faxed report.*
- *Provide to the subcommittee chairmen and to the chair:*
    - *Numbers and percentages for top issues*
    - *A list divided by committee on "other issues"*
- *The executive committee should make a decision on the issues of perceptions of first term pregnancies and how they relate to readiness—also which committee should handle. This had been listed under Quality of Life but the vast majority of the issues are not the 'planned pregnancies' so I believe they should be transferred to Forces. Sue Straughn suggested this. The politically correct thing might be to "consider reviewing research of pregnancy and other health issues and how they relate to readiness."*
- *Prepare both a six month and an annual report for oral briefing at conference and written briefs to the Secretary of Defense.*

Enjoy!
Cc: Liz Bilby (current chairman)
Mary Wamsley (incoming chairman)

The executive committee consisted of the following:

Equality Management Subcommittee
Ginger L. Simpson, Chair
Robert M. Kaufman, Vice Chair
Forces Development and Utilization Subcommittee
Ms. Lori Hunter, Chair
Ms. Mary J. Wamsley, Vice Chair
Quality of Life Subcommittee
Ms. Sue Straughn, Chair
Mrs. Anita V. Elphick, Vice Chair

Installation Visit Coordinator, Vice Chair
Sheila McNeill

The executive committee would also make two overseas trips. One to Europe and one to Asia. The wonderful military staff were as follows:

Carolyn V. Prevatt, Executive Director
Captain Barbara L. Brehm, USN Director
Commander Tala Welch
Commander Deborah R. Goodwin, USN
Operations Officer
Lt. Colonel Kay Troutt, USAF
Lieutenant Colonel Sandy Lewis, ARNGUS
Public Affairs and Protocol Liaison Officer
Captain A. Renee Roberts, USA
Communications Officer
Captain Heather Amstutz, USA
Plans and Logistics Officer
Chief Myra L. Maxwell, USCG
Gunnery Sergeant Brenda L. Warren, USMC
Administrative Assistant
Sergeant Lisa R. Baker, USA 1996
Staff Sergeant James Skoros, USAF
Administrative Technician

As the chairman of the installation visits, I also did the training. Since many had not had experience with the military, I made sure I didn't use any acronyms. I remember one briefing I did say that when they visited an installation they would stay at the BOQ (bachelor officers quarters). All hands came up wanting to know what it was. I was even more careful after that.

My briefing included the following: When you go to an installation you will meet with the commanding officer of the installation. The professional staff will have already briefed him on the protocols but review them again. Tell him or her that you will brief them at the end of the day. There will be no surprises for them later. They will know the issues discussed. The focus groups are divided by rank and gender. You will have five to six different groups. Always begin with the words "If you had five minutes with the secretary of defense what would you say?" Nothing else should be said, no elaboration, no questions. If you ask specific questions, *you* are setting the agenda.

I asked every member to add to the report their top three issues. We had not quantified it this way in the past. When I prepared the report for the Department of Defense, I was able to give them a very accurate—and I think nonprejudicial findings of our committee. Many times, during the in briefs with the commanding officers of the installations or commands I was asked to listen in confidence, and while that installation was never listed, I was able to get a better idea of the real needs of our military. I always gave each commanding officer an opportunity to discuss any issue they wanted to discuss but not have it in the report. I told them I would use the information as "deep background" for my reports but that their name would never be associated with the issue. I was amazed at the officers who talked to be about their concerns.

To give you an idea of the work that went into the annual reports I have included the 1997 CONUS Report:

Defense Advisory Committee on Women in the Service
1997 CONUS (Continental United States) report

In 1997, DACOWITS visited 59 installations and met with more than 3,900 service members from all five Armed Forces and the Reserve component.

This report summarizes the issues most frequently raised by these service members.

The executive committee had two overseas visits:

DACOWITS 1997 OVERSEAS TRIP

COUNTRIES VISITED/STOPS MADE ALASKA, KOREA, JAPAN, GUAM, HAWAII:

1997 DACOWITS EXECUTIVE COMMITTEE MEMBERS and those traveling to overseas:

Dr. Judith A. Youngman, Chair
Sheila McNeill Vice Chair, Installation Coordinator
Hon. Carol G. Micki, Chair Equality Management (my wonderful mentor)
Ms. Ginger L. Simpson, Vice Chair
Ms. Jill Docking, Chair, Forces Development and Utilization
Ms. Elizabeth Bilby, Vice Chair
Dr. Sue Guenter-Schlesinger, Chair, Quality of Life
Ms. Sue Straughn, Vice Chair

We met with the following installations:

Eielson, Air Force Base, Alaska
Ft. Wainright, Alaska

Ft Greely, Alaska
Anderson Air Force Base, Guam (included WESTPAC Vet Services Army, Guam)
Naval Station Guam
CINCPAC—Commander in charge of the Pacific Fleet and those assigned there
Marine Corps Air Station, Iwakuni Japan
Naval Support Activity, Yokosuka, Jap
Camp Kinser, Third FSSG, Okinawa, Japan
Naval Regional Medical, Camp Lester, Okinawa, Japan, including Tenth SG, Army, Okinawa, Japan
Kunsan Air Force Base, Korea
Camp Walker Henry, Korea

The trips were long, but it was a pleasure not to have to transfer planes or deal with civilian airports. The culinary specialist on board were wonderful and had anything we wanted to eat. We were given an area to sit—that belonged to us. My chair had a table and a computer. We were to write up each report as we left the installation. That is the only way it would work. You remember all the comments, but if they are not written down, you could easily confuse the locations.

When I was seated at my place in front of the computer—it was a first. I had never used a computer. I was a good typist, but I didn't know what to do once I had typed it in. They trained me on the Enter button! After that things got a little easier.

Our first stop was at Eielson Air Force Base, Alaska. We were all worn-out, but one of the senior officers offered to pick us up and ride around to see the moose in the area. We were pleased to do that, but at the last minute, we were told it was "improper" for us to accept his offer. In 2017, that isn't unusual—political correctness is at its highest. But I'll bet that if I'd called one of the senior officers in that chain of command they would have scoffed at that. We didn't go. We had dinner and stayed in our rooms.

We flew into Taegu Korea then Marine Corps Air Station, Iwakuni, Japan, and then on to Kadena Air Base.

Lt. General Frank Libutti was commanding general III Marine Expeditionary Force and Commander, Marine Corps Bases, Japan. They were most impressive, and his staff was very gracious to our committee.

We then traveled to Andersen Air Force Base in Guam and a stop off in Honolulu to brief the military leadership on our trip. Coming back through Honolulu, we were met by Kristi Kijek, lieutenant colonel at Hickam Air Force Base—who had the lead on our visit. We hit it off realizing that our paths would not cross again. She was a JAG and at the time chief of Military Justice, Adverse Actions, Labor Law, and Claims.

She later became my niece. She married my nephew, Larry Youngner Jr., also a JAG in the Air Force. She came home with him and we talked but didn't immediately remember meeting each other, but she looked so familiar. Over several visits, she learned I was on DACOWITS and we both realized we had met each other in Hawaii. We even found a picture of us on the airport runway. It is an amazingly small world in these military services.

When I was in Hawaii, I met with RADM Jerry and Rosemary Ellis for dinner. That was very important since he was the one who recommended me for this position.

Dacowits, 1998 Overseas Trip

Sunday, July 12–Sunday, July 26

Countries Visited: Azores, Italy, Bahrain, Saudi Arabia, Turkey, Bosnia-Herzegovina, Germany, England, and Iceland

OVERVIEW: The contrast in weather, in culture, in society were incredible. We were blessed with the opportunity to see the work and meet so many dedicated military men and women. Our prayer was to represent them well as we return to Washington.

Lages Air Base, Azores. This is an island owned by the Portuguese. We arrive one and a half hours earlier because we did not have to stop and refuel. The master chief of the command took us for a tour of the island and the beach. As we were visiting the base, guarded by Portuguese nationals, we were told we would not be able to reenter the base. So much for having special visas to land directly on military bases. After about twenty minutes, they did get approval and we left. On the beach (very limited) there was an even smaller area roped off for military. I supposed to ensure that the American military didn't take over! It was a nice pleasant way to end our first day even if we were gone until about eight thirty. Next day work all day, leaving about two and arriving in Italy about nine thirty.

Sardinia, Italy. It was fun seeing the Simon Lake, a submarine tender, as it had been at Scotland where Arlie and I had dinner on board, and then was in Kings Bay. We ran into a Lieutenant from Kings Bay. When we walked up, I knew he looked familiar, and then he asked about the submarine museum. The commodore was a friend of the captains I know at Kings Bay, so I told him hello. He had a great personality and spent a lot of time telling me the proper way to purchase Oriental rugs. He was a serious silver collector and told me of the places I should go in the States. We had a great lunch onboard and we discussed the museum and the upcoming decommissioning of the ship. The Captain hopes to take it to all the ports where it had been stationed so he hopes to be back at Kings Bay by September or October 1999. I talked with him about the items for the museum. He will save any plaques, etc. We both had milk with our chocolate cake (with icing like Mother makes) and did a little bonding.

As we left the tender that evening, they were announcing DACOWITS departing. Someone asked where Liz and Captain Brehm were. It seems the captain had forgotten them, and they were resting in his cabin. He would not let anyone else go get them, so he rushed back several decks to escort them. Dinner that evening at a local restaurant was wonderful but far too much. There were about four courses with everything but dessert. We then flew all night to Bahrain, Saudi Arabia. I really planned to get a little sleep, but it would not come. I read until 3:00 a.m. when we were served pancakes.

Bahrain, Saudi Arabia. We arrived about 5:00 a.m. and went straight to the hotel. The hotel was equal to a Ritz-Carlton. All marble, with large rooms and baths, but that was where the similarity ended. It was so strange seeing so many Arabs and the women wearing abayas. We were told as soon as the young girls reached puberty—around thirteen—they were required to stop wearing play clothes (very American looking) and wear the robes with the hoods and face covered. Many tried to cover up the fact that they had reached womanhood (started their periods) so they could still play.

We were told not to go around the hotel alone because Arab men did not like "American women" and would spit on them and curse them. I never saw an indication of this attitude. Those I saw in the hotel and later in the gold souks were gracious, perhaps because we were spending money!

We had three hours to check in, unpack, iron clothes, take a shower, rest, and get dressed to meet in the lobby at 8:30. After working all day, we had a couple of hours to go to the gold souks. Our time was limited, so we did a lot of power shopping.

Later that evening, when were given time to rest, Ginger had a friend who offered to have a rug party, sort of like a Tupperware party. About five of us went to her home. I went because I wanted to see the home of a military woman stationed in Bahrain. It was a great home and very large, around 2,500 square feet. There was marble everywhere with five bedrooms with baths. It was bigger than what she needed, but all the homes in the civilian areas were large. The government has to pay an allowance that allow them to live there. The rumor was that the landlords find out the rank and charge the maximum allowed for housing of that rank. Obviously, there was no way out of this, just one of the many situations concerning local nationals we heard of on our trip.

The rug party was great and we were assured by the senior chief that these were the best buys. I, who only came for the tour, ended up buying three and lugging them back home. All of us but Bob Kaufman bought two or three. Security was tight at the base. The Khobar Towers bombing was on June 25, 1996, and was in that command where nineteen US service members were killed, and some five hundred people were injured.

One unforgettable trip was to Bosnia-Herzegovina was a real "what am I doing here moment." where we met with the mayors of the two war-torn villages who, with the military's help, were working to resolve their conflicts and live peacefully together. Meeting in focus groups behind barbwired fences and with soldiers emptying their cartridges as they came into the tent was a trip I won't soon forget.

A couple of us were being escorted by a brigadier general. As we walked around the camp, there were smart salutes by everyone we passed. As we turned a corner, a young soldier did not salute. The general reamed him out, dressed him down, gave him hell… I'm thinking he was being a little too tough—one young soldier who missed seeing him. You could tell the soldier was contrite and very nervous at this point. I had a surprise as we walked away. The general said, "Do you know why I did that? We are in a dangerous county. One mistake could cause a life. You have to be aware of your surroundings. That soldier was not aware and something like that could get him killed." That was a pivotal moment for me.

In Germany, I met with a group of senior enlisted marines. I said the usual, "If you had five minutes to speak with the secretary of defense, what would you say?" There were six minutes of quiet. I sat at the front of the room and about forty marines sat in the audience looking at me. "We will be hearing a knock at that front door in about fifty-five minutes and you are going to wish you had more time." They started to speak up and ask questions. "Do we have to talk about women?"

"I don't know, if that is what you would talk about if you had five minutes with the secretary?"

"No, I'd talk about how we are having to cannibalize our aircraft."

"And I'd talk about pay for our junior enlisted," another said.

As it turned out, this was a time when we were cannibalizing our aircraft to use parts to be able to fly some of them, where maintenance issues were arising as serious issues. Yes, this committee came back from our overseas countries, not with equality issues but with funding issues. We found that the overwhelming majority of those folks we met with wanted the tools and resources to do their jobs and they wanted their families taken care of. It had been a while since there was a significant increase in pay. As long as the person did their job, they didn't care what gender they were! They just wanted their junior enlisted to earn enough pay to take care of their families.

At the next formal dinner in DC, after this European trip in July 1995, I was seated with a service chief (head of one of the services) and an undersecretary of another branch of the military. The undersecretary was really giving me a hard time about the results of the European trip.

The secretary never said another word that evening about our findings. That full story is found in General Dennis Rimer's story.

My DACOWITS trips took me all over the southeast. In January 1997, I had a visit to the USS *John F. Kennedy* stationed at Mayport Naval Base in Jacksonville, Florida (my first "piping aboard") as well as all the installations in Georgia and installations in Europe and Asia.

I was nearing the end of my second year in December 1998. The *Brunswick News* ran a wonderful story in their December 1998 paper:

Sheila McNeill seeing the World as Member of DACOWITS Committee
By Lisa R. Schoolcraft
News staff writer

Sheila McNeill has found herself a world traveler this year as part of her work with the DACOWITS Committee. Mrs. McNeill is in her second year of a three-year appointment to the Defense Advisory Committee on Women in the Services and the quality of life for women (and men—left out) in the armed forces Mrs. McNeill said the committee seeks recommendations on the quality of life on the base, including housing, child care development centers and hospitals. We sit down with focus groups, segregated by rank and gender," she said. "I ask them if you have five minutes with the Secretary of Defense, what would you tell him?" The committee promises complete anonymity and the military personnel are open and honest about conditions and concerns at the various bases, she added. After meeting with the groups, Mrs. McNeill puts together her notes and meets with the generals on the base to go over the concerns. They are not obligated to do anything about it," she said of the concerns. "But we find the generals find them helpful." Mrs. McNeill said she has learned to take notes with her notepad in her lap, and has learned not to make too many requests of base personnel. She said as a DACOWITS committee member, she gets three-star treatment. Once she made the mistake of mentioning she wanted to try a particular pizza and a few minutes later pizza arrived in the room.

In July, Mrs. McNeill, who is vice chairman of the executive committee, went overseas, visiting 18 bases in 16 days. She visited bases in Alaska, Guam, Japan, Korea and Hawaii. "We were completely exhausted by the time we got to Hawaii," she said. On the eighth day of the trip, executive committee members got the day off and went to a formal tea ceremony in Japan, she said.

"We sat on the hard floor in a position a 50-year-old woman should never have to be in," Mrs. McNeill said. "and the members

were so interested in the ceremony, we got the extended version. "She also recalled eating great sushi in Japan. "I thought I understood the service until I went overseas," She said of her trip. "there are not so much gender issues. They need more money to do the mission. They had concerns about people, equipment and money." Mrs. McNeill has been a member of the Navy League for 32 years. She is currently a regional president over Georgia, South Carolina and North Carolina.

"But I never served (in the military)" she said. I guess this is my service. I will feel like I have served after this. I've had to learn about the Army and the Air Force, and the differences between the services. Mrs. McNeill said small instances have been the most rewarding during her appointment on the DACOWITS committee. Once, a female officer in a focus group saluted her and said she felt she was making a difference in the military. Another time, a commander said the base was buzzing with energy and enthusiasm after her visit. "And seeing that United States of America on the side of the plane, you really feel like you are ambassadors," she said of her travels. "This is the hardest work I've ever done. But it's so rewarding" Mrs. McNeill said the appointment is non-paying. "I think people realize you're not some high-paid person doing this—that you're doing this because you care about the service," she said.

In 1998, I sent my last memorandum to members:

Memorandum to: All DACOWITS Members
From: Sheila McNeill

Final plans are being made for our spring conference in Washington. At that conference, you will be asked to give a report on your installation visits made during our fall conference. By receiving a brief on our visits on all issues we will keep our members better informed. However, we do have a concern about our time constraints to address both of these issues I ask you to follow these steps.

1. *Do not mention specific installations and on sensitive issues not give military service branch*
2. *remember these are open meetings and the public and press are present. This should not discourage you from being forthright with all the issues. It is just a reminder so you will be prepared.*

3. *Keep it short. Give only the top three issues and any pertinent information you wish.*
4. *Your report should not take more than two or three minutes.*

Our total visits for 1997 were 59 compared to 48 in 1996 with 20% less members we increased our visits by 23%. This is a great improvement and we welcome the problem of having to limit time because of so many completed visits. Do not let our military down! If you have not completed at least two visits, please look at your schedule and find time to do your part. Remember Capt. Amstutz needs to know your data six weeks out and it helps to give two or three dates. We realize how busy you all are and the difficulty with tying down two or three days but Capt. Amstutz recognizes this and will do everything possible to get back with you in a short time. In the meantime, call me if you have a visit planned and have questions. I look forward to seeing each of you in Washington.

Best regards Sheila McNeill
cc Ms. Liz Bilby
Capt. Brehm, U.S. Navy
Capt. Amstutz U.S. Army

In 1999, after my tour was complete and I had been elected as a national vice president of the Navy League I attended a meeting of DACOWITS in California (that story is in "Women on Submarines" as is the letter I sent to the editor of the *Washington Times* printed on June 2, 2000).

The letter that never got sent:

Suggestion for the Defense Advisory Committee on Women in the Services (DACOWITS) 1999

During the three years I was a member of DACOWITS I saw trends go from gender issues to issues that were non-gender, primarily in the quality of life areas. Recent changes in force restructuring—downsizing, outsourcing and privatization have resulted in issues of retention, recruitment erosion of benefits and lack of resources as prevailing issues. Perhaps DACOWITS should consider changing their name from Defense Advisory Committee on Women in the Services to Defense Advisory Committee on Personnel Issues. There were times when I visited bases the name was divisive. We might concentrate on those issues that affect all military.

This is not to suggest that there are not women's issues, nor to suggest that these issues be removed from the process. There are still those who would abuse and discriminate—both gender and race. We should provide a process for handling these and other single gender issues. The solution could be more effective and less intrusive if these issues result from more gender integrated goals. I recognize the down side of that. The committee would probably lose its funding and be dissolved. Regrettably, in this day of decreasing military funding, a committee to simply listen to military member's concerns would not have the backing that the politically charged 'women's rights' might generate.

There is no question that having this system for giving our service men and women an opportunity to have their five minutes with the Secretary of Defense is healthy and worthwhile. One would only have to make a visit and listen to two or three focus groups to see the incredible process. Beginning with some distrust and resentfulness, my personal experience always resulted in hearing expressions of gratitude, satisfaction and pride.

Without exception, this is a release that comes from being able to express concerns in a process void of retribution. When I started on DACOWITS I wondered how civilians who didn't understand the military could be affective. I quickly saw—particularly as Vice Chair in my last two years that these intelligent, professional concerned citizens are the right conduit for this process.

I'm not sure why I never sent this memo. Perhaps the heavy demands of Navy League or maybe because I was a coward.

After finishing DACOWITS in 1998, I was invited to attend their meeting in 1999 in California. At that time, I was a national vice president of the Navy League and was able to schedule some meetings with Navy League members at the same time. In an airport on the way to the meeting, I ran into RADM Ronne Froman from my DACOWITS days. She was then commander of Naval Station San Diego.

Earlier, I had the honor of attending the ceremony in her office in the Pentagon when she received a medal. I managed to arrange seats on the plane, so we could sit together. We shared many common beliefs about the committee and what we would like to see done. There were many times during the first months of DACOWITS that I felt overwhelmed and wondered if I "belonged" on the committee. RADM Froman always kept me grounded. She was a wonderful mentor as I was training to be a DACOWITS member.

The first person who told me that I was "changing the way the committee does business" was Dr. Schafelin, a DACOWITS member from 1980 to 1982 who attended every conference. She said, "Sheila, the work you did for DACOWITS has started a legacy that has changed the way we do business and will continue for many years to come." Secretary Pang told me the same during that meeting. All those worries of not fitting in and wondering if what I was doing was the right thing all faded away with their comments.

That evening summed up the commitment I had during those three years. The current chairman, Mary Wamsley, had me seated with her at the head table. Her husband, Doug, was also present. And to top off the evening, Secretary Rush told Admiral Donald Pilling, deputy chief of Naval Operations, as the group listened, "Admiral, if you talk to Sheila about the Navy, you *might* be able to get her to be a big supporter. Sheila was the first one to really take hold of the process we use on installation visits and turn us in the right direction. She really worked hard and doubled the number of visits the next year."

The table also included my friend, assistant secretary of defense, Fred Pang. Admiral Pilling was the speaker for the evening. Admiral Pilling was known as a great mind. He was awarded a PhD in mathematics from the University of Cambridge. (Note: The country lost that brilliant mind on May 26, 2008, when Admiral Pilling died of leukemia.)

I did not know him well but enjoyed the time with him. By this time, the Forces Development Committee had had several presentations from the submarine force. Secretary Pang and I had become friends over the years and I always enjoyed an opportunity to talk with him. Imagine my surprise when he announced to the table, "Sheila changed the way we do business at the Pentagon." I assumed this was a result of my instructions to the committee not to determine the agenda but to allow our military members to do that and the process on writing the report. See my story on Secretary Pang.

One of the lessons learned about DoD was you get what you asked for. Many requests were made of DoD during those two years I was on the committee and a few times our request didn't bring us the information we needed to make a decision. It was always what we asked for, but as civilians we didn't always know how to ask for the complete information we needed.

That day Vice Admiral Ed Giambastini, who was SUBLANT (Submarine Forces Atlantic Fleet) at the time, had briefed DACOWITS on women on submarines and I had been invited to attend. Admiral Pilling asked, "So how did the briefing go today. How did we do?"

"Well, sir, if I told you I would have to use an obscenity."

"Go ahead," he replied.

See the story on "Women on Submarines" for my answer.

I am deeply indebted to principal undersecretary of defense Fred Pang. He was my mentor every time I needed him. Assistant secretary of defense for equal opportunity, Bill Leftwich, and principal deputy assistant for Force Management Policy, Frank Rush, were very helpful, and I loved talking with them. We talked a lot—never about politics but the issues and what we could do to improve them. Mr. Leftwich told me, "I think we made a difference—some we had to drag along. We have surfaced things that we have never discussed."

I was at a governor's Military Affairs Committee meeting following one of my DACOWITS visits and a junior enlisted approached me thanking me for my visit to an installation where she was a member of the focus group. I responded by thanking her for taking the time to meet with me. "Oh, ma'am, we feel like we made a difference." That pretty well sums up my feelings about the three years on the Defense Advisory Committee on Women in the Services. That is how we all felt.

ADMIRAL KIRK DONALD AND DIANNE

DIRECTOR OF NAVAL NUCLEAR REACTORS

My favorite story of Admiral Donald was at a submarine ball sponsored by Naval Submarine Base Kings Bay. The ball was at the Hyatt Regency Hotel in Jacksonville in April 2010. Our speaker for the evening was Admiral Kirk Donald. He was then the director of naval nuclear reactors. A big, big job and a position that requires the most brilliant mind and a steady temperament. Admiral Donald was all things proper. Arlie and I were seated at the table with the Donalds and RDML Barry Bruner and his wife, Beth, and both squadron commanders Captains Kevin Brenton and Tracy Howard.

After dinner, and when it was about time for the speaker, Admiral Donald came over to me and said, "Sheila, give me your phone."

"It won't do you any good—I can't get a connection."

"Give it to me anyway."

I had no idea what use it would be, but I gave it to him. To my surprise, he put it in his pocket. He and RDML Bruner walked to the podium. Barry gave him a nice introduction and he began his formal speech. There were close to one thousand in attendance. After about ten minutes into his remarks, he made a slight joke and a phone started ringing and he reached into his jacket pocket and brought out my phone and answered it. As he answered it, the words came up on a screen behind him on the wall.

"Kirk, you are not funny," Diane was supposed to be saying.

The crowd erupted. "Yes, I think I am. I think the audience is really enjoying it." And for that they cheered.

"Well, you are not, and I think you have talked long enough." Were the words that showed on the teleprompter behind him.

A big laugh from several hundred. About this time, Diane was shocked and telling everyone at the table, "It's not me. I'm not telling him anything."

"Well, Sheila likes it."

Now everyone is looking at me as I say, "I don't know where he is getting that—I haven't said a word."

And the crowd is laughing. "And Sheila thinks I'm sexy—she likes my white hair."

Is there anything higher than an eruption of laughter! Everyone was crazy laughing and wondering who this man was who was impersonating Admiral Donald. And then he threw out a lieutenant's name and the tables around the lieutenant erupted. The entire room was crazy as he mentioned others as if they had called him. That is a side of Kirk Donald you don't see every day.

I loved staying at their quarters. Yes, it was in the middle of DC and getting a cab was a breeze and you could get anywhere pretty quickly, but that wasn't the reason. They had a three-story house and *my* room was on the third floor—lots of privacy, but that's not the reason.

And what a selection of scotch! Admiral Donald gave me the okay to sample them all—which I did. To keep it straight, I left the ones I sampled in a row on a table that was out of the way—this was only one time! He "outed" me with the staff! Diane and I were at his office having lunch with everyone after a change of command ceremony at the Navy yard. He told them about my "bottles" and what he had to put up with when he got home. We had such fun. And that was the reason. It was fun and it was always interesting. Everyone was busy, so we didn't have long in the evening, but it was always a 'spirited' conversation and I pulled everything from Kirk I could get. I was always hungry for anything submarine.

When I attended the USS *George H. W. Bush* commissioning in January 2009, I met up with two Camden County friends, Keith Post and CDR Jon Hagemann. I had planned to meet them after the commissioning. I ran into Admiral Mike Mullen and his wife, Deborah, and we all walked together to the reception. We ran into Admiral Kirk Donald and I introduced him to Keith and Jon and added that Jon worked for him. Admiral Donald paused, cocked his head, and said, "You work for me? So what are you doing here?"

"I'm with Sheila," he replied.

Admiral Donald smiled and said, "As you should be—I hope you are enjoying it."

Talk about relief from everyone. We later laughed as we realized how well that turned out and how happy we were that Admiral Donald had a sense of humor.

Charlie and Karen Young came for dinner at the Donald's on May 25, 2010, and it was a night we won't forget. As much as I'd like to share it—that conversation will remain just a fun evening with friends! Diane and Karen worked together with a DC designer, Ann Hand, to design the Dolphin Scholarship Pin. As a member of the board of directors of the Dolphin Scholarship Foundation, I was assigned to the committee to help with the final details. My work was mainly as the cheerleader and an occasion opinion. We had a wonderful time and the pin made lots of money for the scholarship foundation.

We even had a girls' night out at their home in Williamsburg. We went to one of Diane's favorite restaurants. We had a great time with the server. Of course, Diane could not return to the restaurant for weeks. It was a fun weekend and we also managed to get a little work done on the plan for distribution of the new pin they had designed.

I don't see any of them much anymore, but the good thing about friends like that is you can pick up the phone and they would say, "We'll leave the light on for you."

VICE ADMIRAL JAY DONNELLY AND MIMI

COMMANDER SUBMARINE FORCE

We were thrilled when Vice Admiral Donnelly and his wife, Mimi, came to the Submarine Museum for a tour shortly after taking the reins of the commander of the Submarine Forces. In January 2010, both VADM Donnelly and Mimi attended the partnership's "honoring our elected officials." It was a wonderful evening—their presence enhanced the evening for us all.

The Tribune & Georgian had almost a full page on his visit. "I'm a second-generation submariner. It's an amazing collection," he said. "I've got an appreciation for what is here." I received a note from Mayor Deborah Hase. She sent a wonderful note to all the officials about the event.

This was sent to the St. Marys Elected Officials and someone sent me a copy:

> *All, Last night was an awesome opportunity to connect with our military. What a wonderful event! For those of you were there, I am sure that you came away with a renewed understanding of the tremendous asset we have in our community in the form of a Navy base. The fact that a number of high ranking officials (from various Naval positions, and not just Kings Bay) took the time to meet local elected officials demonstrates their interest and the importance in maintaining good relations with the community…*
>
> *However, the most delightful conversation I had was with Mimi Donnell, the Commander's wife. She is such an energetic per-*

son and is so passionate about her work as well as her husband's. She evidently works with promoting the quality of life for the Naval personnel and their families. She expressed her appreciation for the great family-oriented community that we have here as well. She then accommodated me by taking my picture with her husband, so I could use it to impress my son-in-law.

For those of you who were not present, I am sorry you missed it. Take it from those of us who were there we need to take very opportunity we can to nurture our relationship with those who make decisions about the Kings Bay Navy Base, Camden's largest and more important employer.

Deborah Haas (Mayor of St. Marys)

We toured Mimi through St. Marys on a golf cart. She sent one of the best letters:

Dear Sheila,

Thank you so much for the absolutely grand day in St. Marys. It was such a treat to be out and about on that beautiful Georgia morning. I adored the Submarine Museum and think it would be great to go back and spend hours there exploring all the memorabilia stuffed into every nook and cranny. What a terrific way to gain insight into the Submarine Force, both past and present. I have always felt they were a special breed and the things you have there bear that out.

Thank you also for arranging the tour of St. Marys. It is a delightful place filled with wonderful architecture, folk lore and Southern hospitality. Riding around on the trolley was a thrill and a perfect way to see the sights. Orange Hall, the stately oaks, the quaint churches and the lovely little shops add up to one fabulous little town. Thank you also for the lovely lunch. The Crab Bisque was as good as you promised but the highlight was certainly the Lemon Meringue Pie. It was sinfully delicious, and I felt no guilt what so ever as I ate it. (I did a couple of extra laps on the treadmill when I got home.)

Sheila, I believe that you could sell ice to the Eskimos if you thought it was a worthy cause! The Navy League and the Chamber of Commerce are lucky to have you on their team. Whatever you put your mind to just seems to happen. I want to wish you the best of luck in your future endeavors and thank you again for all you did for me on my trip to Kings Bay.

Very respectfully,
Mimi Donnelly
P.S. I was absolutely serious about helping to transcribe Patrol Reports or anything else.

And serious she was: She spent many hours transcribing those trip reports from World War II. She said she could smell the diesel as she typed.

The Tribune & Georgian's Johna Strickland wrote the following:

Navy wife types World War II patrol reports

The USS Rasher (SS 269) commenced its first patrol World War II in October 1943. The vessel, a Gato-class attack submarine, logged eight patrols through 1945 in Japanese controlled waters.

Sixty years later, Mimi Donnelly re-lived their service through the patrol reports. Donnelly picked up copies of the reports for the St. Marys Submarine Museum more than two years ago, The originals—aged to a brown color and words faded to oblivion in places—remain in storage.

"We keep them in plastic because they are so brittle—you touch them, and they fall apart," said Kari Charles, records keeper for the museum. "until you read them, you don't know what World War II was about." Donnelly, whose husband, Vice Adm. John Donnelly, commands the Navy's Atlantic submarine force from Norfolk, Va. Became one of about 20 volunteers who typed the reports into a standard electronic form where they can be read and disseminated. Students enrolled in typing at Camden County High School will transcribe the reports for class, Charles said.

"If I were a wise woman, I'd write a nice book or a movie because there were some dicey things in there," Donnelly said. For two years, Donnelly read about the Rasher's fate as she typed. On the first patrol,"54 contacts were made, resulting in eight attacks. All torpedoes were expended," the report states. The sub was forced underwater by unidentified aircraft and eschewed bright moonlight early in the first patrol, Donnelly typed.

"When 13,999 yards ahead of target, dawn just breaking, dived and made a periscope submerged approach," they recorded on October 9, 1943. "Just prior to firing, observed there were two ships and no escorts so used dived fire. Missed first ship. Sank second." Donnelly told local military advocate Sheila McNeill that she could smell the diesel fuel as she typed.

> *"This was such a labor of love," Donnelly said, noting she used a magnifying glass and other sources to make out the reports. "It was truly an extraordinary experience." She learned about submarines, World War II and the Navy, asking her husband about unfamiliar ranks. Some pages were blurred or faded in the midst of an attack. Depth charges were headed for the submarine, and a blank space later, the attack ended.*
>
> *"We know they survived but we don't know how," Donnelly said. "I felt like I was typing a John Wayne movie. The USS Rasher earned the Presidential Unit Citation for its patrols and nearly surpassed its sister ship, the USS Flasher, for the most tonnage sank by a submarine in history. The USS Rasher downed 99,901 tons of enemy craft and damaged an additional 62,481 tons.*

Doug Cooper was president of the museum at that time.

Thank you, Mimi, for all your work on preserving this great piece of history.

While Jay was head of the submarine force, Mimi took the reins of the Dolphin Scholarship Foundation. It was during that time that I joined as a member of the board of directors.

* * * * *

VADM Donnelly was featured in *Seapower* in March 2009. He was asked, what is the plan to develop a replacement for the Ohio-class SSBN?

His answer was this:

> *In February we commemorated the 1,000th patrol of the Ohio-class SSBN. Since SSBNs came on line 48 years ago, we've completed more than 3,800 strategic patrols. That is the ultimate insurance policy for the nation. The strategic deterrence they provide protects our country and is just as import today as it was during the Cold War. The 14-ship Ohio SSBN class will begin to reach the end of its life in 2027 at a rate of about one per year. We currently are engaged in analyses of alternatives to determine what the follow-on replacement to the Ohio class should be. We have started now on the conceptual design work to determine what the next platform would be.*

* * * * *

I will always be grateful to VADM Donnelly. After he retired from the Navy he went to work with Huntington Ingalls Industries as their corporate vice president for program integration and assessment. We had many talks about the Navy League and how to make it more effective. As busy as he was, he agreed to spend the time as a national vice president of the Navy League. Our Navy League has benefited greatly from Jay Donnelly.

DUNHAM BARRACKS CEREMONY

SUBMARINE BASE KINGS BAY—AUGUST 17, 2007

Rear Admiral Frank Drennan, Submarine Group 10, supported this wonderful event

The Periscope ran this article after the ceremony:

> *KINGS BAY, Ga. (Aug. 17, 2007)—Lt. Col. Andrew J. Murray (left), commanding officer of Marine Corps Security Force Company, Kings Bay, Ga., speaks to Deb and Dan Dunham, the parents of Cpl. Jason Dunham, a Medal of Honor recipient for Operation Iraqi Freedom, after a barracks dedication ceremony for their son here, Aug. 17. Dunham was stationed here from 2001-2003 before joining 3rd Battalion, 7th Marine Regiment, 1st Marine Division in Twenty-Nine Palms, Calif. Dunham received the Medal of Honor for heroic actions in Karabilah, Iraq, on April 14, 2004.*

The citation:

THE PRESIDENT OF THE UNITED STATES IN THE NAME OF THE CONGRESS TAKES PRIDE IN PRESENTING THE MEDAL OF HONOR POSTHUMOUSLY TO

CORPORAL JASON L. DUNHAM
UNITED STATES MARINE CORPS

FOR SERVICES AS SET FORTH IN THE FOLLOWING CITATION:

FOR CONSPICUOUS GALLANTRY AND INTREPIDITY AT THE RISK OF HIS LIFE ABOVE AND BEYOND THE CALL OF DUTY WHILE SERVING AS A RIFLE SQUAD LEADER, 4TH PLATOON, COMPANY K

THIRD BATTALION, SEVENTH MARINES (REINFORCED), ON 14 APRIL 2004, CORPORAL DUNHAM'S SQUAD WAS CONDUCTING A RECONNAISSANCE MISSION IN THE TOWN OF KARABILAH, IRAQ, WHEN THEY HEARD ROCKET PROPELLED GRENADE AND SMALL ARMS FIRE ERUPT APPROXIMATELY TWO KILOMETERS TO THE WEST. CORPORAL DUNHAM LED HIS COMBINED ANTI-ARMOR TEAM TOWARDS THE ENGAGEMENT TO PROVIDE FIRE SUPPORT TO THEIR BATTALION COMMANDER'S AS CORPORAL DUNHAM AND HIS MARINES ADVANCED, THEY QUICKLY BEGAN TO RECEIVE ENEMY FIRE. CORPORAL DUNHAM ORDERED HIS SQUAD TO DISMOUNT THEIR VEHICLES AND LED ONE OF HIS FIRE TEAMS ON FOOT SEVERAL BLOCKS SOUTH OF THE AMBUSHED CONVOY. DISCOVERING SEVEN IRAQI VEHICLES IN A COLUMN ATTEMPTING TO DEPART, CORPORAL DUNHAM AND HIS TEAM STOPPED THE VEHICLES TO SEARCH THEM FOR WEAPONS. AS THEY APPROACHED THE VEHICLES, AN INSURGENT LEAPED OUT AND ATTACKED CORPORAL DUNHAM. CORPORAL DUNHAM WRESTLED THE INSURGENT TO THE GROUND AND IN THE ENSUING STRUGGLE SAW THE INSURGENT RELEASE A GRENADE. CORPORAL DUNHAM IMMEDIATELY ALERTED HIS FELLOW MARINES TO THE THREAT, AWARE OF THE IMMINENT DANGER AND WITHOUT HESITATION, CORPORAL DUNHAM COVERED THE GRENADE WITH HIS HELMET AND BODY, BEARING THE BRUNT OF THE EXPLOSION AND SHIELDING HIS MARINES FROM THE BLAST. IN AN ULTIMATE AND SELFLESS ACT OF BRAVERY IN WHICH HE WAS MORTALLY WOUNDED, HE SAVED THE LIVES OF AT LEAST TWO FELLOW MARINES. BY HIS UNDAUNTED COURAGE, INTREPID FIGHTING SPIRIT AND UNWAVERING DEVOTION TO DUTY, CORPORAL DUNHAM GALLANTLY GAVE HIS LIFE FOR HIS COUNTRY, THEREBY REFLECTING GREAT CREDIT UPON HIMSELF AND UPHOLDING THE HIGHEST TRADITIONS OF THE MARINE CORPS AND THE UNITED STATES NAVAL SERVICE.

NAVAL SUBMARINE BASE KINGS BAY, GA
—Periscope

It was no average summer day Aug. 17, in Kings Bay, Ga., at least not at the Marine Corps Security Force Company's barracks. There was a special feeling in the air for every fellow Marine, sailor, friend and family member of a true American hero.

This hero is Cpl. Jason Dunham, Marine Medal of Honor recipient. The Marines dedicated their barracks to Dunham in a ceremony in front of his family, friends and Marines who served with Dunham during Operation Iraqi Freedom.

"Corporal Jason Dunham is a Marine hero for today's era," said Lt. Col. Andrew J. Murray, commanding officer of Marine Corps Security Force Company Kings Bay, Marine Corps Security Force Battalion, II Marine Expeditionary Force. "He will be a Marine leader to be emulated by Marines here (for years to come)." On April 14, 2004, while serving as rifle squad leader in 4th Platoon, Company K, 3rd Battalion, 7th Marine Regiment, Regimental Combat Team 7, 1st Marine Division, Dunham's squad was conducting a reconnaissance mission in the town of Karabilah, Iraq, when they heard rocket-propelled grenade and small-arms fire erupt approximately two kilometers away. Dunham led his team toward the engagement to provide fire support to their battalion commander's convoy, which had been ambushed as it was traveling to Camp Husaybah near the Iraqi-Syrian border. As they advanced, Dunham's team began to receive enemy fire themselves. Dunham ordered his squad to dismount their vehicles and led one of his fire teams on foot several blocks south of the ambushed convoy. Discovering seven Iraqi vehicles in a column attempting to depart the area, Dunham and his team stopped the vehicles to search them for weapons. As they approached the vehicles, an insurgent leaped out and attacked Dunham. Dunham wrestled the insurgent to the ground and, in the ensuing struggle, saw him release a grenade. Dunham immediately alerted his fellow Marines to the threat. Aware of the imminent danger and without hesitation, Dunham covered the grenade with his helmet and body, bore the brunt of the explosion, and shielded his Marines from the blast. Sacrificing his own safety in an act of bravery which left him mortally wounded, he saved the lives of two fellow Marines. He gave his life fighting for his country.

On Jan. 11, 2007, the president of the United States awarded Dunham the Medal of Honor posthumously for his heroic actions and gallantry.

So here at the Marine Corps Security Force Company barracks, where Dunham served from 2001 to 2003, the Marines dedicated their building, which is now known as Dunham Barracks, to him. General Robert Magnus, the assistant commandant of the Marine Corps, was on hand for the ceremony and offered these words to the audience as the barracks' name was unveiled.

"He knew his mission was to stop the insurgents and protect his fellow Marines. He would stand up in front of those who would bully his fellows," Magnus said. "Dunham (is) courage, honor and commitment. It is with great honor that we dedicate this barracks in memory of Corporal Jason Dunham."

A few of the Marines who served with Dunham in 3rd Bn., 7th Marines, were there as well and they explained Dunham's charisma and sense of pride and how it felt to watch the barracks dedication.

"He was a tough, good-looking, likable young guy with all the charisma in the world," said Capt. Dave Fleming, Dunham's platoon commander while he served with Weapons Platoon, Company K. "The Marines looked up to him. The sense of pride he had, he instilled in them."

"I'm glad I came here to see this; it's beautiful," explained Sgt. Jimmy Moronta, who served with Dunham in Weapons Platoon.

Perhaps no one was more touched by the dedication than Dunham's family, who was there in the front row. "It's an honor and it's wonderful the Marines have the history they do to keep him alive," said his mother, Deb Dunham. "(The Marines) are his family just as we're his family." "It's our family name (up there), but it's about Jason. It's not about us," said his father, Dan Dunham. "Jason was very humble; this would have been something he really respected."

Some say immortality means to be remembered throughout history. For the Marines and Sailors stationed here at Marine Corps Security Force Company, Dunham's memory will last for years to come, inspiring young Marine leaders to carry on the tradition built by Marines like Dan Daly, Chesty Puller, Smedley Butler… and now Jason Dunham.

Invitation:

The Commanding Officer
Marine Corps Security Force Company, Kings Bay, Georgia
Request the pleasure of your company at the barracks dedication in honor of
Medal of Honor Recipient Corporal Jason L. Dunham, USMC (Deceased)
At ten o'clock a.m. at Marine Corps Security Force Company, Building 1061

Naval Submarine Base Kings Bay, Georgia 31547
Officiating Officer will be General Robert Magnus,
Assistant Commandant of the Marine Corps

Assistant Marine Commandant, General Bob Magnus, to recognize an American Hero at Kings Bay.
Excerpts from that article:

> General Robert Magnus, Assistant Commandant of the United States Marine Corps, visited Naval Submarine Base Kings Bay (NSBKB) on Friday August 17, 2007. General Magnus combined his trip to NSBKB and the community, to be here to rename and dedicate the Kings Bay Marine Corps Security Force Barracks in honor of Corporal Jason Dunham. Traveling with General Magnus were Lt Colonel Andy Murray and Major Michael Olness. Michael was such a pleasure to work with as we planned General Magnus's trip.
>
> Many Camden organizations worked together to welcome General Magnus. The Camden Partnership, Camden-Kings Bay Navy League, The Camden County Chamber of Commerce, the Kiwanis Club and over a dozen other local groups all were present for the event.
>
> General Magnus, a very respected officer purposely made his way around the conference room at the reception, shaking hands and talking with everyone. Mr. and Mrs. Dunham, Jason's parents were touched by all that had been done. "We want to thank everyone here on board the base and in the community, that has worked so hard first to support the Sailors and Marines and their families that are here," said Magnus. "We just love the Dunhams, we love everything Jason has done, and his family has done to show Americans what great young men and women go forth to serve their nation." Sheila McNeill, past national president of the Navy League U.S. was especially gratified to see General Magnus visit this facility. "We strongly support the Marines at Kings Bay and around the world," said McNeill. "We were pleased to show the General how strong that support is during his visit."
>
> Lieutenant Colonel Andrew Murray, then commanding officer of the Marine Corps Security Force Company, Kings Bay was very appreciative of what the Dunham family has done for our Country. "The Marines and Sailors of Marine Corps Security Force Company Kings Bay were truly humbled to have

the Dunham family here to represent their son, Corporal Jason Dunham, as we dedicate our barracks in his honor." Said Murray. "His heroism and sacrifice stand as a lesson to us all."

Dunham, whose first duty station was at Kings Bay, was mortally wounded after he held his helmet over a live grenade to save his fellow Marines. An insurgent dropped the grenade during an attack on Dunham's patrol unit near Husaybah, Iraq, in April 2004. The Medal of Honor was posthumously awarded to Corporal Dunham by President Bush in January of 2007

Ed Buczek, public affairs officer for NSBKB said, "This is somebody that we'll take lessons from. His actions now tell the story that will be told to other Marines—sacrifice, honor, courage, and commitment. Those are the Marines' ethics. I think he exemplifies all of them."

REAR ADMIRAL JERRY ELLIS AND ROSEMARY

COMMANDER, SUBMARINE GROUP 10
COMMANDER, SUBMAIRNE FORCE PACIFIC FLEET

Rear Admiral Jerry Ellis was the person who had the most impact in my career. He, Al Konetzni, and Chuck Beers were the three officers I owe so much to.

One of the best opportunities in my life was given to me by Rear Admiral Ellis. He relieved RADM Tom Robertson in 1992. We had developed a wonderful relationship with Tom and Julie Robertson and wondered how this transition would be. Arlie and I connected right away with him and his wife, Rosemary. We have talked about those unbelievably successful years and how much we enjoyed working together.

At a speech he gave to the Navy League in January 1994, he shared with the audience that the first British submarine, the HMS *Vanguard*, would be arriving in the spring and the seventh SSBN submarine, the USS *Rhode Island*, would also be arriving later in the year. He recognized that the chamber traditionally gave a welcoming ceremony for every new submarine.

There would also be the departure of Submarine Squadron 16, the first operational unit to arrive at Kings Bay in July 1979. He talked about the departure and decommissioning of the USS *Canopus*. He assured everyone that they would do all they could to absorb the military into the current commands at Kings Bay, but a large number would be leaving the area. He discussed our strategic forces, the upcoming Submarine Veterans WWII ceremony, and the recent announcement that Presidents Clinton and Yeltsin agree that they would order the detargeting of strategic missiles under their commands in the upcoming Nuclear Posture Review—the first nuclear policy review in over fifteen years.

> *"The traditional doctrine of nuclear deterrence presumes the other side is rational, and that we can identify the responsible parties. In the future, those assumptions may not apply as we face rogue states or terrorist groups of unknown origin or location. Many of the people associated with these states or groups do not think rationally and do not place the same high value on human life that we do. Hopefully all of these considerations will go into our (next) posture review," he said.*

During his tour at Kings Bay we had chief of Naval Operations, Admiral Mike Boorda, as a speaker at Navy League. (My relationship with Admiral Boorda is recounted in another chapter.) His visit was on the same day as Rosemary's birthday. We had a great time celebrating both events and everyone sang happy birthday to Rosemary at the meeting.

In 1995–1996, we had as speakers:

- The British Liaison Office, Lt. Commander Ian Carpenter, Royal Navy
- Lt. Col. Anthony Jackson, Marine Corps Security Force Battalion (Tony retired as a lieutenant general)
- Senator Sam Nunn (see his story)
- Dr. Harold Smith, undersecretary of defense
- VADM George Emory, commander, Submarine Force Atlantic
- Secretary of the Navy, John Dalton

I'm sure having these VIPs coming to the base didn't make life easier for him and it was certainly a busy time running the local Navy League.

In September 1995, Rear Admiral Ellis hosted approximately forty admirals at the Fourth Annual Submarine Flag Officer Conference in Kings Bay. Arlie and I were invited the attend the evening reception.

On July 19, 1996, he sent a letter to the community in response to the allegation of a local group headed by Mr. Linehan on the safety of the weapons associated with the development of the Trident system. Jerry was always one to assess a situation and handle it. Rather than ignore the concerns of the community he addressed them. A part of that response is below:

> *To the Residents of Camden County, Georgia*
>
> *On behalf of the Navy, I wanted to take this opportunity to thank the people of Camden County for your support over many*

years during the establishment and growth of the Submarine Base at Kings Bay. We have experienced unprecedented success in working together to manage the growth of the base and community. During the development of the TRIDENT system, one of the Navy's major efforts has been in the development of systems with assured safety. This has been demonstrated by a long history of safe operations for the TRIDENT system. Designing and deploying safe systems are of paramount importance to the Navy.

And he continues with a full page on information for the community to understand the system and the safety of the systems. He shared the letter with me before the press release. There was no backlash.

There was always clarity with RADM Ellis.

One day he called me and said, "I'd like to nominate you for a defense committee, the Defense Advisory Committee on Women in the Services, but the only problem is you have to get references and it has to be submitted in three days." We talked about the position and what would be required.

It sounded like a great opportunity but also very time consuming. The first meeting of the committee would not be until the following year, April 1996. I knew we had the opening of the St. Marys Submarine Museum planned for March 1996, so the timing looked good. To have a chance to support the women and men of our military was something I would not turn down. I got to work and sent requests (see more in DACOWITS). Everyone responded within two days and Jerry was able to submit the application on time. We waited for a decision. I realized that it was a long shot.

When Jerry and Rosemary left Kings Bay, the Navy League presented them a lifetime membership. The first and only one that I know that has ever been given. I presented the award:

RADM Jerry Ellis
Life Membership Presentation

The Navy League of the United States exists to educate the American people and their elected representatives on both the need for and the value of a strong sea service to our national defense. This is a big job, and one that requires the assistance of many talented and committed individuals, both civilian and military. And every so often, a person is distinguished by his or her efforts on behalf of our mission. We reserve for those very special few, the honor of awarding Life Membership in the Navy League of the United States. And it is my pleasure to represent the Navy League's national president, Rear

Admiral John Fisher, USN (Ret), in recognizing as our newest Life Member, Rear Admiral Winford G. "Jerry" Ellis.

"To fulfill our mission, good relations between our civilian organization and the sea services is vital. No person in recent memory has contributed more to developing and enhancing those relationships than RADM Ellis. And while this is but the latest of many many awards he has received over the years, it nonetheless represents the genuine gratitude we feel deeply for his enormous efforts on our behalf. RADM Ellis, your example has left an enduring impression and I am humbled to be the one selected today to thank you for your contributions. You are truly an ambassador for the Navy."

* * * * *

It is obvious that Rosemary and Jerry became our good friends. His tour went fast, and I learned much from him. One day I received a phone call from Jerry. He said, "Get your moo-moo out, Sheila. We are going to Hawaii." And not just to Hawaii, he was going to be SUBPAC: Commander of the Submarine Forces Pacific. That's a big deal! We hated to see them go, but we knew there was a Navy League convention in Hawaii coming up, so we knew we would see them again.

We stayed in touch and one morning I called Hawaii to talk with Rosemary. Jerry answered, and I asked, "Why aren't you at work?"

"Well, Sheila, it's four in morning and I'm home sleeping. Rosemary is visiting family and will be gone for a few days."

I could have died. I was just horrified—I failed to consider the time change. Quickly I said, "Hang up, Jerry—go back to sleep—we'll talk another time… I am so sorry."

Always gracious (and I think we both loved talking to each other), he replied, "No, no, I'm awake now—let's catch up. What's going on?" So we did just that.

I received word that I had been appointed to DACOWITS—the committee that gave me the knowledge and confidence to later run for national president of the Navy League of the United States. Thank you, Jerry!

In 1998, the DACOWITS executive committee had their annual pacific fleet trip. On the way home, we stopped at Hawaii for us to debrief the PAC fleet commander and others. I had told Jerry and Rosemary that I would meet with them for dinner on our night off, but details had not been made. I received word from Captain Brehm that the admiral had called and wanted to confirm dinner that evening. It was just awesome. I was so pleased that nothing was interfering and we would be able to get together for dinner. After all, he was the one who put me here and now I can give him a heads up on our trip.

The time came for our Navy League convention in Hawaii and the Ellises invited us to spend a few days with them before the meeting. I told them we were bringing my mother and her girlfriend, but we'd be glad to visit them while we were there. They insisted we all come. For weeks, Mother and Louise Raulerson, her best friend and the person who introduced her and Dad, talked about the visit. There was a lot of discussion about how to refer to him. As they told us, they had never met an admiral. They wondered if Rosemary would be happy with so many guests. I assured them in every case they had no worries. The admiral's quarters were on Ford Island. Everyone at that time had to be transferred by boat. It was a beautiful island and their quarters were wonderful.

We arrived and within an hour I heard Louise say, "Hey, Jerry, how about another Mai Tai?" Quickly they had no questions of what to call them and made themselves part of the family very quickly. They loved asking Jerry to do things for them and they loved Rosemary. She was in many conversations over the years, as they fondly remembered this visit. Even months before Mom died, we were recounting this experience, and she regretted that she was never able to cook them a meal.

They hosted the Navy League's executive committee at their quarters. The weather was perfect and we all enjoyed the lawn with the spectacular view. There were about one hundred of the Navy League's top leadership. I was about to close out my tour with DACOWITS and was interested in running for national vice president. Jerry knew this and spent much of the evening walking around holding my hand. It was obvious that Jerry and Rosemary were good friends but to have Jerry let everyone know how close we were meant so much to me that night.

Mother's friend, Louise, was a bit of "cut up" and realizing she was at the headquarters for the Pacific Submarine Fleet she decided to have a little fun. During WWII, she had met and danced with a sailor who was an incredible dancer and very charming. Louise put out the word that evening at the outdoor reception on their lawn that she wanted to find out where he was. We knew she was joking but everyone picked up on her requests to find this sailor. All we had on him was: he was a cute and good dancer, his name was Shorty, and he was on the way to war.

Jerry and Rosemary, being the good sports they were, had Jerry's intelligence officer go up to Louise to obtain the information she had and let her, and mother know they were putting out an alert. It buzzed across the lawn and everyone was asking for an update on finding Shorty. What fun to have them and their staff give Mother and Louise such attention and go along with such a fun request.

The next evening Jerry and Rosemary took us to the Arizona Memorial via his gig. (A small yacht but very important one.) Flying the flag of the admiral every ship's officers and crew stood at attention manning the rail in respect as the gig passed by. Mother and Louise were not the only ones awed by this event. On the way back from the memorial, it was the time for taps. Honors were given as we passed by all the ships. It was all incredibly emotionally and never to be forgotten. Mother and Louise were a part of a ceremony that most people rarely ever have an opportunity to see.

We kept in touch and they were transferred to the Pentagon for his newest job. This job, obviously, was in a small room with everyone wearing dark glasses. I'm sure they had a special knock in order to be allowed. And he wouldn't tell me a damn thing about what they did.

In 2000, the child care center dedicated the Rosemary Ellis playground. This was the song the children sang, and the song was distributed to all attendees:

She'll be visiting our center when she comes
She'll be visiting our center when she comes
She'll be visiting or center
She'll be visiting our center
She'll be visiting our center when she comes.

She will see the new playgrounds when she comes
She will see the new playgrounds when she comes
She will see the new playgrounds
She will see the new playgrounds
She will see the new playgrounds when she comes.
She will see us playing when she comes
She will see us playing when she comes
She will see us playing
She will see us playing
She will see us playing when she comes.

We are happy that our playgrounds are all done
We are happy that our playgrounds are all done
We are happy with our playgrounds
We are happy with our playgrounds

We're so happy, Mrs. Ellis, that you've come!

Washington, DC, fall 2002

Jerry and Rosemary both attended the reception on the *Odyssey*, an elegant cruise ship that takes passengers along the Potomac River. The Navy League had it chartered for the evening. That was the night I was running for national president. Jerry knew me well and could speak to my support of the sea services. I kept running up to Rosemary for updates and she told me she campaigned for me very hard. She told me Jerry was telling "Sheila stories." I looked at the dance floor at one point during the evening and Rosemary and Mother were jitterbugging.

The defense committee changed my life—I have shared some of those experiences in this book. I will forever be indebted to Jerry for not only his confidence in me but for going to such measures to support that nomination and then their support when I ran for national president. And then on April 30, Jerry nominated me for the Distinguished Civilian Award for 2003 in the Naval Submarine League. I didn't make it. I didn't expect to. But what an honor.

You don't get better friends than Jerry and Rosemary Ellis.

* * * * *

Jerry is now chair, Undersea Warfare; professor of practice, Undersea Warfare; director, Undersea Warfare Research Center; naval postgraduate school, Monterey, California

2009 EMORY DAWSON HUMANITARIAN AWARD RECIPIENT

WHEREAS, The late Emory Dawson was a member of many community service organizations, including Brunswick Elks Lodge 691; and

WHEREAS, each year the Brunswick Elk Lodge 691 honors a member of the community who exhibits Mr. Dawson's spirit and commitment to improving the condition of their fellow man, while providing educational scholarship opportunities to disabled or handicapped students, and

WHEREAS, this year's recipient of the Emory Dawson Humanitarian Award is a person who shares the same vision and dedication as Mr. Dawson that of her cheerful service to her community, state and nation; and

WHEARAS, McNeill served as National President of the Navy League of the United States. And in that capacity, Ms. McNeill was responsible for leading the Navy League's 70,000 members who are dedicated to educating American citizens and elected officials about the importance of sea power; and

WHEREAS, Ms. McNeill also served as a national director of the US Naval Sea Cadets Corps, and served as the National Maritime Policy Committee and as a member of the Executive

> Board of the Governor's statewide Military Affairs Coordinating Committee; and
>
> **WHEREAS**, Ms. McNeill was named one of the 100 Most Influential Georgians in *Georgia Trend* Magazine and has received the Secretary of the Navy's Distinguished, Superior, and Meritorious Public Service medals, the United States Armed Forces Spirit of Hope Award, and was the first female recipient of the Spanish navy Leagues' highest honor, the Golden Anchor Award
>
> **NOW THEREFORE, BE IT PROCLAIMED, BY THE** Glynn County Board of Commissioners, in conjunction with the Brunswick Elks Lodge 691, that it honors Ms. Sheila M. McNeill, as the 2000 recipient of the Emory Dawson Humanitarian Award in recognition of her service and leadership, and the unselfish giving of time, talent and love to her country.
>
> **IN WITNESS, WHEREOF**, we set our hands this 6th day of August 2009.
>
> Attest
> Board of Commissioners, Glynn County, Georgia
> Jerome Clark, Chairman
> Tom Sublett, Vice Chairman
> Attest: Cindy S. Overstreet, Clerk

As a result of this award, the mayor and City Commissoners of Brunswick, Georgia, also had a proclamation that concluded,

> **NOW THEREFORE**, It is with great pleasure that I, Bryan Thompson, Mayor of the City of Brunswick along with my fellow Commissioners do hereby proclaim Friday August 28th as "SHEILA M. MCNEILL DAY" in the City of Brunswick.

Note: That is my hometown! Also, receiving the 2009 Emory Dawson Humanitarian Award was Virginia Ramsey who served two terms as Georgia State Representative

My remarks:

> Dan, Wayne and members of the Elks Club. Mayor Thompson, Dr. Hepburn.
>
> Thank you to the Navy League, Nick Hart with the Golden Isles Council and Keith Post for the Kings Bay council for putting up with the former national president for always making sugges-

tion and giving advice. Thank you both for indulging me. Thank you to Woody and Chris our respective chambers who gave me an opportunity to serve and to learn about our community. Thank you to The Camden Partnership, Jim Wells and Marty Klumpp.

Arlie and I have enjoyed our relationship with the Navy, Marine Corps and Coast Guard over the past 43 years. My tour with the defense committee traveling around the world visiting our troops and the two years as national president visiting the same countries has given me the greatest respect for our men and women in uniform. And for that reason, I am stunned and humbled by the representation of each of those services that we support in the Navy League:

RADM. Barry Bruner, new commander of Submarine Group 10 Commander of one of those special submarines, the USS GEORGIA, Captain Mike Brown. To the military officers I've worked with the most over the past couple of years and doesn't seem to mind too much that he is on my speed dial Captain Wes Stevens, commanding officer Kings Bay, Lt. Col. Duanne Whiteside, Commanding Officer Marine Force Security Battalion and his gracious wife, Verona. We can now brag about the Coast Guard at Kings Bay and CDR Joe Raymond, commanding officers of the Maritime Force Protection Unit attended.

So here I am today—finally having something in Brunswick that my mother, sister, daughter and family can witness. Having my Brunswick friends, my Camden friends, my two oldest friends, my Navy League friends and my military friends in one room is amazing.

It just doesn't get any better than that and for that I want to again thank the Elks Club.

SECRETARY OF THE NAVY GORDON ENGLAND AND DOTTY

SEVENTY-THIRD SECRETARY OF THE NAVY
DEPUTY SECRETARY OF DEFENSE
ACTING SECRETARY OF DEFENSE
FIRST DEPUTY SECRETARY OF HOMELAND SECURITY

When I was national vice president, I had a call from Secretary England's office. They asked me to reply to his letter from East Timor. A young Bosnia girl whose brother, Boaz, had cancer had reached out to them. I wrote a note to her and included several items for his birthday, included some patriotic American items and, after finding out the sizes, a few items of clothing for both of them. Tamar sent me a note:

> *Thank you so much for the presents. I have no words! My brother was so happy. You should have seen his face. It takes a wonderful person like you to make the world a better place. God bless you. Thank you! Thank you! You are so cool!!! Tamar*

It was a very fulfilling project and I'm pleased Secretary England's office called the Navy League!

March 2002: Secretary of the Navy, Gordon England, was speaking to members only at the Navy-Marine Corps Caucus on Capitol Hill for an early morning breakfast. I told him I was there as the national vice president for legislative affairs for the Navy League. We were attending to greet the congressional members as they came in and to let everyone know that SECNAV had the support of the Navy League. I didn't sleep all night—just catnaps and questioning my enthusiasm for both the Navy League and the Navy with this crazy decision to greet Secretary England and the congressmen at such an early time.

Major General Corwin, chief of the Marine Corps Office of Legislative Affairs, and Secretary England were there when I arrived. Neither appeared to have any issue with the early hour. Secretary England brought up our last event together when he came to Kings Bay, and we had dinner in the admiral's wardroom. That evening, he was very surprised to see me and asked, "Sheila, what are you doing out of Washington?"

"I live here," I told him.

All this time he thought I lived in the DC area. I let him know how disappointed we were that he had to cancel out on Sea Air Space and asked if he would be at the annual meeting in New York. I told him, "I'll forgive you for missing Sea Air Space, if you'll come to New York." We both laughed, and he promised he would.

"Mr. Secretary, they are really beating you up on shipbuilding, aren't they?" I asked. We had a great conversation and he explained the dilemma he found himself in: No spare parts for planes. No maintenance done on planes, ships, or infrastructure. His plan was to bring all maintenance and spare parts up to speed this year and go for ship building the next year when everything was in better shape. What a common-sense approach. Sure, sufficient funding for both new ships and maintenance would have worked but he knew that wasn't possible. I understood the plan and admired him even more. Here he is, from the industry and asking for more ships seems like it would have been an easy thing to do. He doesn't do easy. I told him, "When else do you have Congress pressing on the Navy for more ships? Hopefully next year they will still be the ones insisting and we'll get those ships."

When I was national vice president for legislative affairs and I was running for national president of the Navy League, I received a call from Secretary England's public affairs officer, Kevin Wensing. I learned a lot from Kevin. He asked if I'd like to join Secretary England and Congressman Crenshaw on a coin toss with the Jacksonville Jaguars. I was thrilled!

Jacksonville, Fla., Florida Times Union Aug. 16, 2002—

> *Congressman Ander Crenshaw (right in baseball cap) and Navy League National Vice President Shelia McNeill (left) join Secretary of the Navy, Gordon England for coin toss at the home opener of the Jacksonville Jaguars pre-season. The Jaguars honored the Armed Forces at the game and through the USO provided 1,100 discounted tickets for military families at each home game. Photo courtesy of the Jacksonville Jaguars. Aug. 16, 2002*

And our local paper, *Tribune & Geor.gian*, August 23, 2002:

> They ran the same picture that Kevin made with this caption: *Local Business woman Sheila McNeill (right) Gordon England, secretary of the Navy (left) and U.S. representative Andre Crenshaw for the coin toss at the August 16 preseason game between the Jacksonville Jaguars and the Tampa Bay Buccaneers at Alltel Stadium. McNeill, national vice president of the Navy League of the U.S. had attended a luncheon earlier that day celebrating the centennial anniversary of the Navy League for the Jacksonville, Fla/ Southeast region. The trio, along with area military honorees, Navy League members and political aides were provided with a skybox to enjoy the game. According to McNeill, the Jaguars won the coin toss, even though they eventually lost the game.*

During the prior years, I had met and became friends with Congressman Ander Crenshaw of Florida's Fourth District. We both caught the same flight going from Jacksonville to DC and back to Jacksonville many times. Secretary England's Public Affairs Officer, Kevin Wensing was usually with the secretary (I'm sure he had something to do with bringing me in). It was an exciting evening. I'll never forget walking out onto the field with them and standing with the players during the national anthem and the prayer. The players were huge. If I put my arms straight out it would have been the height of their hips.

As we walked back among the cheers and excitement of the crowd and the display of lights flashing and the band playing, Kevin noted the "smoke and mirrors" effect of the surroundings and suggested I use the same for my campaign as national president of the Navy League. It seemed like a fun idea! After the toss, I was asked by the Jaguar's photographer if I wanted my picture made with the Jaguar cheerleaders. Secretary England was standing with me and responded, "No, Sheila, don't do it."

I looked at him as if he were crazy and responded, "Of course I'm going to do it."

"You are going to be sorry," he replied.

"Why in the world would I be sorry?" "My wife had her picture made with the Dallas Cowboys cheerleaders. You don't want your face in the middle of all those young girls." I laughed and had my picture made anyway.

Side note: He was right. It is amazing how you look when you are right in the middle of that picture at age 61 and they are 20 with that perfect make up. But I'm still not sorry I did it!

In September 16, 2004, one year into my presidency, Susan Fallon, our development director at Navy League had worked with Secretary England's office to host a barge cruise. We had several civilian guests as well as VCNO John (Black) Nathman and his wife, Sue. Almost as soon as we sat down, Secretary England pulled his menu over and started writing. He handed it to me. He had written, "Sheila's Navy League dinner" and signed it *Gordon England, SECNAV* with the date.

He laughed and teased, "Keep this, one day it might bring you something on eBay." We had a great time with everyone. I knew it was his birthday, but he didn't want me to mention it.

After dinner, we had entertainment and the singer sang old songs, including "Bewitched, Bothered and Bewildered." Gordon asked the singer if she knew who first sang the song and then said he could remember where he was when he first heard it, and her name was Gogi Grant. Obviously, he was older than everyone there—no one else seemed to know!

Later, Gordon, Dottie, and I talked about our grandchildren and he made it a point to tell the group that he had determined that I was fifteen years older than him. I immediately questioned his math and his logic. "Sheila has a grandson, who is nineteen, and our grandson is only five. So that makes me fourteen years younger." In defense, I let them all know that I was sixty-two and was so much younger than Gordon. Everyone enjoyed the teasing and the back and forth. It was a way to relax everyone. He then talked about the Navy League and used the phrase "The sun never sets on the Navy League." He was just returning from Asia and had just met with Navy League members there. That phrase was used by many after that. He told the group, "We appreciate the Navy League. They give support to our sailors and marines and they do what the Navy and Marine Corps needs doing for us."

"May I say something?" I asked.

"Of course," he answered

"The secretary and the CNO are making the hard decisions to take care of current readiness instead of building new ships. I ran into him on Capitol Hill and said,

'How does it feel to have Capitol Hill beat up on *you* for more ships?'" It was a very unpopular stand at the time.

"It was really Vern Clark's idea and I supported it," he added. "When September 11 happened, and the president called to see if the Navy could send six aircraft carriers to the Gulf, he was told we can send eight." What a statement for readiness and what timing!

"And they are taking care of people," I told them. "There was a young amputee I met who had just been fitted with new arms [he had lost both] and he asked me if I thought they would let him go back to his unit." Later, his picture was on the cover of *Navy Times* in his uniform with an article on his new job teaching karate.

We made a good team that evening. We were both passionate and eager to tell the story of the Department of the Navy. Susan Fallon, our development director, had grown up in a Navy family and was a savvy professional. She told me she was proud of the Navy League that night and loved the comments—that the secretary and I were like a team with the back and forth.

A couple of days later, I'm in Brunswick and in the car on the way somewhere with Arlie. I was telling him about my conversation with Gordon about my age. He said, why would you say sixty-two—you are sixty-one. I thought for a minute (I'm a quick study) and realized he was right. I immediately picked up my cell phone and called his office. "This is Sheila McNeill. Is Secretary England available?"

"No, actually he is on a plane going to an official function."

"Could you give him a message for me?"

"Sure, I can," she answered.

"Would you tell him I'm sixty-one, not sixty-two?"

She laughed and said, "Of course."

The next time I saw Gordon, he told me he was on a plane with several people in a meeting. The aide came to the door and said, "We have a message from the president of the Navy League."

Gordon, thinking something was wrong, stopped his meeting and said, "What was the message?"

"She said to tell you she's sixty-one, not sixty-two." He really got a laugh from my message. He never told me who he was meeting with.

In 2003, I was surprised with a huge statue by several of the male Navy League members. It was a pig holding a gavel and read,

MCPFS

With the symbolic presentation of a gavel this award celebrates the election of Sheila M. McNeill at the election of National President, Navy League of the United States.

It also represents the "Male Chauvinist of South Carolina and California who in 2002 served as and continue to serve as her unswerving advocates."

Presented by the Hilton Head Council
September 24, 2004

These gentlemen, Dale, Jim, Rocky, Bob, and Ken (you know who you are as I tell my grandchildren), gave me incredible support during those years. They were the ones who "created" the MCPFS statue. Jim Smith, council president sent a most gracious letter after my visit. Kevin Wensing was in our suite that evening and took a picture of me with "the Pig." Later, I received the picture signed by Secretary England that ended with "Oink!" and then his signature. I'll bet I have the only photo signed with an "oink" with Secretary England's name. That picture has a special place in my home.

We were at the Navy League convention in New York City. VADM Al Konetzni was the speaker for the evening of the Banquet. I kidded Al about toning down his speech that evening since SECNAV England was present. He responded as if he really was going to take my advice. Read Al's story to see if he really took it.

On March 9, Secretary England hosted a corporate gold members' dinner at the Caucus Room, one of my favorite DC restaurants. After a forty-minute cocktail reception, we seated everyone, and I opened the evening with a welcome.

The tables were in a square, so we could all talk with each other. Admiral Mike Mullen, VCNO at the time, was to my right and the secretary was to my left, and seated next to Gordon was General Robert Magnus, deputy commandant of the Marines Corps. We had the senior leadership from BAE, Boeing, Northrop Grumman, Lockheed Martin, DRS, General Dynamics, Maersk Line Limited, KBR, Raytheon, and ATK-Alliant Techsystems. Also attending was our Navy League executive director, Stephen R. Pietropaoli, and our national vice president for corporate affairs, Bob Ravitz. Almost all the conversation was with one person talking and everyone else listening. I was pleased with that. So many times, individual conversations get started and it's hard to pull everyone together. Not that night. Secretary England had their attention. It was a lovely evening.

Years later, I was at a reception honoring Admiral Gary Roughead at a Sea Air Space event and both Secretary England and Admiral Vern Clark were there. I first saw Gordon and made a beeline to talk with him. He was in the middle of a conversation, so I stayed out of his line of vision, not wanting to interrupt. After a few minutes, I heard what he was saying—it was a story about me! So I walked a couple of inches around until he saw me. We were both laughing hard, and he put his arm around me and continued the story. Someone took a picture of both scenes and I have them framed in my office.

Later, I went over to their table. He and Vern were sitting next to each other. They revealed something to me. It turns out that during the time I was president of the Navy League they both told their staff that when I called for an appointment they were to try to work around my schedule. "But I never came that much!" I answered.

"We know, you were out supporting our Navy and Marine Corps! That's why we did it."

Wow, that would have been a powerful thing to have known back then!

VICE ADMIRAL MALCOLM FAGES AND SHIRLEY

Arlie and I met Malcolm when he was commander of the USS *Pennsylvania* (Gold), at Naval Submarine Base Kings Bay. We became good friends with him and his wife, Shirley. There are two identical crews on the strategical missile submarines on base called Blue and Gold. They alternate manning the boat while the other crew is in training.

Soon after becoming friends we had a Navy League party that we all attended. I introduced Malcolm to one of our new Navy League members as Malcolm Fages, Pennsylvania Gold, and she replied, "I didn't know we had a new jewelry store in town." It was at that time that I decided we needed to have a little education program for our new Navy League members. We've chuckled about that incident more than once.

Shirley went with the family to Las Vegas. Mother went as did Irene, Mother's sister, and Louise, her best friend since high school. We had a lovely time. The sisters talked about how crazy and how much fun Shirley was. She started out with dancing on both beds in Vegas as she described the fun we were going to have—and we did.

At that time, I had a retail story in the Kings Bay Village Shopping Center just about a mile from where Mal and Shirley lived. One day I had a call from Cindy, one of the staff at the store. "We have someone out front who is trying to rob us."

"Is he still there?"

"We aren't sure. We just ran to the back."

"Where are you now?"

"I'm under your desk."

"Have you called the police?"

"Yes, they are on the way."

"I'm on the way but it will be about forty-five minutes."

I hung up the phone and called the Fages to see if Malcolm could go over. "Where is Malcolm?"

"At the dock with his boat."

"Can you get him to run by the store? We are being robbed, the police are on the way, but I can't get there fast enough."

"I'll let him know," Shirley replied.

When I got to the store Malcolm reported to me like he might report to his relief as he is turning over command (that's my interpretation, not his!). He let me know that everyone was all right and that the police had come and gone. As it turns out the potential robber came into the store and laid a twenty-dollar bill on the counter and asked for change. When they asked him how he wanted it he added a bag and said, give me all you have. It scared them so they just turned around and ran to the store room and got under the desks. He left with nothing. We gained twenty dollars. But it was a harrowing experience for the two women working.

They found a plain coffee cup and had the following poem on it

"When Cindy was under the desk reading the yellow pages

Who did Sheila think to call but fisherman Malcolm Fages."

We've laughed about that event often as we also thanked God no one was hurt.

Malcolm received his new orders in 1993 as chief of staff of the USS *Theodore Roosevelt*, an aircraft carrier, a long way from a submarine! The ship had a Tiger Cruise—an opportunity for the crew and officers to invite their families to go out to sea for the day. As chief of staff, Mal had a private cabin with a big double bed. There were thousands of family and guests on the carrier that day. It was a great experience and I got to take a nap on that big double bed!

He made flag after this job. We visited the Fages at every command they had after Kings Bay—they couldn't get rid of us! I was really hoping that when he made flag he might be assigned as the group commander at Kings Bay. In fact, I was touting his virtues at a big reception in DC. The senior admiral I was talking to listened as I told him why Mal should come to Kings Bay. He then said, "You are going to like the officer we are sending, but Mal is going to Connecticut to command that group."

I was so surprised. Why hadn't Mal and Shirley told me? So that night I called and talked to Shirley. "I heard tonight that Malcolm has his orders and he's going to Groton, why didn't you tell me?"

"He's going to go where?" Shirley asked. Then she called out, "Malcolm, come to the phone, Sheila says we are going to Groton."

"You mean you didn't know?"

"No, we had no idea."

"Oh no, if I'd known it was confidential I would have kept my mouth shut."

"Well, Malcolm wants to talk with you."

I didn't tell Malcolm who told me but he did call BUPERSE (Bureau of Personnel) the next day and confirmed he was going to relieve RDML Rick Buchannan as commander of Submarine Group 2 in Groton, Connecticut, on August 30.

Arlie and I went to that change of command. Rear Admiral Rick Buchannan was also a friend so it was good to be at the ceremony. (Note: In 2016, Rick's son Captain T. R. Buchannan became Squadron 20 commander at Kings Bay. I am now working with two generations!)

April 12, 2000—Universal Pictures had a showing of their new film *U-571*. One of the papers started out with "What is it about submarines that attracts so many filmmakers?" I was amazed that there were so many movies and that I had seen so many of them. I think every time (okay, there hasn't been that many times) that I've been on a submarine for a number of hours they always watch *Das Boot*. This story begins in 1942 when German subs are devastating British and American ships in the Atlantic. It stared Matthew McConaughey—who was not present that evening. He missed a good time. It's always nice to know people like the Fages and get such an invitation—and they give you room and board too.

With his second star, Mal relieved Rear Admiral Rick Buchanan on August 30, 1996, as Commander Submarine Group 2. Arlie and I went to Connecticut for that change of command. Shirley instantly became "the old broad in the big house." We had a good time teasing her and suggesting she get a less flamboyant color of hair. She didn't do that—she didn't change anything—and that was good!

The ceremony was most impressive. Adm. William J. Flanagan, commander of the Atlantic Fleet, was the key speaker. VADM Richard W. Mies, Commander, Atlantic Fleet Submarine Force, also spoke.

The *Day*, Groton's local paper, reported,

> *Buchanan has earned considerable praise during his 26-month tour for forging alliances with business, community and social groups that have strengthened the Navy's presence in southeastern Connecticut. "Few have made as indelible a mark as he has" wrote US Rep. Sam Gejdenson. U.S. Sen Joseph Lieberman wrote that Buchanan has been an outstanding commander, a superb role model for all sailors, and a good citizen in every sense of the word. 15 retired and active duty flag officers were in attendance—more than 40 cannon shots echoed across the Thames River valley in three formal salutes during the ceremony. The crowd swelled to nearly 1,000 people, including eight state legislators, emissaries from England and France and several high ranking federal officials.*
>
> *Buchanan read his orders to report to Strategic Command in Omaha a few minutes after noon, and his flag—two plain white stars on a Navy-blue background—was taken down from a pole aboard the adjacent USS Hartford. The incoming commander of Group Two, RADM. Malcolm I. Fages, observed that Buchanan had set very high standards for people who follow him in the job. "Rick, you've set the bar very high," Fages said. But he added, "I accept the challenge. Fages said, "When I was an ensign at Submarine School in 1968, we could get two large lobsters at Abbots for $7.95. Basic pay was about $300 per month and we lived very well. I don't think*

$300 will go quite so far but nevertheless Shirley and I are thrilled to be back." Fages said that despite the end of the Cold War, the world can still be a volatile place.

"The world is awash in failed states, regional conflicts and the threat of proliferation of weapons of mass destruction." Fages said. "We are faced with incredibly difficult decisions—which hardware shall we buy? How fast will we decommission ships, and squadrons and wings, and divisions? But he said if the Navy holds to its guiding principles—honor, commitment and courage—"we will navigate safely through the dangerous waters in this epochal period.

In 1996 toward the end of the building of the submarine museum I received a call from Ben Bastura from Connecticut. He told me he had a wide selection of submarine items that the Navy had requested he leave them to one of the Navy museums. But! If I would come, see the items he would give them to the St. Marys Submarine Museum. I called Shirley and found out that his home was about forty-five minutes from Groton. She offered to drive me there if I wanted to come spend the weekend with them. I accepted her offer and Shirley and I started the journey. It was incredible. We arrived at a home in a neighborhood that didn't look like it had changed from the 1950s. Well kept, pleasant, but not what I would expect for a museum. My doubting came to a halt when we went in. Every room was full of submarine memorabilia. He was retired Army but had always had an interest in submarines. I really wanted these treasures for our museum. We spent a couple of hours with Ben. When I got back to St. Marys, I ordered a subscription of the local paper for Ben as well as putting him on the submarine mailing list. We talked from time to time.

When he died, it took an entire tractor trailer to transport his items. It cost somewhere around ten thousand dollars, but we preserved a remarkable collection of history. Thank you, Shirley!

In July 1997, the Navy League had their meeting in Boston to celebrate the two hundredth anniversary of the USS *Constitution*. The commanding officer was CDR Michael Beck and his wife was delightful. We had a great time celebrating. The captain saw Malcolm and Shirley walking by and stopped them so he could introduce us. The captain said something like, "Have you met Sheila and Arlie McNeill?"

"No, I have not but I'd sure like to."

And with that he put his arms around me, dipped me backward and gave me a passionate (very proper really but no one realized that) kiss on the mouth, and replied, "Very nice to meet you, Sheila."

Captain Beck, with his jaw dropping, responded, "You already knew him, right?"

MALCOLM GOES TO DC AS DIRECTOR OF SUBMARINE WARFARE

This job increased our chances of seeing them more often. In fact, many of my trips to DC meant spending the night with the Fages. I remember one time I was so exhausted I stayed over a Sunday and spent the entire day on their sofa. Shirley came and went all day and prepared lunch at some point but I just wanted to rest! These times in DC also gave us several opportunities to join the Ptomaine Club for dinner. It was a great time.

There was a new Navy Heritage video sponsored by the Navy League. I called Mal and Shirley and they were going. Shirley picked me up at the hotel. It was a very impressive group. Malcolm made sure I met secretary of the Navy Richard Danzig. When he introduced us, he said, "Sheila will be the first woman president of the Navy League."

I was surprised and said, "Malcolm, don't do that."

Secretary Danzig laughed and replied, "He might jinx you, huh?"

Later as we passed Secretary Danzig he and Jack were sitting in the front row of the auditorium seats I could hear Jack him telling him about me and that I was national vice president but could not hear the rest. Thanks, Malcolm, for putting that bug in their ear.

In 1999, I flew to New York for Meredith's tea to honor her graduation from Columbia University. What a poised and beautiful young woman she is! She had recently had her stage debut in the Charleston Ballet Theater's *Nutcracker*.

In 2000, the submarine force celebrated their one hundredth anniversary. As director of Submarine Warfare Mal sent an invitation to us, and of course, we attended. It was at this event that he introduced me to former chief of Naval Operations Frank Kelso. That story is told under Admiral Kelso's name. One more time Malcolm put a bug in someone's ear. The event's theme was "Fast Attacks and Boomers: Submarine in the Cold War" and was held at the National Museum of American History in DC. It was a wonderful event. I still remember that display of a head on a submarine with an actual toilet and a copy of *Playboy* magazine. I loved the fact that it was there.

March 21, 2001: Malcolm was nominated for his third star. He had been on Capitol Hill all day on his confirmation. I was staying at my usual abode the Ritz-Carlton, Pentagon City. Malcolm and Shirley came to the hotel and we had refreshments at the club level. We waited for his confirmation.

After a while, I tried to get Malcolm to call his office and see if they had received word. He was stubborn and wouldn't call. "They will let me know as soon as they know," he said. We waited about an hour and then Malcolm said, "I think it is time to call." I'm not sure now who he called but when he did, it was great news and it was fun to see him excited. I announced, "We need some champagne" and the attendant heard us and right away we had a glass of champagne. The rest of the evening Mal and Shirley talked about the logistics of how they would leave in twenty-four hours. We talked about his frocking the next day and how it would fit into the CNO's schedule with such short notice. They agreed to call me when they had a time. We finished dinner (cocktails and appetizers) and they left.

I received the call the next morning. It was at twelve thirty. I had meetings that morning, so it was a frantic rush to make sure I was on time. However, I got to the Pentagon thirty minutes early bringing the script and bios for an event later that day. I knew most of the officers who were present: Admirals Ed Giambastiani, Skip Bowman, and Gerry Talbot arrived, and we were shown into the CNO's office for a short ceremony. It was very impressive. Admiral Clark did everything off the cuff and so did Mal and Shirley. Shirley's comment "The question is, is Europe ready for Shirley?" got a laugh, and we all agreed with her.

We had lunch—the three of us in the OSD dining room. They now have four hours before they leave. Back to Mal's old office and then they showed me to RDML Gerry Talbot's office. He had asked at the frocking if I had a few minutes to talk about Kings Bay. I left the Pentagon at two thirty and walked through the parking lot and construction for a taxi and arrive at headquarters at three. The next day the following press release was sent.

> *Secretary of Defense Donald H. Rumsfeld announced today that the President has nominated Navy Rear Admiral Malcolm I. Fages for appointment to the grade of vice admiral with assignment as deputy chairman, Military Committee, North Atlantic Treaty Organization, Brussels, Belgium. Fages is currently serving as director, Submarine Warfare Division, N77, office of the Chief of Naval Operations, Pentagon, Washington, D.C.*

When I was on the cover of *Georgia Trend* magazine in July 2001, Shirley and Malcolm were one of the couples I sent a copy to. On July 29, I received the following e-mail from Shirley:

> *Good Morning Admiral*
>
> *Saw the article—thought the magazine was clever to picture you with a large phallus behind you! Noticed that the writer gave you only "a couple of stars." I told Malcolm that two wasn't enough. Seriously, it was a very complimentary article and I've sent it to a couple of people. Meredith was impressed, she said, "the Georgia Trend article is so cool! She's your friend..." We're pretty impressed too. And hopefully the Navy League is as well. Some nice stuff about Walt, too.*

Weekend in Paris was nice. Weather not great but we walked a lot nevertheless. Train ride is only 1 hour 20 minutes from Brussels. Mal's trip to Moscow last week went well. He's helping to negotiate with the Russians to establish a NATO mission there. He saw several people there that he worked with when he traveled there in '95-'96 and thought there was some progress made. He and Rick went to the Bolshoi Ballet and enjoyed that. Mal thought Moscow had changed somewhat—more evidence of prosperity in the people, cleaner streets, people better dressed, nicer merchandise in stores, etc.

Hope you had a nice relaxing weekend. Talk to you later. Shirley

September 26–October 3, 2001

Fifteen days after the September 11 attack on the World Trade Center, Arlie and I left for Brussels to visit Mal and Shirley. It was an incredible time to be visiting Brussels much less traveling to any foreign county. The security at every airport was tight. We were glad for that.

Even more we were amazed at the security Mal had to have. He was given guards and a "hard car" every time he traveled. His car was so heavy it was an effort to open and close the doors. Mal was still into bike riding so when he biked he has a series of people who would follow him by bicycle and with the car. They had a dinner party with friends from Portugal and Canada. Everyone was so sympathetic and loving to the Fages and to us. It was like we had lost a beloved family member and they consoled us. We met Robert Bell who works for NATO and had been a staffer for Senator Sam Nunn and President Clinton. Malcolm made arrangements for Shirley, Arlie, and me to be present when NATO confirmed Article 5. This article states that any armed attack against one or more of the Allies in Europe or North America shall be an attack against all. It was amazing to be in the audience when the Secretary General presented the evidence against Osama bin Laden and the Taliban.

Invocation of Article 5 confirmed:

Frank Taylor, the US Ambassador at Large and Co-coordinator for Counter-terrorism briefed the North Atlantic Council—NATO's top decision-making body—on 2 October on the results of investigations into the 11 September terrorist attacks against the United States. As a result of the information he provided to the Council, it has been clearly determined that the individuals who carried out the attacks belonged to the world-wide terrorist network of Al-Qaida, headed by Osama bin Laden and protected by the Taliban regime in Afghanistan.

At a special press conference, NATO Secretary General Lord Robertson announced that since it had been determined that the

> *attacks had been directed from abroad, they were regarded as an action covered by Article 5 of the Washington Treaty. When the Alliance invoked the principle of Article 5 of the Washington Treaty on 12 September, it stated that it needed to know whether such actions had been conducted from abroad before the Article could become fully operative. This has now been determined, but Lord Robertson explained that, at present, it was premature to speculate on what military action would be taken by the Alliance, be it individually or collectively.*

It was a wonderful few days visiting with Mal and Shirley and a historic time to be in Brussels.

When Malcolm was planning his retirement in 2004, he sent me this e-mail:

> Sheila, delighted that you will be able to come (to the retirement ceremony). I have something for you to consider that would really embellish your resume… far more so that a mere Navy League presidency. Would you be willing to participate as an honorary sideboy? No speaking part and swords not allowed. You would be one of the contingent of eight honorary sideboys through which Shirley and I would depart at the completion of the ceremony.
>
> This might be a little out of the ordinary, but we'd be delighted if you accept. The sideboys would be John Redmond, shipmate from my first sub; Bob Boyce, my skipper on Sea Devil when I was his Exec; Jim Fletcher, we served together on Von Steuben and were in sub school together, Dan Bruce, my Flag Writer from CSG2 and N77, representing our Navy enlisted; Walt Yourstone, Exec from Pennsylvania, Jon Yuen, Supply Officer when I commanded Narwhal, Army Sgt. James Saiz, my driver/Enlisted Aide/all around great soldier, representing joint service and my staff at NATO and Sheila McNeill, who shared my bed on Theodore Roosevelt*, caused a lot of mischief in Kings Bay, and represents the finest of those who support our sea services (was that smacky enough?) Hope to hear from you soon.

*Sheila's note: obviously at different times!

I answered: "Malcolm, I would be honored, and you are right—the Navy League presidency pales by comparison."

The presiding officers was Vice Admiral Kirkland H. Donald, USN, commander of Naval Submarine Force, and his guest speaker was Vice Admiral John J. Grossenbacher, USN (ret.). The surprise for the dads was Shirley's remark. She had written a letter to Vice Admiral John Grossenbacher, commander of Submarine Forces, and shared these works to us:

> *Dear John, This is an emotional time as we happily prepare to return to D.C. on April 1st, but in doing so must sadly leave this special place and special friends. But hasn't it always been so? As Navy families, we hopefully bloom where we are planted and then are yanked out of the ground replanted in new soil, watered with tears, fertilized with new experiences and new friends and slowly we seek our roots and bloom again. The plant grows a bit stronger with each replanting or, so I choose to think.*
>
> *Mal and I embarked on this journey together nearly 32 years ago. I was almost 21 and Mal was (of course) much older, already a lieutenant on his first boat, Gato. We started out in Pascagoula, Mississippi and are now finishing in Brussels, Belgium at NATO. The list is long with stops in between… Spain, Charleston, Hawaii, Norfolk, Orlando, Kings Bay, New London, D.C. (several more than one time)… How far we have come in every sense!*
>
> *Mal recently came across a journal he 'd saved that I'd written during a patrol as engineer on Von Steuben in 1977. He'd left only days after the birth of our sweet Meredith and I wanted him to experience the wonder of this new baby as well as give him a glimpse of "normal" life. I was struck, rereading this journal, that in only a few pages are recounted a story that could have been written by any of the women doing what I was doing—raising children, taking care of the car, house, etc., helping each other cope with loneliness, problems, crisis and sometimes tragedy; preparing for half-way night or homecoming, laughing crying, sharing, waiting. I was not unique and sometimes I was not good at it; but I learned and, like cheese and fine wine, got better with age and the help of many mentors. The hardships were many, but the rewards great. We forged bonds and many of those friendships from even those earliest days have lasted. And many of those friends will gather with us at Malcolm's retirement ceremony to celebrate and remember our history together.*
>
> *Our daughter grew up and she, too, flourished due in part to the Navy lifestyle. She learned to adapt, to be self-reliant, to challenge herself, to make others feel welcome, to be a friend and to value friendship, to be expressive, to listen—in short, she learned to be*

graceful in all the connotations of the word. She waved goodbye to her day too often and was comfort and company to her mom. Meredith is the best of both of us and so much more.

I leave Mal's professional contributions to the Navy and the Submarine Force to his peers to recount. He is a talented, forward thinking, smart, well spoken analytical officers who tried to do the right thing even when it wasn't easy, expedient or politically correct. He has succeeded far beyond his own dreams or expectations. I heard him say recently that there were times he wasn't sure he was going to make it to commander, let alone flag. And I know he is grateful. But I also know he earned his success and the respect of those he has served with. I am prouder of him than I can possible convey. I am proud to be his partner for life and love him with all my heart. Life is not a journey to the grave with the intention of arriving safely in a pretty and well-preserved body, but rather to skid in broadside thoroughly used up, totally work out and loudly proclaiming… wow what a ride.

That quote was recently sent to me by a friend and it sums up nicely my attitude about our life in the Navy. Ultimately, the experience has been less about the destinations that the journey. We have endeavored to enjoy each place we have been stationed fully and to give as good as we got. To be sure there have been some jobs Mal has enjoyed more than others but there are none that we would look back on and fail to find some memory to smile about. The people were and are what mattered most—without friends and family and their support and ever-present place in our hearts, we could not have lasted. I am proud of our contribution to the submarine force, to our service and to our nation. Wow, what a ride it has been… so far! And it ain't over yet.

John, Mal and I are so happy that you (and hopefully Kathy) will be with us for this special day. Mal has so much admiration and respect for your professionalism and is proud that you will stand up for him. For my part, I just always feel a warmth and caring and a real genuine-ness (not sure that's a word) from you both. We look forward to seeing you very soon.

Love, Shirley

It was a wonderful ceremony.

When Malcom retired, he and Shirley moved to London where they had a spacious apartment. Arlie and I went to visit (of course, we did) and had a great time.

Arlie kept Shirley busy a full day by going everywhere to cash in some old British currency to the new pounds that Arlie had held onto for years. We visited Peter and Marica Turner in Desborough. This was a wonderful opportunity for us. They and about ten others of their family had visited with us about twenty-five years ago. Although we stayed in touch through letters and Facebook nothing could replace sitting down in their home and catching up. On February 1, I went with Mal and Shirley to see Meredith dance at the Virginia Ballet Theater. She was incredible!

Shirley and Malcolm remain good friends. We expect to show up at their home any day.

FEDERATION OF NAVY LEAGUES

OCTOBER 5–7, 2004

The Twentieth General Assembly of the International Federation of Maritime Associations and Navy League organizations was organized by the Navy League of Chile with the theme: Pacific Ocean in the twenty-first century. The general secretary, Jesus Peior Artal via letter, invited me to speak (as the national president of the Navy League) at the annual conference to be held in Santiago, Chile. I accepted and called Commander (at that time) Dennis Moynihan and asked him to connect me with Dr. Perett, for a protocol briefing.

The organization arranged for an interpreter the entire time and a system where I wore earphones while others were speaking, and all others wore phones while I was speaking. I went directly to the Hotel O'Higgins in Vina del Mar. Within an hour, I was on a bus touring Turistico por Valparaiso and it never slowed down. Sr. Hernan Gonzales Fernandini was the secretary general. He was most gracious. It was interesting that in four full days I was there I met *no* Americans. Fernando Claudio Morales, the general secretary of the Argentina Navy League was also most helpful. They had interpreters for the meeting. Joan and I stayed at the same hotel and she was with me during tours and meetings outside the conference area. We also met with the Chilean Naval Academy at a special ceremony. It was amazing talking to Navy League leadership from several countries. They were so pleased that the American Navy League was present.

The countries in FIDALMAR were Argentina, Brazil, Chile, Colombia, Cuba, Curacao, Spain, Holland, Italy, Mexico, New Zealand, Peru, and Panama. My remarks were on public education and the Future Naval Challenge in the Pacific. Representatives from Chile, Peru, Brazil, and the Dominican Republic were all on the agenda to speak. The evening of October 8, there was a social. Buses left the hotel at eight for the Casino Municipal De Vina Del Mar. I couldn't believe that the very first bus to return was at 1:20 a.m.

The banquet the next night was elegant and well attended. Especially gracious during my visit was Eri Solis Ayarzun who was the president of Liga Maritime Chile. I could not believe that I was seated with the chief of Naval Operations, Admiral Miguel Angel Vergara Villablobos, and his wife, Sra. Maxie Iturriaga de Vergara. Later Admiral Vergara and I exchanged coins and talked at length about our military. He was most gracious and spoke well of Admiral Clark. On my right was a former senator Sr. Beltran Urenda Zegers and to my left was Vice Almirante Sr. Maurice Poisson Eastman. He was my interpreter for the evening and he was most interesting. At some point he just said "blah, blah, blah" into my ear. I almost laughed but caught myself. He also told me that evening that he was a former Army official who called his officers and said, "We are going to overthrow the government…" and they did. He kept me engaged all evening and I loved his stories. He was the editor of a major newspaper in Chile. When I arrived home, I researched the government overthrow and was amazed.

He wrote a column March 12, 2001, that I didn't see until years later. This obviously was translated from Spanish to English and is not as easy to read as I would like but it certainly tells the story.

> ***Military Government***. *A sense of decency and a deep gratitude to those who made possible the 1973 military coup has prompted me to write these lines.*
>
> *In September of that year, the Chilean Marxist getting ready to remain in power. The military demanded by much of the active population, opposed it. Making them the front, caught them by surprise and completely neutralized within a few weeks into the movement. There was opposition of wills and struggle, sometimes violent, unlike the Armed Forces managed to pacify the country. Then came a military government, possibly for some lasted too long, during which the military brought progress and modernization is not unquestioned. Later, to the surprise of his detractors, the military government handed power to his successor, elected in a vote whose correctness and freedom no one has been questioned.*

Years later I read a short notice of the death of Admiral Poisson:

> Editor of "El Mercurio" Died—Admiral Maurice Poisson
>
> His funeral will be today, after a Mass in the naval chapel in Las Salinas. At age 79 following cardiac arrest at 9:00 pm yesterday died in Vina del Mar, Vice Admiral Poisson Maurice Eastman former Chief of General Staff of the Arm and editor of "El Mercurio" since 1988.

He was a fascinating man and I am blessed to have had the opportunity to make this never forgotten trip. When I returned home, I received a letter from the president:

Dear Sheila,

The Chilean Maritime League would like to express its extraordinary satisfaction for your attendance to the 20th Assembly of the International Federation of Navy Leagues recently held in Chile. As well as giving prestige, charm and enhancement to our event, your participation in the Conference Program instructed our audience about "Public Education and the Future Naval Challenges in the Pacific." We expect the short visit you made to our country has been beneficial in professional and personal terms.

Eri Solis Oyazun, Rear Admiral, President

Their extraordinary satisfaction is equally matched by mine.

REAR ADMIRAL EUGENE FLUCKEY AND MARGARET

MEDAL OF HONOR RECIPIENT

How in the world we were able to get Admiral Fluckey is beyond me! It was a simple letter to a remarkable man. His book *Thunder Below* was just published four years earlier and he was a Medal of Honor recipient. He was an incredible man. At the time, he came for the commissioning of the museum he was eighty-four. I was fifty-three at the time and was amazed at his energy. Over the years, folks have commented on my energy so I thought I was pretty good in that sense. I was nothing compared to Gene Fluckey.

The day of the commissioning I went with Gene as he signed books at the base commissary He spoke at the commissioning of the museum and took as many pictures as anyone requested, and there were many. He autographed books and later joined us for dinner at RDML Chuck and Susan Beers quarters.

The St. Marys Submarine Museum and the commissioning are covered in another story.

It was a wonderful day and evening but that evening I was running out of steam. It had been an incredibly busy and fulfilling day. The museum was built! The museum was commissioned in style! It was done! We laughed, talked, and had a wonderful dinner. Around ten, Margaret told me, "Sheila, it's late we have got to go." I understood and helped her end the evening, but I really didn't want to—I was beat—and he should have been also!

12 April 1996
Dearest Arlie and Sheila,

We do appreciate so very much all these precious historic St. Marys events and your very kind letter plus publications. Yet, somehow your wish list was missing. I know some of the museum people, re submarines particularly, I have been impressed with the USS COD museum in Cleveland where I gave the rechristening speech. Two civilians John Baker, President and Paul Sarro, his cohort does seem to have the best knowledge of submarine parts in the U.S. So, I await your "wish list."

Your publicity was fantastic as is the museum. The annual Submarine Veterans of WWII in Milwaukee, August '96 I am the memorial and banquet speaker—so I can see what they have. Also, I can check the Navy Academy Museum and Nautilus Museum at Groton, Conn. We had so much fun with you. Thanks, a heap in which Margaret joins. She dropped you a line via Sue Garwood.

Good luck and God Bless,
Gene Fluckey

What an honor to know Gene and Margaret. Later the building 1063 that houses the offices of base personnel and Group Ten was named Fluckey Hall.

STEVE FORBES, FORBES MAGAZINE, ON OUR ENVIRONMENT

We had dealt with some of the environmental issues when I was national vice president for legislative affairs. One of my meetings at that time was with the head lawyer for the Navy, we discussed the challenges of proper balance.

My first president's message was in August 2003 and was titled "Rebalance Security and Environmental Needs" published in *Seapower*. That message closed with "Our nation need forces that are humane and highly skilled and fight with the precision that Americans expect. To achieve that end, we need to correct the imbalance between our environmental laws and national security requirements. Congress can help in several ways. For example, the Marine Mammal Protection Act's vague definition of 'harassment' of marine mammals which includes 'annoyance' and 'potential to disturb' mammals, should be changed to encompass biologically significant behavior. The sea services—and the nation—would benefit greatly if Congress would allow our military forces to substitute Integrated National Recourses Management Plans for critical habitat designations. A pending change to the Endangered Species Act would require that such a plan be prepared in cooperation with the U.S. Fish and Wildlife Service."

Those changes to existing laws are contained in HR 588, the 2004 Defense Authorization Bill, which in mid-July was before a House-Senate conference committee to resolve differences in House and Senate versions of the legislation. We urge Congress to support these changes.

This part of that message was picked up by *Forbes* magazine, September 2, 2003:

> Balancing Act
>
> These are perilous times. Our (armed) forces must continue to prepare for the kaleidoscopic array of asymmetric threats that will confront them. There is no doubt that military training disrupts the environment. War is a violent enterprise. But in recent months we have witnessed the extraordinary national benefits of maintaining a well-trained force that prepares for our defense in areas carefully selected and set aside for that purpose. Over the years, the Navy and Marine Corps have been excellent stewards of our environment. Their two million acres of land are home to about 185 threatened and endangered species that are protected by 130 full-time natural resource specialists. Our nation needs forces that are humane and highly skilled and fight with the precision that Americans expect. To achieve that end, we need to correct the imbalance between our environmental laws and national security requirement. It was only 22 months ago that the very worst environmental criminals of our time leveled the World Trade Center, set the Pentagon ablaze and slaughtered 2,976 of our citizens and friends in cowardly sneak attacks. We learned again the great value of military preparedness. Our sea services need our help and support. Let's give it to them.
>
> National President Sheila McNeill
> Navy League of the United States *Seapower* Magazine

At this time, Randy Hollstein was national vice president for legislative affairs and Jeremy Miller was director of legislative affairs. Randy spearheaded an effort for the National Capitol Council to blanket the Hill with a letter to Congress on encroachment. Randy told his council, "We need to get the word to our elected representatives that there are people in their districts and state that support the military's side of the encroachment issue."

Washington Times ran an editorial written by John McCaslin that expanded on the issue and quoted part of the president's message. I received a letter from Steve Forbes that said, "You might be interested in one of the items on page 28 of the enclosed *Forbes* magazine." I in turn sent a response to Mr. Forbes:

September 23, 2003

Dear Mr. Forbes, Thank you very much for quoting our commentary in your "Other Comments" department in the September 15 issue of Forbes.

It is terrific to be quoted by Forbes, and I am particularly pleased that you excerpted our message about the need to rebalance the nation's national security and environmental efforts. It is an important issue in Washington, and I am delighted that Forbes spread the work to its tens of thousands of readers.

Please accept a complimentary membership in the Navy League of the United States. Now in its 101st year, the League remains dedicated to the education of the public and Congress about the needs and accomplishments of our sea services. Our task is especially vital in these uncertain times.

All the best, Sheila M. McNeill

Then on October 1, 2003, he wrote,

Dear Ms. McNeill,

Thank you! I'm flattered! You might get a chuckle out of the enclosed scarf which has on it the motto of Forbes Magazine.

Sincerely,
Steve Forbes

It was a lovely scarf with capitalist tool written all over. It was great to have our message in the mainstream media. And one day, I'm going to wear that scarf!

GEORGIA MILITARY AFFAIRS COORDINATING COMMITTEE

The February 16, 1994, *Tribune & Georgian* had the following article:

> *Governor Zell Miller has appointed 34 members to the newly-created Military Affairs Coordinating committee. Governor Miller formed this committee, composed of representatives of Georgia bases, the surrounding communities, business executives, and defense experts to advise the Governor's Development Council on a variety of defense-related issues. Sheila McNeill has been appointed to this new committee.*
>
> *This committee is an integral part of the Georgia Defense Initiative, launched by Governor Miller last September to provide a statewide focal point for efforts to protect Georgia's defense bases and stimulate private-sector spinoff from defense technology. Citing the 1993 base closure experience, the governor said, "As the saying goes, nothing concentrates the mind like the sight of a hangman's noose. While our minds are still concentrated, it's time to begin preparing not only for the next round of base closings scheduled for 1995 but indeed for the role our bases can play for years to come."*
>
> *General Edwin Burba, former commander in chief of the Armed Forces Command at Fort McPherson, will serve as the chairman of the committee. Governor Miller called General Burba "the ideal person to head up this advisory group. He commands universal respect in all branches of the armed forces, and he is intimately familiar with the resources and missions of all Georgia military facilities."*
>
> *Committee members will advise the Governor's Development Council on military civilian relationships, assist in the development of regional strategies regarding the 1995 BRAC hearing, study the quality of life issues for military personnel in Georgia and evaluate strategies to add value to Georgia's defense installations.*

December 2000: The committee is going strong and I'm between visits to DC, so I caught a ride with Woody Woodside the president of the Brunswick Golden Isles chamber. I received my community training under Woody by serving as vice president for three years with that chamber. The years with Sam Cofer, who was chairman of the Legislative Affairs Committee, gave me the most pleasure. It was when I got my toes wet on legislative affairs and I've had a passion for it ever since. I loved working for Sam. He had a lovely wife who smiled at his nonsense. When we were traveling, and a pretty young woman came up, his typical line was, "If my wife wasn't so narrowminded, I'd take you home with me."

It was taken in the vein it was meant and always got a laugh.

GEORGIA STATE NAVY LEAGUE MEETING HELD AT KINGS BAY

When Arlie was state president he planned a state meeting at Naval Submarine Base Kings Bay. I worked with him on the agenda and the special guests. Captain Nuremberger insured that the event would be as successful as possible. We invited and they responded affirmative:

- Rear Admiral W. Ted Leland, chief, Office of Law Enforcement and Defense Operations USCG
- Captain Dean M. Hendrickson, commander, Carrier Air Wing 17, USN
- Colonel Paul J. Kern, Second Brigade commander, Twenty-Fourth Infantry Division (Mechanized), USA
- Captain John Nuremberger, commanding officer, NSBKB

Rear Admiral Leland, Captain Hendrickson, and Colonel Kern all served in the Persian Gulf and spoke on "Lessons Learned in the Persian Gulf." Colonel Kern had recently returned from Operation Desert Storm.

The base provided a tour of the waterfront facilities, base and a submarine.

The meeting was covered by the *Southeast Georgian*, Jackie Stanfield, staff writer.

> *U.S. Victory in the Gulf War took place swiftly, but high ranking military officers hope the public does not have a fairy tale viewpoint of the ease of that victory.*
>
> *"Desert Storm was not a 4-day fight, not a 100-hour war, but a 15-year fight in getting the equipment and training," said Colonel Paul Kern emphasizing this point more than once at the Georgia state meeting of the Navy League. The gist of the League's state gathering at Kings Bay on April 20 was to remind the audience that we cannot take our Desert Storm victory for granted. Kings Bay and Regional Navy League Vice President Sheila McNeill organized Saturday's seminar and introduced military speakers. Arlie McNeill, Navy League Georgia State President called the seminar to order.*
>
> *Relaying lessons learned in Persian Gulf actions, guest speakers explained how these lessons will color the U.S. armed forces in their preparedness against similar hostile forces. Along with Kern, RADM W. Ted Leland and Captain Dean Hendrickson conveyed their unit's roles in the Gulf war. The officers pointed out the U.S. strengths and*

weaknesses as the Gulf crisis ignited and grew to full-blown war. Major strengths included fast deployment, accurate use of weapons, and the destruction of Saddam's communication network. The 24th Division had the end run, said, Kern, and their strategy was right on target. They cut off the Iraqis from the rear, so they could not cross the Euphrates River to the north. They completely surprised the Iraqis who never expected the infantry to go so far west. "We went four times as far, twice as fast as General Paton went across Europe," Kern remarked. Tanks that maneuvered through sandstorms, known as raging shambles, were able to use hand-held LORANs to continue moving in blinded situations. Problems included culture barriers, such as not knowing foreign languages of the allied forces, and initial unawareness of Islam regulations for attire and actions expected of females.

Nine hundred women served in the Gulf, living just as the male soldier did, Kern said, but when they went into town, Saudi patrol stopped women for driving vehicles and males were given the wheel. Assessing bomb damage presented problems, since photographs were taken at the same time bombs were activated and creating clouds. Before relaying what it takes to be in ready mode against dictators such as Saddam Hussein, Hendrickson expressed concern that the public will focus only on preparation for duplicate threats, when support for all possibilities is needed. We tend to focus on Desert Storm as being the way we ought to be prepared. I just want to be sure that you support us when we go out to Congress, and remind people that we could have a civil war in the Soviet Union next month. We could have a war at sea on our hands in three months. "These are not missions that we can forget about. What we call the con-ops in the Mediterranean, those air strikes, those individual one-night kind of events are not things of the past. They could be part of the future, but should not be the only vein of our focus." cautioned Hendrickson Besides acquiring additional ships, weapons, and ensuring training has taken place in preparation for potential conflicts, there will be a different trend in military personnel as a result of the successful use of reservists in the Gulf," says Leland "Reservists were plucked out of civilian life, many of them playing it on the run for the first time, and we are pleased and proud of this country's reserves" stated Leland. "Our military forces will reduce with confidence because of our successfully-tested reserves."

The Navy League received due credit also, as Hendrickson expressed gratitude for vital support given to the armed forces during

Desert Storm. McNeill express her thanks for the officers in accommodating a speaking engagement so quickly upon the return of the USS Saratoga to Jacksonville and the 24th Infantry to Ft. Steward.

I sent the following letter of thanks to Colonel Kern:

April 25, 1991
Dear Paul,

Thank you so much for participating in our Seminar at the State Meeting. I understand how very precious your first few weeks back home are and appreciate so much your sharing your experiences with us. You were quite a hit! It's interesting hearing all of the praises for an "Army Man" at our Navy League function. Of course, we have always supported every branch of the military and continue to support a strong national defense. Your talk strengthened our stand and made us even more proud of our country.

We feel that we have found a friend. I do hope the bell plaque doesn't look too out of place with your other memorabilia. We hope it will serve as a tie between you and the Navy League and a reminder that both our councils and Arlie and I personally are available if we could ever be of help.

Sincerely, Sheila

I look back on these speeches, these briefings, these opportunities to talk directly to our military leadership and wonder why we have such a difficult time enlisting the public in joining us and working to make a difference.

About five years later I was waiting on the tarmac at NSB Kings Bay waiting for secretary of defense, William Perry, to arrive. When he arrived, he had someone with him. It was Paul Kern, now a lieutenant general! What a thrill that was! We hugged and talked as if it had not been yesterday. And then some twenty years later I see him again as we were seated at the same table with the commandant of the US Marine Corps, General Robert Neller, during Sea Air Space.

Only in the military…

GEORGIA TREND MAGAZINE

Georgia Trend is a state magazine that is read by every chamber, economic development agency and state leadership. Neely Young has been the editor and publisher for the many years I've been reading it. The magazine cover was enough of a thrill to last me a lifetime. That first call came to Navy League headquarters in DC on May 14, 2001, when I was national president. They spoke to Ramona Joyce, our public affairs director. They told her I was included in the one hundred most influential Georgians. Ramona called me to see if it was all right to give them my age. When she told me why they were asking I was delighted to give my age.

The next day Carla Carper and I were in a cab in DC. She had come in town early to prepare for the community group's first fly-in to advocate for the SSGN conversion. Carla had had recent surgery on her hand and was a trooper to be doing all of this travel and preparations for everyone. I felt like my feet were one mass of pain—my back hurt and I had an upper respiratory infection. I felt completely disoriented at times—it was a tough afternoon. I called my assistant Amanda Gross. She said that *Georgia Trend* magazine had called and wanted to make an appointment for me to meet with the photographer to take a picture of me with a submarine for the *cover of the magazine.* I thought there must be a mistake, probably a picture inside with the story and that would be an honor so, okay. I called, and they said *cover.* As we were riding in the cab, Carla would say *cover* and we would smile. Then I would say *front cover* and we would smile. I was so glad I was with Carla who could really appreciate the *cover.* I'm glad it is with a submarine because that was the story we wanted told. The cab driver thought we were crazy.

It was an exciting time. There is nothing quite like it. When they asked me how many copies, I said 165! I later calmed down enough to order enough magazines for all my friends! The article is included in the book. Three weeks later I had an invitation to a breakfast in Atlanta to honor the one hundred, but I had to be in California to speak at two councils and the regional meeting. If there was any way I sure would have loved to have been there. I consider this one of my highest honors and will be grateful to the magazine and Mr. Young for recognizing my work. A year later Mr. Young referred to me as one of the "big mules" in an article.

> On May 13, 2002, I sent him a letter:
> Mr. Neely Young, Editor and Publisher
> *Georgia Trend*
>
> Dear Mr. Young,
>
> I was quite surprised and truly flattered to find myself included in your May 2002 article on Georgia's "Big Mules." I'm not so sure about the term "Big Mule" but being a true Georgia girl—and not too far removed from the farm I understand the compliment. Even the biggest mule cannot accomplish very much without guidance and assistance and I am quite fortunate

to be surrounded by a very dedicated group of folks in Camden County who like to get things done. Thank you so much for this honor!

Sincerely, Sheila

I still have some of those magazines if anyone wants one. I'll have them at my book signings!

ADMIRAL ED GIAMBASTINI

VICE CHAIRMAN JOINT CHIEFS OF STAFF

When I became national vice president of the Navy League I received a note from Vice Admiral Giambastiani on July 28, 1999:

Dear Sheila, A quick note to extend my personal congratulations to you for your recent selection as a national vice president of the Navy League. You can be justifiably proud of this significant achievement. Again, Congratulations and best wishes for continue success. Ed

He added this message: "We're proud of you. Pretty impressive but I'm not surprised."

Ed was never stationed at Kings Bay but many of his jobs took him there. We had known each other for many years and I always enjoyed talking with him. He was deeply involved with the conversion of the SSBNs to SSGNs and I was always trying to get more information than he was willing to give. That didn't stop me from trying!

When I was national vice president of the Navy League, I traveled to San Diego and joined the Defense Advisory Committee on Women in the Services at their annual meeting. One of the big issues was women on submarines. Ed was a two star and serving as director of Submarine Warfare at the Pentagon—he was briefing the committee on submarines as well as answering questions that they submitted to the Navy. He was amazingly direct and clear with answers. Every question that was asked he answered. There was no "let me get back with you." This was the case in many times when I was serving on the committee. We interacted with all branches of the military and sometimes we would submit questions that only resulted in the service asking for clarification. Sometimes it would take several meetings to get an issue clarified. But not the Navy that day. See my story on "Women on Submarines" to read my response to Ed's briefing.

On April 8, 2000, when VADM Giambastiani was commander, Submarine Force Atlantic Fleet (SUBLANT), he attended the Kings Bay Submarine Ball on Jekyll Island. Admiral and Mrs. Vern Clark were also in attendance. That evening it was announced that Admiral Clark was to be the next chief of Naval Operations. I was seated between the two of them. It was quite a heady night!

In 2002, as the senior military assistant to the secretary of defense, Vice Admiral Ed Giambastiani Jr., spoke at the submarine birthday ball at the Adams Mark Hotel in Jacksonville. He was introduced by the group commander Rear Admiral Gerald (Gerry) Talbot. I was seated with him, so I grilled him all evening.

He has had one of the most versatile careers.

The *Washington Post* covered secretary of defense Rumsfeld's announcement of military changes with the headline:

> *Rumsfeld's Next Battle*
> *After Iraq, his priority is reshaping the military*
>
> *… as key positions came open, Rumsfeld has been able to fill them with his own picks. Three in particular stand out. Rumsfeld has turned what was once a military backwater, the Joint Forces Command into his agent of change in the uniformed military. Last year he displaced his military assistant Adm. Edmund P. Giambastiani Jr. to take over. Now Giambastiani, a former submarine commander has been put in charge of assembling the 'lessons learned' in the Iraq war—a function that in the past was done separately by each of the services. The document he produces is expected to shape next year's defense budget and effectively has made him one of the most powerful figures in the military establishment.*

> *November 2004*
> *Dear Sheila,*
>
> *I would like to thank you for your support and that of the Navy League in fostering communication of the untold stories of our service members in Iraq and around the world. It's an important story to tell and your efforts of empowering the hundreds of Navy League councils throughout America to get out the message is appreciated. I always wanted to personally express my thanks to you for the fine article Hunter Keeter wrote for Seapower magazine in September. I'm not used to having my picture on the front cover of a magazine, but I have to say I received many favorable comments regarding the article.*

The Navy League truly supports this nation's service members and their families, and I know you will continue this great tradition of support. Your personal attention is greatly appreciated and dramatically increases the effectiveness of the Navy League's outreach programs. Thank you for your continuing support of this great military.

Sincerely, Ed

When I "retired" from the Navy League in June 2005, I asked Ed to speak at the last banquet. He was then commander of Joint Forces Command in Norfolk.

I sent him a letter at the end of that convention:

Dear Ed,

Thank you for speaking at the Navy League banquet during our 103rd National Convention in Norfolk, Virginia. I know what a challenge it was for you and your staff to join us for what has become a signature event at our annual get-together, and deeply appreciate the extraordinary measure taken to make it possible. Your presence as the keynote speaker and your assistance in the presentation of the Secretary of the Navy Public Service Awards meant a lot to our members and the Award recipients—including myself. Your excellent remarks on the areas currently being focused on by the Navy provided a powerful message for attendees at this event. Your points will be very useful to our leadership in their interactions with the public and their legislative representatives. I thank you for your support and friendship during the past 15 years. Your personal encouragement during my term as president was so much appreciated. I cannot think of anyone better to speak at my "retirement." Your remarks made my mother and family proud and filled my heart… what can I say.

Thank you, sir.
With appreciation and best wishes
Sincerely, Sheila

I don't know of any who has had a more interesting career. I saw him often in the news when he was the senior military assistant to secretary of defense, Donald Rumsfeld—at that time both Rumsfeld and President Bush referred to him as Admiral G. Previously he served as NATO's first Supreme Allied Commander of transformation and as commander of the United States Joint Forces Command where he led the transformation of NATO and US military forces. His last assignment in the Navy was as vice chairman of the Joint Chiefs of Staff. "A veteran of the submarine service who became a leading Pentagon strategist," the *New York Times* reported in June 2007.

Ed retired in 2007 after thirty-seven years of service. An interesting man with an incredible career.

VICE ADMIRAL TIM GIRADINA AND MISSY

COMMANDER SUBMARINE GROUP TRIDENT

I don't know how he did it. Rear Admiral Tim Giardina was Submarine Group 10 Commander at Kings Bay as well as Submarine Group 10 Commander at Bangor, Washington. He had quite a commute—three thousand miles! They made the decision to live in Washington state, but Tim was often at Kings Bay and involved with the community. And we did get to see Missy from time to time, but I know it had to be hard on them. Yes, even with all this responsibility, he still managed to meet with and keep in touch with the community. Even as I "fussed" with Navy leadership about not have a flag officer at Kings Bay I continued to brag on Tim for the support he was giving.

It was a busy time for him and the submarine force. The one thousand Trident patrol was celebrated during his tour and there were the most significant number of VIPs of any event since Kings Bay existed.

The program:

1000th Trident Patrol Ceremony Schedule of Events
19th February 2009
Arrival of Official Party
Parade the Colors
National Anthem
Invocation
Opening Remarks: RDML Timothy Giardina, Commander, Submarine Group Trident
Welcoming Remarks Rep Jack Kingston, State of Georgia

Guest Speakers:
VADM John Donnelly, Commander Submarine Force
Gen. Kevin Chilton, Commander, U.S. Strategic Command
Adm. Gary Roughead, Chief of Naval Operations
PRINCIPAL MILITARY SPEAKER

Gen. James Cartwright, Vice Chairman of the Joint Chiefs of Staff
KEYNOTE SPEAKER
The Honorable Donald C. Winter, Secretary of the Navy
Benediction
Departure of the Official Party

Even with events like the one thousandth patrol he managed to reach out. He had several flags attending: Vice Admiral Jay Donnelly and his wife, Mimi, and Rear Admiral Steve Johnson, Vice Admiral Mel Williams, two British admirals, and two gentlemen from the Bangor community. Guy Stitt was president of Olympic Council of the Navy League and Jim Nall was president of Puget Sound Naval Base Association. Tim had reached out to them and made introductions to us all to bring leadership in both Trident bases to work together to make us all more effective. We met for a no host dinner at Marianne's in downtown St. Marys and Arlie and I attended. What a wonderful, relaxed evening.

Keith Post and I even convinced him to come to St. Simons Island for dinner and talked the entire night. Keith was able to cover all the submarine museum issues and we discussed the submarine force and what was happening in the community.

The command was split at the end of his command. No more traveling from Washington State to Georgia to go to work. Yes, in 2009, it was announced that Kings Bay would, once again, have a flag officer at Kings Bay. Rear Admiral Barry Bruner was to relieve Tim as commander of Submarine Group 10 at a ceremony held June 26, 2009. To show the terrific amount of respect he had for the community and the connections he had made he sponsored a reception "In honor of Kings Bay Community Leaders" two days before his change of command. I will always be grateful to Tim for his words at that ceremony. He recognized Arlie and me for the support and my work on the Return to Service as "nothing sort of spectacular"!

Tim was brilliant and had a great way with words. I must admit I called him a couple of times when I was introducing top military to get a better slant—to have something different from just reading the bio. We would share common stories and before the call was over I had a great introduction. He was also very interested in gems and antiques. You could talk with him about most anything! Of course, I knew him when he was commanding officer of the USS *Kentucky* so that helped!

Since Missy lived in the Bangor area we did not have the time with her that we would have liked. She was great fun to be with and had a knack of getting people to open up—to relax and talk with her. She was a great asset to Tim. I was pleased to have a little time with Missy and with Beth Bruner when we spent June 25, touring the area and having a community leadership lunch in their honor.

ADMIRAL JONATHAN GREENERT AND DARLEEN

CHIEF OF NAVAL OPERATIONS

When Admiral Greenert spoke to the Camden Kings Bay Navy League on February 11, 2001, he was vice chief of Naval Operations working for Admiral Vern Clark. He was on the short list for chief of Naval Operations, but I didn't want to mention it—I was afraid to jinx it.

I had the honor of introducing him. I gave the usual introduction with his former commands and mentioned the fact that he was a recipient of the Vice Admiral Stockdale Award for Inspirational Leadership.

What the admiral didn't know is that I called some of his friends to get some of the more personal aspects of his career. Rear Admiral Tim Giardina a former group commander at Kings Bay had worked for him and he gave me a little scoop that helped in the introduction:

> INTRODUCTION: ADMIRAL JONATHAN GREENERT
>
> Tonight, I have the pleasure of introducing our guest speaker, Admiral Jonathan W. Greenert, Vice Chief of Naval Operations.
>
> A graduate of the United States Naval Academy, Admiral Greenert has successfully commanded at all levels including the USS Honolulu where he earned the "Vice Admiral Stockdale award for Inspirational Leadership" (which I might add is a Navy League award), Submarine Squadron Eleven, Commander Naval Forces Marianas, Commander U.S. Seventh Fleet and Commander U.S. Fleet Forces Command.
>
> Now if he had his way—that official introduction is all he would have. But he is not going to have his way—and I am sure that is rare at this point in his career. I can't say enough good stuff about Admiral Greenert. He is one of those "scary smart" folks—you know the kind with a green visor over his eyes as he peers deep into the budget. But then, you'd hardly know this because he is so "normal." Who would believe that a finance guy would also be so normal? As the Navy budget officer, he was a natural. But then he has been a natural in his command positions also. I remember meeting with him when I was Navy League national president and was on my trip to Asian back in 2003. He was most gracious.
>
> Successful at every level he doesn't mind rolling his sleeves up and facing the tough issues. At USFFC he took on the Navy's

Individual Augmentee policy and processes. Everywhere he visited, he talked to both leadership and anyone who had done an IA. His wife Darlene met with spouses separately or they engaged the families as a group.

He takes full responsibility for any issues with "the buck stops here" tone. And the guy has a great sense of humor, too.

He listens and fixes the problems. That attitude will come in handy with the fiscal challenges of our Navy and the hard choices we will need to make through these troubled times. No one I know is better able to get us through the turbulence.

We are honored to welcome Admiral Jon Greenert.

He learned a few days after his visit to Camden County that he got it! He was to be our next Chief of Naval Operations. The *Washington Post* sent out a short announcement:

Longtime Submariner Will Be Next Navy Leader
By Craig Whitlock

Adm. Jonathan Greenert, a longtime submarine officer has gotten the nod to become the new leader of the Navy. Gates told reporters he would recommend that President Barack Obama nominate Greenert to become Chief of Naval Operations, replacing Adm. Gary Roughead, who is scheduled to retire when his four-year term ends in September.

Greenert, a 1975 graduate of the Naval Academy in Annapolis, Md. Is vice chief of Naval Operations and is considered an expert on the Navy's budget and financial management. "He has extensive experience in the money world which is now facing all of us," said Adm. Mike Mullen, chairman of the Joint Chiefs of Staff, referring to spending cuts faced by the Pentagon.

Greenert has two decades of experience as a submariner, including assignments on the Fly Fish, the Tautog, the Michigan and the Honolulu, which he commanded. He has also served as commander of the U.S. 7th Fleet in the Pacific and as commander of the Navy's Fleet Forces Command.

When I was national president of the Navy League, it was protocol to stop by and talk with the commander of the Pacific Fleet before you travel into his area of responsibility (AOR), especially when you planned to meet so many of those he deals with. Admiral Walt Doran was the commander US Pacific Fleet at the time and

Admiral Greenert was his deputy. I was amazed and gratified that Admiral Doran took the time to meet with Arlie and me. He asked me to pass on his appreciation to these military leaders in Asia for the partnership they have with the US military. That's what I thought happened but when I ran into Rear Admiral Greenert in July 2003 at the USS *Ronald Reagan* commissioning I heard a little different story.

"Sheila, remember when you came out to PACFLET and had a meeting with Admiral Doran before you made your Pacific trip?"

"Yes, everyone was so nice to me. I really enjoyed it."

"Let me tell you what was happening. We had planned your visit as a nice Navy League president social visit where you would visit for a bit and be on the way. We learned after a little discussion that you had already met with the CNO (chief of Naval Operations) and the protocol director from the Pentagon. You were seeing some of the same people the admiral worked with. And you had many questions about this upcoming trip. We kept bringing in the experts on those particular countries. Did you notice how the crowd got larger as you and the admiral talked?"

"Yes, but I thought it was because another meeting had ended, and they were just listening. I was a little surprised but didn't think much about it."

"You were asking the same questions we would ask if we were meeting with them. When you left, my staff said, 'Who was that woman?' I answered, 'That gentleman was the Tasmanian devil!' I must assume since you are smiling that you mean that as a compliment?"

"Yes, I do," he replied with a smile.

On March 2014, I was pleased—no, I was overjoyed—when Admiral Greenert agreed to speak at the annual partnership event, the Community that Cares. I sent an e-mail to our community leadership:

Hello Everyone,

I have good news for TCP, for Kings Bay and for the Navy. Adm. Jon Greenert has been selected as the next CNO. Some of you may remember that he was our speaker at the Sailor/Marine/Coastie of the Year banquet and I had the honor of introducing him. He has been a friend for a number of years and he is the one I briefed at the Pentagon on the proposal discussed at our meeting.

He is a submariner and certainly knows Kings Bay and our capabilities. Don't think he will relieve Adm. Roughead until late September. This is the third individual that we've had speak in our community: Admiral Mike Mullen, CNO who became CJCOS, Admiral Bob Papp who became Commandant of the Coast Guard, and now Admiral Greenert who have had BIG promotions after their visit. We've had a good time with this point.

Note: We have shared the fact that to speak at the partnership's Community That Cares Event can only be great for your career!

We began to prepare for Admiral Greenert's visit. We sent invitations and received positive responses from Senator Johnny Isakson, Senator Saxby Chambliss Congressman Jack Kingston, Congressmen Ander Crenshaw from Jacksonville and former Secretary of the Navy Will Ball. The biggest group of heavy hitters The Camden Partnership had ever assembled at one event. There were so many dignitaries that I couldn't sit at the head table! It was wonderful. The group commander at the time was Rear Admiral Chas Richard. Thank goodness, he was a savvy officer, so he took it all in stride.

Before the event we did the "Where's is the admiral?" version of "Where's Elmo?" We had the picture blown up, so his face was about three feet high and several carloads of us took it to every place in the community: the hospital, the schools, the police and fire departments, etc., and shared a scrapbook of all "his" adventures. I kept that big poster and it is on the wall of my office. It stops people in their tracks. It's fun waiting to see if my guests will say anything!

A couple of billboards and the marquees around town told everyone the top man in the Navy was on the way.

Attending with him were his public affairs officer, Captain Danny Hernandez, and protocol officer, Mrs. Wendy Boler. MCPON Mike Stevens who met with the chiefs during the luncheon and a great photographer that I had met several times MCCF Peter Lawlor.

President of the council Dave Burch and Keith Post, executive director of the St. Marys Submarine Museum and I met the admiral when he arrived at the conference center.

Local attendees included commander of the Submarine Group 10 RADM, Richard; Captain Harvey Guffey, commanding officer of Kings Bay; mayor of St. Marys, John Morrissey; mayor of Kingsland, Kenneth Smith; mayor of Woodbine, Steve Parrott; and the chairman of the Camden County Commission, Jimmy Starline. Our cities and country proclaimed it Admiral Jonathan W. Greenert Day and presented the following proclamation:

A PROCLAMATION by the cities of Kingsland, St. Marys, and Woodbine; and the County of Camden, Georgia designating Tuesday, the 18th of March 2014 as ADMIRAL JONATHAN W. GREENERT DAY.

WHEREAS, today, on behalf of all Camden County citizens, we welcome the 30th Chief of Naval Operations of the United States Navy to Camden County; and

WHEREAS, Camden County has an exceptional supportive relationship with all the military services based in and around Naval Submarine Base Kings Bay; and

WHEREAS, we live in freedom thanks to the contributions and sacrifices made by the extraordinary men and women of our armed forces, as well as their families, who serve our nation in times of peace, war and national peril; and

WHEREAS, Admiral Greenert has served our nation for nearly 39 years since graduating from the United States Naval Academy in 1975, in sea assignments which have included USS FLYING FISH (SSN 673), USS TAUTOG (SSN 639), Submarine NR-1 and USS MICHIGAN (SSBN 727) (Gold), and culminating with command of USS HONOLULU (SSN 718) from March 1991 to July 1993; and

WHEREAS, Admiral Greenert has served in numerous fleet support positions including Deputy Chief of Naval Operations for Integration of Capabilities and Resources (N8); Deputy Commander, U.S. Pacific Fleet; Chief of Staff, U.S. 7th Fleet; Head, Navy Programming Branch and Director, Operations Division Navy Comptroller and most recently served as the 36th Vice Chief of Naval Operations from August 2009 to August 2011; and

WHEREAS, Admiral Greenert is the recipient of the Vice Admiral James B. Stockdale Award for Inspirational Leadership, the Distinguished Service Medal (Six Awards) the Defense Superior Service Medal and the Legion of Merit (Four Awards); and

WHEREAS, the people of Camden County are honored and privileged to welcome, salute and pay tribute to this distinguished military leader and we are grateful for the opportunity to host Admiral Jonathan Greenert in our Camden County-Kings Bay Community.

NOW, THEREFORE, we do hereby jointly and proudly proclaim Tuesday, the 18th day of March 2014 to be:

ADMIRAL JONATHAN W. GREENERT DAY IN CAMDEN COUNTY, GEORGIA

James H. Starline, Chairman John F. Morrissey, Mayor Camden County Board of Commissioners City of St. Marys Kenneth E. Smith, Sr., Mayor Steven L. Parrott, Mayor City of Kingsland City of Woodbine

In his remarks, he said, "The main strategic deterrent to nuclear conflict are the submarines home-based at Kings Bay Naval Submarine Base, and there is money in the budget to design the replacements for the Ohio-class subs that will begin going offline in fourteen years."

Darlene spent the time meeting with Lisa Richard and Wanda Guffey touring family housing, Navy Exchange, and the Commissary Complex. She was a former naval officer so when she listened, she understood exactly what our Navy was talking about.

The *Florida Times Union* reported:

> **Kings Bay's key role for Navy reaffirmed by Chief of Naval Operations**
>
> By **Terry Dickson**
>
> Adm. Jonathan W. Greenert says base is deterrent to nuclear conflict
>
> ST. MARYS—The main strategic deterrent to nuclear conflict are the submarines home-ported at Kings Bay Naval Submarine Base, and there is money in the budget to design the replacements for the Ohio Class subs that will begin going offline in 14 years, Adm. Jonathan W. Greenert, chief of Naval Operations said Tuesday. That was good news to an appreciative crowd that gathered at a luncheon to thank Greenert, who visited sailors at Kings Bay at noon and Mayport later, for his continued support of the base. The Camden Partnership hosted the luncheon. Among other things, Greenert came away with a resolution from Camden County, St. Marys, Kingsland and Woodbine declaring it Jonathan W. Greenert Day. Most of the talk, however, was a serious discussion about the Navy's needs, especially the new class of subs for Kings Bay. Kings Bay has eight Ohio Class subs.
>
> Although Greenert cautioned the Navy needed "money help" in getting the replacements done on time, he said, "It will happen. It has to be done right." Some of the costs will be reduced because the U.S. is working with the United Kingdom to design the missile compartments for the submarines, Greenert said. When the boats are complete, the U.S. and Great Britain will be capable of firing each other's missiles, Greenert said.
>
> U.S. Sen. Saxby Chambliss, R-Ga., who greeted Greenert at the luncheon, said simply of the $1.2 billion in design funding, "That's huge. We've got to keep it going. That's full funding." Chambliss also gave the same weight to Greenert's description of Kings Bay in the Navy's plans. "When he says Kings Bay is the No. 1 base in the U.S. for strategic deterrence, that's huge,"

> he said. The man who is running to replace Kingston, U.S. Rep. Jack Kingston, R-Ga., said Congress has to make sure there is continued funding for military programs such as Kings Bay's key mission as money gets diverted. He pointed to President Barack Obama's proposal to increase the funding for administration of the Affordable Care Act from $5 billion to $23 billion in a single year. "That's just for the bureaucrats. That's not one dime in medicine," Kingston said.
>
> **CUTS STILL A DANGER** Protecting Kings Bay's subs doesn't mean Obama won't cut other military funding, Kingston said. "He doesn't have trouble finding money for programs he likes, but when it comes to the military, we're out of money," Kingston said. Even if all the money is there, Greenert said there could be trouble finding the companies and labor force to build the replacement submarines and other ships. The Navy needs major ship builders to construct the submarines and other replacement ships and their numbers have fallen from 10 in the 1990s to five now with another going out of business, he said. "Imagine losing one more," he said.
>
> In addition to building a new class of submarines, the Navy must also modernize its fleet of 22 cruisers. Eleven already have been modernized but the rest must undergo the same transformation, or they'll be obsolete in five or six years, he said. He also said the Navy is still suffering the impact of sequestration under the Budget Control Act of 2011. The reduction in funds slowed the maintenance of ships so that others had to remain on deployment longer than they otherwise would have, but the Navy is finally catching up, Greenert said. He made one announcement that should make Navy spouses happy. By 2015, he said, "we're looking at a stable eight-month deployment." That depends, however, on stability, and should the "world go crazy" more ships would have to be deployed, he said.
>
> Former state representative Charlie Smith of St. Marys advised Greenert the Navy could save a lot of money by moving "a squadron of fast attack submarines from the icy north to Kings Bay." "Well, Mr. Smith," Greenert joked, "I hadn't thought of that." After leaving Kings Bay, Greenert was due to visit Mayport.

When we were working on the Triad event at Kings Bay I heard at Electric Boat's Submarine Industrial Base conference that the secretary of the Navy had not approved the event. That evening I made a list of the reasons why the event should happen—listing about a dozen reasons. That evening at the reception everyone was trying to get a moment with Admiral Greenert, so I asked Darleen if she would give him my list. She urged me to stay for a few minutes and talk with him. I talked with Jon about the last-minute notice on the Triad. We had been waiting for approval for months and many of the arrangements had been made. I left my list of issues on "why nuclear deterrents aren't that important" with him as well as all the admirals that were at the reception that evening. The next morning, he shared that list with VADM Breckenridge after a morning meeting. I received a call that afternoon that the event was reinstated. I'm pleased that Jon saw the value in the Triad event at Kings Bay.

Skip Witunski, the new national president of the Navy League, invited me to join him and VADM Jay Donnelly—then a national vice president of the Navy League for a call with Admiral Greenert right before he retired. We could tell that many of his memorability had already been removed from the office. I kept looking at all the great items and picturing them in the St. Marys Submarine Museum.

After our visit, I tentatively (as well as I do tentative) mentioned that he should remember the museum if he had items he didn't have room for at home. He told me to pick out what I wanted. They continued to talk as I walked around the room. As I touched an item, I watched his reaction. He got in the spirit and flinched at each of the items. A slight flinch and I put it on the table to take with me. A stronger flinch and I left it alone. I picked four items. As we left I gave one to Jay and one to Skip to carry out. Jay made it clear that if security had any questions as we left the Pentagon he was going to blame it all on me.

Thank you, my friend, for being so gracious to me and for doing it all with a sense of humor.

CAPTAIN, JON HAGEMANN AND CINDY

COMMANDING OFFICER NAVAL SUBMARINE SUPPORT CENTER (NSSC)

I had known Jon and Cindy for several years. Cindy was very active in the community and helped me with events we had at the St. Marys Submarine Museum. I was surprised and honored when he asked me to speak at his change of command on May 11, 2007.

The chief of staff of Submarine Group 10 at Kings Bay was Captain Dave Volonino. I had become particularly fond of his wife, Naoko Yokomura of Tokyo, Japan, and convinced her to help us out at the store. Jon was being relieved by Commander Mark B. Guevarra. Jon began with welcoming remarks and introduced me. Captain Volonino also had remarks and presided over the award presentation.

My words indicated the respect and admiration I had for both Jon and Cindy. He was the first commanding officer for the new command at Naval Submarine Base Kings Bay the Naval Submarine Support Center.

As a change of procedure, Jon introduced me and gave me the best introduction I've ever had.

> *Today's guest speaker really needs no introduction. Sheila McNeill is truly an institution. I asked Sheila to speak today because of her role in support of the sea services and in particular the role that she plays in direct support of Kings Bay. In many ways, Naval Submarine Support Center intertwines closely with the objectives that Sheila has been so directly involved with for more than 40 years. Sheila's biography would take hundreds of pages and would be compiled in many volumes. The biography in today's program only touches on her extraordinary accomplishments. The direct and positive impact that Sheila has had on our sea services cannot be overstated. Whether it has been while serving as the first woman National President of the Navy League of the United States, on the executive board of the Defense Advisory Committee on Women in the Services, on the State of Georgia executive board coordinating military affairs, or in the many other leadership roles that she has taken on, she has met and influenced men and women in the highest levels in countries all over the world. Ladies and Gentlemen, not only is she one of the 100 most influential Georgians, but she may well be the most influential woman to ever grace this base. Ladies and Gentlemen, my very special friend, Sheila McNeill.*

These were my remarks:

> *It is a privilege and an honor to be with you all here today and to be given an opportunity to participate in the time-honored tradition of the change of command of Commander Jon Hagemann and Commander Mark Guevarra.*
>
> *When Jon first approached me about speaking today I was reluctant… not because of any lack of respect for Jon… I guess it would be the opposite. I go to a lot of change of command ceremonies. In almost everyone in the past two years one person is usually mentioned in everyone's recognition of those who helped in their command—Jon Hagemann. A naval officer who affects so many people and so many missions at Kings Bay deserves more than this lady can convey—yet here I am and here we go.*

Let me begin by telling you a little about why I have such a deep and abiding respect for the military.

Arlie and I joined the Navy League in 1966 and have remained active for these 41 years. For the past ten years, I have traveled in support of our military. We found that the citizens in foreign countries have a deep respect for our military.

When I traveled in Europe as National President of the Navy League one of our visits was in France where an elderly gentleman wore a cowboy hat in our honor and wept as he described the liberation of his country by Americans more than half a century ago. The next day when I laid a wreath in the shape of an American flag, men in French WWII uniforms stood in line to hug us and kiss us and thank us for our American Navy with comments like, "it is your country that is supporting us and we are so grateful. Please thank your Navy." Another trip in another part of the world I was speaking to our military, Navy League members and citizens of South Korea and again and an older gentleman had tears as he shared with me and the commanding general his story of the sacrifices of our U.S. Marines in his country during the Korean War.

And as Arlie and I stood at the DMZ and hear briefings, I was aware of the military's diplomatic efforts to ensure peace and that any unification should preserve economic stability in this part of the world. One of the guests at the DMZ had flown in from the US to meet us and told us that his grandfather, brother and uncle were still in North Korea, 50 years after the war's end. It certainly brought home to us the tragedies resulting from the past conflicts in this part of the world; the pain that still exists and the need to make certain the many tension that remain are resolved peacefully. What a force for peace we have in our military. I believe there are some things we can be fairly certain won't change… We can be certain for example that the global economy will continue to depend upon the world's oceans, as the primary means of transporting goods and materials at a reasonable cost.

We can be certain… that 80 % of the world's population will continue to live within 500 miles of the coast. And sadly, we can be certain… that our adversaries… be they rogue nations, Global terror networks or modern-day pirates with no regard for life or property. We can be certain these adversaries will understand the strategic and economic importance of seaborne commerce. And will focus their attacks in that direction. And we can be certain… as long as we have Naval officers like Jon Hagemann our country is in good hands.

Commander Hagemann is a native Texan. He is married to Cindy Rusho of Sanford, Florida and they have four children, David, Amanda, Jared and Carly. Three years ago, there was no command to turn over. He is the first commanding office of Naval Submarine Support Center, Kings Bay, but let me tell you a little about Jon's past. Before this challenge, Jon showed his mastery of diverse tasks he was an ROTC instructor, he is an administrator, he is a seasoned seaman having last served as Executive officer on USS Dallas where his command earned two battle Efficiency "E" awards, and he is a foreign logistics expert serving with Joint Special Operations Task Force, Crisis Response Element, horn of Africa in 2003 in support of Operation Enduring Freedom.

Let me tell you a little story about Jon's work during that time. I asked Captain Ken Perry a former commanding officer at Kings Bay who was aboard the USS Enterprise sailing in the Arabian Gulf. These are his words: "I was assigned to the ENTERPRISE battle group and aboard the flagship USS ENTERPRISE. During our deployment, we became involved in a sensitive real-world operation taking place in the CENTCOM theater. It involved special forces, Marines, and expeditionary strike group—and an SSN. When I wanted to learn more about this operation I asked the headquarters staff at U.S. Fifth Fleet for the "point man" who can explain the details" and they pointed me to CDR Jon Hagemann. At that time, Jon was stationed in the garden spot of Djibouti, along the Red Sea on the Horn of Africa, farther from Kings Bay in distance and comfort than practically anywhere on earth. Even Flying Teeth can't survive there! He was probably the only submariner for hundreds of miles—and he was absolutely the right officer at the right time for the right job.

This operation required not only a special set of submarine skills (which Jon had become expert in while XO of the Dallas) but also the critical ability to work well with a joint force team that had been quickly assembled, in harsh conditions, to execute a new and dangerous War on Terror mission. It involved air and surface and ground and submarine platforms as part of a joint forcer to identify and attack key targets. From a base that has been called "one train stop beyond hell" Jon put his competence and leadership and personality on the line to help make this mission the success it was. He ensured the submarine was well positioned to exploit the full range of its powerful capabilities, while also making sure it fully supported the needs of the naval and joint force commanders afloat and ashore.

He did a great job, and you'll have to trust me on this: It was a big success."

Just one of the examples of stories about Jon most of us won't ever know about.

So, after a long career in the Navy, Jon gets this new assignment: He had the responsibility to get this new organization running efficiently and effectively based on lessons learned from other NSSC commands. It's a good thing that Jon has always had a thirst for knowledge, for learning something new and different. He looks for change as a chance to grow. And take it on he did, he hit the ground running. During his tour, there has been marked improvement for the support for the subs and ships that come into Kings Bay as well as improved maintenance availability planning and material support.

Jon invited me to the waterfront to get a close and personal view of what they do every day. Being a longtime fan of the Coast Guard I was able to observe the strong relationship between the Coast Guard and NSSC in our emerging partnership for Force Protection of our vital strategic assets. The professionalism and pride of workmanship are the principle factors in the ability of NSSC to do superb work. They each play an important role in support of the Trident mission scheduling and coordinating over 850 operational events that included personnel transfers at sea, arrivals, and departures for all submarine movements in Kings Bay, Mayport and Port Canaveral. If you want a demonstration in synergism look closely at this point who have experienced a 53% synergism look closely at this group who have experienced a 53% increase in operational tempo from 2005–2006. Each member works hard to improve the quality of life for our sailors and their families and to keep our tridents at sea. They did all this with a 20% savings to the government—meaning us taxpayers—with no degradation in support to the operational units. They are unbeatable.

They execute their job with a sense of duty and a realization of how important their work it. We have come to expect no less from our men and women in uniform and NSSC has risen to the challenge. And Jon is the ideal temperament for this job. A level headed, never lose your cool, compassionate man. One of the missions of NSSC is in family support, American Red Cross response and direct OMBUDSMAN support. The success of this relationship was evident in the emails I received from wives of men who were deployed on Tridents from Kings Bay. One email said, "I'm writing to tell you why I think CDR Hagemann is so wonderful. During Dean's three patrols, CDR Hagemann was my constant. He was always available (night or day) no matter what the reasoning. He assisted me and the Ombudsman in more ways than I can convey. He was my point of contact for practically every issue. His kindness, compassion and willingness to listen saved my sanity more than once! I know I speak for my husband, CDR Dean Nilsen, Tennessee Gold in saying that Jon was invaluable to the families and crew. He and his Command Master Chief MC Prince went above and beyond to help us through each patrol. I knew I could call on him for sound advice, direction, and a friendly "ear." He always told me "Maria, you can call me any time." Some people that say that don't really mean it; he did. I put it to the test more times than I can remember. I knew I could trust him to keep my confidence and give me the straight scoop."

What a tribute to Jon from the wife of one of our Trident command officers. Let's talk about Jon Hagemann the man—the father, the husband and the friend. First, I just plain like the man. I like the fact that he is the same man on Saturday night as he is on Monday morning. I like a man who shows respect to others. His compassion and dedication to service is evident in the partnerships with the submarine museum and Sugarmill Elementary School. I saw firsthand the work that the sailors at NSSC did for the submarine museum. Without their help, we could have never pulled off the 10th anniversary event. Jon invited me to attend one of the ceremonies of the Junior sailor of the month at Sugarmill Elementary. What an impressive event that was and what a wonderful way to recognize those young children for their good citizenship.

I am moved by the reverence and tenderness and the unabashed love Jon shows for Cindy. Of course, their meeting was something out of a romantic novel—on Valentine's Day, no less. With those looks and a cowboy hat on, Cindy didn't have a chance. They fell in love and married and have been a perfect match. Jon follows the old saying that if you fall in love with a thoroughbred you ride with a loose rein. Cindy, a force in her own right has contributed so much to this community. To quote her boss, Tonya at Kingsland Convention and Visitors Bureau: "Cindy is one of the most aware of the players in the Kingsland community—she knows everyone and bridges those gaps between the political boundaries and the communities. She really sees the big community picture and sees her role as a public servant to assist and grow community development. There is really going to be a void when she leaves."

My husband, Arlie has worked with Cindy many times over the past years with the Dolphin Scholarship Auction. Her organizational and people skills have contributed greatly to the funds raised for scholarships for our submarine children. Arlie always knew if Cindy had a hand in it it was done right. He always admired Cindy's spirit and zest and she's not too bad to look at either! I have known Cindy and I have admired her energy, her commitment and dynamic personality since the first time I met her. She's fun to be with—always has a smile for everyone and goes out of her way to make folks feel welcome. This has been her community and she embraces every newcomer and makes them a part of the family.

I am sure that it will be very hard for this family to leave the friendships and the involvement with the community behind. Cindy tells me they have grown to love this community and the people in it. She says that it was the first place in their Navy career that felt like home… that the community embraced her as a Navy wife and that she never felt like an outsider. And what a wonderful family! Carly moved here as a five-month-old baby and is now 14 and has only known Camden County as her home. So, we will always be able to call her a native and expect her to come home. Jared, a high school senior is the politician—friends of ours who just happened to meet Jared couldn't believe his political acumen. What charm and poise in one so young. Amanda started kindergarten just after they moved here and graduated from Camden High School last year. Not too many military kids can start school in the same place and continue through graduation. Amanda now lives in Jacksonville and attends the University of North Florida majoring in graphic design. Thanks for the pictures for the museum brochure, Amanda.

And the oldest David. A graduate of the University of Central Florida with a degree in healthcare administration he has returned to school to get his certification in physical therapy.

Your mom and dad are very proud of each of you as they should be! You are a tribute to the Navy family and what our Navy culture can produce. This family has become such a part of this community, this is home and we get that sense that they might eventually come back home.

It is a privilege to help to celebrate the spirit of this wonderful family and to express our gratitude not only from our country but from our community. For coming in and adopting the community for your own and for leaving it a better place than you found it.

And to Commander Gueavarra's children Amanda and John and to his fiancé, Ann Marie: You couldn't have a better family to tell you all about the benefits and charm of this community. Mark, I know that Jon has given you the best turnover possible. And you certainly aren't new to this area, as deputy squadron 16. What a varied and interesting background you bring to this job. From combat operations conducted in support of Operation Iraq Freedom, to working with the Iraqi government on the development of the Iraqi Constitution, to assistant to the President of the United States during the 54th Presidential Inaugural (let's see how many of you can figure out which that was) to the joint staff and working with Iraqi, and your share of tours on SSBNs and SSNs you bring a wealth of knowledge and experience to the job. Welcome to Naval Submarine Support Command.

In closing let me remind you that America is defined not only by its power but by its ideals. One of the strengths of Americans is the desire to serve a cause bigger than ourselves. Jon is one of the finest men I have known in my life and he shares this bond of service and it is with great pride and respect that we thank him for that.

Fair winds and following seas to the Hagemann family and welcome to the Guevara family.

God bless the officers and crew of NSSC, God bless our military and God Bless America.

They are a wonderful family and I check up on them often!

GENERAL MICHAEL HAGEE AND SILKE

COMMANDANT, US MARINE CORPS, JANUARY 2003–DECEMBER 2005

General Hagee was the commandant of the Marine Corps the entire time of my presidency. As most of the Marine Corps officers I have known he is reserved, dignified and not one to kid around. He didn't have much to kid around about during his tour. During the beginning of his tour we had twenty-three thousand marines in the Persian Gulf area. Before he became commandant, he helped plan the invasion and advance on Bagdad. As I came to know him better, I think we both relaxed a little and were happy to run into each other. His great asset was his wife, Silke. She has a wonderful personality and reaches out to those she met. I read an article about them in Stars and Stripes and recall her advice about marriage: "Let each other live. You have to allow your partner to do his or her own thing." A good philosophy and one I could really relate to with a husband like Arlie

When I was national president, I had gotten to know them fairly well when I attended a Marine Corps Association event on Capitol Hill. Most of the retired marines who were there were older (as was I) and tended to stand in groups of old friends. I wandered around and tried to make conversation but for the most part walked around looking at everyone. Something I enjoy but rarely have the opportunity. I was called over to stand in line to greet the commandant and his wife when they arrived. What a wonderful surprise when he got to me he gave me a big hug as did Silka, and we stood and talked a few minutes before he moved on. Wow, did that make me more popular. In fact, a group of them asked if I would join them for a picture with the commandant, and I was very hesitant as I hated to bother him, but I agreed. As we were waiting, one of the gentlemen approached General Hagee and said, "Sheila would like to have a picture with you—could you join us?" Now that was a big surprise and I never did see that picture!

My favorite story was at Sea Air Space in 2005. All three service chiefs and the maritime administrator were there. I was seated with Admiral Clark who had spoken several times during the three days. (Recollections of those days are in my memoirs of Admiral Clark.) I looked up and down the front row of tables. Suddenly, I noticed that the commandant of the US Coast Guard Admiral Tom Collins was at a table on the second row! I immediately lost my appetite. To this day I don't know why I took it so hard. I didn't eat another bite but did get up and ask the staff why this had happened. The staff was the best, most professional there is, so a glitch like this was rare. To this day I don't remember the answer but I do remember my exaggerated response.

When it was time to begin the ceremony, I went to the podium. We had about 1,200 in attendance. After a welcome and a few announcements, I introduced our principal speaker for the evening, General Mike Hagee. The introduction went well and as I was finishing my eye caught Admiral Collins and I ended the introduction with, "Help me welcome the commandant of the greatest fighting force in the world, the commandant of the United States Coast Guard, General Mike Hagee. There was thunderous applause as he walked up to the podium. By then I was horrified and was looking a little woebegone. As he walked to the podium—all 6'4" in formal Marine dress, he walked up to me, pointed his finger sternly and leaned into the speaker on the podium and said, "Sheila, down and give me ten."

"Sir, if I could give you one I would."

We had to wait for the crowd to calm down.

He reached for the microphone.

"No, not yet," I said as I realized I had failed to recognize the chief of Naval Operations, Admiral Clark. This was not my best night.

He turned to the back of the podium and stood straight behind me as the crowd cheered again.

I begin introducing Admiral Clark, when I realized General Hagee was walking back and forth behind me. I stopped and turned to him.

"General, are you pacing?" "Not any more I'm not!" He said as he abruptly stopped pacing and stood at attention. The crowd cheered once again.

Finally, he was able to take over the microphone and he did a magnificent job. I'm sure he must have but I sat on a chair at the back of the podium and couldn't hear every word he said for being so horrified by my screw ups in the introductions. As we left the podium, we were met by his aide who said, "Sheila, when did you and the General work that out? It was great!" Tongue in cheek, Silke came up and said, "Sheila, thank you for making my husband look like he had a sense of humor." It turned out to be a wonderful end to a fun evening. It could have gone either way! Years later I still have people who come up and talk about how much fun they had listening to our banter. With the responsibility, the general had I'm glad to say we participated in a fun evening for us all. And to this day, I am thankful that this Marine Corps commandant had a good sense of humor.

Years later I had to call General Hagee and during the call we discussed that evening. "There were several times people referred to me as admiral and I could tell them not to worry, Sheila introduced me as the commandant of the Coast Guard," he told me. Thank you, General, for allowing me to share my worse screw up and my best story.

After his retirement from the Marine Corps, Mike headed the Admiral Nimitz Historic Foundation that runs the National Museum of the Pacific War in Fredericksburg, Texas, Fleet Admiral Chester Nimitz's birthplace and hometown.

COMMANDER DAN HURD AND ERIN

UNITED STATES COAST GUARD

I was on the Defense Advisory Committee on Women in the Services. The committee dealt with women's issues of utilization and discrimination but also on quality of life issues for all military members. There was an incident at an Army base with recruits. Our committee was assigned to visit all the military training bases. I choose the Coast Guard Training Center at Cape May, New Jersey. It is the sole accession point for the entire enlisted workforce. I was there for two days, October 7–8, 1997. Bootcamp graduation was on the eighth. My visit report showed that I met with thirteen women and sixty-nine men in focus groups.

The captain was very impressive and embraced the visit. We were at a breakfast for some of the recruits and Dan was placed at my table. As we talked, I learned he was from Atlanta. Later a private meeting was set up with Dan with the explanation that he was a Georgia boy, and they thought he would be able to answer any of my questions. We talked for a while about his experiences at boot camp—he says it was forty-five minutes, but I doubt that. He did not know where his first assignment would be. I was impressed with him, but considering the fact that I visited forty-five different installations in those three years, I didn't expect to ever see him again. The captain approached the door and Dan was very much aware that the captain was waiting for him—a recruit—to finish. I then gave my brief to the captain and was a speaker at graduation. It was a great visit and the recruits were in good spirits.

A few months later I am at a Coast Guard picnic at Coast Guard Station St. Simons. A young man came up to me with a quizzical look, "Mrs. McNeill?" he asked. Well, it was Dan. I invited him to come to the house anytime and we made a date for lunch. We saw each other frequently. At one of our Navy League meetings, we had Rear Admiral Pat Stillman as the speaker. Arlie and I picked him up from the airport in Jacksonville, but I asked Dan to take him back the next day. I thought an hour with an admiral wouldn't hurt his career. If he behaved—and I told them that.

A few months later, Dan made a decision and called me for lunch. He was going to leave the Coast Guard when his first tour was completed. Obviously, I couldn't let him do that. I convinced him to apply for officer candidate school and let me write a letter of recommendation. He was approved. By the time he finished OCS, I am national president of the Navy League and Arlie and I planned to attend the graduation ceremony. He asked me to pin him. At first, those in charge of the ceremony told me that since I was not family and not former military, I would not be able to pin him. But when Rear Admiral Richard Houck, USCG arrived in the room reserved for speakers and heard this he reversed that decision and I had the honor. I was presenting the Navy League Award and was seated on the podium, so I didn't have far to go!

He was sick as a dog that day! He came from the hospital to walk across that stage. We didn't have an opportunity to visit much that day. He went right back to the hospital. It was an honor to be able to pin him that day.

He always called me and asked for my suggestions. I liked to tease him about not taking my advice, but later he reiterated each of his career decisions and sure enough—we both had liked the path he was taking. He does well in his career, but one day I received a call that he has decided to apply for flight training. I thought, *Here we go again, pushing his luck.* But I didn't argue with him. So, to the good fortune of the surface fleet Dan went into aviation. (I just couldn't resist that.) As it turned out, it was a great decision.

When he graduated, I receive another call. He said, "Sheila, I have my orders. I'm going to be the pilot for the commandant of the Coast Guard and the secretary of Homeland Security."

"Damn, I wouldn't fly with you!" I said.

"I know you wouldn't, but don't tell them that."

I talked with Admiral Papp a week or so later and told him the Dan story. I understand that when Dan first met Admiral Papp he was in the pilot's seat and Admiral Papp came to him and said, "I think we have a mutual friend."

The Papp's loved him like we do and he became Admiral Papp's aide for the admiral's last year. Linda was most comfortable when Dan was flying them. I always wanted to question her on that one.

I remember sitting in the commandant's change of command and seeing Dan in his uniform standing straight and very formal. I tried a little smile but got no reaction. I was very proud of him that day. But then, the biggest change ever! He is sent to Washington. Yes, the most politically correct arena for a member of the military. Dan is a driving force. His personality will work in many ways, I thought. He has never met a stranger. He is smart. He loves the Coast Guard. But Capitol Hill for this renegade? Do I need to worry?

Obviously not. He served successfully as the US Coast Guard fellow in the office of Senator Bill Nelson (FL). I've rarely seen Dan in an official capacity. Dan is a great storyteller—in fact, many of my friends that may have heard some of our stories realize he likes to push the limit with me. But I hear about him it is always wonderful news. Everyone I've ever talked to respects Dan and his ability to make things happen. He has touched the lives of many and for some reason we all love Dan Hurd.

Arlie and I attended his retirement on February 1, 2017. The room in the Russell Senate Office Building was packed. It was a wonderful time to see some old Coast Guard friends and to see Dan's family again. The three years Dan had worked as the military liaison for Senator Bill Nelson from Florida went well. Senator Nelson spoke that day on Dan, his "exquisite and charming" personality and how much he had taught him about the Coast Guard. He thanked Dan for his protection and projection of the national interest. Admiral Bob Papp spoke eloquently of Dan's service under him and of his integrity and courage throughout his career. He used the theme of the song by Garth Brooks if tomorrow never comes.

Sometimes late at night
I lie awake and watch her sleeping
She's lost in peaceful dreams
So I turn out the lights and lay there in the dark
And the thought crosses my mind
If I never wake up in the morning
Would she ever doubt
The way I feel about her in my heart

It was a very poignant reminder for each of us to let our friends and family know just how we feel about them.

And I was honored to read his citation:

CITATION TO ACCOMPANY THE AWARD OF
THE MERITORIOUS SERVICE MEDAL
(GOLD STAR IN LIEU OF A SECOND)
TO
LIEUTENANT COMMANDER DANIEL G. HURD
UNITED STATES COAST GUARD

Lieutenant Commander Hurd is cited for meritorious service in the performance of duty as a congressional fellow detailed to Senator Bill Nelson's personal staff from July 2014 to February 2017. As the first Coast Guard officer ever assigned to Senator Nelson's staff, he singlehandedly elevated the Coast Guard's importance among several influential Senate leaders. By enthusiastically leading the Senator's participation in over thirty-seven visits to Coast Guard units, including one multistate trip accompanied by three other senators, he fostered an enduring relationship between congressional decision-makers and the Coast Guard's workforce and executive leadership. Following the tragic shootings at the Pulse Nightclub in Orlando, Florida, Lieutenant Commander Hurd provided critical information and recommendations that aided Senator Nelson's efforts to direct federal resources to victims and their families. Demonstrating exceptional professional expertise, he crafted the 2016 Disaster Assistance Improvement Act, a bill sponsored by Senator Nelson to reform the federal government's ability to assist local government recovering from natural disasters. He also provided careful analysis and insight to the Everglades for the Next Generation Act, which will authorize a 337-million-dollar harbor deepening project to sustain the port's 28-billion-dollar annual business activity. Lieutenant Commander Hurd's dedication and devotion to duty are most heartily commended and are in keeping with the highest traditions of the United States Coast.

Erin, his lovely and patient wife, is perfectly suited for Dan. She is a teacher and I think that helps with Dan. She is used to dealing with willful children. They have two beautiful daughters, Lilly and Delaney. They are a wonderful family and I'm proud to know each of them.

I love you, Dan—it's nice to get the last word.

UNITED STATES SENATOR JOHNNY ISAKSON

There is no better senator than Johnny Isakson. He has listened to the concerns of his constituents with patience and understanding. He has the respect of his constituents as well as his colleagues. As chairman of the Veterans Committee in the Senate he has made a difference in the lives of many of our veterans. I have never written a letter to the editor in response to another letter. But one day I picked up the paper and read what I considered criticism of this great statesman, so I wrote the following:

> The Brunswick News
> April 24, 2013
> Letter to the Editor
>
> Recently I watched with pride as Senator Isakson gave an interview on his dinner with the President and a dozen senators. I thought, what a great way to handle this and I was proud that our own Georgia Senator was selected to choose 11 of his fellow senators to meet with the President.
>
> When I heard some criticism of this action in various settings I was frustrated with the remarks. We should all understand civility—we should all understand negotiations and compromise. What has happened to the respect we used to give to our statesmen who stood for their party beliefs but were still able to cross the aisle and reach a compromise that was in the best interest of our county? When did compromise get to be such a negative when all successful issues in business and politics are settled this way? Statesmanship is what Senator Isakson showed. How could we possible expect that any good would come from walking away from that dinner and immediately insulting the President and questioning his intent with the invitation?
>
> We need to salute our elected officials who are willing to be statesmen and are willing to work together in a common ground to do what is right for our country. The county needs that.
>
> Sheila McNeill

I hope Senator Isakson continues to serve for a long time.

CAPTAIN RHETT JAEHN

COMMANDING OFFICER, USS *GEORGIA* (729) GOLD

Lt. Rhett Jaehn was aide to Rear Admiral Tom Robertson and returned twenty years later as commanding officer of USS *Georgia*. After an event at Kings Bay, I Introduced him to Dr. Valarie Hepburn president of the College of Coastal Georgia. As they shook hands, Rhett told Valarie, "Sheila may call me captain but to her I'll always be a lieutenant."

I thought, *Wow, he's right*. Not that I don't have enormous respect for him. I do but I also remember him as a young man just starting out, married to his wonderful Dinah.

In January 2014, the Atlanta Navy League councils sponsored an event at the Georgia Capitol. That story was covered in *Seapower* magazine:

> *Atlanta Honors USS Georgia Commanding Officer, Crew*
> *By Peter Atkinson, Deputy Editor*
>
> *The Atlanta Metropolitan Council hosted a reception at the Double Tree Hotel in Atlanta January 29 for Capt. Rhett Jaehn, commanding officer of the Ohio-class guided-missile submarine USS Georgia Gold Crew and several top crew members. In attendance at the reception from the council were President Jeff Alexander, Don Giles, vice president Legislative Affairs, Diane Ritter, vice president, Public Affairs, Paul Ritter, Denny Holmes, Vice president Members, Allen Legel, vice president, Operations; Lt J.G. William Golden, U.S. Naval Sea Cadet Corps (NSCC), vice president, Education, Darlene Golden; Danny Camp, the council's photographer, Lt J.G. Eric Farland, NSCC and Cindi Farland.*
>
> *A contingent of officers of The Camden Partnership, Inc., a nonprofit organization in support of the Naval Submarine Base Kings Bay; where Georgia is homeported also attended. They were led by President Sheila M. McNeill, past Navy League national president and a member of the Executive Board of the Governor's Military Affairs Coordinating Committee in Georgia.*
>
> *Joining Jaehn from Georgia for the reception were Mark Kelly, master chief of the boat. Yeoman 1st Class Michael Alsbrooks, Petty Officer 2nd Class Don Paul and Electrician's Mate 1st Class Cody Brooks.*
>
> *Alsbrooks, a former Sea Cadet was presented with the Sailor of the Quarter for 1st Quarter 2013 during the reception. On behalf*

of the offices and crew of Georgia Jaehn presented a plaque to the Atlanta Metropolitan Council for its support and sponsorship. He also honored Alexander as an "Honorary Crewmember of the USS Georgia (SSGN 729)."

Jaehn was in Atlanta to participate in the "Georgia Institute of Technology (Georgia Tech) Day" January 30 at the state Capitol with Governor Nathan Deal and Georgia Tech President Dr. G. P. "Bud Peterson, Jaehn, a native of Ohio is a graduate of Georgia Tech and was honored for his work and long service to the Navy. While at the Capitol, Jaehn introduced his attending crew and answered questions from members of the Senate and House of Representatives about the submarine. Jaehn took command of USS Georgia on May 18, 2012. It was one of the first four submarines to have female crew members. An Atlanta Council sponsored boat, Georgia recently was awarded the coveted Battle Efficiency or Battle "E" award for 2012

When Rhett's tour was over he came to my office with a book entitled *Peak of Limuria: The Story of Diago Garcia and the Chagos Archipelago* with this inscription in the book:

Sheila,

You are a blessing to me, the men and women if USS GEORGIA (SSGN-729) and all the military families in the Kings Bay area. Your personal leadership and relentless devotion to the Submarine Force and the Navy is an inspiration to all. You championed the 'rogue 'concept of the SSGN when no one else would. I am honored and humbled to command one of your boats. On Georgia, we find, fix and finish. Find the enemy. Fix their position and Finish them off. Our ability to take the fight forward and change the geo-political environment in real time is unmatched by any platform in any Service in the Country. Thank you for your support, thought and prayers over these years. May the Lord bless you and keep you. May his light shine upon you.

Sincerely, Rhett Captain, USN
Diego Garcia, BIOT is our home away from home
June 2014

My response:

> *Rhett, I hope you enjoy this book showcasing the art of students across the state. This was part of the Return to Service Ceremony. The CO of the Georgia!! Hard to believe after all these years we've known each other, and we have this connection. The book and your inscription on Diego Garcia is a treasure to me. We were blessed to have you as a CO of the Georgia. You got it! You always "got it"... the outreach and how important it is to Georgia. Thank you for your tour—it was incredible. I love you and your precious family. Sheila*

It has been a joy and a blessing to have known this military officer and who would have expected I would see him again twenty years later.

ACTING SECRETARY OF THE NAVY H.T. JOHNSON

When Gordon England left his post as secretary of the Navy for the Department of Homeland Security, he left behind the best-organized and most effective leadership team among the military services Our Navy and Marine Corps team was blessed to have one of England's key advisors, Hansford T. Johns designated by President Bush to take up the task of serving as acting secretary. Along with the outstanding uniformed leadership of Admiral Vern Clark and General Michael Hagee, Johnson immediately got to work insuring that America's sailors and marines and the materials they need for war and that their families had what they needed on the home front

Holding down three jobs at once, as acting secretary, assistant secretary of the Navy (installations and logistics), and unofficially, the gapped undersecretary position, Johnson, a retired four-star Air Force general got cracking as war in Iraq loomed. As a career military officer with more than four hundred combat missions during Vietnam and the person responsible for the largest and fastest logistic effort in history during the first Gulf War when he commanded the United States Transportation Command, Johnson recognized the importance of remaining close to the sailors and marines on the front lines and communicating with their families at home.

I met with Secretary Johnson many times. A couple of the visits that stand out is one about the Base Realignment and Closure Committee (BRAC) that was approved by Congress for and the list released in May 2005. When the list of those installations slated to be closed is released all of the communities that support those installations start working to turn it around. No one wants to lose their base. However, the Navy League's mission is to support the services. I had written a letter to go out to our seventy thousand members to ensure that no one use the Navy League name in their quest to "save the base." I went by to see him at the Pentagon. I knew that

Captain Walt Yourstone was assigned as his assistant, but it did seem strange to go into his office and see Walt!

H. T. read my letter and thought it was a little strong. He told me I was "a *mean* woman." He said it with a big smile and added how important it was that I had taken this stand and written the strong letter.

The first of the more than sixty-five thousand miles traveled as acting secretary over the past seven months took him to the desert camps in Kuwait and facilities in Bahrain and Qatar. There he met with thousands of Sailors and Marines in the desert and at sea. Johnson understands that the people who are the Navy and Marine Corps are its most precious asset. His special way with people made him a popular figure with all he met. Johnson treated each and every person he met with dignity and compassion. From deck plate sailors to marines and corpsmen wounded in combat Secretary Johnson's special way with people endeared him to those who wear our nation's uniform and their loved ones.

The service of these men and women, appreciated by all American's had a very personal interest from H. T. and his wife, Linda. Their own son, a Marine Corps Reserve officer was one of the tens of thousands of brave military personnel assigned to Operation Iraqi Freedom. Johnson found them ready and in high morale and he reported his findings to Congress a few days after his return.

Not only did Johnson work as acting secretary to ensure that our frontline troops have the supplies and weapons they needed but on the home front Johnson continued the work he began as the assistant secretary to advance and accelerate public-private housing projects. At bases around the globe, including Kings Bay, hospitals, and other facilities, long overlooked are quickly coming up to modern standards.

When he came to Naval Submarine Base Kings Bay Rear, Admiral Jerry Talbot invited me to attend the dinner held the evening of March 10. Secretary Johnson is a gracious, outgoing gentleman, and we would grow pretty close over the next few years. Captain Kevin Wensing, his public affairs officer and my good friend was with him for the visit. Also accompanying SECNAV was Captain William Toti and Colonel John Kruz. Kevin later sent me the great pictures made that evening.

Secretary Johnson, who later became H. T. to me, wrote wonderful letters. He came to Naval Submarine Base Kings Bay. Thanks once again to Kevin Wensing, PAO, for his assistance. After the dinner, I received the following letter.

Dear Sheila,

It was great to see you at the dinner in Kings Bay. Congratulations on your recent election to President of the Navy League. Our Sailors and Marines and all of America's sea services are blessed to have the strong support of patriotic Americans like thousands of League members around the world.

Whether it is a port visit in Singapore, Fleet Week in New York or the upcoming commissioning of the USS Ronald Reagan, the Navy League plays a key role in our daily lives. The new Safety awards established by our good friend, Gordon England, in the names of Vern Clark and Jim Jones and administered by the League, is another example of the close cooperation that directly benefits the men and women who wear the cloth of our nation and their families.

Best of luck as you prepare to take on your new responsibilities this summer. I look forward to eyeing you at the Sea, Air, Space Convention in April. Please let me know how we can work together to enhance the effectiveness of the Navy League and the readiness and quality of life for our Navy Marine Corps team. God bless you and your fellow members for your unfailing support. With deepest respect and admiration.

Hansford T. Jonson
Acting Secretary of the Navy

In August, President Bush again chose Gordon England to serve as the Navy Department's leader. Thanks to his loyal friend and colleague H. T. Johnson and the outstanding work of Admiral Clark and General Hagee, England will return to a Navy and Marine Corps team that continue to prove itself the best in the world on the battlefield and at sea and which continues to transform itself while building the kind of quality of service for its people that has maintained the highest retention and recruiting levels in history. The Navy and Marine Corps has been blessed with great leadership and the results have set a high mark for the services. America is likewise blessed to have these selfless public servants working day and night to ensure our freedom.

And although we missed H. T. Johnson, it was good to have Gordon England back home.

NAVY LEAGUE PRESIDENT CAPTAIN BILL KELLY AND NANCY, REAR ADMIRAL RAYMOND AND JUNE COUTOUR

The time when Bill was president of the Navy League of the United States was incredible. He is such a gracious man and Nancy such a lovely woman they made a great "first couple." They had a real appreciation of what the Navy League should be doing and neither had an ego. We were friends with them and with Rear Admiral Raymond Contour and his wife, June. Raymond, a former Navy JAG, was also the Navy League's JAG. They all "took me under their wing" at the first Navy League meeting I attended with Arlie (he had been attending for years) and have protected and loved us ever since.

With Raymond and June, we enjoyed the perks of Bill's presidency. We had always gotten together for dinner, ordering pizza at least one night and using our hotel rooms as best we could. Now "we" actually had a dining room table! No matter how hard Bill tried to be on time for our dinners someone was always wanting to speak to him about an issue. One of the evenings, we had been waiting a while to have dinner, we put on the white terry cloth robes furnished in the suite, and all were in his huge bed when he got to his room. Nothing seemed to surprise him and we all had a good laugh. Memories are made of the dinners and conversations we had during those thirty years. We remember the wonderful dinner at Coronado in California with the Contours and the visits to Cape Cod and the lobster dinners.

When Bill was national president, he had a wonderful attitude. He was very busy with all the travels, but he accepted our invitation to come to speak at Naval Submarine Base Kings Bay to the Camden Kings Bay Navy League Council. Captain Chuck Ellis was commanding officer of the base and his wife, Judy, was treasurer of the council. (Note: When Chuck retired, he served as our council president.) The commanding officers were very gracious. Captain Jim Hamburg, CO of the USS *Pennsylvania*, and Captain C. J. Ihrig, CO of the USS *Canopus*, both gave tours and briefs of their ships.

The Ellis's were from Texas, so they knew a special game called, "Finger in the hole." This many years later and I can't remember how it is played (other than on the floor), but the title was provocative, and we had a lot of laughs playing the game with the Kelleys when they visited at the admiral's quarters.

Rear Admiral Tom Robertson was the group commander, and he and his wife, Julie, invited us all to have dinner at their quarters. I believe this might have been an evening offered for auction at the Dolphin Scholarship Auction. I'm realizing this since the admiral wore a chef's apron and Julie worked hard in the kitchen as Tom entertained us with his waiter protocol and his limericks. We could hear the women in the kitchen or wenches as Tom called them. Read that story in RADM Tom Robertson's story.

They all encouraged me to run for national office. How could I miss with such good tutors! After serving for four years as national vice president, Nancy was the first to encourage me to run. All four were critical to my election. They critiqued my platform and had many trial questions to prepare me for the nominating committee. Bill and Nancy were a wonderful gracious couple. We were blessed to have them serve as our national president and president's wife. Bill was a great speaker and very articulate. He understood the issues and reached out to others to make things happen.

Bill and Raymond both served on the board of directors for the USS *Constitution*. Raymond arranged for me and Arlie to be on the annual turnaround on the Fourth of July. Not only that but by this time I was national president, so he also arranged for me to be piped on board. It was an incredible honor. The only time that had ever happened before was when I was on DACOWITS and had an official visit on the USS *John F. Kennedy* aircraft carrier.

We miss those early days in the Navy League with these wonderful friends.

ADMIRAL FRANK KELSO

CHIEF OF NAVAL OPERATIONS
JUNE 29, 1990–APRIL 23, 1994

The evening of the one hundredth anniversary of the submarine force reception at the Smithsonian Museum in DC Admiral Frank Kelso was in attendance and *everyone* wanted to talk with him. Instead he came over to me and asked if I had time to sit down with him and talk. I was taken aback. Vice Admiral Malcolm Fages had been talking with him earlier and told him I was going to be the first woman president in the Navy League. Malcolm told me Admiral Kelso wanted to talk but walking away from everyone for a private conversation surprised me.

He asked if I would come talk with him. We went over to a table away from the crowd, and he asked me about the Navy League's national presidential election. We talked for about fifteen minutes. During that time, many guests kept coming up but left when they saw he was talking. He felt a great urgency for my election.

He told me, "Sheila, the Navy League has got to change." He made the following points:

- The Navy League will not grow with the current structure
- Conventions are now opportunities for old men to get together and see friends although this is not a problem it should not be the focus
- The Navy League wants the CNO to tell them what to do but that isn't his place—unless the CNO is "smarter than I was."

- We must have young people and "women like you."
- If someone doesn't have the passion and drive that you show, it's not going to happen.
- I think the Navy League is ready for a woman—it would certainly show they were ready for a change
- I believe Jack (Fisher) wants to make a change, and evidently, he knows how—he gave you this job.
- Probably governance is the way to begin
- Sea Power ambassadors is a good way to begin, but it must expand its audience to those who don't already support the services—you must go to organizations that might throw tomatoes at you.

While we were talking, Admiral Trost, also a former CNO, interrupted with apologies to tell Frank a funny story about a mutual friend who had his seven-year-old grandson on a tractor on a farm. I took notes while he talked but could hardly wait to leave to expand on those notes. He gave me his home phone number and asked that I let him know how the retreat I was planning went. This discussion with Admiral Kelso gave me such a boost. The campaign was tough and this helped my morale every time I thought about it.

The morning after my election I called him at home from the airport and gave him the news. He was so pleased. Admiral Kelso died in 2013. I am grateful for his guidance.

REAR ADMIRAL MARK KENNY

COMMANDER SUBMARINE GROUP 10
NAVAL SUBMARINE BASE KINGS BAY

I was at Sea Air Space, the premier event of the national Navy League. There must have been well over one thousand attendees at each event. In between introductions that I gave I would receive comments from those I was introducing that my term was coming to a close.

Rear Admiral Mark Kenny, commander of Submarine Group 10 at Kings Bay, approached me after one of those events. I was pleased that he had taken the time to come to Sea Air Space. We talked a bit and then he told me that he would like to give me a welcoming party at group headquarters when my tour as president was completed. I was thrilled—that was really something to look forward to. I still believe he "stuck his neck out" when he did this. It seems that the military officers that I had special relationships with made decisions based on what was the right thing to do.

Many would not have chanced hosting this reception. That made me appreciate it even more.

It was a wonderful night. The offices, board room, and every cranny around the stairways were full. That is the event where I heard the unbelievable words about a pretty unbelievable Navy Leaguer from Mike Altiser. That story has been told many, many times over the years and is found in this book. It is so reassuring to have friend like Mike who are willing to step up when an injustice is done. I was not able to support Rear Admiral Kenny and Cheryl while they were at Kings Bay—I was rarely in town, but we did seem to meet at various events, and we always took the time to sit down and talk.

The base paper, the *Periscope*, sent out a press release. The release as well as the party were certainly not a usual event for a Navy base to support. I am grateful to Rear Admiral Kenny, for all the JAGS who said, "approve" and all the wonderful staff who worked to make it happen.

LOCAL WOMAN RETURNS TO KINGS BAY AFTER TENURE AS NAVY LEAGUE NATIONAL PRESIDENT NAVAL SUBMARINE BASE KINGS BAY, GA.

It's been a busy two years for Sheila McNeill

The local business owner and longtime advocate for members of the United States sea service recently retired from her two-year term as the National President of the United States Navy League.

McNeill's service to the men and women of the sea services was celebrated July 8 at the Group Ten headquarters aboard Naval Submarine Base Kings Bay. Group Ten Commander RADM. Mark Kenny was joined by Kingsland Mayor Kenneth Smith, Representative Cecily Hill and others in welcoming home McNeill and thanking her for her tireless efforts on behalf of the Navy and in particular, Kings Bay.

"We are honoring a tremendous woman," said Kenny. "Sheila has spent the last 39 years supporting Sailors and working to improve our lives. We are glad to welcome her home and thank her for a job extremely done." McNeill was sworn in as national president June 2003 during the League's annual convention in Honolulu. Serving as national president was the logical next step, who has devoted nearly 40 years of her life to proclaiming the importance of maintaining a strong sea presence to our national leaders and citizens alike.

> "The Navy League has a proud tradition of dedication," said McNeill. "It does not matter where you go—mention the Navy League and someone will have a story about what Navy Leaguers have done for them. This was an opportunity for me to serve my country by serving the men and women of the sea services. Improving quality of life of our sea-service families is a priority for me." McNeill is a longtime friend of Naval Submarine Base and during her two-year term she was a driving force behind the successful efforts to have two SSGN submarines, USS Florida and USS Georgia, home ported in Kings Bay. McNeill the first woman to serve as national president in the organization's 100-year history, said that her passion for the submarine forced started in Kings Bay. "That passion started with my first visit to the base," McNeill said. "When I saw what submariners do, I couldn't help it! My first leadership position in the Navy League was here in Kings Bay and I feel like I have come full circle tonight."

I was so disappointed when I had to miss his retirement ceremony at the Naval Academy in October 2009. I sent him the following note:

> *Mark, I received your invite to your retirement. I can't believe it's already here and I know you feel that way! I will be in D.C. that day and I have a lunch date with Admiral Roughead and you can imagine how long we've worked it to make that happen. I wish you the very best. I always smile when I hear your name and will be forever grateful for your friendship and the wonderful party you had for me at Kings Bay. Let me know where you two will be settling down and your contact information. I want to make sure I can always reach you!! Sheila*

He replied,

> *Lady, thank you for the kinds words and understand completely your schedule. Glad you smile when my name is brought up, means a lot to me. I love the Southeast Georgia family, one of the happiest times in the Kenny family history. Thanks for what you have done and continue to do for our submarine force, the Navy and the nation. You have been our secret (and not so secret) weapon!!! God Bless and all the best, Mark.*

I will always be grateful to Mark Kenny.

KINGS BAY'S 35 YEARS IN CAMDEN COUNTY

The thirty-fifth anniversary of Naval Submarine Base Kings Bay was held on Thursday May 23, 2013, at the World War II Pavilion. RDML John "Jack" C. Scorby, commander, Navy Region Southeast, began the program with remarks for the Memorial Day commemoration, including remarks on the Battle of Midway. Vice Admiral Albert Konetzni then spoke on the history of Kings Bay. Senator William Ligon read the senate resolution recognizing and honoring the thirty-fifth anniversary.

I wrote a column on the thirty-fifth anniversary of the base and included comments from local citizens. This is a reminder of why I continue to stay involved. The column appeared in the May 13, 2013, base paper, the *Periscope*, the *Tribune & Georgia*, and the *Florida Times Union*. I was thrilled when U.S. Undersea Warfare picked it up from the Florida Times Union for distribution.

Thank you, Kings Bay, for thirty-five years.

This is a momentous week for Camden County. We are celebrating thirty-five years that Naval Submarine Base Kings Bay has been in our community. What an impact that base and the military, civilian, and contracted employees have had on our community. Those who work at Kings Bay shop in our stores, patronize our medical services, eat in our restaurants, and worship in our churches. They are a very large part of our community. The number of volunteer hours our military donates to our churches, schools and various non-profits is impressive.

On a recent radio talk show in Glynn County someone called in and asked the host, "What is Camden County putting in their water?" He was referring to the high-test scores that were recently released from the Camden County School system. Another caller said he had the solution: "The Navy base. Those parents are involved and that's what it takes." A state official said to me this past week that many districts have to apologize for their school systems, but ours is a positive factor in promoting our community.

The citizens of this country receive a significant return on America's investment in our submarine force. We have one of the best examples of that significant return with our boats at Kings Bay—our SSBNs and our SSGNs. We sleep safely and pursue our dreams and see our families every day while they stand the watch and protect us. We also appreciate the efforts and contributions of our civilian employees and our defense contractors and the part they play in our nation's defense and in the economic impact of our community.

Through the Georgia Military Affairs Coordinating Committee, our state is constantly improving our support of our military. Two new bills have been approved in the legislator in the past year that will positively impact our military families.

The chamber's annual Chick-Fil-A Leadercast held last week had included in their program special recognition for our military. I had the opportunity to speak about Kings Bay and its impact. I shared with them the pride that our community has in the role that our military has in national security. I talked of the power in economic development that brings to our community ($1,142,000 in goods and payroll), and I talked about the partnership we have with our military and community making it a great place to live and work.

Each of the attendees was given the opportunity to thank our Sailors, Marines, and Coasties in post cards that were provided. I would like to share some of those comments:

> *As an educator in Camden County for 20+ years it has been a pleasure to teach your children. Please promote strengthening educational and resource partnerships for all our Camden County children. Our non-military/civilian students learn from your expertise and our military students are benefitted by living in a community that cares about families. Thank for your military service and sacrifice and/or your civilian specialist/contractor support for our community*
>
> *A thank you cannot even begin to express the gratitude felt towards those of you in the military. We are so blessed to have people like you to care about our freedom and well-being God Bless!*
>
> *Thanks for your contributions to our community and to our country. The time away from your family does not go unnoticed. We appreciate all that you do! God bless you and your family*
>
> *On behalf of myself and my entire family, thank you for your selfless commitment to protecting and securing this great nation of ours. Your sacrifice and honor are a true inspiration to us all*
>
> *Thank you for your service to the greatest country on earth.*
>
> *Thank you so much for your service to our county, community and world. You will never truly know the impact and positive influence you have on all of us. We are eternally grateful. I can't say thank you enough*
>
> *Thank you for dedicating your life and yourself to keeping this country safe. The work that is performed on base provides a tremendous service*
>
> *Thank you for your dedication and support in keeping our country and our community safe. Without your attention to the details that must be accomplished properly and thoroughly this submarine base would not be as successful as it is*
>
> *Thank you for the service that you provide to this community and country. Because of what you do millions sleep well at night with minimal worries. I am sure that you have your moments and want*

to throw in the towel. Maintain the course, hold your head up high and get-r-done we are depending on you

Thank you for all you do. You offer a stimulus to a small town that otherwise wouldn't get your time and your efforts are appreciated you are a leader in environment. Thank you to all the brave men and women who sacrifice so much for our country and to protect us. We care. We know you are there. Stand strong and God bless.

We are so proud of you for what you do for our country. We are grateful for the positive impact you bring to our community. We cannot thank you enough. We know our lives and community are enriched because of you thank you so much

Thank you, Kings Bay for being a part of our community

Sheila M. McNeill
The Camden Partnership

UNITED STATES CONGRESSMAN JACK KINGSTON, DISTRICT 1 1993–2015

Jack had been our congressman for twenty-two years when he resigned in 2014 to run for the Senate. He is a wonderful man and was an effective congressman. As the First District congressman, he was a senior member of the powerful House Appropriations Committee and several other very important committees. He was a great asset to Camden and Glynn County.

Jack and I were intricately entwined. We worked together on the conversation of the submarines from SSBN to SSGN. We worked together on funding for Kings Bay and Camden County. Any issue that involved Camden County involved Jack Kingston. I became friends with his wonderful staff and called whenever I needed to. I rarely asked for Jack—I knew he was busy—but I also knew that his crackerjack staff would get the word to him. He is a special man and I'm proud he is my friend.

Rather than try to put all those twenty-two years in one story, his name is found throughout this book. I did want him to have his "special" place along with my other special people so here it is.

On September 11, 2003, he wrote a poignant column that appeared in the *Brunswick News*. It ended with this:

Here at home we must show the same courage, and steadfastness as our soldiers in the field. We must remember those who died on that clear September morning because they went to work or got on a plane. We must remember those who have sacrificed since because they were doing their duty far from home. Most of all we must remember that in this war against terror there can be no excuses, no negotiations and no choices except to win.

Jack Kingston

Jack has been listed in *Georgia Trend* many times as one of the one hundred most influential Georgians. The *Georgia Trend* January 2004 issue was no exception. This was what they wrote:

> *According to six term Congressman Jack Kingston, his GOP politics may have been a result of indoctrination at an early age. "My mother was the chairman of the Clark County Republican Party and instead of getting a baby sitter she would drag me to meetings," jokes Jack Kingston. However, it occurred, Kingston is considered a rising star in Republican politics after ascending to the chairmanship of the Appropriations Subcommittee in mid-2003. The position is so powerful that the chairman is referred to as the House "Cardinal."*
>
> *Such trappings don't add up too much for the plain talking Kingston, who believes the greatest challenge facing the U.S. is the size of government and citizens' view of what the federal government should do for them. "It doesn't sound sexy or glamorous, but I don't think the Founding Fathers intended the federal government to have a federal cat litter policy!," he says As fond as Kingston is of talking about philosophical and ideological convictions, he is also convinced that pragmatic teamwork is the key to getting things done in Congress. "I try not to be in someone's face," Kingston says. "But I won't back away (from my position) and I hope you won't back away from yours." At the end of the day he concedes, "I want to win, but I know there's going to be a split, 70/30 60/40… I can live with that."*

In October 1997, Jack visited Kings Bay for an official tour. The base paper *Periscope* covered the event with the heading "**Just stopping by**." And Jack did that frequently.

In February 1999, we hosted a "coffee and chat" for Jack. It was a good informal way to hear from key local leaders on issues of concern in Camden County.

He and Senator Cleland were the head legislators who supported and worked toward the SSGN—their names and influence can be found in the SSGN story.

In April 2000, Jack brought the Honorable Dennis Hastert to our community for a fund-raiser. It was a good chance for many of us to meet the speaker of the house. Jack was always good about that—reaching out and making sure we met the right folks.

He sent the following letter:

> Dear Sheila, Thank you for all your support of the fundraiser with Speaker Denny Hastert. Thank to friends like you his entire visit was a success. We raised more money than we ever had on a single day. Now the campaign season is getting under way. From the President on down, it will be a very competitive year. I plan to work hard and continue my vigorous schedule of work in every First District County. I'm lucky to have friends like you who make it possible. Thanks for everything.
>
> Sincerely,
> Jack

Arlie and Sheila, thank you for all the help over the years. You've been good friends.

In 2002, Congressman Kingston was asked if he would be interested in flying with President George Bush to Ft. Stewart. He was told there would be several Georgia legislators on the trip. Deputy secretary of defense, Wolfowitz, would be flying with them. They were also told that there would not be time to talk with the president. After the plane got underway they approached the congressional members and told them that they could have three minutes to discuss any issue with the president. "What can I talk about? What would be significate that I could convey in three minutes?" he told our fly-in group. He told us he then thought, "What would Sheila do?" And then I had it: "SSGN!" He then used his time to tell President Bush about SSGN.

President Bush responded, "I don't know about this."

"We'll get you a brief as soon as we return to the White House," Secretary Wolfowitz told him.

Weeks later, I was driving to Atlanta and received a call from a New York newspaper who asked for my comments on the president's remarks that morning at the Naval Academy. I told him I'd call him back and quickly called Navy League headquarters to find out just what was said. President Bush said in his remarks, "Future commanding officers may command modified Trident submarines carrying hundreds of next generations cruise missile." It went viral. The *Bremerton Sun* reports, "Nearly scrapped a year ago, the four older Trident submarines are now a top defense priority in Congress and the Pentagon."

Thank goodness Jack is on our side!

In March 2002, LCDR Tom Prusinowski, who had transferred from Trident Training Facility to the USS *Theodore Roosevelt*, sent me an e-mail.

Sheila,

LCDR Tom Prusinowski here. I am writing today as we make our way towards Norfolk. Our ship, the USS THEODORE ROOSEVELT is finishing her deployment that took us to the War on Terrorism. We were off the coast of Afghanistan for nearly 140 days as we bombed various sites. During that time, Congressman Jack Kingston came aboard the ship. I was chosen to escort him around. We talked at great length during the visit. He was surprised that I knew you. He spoke very highly of you and everything that you have accomplished. I was so proud to say that I knew you. I'm going to be in town April 6th and I was wondering if you might be there. I would love to stop by and talk for a little bit and to just say hello.

I hope all is well. Please tell Mr. McNeill that I said hello.

Your Friend
Tom Prusinowski

I loved Tom's "travelogues." His deployment with the *Roosevelt* was the longest deployment ever for a carrier.

In 2003, the Defense Department would not initially support this SSGN conversion and now Secretary Rumsfeld was calling it the most revolutionary platform in the Defense Department.

July 2007: I find it hard to think of a way that Jack Kingston could be criticized but in politics someone is always there. Someone sent a letter to the editor to the *Brunswick News* with criticism of Jack and his lack of military experience. A week later my response to this nasty letter ran.

July 13, 2007:
KINGSTON STANDS BY MILITARY

I am writing in reference to the July 6 letter to the editor, "Military service should not be questioned." I am stunned that anyone would question District 1 U.S. Rep. Jack Kingston's patriotism and dedication to the military. I have known and worked with Jack Kingston, R-Ga since he was elected. For about 13 years I have traveled with Camden County leadership to Washington, D.C., every year for our fly in to discuss Camden County and Naval Submarine Base Kings Bay issues. We have marveled at the grasp of information and concern he has shown during our meetings. He understands the military and he supports Kings Bay. With his support, we have watched Kings Bay expand and gain new missions.

The new SSGN, known as the transformational issue for the Navy was developed and deployed and Kings Bay and the SSGN have become a large part of the Navy's future plans. Jack Kingston deserves much of the credit for this. Jack Kingston not only supports but also truly cares. Jack has also been a big supporter of our veterans. He has helped boost spending for veterans and has brought planned outpatient clinics to Glynn and Camden County. Disagreeing with someone politically is a right our military fights for every day, but making unsubstantiated personal attacks against Jack Kingston and our military is uncalled for.

Sheila McNeill
Brunswick

Editor's note: The writer is a former president of the Navy League of the United States

Jack sent me this handwritten note.

Dear Sheila, Many thanks! It's not often friends stand up for a politician, especially in today's climate of abundant criticism. Thanks for the great letter. And with or without our critics we will continue to work for the base, the Navy and all the good folks in uniform. The Defense Apropos bill is on the floor next week. We've had lots of hearings and many hours of work. Despite our divisions on Iraq I think the final product is a good bipartisan package. Thanks again, Jack

When he decided to resign as US congressman and run for Senate, there was a huge article in the *Brunswick News*—part of that article is covered below:

BELOW THE SURFACE
By Gordon Jackson

***ST. MARYS**—Few would dispute that U.S. Rep Jack Kingston, R-1, is a staunch supporter of the military.*

His congressional district that stretches along the coast and inland has four bases—Naval Submarine Base Kings Bay in Camden County; Fort Stewart at Hinesville, Moody Air Force Base near Valdosta and Hunter Army Airfield outside Savannah.

But his announcement Thursday that he will seek the Republican nomination for U.S. Senate seat held by retiring Sen. Saxby Chambliss, R-Ga., has some people wondering how bases in his congressional district and the state will be affected if and when the Base Closure and Realignment Commission meets in 2015. "There's always reason to be nervous," said Tony Wege, professor of political science at College of Coastal Georgia.

President Barack Obama has included a so-called BRAC in 2015 in his proposed budget for fiscal 2014, which begins Oct. 1 and runs through September 30, 2014. He had proposed one in his current budget, but it was shot down by Congress. There may be little will in the House of Representatives or the Senate to balk this time around given pressure in Washington to cut spending and reduce the federal deficit.

… Former national Navy League President Shella McNeill, who lives in Glynn County, said her concern is the district will lose a congressman who has the influence and respect to help protect Kings Bay… I know he has been a powerful voice over the years."… If he wins a nomination and fall election in 2014, Kingston would be considered a junior senator, which means it's unlikely he would be given important Senate committee assignments. But McNeill said Kingston's experience in Congress for two decades will still be influential when it comes to military matters.

Jack was a major factor in the SSGN program. All of that is in the SSGN story.

In March 2002, Jack told our fly-in group, "Sheila is in D.C. every week—we see her frequently—she knows she has a place to stop… She's starting to rearrange our furniture. Sheila has been your lobbyist in the past and she now has included the national Navy League as its national president."

I worked with Jack on the reduction to the Coast Guard budget in 2010 for FY 2012. This was a time when earmarks were a big issue on Capitol Hill. The Republicans had made a commitment they would not support any earmarks.

In our briefing to Jack I was passionate that he not consider this issue an earmark. Earmarks are Senator Byrd's road to nowhere; Senator Murtha's airport and Senator Stevens bridge to nowhere. We have a constitutional mandate (section 8) to defend for our county and that protecting our homeland was *not* an earmark.

He has a great sense of humor and that is throughout the book. We were having one of our annual DC fly-ins. We always had dinner at a nice place in DC. Rear Admiral Cecil Haney was the admiral at N97 that we visited in the Pentagon. He came for dinner that night and brought his wonderful mother. Jack was late arriving and quickly sat down and leaned over to Cecil and said, "Admiral, I've been trying to get Sheila to fight for a fast attack squadron in Kings Bay, but I can't convince her it's a good idea."

Time stood still. Cecil had not met Jack. He paused, looked at me, and said, "He is kidding, right?"

"Right!" I told him.

In March 2008, Jack was one of the principal speakers at the return to service for the *USS Georgia*. In his remarks, he told everyone he stood up to speak to President Bush about the SSGN: "I'd rather have the president on my back than Sheila." It got a big laugh!

So look for Jack's name and some of these references throughout the book.

VICE ADMIRAL ALBERT KONETZNI

COMMANDER, PACIFIC FLEET

Al has always been a renegade—albeit at the end—a three-star renegade. One of the harder friends to write about was Al Konetzni. Arlie and I have known him since 1986 when he was Squadron 16 commander. That command has been decommissioned and recommissioned since those days.

When we met, I had a small gift shop in St. Marys. I had just become active in the Navy League. It was an incredible time. The captains at the base at that time all became good friends. There is a little joke that gets mentioned in a lot of memoirs. This was before there was an admiral. It was a time when everyone reported to pretty much the same person—all were equal—and all were exceptional. They also did things that were perfectly accepted then but would not be allowed in this politically correct world.

Al, as squadron commander, had a gig. Arlie and I were invited several times to join other military on the gig and go to Fernandina for dinner.

He was always looking for ways to support the young sailors. He has a nickname that is known throughout the world. I've never asked him what he thinks about it, but you hear it every time his name is brought up: "Big Al, the Sailor's Pal."

And he was. I remember one day when we had a reception on the submarine tender USS *Canopus*. He had left the crowd for a while, and later, when I ran into a sailor he had spoken to, the sailor said, "I've never been hugged by a commodore." Al had stuck again.

His father was a designer with Disney Studio and they were close. He just died in 2016.

As a Captain Al Konetzni was one of the three Navy officers who influenced my life the most. He would ask me to join his leadership at Squadron 16 for lunch. They would discuss issues and the lunch would often end in interesting conversations. And they let me listen. Of course, nothing sensitive or classified was discussed, but I learned the lingo of the submarines force and all about submarines.

He was also the person responsible for the first submarine museum in Camden County. He used the building at site six to begin accumulating historic items and displaying them. One of the popular displays was the bar that came from Squadron 16 in Rota, Spain. The squadron moved from Rota to NSB Kings Bay.

Everyone got along famously—except maybe the time the commanding officer of Naval Submarine Base Kings Bay walked into his office and surveyed his base and realized the playground equipment for the base children was gone! He put the word out and it was found at site six. Seems that Al had tried to get funding for the equipment but was not successful. This was the site where the submarines would come in after months at sea to be greeted by their families. Al thought the children needed playground equipment while they waited for their father.

It was during this time that Arlie and I planned a weekend for the commanding officers in Glynn County. We made arrangements with the hotel at the Glynn Place Mall and they comp'd rooms for everyone. And somehow, we got a large transport van that took us around the city and the islands for a tour. Imagine today convincing eight or so captains and their wives to get together for a weekend with civilians!

The Konetznis gave a party at their home in Camden for every crew that returned. They cooked many meals. Several times Arlie and I attended, and we just spent the night. It was so relaxing, Arlie and I found ourselves oversleeping several times. Dinner many times included Robert and Alma Edenfield and Kenneth McCarthy. Until Kenneth's death, VADM J. D. Williams still came every year to go hunting with some of the "good ole boys" from Camden.

When Arlie was state president he had a statewide meeting at the base conference center. Al was then a member of the chief of Naval Operations (CNO) Strategic Studies Group. It was an amazingly knowledgeable committee. The Navy League felt honored to be able to hear their briefs on issues that the CNO was having them work on.

Al's first job as admiral was assistant chief of naval personnel for Military Personnel Policy and Career Progression. He spoke to our council in May 1995. It was our Sailor of the Year banquet and he spoke from the heart to our sailors and marines.

> *The bottom line is we can't continue to promote the concept that 'survival of the fittest' is the key to success in the Navy. Our goal must be to build the strongest teams we can so our young sailors will feel that their job is every bit as important as the old man's (captain's). Nobody in the world can tell me that after all the screening these kids go through and all the money we spend to screen them, that we should lose 15% of 55,000 recruits each year. I know we can do better. We need to make these folks feel welcome and important to the organization from day one. We need to quit bringing these young people down to their knees before bringing them back up again. Sometimes the diverse talents they bring with them can be lost in that process. Maybe our goal should be that everyone brings good stuff to the table and to make sure together that the team works. You are all winners. But that isn't enough. You've got to make the rest of the crew winners too or we're not going to make it. As leaders, we need to focus on positive motivation from the day a person enters boot camp or reports to a ship. Our job as leaders is to make an environment where newcomers can succeed, and this Navy doesn't do that very well. We've led by humiliation and threats when we should motive our sailors through higher self-expectancy and optimism.*

This was Al Konetzni at his best.

When I became national president, I often called him for advice. When Al received his second star, he was also given the command of the Commander Submarine Force, Pacific Fleet. Many famous admirals have served in that command:

And I knew every one of these—some better than others:

- RADM Eugene Fluckey, 1964–1966
- RADM Henry C. McKinney, 1991–1993
- RADM William G. Ellis, 1996–1998
- RADM Albert H. Konetzni Jr., 1998–2001
- RADM John B. Padgett III, 2001–2003
- RADM Paul F. Sullivan, 2003–2005
- RADM Joseph A. Walsh, 2006–2008
- RADM Douglas J. McAneny, 2008–2010
- RADM Frank Caldwell Jr., 2010–2013
- RADM Philip G. Sawyer, 2013–2015
- RADM Frederick J. Roegge, 2015–2018

Several are mentioned in this book.

When I was national president, I was preparing for my trip to Asia and called Al on his advice. As commander of the Submarine Force, Pacific Fleet, he knew all the players in Asia. I was to meet with Fred Harris at some point on my trip. Obviously, he was an important man because every time his name came up when I was talking with anyone who had served in the Pacific they had wonderful things to say about Fred. When Al called me, to ask, "Are you going to see Fred Harris when you are in Japan?"

I said, "Yes and he is going to be my best friend!" I repeated that story at a national Navy League meeting with I introduced Fred. Al left an inedible mark in Japan and Korea and has returned several times since his retirement to speak to various groups.

As PACFLEET, he spoke at the Sailor of the Year banquet sponsored by the Navy League in May 1995. He also wrote many papers on the need for more submarines. One was entitled, "The Good, the Bad, and the Ugly." He was interviewed by Paul Gagnon, the president of the Honolulu Council in *Fore & Aft* magazine in the February/March 2000 issue.

> COMMANDER SUBMARINE FORCE
> UNITED STATES PACIFIC FLEET
> PEARL HARBOR, HI 96860-4664
> 06 October 1999
>
> I'm sending out an S.O.S. This is a distress call to save our submarines! Over the next ten years our country plans to prematurely lay to rest more than 190 submarine years. That's throwing away more than six perfectly good submarines!
>
> While we may save some money in the near term, what we as a nation lose is priceless capability—a capability that statistically has been steadily on the rise. Knowing this, its penny-wise, but pound-foolish.
>
> At the same time submarines are being cut up early, the national tasking for submarines has more than doubled. And if trends remain unchanged, increasingly more critical requirements will go unfulfilled. There is *already* a deficit in the number of submarines required to satisfy national interests in the Pacific, and we can no longer meet the high-priority tasks assigned by national leadership.
>
> But we do have a chance to stem the tide, but only with *immediate* action. Today, we have the opportunity to salvage eight Los Angeles class fast-attack submarines currently slated for

> early retirement. Additionally, our country has a once-in-a-lifetime chance to convert four of the most capable, stealthy Ohio-class submarines to undersea battleships, capable of carrying 154 Tomahawk cruise missiles and dozens of Navy SEALs.
>
> One of these submarines could single-handedly relieve an entire carrier battle group of Tomahawk responsibilities, which in turn would be available to protect our interests in other important areas.
>
> Make no mistake about it *this is a distress call.* We need your assistance now to help support making an investment in our collective future by helping us navigate in these perilous waters. Together, and with immediate action, we can stay the course.
>
> Help Save Our Submarines.
>
> RADM Al H. Konetzni
> Commander Submarine Force, U.S. Pacific Fleet

At a Navy League meeting in New York Al was the principal speaker. One of the attendees that evening was a fairly new secretary of the Navy, Gordon England. I went over to Al and said, "You need to be careful with what you say tonight. You don't want to screw with a secretary of the Navy."

Al said, "Sure, Sheil. [He is the only person who managed to shorten Sheila.] Don't worry." That evening Al was the worst he has ever been or the best depending on your point of view. He didn't hesitate to say what was needed in our submarine force; he talked about funding, he talked about numbers of submarines and the needed for more. But all in the strong, direct "renegade" style, he was famous for. When Al completed his remarks, I asked Secretary England, "Does Al still have a job?"

"Yes, don't you just love that guy!"

I then went to Al and told him the secretary's response and brought him over to Gordon and introduced him.

As deputy commander and chief of Fleet Forces Command where he had a big role in aligning the requirements for our fleet in the Atlantic, Europe, and the Pacific.

An article appeared in the base paper, the *Periscope*, on October 28, 1998:

> **All in the Family: Military ties help family find happy home in Georgia.**
> By Lt. Cmdr. Dave Werner
> Submarine Forces Pacific Affairs

> *Kristen Konetzni-Uprichard, the daughter of Rear Adm. Al Konetzni, Jr. who currently serves as the Commander for the Submarine Force Pacific in Pearl Harbor, Hawaii, has traveled around the world as a Navy brat. She has lived in Annapolis, Md., Groton, Conn; Washington, D.C., Charleston, S.C., Pascagoula, Miss, and of course Kings Bay, Ga. She wound up here when her father served as commander of Submarine Squadron 16 on the submarine base. "After I graduated from Camden County High School, I really wanted to go to school here in Georgia," she said. "My dad and I reviewed my options and I ended up entering the Universality of Georgia." After earning her undergraduate degree in 1992, she graduated with honors from the Medical College of Georgia as a Doctor of Dental Medicine in 1996. She finished per postdoctoral residency in pediatric dentistry this past spring.*
>
> *She isn't alone in finding a home here. Her two brothers also call Georgia home. Al graduated from Valdosta State university and Kyle is a junior at Augusta State University. Rear Adm. Konetzni who still owes a home in Woodbine, attributes the sense of community as the reason three of his four children have chosen Georgia.*
>
> *"I think it was one of the best places we've ever lived because it's so family friendly" he says.*

Al remained an advocate even after his retirement. He spoke before the Projection Forces Committee of the House Armed Services Committee:

> *I would not be here today unless I was convinced that the declining number of submarines has put our nation's security and prosperity at great risks… I am convinced that our Navy and the nation have been lulled into a false sense of security by strike intensive conflicts… conflicts that have completely lacked serious opposition at sea. Unfortunately, we American's too often ignore history. History tells us that this is a condition that is unlikely to continue…*
>
> *If you stop the carriers… you stop the United States of America*
>
> - *OIF (Operation Iraqi freedom)—70% strike sorties from the sea*
> - *OEF (Operation Enduring Freedom)—50% strike sorties from the sea*
>
> *If you stop the flow of equipment. You stop the United States of America*
>
> - *OIF/OEF 95% of the vehicles and equipment went by sea*
>
> *If you stop the flow of commerce… you cripple the United States of America*

- *About 95% of imports and exports still travel by sea*

  Sometimes I worry that we have forgotten that job one for the U.S. Navy is to ensure that no nation is ever capable of denying us such access. It is my belief that the U.S. Navy's first obligation must always be to secure the maritime commons for the security and prosperity of the American people.

  Our responsibility with regard to submarines: There are over 400 submarines in the world today. I believe this global proliferation of submarines clearly poses the greatest threat to that maritime security… a threat that has gone too long with too little focus, investment and training.

There was never the issue of trying to figure out what Al meant—he was very clear and so right!

When we opened the St. Marys Submarine Museum he sent eight hundred pounds from Yokosuka, Japan, where they were closing the "sanctuary."

He remains the best advocate for the submarine force and for our military and their families and such a dear friend.

TALAXE AND GLEN LAWSON

AND THE NINTH AIR FORCE F-16 DEMONSTRATION TEAM

May 10–11, 1997, at the Blue Angels show in Brunswick.

"Come on, I want you to meet someone"

"No, I would be embarrassed to go over there and I'm not interested in meeting any of the pilots."

"This isn't just a pilot, he's very nice… and good looking and it's just a hello."

Arlie and I had been invited to have dinner with the pilots and crew of the United States Navy Blue Angels and United States Air Force Ninth Air Force F-16 Demonstration Team before their performance on May 12. I happened to be seated next to Captain Glen "Lunar" Lawson, the Air Force F-16 Demonstration pilot. He was an interesting young man and I really enjoyed the evening. The next day we took our grandson, Ryan, with us for the show. He was twelve years old and loved it!

After the show, I got up to tell Glen how much I enjoyed the show when I spotted Talaxe Vasquez. She is a more than a beautiful young woman—she is breathtakingly beautiful. Let me tell you a story about Talaxe.

A month or so earlier Arlie and I had a cocktail party at our home and Talaxe was a guest. She was someone you can't meet without noting her beauty. Of course, we look nothing alike, but I enjoyed going around the room introducing her and to watch their mouth drop or their eyebrows would rise. I would reply, "Yes, it's remarkable how much we look alike, isn't it? She is my cousin."

She had been around the world creating Georgia's Scarlett O'Hara as a lookalike of Vivien Leigh, who played Scarlett in the popular movie *Gone with the Wind.* She was often asked about her name. Her parents were named Mary and Joseph, so it didn't come from either family. In fact, her mother and I are cousins and no one in our family has a name like Talaxe.

Her website has the following message:

> *Born and raised in Georgia, moonlight and magnolias have long since been a big part of my life… not to mention, "Gone with The Wind." Some of my earliest memories include our family crowding around the television each year when "Gone with The Wind" would air. In the early years, my favorite scenes included Bonnie and her kitten, however, as time passed I began to fall in love with Scarlett's character and wished I could jump into the television screen and have Mammy help me put on that BBQ dress! It is not hard to see why I am so grateful to portray Scarlett O'Hara. It truly is a dream come true. I love to bring a little bit of our Southern hospitality to people all over the world.*

Talaxe was a true Glynn County resident with no plans to ever leave Brunswick. At the time, she was serving as a staff member for our wonderful Congressman Jack Kingston.

So back to that day at the Thunderbird event. She finally reluctantly but more because she was being gracious and went to meet Glen. We took pictures of them and talked for a while and left them. It turns out they did enjoy meeting each other as she agreed to join him for dinner the following evening. A week later I received an e-mail from Glen:

> *Sunday May 18*
> *Dear Mrs. McNeill,*
>
> *It was a great honor to meet and talk with you and Mr. McNeill at the airshow last weekend. Brunswick and the surrounding areas are unique in the people and the area geography. Good friendly southern people. My team and I had a great time. The insight into the happenings in your field of work were equally interesting. It is an important area of human interaction which unfortunately many people do not understand or pay due attention to. Thank you for giving me some insights!*

Most of all, though thanks for introducing Talaxe to me. I was initially left speechless when first introduced. Since then we have spent some time together and talked quite a bit via telephone and email. She is an amazing person with values and ideas not often found. I only hope I don't let her down. Currently I am in Montreal performing for the folks up here. Interesting culture! Next weekend we are off to NAS Patuxent River. I plan to be down in your neck of the woods soon. I'm going to visit if only for a short time. Once again thanks.

Sincerely,
Glen K. Lawson, CAPT USAF, 9th AF F-16
Demonstration Team Commander

Five months later, Talaxe sends the following e-mail:

It was Saturday… Around 3:20 (October 4, 1997) he was staged from another airport because the runway at the show site was too short. So, I flew with him to drop him off at the other airport, then flew back to the air show in order to see him fly. I suspected nothing! As usual, I stayed at show center with the other pilots (Rags & Psycho, the narrators) and the rest of the team. (p.s. they always tape his show in order to debrief later, so this is all on tape) so… the show begins… except he starts speaking to the crowd at a part of the show that he normally does not. I am thinking, well that's kinda weird. He says, "Good afternoon ladies and gentlemen, and welcome to the Chester County airshow! It's a beautiful day up here in the cockpit of the F-16. I would like to mention two special guests here today… Capt. Mike "Psycho'" Synoraki—this is his last show with us here today… and Miss Talaxe Vasquez from St. Simons Island, Georgia" At this time, he does another maneuver. Then he comes back on the radio… "I would like to tell everyone here a little about Ms. Vasquez… I met her about five months ago in Brunswick, GA, at the airshow…" And then he cut off again… at this point my mind is going crazy! Then he flies around a little bit more… then says… "I would like to ask you all here today to help me in persuading Ms. Vasquez to make me the happiest man on earth. Talaxe will you marry me?" At this time, the crowd is going wild! Rags hands me a card in which he had taped the ring. I am crying, everyone is yelling and whistling,

> everyone is hugging… in the meantime… Glen is up there with no answer… so Psycho held the microphone up to my mouth while someone else held the radio to the microphone (so Glen could hear) and Psycho said… "well, say something… say YES!"

I said, "Yes, I will!"

The crowd went crazy! But what we didn't realize for about a minute was that the guy holding the radio didn't have the button pushed all the way down so Glen never heard an answer. Meanwhile he and Ed Shipley (owns a P-51, which I have flown in) are up in the sky talking back and forth to each other from F-16 to AP-51, saying, "Well? Well?" So Ed radioed back down to show center and said that they never heard an answer. So I said *yes* once more. Something was wrong with the radio that we were using because it went through, but not very clear. So Glen and Ed flew back to the airport, left the F-16, Glen jumped in the Mustang with Ed and they flew back to the airshow. All the way there Ed said that Glen kept saying, "Did she say yes? I couldn't tell, do you think she said yes?"

Ed said, "Oh yeah! She said yes! I heard her clearly!" But in his mind Ed was saying, "Oh God, please let her have said yes!" But when they got back, and Glen jumped out of the plane and saw the ring on my finger he knew. Then we had a big party in Ed's hangar.

They were married March 7, 1998, about ten months later It was a beautiful wedding. The television show *A Wedding Story* on TLC was on hand to tape the wedding. To this day, I have people come up to me who saw that show and heard our story about the first time they met.

Talaxe sent us a note that Christmas:

Sheila and Arlie. You have given me the best gift ever—Glen!

They now have two children Gabriel and Savannah. After tours in Korea, Texas, Las Vegas (USAF Thunderbirds), Phoenix, Iraq, Virginia, Romania, and Washington, DC, they now live in Orlando, Florida, following Glen's retirement after thirty wonderful years in the United States Air Force.

I'm so glad we talked her into meeting him.

LAWSUIT: SEX DISCRIMINATION

I have always abided by words written by Elbert Hubbard and was the creed of the American Business Women's Association.

> *If you work for a man, in Heaven's name WORK for him. If he pays you wages which supply you bread and butter, work for him; speak well of him; stand by him and stand by the institution he represents. If put to a pinch, an ounce of loyalty is worth a pound of cleverness. If you must vilify, condemn and eternally disparage—resign your position and when you are outside, damn to your heart's content, but as long as you are part of the institution do not condemn it. If you do that, you are loosening the tendrils that are holding you to the institution and at the first high wind that comes along, will never know the reason why.*

I made speeches based on this. Particularly with my position at Concrete Products Inc. (CPI), this was especially important. Respecting and supporting management was ingrained in me.

In 1964 two or three years after Arlie finished John A. Gupton, mortuary college at Vanderbilt University in Nashville, Tennessee, we returned to Brunswick. I went to work as an accounting clerk at Concrete Products Inc., a manufacturer of wood fiber roof decking with offices in Brunswick, Woodbine, and Terry, Miss.

I stayed for seventeen years and worked under four wonderful men who allowed me—sometimes cautiously—to climb the ladder in the company and create an up to date industrial relations department. I had great bosses: Bob Brown, Walter Berry, Evan Mathis, and Chuck Breslauer. With each new boss, I took on more responsibility.

I loved the men who worked in the plant and the men and women who worked in the office. I became a skilled negotiator. We had labor contracts in all three plants, and I had a positive relationship with both the skilled and unskilled workforce. They began to trust me as did their union leadership.

One story that will always be remembered as a positive event in my career at CPI is when we were having trouble keeping employees in the Mississippi plant. I did a survey in the Terry, Mississippi area and found that we were losing employees to jobs with higher wages. I found that most plants paid more than we did for the same type jobs. I then studied our insurance plan to see if there was a way we could change companies and could improve benefits without a large increase in premium. The company also agreed to several other issues that would improve life for our plant employees.

With leadership approval, I called the union president and told him I wanted to reopen the contract but did not want to make this awkward for him so why didn't he ask that we reopen it? We reviewed the additional wages and benefits that the company would add. I went to Mississippi and met with the union leadership and senior employees. We were meeting in a conference room at the local hotel where I had a room.

At some point during the meeting the union president said he wasn't feeling well and asked for a half-hour break. I went to my room while we waited. In just a few minutes, I had a call from the union president, who said, "Sheila, I don't remember what I'm supposed to ask for next!"

We reviewed the list and then continued "negotiations." The union was happy, the employees were happy, and the company management was happy. We ended up taking better care of our employees and reduced turnover—it was good for employees and the company.

Concrete Products Inc. was locally owned. During those years, I worked for Bob Brown, who was the most senior employee and ran the plant. He was a brilliant, professional man who appreciated my efforts. I was a young woman of twenty-one or twenty-two when I started work. but from the beginning I wanted the responsibility and loved the work.

It was sold to W. R. Grace and Company and an executive of about twenty years with Grace came to be our president. I thought that might create a change in my responsibilities but it did not. He, too, was a wonderful man to work for and encouraged me to take even more responsibility. His name was Chuck Breslauer. In later years Chuck became a close friend and helped me with many projects. He was of special help when I ran and won the election for national president of the Navy League. With his construction background, he was one of the experts I called when I took over this huge responsibility of building the Navy League's new five-hundred-thousand-square-foot building occupying an entire city block in Arlington, Virginia.

One day I took a proposal to Bob and Chuck. I was still payroll clerk and that job included interviewing for the plant hires. I gradually created what is known today as an industrial relations department. I took a proposal into Bob Brown and Chuck Breslauer about officially creating this department.

Bob Brown was a friend by that time and had always supported me. But he wasn't sure what to do about this aggressive young woman who wanted to make so many changes, so he sent me to a firm in Savannah, who employed psychologists who would evaluate me and my plan. They came back with a report that recommended that I continue with my plan and assume more responsibility until "someone with more education" can take over the responsibility.

For the next few years it was seamless. I worked harder than I have ever worked. Mother kept Leslie until I got home and Arlie was very supportive of my work. Working under W. R. Grace, I was able to enhance my education. Attending several seminars and training in Boston, Massachusetts, expanded my knowledge of industrial relations. But there is always a but. W. R. Grace and company made the decision to sell the business to a group of local businessmen. Chuck was offered the position as president but decided to stay with Grace and was transferred to Florida. Bob Brown had retired and the new president was hired.

As I talk about the three military men who most influenced my life, this new president—the one who did not want women in management—was the one civilian who had the most influence. It was a hard lesson and a terrible time, but it did influence my life from that moment on. The new president came on board right after the wonderful experience with the Terry, Mississippi, plant. He let me know that he didn't like me. At the time, I couldn't figure it out. I'd work anytime he wanted me to and tackled anything he had me do. I found that that when my name was on a report or recommendation it didn't matter if it was good or bad he would not accept it. So I began to submit proposals as other's ideas (with their permission). One idea was in revamping the maintenance department. I made suggestions on job classifications, production rates, and salaries. I worked with our maintenance supervisor, Eddie Ricks, to put this together in a complete program. We signed only his name. Bob told me after he had read the changes, "By the way, I know this is your work, but I approved it anyway. You aren't getting anything over on me!"

He was angry with me another time when he went to DC and the senators told him to give me their regards after making sure I still worked for Concrete Products. He said, "I represent the company, not you." As if knowing legislators in DC was a negative! No matter how much I tried to please him, one day it happened.

I had been out of the office that morning of June 30, 1981. We had a senior employee from our Jackson, Mississippi, plant in town and I was asked to help him, and his wife find a place to live. The president called me into his office when I returned and told me that I had not had permission to leave the office and help find an apartment for this employee. It didn't matter that I had not only had two senior employees asked me to do this, and that I had also stopped by *his* office and told him that very morning.

Of course, it had nothing to do with me leaving the office to help a senior member of the team. It had everything to do with the fact that I was a woman, and he didn't want me on his team. He didn't want a woman in management, he didn't want a woman negotiating his union contract, and he didn't want a woman wearing a hard hat in his plant. He told me he was firing me because I had gone to help this employee and his wife from Terry, Mississippi, find an apartment.

"I'm going to ask you to leave but you don't have to tell anyone we had this conversation. You can take the next month and look for something else." I was devastated and told him I would leave that day and that I *would* tell everyone why I was fired. It was an awful day and as I write this thirty years later it is still painful. I'm glad I wrote many of my thoughts down after it was all over so that details are remembered.

I called Arlie and he met me at the house. I was a member of an industrial relations group representing all the large plants and businesses in Brunswick. I called them, and they were all shocked but also encouraged me to fight this kind of discrimination.

I called Amanda Williams a new lawyer that I had heard great things about. We didn't know each other, and my story sounded far-fetched. I had a copy of my file and it only included excellent reviews. She asked for a few days to find out if I was legitimate. (Of course, she didn't put it that way.) The first thing she did was to call Jim Gilbert, who graduated with me from high school and was the Concrete Products attorney. They went together to Concrete Products and looked at my file. Bob was on an overseas trip. Amanda expressed surprise that, indeed, there was nothing in my file to indicate I had been anything other than a stellar employee.

Jim admitted he had known me most of my life—since age thirteen or so and knew that I was respected in the community. Amanda was ready to take on the case and go to court. She called Fletcher Farrington, a well-known lawyer in Savannah, who had been successful in other sex discrimination cases and he agreed to assist.

In discovery, no surprises came up to change her mind, but there was a trend. Since I was the only woman in many instances through the years, the president was going to attack me for being promiscuous and dishonest. We talked about the trial and how hard that would be and if I wanted to be put through that. We waited first for word from the National Labor Relations Board for their opinion on the merits of the case and approval to proceed. We continued to plan. It was such a stressful time for the hours upon hours with both lawyer teams and the grilling on everything I had done for seventeen years. It consumed our lives for a year.

In the meantime, the president had completed my discharge papers with the Department of Labor and said I was dishonest and a liar. I was so concerned about my reputation that I relented and told them if he will tell the truth on the separation notice I'd withdraw my lawsuit. He would not agree! So the process continued. It was a three-day trial and he did everything he said he would do. As I said during the trial, it was like a death in the family. The men from the plant and other friends brought covered dishes to the house and tried to console me. The union president came by and told me he wanted me to represent them in the contract negotiations coming up. I had to tell him that it was a conflict of interest. But I so wanted to.

The case would be heard in federal court and the judge was Anthony Alaimo. A man that I had much respect for. I had met Judge Alaimo many times but did not know him personally but had always admired him. I was satisfied when I heard he would be the judge. The transcript of the trial is in three volumes—I believe I could write a book on all that happened during that three-day trial but instead I'll just share with you some of the actual transcript.

Opening statement by one of my attorneys, Mr. Fletcher Farrington:

> Members of the jury, I am Fletcher Farrington with Amanda Williams. We represent the Plaintiff in this case, Mrs. Sheila McNeill. At the other table is Mr. Griffin Bell and Mr.

Jim Gilbert, who represent the Defendant, Concrete Products, Incorporated.

In 1964, Congress passed a law making it unlawful for an employer to treat persons differently in the work place because certain reasons, race, religious affiliation, national origin, and sex. Of course, an employer has a right to hire and fire who he wants to, he has a right to promote who he wants to, he has a right to get rid of people he doesn't like or that he can't get along with. But he cannot fire someone because she is a woman, cannot pay a woman less just because she's a woman. So, consequently, in any case like this, we are called upon to examine the state of mind of the officers of the corporation, whether in the mind of the president or the vice-president there was an intent to treat women differently.

Also, in 1964, Plaintiff, Sheila McNeill, went to work for Concrete Products. Concrete Products is a relatively small company. It employs about 200 people. It's been in the Brunswick area for thirty or so years, maybe closer to forty. What it does, it taken excelsior, which is paper made out of wood pulp, and coats it with a Portland cement mixture, and puts it in a mold where it dries; then they cure it, trim it, and they use these slabs, concrete/paper slabs for roof decking. It's called Permadeck (Phonetic). There're also another couple of products that they make; but primarily, they make these roofing decks for sale to contractors in building buildings. They have three plants. They have a plant down in Woodbine called Ex-Co (Phonetic) that manufactures the excelsior; and they have two concrete plants, one here in Brunswick and one in Terry, Mississippi, which is just south of Jackson.

Mrs. McNeill went to work as a clerk in the accounts receivable department, where she was, of course, responsible for sending out the bills and collecting the money for the concrete products that were sold. After a while, she was transferred to a clerk. There was not really a personnel department, so you couldn't say she was transferred to the personnel department, but she began doing clerical work in connection with the personnel functions of the company. And not long after she had been there, she realized that the company really didn't have any personnel policies. They didn't have a standard application form. There were a lot of things that they didn't have, so she began setting these things up. And, eventually, she worked her way up to personnel manager. During her tenure, Concrete Products has been owned by a number of different persons. It's been sold, and resold, and resold. And, consequently, there has been different managements. Mrs. McNeill has worked under at least four different managements. Sometime in the sixties, a company called. W. R. Grace brought Concrete Products. Grace is a very large conglomerate corporation. I remember them as owning a lot of ships. But they decided that they wanted to buy Concrete Products.

While Grace owned the company, it began to promote women into jobs that men had ordinarily held, and it took a great deal of pride in that. And, ultimately, three women held jobs in management at Concrete Products, Mrs. McNeill, who was the personnel manager; Phyllis Johns, who was the traffic manager. The traffic manager was responsible from the time the slabs came out of the mold, out of the curing. She was responsible for trimming them, putting them on the trucks, getting them to the customers, being sure that the customer was satisfied. She supervised more than twenty employees. All of them were men. The third woman in management was the accounting supervisor, whose name is Jan Brinson. She did not supervise any men, because only women worked in the accounting department.

Sheila McNeill had a variety of responsibilities as personnel manager. She negotiated for the company with the union. Every three years when the contract came up for renewal, Mrs. McNeill, along with the plant manager, would meet with the union, they would sit down and negotiate, and sign the contracts. She also negotiated with insurance companies. This company, like every other company, has benefits for its employees. It also requires liability insurance and a variety of kinds of insurance. She negotiated rates with the various insurance companies. She set up various systems for the operation of the personnel function of the company. She interviews applicants for jobs. She made recommendations about who to hire, not only for people in production but for other jobs as well.

In 1979, in April Concrete Products underwent another management change. Mr. Bob Bledsoe came down from South Carolina to take over as president of the company. Now, Mr. Bledsoe had a different idea about running things than the previous management, as you would expect. Most people have different ideas about those things. But Mr. Bledsoe also had another idea about women. He did not believe that women should work where men worked. He did not believe that women should be in management. He didn't believe they should be in the plant. He didn't believe they should be out on the road selling. And as a result of his beliefs, Phyllis Johns left the company, because he took all of her responsibility away from her. Shella McNeill was stubborn and wouldn't leave, so he fired her. Determining what is in somebody's mind two or three years ago is never an easy task. It will not be for you. Of course, nobody admits to breaking the law. Mr. Bledsoe's not going to get up on the witness stand and say, "Well, yeah, I fired her because she is a woman." So, you will have to look at all the evidence that is introduced and draw your own conclusions about what was in his mind. And some of the evidence that you will hear is statements made by the vice-president of the company about how Mr. Bledsoe didn't want women in the plant.

You will find that one woman who was working as an assistant traffic manager came in one day and found her hard hat gone. She asked the vice-president where her hard hat was, and he said, "Well, you know how Bledsoe feels about women in the plant. He made me take it away from you. You can't go back in the plant." Although women have applied for sales positions, productions positions, there are no women in any of those places.

The evidence will also show that women receive substantially less money for doing the same things that men do. After Mrs. McNeill left, her functions, what she had been doing were parceled out to several people, most of them men and all of them making substantially more money than she did. This is evidence, of course, we will contend shows what the state of mind of the officers of Concrete Products was when they fired Mrs. McNeill. But, of course, as the judge told you, there are two sides to every story. Concrete Products will say, "No, no, we had good reasons to fire her." Mr. Bledsoe will tell you what those reasons are. And we believe that the evidence will show that those reasons are not true, that the evidence will show that there was no reason at all to fire Sheila McNeill except because she was a woman. At the close of the evidence and after our arguments, you will be asked to decide these questions. You will be asked to decide how much money Concrete Products would have paid a man for doing this particular kind of work, if you find that Concrete Products treated Mrs. McNeill differently because she was a woman.

Although what I say here and what Mr. Bell says is not evidence, I ask you to remember what we have said in our opening statements as you listen to the witnesses, and at the end of the case, remember which of the statements is supported by the evidence. We believe that after the evidence is in, you will agree with us that Concrete Products had on its mind or on the mind of the officers an intention to treat women differently in violation of the law. Thank you.

Opening statement of Mr. Griffin Bell:

May it please the Court, ladies and gentlemen of the jury, the sole issue in this case is whether Mrs. McNeill was discharged because she was a woman. That's the issue that's going to govern this case throughout. You're going to hear a lot of evidence that will touch on it one way or the other. The issue in this case is not going to be whether Mr. Bledsoe, who is the president of Concrete Products, whether he discharged her for a good reason, a bad reason, or no reason at all; but the issue is whether he discharged her for an unlawful reason, that is, because she was a woman. Another way of saying that: Would she still have her job today if she were a man? That's what is case is about.

Now the two central figures in this case, the two major witnesses in this case are going to be Mrs. McNeill—Why? Because she was discharged, and she's brought the lawsuit—and Mr. Bledsoe, who's sitting over there next to Mr. Gilbert. He is the president of the company.

The time involved is this, it really starts in early 1979, and it goes through their relationship, her working for him till June 30th, 1981, which is a little over two years, I believe. Now, we're going to ask that you focus on that period of time and the relationship between the two of them. That's what this case is about.

Now, they're going to be a variety of witnesses in this case. They'll bring more witnesses than we bring. They're going to bring a number of witnesses who do not work with Mrs. McNeill and have not worked with Mrs. McNeill but have known her in other aspects of her life, and they will testify to her competency, ability, to perform, good character, et cetera. We also will have witnesses who will come from the working relationship between Mrs. McNeill and Mr. Bledsoe. Another thing I'd like for you to keep in mind is that Mr. Bledsoe came to Concrete Products as president in early 1979. The reason he came is because the company was on the rocks. Bearing in mind what Mr. Farrington said, is that it consisted of a plant here, a plant in Woodbine, and a plant in Terry, Mississippi. All three of them are small plants and they are manufacturing plants. And he came in 1979 because the company was just about to close the doors. His purpose and his mission given to them by the board of directors was to do whatever was possible to turn this company around. There were several hundred people who were going to lose their jobs. This is what the evidence is going to show. There were already people out looking for a job and thinking about looking for other jobs. His mission was to try to save the company and thereby save the jobs.

Now, in order to come into this trying circumstance, he needed all the support he could get. He needed a change in attitude among the employees. He need a positive attitude. And he had to do certain things. And what does a person have to do when they come into a desperate situation? It's no different from a new football coach taking over a team that hasn't won a game the previous year. He has to make changes. He has to make a lot of hard decisions. And he needs support.

Now, that is the background to his beginning of his relationship with Mrs. McNeill. Mr. Bledsoe was the president of the company with his, with this burden, really. Mrs. McNeill was on his staff. She was the personnel manager. He had really two departments, two people on his staff that were heads of departments. He had the accounting manager, Jan Brinson, and she will be here to testify; and he had Sheila McNeill, who was the personnel manager. Jan supervises, I believe five or six people. Mrs. McNeill supervised one, perhaps two. And the position of the staff, it was their duty to support him. One support him magnificently, Jan Brinson. Mrs. McNeill did not, and that's why we're here today in this case.

Now what happened was a relationship that deteriorated, a relationship over a period of time in which he lost confidence in her. This is what the evidence is going to show. It's going to be very important for you to listen to the testimony of these two major witnesses, Mrs. McNeill and Mr. Bledsoe. They're directly opposite on certain things that happened.

The judge charged you that you're the judges of the credibility. And one of the best things he said is: Use your common sense. That's what's necessary in trying to separate all these facts in the case that aren't relevant and some that are relevant.

The relationship deteriorated over a period of time, over a period of these two years to the point that he no longer had any confidence in her. The incidents that occurred weren't, by themselves, major incidents. There was incident concerning union negotiations, where she withheld information, didn't tell him about it for two years, didn't provide that support. There was an incident—The straw that broke the camel's back concerned showing an employee who was being transferred from Terry, Mississippi, to here, showing him, doing something she should not have done. That in itself, that last straw, was not by itself something that you would fire someone over. You would reprimand them, or, as we say in the Army, you'd chew them out. But given all these other things, it resulted in her discharge.

Now it's our contention, and I think Mrs. McNeill is going to testify, actually, that she did not feel that Mr. Bledsoe, discriminated against women in any area other than management, that she only said that he only did not want women in management. There were really—and you're going to have further testimony to the effect that she doesn't hold him responsible for Phyllis Johns, the traffic manager that was mentioned by Mr. Farrington.

You'll hear testimony from Jan Brinson, the other manager, who is a lady, and you'll hear testimony that not only has he treated her well, pays her a good salary, he relies heavily on her, he has confidence in her, but he even made her an officer of the company, Concrete Products. You'll hear testimony from several other people, people who have worked in a close relationship not only with Mr. Bledsoe but Mrs. Mc Neill

The point in this case is not whether Mrs. McNeill did her job. She was qualified. She did her job, maybe not as well as Mr. Bledsoe wanted her to. But that's not the point. The point was whether she provided him with the support that he could do his job. And that's what I'd like for you to be careful of and be aware of when you hear the evidence in the case.

Now, we expect the evidence to show, contrary to what Mr. Farmington said, that we do like and encourage women working for Concrete Products. There are women working in all areas of Concrete Products. We've had as many—Part of what we do—not only do we manufacture the product, but we also install it in the south. And we've had as many as ten out of thirty people, ten women out of thirty people total working on these installation crews, putting in these concrete slabs on commercial buildings. It varies, of course. We've had women—There's going to be a good bit of testimony about whether or not there was a rule concerning women going down into the plant. You will hear all—In fact, there'll probably be too much testimony about that.

Now, as to the burden of proof, the burden of proof in a discrimination case is somewhat different than it is in just another case, in other cases."

The court said,

Mr. Bell, I will instruct them as soon as you get through

Mr. Bell replied,

All right.

The court said,

On the burden.

Mr. Bell replied,

Remember one thing, Mrs. McNeill initiated this action. She filed the suit. What she is asking for is money. I think you've heard all the evidence, you'll find that she has not carried the burden of proof, that instead, we have, in fact proved that there was no discrimination in the case, and we don't even have to prove it. The burden of proof always remains with her. And in order for her to recover any money in this case, she must prove her case. After you've heard all the evidence, I think that you will find that there is no discrimination in this case. You will find that you don't agree with Mr. Bledsoe and his reasons for having discharged her. I do. But you may not. But that's not the point. The point is whether he fired her because she was a woman or for some other reason. And one other thing I'd like to ask you to do is, the case may last two to three days. You may get bored with it after a while. Please keep an open mind. The plaintiff puts on its case, her case first. And then after a day or so we'll put on our case, we'll tell our side of the story. Please don't make up your

> mind and please keep an open mind until you've had a chance to hear both sides of the case. And when you do, I feel confident that you'll find that she was not discriminated against and you'll return a verdict in favor of the Defendant. Thank you.

I've tried to present this part of my life in a balanced way. The reasons he used for my transgressions were unbelievably minor and distorted. Where I would approach him with a suggestion, he would testify that I was against it. The silly idea of firing me because I took an employee to look for a house doesn't hold up in any way you look at it. One difficult thing about the lawsuit was that I had to put employees on a spot. Most talked to me later and were glad to get it in the open.

I will always be grateful for so many who wanted to testify on my behalf. Some of those came to the trial and waited outside the door just in case I needed them. The local industry and business community was very supportive. As personnel manager of Concrete Products, I was invited to be a member of the Coastal Industrial Relations Group. We were certainly a small fish in a large pond. The large plants Brunswick Pulp and Paper Company, Hercules, and Babcock & Wilcox—all with more than one thousand employees, yet they invited me to join.

Wayne Reynolds who was the director of personnel and labor relations for Babcock & Wilcox Company, Brunswick plant was a member of that group and one of my colleagues who testified on my behalf. He added a good bit of credibility to my testimony. Two of the past presidents testified on my behalf and others were waiting to see if they were needed. Two of those employees who testified for the defendant were still employed by the company which put them in a terrible position, but they told the truth anyway. I believe one part of the trial helped. When Mr. Bell tried to tell the jury, I was doing this for money, he later asked me that very thing. He asked if it was true I was doing this for money. I replied something like "I don't want any money—just tell him he was wrong, and I'll be happy." I later found out that the jury listened to that.

On the third day, Judge Alaimo charged the jury.

They deliberated for about three hours and then came back for a question. My husband, Arlie, and both my mother and grandmother attended the three-day trial and were waiting with me and Arlie in the courtroom. My pastor was there also.

When the question came from the jury, Amanda Williams, my attorney, tried to help prepare me. She said, "This may not be good." She and Fletcher went up to the judge with Mr. Bell. She turned and thrust her arms in the air! She told me, "They want to know how much they could give you!" Evidently the decision must have been made!

I was paid seventeen thousand dollars a year. During the trial, my lawyers said that I should have been making twenty-five thousand to thirty thousand dollars. Five minutes later the jury returned to the courtroom with this verdict:

- Was Mrs. McNeill's sex a substantial factor in Concrete Products decision to fire her?
- **Answer: Yes.**
- What would man have been paid performing Mrs. McNeill's job?
- **Answer: Thirty thousand dollars.**

The decision was that sex was a substantial factor in my firing, that I should be reinstated and awarded thirty thousand dollars.

As we left the courtroom, that night Arlie gave me a dozen red roses. I asked him, "How did you know we were going to win?"

"I knew that you deserved the roses no matter what," he answered.

Walking out that door with him holding me and carrying those roses is a moment I'll never forget.

Over the next few years I had many calls. Companies called to say if this could happen to me it meant they should review their policies and their "attitudes" to make sure this wasn't happening in their company. Individuals told me they received salary increases after this trial. It was the first sex discrimination lawsuit in the district and it remains the only one to this date.

For the most part I never talked about this case. That was especially true in the Navy League. I was always afraid that if it came up there might be the assumption that others had to be "careful" around me—that I might sue them for any minor comments. Of course, that was not true and that certainly was proven as I was appointed to a defense advisor committee and I climbed the ladder of the Navy League as the first woman to be national president. I thought of the Concrete Products president with each of those appointments.

A couple of months after the trial Arlie and I were at the Cloister on Sea Island. There was a great band and when I ran into Judge Alaimo he asked me to dance. The president walked in. I was stunned and pointed him out to the judge. He said, "Sheila, I tried to tell him before we went to trial that he should settle."

Several years later I stopped by to see Judge Alaimo. I had called him and told him he should call his publisher and let them know all the local bookstores were out of his book. He suggested I come by for an autographed copy from him.

We had a lovely chat about my trial. He thought Amanda was very good and fair and that she was smart to bring in Fletcher. It seems that Fletcher had died just five years before and Judge Alaimo went to his funeral.

When we were reminiscing about the trial, I asked him if he knew that Bill Jones III was in the courtroom every day. He was surprised. I reminded him that Sea Island Company was on the board of directors for Concrete Products. What I didn't tell him was that after the trial Bill came up to me and said he was sorry I had to go through what I did!

Judge Alaimo said there was one thing that the plaintiffs brought up that was a real mistake: When Griffin Bell or one of the associates said, "Isn't it true that you are doing this just for money?"

My suggestion was not to give me any money—just find him guilty. And they not only found him guilty but also awarded me back pay with an adjusted increase. One of the more damaging things he said during the trial was "working women is a bitch." Years later I was in a meeting and someone who was in the court during that time sent me a note with this on it and "Do you remember this?" Yes, I will always remember that statement. It was an awful experience but I'm glad I fought him.

LEGISLATIVE AFFAIRS VICE PRESIDENT

Jack Fisher finally appointed me to vice president of legislative affairs in 2000, and I stayed in that position for a great three years. I immediately called Rear Admiral Chuck Beers asking him to take on the chairman of the national Legislative Affairs Committee. I offered to Chuck that I would do most of the work if he would just brainstorm with me from time to time and head the committee meetings but he was all in! He agreed, and we changed the legislative program in the Navy League. The others on the steering committee during 2001–2002 were as follows:

Jack Fisher, Chairman, Advisory Council
Mel Burkart, Education and Information Technology
Ed Carter, Finance and Administration
Mike Wilson, Corporate Affairs
Richard Kennedy, Treasurer
Glen Huber, Development
Jerome Rapkin, Corporate Secretary
John Panneton, Sea Service Liaison
Brad Nemeth, Council Matters
Richard Saliterman, Judge Advocate
Jim Ward, Youth
Ron Weeks, Membership

My first trip was to Capitol Hill to meet each of the legislative heads. I met with Rear Admiral Patrick Stillman as assistant commandant for governmental and public affairs for the Coast Guard (Captain Bob Papp was the 06 working for him), Rear Admiral Cutler Dawson was chief of legislative affairs for the Navy, and BG Tony Corwin with the Marine Corps. Later it was Rear Admiral Gary Roughead for the Navy and Rear Admiral Kevin Eldridge for the Coast Guard. We couldn't miss!

The legislative directors during that time were Jeffrey Redinger, Shannon Graves, and later Jeremy Miller—most of the time I was serving was with Jeremy. The first objective was to write a platform. We did a two-pager—front and back—of the issues of each of the services on issues coming up with the legislature that session.

The meeting with General Corwin was an interesting time. I had not met him and was asking him to give me a list of all his funding needs. We talked for about an hour. We continued to reach out to all the legislative offices and were at all the hearings that affected our sea services. I made another appointment with BG Corwin. When we sat down to the table I began to repeat my pitch about needed his issues. My jaw dropped as I looked at the paper in front of me. "Are these your issues?"

"Yes, they are," he answered.

"Are they for me?"

"They are—look at the date."

It was dated that day. "Yes, ma'am, this report was made for you and the Navy League."

My reception from the Coast Guard was about the same. No one knew what to expect from the woman demanding so much and, I believe, offering so much. But we proved ourselves. We had amazing receptions during those three years. Receptions with hundreds of attendees. Many of the stories in the book and individual stories were from those receptions and breakfasts. Over the years, it is fact that the people you meet in the military continue to show up with other commands and you feel like you are seeing an old friend when you run into them. One of the most significant was a breakfast on Capitol Hill for new members of Congress. As I listen to the news, now I hear from some of those new members—like Representative Darrell Issa (R-CA 49). He was brand-new that day and look at him now! Congressman Ed Schrock was president of that freshman class in the 107th Congress and was a retired Navy captain. He was a joy to work with. Service chiefs who attended were Admiral Vern Clark, CNO; Admiral Jim Loy, commandant of the United States Coast Guard; and General Jim Jones, commandant of the United State Marine Corps. I couldn't believe we were able to convince all three to come. And all the new members of the class of 2001. What a wonderful opportunity to reach out to these new members at the beginning of their term. I spoke at that breakfast and introduced the service chiefs.

After the remarks were over a Navy admiral by the name of Jay Cohen came over to me and complimented me on my delivery. You voice is like sweet nectar. He was really giving me a great moment. Then Rear Admiral Chuck Beers (retired) came over to us and said, "Sheila, don't believe anything he is saying, he is full of s——." I laughed thinking obviously, they are good friends, and they were, but I continue to tell myself that he was sincere! Jay and I became good friends that day.

In June 2001, we had a welcome-back reception in the Rayburn Building of Capitol Hill. There were approximately seven hundred who attended over the two hours. All the service chiefs were there. (Look for more details in the book!)

At this reception, many of my friends and connections were made: Rear Admiral Gary Roughead, Office of Legislative Affairs; Major General Tony Corwin, Marine Corps Legislative Affairs; Secretary of the Navy, Gordon England; commandant of the Coast Guard, Jim Loy; Fleet Forces Command, Bill Fallon; and Senator Susan Collins. That was the evening I met General Shinseki and had a chance to talk with him about SSGN—thanks to Jack Kingston's military legislative assistant who introduced us; Rear Admiral Chris Weaver with his newly formed career in the newly created Installation Command was there; the top enlisted for the USCG Vince Patton and USMC Alford McMichael. It was our first legislative affairs reception. When I was talking to Senator Susan Davis, she mentioned the chocolate submarines and asked her legislative assistant, Mike Velasquez, if the staff had left her one. I was so surprised and told her I was with that group who left the chocolates!

Later I worked with Rear Admiral Karl Schultz as the Coast Guard's head of legislation and public affairs and Rear Admiral Pat Stillman, the program manager for the recapitalization of the US Coast Guard on supporting that recapitalization.

There was also someone I met while on DACOWITS. He was then a two-star general and when we saw each other it was like old home week. He then introduced me to someone. He said, "This is Sheila McNeill—she visited my base when she was on DACOWITS and scared the shit out of me." Imagine a 6'5" general saying that! He'd probably not care if I used his name and service but just in case I don't think I will. Loved that man!

One of the congressmen I enjoyed working with was Representative Floyd D. Spence, a South Carolina Republican who was chairman of the House Armed Services Committee. He always made it a point to come up to me if I didn't see him first and he always saluted me. I have a great picture that someone caught at one of our receptions. Obviously, he was smart, but he also had the common sense needed for someone fighting for our military's budget and a national missile-defense program. He died in Jackson, Mississippi, after emergency brain surgery on August 16, 2001. He was seventy-three.

STATE SENATOR WILLIAM LIGON

William is one of the most level-headed gentleman you could ever meet. I had known his family but did not know him well when he decided to run. He came to my office and we talked. It didn't take long to determine how blessed we would be to have this man in our state legislature. I agreed to support him. Later he asked if I would be willing to make this public. I made a very rare decision to do just that. During the campaign, the following ads were in the local papers:

William Ligon is a proven public servant who understands the US Constitution. He has the legal experience and the right temperament to represent the people of Georgia. He is a smart, hardworking man of integrity who has the courage and the character it takes to do the job.

Join me in supporting William Ligon as our next Georgia State Senator from the Third District.

Sheila McNeill
Past National President, Navy League of the United States

Ligon means leadership

Picture: Sheila McNeill and William Ligon at the Pentagon in Washington, D.C. earlier this year. The two were part of a delegation that met with Pentagon officials regarding Kings Bay Navy Base and its importance to the people of Camden County, coastal Georgia and our nation. He has an amazing family. I've met each of his five children and am impressed with each of them. Kim and William have done a remarkable job with parenting.

He is always willing to listen. He continues to use good judgment and he continues to be the blessing for our communities that I would he might be.

ADMIRAL JIM LOY AND KAY

COMMANDANT OF THE US COAST GUARD 1998–2002

Admiral Loy was the Commandant of the Coast Guard when I became vice president for legislative affairs. He made sure that I met with Rear Admiral Pat Stillman, program executive officer (PEO) of the Integrated Deepwater Project; and Rear Admiral Kevin Eldridge, legislative affairs and public relations as often as I needed to support this recapitalization of the USCG. I teasingly said that I became known as Sheila Deepwater McNeill because I talked about this recapitalization every time I spoke to organizations and our councils. I always enjoyed meeting with Admiral Loy. I could always get a straight answer.

Admiral Loy and chief of Naval Operations, Vern Clark, were very close. They both shared with me some of the insights and experiences during the attacks

September 11, 2001. When the homeland is attacked, the USCG is in charge. As the United States Coast Guard commandant, Jim, had the lead to respond to the attacks. As soon as the attacks occurred Admiral Clark called Admiral Loy and said, "Jim, this is Vern Clark, what can the Navy do to help?"

> *The evacuation of New York during that day was massive. The Coast Guard and the gathered assets of the local maritime community evacuated over 500,000 citizens from Manhattan. Immediately after the first attack, the captains and crews of a large number of local boats steamed into the attack zone to assist in evacuation. These ships had responded to a request from the U.S. Coast Guard to help evacuate those stranded on Manhattan Island. Estimates of the number of people evacuated by water from Lower Manhattan that day in the eight-hour period following the attacks range from 500,000 to 1,000,000. Norman Mineta, Secretary of Transportation during the attacks, called the efforts "the largest maritime evacuation conducted in the United States." The evacuation was the largest maritime evacuation in history by most estimates, passing the nine-day evacuation of Dunkirk during World War II. As many as 2,000 people injured in the attacks were evacuated by this means. (Google)*

Early in 2001, I received the Secretary of the Navy Superior Public Service Award from the Navy and Jim sent a nice letter congratulating me with an invitation to join him and Kay at Quarters One for dinner. Arlie and I both attended Sea Air Space in 2001. We always showed the VIPs around the booths before the banquet. John Thorne, public affairs officer for the USCG, knew my great admiration for Admiral Loy and asked Linda Hoffman if Jack Fisher, the president, was not available to escort the commandant, John would like for me to do it. Wow! I was thrilled. Jack wanted to join us for the beginning and then leave to escort the chief of Naval Operations. We waited with the large delegation including RADM. Stillman, RADM Etheredge, several Navy League vice presidents, two photographers, and half the staff who were greeting at the door. I let the commandant know I would be pushing him so we could get to as many of the booths as possible and gave him a signal to give me if he didn't want to leave a booth. At the very last I said, "Sir, the next booth has nothing to do with the Coast Guard, I just want to impress one of my friends by taking you by his booth. Is that okay?" With his wit and personality, I knew he would be okay with that, and sure enough he said, "Sounds like fun, lead on."

The big news when we got home: Arlie told me that Jim's wife Kay told him, "Sheila is going to be the best president. There is no one else that stands a chance or could do it better. I hope you'll enjoy the travel as much as we did." Amazing. As the saying goes, from her mouth to God's ears.

Jim sent me a wonderful letter concerning my dinner with Secretary Mineta and his wife as well as undersecretary of defense, Fred Pang, and his wife.

The Admiral Arleigh Burke Leadership Award was presented to Admiral Loy on June 27, 2002, at the New York Athletic Club. It was a big deal with secretary of transportation, Norm Mineta; former secretary of the Navy, John Lehman; Admiral Vern Clark, chief of Naval Operations; and his relief, Admiral Tom Collins, the new commandant of the US Coast Guard.

In 2002 at the end of Admiral Loy's tour, John Thorne, public affairs officer, asked if I would like a little face time with Admiral Collins. I was pleased and made an appointment. At that time, I was vice president for legislative affairs, and with the recapitalization of the Coast Guard fleet, it was important that I stay "connected." The morning of my appointment I was a few minutes early and sitting on the couch outside of the commandant's office with John and RADM Eldridge. About that time, the door opens to the conference room and Adm. Loy walks out with several of his flag officers following him. Suddenly I felt like I was betraying him. He looked at me and said, "Sheila McNeill, my body's not even cold yet and you are already sucking up to the next man."

It immediately lightened the situation; I laughed and said, "Yes, that is just what we do in the Navy League, sir."

Admiral Loy continued to have an amazing career after his retirement from the Coast Guard.

In May 2002, the secretary of the Department of Transportation Norman Mineta, appointed Admiral Loy to become the deputy undersecretary for the new Transportation Security Administration. This was when all the new airport regulations had started. He took such a common-sense approach to the security issues. I loved giving him a hard time recanting any issues I had during any of my airline travels, even sharing with him my angst that I might have to remove the wiring from my bras to avoid constant delays.

To show how common sense he was, he eliminated the rule that ticket agents had been required for years to ask passengers two questions: "Has anyone unknown to you asked you to carry an item on this flight?" and "Have any of the items you are traveling with been out of your immediate control since the time you packed them?" I always thought if they were going to hijack the plane they would have no problem about lying to this question. There were other common-sense regulations enacted during his tour. The Coast Guard had always reported to the Department of Transportation. While the former secretaries that I met, especially Secretary Norm Mineta, were very supportive it made more sense to transfer responsibility through its creation and subsequent incorporation into the Department of Homeland Security. That issue was something that I worked on during the time I had legislative affairs responsibilities. The Coast Guard presented me with a copy of the bill transferring the USCG from the Department of Transportation to the Department of Homeland Security.

In 2004, Rear Admiral Kevin Eldridge gave me a copy of Admiral Loy's book, *Character in Action.* It had story after story of examples of leadership. I couldn't put it down and read it all in one day of multiple airline flights. It was so intense and so inspirational that I made it my Christmas gift for everyone on the Navy League staff that year—about fifty copies. Jim was always appreciative of the Navy League and our legislative program and the staff recognized that. There couldn't have been a better gift to give them.

I continue to call for advice from Admiral Loy. In 2010 when we faced the three hundred thousand dollars cut to the Coast Guard budget by the administration I called Jim to review the paper I was taking to Congress. Admiral Loy and Vice Admiral Jim Hull ensured that all the figures I used on the paper were factual. In April 2010, I attended the Coast Guard Ball on behalf of VT Group. There were about seven hundred in attendance that evening honoring Admiral Bob Papp, the new commandant of the Coast Guard. The speaker for the evening was Admiral Loy. He spoke with great passion and said, "Bob, know you have my support and if you need one damn office on Capitol Hill visited, just let me know me and Sheila know." It got a big laugh and I was thrilled.

CAPTAIN BRIAN MCILVAINE AND SHIRLEY

COMMANDING OFFICER
USS *GEORGIA* (SSGN 729) BLUE

Captain McIlvaine asked me to speak at his change of command in 2008. That was quite an honor. I shared the stage with Rear Admiral Bruner who was Submarine Group 10 commander. These were my words:

Captain McIlvaine, thank you. What a privilege and honor it is to speak at your change of command. Good morning, Admiral Bruner—it's nice to share the podium with you. And welcome, Captain McDowell and your family. You are going to love it here. The USS *Georgia*—won't that always evoke the best memories?

Well, maybe not for Captain Stevens and Bud Lett and his security team and maybe not Melody, Chuck, or Todd Sullivan! But if you convinced them to fess up, they thought it was awesome too. And can you believe it's been two years! USS *Georgia* return to service was—to quote our vice president—a really big deal to Camden County and to the state of Georgia. I've worked with the military for forty years and have never seen a more unifying project. The state of Georgia, our three cities and our county responded quicker than I could imagine.

The flag project! Were we out of our minds? Oh my, with 159 counties. The logistics issues were gigantic. First, the governor had to make time to meet with us. Then folks from all over the state did a tag team carrying the flag from county to county. Each volunteer received the flag, sponsored an event in each county, and then hand-delivered it to the next county. Without the work of Don Giles (Atlanta Navy League council) and the Navy League councils throughout the state it would have never happened. Many of you here today were part of that project. There were ceremonies where veterans, active duty, children, and just plain folks joined together to celebrate *Georgia*'s return to service. In many ceremonies, there were tears and renewed appreciation of our military and in particular our submarine force.

Then Keith decided we needed to get our school children involved. So we had three weeks to develop a plan, sell it to Dr. Hardin, then the Governor and the State Superintendent of schools. Again, we had 159 school systems to contact and communicate with. All of those Georgia school children, surfing the internet, finding out just what a submarine was and what it did. Did you know that many of them are yellow and have nice windows? However, the work from our more-senior students in the state was magnificent and depicted the right kind of submarine! Dean Slusser was chairman of the art project. As director of the arts program at the high school, this was the first "military project" and he did a superb job. Thank you, Dean.

We never found a PR person, but between Keith, Marty, and me we got the word out on the return to service. Thank you, Keith, Marty, and Chris. And we did get lots of publicity through the state and the country and we actually had someone produce a documentary, *Tale of Two Georgias*, that told the SSGN story.

But early on while we were working some of this we are talking about the commanding officer who was due to report as the commissioning commanding officer of the *Georgia*. We were apprehensive—that may be too strong a word—but we were only cautiously optimistic awaiting Brian McIlvain's arrival. What would he be like? Would he understand how important the Georgia was to us? Would he not only endorse this but enthusiastically support our projects? Is he just a brilliant guy—what kind of a guy was he to command such a ship. Could he be CO and ambassador? Brilliant doesn't always equate to personality and charm—well, we had no worries. Of course, during this time, *we* were wondering we never thought about his thoughts and concerns. Who are these people? Am I really going to have to put my career on the line with some of the far-reaching initiates? Do I have to be concerned not only with a new boat with a new mission but with 140 new crew all who had zero experience on an SSBN? And by the way, a new boss, a new community, and a new home for the family with new schools and new friends. But look at how it worked out. I think we were all happy. Captain McIlvaine was a shot in the arm for us. He took us to a higher level with his graciousness and willingness to do *almost* anything we needed. I know that when we were a week out and Captain McIlvaine was speaking at the flag ceremony he made a comment that after meeting and having dinner that first evening he was a little concerned about having to go to admiral's mast before it was all over. Admiral's mast is equivalent to us going before a judge for an infraction of the law. Not a fun thing to do. It's a good thing he had the temperament he did. He is a levelheaded; never lose your cool, compassionate man. And don't you just like the man? I like the fact that he is the same man on Saturday night as he is on Monday morning. I like a man who shows respect to others.

He loves his Shirlee and his children. In talking with Shirlee about this move she said, "Brian would like to live near the beach and enjoy the casual living and walks on the beach. But he wants to make me happy. I just want to live near a good school for Casey and make him happy. So we'll live where there are good school and we'll all be happy. Jenny will be entering college after spending her last two years in a new school with new friends during one of the most important junctures of her life." We wonder why our Navy children seem to succeed more than their counterparts and maybe this ability to adjust and bounce back is what gives them the resilience in future years to succeed and be happy.

I like the fact that no matter what we asked of him he was there—he would just smile and do what we asked. I like the way he showed Shirlee off that first night she arrived, tired after fourteen hours of travel but still there for our Navy League meeting honoring the *Georgia* and her crew. After all he had to be an ambassador for Georgia as well as have those leadership skills to take 140 or so men he had recently met to go to sea on an entirely new class of ship. And let me tell you how that new crew and the new CO worked out. That ship won the battle E award.

Governor Perdue sent a letter to the crew and I'd like to share with you some of his words:

> **Not only does this award recognize the hard work, dedication and effectiveness of your team, but it also indicates the high honor and integrity through which you represent our state and nation. We recognize that our freedom comes only from the courage and resilience of our military. Thank you, not only for your service and sacrifice, but also for the honor and the spirt with which you serve our state and our nation.**

And what did that boat mean to Georgia? Our namesake. I don't think many Georgians knew of its existence until she came to Kings Bay. Having our namesake in the state has opened many eyes to the advantageous of our submarines and the security they bring to our nation. I know that our CNO (Chief of Naval Operations) talks every chance he gets about our submarines and the briefs he gets that are so important to him and to the nation.

The USS *Georgia* has energized an entire stare. The SSGN program, a platform that was not destined to be built has succeeded, surpassing all expectations. We hope that when Brian and Shirlee tell their stories of their Navy career to their grandchildren, they will be able to convey to them the tremendous impact they both had on our state and our community. And, Captain, you will always have a place in our hearts and will be forever immortalized as the commissioning commanding officer of the USS *Georgia*.

We wish you success as you uproot your family for yet another adventure. Don't forget us!

What great publicity. The base paper article was picked up by the Navy and appeared on the Navy website:

Success of Georgia Inspired by Top "Dawg"
Release Date: 6/9/2010 11:16:00 PM
From Commander Submarine Group 10 Public Affairs

KINGS BAY, Ga. (NNS)—USS Georgia (SSGN 729) (Blue) held a change of command ceremony at the Naval Submarine Base Kings Bay Chapel June 9. Capt. Brian McIlvaine was relieved by Capt. J. Kelly McDowell as commanding officer of the Georgia Blue "bull dogs."

Sheila McNeill, president of Camden Partnership, and Rear Adm. Barry Bruner, commander Submarine Group 10, served as guest speakers. "I don't think many Georgians knew of its (USS Georgia) existence until she came to Kings Bay," said McNeill. "Having our namesake in the state has opened many eyes to the advantageous of our submarine and the security they bring to our nation. USS Georgia has energized an entire state. "McIlvaine led Georgia through its March 28, 2008 return to service, following its conversion from a ballistic-missile submarine to a guided-missile submarine, and its maiden SSGN deployment in August 2009.

"He prepared his crew and submarine for battle. By doing so—his efforts will be felt for generations in the future. There is no greater measure of a commanding officer than that of the legacy that he leaves behind," said Bruner. "Brian's legacy is that of a commanding officer who has no comparison—one who treats everyone with great dignity and honor and one who gets the mission done."

McIlvaine led the Georgia blue crew through two arduous modernization periods, Naval Special Warfare Certification, and Pre-Overseas Movement Certification that transformed his Sailors into a unified combat-ready crew. Through his leadership and guidance during Georgia's maiden deployment, McIlvaine flawlessly delivered mission capability in Tomahawk strike, SEAL delivery operations, and battlespace preparation. The blue crew earned the Commander, Submarine Squadron 16, 2009 Battle Efficiency award, or Battle "E," Engineering Red "E," Navigation Red and Green "N" and the 2008 Supply Blue "E."

"It is difficult for me to objectively state the amount of respect I have for this crew," said McIlvaine. "I appreciate the hard work of this crew defending America against her enemies and sincerely appreciate their families for supporting their Sailors."

McIlvaine lists key personnel accomplishments, including retention readiness for three years, no driving under the influence incidents in the past two years, no alcohol-related issues in more than a year, and no Sailor attending Captain's Mast during his command tenure for procedural compliance, tag out, or other operational misconduct. Georgia's high standards continued during the last exam cycle when the Georgia Blue Sailors taking the petty officer third class exam averaged 15-percentage points over the Navy average. In addition, every junior officer passed the engineer's exam the first time. These accomplishment "provide you with a sense of the level of effort and more important the level of accomplishment these fine young men achieve on a daily basis," said McIlvaine. "I remain fiercely proud of them and their ability to man this ship. "McIlvaine's next assignment is the director for operations at Commander, Submarine Forces in Norfolk, Va.

McDowell arrives to Kings Bay from Chief of Naval Operations staff as director of the Information Management Division and chief information officer for the Chief of Naval Personnel where he developed and implemented a strategy for modernizing Navy's legacy pay, personnel, and training information systems. He is a native of Vineland, N.J. and received his commission through the NROTC program at the University of New Mexico in December 1984.

"I am both honored and humbled by the opportunity to join Team Georgia and lead the Georgia Blue. During my turnover, I have had the opportunity to observe the crew in action and I am very impressed by their level of talent, professionalism, and teamwork that has produced outstanding results," said McDowell. "I look forward to continuing this tradition of excellence on Georgia and to continuing the close relationship that Georgia has established with the local community."

Georgia is an Ohio-class submarine and the second ship of the U.S. Navy to be named for the fourth state. Commissioned as a fleet ballistic-missile submarine (SSBN) in February 1984, it conducted 65 strategic deterrent patrols before its conversion to a SSGN. Georgia is homeported at Naval Submarine Base Kings Bay, Ga.

Working with Brian McIlvaine and his Chief of the Boat, Richard Rose was an honor.

CAPTAIN MIKE MCKINNON AND RHONDA

COMMANDING OFFICER NAVAL SUBMARINE BASE KINGS BAY USS KENTUCKY GOLD

The Cloister Award for 2000 was awarded to Mike's crew when he was commanding officer of USS *Kentucky* Gold. His chop sent the following note:

> *Dear Sheila, I wanted to thank you again for the wonderful meal and award ceremony at the Cloister for the USS Kentucky Gold. The food was great the company outstanding and my guys will remember Monday evening for the rest of their careers. Being able to attend an event like this has become more important in the last few years since the awards to celebrate and send sailors to special events have become scarce. I hope this event can continue for many years to come. I enjoyed our conversations on the Navy League and your stories. Definitely consider us when you need anything from the Kings Bay submarine community or the USS Kentucky. I intend to keep in touch with you and I hope I can repay you for your efforts on behalf of our fine Navy. Thank you!! Very respectfully, W.A. Clark "Chop" 737 Gold*

In spring 2004, when I was national president, I had a trip planned for Europe, which included Naples. Captain Mike McKinnon was stationed in Naples, Italy, working as the commander of the Submarine Group 8, assistant chief of staff for plans and operations. I gave him the date the evening a big party was planned with General Jim Jones and told him to please come. I was really looking forward to seeing him, but when I got there, Mike was missing. Where was he? As I met everyone coming in, I kept asking, "Have you seen Mike McKinnon?" and "Do you know Mike McKinnon?" They all knew him but didn't give me any idea when he might arrive. Finally, one of the admirals came over and told me "Captain McKinnon is running a little late but he is on the way." When Mike arrived, he told me that he had mentioned to his seniors that I was expecting him to be there. He was told that others were coming, and the Navy would be represented well. They just had not expected me to continue to ask for him. I apologized to Mike for making an issue of it and asking about him so much. It turned out that he was especially pleased I had asked for him since he had told his seniors I would do just that!

Mike received orders! He would be returning to Naval Submarine Base Kings Bay as the subase commanding officer. Mike as CO and Rhonda as First Lady—it doesn't get any better.

When he was in the store one day making a purchase, he started a conversation with an employee running the register with me standing right there and listening. He was teasing her about not getting a discount. I chastised him and said, "Don't tell me how to run my business, do I ever try to tell you how to run… never mind." We both had a good laugh. Rhonda was his greatest strength—she was the COW—the commanding officer's wife! They both believed in working hard and playing hard. Some of the most fun I've had has been with Mike and Rhonda. One of those times was at Seagal's, probably for one of Barbara Ryan's *St. Marys* Magazine parties. We were trying something new: Okefenokee champagne. Only the best when we are together. I believe that was the night Mike insisted Keith drive me to my hotel room on the base. I really was fine, but it's hard to disagree with the commanding officer of the base when you are staying at his hotel.

I got to the hotel, put some popcorn in the microwave, and took a quick shower. When I opened the bathroom door the room was full of dark smoke. I called the front desk as the alarm was blaring. "My alarm is going off but there is no fire. There is no need to call the fire department." Too late, they were on the way. I was in my pajamas and had no makeup, and the room was filled with black smoke. They came in fully loaded with everything they needed for a fire. It took a while to get the alarm off. Every guest was evacuated. They were standing all around the buildings. I was hoping no one would know it was me. I was so embarrassed.

I asked the fireman in charge, "Is Captain McKinnon advised of this… or since it wasn't a fire maybe he won't know?"

"No, ma'am, he gets a report every morning on any calls we have."

"Thank you all, I sure hated you had to come out for this."

"That's okay, ma'am, but next time I'd recommend crunch and munch!"

I called Mike at home and confessed everything. I've never popped popcorn in one of those rooms again.

On May 4, 2007, Kings Bay received the commander in chief's Installation Excellence Award at the Pentagon. Mike sent me a letter with an invitation to join them for the ceremony. I was the speaker at a graduation at Thomas University in Thomasville during the same time. I sure hated missing that event!

Mike spoke to a combined meeting of the Navy League and the Military Officers Association in May 2007 NSB Kings Bay.

> *I would like to start out tonight with a tremendous thank you to both MOA and the Navy League. Your support of the active duty military through your organizations have made a difference… a lasting difference to our current military readiness, capabilities and quality of life. I wholeheartedly believe that the work the Navy League did just prior to and during Sheila McNeill's term as the Navy League's national president resulted in the Navy's adoption and pursuit of turning four Trident submarine that would have been scrapped and decommissioned, each at a value of four billion dollars to our taxpayers, into the SSGN platform that Kings Bay is now honored to home port. The USS Florida and USS Georgia bring to the table a military capability that far exceeds the fire power that a carrier strike group can bring to a numbered fleet commander. Its 154 tomahawk missiles, ability to inconspicuously gather electronic intelligence and then plan and direct the covert insertion of 66 special operations forces provide an unmatched force for any enemy we may face. This capability simply would not exist today without the Navy League's lobby efforts to help congress and even our own Navy leadership to see the light…*

He eloquently talked about leadership:

> *First of all, leadership is about influence, nothing more, nothing less. It's about getting people to do what they sometimes don't want to do. And finally, leadership is about harnessing the genius of your people through teamwork and honest and open communication. Simply put, the power of any organization is not in the talent or wisdom of the chief executive… because talent alone is simply not enough. Real leadership recognizes the real power of an organization is in the genius of its people, and those leaders who can harness that ingenuity with the right attitude are the ones who will succeed. Basically, you win or lose with people. With the right attitude and people on your side, you will win—without them or with poor attitudes you will lose. Entrepreneurs will tell you the one skill that separates the successes from the failures is skill with people. Top sales persons will tell you that people knowledge is more important than product knowledge. The bottom line is that people skills make the difference between those who excel and those who don't. For every*

success or achievement, I've enjoyed, and I bet if you looked back, for every success you've enjoyed, you can see an important relationship that made it possible.

On July 6, 2007, The Camden Partnership, led by Captain Walt Yourstone, US Navy, retired, gave a farewell party for Mike. The local papers carried this story:

The Camden Partnership to salute Kings Bay CO

"Fair winds and following seas" to Capt. Mike McKinnon commanding officer of Navy Submarine Base Kings Bay. The public is invited to join The Camden Partnership at the St. Marys Police Department at 8:30 a.m. Thursday July 12, to wish this outstanding leader all the best for the future as he introduces the community to his relief, Captain Ward Stevens. This will take place at the regular Community Action Group (CAG) meeting.

Special invitees include all members of the Camden-Kings Bay Navy League, The Camden County Board of Commissioners and Board of Education, the cities of Kingsland, St. Marys and Woodbine., and Camden County, The Rotary Club and Democrats and Republicans of Camden County, The Camden County Chamber of Commerce, The Camden Black Business Association, Woodbine Lions Club, Camden County Joint Development Authority, NSB Kings Bay—Fleet and Family Support and MWR.

For more information please call Marty Klumpp, director of The Camden Partnership

He was presented:

Community Appreciation Award
Presented to Captain Mike McKinnon
Commanding Officer, Kings Bay Naval
Submarine Base Georgia
In conjunction with
"Installation Excellence Award"
and encompassing everything Camden County stands
for, we would like to recognize you for your out-
standing relationship with the community
"One team, enhancing readiness, transform-
ing challenges into achievements"

Mike McKinnon, on May 29, 2007 was quoted from a speech at Federal Law Enforcement Training Center for Global War on Terror.

His change of command was on July 27 at the Submarine Veterans of World War II Memorial Pavilion

The Tribune & Georgian
By Ashley Smith

Capt. Mike McKinnon commanding officer of Naval Submarine Base Kings Bay, will be retiring July 27 after 26 years in the Navy. He said that he wants to be remembered as a captain who, through his compassion and understanding, molded the lives of his people and impacted them positively. "I truly care about them. Take care of your people and they'll take care of you." He said. And his people agree that he has been an excellent commander, and has taken very good care of them. "He is an outstanding captain, he is the best one I've had in 17 years. He is very supportive. He is most definitely a people person. He backs his chiefs 100%, and he lets us do our jobs. He is an awesome guy." ENC Willie Thornton said. He remembers McKinnon donating the chief petty officer building to the chiefs when they were in jeopardy of losing the old one, which Thornton is very grateful for.

MM2 (SS) Douglas Sommer said that McKinnon has been a good listener. "He's real open-minded; he'll listen to anything you have to say. He shows respect for his guys. He puts his guys first, and the man worries about his guys; if you have a problem you can let him know. That's what makes someone a good or bad person, if they stay behind their guys and worry about what they think. And he's funny too," he said. Sommer remembers gratefully how McKinnon helped his stay in the Navy when others were trying to process him out. "Because of him, I can now stay in the Navy and serve my country," he said.

And the *Tribune & Georgian*'s editorial (a rare occurrence) was about Mike:

OPINION
MCKINNON WILL KEEP UP HIS GOOD WORK

> The Navy may be losing one of its top commanders, but the Camden County Community will be fortunate to hang on to Captain Mike McKinnon. Following 26 years of distinguished service to the United States of America, McKinnon will be retiring from the Navy on Friday and entering civilian life for the first time since he was a teenager. The Sailors who worked with him and under him for the last three decades will remember him first and foremost as a compassionate and understanding leader who knew what it took to shape people's lives in a positive way. McKinnon will be remembered as a caring and supportive commander who took care of his people and allowed them to take care of him by doing their jobs to the best of their ability. His faith in his people was well regarded as the sailors at Kings Bay have won nearly every major Navy and Department of Defense award under his tenure. McKinnon knew everyone he works with and always managed to make their needs a propriety It never hurt that he was a pretty funny guy too. McKinnon's compassion also ran deep with the families of his Sailors and with the Camden County community at large. He was a smiling public face for Kings Bay throughout the county and an "A-list" guest for every community function. McKinnon had his share of mentors during his rise through the ranks from the congressman who nominated him for the Naval Academy to the commander who inspired him to truly love his naval service and to serve with pride, humility, integrity, and humor—that it was possible to both do things right and have fun. It is with those traits that he will enter the civilian world and embark on the next phase of his life. Camden Count is his home. He loves the community's patriotism, support of the Navy and the friendly helpful attitude. It's a place that would be hard to leave. Whenever McKinnon lands in Camden County and whoever he works with one thing is certain: we should all be lucky enough to have a boss or co-worker like him. May he always have fair winds and following seas.

The week before his change of command and retirement I went out to dinner with Mike and Rhonda and Hunt and Alyce Thornhill. We rode a golf cart around town and relived memories. The details of that evening will never be shared.

MILITARY CARD AND GIFT SERVICE

I can't take credit for thinking of the Military Card and Gift Service when I had the Hallmark store. Jennifer Fullmer tells it well. We saw a need for bringing in appropriate holiday cards to have enough for the season and for the submarines going out before the new seasons cards were received. The Hallmark Company questioned our reasoning when we had surplus left over after inventory of seasoned cards. When they found out why, they worked with us to have all we needed early.

Bonnie Dumont, wife of CMC Roger Dumont, master chief of Squadron 16, came to the store one day and we were talking about this. She inspired us all to ramp it up. We had an entire section of military gifts and seasonal cards months before most customers would even be thinking of that holiday. When the sailors came in, I would encourage them to buy two to three less expensive cards rather than one large expensive one. The thrill was the card when they opened their mailbox—not the value of the card. And then there were times that I just said, "You've got to send them one." And there would be no charge. There never was a charge if I had someone who didn't have the money to pay. It was just important that their wife and children heard from them. We went straight to the submarines at the waterfront many times. We would sit in the crew's mess or anywhere they had room for us and sit two to four hours bringing cards for every occasion possible. The program didn't break even—it lost in dollars but was successful to all of us in the store who had an opportunity to hear the appreciation from the sailor and the families. We also had a program for mothers and fathers to be. If a wife was having a baby while the husband was at sea, the husband could come in the store, pick out a gift (usually a large stuffed animal), maybe candy and a card, and have a friend call me when the baby was born. I would go to the hospital and take the card and presents to the new mother. I would say, "You don't know me, but your husband sent me." On one visit, the new mother's parents were sitting with her. They cried, she cried, and I cried. I knew how much it meant to have something you didn't expect from the new father who was missing such a beautiful event. There was no charge for the gifts, etc. I just loved to do it.

This column appeared during that time:

Camden County Tribune
Wednesday, March 3, 1993

TIDE TREASURES BRINGS HAPPINESS TO 'SUBMARINE WIDOWS'

By Jennifer K. Fullmer

I would like to take this opportunity and speak on behalf of the Navy wives of Camden County and thank Tide Treasures Hallmark for caring. Before submarines depart on patrol, owner Sheila McNeill and the lovely ladies from Tide Treasures offer special cards to the sailors. They have boxes of cards for each holiday that will be missed such as late birthdays, or just cards that say, "I love you and miss you."

After purchasing the card, the men sign and return them to the Hallmark store, marked with the date to be sent. Tide Treasures mails them to the wives, girlfriends or families who miss their husbands and sons. There is no correspondence during patrol. When sailors are gone, they are gone. There is no one-sided correspondence, since wives, friends, families, and girl-friends can send eight "family grams," 38-word letters that end up reading like police reports. "House fine. Kid fine. Dog spastic. Money okay. Weather nice. Cat ate bird. Paid taxes. Lonely. Miss you. Love you. Honey" They may appear unromantic, but the men love them. They are out there in some unknown location, floating along under the surface of the ocean. They have lost track of the date, working practically around the clock, and only know whether its morning or night by the meal being served.

They get lonely, and often depressed. Family-grams are the highlight of their weeks, bringing messages of love from loved ones whose images never leave his head. Family-grams keep the sailor connected, knowing there is someone at home who loves and cares for him and is awaiting his return. Police-reportish, maybe, but to a sailor concerned whether his wife is healthy, the kids are okay, the car is still running, and the money is holding out, they are blissful live love notes he can carry in his pock et and read over and over. Families at home are not so lucky. The submariners cannot send family-grams, letters or messages of any kind. As patrols neared, Sheila noticed many men and women coming to her for help choosing cards for upcoming holidays. Quite often these cards were not yet on display, the season to purchase them still to come. She began collecting holiday and birthday-type cars, as well as romantic loves notes for any occasion and saving them for the patrols.

The idea has been successful since she has convinced many of the sailors to participate. Some men give their wives all the cards at once, but many of the women would rather they didn't she told me. They like to receive them in the mail. Just looking into the mailbox and seeing the handwriting can be the biggest thrill of your week. Reading their messages and seeing their names with "I love you" written beside it may inspire the warmest memories. It may sound small and insig-

nificant, a card, but to wives lonely for their husband, it is utterly the most touching and romantic gift possible. Next to having him arrive at the doorstep, that is. This kind of excitement and romance is hard to understand for non-Navy couples, who see each other daily. Imagine going to work tomorrow. You are in your office building, except there are no windows and the phones have been removed, and you will have to stay there until, say June. I couldn't do it.

Patrols have been described as a divorce and remarriage every so many months. To an extent, this is true. When he is gone, the wives are totally on their own to make ends meet, take care of the house, the children, and keep their spirits up. Something as simple as receiving a card to show he remembered and cares makes it all worthwhile. And Sheila and the staff of Tide Treasures Hallmark cared enough to make it possible. Thank you.

My sales representative with Hallmark was also interested in this program. She submitted it to Hallmark headquarters for their newsletter. This story was listed as a "Create Crown Moments."

Create Crown Moments—Creating a Store for Navy Families

For the families of King's Bay Submarine Base in St. Marys. Ga., it's a Crown Moment every time they walk into Sheila's Hallmark. Sheila McNeill, owner of the store, Dinah Ulmer manager, and their staff do a lot to support the Navy families that are stationed nearby. They display cards for upcoming holidays several months in advance, so that husbands and wives can buy for each other before the spouse spends two months at sea. They then mail the cards on specified dates while the sailors are away. They have sold tickets to all the local events, including school plays, band performances, raffles and the Navy ball. They provide wedding registries for brides-to-be. And they provide constant counsel to sailors on how to keep in touch with their families while at sea.

But one of the biggest contributions comes with the birth of a new child. Staff members invite fathers-to-be who will be at sea when their child is born to come into their store to pick out cards and gifts for their wife and child. A friend notifies the store when the baby is born, and Sheila personally delivers the beautifully wrapped gifts to the new mother in the hospital saying, "You don't know me but your husband sent me." "All of this is done at no charge to the sailor. I work with the Navy a lot, and

I'm very aware of the issues these families face." Sheila says. "This is a way to for me to use my business to help out these brave men who fight for the freedom we all enjoy" Sheila has really taken the plight of Navy families to heart. She is a member of the National Defense Advisory Committee for Women in the Services, a national director of the Navy League of the United States, a member of the governor's Statewide Military committee, and chairwoman of the civilian group Friends of Kings Bay.

Although her work on these committees and the support she gives to Navy families genuinely comes from the heart, it also makes good business sense. "our store had a reputation as being honest and caring." Sheila says. "Our customers know we give a lot back to the community, and they're loyal to our store. They tell their friends about us, so our customer base is constantly growing. It's a very exciting place to be."

SECRETARY OF TRANSPORTATION NORM MINETA AND ASSISTANT SECRETARY OF DEFENSE FRED PANG

It was 2001 and I am at an event on Capitol Hill sponsored by the Navy League. I had heard that Secretary Mineta would be attending. He was the secretary of transportation under President Bush and President Clinton and in that capacity had the responsibility of the Coast Guard. He served six years—the longest serving secretary of Transportation in the history of the Department of Transportation. I found myself right in front of him. I tried to do what Congressman Jack Kingston described when he had five minutes with President Bush. I remembered his name coming up in my conversations with Secretary Pang. I knew they were friends. Secretary Pang was several levels up from the Defense Advisory Committee on Women in the Services that I was serving on, but we had had several great conversations. As it turned out, in his younger years, he had worked for Senator Sam Nunn and we had met during that time. I'm always amazed when you've been involved with the military or Capitol Hill for years you always run into old friends and life is good when you have a chance to catch up.

After we talked two or three minutes and I knew he had to go on to others, I said, "I think we have a mutual friend, Secretary Fred Pang."

Boy, did he react. "He's my best friend" he said.

"I have his card and had planned to call him to buy me lunch," I told Secretary Mineta. We talked about Navy League and the Coast Guard's Deep Water project, and I told him the commandant was really pleased he was the new secretary and how much his support was going to help the Coast Guard. Later as I was passing him—he was always with a crowd of people, he called out,

"Sheila, do you think I could join you and Fred for lunch? I tilted my head as I considered the request.

"I don't think so sir." He was a little surprised.

"I don't think we'll get him to pay for three lunches."

He laughed and said, "What if I pay for my lunch?"

"Sounds like a plan. we'll call you."

"That's a deal."

Later that week, I called Secretary Pang and told him of my conversation with Secretary Mineta. He was happy to meet with us both and called later to change the lunch to dinner at the Army Navy Club.

I could not wait to talk with Secretary Mineta about the Coast Guard. This was during the effort to recapitalize the Coast Guard and replace those "legacy" ships. He had no idea that I worked hours each week in support of the Coast Guard and had been doing so for a number of years so I thought I could enlighten him. Boy, was I wrong. This man knew more about the Coast Guard than anyone other than very senior officers that I had ever met. He could not only tell us the latest ship that had confiscated drugs but the name of the ship, the commanding officer, and the tonnage they confiscated.

We had a real blast at dinner. I can't relate a lot of it because so much was personal—and funny. He and his wife have a great sense of humor as do the Pangs.

I called Admiral Jim Loy, commandant of the Coast Guard, with my tales about the knowledge of Secretary Mineta on Coast Guard issues. He sent the following letter:

> Sheila,
>
> I appreciate your taking to time to tell me about your recent dinner with Secretary Mineta, Mrs. Mineta and the Pangs. With such a distinguished group choosing such a fascinating subject as the Coast Guard, the conversation must have sparkled! You are absolutely right about Secretary Mineta's active interest in the Coast Guard. His energetic leadership has already encouraged and impressed all of us at Coast Guard Headquarters. His choosing to seize yet another opportunity to learn more about his service secretary role confirms anew the seriousness with which he views this part of his responsibilities.
>
> Thank you for filling him in on the Navy League and the great public service you perform on our behalf. I look forward to seeing you at the Navy League's national convention in Reno.
>
> Sincerely, Jim

Later, as national president of the Navy League I received a request to talk at the annual meeting of the AFL/CIO. Our Merchant Mariners were greatly affected by the group. Admiral Al Herberger, former maritime administrator, I'm sure made that happen. He went with Arlie and me to the event in Los Vegas where the convention was being held. We arrived at the ballroom where the panel would speak. It was quite a list of speakers:

Secretary of Transportation, Mineta
President AFL CIO, John Sweeney
Congresswoman Loretta Sanchez
Congressman Norm Dicks
And the president of the Navy League

When Al, Arlie, and I arrived, it was just like a Navy League reception or a party at the church. Everyone knew each other, and everyone talked to those they knew. I have spent many of these events pulling people out of their comfort zone and talking to others. I wasn't so successful mingling at this reception. Of course, everyone knew and respected Admiral Herberger.

We sat down—it was almost time for the opening. About that time Secretary Mineta walked in—everyone stopped talking and looked toward the Secretary of Transportation. He saw me and came toward me with his arms out saying, "Sheila, I didn't expect to find you here!" We hugged, and he went to his seat. As each speaker was introduced a picture came up behind the dais—a picture about 8' × 12'. John Sweeney, President of AFL-CIO praised the work of the Navy League as did Congressman Dicks, Congressman Sanchez

It was my time to speak and the big picture came up behind me. They couldn't miss me and I thought maybe I needed to touch up that official photo. The remarks went well and at the reception everyone accepted me… a lot because of Norm Mineta!

Many later praised the two president's messages concerning the Merchant Marine and sea power in general. Robert Martin and Lou Marciello of Marine Engineers' Beneficial Association were particularly interested in our past coverage and said they would send a letter to the editor Rich Barnard.

Fred Pang worked for Senator Sam Nunn on the Senate Committee on Armed Services. And as he was doing that he completed the National and International Security Program at Harvard University. He was appointed by President Bill Clinton as assistant secretary of the Navy for manpower and reserves but by the time I met him he was principal deputy undersecretary of defense for personnel readiness. With that position came the Defense Advisory Committee on Women in the Services. And that is how we met. We found out that we both had enormous respect for Senator Nunn. He humored me by listening to my Sam Nunn stories.

Secretary Pang, through Captain Carolyn Prevatte, who was the director in charge of the Defense Advisory Committee on Women in the Services, offered me the possibility of a job on a Senate Committee. At the same time, she urged that I not leave the committee. I had made a commitment for three years and should finish that commitment. I was really working to streamline the visits and produce more specific results—results that gave a better idea of the concerns of our men and women in uniform. I often wondered if that was the best decision, but I will always be grateful to Secretary Pang for his support all of those years.

He told many people, who in turn passed the compliment on to me that I had changed the way they did business in the Pentagon—referring to my work on DACOWITS. Those three years I devoted much of my time to the work of the committee and hearing this from so many was so gratifying. I will always be indebted to Secretary Pang

The Camden Kings Bay Council of the Navy League was pleased that he agreed to come speak to our council several years later and we had a great time catching up. It's always easy with friends.

I'm glad that two old friends became my friends.

CHAIRMAN JOINT CHIEFS OF STAFF ADMIRAL MIKE MULLEN AND DEBORAH

CHIEF OF NAVAL OPERATIONS CHAIRMAN, JOINTS CHIEFS OF STAFF

I can't remember when I met Admiral Mike Mullen, but it seems that I have known him forever. When Admiral Mullen was vice chief of Naval Operations, he made sure I had any information I needed to better serve the Navy. He was concerned about the time it took me to go through security and get back in. He told me if I wanted to see any of the admirals I should let him know and he would have them come to my office! Of course, I never did that but it is indicative of the amount of support he gave me during that time.

I was in the Pentagon when I was national president. I was with Steve Petropolis waiting to meet with an admiral. We were waiting a few minutes, so I walked to the door. As I was standing there, Admiral Mullen walked by with about a half dozen naval officers. We were both surprised to see each other. He was stationed in Europe and was in town for a few days. He turned to the group he was with and told them to go ahead he wanted to talk with me and guided me to the office just a couple of doors down from the office where we were meeting. We had a wonderful chat and I lost track of time.

Mike was being considered for CNO and I asked him about this, but he had not had word (or wasn't talking). His job then was commander, Allied Joint Forces Command, Naples. He had responsibility for NATO missions in the Balkans, Iraq, and the Mediterranean, and he was commander US Naval Forces Europe. After about ten minutes we parted, and I slinked into the office where we had the appointment. Everyone wondered where I had been.

He did later hear about his selection as CNO and assumed those duties on July 22, 2005, just a few days after I left office as national president. And he followed that as the seventeenth chairman of the Joint Chiefs of Staff from October 1, 2007, until September 30, 2011.

When he was CNO the community really wanted him to come speak at our annual Camden Partnership's Community That Cares luncheon. I asked for time to see him and he answered I should come and that he would ask his wife, Deborah, to join us. Walt Yourstone and Marty Klumpp were with me. They visited with some of the folks Walt had worked with when he was administrative assistant to acting secretary of the Navy, H. T. Johnson (see a section with Secretary Johnson's stories), while I met with Admiral Mullen. After lunch, I met up with Walt and Marty in the Chairman's waiting room. Although his waiting room was literally full of admirals, most of which I knew, he still took the time to take us in his office for a photo op.

During lunch, I was trying my best to convince him on why he should come to Kings Bay. I had a list of individual organizations, cities, and entities that jointly would sponsor his visit. I knew and agreed that he should not just speak "to the choir," but that it was important to speak to a variety of citizens. I also mentioned the SSGN and reminded him that he had not toured one as yet. Deborah asked, "What is an SSGN?"

Mike, in his understated, sarcastic, aloof way, he said, "Sheila?" indicating I should explain it.

Well, I did. I gave the full story of the reduction, the plan to save, and the benefit of the SSGN ending by saying, "They have the equivalent fire power of an entire battle group."

At that point he corrected me, "Sheila, that's submarine lore."

Perhaps I should have said "some entire battle groups," but I could see his mood and he was enjoying giving me a hard time. Then I wondered what to say. Should I argue with the chairman in front of his wife? Could I win? So I smiled and said, "Sir, do you want accuracy or do you want enthusiasm?"

He smiled and answered, "Enthusiasm."

I repeated my earlier description without another interruption from him.

He and Deborah later came to Kings Bay. We had quite a time preparing for his visit. It was a major event for the entire community. We declared "Mike Mullen Day" throughout the community with billboards, marquees, banners, and a proclamation from each of the cities and the county. Mike told me he was coming in the night before in time for dinner and asked that Arlie and I join him and Deborah. The day before he arrived I had a call from his security folks at NCIS who wanted to know the name and location of the restaurant where we would eat. They would get with the security folks on base and cover his route and "sweep the restaurant" before he arrived. They wanted to know if there would be any other stops on the trip. I told him I'd love for them to "sweep" my retail store. The staff would love it. The agent said, "Ma'am, you know we don't do this with a broom?" I assured him I knew the difference, but I don't think he was sure.

Deborah took some well-deserved rest time—she also knew Mike and I had a lot of catching up to do so she decided to have a little down time while we had dinner. Arlie, Mike, and I had a very nice dinner and caught up on all our friends and the latest on what he was doing. He told me he missed his friends in the Navy. His time was now divided between all the services and with the war he spent more time with the Army and Marine Corps.

We could almost forget in that small restaurant that only seated about twenty people that the three of us were having a secluded dinner. The fact that two black vans were parked outside, that the tables had NCIS agents with a few locals who wondered what was going on made it a little less casual and intimate!

Keith Post just happened to come by. Of course, he knew we were meeting for dinner, so we laughed about this "coincidence" later.

The day of the luncheon was just perfect. He was impressed with the work we had done on this event and told me this was his first ever "Mike Mullen Day." Kevin Dalton had arranged for a miniature billboard, and it was sitting as a place card. Mike asked that I be sure to give it to his aide when they left. He planned to put it on his kitchen table to impress Deborah. That day Deborah spent all day meeting with the submarine officers' wives and Fleet and Family Support.

When he became chairman, I visited him several times. It was never easy—his schedule was unbelievable. I read an article in the May 2010 edition of Fast Company and that made me even more appreciative of having any of his time. I tried to wait until a few days out to ask for an appointment. It seemed presumptuous for me to ask his staff to block out any time in the future. One of the times I was in DC. I called from Capitol Hill to see if he had a few minutes. The staff was so nice but turned me down. About an hour later when I'm meeting with a congressional office, I received a call and time had opened up, so I took off shortly for the Pentagon.

When I met with him, I talked with him about the funding for the SSBN X. We discussed the costs and the timing. When I told him, I planned to add to our papers the request to make this funding a top-level funding over the defense budget. I said this is a strategic issue and should not have to be all funding by the Navy but should be shared by all services.

He replied, "Sheila, this was my idea in the first place."

"Well, I know I read it somewhere. So now you won't be PO'd at me, right?" He smiled.

After the visits, he walked me out of his office. I said, "Admiral, I didn't ask you, did you have anyone interesting or famous in your office today?"

"Yes," he answered stoically with that wry smile.

"Are you going to tell me who?" I asked

"No," he answered.

"Are you answering that way because it is confidential or because you are being difficult?" I asked with all the staff waiting to hear his answer.

"Both," he answered.

We all laughed, and I was escorted to the security entrance.

One Sunday night, I read in the local papers that he and the president would be traveling to Russia on the Start treaty. I got directly up and sent an e-mail that said, "Don't give away any of our submarine capabilities! I told him that I had invited President Obama to speak at Kings Bay and if he had a chance he should encourage the president to accept our invitation. After all I told him, it's a big deal to get your name on the marquee of the waffle house. The next morning, I woke up to an answer: "About an hour out from Moscow as I write. The job does call for a little travel."

On December 7, 2007, I spent the night at Keith's house. After a long conversation with them about his gratitude to Admiral Mullen, I got up and sent Mullen an e-mail telling him that my friend, a retired submariner, and his partner wanted to thank him for all he was doing with "Don't ask, don't tell." I told him that Keith was in the submarine force for twenty-two years, and the policy created a lot of pain for him. He chose to retire rather than move up to his next job as chief of the boat with a requirement to enforce DADT. I added that the month before the Navy and the Coast Guard both presented him with Distinguished Service Medals for his work with the Navy League. I told Mike he would go down in history as one of the great ones but also reminded him he was too young to "go" any time soon. I later forwarded a letter Keith wrote to him. He e-mailed me back and said he was actually on the way to Capitol Hill on a DADT hearing.

One of my later e-mails demonstrates how he is a man of few words. Mike was the oldest of five children. His father was Hollywood press agent Jack Mullen who worked with Jimmy Durante. It always seemed so unlikely that a young man from a theatrical family, born and raised in California, could have his very distinguished career. When I received an e-mail from him in 2014, it had the signature "Mike Mullen, MGM."

I wrote back, "Seriously? MGM—is that some kind of new weapon or are you really in show business?"

He replied, "My initials—seriously, Mike—I wasn't being funny, just stupid."

I am very proud to call Mike and Deborah Mullen friends. They had a great world tour. You could tell that both President Bush and President Obama had great confidence in him. Deborah was a staunch supporter of our military families. I don't know how they kept up the pace for six years.

NATO ON JEKYLL

1997

Woody Woodside, president of the Brunswick Golden Isles Chamber of Commerce, called me one day and said he had a request that the community assist in a visit from US Joint Chiefs of Staff General John Shalikashvili. The General was finishing a brief stopover in South Georgia as part of the National Alliance Treaty Organization (NATO) annual meeting. He asked me to help with that visit. The *Times-Union* reported that "NATO is a defense alliance formed in 1949 at the beginning of the Cold War. It served as a buffer against the expansion of the Soviet Union into Western Europe. It originally consisted of Belgium, Canada, Denmark, France, Great Britain, Iceland, Italy, Luxembourg, the Netherlands, Norway, Portugal and the United States. Greece and Turkey were admitted to the alliance in 1952, the former Federal Republic of Germany 1955 and Spain in 1982. NATO's purpose is to enhance the stability, well-being and freedom of its members by means of a system of collective security." (In 2001, Arlie and I visited Malcolm and Shirley Fages when he was assigned to NATO.)

They arrived on Monday, September 15, 1997, so we planned a reception for that evening. The committee gets together once a year in different parts of the world for meetings and to observe military operations. The last time the committee met in the United States was in 1991, so it was important that we made a good impression. Having the meeting at the Cloister made our preparations easy. At least one of the members was to visit Kings Bay but the great majority would be in meetings the entire two days. Arlie and I really hit it off with General Sir Charles Guthrie who was minister of defense for Great Britain. He and his wife were wonderful dinner partners. We later had a very nice letter from General Guthrie thanking us for our hospitality to the British ships and crew who came to Naval Submarine Base Kings Bay. Lt. General Wiseman was his assistant and was very interesting to talk with.

(Three years later I am with Linda Hoffman and her husband Jim at the club level of the Ritz-Carlton. We kept looking at each other wondering who the other was. He came over and told me he had met me on Sea Island at the NATO conference. What a surprise that was to both of us. He sent his aide to his room to get one of his cards and we talked. The next morning, I joined him for breakfast and he invited Arlie and me to come visit him in Brussels. He said I would enjoy the dinners he gives three times a week and empha-

sized how inexpensive the trips from DC to Brussels were. If I had not had so much travel with Navy League I would have taken him up on that!)

General Shali's retirement was later that year in October. The defense secretary at the time was Secretary William Perry who had high praise for the chairman. He later sent a nice letter to Henry Bishop who was chairman of the chamber asking him to thank Woody and me for our help. His gift of an engraved box still sits on my coffee table.

The letter was this:

> Mr. Henry Bishop
> Chairman, Brunswick Golden Isles Chamber of Commerce
>
> Dear Mr. Bishop,
>
> Please extend my appreciation to the members of the Chamber of Commerce and the Friends of Kings Bay for their support during the recent NATO Military Committee Fall Tour. Our three days in Georgia were delightful!!
>
> I would like also to extend my personal gratitude to Mr. Woody Woodside and Mrs. Sheila McNeill for their many hours they spent to ensure our visitors received a warm Georgia welcome. And a special thank you to everyone who hosted us at the reception at The Cloister. The NATO Defense Chiefs and their wives had the highest praise for the quality of service as well as the facility As exceptional, many of our guest described the visit to the Golden Isles—the highlight of the tour.
>
> Please accept my gratitude for your superb support in helping make the 1997 NATO Fall Tour an overwhelming success.
>
> With best wishes,
> Sincerely, John M Shalikashvili,
> Chairman of the Joint Chiefs of Staff

I must remind readers that I did not pay for the club level at hotels—sometimes I just got lucky! So many events happen like this when you work with the military. You meet them, believing you will never see them again but you usually do. It's always a pleasure.

NEY AWARD AND MY PROMISE

NAVY CAPTAIN EDWARD F. NEY MEMORIAL AWARDS FOR OUTSTANDING FOOD SERVICE

In 1995, I was on an underway with the USS *Tennessee* SSBN (734). I spent part of the day hanging out with the mess specialist now known as culinary specialist in the dining room. Master Chief Coogan and I were playing cards and talking. I brought up some of the better restaurants where he had dined. We talked about which restaurants were the best and which ones we wanted to go to. The Cloister was on the top of the list, especially for Master Chief Coogan. I knew that they were competing for the Ney Award—Captain Edward F. Ney Memorial Award for outstanding food services. I got caught up in the enthusiasm and promised them if they won the award I would treat the food services team to dinner. Squadron 20 submitted USS *Tennessee* as the winner of the squadron and ultimately the base. It was then sent to compete nationally. I received a call a few months later from Master Chief Coogan, "Sheila we won the Ney Award!"

"You're kidding me!"

"No, seriously, we won!"

"Then let's get together and determine a date."

Who would have thought they would be the winners? Not that they are not great but there are so many ships in the Navy. I first called Rear Admiral Chuck Beers. He later expanded the outreach with the Cloister.

I called Bill Jones, president of Sea Island Company, and told him I was bringing the mess specialists from the USS *Tennessee*. I told him I didn't want a "discount" The only thing I was asking for was that I wanted the Cloister chefs to know they were coming and treat them like the visiting chefs they were.

Arlie and I invited the officers and crew to come by our home for a pre-reception. We then left for Sea Island. You should have seen the response with those white bell bottoms mixed with chiefs and officers walking through that dining room with everyone standing up and shaking their hands as we traveled to the private room. We were then taken to the wine cellar and were amazed at the assortment—then a trip to the kitchen where tips were given by the chefs and questions were answered.

At the end of the evening they brought me the bill—I was expecting about two thousand dollars (and that is back in 1995), but there was a note from Bill. "Thanks, Sheila, for bringing them—and it's on us." Wow, amazingly generous with so many guests.

It was such a success that the Cloister offered to sponsor the top submarine in food services at Kings Bay every year! The *Brunswick News* ran a story on February 28, 1997, which included the following:

Navy League Teams up with the Cloister in Presenting Culinary Excellence Award

Instead of having to prepare and serve the meal themselves, the food service team of USS Rhode Island (SSBN 740) (Blue) was recently treated to an outstanding meal at The Cloister. In addition to the meal prepared and served by the award-winning chefs at The Cloister, the food service team also received a mirror engraved with the name of the award, the submarine name and participant's insignia.

Guests were MSC (SS) Kenneth Winslow, MS1 (SS) Richard Bryant; MS1 Charles Csicsek; MS1 (SS) Patrick Rameriz; MS2 (SS) Timothy Gosser; MSSN Angel Rivera and MSSA Ervin, Rhode Island Blue's command officer Cmdr. Gregg Balzer, and supply officer, Lt. Cmdr. Mark Jones were at the dinner to support the award-winning food service team as were Hugh Mayberry, National President of the Navy League, Howard Jones former chief executive officer of the Cloister, Camden County Navy League Council President Jack Mead and Vickie, Rear Admiral Chuck Beers and Susan, of course, me and Arlie.

Captain Balzer sent a very nice note later:

On behalf of the RHODE ISLAND, I thank you for your collaboration with the Navy League's presentation of the highly prestigious "Cloister Award for Culinary Excellence." Your time and effort to take and develop the pictures of this spectacular event were greatly appreciated. Thank you again for your generosity and making this event a memorable one.

Sincerely,
Gregg Balzer

They did it right—thank you, Sea Island Company.

From 1997 to 2001, the Cloister continued to host the top Ney Awardee at NSB Kings Bay. I have listed those from 1995:

2000 USS *Kentucky* (SSBN 737) (GOLD)
1999 USS *Pennsylvania* (SSBN 735) (GOLD)
1998 USS *Tennessee* (SSBN 734) (GOLD)
1997 USS *Nebraska* (SSBN 739) (BLUE)
1996 USS *Tennessee* (SSBN 734) (GOLD)

1995 USS *Rhode Island* (SSBN 740) (BLUE)

In February 2001, I went to the Cloister for the annual Ney Award, Arlie had his state board meeting in Macon. Master Chief Coogan came from Norfolk to be the guest speaker and told the story on how the Cloister Award and the dinner started.

That event included commander, Submarine Group 10 RADM. Rich Terpstra and his wife, Sue, and the commanding officer of USS *Kentucky*, Captain Mike McKinnon and his wife, Rhonda.

Awardees were the following:

MMCM Bradley, Chief of the Boat
ENS Michael Ogden, Supply Officer
MSC Cameron, Leading Mess
Management Specialist
MSI Juarez
MS2 Babcock
MS2 Fritz
MS3 Taggart
MS3 Murray
MS3 Shackelford
SKCS Rinderer, Leading Storekeeper
SK2 Pollard
SA Witham
Lt. Ezelle, Supply Officer, Group 10
MSC Harrell, Leading Mess Management Specialist, Group 10 (Note: Master Chief Harrell later served in the White House and is now teaching at the local college)
Lt. Clarke, Supply Officer
SKCM Johnson, Leading Storekeeper, Group 10
MSCM Coogan, SUBLANT Mess Management Specialist, Group 10
JO2 Kempton, Photographer for *Periscope*
CDR Davis, Chief of Staff, Submarine Squadron 16
LT Abrams, Supply Officer, Squadron 16
MSCS Houston, Leading Amess Specialist, Squadron 16

Yes, there was a great group: Commanding Officer of NSB Kings Bay Frank Stagl and his wife, Mary, and the above crew. I enjoyed spending time with the young enlisted and their wives and dates. It was a really big evening for them and the young women were dressed as if for prom. I sat with James Gilman our Navy League council president and Michael Johnson, Manager of the Cloister and his wife. And the celebrity of the evening Chef Todd with the Cloister. RADM Terpstra and I had a spirited discussion.

Note: My work with Navy League may have let this program slip. In May 2016, I met the new president of Sea Island Company, Scott Steilen, at the radio station where we both we waiting to do interviews. I told him this story. He said, "Sheila, we'd love to do that again if a submarine from Kings Bay is the recipient—just let me know." I love Sea Island Company and I know Glynn County realizes the strong support they give this community.

CAPTAIN JOHN NUERENBERGER AND SUE

When John and Sue were at Kings Bay it was a different time. It was a wonderful time.

It was a time when an admiral at Kings Bay was not even being considered. Rear Admiral Arleigh Campbell and his wife, Bonnie, lived in Charleston and made regular visits to Kings Bay. The Dolphin Scholarship auctions were held in Charleston and Arlie was auctioneer during those years too. The Campbells were so gracious they opened their quarters to us many times, and we would spend the weekend with them. They were followed by Rear Admiral Tom Meinicke and his wife, Alice. One of the first events I had with Alice was an underway on one of the submarines at Kings Bay. It was an all-woman group and we had a wonderful time. At some point one of the crew asked me my name and I replied, "Alice Meinicke." I quickly told Alice and explained that is was a moment's decision without a lot of thought. She loved it. She said her entire husband's career she could do and say most anything, and if anyone complained, she could say, "It was Sheila pretending to be me!"

Everything was new and exciting. The incoming military didn't know what to expect but were pleased with what they found. Of course, there were a lot of exaggerated stories about the wildlife and less exaggerated but true stories about the lack of businesses and "things to do" in the county. When they realized that the "things to do" that they missed were only a pleasant thirty-minute drive—a drive they made daily in larger communities—they appreciated the quieter, beautiful area of Camden County.

John was commanding officer of Trident Training Facility (TTF) taking command on July 10, 1987. He relieved Captain Bill Ramsey as Commander of Naval Submarine Base Kings Bay on July 21, 1989. The ceremony was held in the gym where over four hundred guests attended. The speaker was Rear Admiral Kenneth C. Malley, director of Strategic Systems Programs. We began working together a little more. He was well respected by his staff and the other commands.

On October 21, 1989, he invited the public to visit NSB Kings Bay in honor of the Navy's 214th birthday. The presentation was given in the auditorium of the massive Trident Training Facility and a historic submarine display was in the lobby. Tour buses ran every ten minutes from the training facility parking area to the port services area and return. At the port services area, there was a display of various environmental control equipment, tugboats, and other small craft.

During this time, there were seafood buffets at the "clubs of Kings Bay." The buffet was a huge selection of every kind of seafood possible. It was both beautiful and delicious. Almost every Friday night, Arlie and I would join our friends at the club. It truly was a magical time. That was the place to go because there was nowhere else to go. Everyone was there. Every Friday night. You could catch up with any officer you were working with. We made friends during that time that remain friends to this day. We had a great time suggesting ideas to John when he and Sue had an upcoming wedding anniversary. Several times we had teased Sue about the fact that she was the only one who had never stayed at the BOQ. And that is just what he did. He packed some clothes for them both (without her seeing him) and added a few amenities in the suite, and after having dinner, he drove straight to the room.

When they received his orders for Naples, Italy, I had a shirt printed for Sue with "I slept with the commanding officer of Kings Bay at the BOQ" and presented it at a party we gave at our home. Sue had been working with Trident Refit Facility in accounting, so these new orders were it a big change for both. They invited us to visit them in Naples, and we set up a time a few months later. We had a wonderful time. John was working most of the time and Sue would go with us when she could. She was a great guide. When we returned home, one night it was pretty late. John said, "Hello, I'm going to bed." Or something equally as short. I stopped him and told him he should be more gracious.

"What do you want me to say?" he asked he asked with a grin in his attempt at being unhospitable.

"You should ask what we did today."

"What did you do today?"

"We toured."

"You should now ask if we had a good time."

"Did you have a good time?"

"Yes, we did, thank you."

"And now, you say, 'I'm going to turn in.'"

"I'm going to turn in."

"Now wasn't that more gracious?"

On Sunday, they asked us what we wanted to do. I replied, "We are going to all stay in but we can't talk to you or you to us. You do whatever you usually do on Sundays, we rest and read and tonight we can ask each other how the day was." It worked—and was fun. We had a wonderful time taking day trips and staying overnight on some of those trips

Sue took the time to take us to Pompeii. On the return trip, we found out that the motorway was shut down. She managed to figure out another route home so we arrived safe and sound late that night. She also helped us arrange a few days on our own. We stayed in a hostel one night—very barren where one fairly large room had the shower in the middle of the ceiling—no tub—just wash and let the water fall into a drain in the middle of the floor. What an experience.

The entire week was a range of wonderful experience made possible by the Nurembergers.

* * * * *

Every year they bring in friends to share the accommodations of their timeshare in Moncrieff (Black Mountain), North Carolina. We joined them in November 2009 with Marcia and Jim Fletcher, Malcolm and Shirley Fages, Chuck and Greer Meyer, Mary and Joe Setser, Rick and Reenie Adams, Ray and Ellie, and others. There must be about fifteen couples in total but it seems to work out that most get to attend when they can. It was a great gathering of friends. Some of the days everyone would split up, some would play golf, others would tour and others, like me would stay at the house. Neither of us played golf. Arlie would do some touring but I was content to sit with a book while everyone got exhausted during the day and visit when they returned for happy hour.

John and Sue live in the Charleston area now. And yes, we've been to their house and spent the night several times. The always let us in.

UNITED STATES SENATOR SAM NUNN, COLLEEN AND MICHELLE

MICHELLE NUNN

Arlie called me a few weeks after I had decided perhaps this book should be named "What are you doing here?" He said, "Remember when you were in Japan and ran into Senator Nunn he asked you the same thing?" That clinched it! the name of my book would be "What are you doing here?" One of my favorite stories is about Senator Nunn is when I was president of the Camden Kings Bay Council of the Navy League. I had written several letters to Senator Nunn asking him to speak at our council.

In March 1994, I finally wrote a letter that got his attention. I received a call in late March that he could speak the next week on March 31. Wow! I had less than a week to prepare. In fact, I had to call the local newspaper the *Tribune & Georgian* and say to the editor, Linn Hudson, "hold the presses." The paper was published weekly, and it was the only issue we could get it in so they held it up long enough to add the story. We used every means we had to get the word out to everyone and had the biggest luncheon we ever had.

> *Hudson, with the Camden County Tribune had this report:*
> *For more than two years Sheila McNeill pursued a southeast Georgia visit by US. Senator Sam Nunn. Finally, McNeill's persistence is paying off. Considered one of the nation's leading authorizes on national defense, Nunn will visit Kings Bay Naval Submarine Base on March 31. Nunn will be the guest of the Camden Kings Bay Council of the U.S. Navy League and the Federal Managers Association at 11:30 luncheon at Kings Bay McNeill said she has been in contact with Nunn's office on numerous occasions in attempt to bring the veteran senator to the area. A recent three sentences, 12-word request seemed to catch the attention of Nunn's staff. "They said they are used to getting four page letters on requests), said McNeill local Navy League president…*

The day came, and it was sold out. Right before I introduced Senator Nunn as we sat at the table he asked if anyone had seen my letter I told him no. He asked permission to read it to the audience. I laughed as I gave him permission. To the audience, he said, "I was on a plane traveling to the next event and reading my correspondence.

There was a letter from Sheila that said, "Dear Sam, we are good, we are your constituents, enough is enough—we want you to come." The senator asked his staff to give him the full letter from Sheila.

They replied, "That is her full letter, sir, in its entirety."

Senator Nunn answered, "Then give her a call and tell her we are coming." The base paper, Kings Bay Periscope had the following article on the first page:

NUNN VISITS BASE

> *Approximately 300 people squeezed into the Clubs of Kings Bay March 31 to hear Sen. Sam Nunn, D-Ga speak at a luncheon sponsored by the Camden Kings Bay Council of the U.S. Navy League and Federal Managers Association. Prior to the luncheon, the veteran politician visited St. Mary Elementary School and toured USS Georgia (SSBN 729). Chairman of the Senate Armed Services Committee, Nunn is considered to be one of America's leading authorities on national defense.*
>
> *During his speech, Nunn comment on how pleased he was to see Kings Bay sailors volunteering their time to the community. "The*

community means so much to the spirit of the people who are stationed here, and the people stationed here mean an awful lot to the community," said Nunn, who was named one of the five most respected senators in a 1990 survey of senior congressional aides. "It was a pleasure to see the Navy volunteers out at the St. Marys school relating to the young people. These volunteers are doing something about the internal security of our nation. They play a tremendous role in protecting America's future just as they do when they go out on patrol." Nunn has watched the relationship between the community and Navy grow over the years and said Kings Bay will be around for years to come

"My general assessment here at Kings Bay is that you'll have a pretty stable mission here, said the Perry native. "the Base Closure Commission meets in 1995, but I don't see a threat to Kings Bay. I think it's one of the most stable bases in the country." With the military drawdown affecting all the armed services, Nunn stated that there are still many national security challenges to be faced, especially for the Navy

The military budget has been reduced by one-third in the last eight to ten years," Nunn said. "I think it's going down too much and too rapidly. Last year, the Navy faced at least six major operational crises with each one requiring extensive mobilization of forces. Since the end of the Cold War a lot of groups who hated each other over the years feel that they can now unleash their hatred without being reined in by the superpowers... this is clear when you look at the tragedy that's happened in the former Yugoslavia." Nunn went on to state several challenges the military faces today. Maintaining the quality of personnel, maintaining the readiness of military forces and paying attention to relationships with Russia are a few Nunn stressed. "We have at the Armed Services Committee put up $400 billion the last three years, so we can help the Russians get control of their own nuclear weapons," Nunn said. "The possibility of Russian nuclear weapons getting into the hands of Syria, Iraq, Iran Libya, North Korea or other countries like that is a profound national security challenge." Nunn also express other international concerns—North Korea, Somalia, NATO—and how the U.S. as the only residual superpower will deal with peacekeeping in this new world. After the senator's speech, a brief question and answer session followed. Nunn, who served in the Coast Guard and later graduated from Emory Law School with honors, and elected to the U.S. Senate in 1972 after serving five years as a state representative.

When I was nominated by Rear Admiral Jerry Ellis for DACOWITS (Defense Advisory Committee on Women in the Service), one of the first people that I sent a request for a recommendation was to Senator Nunn. He was able to get it back to me within the three-day limit that I had been given. He wrote on August 16, 1995,

> *Dear Admiral Ellis,*
>
> *I was pleased to learn that Sheila McNeill is being nominated for a position on the Defense Advisory Committee on Women in The Services. As her record indicates, Sheila has a long history of services to the Brunswick and Kings Bay communities. Sheila serves as president of the Georgia chapter of the Navy League of the United States and Director of the Camden County Chamber of Commerce. She has held several distinctive positions within numerous professional and civic organizations in Georgia including the American Cancer Society, United Way, Georgia PTA and Women Business Owners. In addition, she is the recipient of many honors, including the recipient of a "Points of Life" designation for support of the military in the Persian Gulf and the Submarine Lady of the Submarine Force Award. Sheila's record clearly indicates a dedication to the support of our servicemen and women and the community in general.*
>
> *I am pleased to endorse her nomination to serve on the Defense Advisory Committee on Women in the Services and would express to all concerned my hope that her nomination be given every consideration consistent with the established procedures of the Committee.*
>
> *Sincerely, Sam*

When I read this letter years later, I was reminded of how green I was at the time and how my affiliations look twenty years later. Thank you, Sam Nunn, for having faith in me at that time.

Later as a member of the executive committee, I was in Japan going into the lobby of the hotel where we were staying. The hotel had bungalows that were separate from the main building. I saw Sam walk by with six or eight gentlemen. I quietly followed him down several pathways and was the last person to walk into his bungalow. I certainly gave him a surprise and he said, "Sheila, what you are doing here?"

I told him, "It's because of you, sir I'm on a DACOWITS trip."

When Adm. Frank Kelso, chief of Naval Operations and nearing his retirement, there were hearings on Capitol Hill to determine if, after Tailhook, he should retire with three or four stars. Arlie and I happened to be having lunch with Senator Nunn and a few others. As he got up to leave, he told me what they were about a to vote on. It was if Senator Kelso would retire with three or four stars.

I said, "Four stars, Senator, four stars. There is no better supporter of women than Admiral Kelso."

"You may be the only woman in this building that says so, but thank you."

Arlie and I went into the galley and watched the proceedings. As all the discussion went on a woman sitting behind us asked her husband, "What is Tailhook?"

"Oh, some women's lib thing," he replied.

I was shocked that something with that much publicity would be totally unheard of by American citizens. I know sometimes when you're in the news and visible to so many people you think everyone is talking about it and everyone knows about it. Obviously, that isn't so. As it turned out every woman in the Senate marched in together asking that Admiral Kelso, one of the most supportive of women military officers, should retire with three stars. The Congress made a great decision. Admiral Kelso retired with four stars.

In 2014 Arlie and I were with my grandson and his family at Long Boat Key when I received a call from Senator Nunn. His daughter Michelle was running for Congress, and he wanted to get her up to speed on our strategic missile submarines. Since it was hot in the campaign cycle the base could not be involved and Sam was well aware of that so he asked me to brief her. Right after that I received a call from Linda Victory and Reenie Adams both active in the local Democratic Party wanting to discuss a reception for Michelle. They decided on the PSA building—they were able to accommodate a small room for the briefings and a larger room for the reception.

This was a wonderful opportunity for Camden to get their issues out as well as our military, so we started planning. Attending were Dr. Will Hardin, superintendent of schools; county manager Steve Howard, on Spaceport; Mayor John Morrissey (St. Marys); Mayor Kenneth Smith (Kingsland); Mayor Steve Parrott (Woodbine); Tonya Rosado, the Camden County Chamber of Commerce; Jimmy Starline, chairman, Camden County Board of Commissioners; Joel Hanner with Georgia Power and chairman of The Camden Partnership; Charlie Smith Jr., chairman of the Joint Development Authority; and Bill Gross with W. H. Gross and Company. With my job I'm always careful about nonpartisanship so we made sure we invited others running for the Senate to come to Camden but Michelle was the first to recognize the value. After the event, we had the following notes concerning Michelle Nunn's visit to Camden:

From Sally Rossier: "I spoke with Sam Nunn about the events in Camden County today. He said that the briefing was 'exceptional, the ultimate in what they could be. You guys were wonderful, and he gave you full credit for an amazing day. And he just kept talking about it. I am proud to know and work with each and every one of you."

From Michelle Nunn: "Thank you so very much for organizing such an informative briefing on St. Marys Submarine Base and Camden County, especially the Spaceport, and to see how closely the Navy and the community are working together. I look forward to reviewing the briefing book that you thoughtfully took the time to prepare for me. You know St. Marys holds a special place in my family and I know that with your leadership every day will continue to be military appreciation day in Camden County. Thank you for everything that you have done and continue to do."

From Sam Nunn: "Thank you for the excellent preparation for our recent visit to Camden County and our discussion on Kings Bay. The key players were all sitting around the table and I thought the briefing was on point and very helpful on both the military as well as the community issues. Only you could have pulled this off and all the Nunns are grateful."

On Michelle Nunn's blog: "In the last few weeks, I have had the opportunity to talk with folks at military bases and communities all over Georgia. Ron and the kids joined me as we traveled throughout South Georgia from Savannah to Moultrie to Vidalia. We have been to barbeques and fish frys and food pantries and business incubators and we have seen the best of Georgia. I am so glad that my children are getting to experience Georgia's spirt of leadership, cooperation, and innovation.

We have met people in diners, taverns, parks, and community centers. I have been newly inspired by the hope and sense of possibility that I experience.

I also want to take a moment to share a few of these stories with you. In Camden County, I met dedication. The community and business leaders I met with are committed to working together and support the men and women that serve at the naval base at Kings Bay and to expanding the base's capacity to continue to fulfill and extend its critical mission of nuclear deterrence. Community members are working together to ensure that businesses continue to invest in Camden and to create the conditions for big new opportunities. The folks in Camden are rallying together with a big vision and a cooperative spirit."

What a gracious and intelligent woman. You could tell she was Colleen and Sam's daughter! Sam Nunn's remarks to the community reception/briefing group at the same event: "I'm looking at Sheila's background I saw that she was one of the (*Georgia Trend*'s) 100 top influential Georgians. I think you should remove one of those zeros."

In June 2016, I was pleased to help arrange a tour of Kings Bay for Sam and Colleen and their family. It was great to be with him as he was briefed on board one of our SSBNs, the Trident Training Facility and then delicious lunch at the base galley. "President Jimmy Carter and Senator Nunn's part in the creation of Naval Submarine Base Kings Bay is usually a point of discussion with visitors touring for the first time," Public Affairs Officer Scott Basset shared with the senator and his family. It was a pleasure for all of us to be a part of that that tour. Sam sent the following e-mail that I forwarded to those mentioned.

Dear Sheila,

All of the Nunns and the Lauers thank you—our tour was perfect!!! I hope that you will express our appreciation to Captain Jenks, Captain McKinney and Scott Bassett and their teams for a terrific day. For me, the memories were many and moving—for the young crowd, and Peter—this was a thrilling dream come true. Much of the information was new—even to me—and encouraging. I drove away from Kings Bay even more confident in our Navy's leadership and our nation's deterrent. I also came away—as always—inspired by the local community support and your outstanding leadership. With great appreciation,

Sam

Senator Nunn and I have kept in touch through the years—mainly me trying to get him to speak somewhere or wanting his opinion on something. We ran into each other on planes, airports, and restaurants!

I sure respect that man and I feel fortunate to have known him these thirty years.

CAPTAIN JOHN O'NEILL AND SHELLY

COMMANDING OFFICER, NAVAL SUBMARINE BASE KINGS BAY

I first met John when he was aide to RADM Tom Robertson in the early nineties. I met Shelley a few months later. John had brought her, she was his fiancée then, as his guest to the Dolphin Scholarship Auction where, as usual, Arlie was auctioning. I sat with Shelley and we had some time to get acquainted. She asked what I did and I said, "I have a card shop—I sell cards."

"Well, at least you don't sell caskets," she replied.

I paused a moment and said, "No my husband does that." When she realized I was serious, she got a little embarrassed and asked me not to tell anyone. I told her *then and there* that I had to tell it. It was just too funny.

Years later *Captain* John O'Neill returned to St. Marys. He was at a chamber function within a week of taking over the reins as commanding officer of NSB Kings Bay. He was impressed with the way the county had grown and the reputation of our schools. Their son, Connor, was in his senior year of high school and played football. The state is supportive enough to allow military families who have children transiting into the system to be given the opportunity to try out for sports even if they have missed the deadline. They also will accept immediately a military family student who is in advanced classes. Of course, they require the necessary documentation but in the meantime the student doesn't miss out.

Connor tried out and became a member of the team. His first day of school, he boarded school buses with a hundred or so kids he didn't know and went off for a week of football camp. How is that for tough! All three were at the age that made changes hard.

He was a wonderful commanding officer. Warm, kind, smart, approachable, analytical, always ready to work with you on solving any problem—all the attributes of a leader. Shelly was a great First Lady. She knew many of those in Camden County and reached out to those she didn't. With three children: grade school, middle school, and high school—they all made us proud. There is no better way to tell about John's tour than to use John's own words at his change of command. Many of those he recognized that day are still at the base several years later. They are magnificent folks to work with.

July 6, 2010

Good morning and EDICCIMAD. Admiral and Mrs. Robertson, Admiral and Mrs. Bruner, Admiral and Mrs. Tofalo, Admiral and Mrs. Scorby, Mr. Cwalina, Mr. and Mrs. McNeill, Mayor DeLoughly, Mayor Smith, Mayor Parrott, friends, family and shipmates… thank you for joining us this morning for this time-honored Navy tradition that marks the change of command of Submarine Base Kings Bay. Captain Guffey and I are honored and humbled by your presence and are grateful for your support. Let me start by welcoming the Navy Region Southeast Band. As always, your support of Subase Kings Bay is exceptional and your performance truly makes the event.*

It is my privilege today to introduce my boss and our guest speaker Rear Admiral Jack Scorby, Commander Navy Region Southeast. Admiral Scorby's distinguished career included tours as Officer in Charge of Patrol Squadron Special Projects Unit One and Commanding Officer of Fleet Air Reconnaissance Squadron Two. Ashore he has served on the staffs of the Bureau of Naval Personnel, NORAD, and the Chief of Naval Operations. Most recently in the installation world, he served as Commanding Officer of Naval Air Station Jacksonville and as Executive Assistant to the Assistant Secretary of the Navy (Energy, Installations and Environment). He took command of Navy Region Southeast—the largest Region Command in the Navy in August of 2011 where he oversees 16 installations from Texas to South Carolina. Ladies and Gentlemen, please join me in welcoming Admiral Scorby. Admiral Scorby, thank you for your kind words and for the tremendous leadership and support you have provided over the course of this tour. We are so pleased that you and Chris could join us today to be a part of this ceremony. Distinguished guests, friends, family and shipmates—thank you again for joining us this morning. It was exactly two years ago today that we began our household goods pack out in preparation for our move to Kings Bay. I have to say that in July of 2010, Shelley and I had no idea and could never have imagined what a great two years were in store for us and our family. Those two years have flown by and as we reflect on them, they will go down as two of the most wonderful and significant years of our twenty-two plus years together in the Navy—both on a personal and professional level.

We arrived in Kings Bay at about 2200 on Saturday, July 10th following a painfully long day on I-95. The next morning at 0630 we dropped Conner off at Camden County High School where he boarded school busses with a hundred or so kids he didn't know and went off for a week of football camp. That began our induction into the Camden County way of life. From the moment, we arrived at the Stimson Gate that Saturday night—for those of you who have trouble with the gate names, that's the one by the Commissary and Exchange—we were welcomed to Kings Bay and Camden County everywhere we turned.

Of course, there is some trepidation when one moves a rising high school senior, a junior and a seventh grader from a location that is comfortable, supportive and well known to a location that is completely unknown. Let alone, moving to a job—installation command—in which you have had no experience during your twenty-five years in the Navy. Our concerns and fears were quickly laid to rest as we met more and more people in the community and on the base and we jumped head-long and whole-heartedly into our new lives.

Let me talk first about the people of this community. Nowhere in the Navy is there a community that is more supportive of its base and of its Sailors, Marines, Coastguardsmen and their families. I began this morning with the word EDICCIMAD—Every Day in Camden County is Military Appreciation Day. And while it sounds like a greeting, it is really a mentality. It is the result of the efforts of The Camden Partnership led by Chairman Joel Hanner and President Sheila McNeill. They, along with a board of community leaders strive to support Naval Submarine Base Kings Bay and promote the economic development of Camden County. They are a dedicated group of individuals from all facets of the community. And they are not the only dedicated group of individuals that support the base and the community—the Camden County Chamber of Commerce led by Chris Daniel does incredible work for us in many ways. The Chamber's IA Family Adoption program is but one example of their efforts to support our Sailors and their families. The Camden-Kings Bay Navy League led by Council President Hunt Thornhill, Georgia State President Keith Post and South Atlantic Coast Region President Dave Reilly are some of our strongest supporters. From Toys-to-tots to the annual Sea Service member of the Year banquet, the Navy League leads the way in promoting our sea services and supporting our service members and their families.

It is not just organizations that support SUBASE Kings Bay—the local communities and municipalities are intimately involved as well. As you heard at the beginning our three mayors—Saint Marys, Kingsland and Woodbine are here as well as a number of city council members and county officials. School Board President Herb Rowland and Camden County School Superintendent Dr. Will Hardin are tremendous supporters of our military families and their efforts are greatly appreciated.

And venturing outside of the county, the Georgia Military Affairs Coordinating Committee Executive Director, Colonel Bill Cain travelled from Atlanta to join us. Bill is a strong supporter of our military installations in Georgia and I am proud to say that due to his efforts and those of our local GMACC board members, last month, the Governor signed the Interstate Compact on Education for Military Families, aligning Georgia now with 42 other states supporting military families who, due to their careers, are forced to uproot their families and place them in new school districts across the country every two to three years.

Congressional leadership and support abounds as well. Jared Downs from Senator Isakson's office, Kathryn Murph from Senator Chambliss' office, Jackie Smith from Congressman Crenshaw's office and Tim Wessinger from Congressman Kingston's office are all ardent supporters of SUBASE Kings Bay and participate in almost every major event we have.

And before I leave the subject of community supporters, let me talk briefly about our number one community supporter—Sheila McNeill. Shortly after the Change of Command ceremony at which I relieved Wes Stevens, some from the local community took comments about Sheila that were made in good humor and twisted them. Wes joked that we all work for Sheila and some people jumped on that. Let me set the record straight—those who took that seriously don't know Sheila. If they knew her, they would recognize that no one works for Sheila—rather Sheila works for each and every one of us—she works tirelessly for her community, for SUBASE Kings Bay, for the United States Navy and for our Nation. There is no one I know with a greater heart, a greater love for her community and a greater love for her Navy and her Nation than Sheila McNeill. She is a true patriot and Shelley and I are proud to consider her and Arlie our good friends. As I scan the audience, I see many others deserving of recognition and I could go on and on—but my goal was 50 minutes for the ceremony and then get on with the party. So let me move inside the fence-line so to speak now.

I will start with Navy Region Southeast—I have had the great fortune to work for two incredible leaders—Admiral Scorby and his predecessor Admiral Tim Alexander who is now serving as Commander Navy Region Mid-Atlantic. Mr. Bruce Cwalina, the Region Executive Director is easily one of the foremost experts on installation management and that expertise combined with a refreshingly common sense approach to doing business make him a national treasure in the installation world. Chief of Staff Captain Steve Blaisdale and all of the Region Program Directors, some of whom are here today, provided sage advice and tremendous support to me and the entire Kings Bay Team while providing us the resources and allowing us the freedom to execute our mission. To all on the Navy Region Southeast staff—thank you for your tremendous support over the past two years.

And now to the Kings Bay Team. With 42 tenant commands onboard Kings Bay, I can't recognize everyone, but a few standouts must be recognized today. Navy Branch Health Clinic led by Officer in Charge CAPT Danny Denton, senior dental officer CAPT Tom Cade and Senior Medical Officer, CAPT Phil O'Connell has provided amazing support to the base and to our service members and their families. The Navy Marine Corps Relief Society, led by interim director Bill Kennedy and now director Brandi Frazier along with her dedicated staff and volunteers do great work to help our Sailors, Marines and their families both in times of need and in helping them establish solid financial footings. The Kings Bay PSD, led by Ms. Marcia Love, leads the Navy in customer service. Our housing

Public Private Venture Partner, Balfour Beatty led by Ms. Paula Cook and Kings Bay Community Manager Tony Cartagena has provided a quality community for our families.

Our local NCIS office, Nick Mancha lead agent, provides tremendous support to all of our local commands and the local community. Our Base Operating Service Contractors, VT Group and now Kings Bay Support Services maintained the base complex in outstanding condition. I would be remiss if I did not recognize our contract security force as well. The folks you see at our entry control points, patrolling our perimeter, checking the security of our buildings and providing support to our SUBASE Navy Security Forces are the first impression one has of SUBASE Kings Bay. It is always a pleasure to drive up to the gate where one is greeted warmly, and you can sense that our first line of defense is solid. I especially want to recognize Mr Robert Sykes who has been involved in the security of this installation for a couple of decades and who happens to be one of the most interesting individuals you will ever meet—simply stated, he is a true American Patriot.

One of my greatest pleasures has been working with our local Flag Officers and the Major Commanders responsible for the operational mission of SUBASE Kings Bay and our submarines. Admiral Barry Bruner former COMSUBGRU 10 and current COMSUBGRU 10 Admiral Joe Tofalo lead an amazing group of individuals who execute the vital mission of the strategic defense of our nation. They have both been tremendous neighbors and friends as well. As Admiral Tofalo often states, the Kings Bay Machine churns out a submarine ready for national tasking every two to three weeks. From the outside, it is almost impossible to comprehend what goes on inside Kings Bay to make that happen. It takes the professional and talented craftsmen of Trident Refit Facility led by CAPT Rich Verbeck to repair and modernize these beautiful boats with an average turnaround of about 28 days. The crews are expertly trained and are able to maintain their proficiency while ashore due to the superb training facilities and instruction provided by CAPT Rod Hutton and his Trident Training Facility staff. The strategic assets are built and maintained by Strategic Weapons Facility Atlantic led by CAPT Chris Schofield and those assets and our waterfront and submarines are protected by the 900 dedicated Marines and Sailors of Marine Corps Security Force Battalion led by LtCol Wendy Goyette and now LtCol Kevin Moody.

And when our submarines leave our secure waterfront area, they are protected by the United States Coast Guard Maritime Force Protection unit led by CDR Steve Love. Then there are the submarines themselves. The Guided Missile Submarines of Submarine Squadron 16 under Commodore Steve Gillespie and the Ballistic Missile Submarines of Submarine Squadron 20 under Commodore Chris Harkins are the reason we all are here. They are the forward presence leading a Global War against Violent Extremism and Terrorism and the strategic deterrence critical to our national security.

And it is SUBASE Kings Bay's mission to enable those warfighters and care for their families. In my completely unbiased opinion, no one does it better than the SUBASE Kings Bay Team. The 486 civilians and 230 military members I have been privileged to work with over the past two years are true professionals and they are fully dedicated to their mission to provide support to the fleet, fighter and family. Admiral Scorby mentioned some of the accolades that team has earned over the past couple of years. It really is a remarkable group of individuals, but more significantly it is a remarkable TEAM.

It starts on the deck plates with enthusiastic and dedicated Sailors and a strong Chiefs Quarters. The SUBASE Chief Petty Officers are adept at running the day to day operations and taking care of our great Sailors, mentoring and leading them and facilitating their professional and personal growth.

Then there are our dedicated SUBASE civilians. They are our continuity and provide the expertise in areas that our military cannot. There are a good number here today who have served this base from its beginning. They, probably more so than anyone else have dedicated their lives to our mission and working with them you quickly recognize the pride they take in their jobs and the passion they share for the submarine force, the service members and the families.

Civilian and military—an amazing team with some amazing leaders with a focus on service. Admin—led by CDR Mike Altiser and now CWO Chris Melody kept me and the entire staff on track, Security—led by CDR Rick Gilbert and Mr. Bud Lett, two security experts set the standard on force protection at this rather unique installation, Unaccompanied and Family Housing—led by Mr. Paul Petroski has ensured quality accommodations for our service members and families, Port Ops—led by LCDR Sean Farrell and now LT Dustin Dooley maintains the waterfront in a rather unique operat-

ing environment; SUBASE Safety, led by Ms. Lori Newman is simply the best in the Navy and our Fire and Emergency Services, led by Chief Freddie Thompson stood up the department from scratch last fall after a change in contract operations, Public Affairs Officer, Scott Bassett and Community Relations Manager Kelly Wirfel have excelled in community engagement; our Information Technology department led by Mr. Jeff Willadson, has always kept us connected and has done amazing work to support a number of significant events over the past two years; our Explosive Ordnance Disposal Detachment led by LT Bruce Batteson has been in high demand and our SEABEE detachment has provided numerous base improvements; two of the Navy's best Public Works Officers, CDR Jeanine Avant and CDR Shawn Follum, expertly managed our facilities sustainment, construction and utilities; our five galley operations, led by CWO Scott Matts and now LT David Mahoney, provide a great product and great service to our Sailors and Marines; the best Fleet and Family Support Center in the Navy, led by Ms. Debbie Lucas, leads the way in promoting family readiness; serving the spiritual needs of our service members and their families is a great group of Chaplains, led first by LCDR Dedra Bell and now CDR Ted Fanning; and our Morale Welfare and Recreation organization, led by Mr. Bob Spinnenweber, is one of only a handful of 4 star accredited MWR organizations leading the way for the entire Navy.

Emergency Management Director Dave Ford, when not coordinating major national level exercises, has lately kept busy handling a couple of unusually pesky tropical storms; In a time of tight resources, I have been fortunate to have an incredibly talented Financial Manager, Ms. Jacque Williams who kept everyone in line and somehow managed to come up with the money we needed, when we needed it.

Business Manager, Karen Dotson is one of those individuals who has been here for quite a while. She has expertly managed the installation and workforce and along with union president Mark McCabe has facilitated an environment where all team members can excel and grow to their potential.

Finally—the front office staff—LT Jessica Burrell has led the legal office. Let me just say that is GOOD to have a good JAG—and Jessica is the best, providing sage council and handling all legal matters deftly and professionally.

Then there is the person who has really kept me on track over the past two years—Ms. Monique Gregory. You could not ask for a bet-

ter administrative assistant—or sometimes more accurately—"gate keeper." Monique is a treasure and Harvey; I know you will quickly appreciate working with her as much as I did. Monique—thank you for all that you have done to make this such a rewarding and pleasant tour for me. I will really miss seeing you each morning!

Command Master Chief Jimmy Schubert. What can I say about Jimmy Schubert? Well, I can say that there is simply no one that I have ever come across in my 27 years in the Navy who has a bigger heart and who is more dedicated to his Sailors (and his Marines and Coastguardsmen) than Jimmy Schubert. Master Chief Schubert is the quintessential Command Master Chief—he handles things—he makes things happen—he leads—and there is nothing that he is not involved in. He is an integral part of this community and of this base and when he retires this fall, it will be a great loss to the Navy. Master Chief, it has been an honor to serve with you these past two years.

Finally—the XO—CDR Jeff Pafford. Every Commanding Officer should be so fortunate to have an XO like Jeff Pafford. While he may appear a little gruff at times, he too has a tremendous heart. Let me say in no uncertain terms, Jeff runs the base—and he runs it well. He is simply the most talented, compassionate, professional and dedicated Naval Officer I have served with. He will someday soon be a Captain and when he takes command, it will be a fortunate day for those who will work for him. Jeff—thank you for a great two years. We certainly have had a lot of fun—probably more than we should have. Shelley and I wish you and Patti the best and we look forward to continuing our friendship.

Finally, I need to address my family and our great friends. We have friends in attendance today that span decades of our lives and Naval service. The Bugajs and the Reuters from Texas, the O'Briens and Wagners from Norfolk, and the Sinnetts from Tallahassee. And from just down in Amelia Island, RADM Tom and Julie Robertson.

I was Admiral Robertson's Aide a little over twenty years ago right here at SUBGRU 10. Admiral and Julie thank you for coming and sharing this day with us. And of course, our Saint Marys friends. You all have made these two years very special and we will miss you greatly. Thank you for your support and for showing us what a special place Camden County is. My mom Susan and my sister Nancy and Shelley's parents Kay and Leon have always been our greatest supporters and I think they too have enjoyed our tour and their visits here to Kings Bay. Finally—Shelley, Conner, Carey and

Cullen. As always—thank you for your steadfast love and support. I am so proud of all of you and I am excited and looking forward to embarking on our next Navy adventure with you! Harvey, I cannot think of anyone I would rather turn over this command to than you. I know you and Wanda are going to love this job and this community as much as Shelley and I did. You all are the perfect fit and we wish you the best.

As I stated, at the beginning, these have been two of the most wonderful and significant years of Shelley's and my twenty-two plus years together in the Navy. Both on the personal and professional level—it has been the people we have worked with and played with that have made it so special and so hard to leave Kings Bay. To our friends in the community—thank you for welcoming us into your lives. To the members of the Kings Bay Team—thank you for what you do every day to support the mission—keep up the great work. This is a special place. SUBASE Kings Bay and Camden County will always hold a special place in our hearts—and you just never know—you may see us again down here.

*The remark John refers to is one that Captain Wes Stevens made when he relieved Wes. It was, and still is, one of the best compliments I've ever had. It was meant that way, recognizing my sense of humor and the kind of relationship that Wes and I had. Certainly, the relationship continues with John, whom I had known for twenty years. When you are in the public there is bound to be people who will have inappropriate, hurtful remarks. They wrote a letter to the editor that the captain was more concerned with "making me happy" than taking care of anything else. This was response meant to be negative, taken completely out of context, by an unhappy person. That did not in any way take from my pleasure at receiving both the remark and the explanation. It is keenly satisfying to have two successful military officers take up for you!

On July 9, Stephanie Muth sent me the following e-mail:

Sheila—I was really touched by what Captain O'Neill said about you today. Thank you for all that you do for the sailors and families stationed here at Kings Bay, for your work through the Navy League and all that you do for Camden County. You are an amazing role model.

All the best,
Stephanie Muth

Stephanie is married to a great guy, Sean Muth, commanding officer of USS *Rhode Island* (G). I wrote back,

> *Dear Stephanie, I was so taken back by his remarks and it affected me far more than I would have thought. It touched my heart so and I found myself filling up with tears. It was hard to stay composed. And I didn't want everyone to know I was crying. It was such a sweet, personal thing he did. I love what I do for the base and it is never done for recognition but it sure can be wonderful when it happens. You know sometimes you wonder if you get kind of 'pesky' and in their face—you hope you don't step over the boundaries and then I hear the Captain today and I was just crushed with so much emotion and assurance that what I was doing was really appreciated Thank you, Stephanie, for taking the time to write. Your words that again made me tear up. I swear tomorrow I'm getting back to my old tough self but this has been a great day and your note was the sweetest way to close out that day.*
>
> *Sheila*

John, your words continue to inspire me. Thank you.
"Every day in Camden County is Military Appreciation Day."

OVERSEAS TRAVELS FOR THE NAVY LEAGUE

When I was national president, each year Arlie and I traveled overseas. Thank goodness, I wrote an article for *Seapower*, and it was published so I had most of the names and events documented. When I talked with editor, Rick Bernard, about putting my article in *Seapower* he told me it would have to be limited to one page. That was hard to do so I gave him the article and told him I would be okay with whatever content he deleted. I was pleased that it remained intact

I met with Dr. Perett the Pentagon protocol officer before each of the two trips.

The tour of our Asia-Pacific councils revealed strong sea service support. These members, residing in another country, must not only be supportive of our sea services, they must develop a strong relationship with the local nationals and governments. This they do—and do it well. This was more evident than ever when Arlie and I visited the councils in the Asia-Pacific region. Our tour included briefings with our Navy, Marine Corps, Coast Guard, and Merchant Marine as well as foreign military officials, defense ministers, ambassadors, homeland security officials, governmental leaders, and governors—all of whom spoke of a constant continuing dialog with our

Navy League leadership. Never has it been more important to nourish and cultivate our partnerships in this region of the world, as current events so strongly indicate.

On our way to Asia, we visited San Diego where Pamela Ammerman, Pacific Southwest region president, and Curtis Beauchamp, San Diego Council president, organized a great reception. Commander, US Pacific Fleet, as well as a briefing from the Navy and Coast Guard.

We visited with PACFLEET Admiral Doran. (Some of that visit is in Admiral Greenert's story.)

Japan: Our first stop was Japan, where we were met by Scott Hancock, Tokyo Council vice president, who accompanied us for the entire Japan visit. Our first brief was with Captain Tom Arnold, chief of staff of US Naval Forces Japan. Cmdr. John Wallach, spokesman for commander, Naval Forces Japan, gave an excellent briefing on Japan geopolitical issues and the installation mission.

RADM Jamie Kelly, commander, Carrier Strike Group Five, met with us before our tour of the carrier USS *Kitty Hawk* at Fleet Activities Yokosuka, *Kitty Hawk*'s forward-deployed operating port. Cmdr. Brenda Holdener, the ship's navigator, gave us a tour of the bridge and gave me an opportunity to thank the men and women of Kitty Hawk on behalf of the Navy League for all they do. We were interviewed on the deck of the ship and *Navy News* carried the story.

We then traveled to Japan Maritime Self Defense Force (JMSDF) Yokosuka District and toured JMSDF ships, including the newest destroyer, *Makinami.* During that interview, I learned of the Japanese plans to build a nuclear qualified pier. This is brand-new news for me—nothing had been in the American press, and I had heard nothing about this in briefs. Later I was able to pass this on to Navy officials. That evening a reception was held with Navy League members; ships crews; US commanding officers; Japanese flag officers and spouses; RADM Frederic Ruche, Commander, US Naval Forces, Japan; and submariner RADM Dave Gove and his wife. We were pleased that Tokyo Council president Fred Harris, a recent recipient of the secretary of the Navy public service award, was able to join us. He was recently hospitalized but had very much improved. When we arrived at the hotel the first night, we were greeted with a welcome from Fred. Our small hotel room turned into a spacious suite.

Our next visit was to Sasebo, where President Gerald Havens runs the award-winning Sasebo Council. As in Tokyo, we were impressed with the number of Japanese nationals working hard as Navy League members. At the mixer on Sunday evening were VADM Seizo Nakao, commandant Sasebo District; and RADM Katsutoshi Kawano, chief of staff, Headquarters Sasebo District. Also in attendance were Captain Michael James, commander, Fleet Activities Sasebo, and his wife along with base commanding officers and many council members.

The following day we had an excellent meeting with Capt. James Takeshisa Seki, vice president of the council, who checked out of the hospital for a few hours to join us at the council reception. Arlie and I visited him at the hospital a few days later before we left Japan. A tour of Nagasaki Peace Park with Toshio Maeda finished up our visit to Sasebo.

Korea: The following day we departed for Korea, where Navy League Area president Paul Chung and the Republic of Korea (ROK) Sea Power League had planned a full five days of meetings, tours and briefings. Within an hour of arriving in Korea, we were hosted by Adm. Youan Nam the ROK Navy Club. We were able to discuss and solidify the memorandum of understanding between the Navy League and the Sea Power League, "strengthening the bonds of friendship, cooperation and understanding" between the two leagues and fostering support of robust programs for Sea Power.

The next day, the Sea Power League flew us to Gimp Airport where we traveled by land to Jinhae. We were hosted at a luncheon by RADM Choi Ki Joo, deputy commander, naval training command.

Arlie and I were met by several black sedans and vans at the airport and had an impressive motorcade from the airport to the Naval Academy. We arrived, someone opened the door and introduced me to RADM Choi Ki Joo. We were ushered quickly to the building, thinking we will go into a room to discuss the events about to take place, I held off of some of my questions. RADM Choi Ki Joo told me that after my remarks some of the students would come forward with flowers and that some of them would greet me with a salute. I quickly let him know that I was a civilian and didn't salute. He was crestfallen. He told me they had been practicing for weeks and could I salute this one time. Not knowing what to do I told him, I would salute the students if he promised not to have anyone taking pictures of the salute. I did not want that picture to get back to the US! All of a sudden, they opened a door and motioned for Arlie to follow another group of officers, and I found myself on the stage. It was quite a surprise.

One of the highlights of my trip was being invited to address the more than six hundred midshipmen at the Korean Naval Academy. Over the entire trip I had to speak at every event and sometime two or three times during a dinner. There were numerous toasts and responses to toast and this was challenging but enjoyable. This event was one of only two where I had prepared remarks. I had been asked to send these remarks to the academy before my visit and they were provided to every cadet. It turned out that my speech was considered a civics lesson, a government affairs lesson, and an English lesson. As I was speaking, I kept hearing a *swoosh* sound. It took me a while, but I was hearing seven hundred people turning their page as I spoke.

My remarks were followed by lively and informed questions from the midshipmen. All were easy and I felt comfortable answering them. The last question had to do with the conflict between North and South Korea and America's position on a situation. I thought for a second or two and said, "You will all be in the Navy soon. You will be naval officers. There is one phase you will learn in your first few months and that is 'That is way above my pay grade.'" There was a chuckle and I got out of that one.

Sure enough, after a standing ovation, about six students came to the front with a bouquet of flowers and stood straight and saluted smartly. I was prepared and gave them a return salute. It wasn't bad if I have to say so myself. And I'm proud to say there were no pictures.

I then had a separate meeting with eighty female midshipmen. The academy opened its enrollment to women just three years before, and it was an opportunity to use my newly honed DACOWITS skills. It was a great opportunity to discuss the unique challenges faced by these female midshipmen in their new environment. They were in a smaller auditorium and seemed anxious to discuss issues. I noticed Rear Admiral Choi Ki Joo had slipped in the back of the auditorium to listen. I began "straight talking" with them.

Afterward the admiral was very pleased. He told me the issues I brought up were the issues they were experiencing and to have another female give them the same advice as their seniors really helped to solidify their training. He also said there was no way any of them could have talked with the female cadets so frankly and he was very pleased.

RADM Choi Yun-Hee, vice superintendent of the ROK Naval Academy, had just taken command the day before my arrival, and his introduction before my remarks was the first address to his midshipmen. That afternoon we visited ROK fleet ships, including the submarine Chang Bo Go and the newest Korean destroyers during a tour of the naval port.

Chung and Admiral Yu arranged for us to meet with the Korean Minister of National Defense, Yoon Kwang Ung. We had an informative half hour. At first everything was done by interpreter with a room full of ROK senior officers. At one point, I made a funny remark and he laughed before the interpreter had a chance to translate. I lifted my eye and asked if we could just talk without the interpreter. (I understood that, even with very good English, most Asians were reluctant to show anything other than perfection—while I was impressed by their command of the English language.) He agreed and began a little chitchat. He told me we were the same age mentioning that I was sixty-one. We had an informative half hour as we sipped tea, discussed the mission of the Navy League, shipbuilding, the importance of the partnerships between Korea and the United States, and the interoperability between fleets of both countries. There were some items he wanted me to pass on to "my government," which I did. He complimented RADM Fred Byus, commander, US Naval Forces Korea, on the many changes he had implemented during his tour.

When our meeting was over, the Minister of Defense asked if we would wait a few minutes. He wanted to bring in the joint chiefs for a picture. Yoon introduced General Kim Jang Soo, chief of staff of the Korean Army, and Adm. Nam Hae II, chief of Naval Operations. I said our goodbyes and the defense minister, Yoon

Kwang Ung, announced to us that he would be walking me to my car. We talked the entire trip down and to the car. He asked me if I might consider coming to work for him. He told me I would be his assistant and we would be able to accomplish many things. I was so flattered. When we were in the car, Admiral Yoo told me that it was most unusual to have the minister of defense walk someone to the car. In fact, it was unheard of. He had the same job at one time and stressed to me the honor that was. We were pretty blown away by the entire visit.

The next day we had lunch with Youngsan Military Compound sailors and marines and later dinner with retired and active duty flag officers of the ROK Navy.

Songhanksan: On Sunday, we traveled to Songhaksan to visit the Observation Point at the Demilitarized Zone with the ROK Marine Corps. We met with Colonel Byung Hoon Jun, commanding officer of First Regiment, Second Marine Division, who joined us for the lunch. The brief was given by Cheol-Jae Seo, vice chairman of the ROK/US Marine Corps Friendship Association and many of his senior leaders, who joined Arlie and me. He told us that his uncle and cousins were in North Korea. Later, when I talked with the briefer and we discussed this same thing, he said it was the very first time he had briefed anyone that had relatives in North Korea. We were told that five years ago the North Korean forces were 30% forward-deployed, and today they are at 60%. South Korean officials we talked with continue to work in diplomatic efforts to ensure any reunification preserves economic stability.

One of the guests as the briefing who flew from Chicago where he now lives to meet with us told us that his grandfather, brother, and uncle were still in North Korea, fifty years after the war's end. I couldn't help but ask, "So those young men pointing their guns at South Korea could very well be your nephews?" He nodded somberly. It certainly brought home to us the tragedies resulting from the past conflicts in this part of the world; the pain that still exists and the need to make certain the many tensions that remain are resolved peacefully. Our military continue to have a key role in achieving this.

The next day, Paul Chung had arranged for the historian of the Eighth Army to take us on a tour of the site of an incredible piece of history—the Green Beach point of the Inchon Landing of September 15, 1950. We toured MacArthur Park and the monument to marines, sailors, and coast guardsmen that was sponsored by Chung and the Korean Council. It was at Inchon Landing that I experienced my most interesting toilet!

That evening event was outstanding. There was an overflowing crowd of sailors, marines, coasties, and Navy League members. Major General John E. Goodman commander, US Marine Corps Forces, Korea, and I had the opportunity to talk with a Korean gentleman who told of the horrors of the Korean War, the fear when the Chinese invaded, and his gratitude for the US Marines.

Sitting next to him, I thought, gave me an opportunity to be a little irreverent with General John Goodman. While he was very nice there was a definite formality with our conversation. I asked him if he knew the Rusty Puller story about fighting the Chinese. He answered with a wry look and said, "Yes, but why don't you tell me." I proceeded to relate the story as I had heard it: I believe it broke the ice and we had a pleasant evening.

That story went as follows: During the Korean war Colonel Puller received a call from the field:

"Sir, we are being attacked by the Chinese," a Korean commander screamed.

"How many Chinese?" Puller asked.

"Many, many Chinese," he answered excitedly.

Puller again asked the question and received the same answer: "Many, many Chinese."

Puller replied, "S——! Let me speak to someone who speaks English."

An American voice came on the line and Puller asked, "Exactly how many Chinese you got up there?"

The American answered, "Colonel, we got a shitload."

Puller replies, "Thank God, someone who knows how to count.

(Note: Lt. General Puller joined the Marine Corps in 1917 and is the most highly decorated Marine in history and a legendary figure among his fellow Marines. To this day, Marines at Parris Island end their day by saying, "Good night, Chesty Puller, wherever you are!")

General Goodman smiled and said, "Yes, that's just about right!" We continued eating and had a great conversation. After dinner, there were remarks from Goodman and RADM Fred Byus, who said, "All of us who are here in uniform understand the value of your kind assistance. To those of us so far away from home, you do make our lives much better. We are very thankful for the way you have opened your arms and your heart to the Sailors and Marines of the United States based in ROK." What a wonderful end to a great visit.

Singapore: When we arrived, Jack Miller, Singapore Council president, had a full three-day schedule planned for us. Our first stop was with US Navy Logistics Command Western Pacific (COMLOGWESTPAC), where we met with Rear Admiral Kevin Quinn, who wears many hats including commander, Logistics Group Western Pacific and staff from Naval Regional Contracting Center Singapore and the US Coast Guard on the role of the military in Singapore. We received briefings on the recent tsunami relief efforts and the great successes of our military in responding so quickly to the needs of the people in this terrible tragedy. COMLOGWESTPAC is the US Seventh Fleet's principal logistics agenda and bilateral exercises coordinator for Southeast Asia.

We also heard of the challenges and many successes of the US Coast Guard in Singapore from the briefing by Lt. Cmdr. Glen Martineau. We called on the American ambassador to Singapore, Frank Lavin, who was a Navy Reservist and is a Navy League member. I was very pleased when he asked what the Singapore council could do to increase our support of the sea services in Singapore. We then met with a US Department of Homeland Security representative, US Customs Service attaché, Matt Kings, who discussed the issues with port security.

That evening we had a reception honoring the COMLOGWESTPAC Sailors of the Quarter and Year. I had been told that the Singapore chief of Naval Operations, RADM Ronnie Tay, would be at the dinner. I had just arrived in the room when he joined the group I was talking with. The waitress came up and took our drink order. I thought I would be gracious and told them I would have whatever the admiral was having. He looked so young I wanted to get some tips from him on staying youthful. What a surprise when I received a cup of warm water. Yes, warm water. "Warm water is good for your digestion, that's all I drink," he said. So, for the rest of the evening instead of my favored scotch I drank warm water with the admiral. The next day he met with us at his headquarters. As the young officer was taking orders—I was looking forward to a cup of coffee. Rear Admiral Tay instructed the officer to take orders but said, "Ms. McNeill will have what I have." He got a big kick out of "getting me."

The briefing was followed by a tour of the Singapore Naval Port. We also toured Changi Navy Base and had an excellent briefing.

While I spoke about twenty times during this trip I only had two speeches prepared—one for the ROK Naval Academy and one for the Defense Technology Asia 2005 conference. This was a unique opportunity to speak to these expert active duty and civilians. My subject was "Future Maritime Challenges"—the challenge to maintain and promote a healthy exchange of human capitol, investment, and tradable goods, while improving security on the high seas.

Nowhere is this vulnerability better illustrated than the Strait of Malacca. We were provided a first-hand look at just how narrow the strait is and the vast amount of trade that flows through it every day. Modern day pirates are a reality in this region. Everywhere we went we were reminded of the strategic importance of the Pacific Fleet. I told the conference attendees of the vital role civilian organizations such as the Navy League serve in developing support for a strong maritime force through the education of the public and their elected officials.

Guam: A 2:00 a.m. wake-up call and on to Guam. Council President Thomas Ahillen met with us that morning as we discussed with the governor of Guam, Felix Comacho, the desire to support the Navy and Coast Guard in Guam, the most forward-deployed American facility in the Pacific, and the opportunities Guam offers for national security.

Lee Webber, greater Pacific area region president, planned for me to have interviews with local media as well as the base paper. It was probably fairly easy since he was the owner of the local paper. We had dinner that night with the Navy League. The following day we went to Navy Base Guam and were provided a helicopter tour of the facilities.

The Coast Guard briefing was given by Luann Barndt, deputy commander, Marianas sector. Sector Guam serves the people of Micronesia, saves lives, protects the environment, enforces law on the sea, facilitates commerce, and guards the homeland—a lot of responsibilities for a small number of Coast Guards men and women. We toured he USCGC Sequoia with Lt. Cmdr. Matthew Melstrup, commanding officer. Dottie England, wife of outgoing Navy secretary Gordon England, was sponsor of the Sequoia. It was fun to see "Dottie's ship" and see one of the newest cutters in the fleet. The set of dishes she gave the crew was a lovely gift and they had made good use of them.

We then met with RADM Arthur Johnson, commander of US Naval Forces Marianas, and discussed the variety of issues and challenges of the region, which is a very important strategic location and has proved to be essential in our war on terror.

I was pleased to be invited to tour the USS *Petersburg*, my first visit on a maritime prepositioning ship. We enjoyed lunch with the crew. We also met with the cadets and leadership of the Naval Sea Cadet Corps, commanded by Lt. J. G. Jeffrey E. Brown, NSCC, and presented awards to the top cadets. We could not believe that during that Sea Cadet brief Arlie looked across the room and recognized someone he knew from Darien, Georgia! She and her husband were volunteers with the Sea Cadets and had been in Guam for a number of years. What dedication these two have. After a number of years, they returned to Darien to retire and Arlie sees and speaks to them from time to time.

Lee Webber was very gracious during my trip. He asked that I do an interview for his paper. Coming into Guam early morning with no sleep and having breakfast with local dignitaries, then going on a helicopter trip and having to wear a hard hat was a challenge! It was a lovely tour of Guam and we saw just what the plans might be if the plan to bring submarines into Guam and increase the presence of our military might be. However, when we landed, I asked if anyone could get me a ball cap. It was hot on the helo and my hair was plastered to my head. I wore that ball cap the rest of the day.

The last days of our trip included a stop in Hawaii to meet with members of the Honolulu Council at the home of Shirley and Ed Carter. Guests included council president, Kraig Kennedy, and his wife; Harold and Doris Ester; Dick and Susie Macke; Adm. William Fallon and his wife; and VADM Gary Roughead. I was so pleased at Admiral Roughead's insight. He told Admiral Fallen, "Sheila made the same trip we did, saw the same people, but did it on commercial flights and without an aide!"

Then it was on to Hilo where I spoke to the council, participated in a radio interview with Hilo Council president, Dan Coates, and did an interview for *Now Hear This* with area president, Dee Coates.

Wherever we went, we found our councils highly respected and well connected. The local nationals were most eager to show their strong support. History was very much a part of today in Asia, and I certainly now have a better appreciation of what a force for peace we have in our military. As everyone realizes when you travel overseas for several days, you can get out of touch with what is happening back home. There was also much going on abroad during this visit: The pope died and a new one was named, Prince Rainer died, Secretary England was announced as deputy secretary of defense, General Peter Decker was announced as Chairman of the Joint Chiefs, Admiral Ed Giambastiani was named as vice chief of the Joint Chiefs of Staff, and lastly, Prince Charles married Camilla!

European Visit Highlights Foreign Councils Unique Challenges

The first six months of my presidency were predominantly spent in Washington meeting folks and learning the ropes. Most of 2004 has been spent visiting our councils. I continue to be amazed at the dedication and professionalism of our members. They continue to perform our mission and take extraordinary care of the men and women who visit their ports. They *are* the vital link between our citizens and our sea services.

The link was never more evident than when Arlie and I visited our European councils in May. The unique challenges our councils face in serving the Navy League missions include great distances from US military installations, infrastructure, and sea service populations, shifting political and social climates that can be less than friendly to the US military presence, and a small population base from which to draw membership.

This was an interesting time to be visiting France, Italy, and Spain. As we were traveling to the first council meeting in Cannes we had to wonder about our reception, given the tension between France and the United States over the war in Iraq. Of course, I knew that, for the most part, those present supported the sea services and the Navy League. Phil Temple was the European Region President and joined us for the meetings. He was an enormous help to me during my presidency.

Cannes, France: Avery Glize-Kane, president of the French Riviera-Monaco Council, said the distinguishing character of the council was the dedication shown by its members, including many French citizens, to the men and women of the Sixth Fleet and their eagerness to express their gratitude for the role the Sixth Fleet plays in preserving freedom in that part of the world.

As we arrived at a reception in Cannes with Avery and Deborah Cozzone, northern Europe area president, one of the first guests was a gentleman who wore a cowboy hat in our honor and wept as he described the liberation of his country by Americans more than half a century ago. I was amazed at the number of foreign nationals—about 80% of the group. The next day, Avery had arranged for me to lay an American flag wreath in a ceremony at the memorial commemorating the liberation of France during World War II. It was heart wrenching as we watched dozens of soldiers in their WWII uniforms standing at attention during the ceremony. Arlie and I had no idea we would be in a receiving line, but the French started lining up after the ceremony to speak to us. They kissed us, they hugged us, and they told us of their enormous gratitude to the United States. What an incredible experience.

Italy: The next stop was Naples where new European region president, Betty Reese, had organized the first European region conference in recent memory. Almost every council president in Europe attended, and the next few days were full of training and the sharing of ideas and concerns. It began with a dinner with speakers Adm. Gregory "Grog" G. Johnson, commander, US Naval Forces Europe; General James L. Jones Jr., commander, US European Command, and Supreme Allied Commander, Europe; and RADM Stanley D. Bozin, commander, Fleet Air Mediterranean Navy Region Europe. One person missing from the meeting was John Graham. As we were having dinner, General Jones said, "Where is John Graham?"

"Oh, sir, he is busy preparing for your visit to Parma next week."

"Did John tell you that?"

"That was my understanding," I replied.

The general pulled out his phone pressed a number on his speed dial and got John on the phone. Obviously, they were good personal friends and it was fun hearing him give John a hard time. Another person there was Captain Mike McKinnon. How that came about is in his story.

Since those present at the region meeting were Navy League leadership, they shared with me the unique challenges they meet each day, especially with limited ship visits. This, of course, is a common lament even throughout the United States as our sailors, marines, and coast guardsmen are on deployment in support of Operation Iraqi Freedom, Operation Enduring Freedom, and the global war or terror.

Barcelona, Spain: We met with the Navy League's Barcelona Council and business leaders at an amazing opera house in that beautiful city. What an incredible dinner. It was easy to feel like you were in another world, another century. Even the hotel was different—but in an opposite way, more modern, sleeker. Council president, Tim Cashman, and vice president, Dr. J. Garcia-Reyes, gave us an excellent briefing on the Port of Barcelona. They grappled with the issues of a small council dedicated to meeting ships and welcoming sailors and marines—and continually looked-for ways to interest Spaniards in supporting the US Navy, Marine Corps, and Coast Guard.

We had an opportunity to share our mission with Juan Alsace, US counsel general, and he assured us of his support.

Altea, Spain: The members of the council formed a line along the entrance and each member rang a bell as we entered the building. During lunch, I walked to each table and talked to everyone! I was amazed that at every table there was at least one and usually more who were from another county. What a United Nations in that one room!

I had the opportunity to sit with Hampton Terry, president of the Valencia Council. He shared with me the fact that Valencia is the newest council in Spain, that it was chartered to meet the needs of the sea serves in this important Mediterranean port. With few US citizen resources, the council is bolstered by committed affiliate members from the local community and the newly established NATO Rapid Reaction Force there.

The Levante Council comprises people from many nations, as is true of most of the overseas councils. They work together as a team to promote unity among national groups in the area. Americans are in the minority there but respected by the locals. By working together, they put the message of unity across to the local people.

Ron MacMaster, Levante Council president, and I did a radio talk show at one of the only English-speaking radio stations in the Mediterranean with about fifty thousand listeners. The show expanded from the planned thirty minutes to an hour. What a wonderful opportunity to share the word about our work.

Palma de Mallorca: We traveled to this beautiful island where council president John Graham and his wife, Giovanna, spent the next few days introducing us to members of the Spanish Navy League, community leaders, port and embassy officials, and elected officials. The city council hosted a reception in our honor at Castillo Bellver.

One gentleman, who said he was the oldest living Spanish Navy League member, showed us a coin he had received forty years earlier from a national president of the Navy League of the US. I made sure he had one of my president's coins after seeing such interest and pride! Southern Europe area president, Ciro Armellini, was present and thanked the city for its generosity. John Graham was once a member of the Moody Blues, most famous for "Nights in White Satin," and he and Arlie enjoyed "jamming" one evening at Ciro's home where we enjoyed a wonderful meal. It was a good thing John liked Elvis because that is the one artist that Arlie knew the words to the songs—that and gospel but John did not know gospel! They both took turns singing solos and had a great time! What a diverse group we have leading our Navy League.

Madrid, Spain: Arlie and I were joined by James Frances, council president; president-elect Joan Eischen; and James Dodson for a meeting with George L. Argyros, the American ambassador to Spain. The United States has a submarine base at Rota, Spain, and a great Navy League council who has worked intricately with the Spanish Navy League. Ambassador Argyros was a great friend of the Navy League, agreeing to serve as the Honorary President of the council with Joan Eischen as President.

Ambassador Argyros was very easy to talk with. We had a fifteen-minute meeting scheduled and as usual, I wanted to make the best use of those fifteen minutes! We began talking and it didn't stop. The ambassador told a funny story of his trip to Cannes for the car races and we each shared experience while traveling. I was a getting a little anxious to talk about the Navy League in France and looked at my watch and commented about our time running out. He answered, "We have all the time we need. I told my secretary fifteen minutes in case I was bored but don't worry about the time. We both shared stories for another forty-five minutes and the conversation led to the reception that evening. Each year, the embassy hosts the Madrid Council and its sailor of the year event. Argyros told me he planned to introduce me that evening and asked if I had anything I wanted to make sure he covered. I made a flip remark about just telling them how wonderful I was. We eventually wrapped up our discussion and went back to the hotel to prepare for that evening. And what an event it was.

When I met his wife, Joan, she told me, "George had such a great visit with you today. When he came home tonight he said, 'It's a girl, it's a girl!'" The Navy League national president is a girl! He had not read my bio, assuming I was a man, so evidently, it was a great surprise. Joan then caught herself and said, "I hope you are not offended by that."

"Offended? I'm sixty-one years old I love to be referred to as a girl," I answered.

We joined the receiving line that included the ambassador and his wife, James Frances, Arlie, and me. We then joined about 180 guests for a cocktail reception.

It was an interesting mixture of military. The recent elections were quite contrary and for the first-time cell phones played a big part. Right before the election everyone received a phone call asking for support of Jose Luis Rodriguez Zapatero and he had a surprising win. President Zapatero was in attendance as was the current chief of Naval Operations, Adm. Sebastian Zaragosa Soto, the vice chief, and the chairman of the Joint Staff, as well as those who had just recently held those positions under the leadership of former Spanish president, Jose Maria Aznar. In Spain, when there is a new national president, it was my understanding that when he is elected he replaces the military with his own choice.

I had a great time walking around during the reception and talking to the attendees. The Spanish Navy League are great supporters of the US Navy League, and they were anxious to make my visit the best it could be. They made sure I met everyone! The honored guest for the evening was a sailor from the Navy base at Rota, Spain. He was to be given his Sailor of the Year award by some of the dignitaries there.

While I didn't know who would make the presentation I insisted the recipient follow me over to meet the new Spanish chief of Naval Operations. The admiral was standing with his arms folded and his legs stiff and a stern look on his face. I tried to introduce him to the young sailor, but he remained standing with his arms crossed. We just kind of eased out after we had no response It was then time for the ceremony. In the ambassador's remarks, he commented on the change in government and said, "I don't know about this new regime," and continued in that theme for a while. He then introduced me and somehow managed in the afternoon to memorize my bio and covered most of it. I had planned to say just a few remarks, thank the ambassador, and congratulate the Sailor of the Year from Rota.

What do you say in Spain when asked to make remarks to such a diverse group? I looked out over the crowd and still marveled that the military who had been relieved and their replacement were all in the same room. Well, you recognize that all of those present have a common interest in maritime issues—you emphasize the importance of keeping sea lanes open—not only for the freedom of nations but also for the world's economic survival. You emphasize that no civilized country wants war—that no country wants to send their sons and daughters to war. Our military's mission is to build maritime strength so that we might avoid wars. You point out the importance of our country's friendship, and you encourage everyone to work with our Navy Leaguers to expand that friendship and working relationship. You point out that the Navy League is respected throughout the world. And you thank them for their support of our ships and for their hospitality to our military men and women who travel and serve in their country.

None of this was planned, but as I looked at the older members of the Spanish Navy League and saw tears running down their faces, I knew we were okay. Shortly after the program, the new chief of Navy Operations was standing close by and the ambassador said, "Admiral, have you met Sheila."

He answered by putting his arm around me and said, "Oh, yes, good friends, we are good friends!"

The next day the Spanish Navy League took Arlie and me out to lunch. After lunch, they presented a very significant statue of Admiral Farragut. It was inscribed as follows:

David Glasgow Farragut 1801–1870 1st United States Navy Admiral
Adopted son of Cindadela Menorca Spain
Presented to Sheila M. McNeill National President
From Madrid Council United States of America

Then two of the gentlemen presented me a book entitled *Travels of Christopher Columbus*. A book that was replicated exactly like the one Columbus wrote—with the same type of paper, writing, and imperfections: Testimonia 500 1492–1992 Quinto Centenario—Cesar Olmos Pieri, editor, impresor y director tecnico-artistico de la coleccion—Tabula Americae-de Testimonia Companfa Editorial. S. A.

I was told to carry it with me on the rest of my journey—not to leave it in my luggage. Both the book and the very heavy statue were treated with extreme care and I did carry them from plane to plane. Another book was sent to me two years later.

By the time they presented me with the Spanish Navy League's highest medal, the Golden Anchor, the first ever presented to a woman recipient. I was overwhelmed.

They continued to thank me for my words and for my visit. It is something I will never forget.

The Spanish Navy League cherish the relationship we enjoy and we talked of ways to enhance it. I was overwhelmed with their hospitality.

ADMIRAL ROBERT PAPP AND LINDA

COMMANDANT OF THE UNITED STATES COAST

I received the following letter from Rear Admiral Robert J. Papp, commander, Ninth Coast Guard District, written on October 14, 2004:

> Dear Sheila, I want to add my congratulations to those of the rest of the Coast Guard for your recent presentation of the "Spirit of Hope" Award. I have been working with the Spirit of Home organization over the past few months after having met some of its officials at a USO event in Chicago. I have known for weeks that you were to be this year's recipient and it has been hard to keep it a secret. I can't think of a person more deserving of this award. From our days of working together advancing the legislative concerns of the Naval Service through your service as National President of the Navy League, you have always given equal consideration to the Coast Guard as you have carried out your responsibilities. Thank you for being such a great friend of the Coast Guard. I am very proud of you and your contributions to the welfare of our Services. Best wishes for continued success and I look forward to seeing you soon.
>
> Fair winds,
> R.J. Papp, Jr.
> "great talking to you!"

I introduced him when he was commander of Atlantic area (LANTAREA). We were thrilled to have Bob or R.J. as Linda calls him as the speaker at the Camden Kings Bay Council Sea Services Recognition Banquet on May 14, 2009. He just blew everyone away. You always came away inspired when you heard him speak. As I told the audience this meant, he was responsible for US Coast Guard missions within the eastern part of the world. From the Rocky Mountains to the Arabian Gulf and spans an area of responsibility including five Coast Guard districts and forty-two states with over fourteen million square miles and serves more than fifty-one thousand military and civilian employees and auxiliarists. As if that were not enough to fill his day up he serves concurrently as commander, Defense Force East, and provides Coast Guard missions support to the Department of Defense and combatant commanders.

Linda, Bob, Arlie, and I had dinner that next evening in downtown St. Marys. It was a wonderful relaxing evening and we caught up with who was where in the Coast Guard and our families. I told him I had heard rumors that he might be our next commandant. He smiled but had not heard any definite news. However, that turned out to be good intel!

PAPP TAPPED FOR COMMANDANT

The White House nominated VADM Robert Papp on December 23 to succeed Adm. Thad Allen as commandant of the Coast Guard. If confirmed by the Senate, Papp would relieve Allen on May 25. Allen plans to retire July 1 after thirty-nine years in the Coast Guard. The Senate likely will decide whether to approve the nomination in March, said Cmdr. Mark Fedor, special assistant to the commandant. If approved, Papp would serve a four-year term. Papp, fifty-seven, is commander of the Coast Guard Atlantic Area and Defense Force East, functioning as the operational commander for all missions with the eastern half of the world.

When it was announced that Bob was selected by the president to become the next commandant of the USCG, he, as all those before him, had to go to members of the Senate for an interview for confirmation. He called me while he was on Capitol Hill. "Sheila, I've been visiting members of the Senate before my confirmation hearings and they didn't know your name, they didn't know who you were with, but they got your message." I had assurances from each one of them—yes, everyone mentioned it—that they would restore that three hundred million dollars to the USCG budget. (That story can be found under USCG budget.)

On January 4, 2010, the following article was in *Navy Times*:

PAPP CONFIRMED AS COAST GUARD COMMANDANT

> *Coast Guard Vice Adm. Robert Papp has been confirmed by the Senate as the service's 24th commandant. He will assume command May 25 when Commandant Adm. Thad Allen retires. Papp had been commander of the Coast Guard Atlantic Area/Defense Force east since July 2008. He was frocked to his new four-star rank on April 30. Vice Adm. Robert Parker, the director for security and intelligence at U.S. Southern Command, assumed Papp's command April 30.*

> The Senate also confirmed the following promotions: Rear Adm. Sally Brice O'Hara to vice admiral, and Rear Adm. Manson Brown to vice admiral. Both incredibly impressive folks.

I would later go to DC to attend the change of command where Admiral Papp would relieve Admiral Thad Allen as commandant.

On January 26–28, 2011, I arrived in DC in the middle of a snow storm with predictions of worse weather as the day progressed. While in baggage claim, I had a call from Coast Guard headquarters advising me that they would most likely have to close headquarters. Rather than cancel the meeting, as I was expecting them to do, they canceled others and moved my four o'clock appointment to twelve. I had expected a generous thirty minutes but actually had about fifty-five minutes with Admiral Papp.

Half of the hour was in personal conversation and catching up. The budget continues to be embargoed until February 14. I asked Admiral Papp if the funding was there would he continue the Maritime Safety and Security Teams (MSSTs). His answer was a very firm and resounding yes. He told me he considers these teams essential and effective. We discussed the time when the budget would be released. He gave me his personal e-mail address and we agreed that I would e-mail him, and he'd let me know if the MSSTs were in the budget. I then asked him to be our speaker for our annual Community that Cares. I assured him we would make every effort to have a cross section of the community and not necessarily those who already attend meetings to support the military. We talked about anywhere from March through June and for breakfast, lunch, or dinner. His scheduler was on vacation but would get with me when she returned. He invited me to come to dinner at their new quarters. Under a public private venture, a four-star commandant's quarters were built near Coast Guard headquarters at Bolling Air Force Base. They have only been in two weeks, but he was pleased with the amenities that will make the required entertaining easier.

April 30, 2012—commissioning of the USCGC *Stratton* (WMSL 752) in California.

The biggest event—other than the commissioning was the Friday night event. I was standing alone for a moment and Linda Papp came up, hugging me, and saying in thirty years of military they had never had anything like what Camden County did for them. They were all laughing about Flat Stanley and told me that Admiral Papp showed everyone who came to his office his scrapbook. That just made my day!

A year or so later, I attended the Coast Guard Birthday Ball in Norfolk and had a chance to tell him about Dan Hurd (be sure to read his story!). Days before, Dan had received orders as the commandant and the secretary of Homeland Security's pilot.

Admiral Papp was our honored speaker for the March 16, 2012, Community that Cares. I had also talked with him about the designation that we were requesting to be a Coast Guard City. I told him that we were three cities and a county and the designation only called for a city. Since the application goes through Coast Guard headquarters and then, if submitted, to all of the committees in Congress who have oversight over the Coast Guard it is quite a process and here I am wanting to change the designation. Everyone was excited. Our community really knows how to pull together when it's needed! We brainstormed and came up with great ideas—plans were developed, everyone had their responsibilities, and then we waited.

When the call came that Admiral Papp and Linda were coming we all knew what to do and the rest was fun, exciting, and exhausting. Linda and Admiral Papp arrived with festive flags greeting them at the entrance of the base conference center, the electronic boards cracking with the "Welcome Admiral Papp" message, a billboard awesomely displayed on Highway 40 and marquees all over town welcoming his visit.

Camden County Commission chairman, David Rainer, joined St. Marys mayor, Bill Deloughy; Kingsland mayor, Kenneth Smith; and Woodbine mayor, Steve Parrott in officially welcoming Admiral and Mrs. Papp at the reception when they arrived. Local sea service leadership in attendance included: from the Navy, RADM and Mrs. Joe Tofalo, COMSUBGRU 10, and Captain John O'Neill, commanding officer, Naval Submarine Base Kings Bay; from the Coast Guard, Commander Steve Love, commanding officer, Maritime Force Protection Unit, Kings Bay, and LCDR Matt Baer and his wife, Laurie, from the Maritime Safety and Security Team; and from the Marine Corps Lt. Col. Wendy Goyette, commanding officer, Marine Corps Security Force Battalion. There were commanding officers, executive officers, chiefs, and master chiefs. There were greetings from community members as they recognized the military present as members of their churches and organizations. It was a sea of white, blue, and khaki. Our military mixing with community leaders from across the county. These was such a festive air in the room. And the room itself was festive, thanks to committee members.

The Camden Kings Bay Council headed by Hunt Thornhill was in attendance as was his wife, Alyce. Keith Post, Georgia State president, presented the proclamation "Admiral Robert J. Papp Day" along with the mayors and chairman of the county commission. Of course, the admiral didn't leave without an EDICCIMAD (Every Day in Camden County is Military Appreciation Day) to always remember this community.

As it turns out one of the most enjoyable and effective events was Cheryl Aston's idea to have a Flat Stanley event after a children's book with that name. Cheryl produced pictures of Admiral Papp, Keith organized the rally and over one hundred men and women in Camden helped us escort Admiral Papp (poster picture of him) to various landmarks and official locations in the cities and country including our law enforcement and fire departments. It looked impressive with all of those cars arriving at the same location. Very significant was the scrapbook prepared by Julie Swick and Katie Bishop. They did a bang-up job of capturing the events leading up to the Community that Cares and the day itself. (I was told that Admiral Papp had the scrapbook displayed in his office for all to see!) The three cities and the country presented a proclamation:

PROCLAMATION
ADMIRAL ROBERT J. PAPP, JR. DAY

A PROCLAMATION by the cities of Kingsland, St Marys, and Woodbine; and the County of Camden, Georgia designating Friday the 16th of March 2012 as ADMIRAL ROBERT J. PAPP, JR. Day.

WHEREAS, today, on behalf of all Camden County citizens, we welcome the 24th Commandant of the United States Coast Guard to Camden County; and

WHEREAS, Camden County has an exceptional supportive relationship with all the military services based in and around Kings Bay Naval Submarine Base; and

WHEREAS, with the commissioning of the Maritime Safety and Security Team Kings Bay (MSST 91108) in August of 2003, the commissioning of the Maritime Force Protection Unit Kings Bay (MFPU) in July 2007, and the commissioning of the cutters USCGC SEA DRAGON (WPB 87367) in January 2008 and USCGC SEA DOG (WPB 87373) in July 2009, the Coast Guard presence in Camden County has dramatically increased; and

WHEREAS, we live in freedom thanks to the contributions and sacrifices made by the extraordinary men and women of our armed forces, as well as their families, who serve our nation in times of peace, war and national peril; and

WHEREAS, the people of Camden County are honored and privileged to welcome, salute and pay tribute to a man who has served his nation with distinction for more than 36 years following graduation from the United States Coast Guard Academy, which has included critical assignments such as the Commander, Coast Guard Atlantic Area and Commander, Ninth Coast Guard District; and

WHEREAS, Admiral Papp is the 13th Gold Ancient Mariner of the Coast Guard which is an honorary position held by an officer with over ten years of cumulative sea duty who has held the qualification as a Cutterman longer than any other officer; and

WHEREAS, we are grateful for the opportunity to host Admiral PAPP in our Community;

NOW, THEREFORE, we do hereby jointly and proudly proclaim **Friday, the 16th day of March 2012** to be:

ADMIRAL ROBERT J. PAPP, JR. DAY
IN CAMDEN COUNTY, GEORGIA

David L. Rainer, Chairman William T. Deloughy, Mayor

Camden County Board of Commissioners City of St. Marys

Kenneth E. Smith Sr., Mayor Steve L. Parrott, Mayor
City of Kingsland City of Woodbine

This was my introduction:

> Admiral Bob Papp was meant to be a Marine—there were early signs—and his father was a Marine. But he made the decision to serve his country in the United States Coast Guard. And that seems to have been a good decision. We are pleased to welcome back Adm. Papp who honored us as guest speaker for our Military of the Year banquet two years ago. Admiral Papp is a ship driver who has a great fondness for his shipmates. But his definition of a shipmate is broader than most. In fact, I am a proclaimed "shipmate" of Bob Papp's. We all wondered who the next leader of the Coast Guard would be. Some folks had him pegged—and thought they had him all figured out—but he could not be pegged. Now we all hear how approachable he is and that he is seriously smart. Where others see problems, he sees challenges. And with what is this country is facing we are blessed to have him at the helm of our Coast Guard.
>
> And welcome to his wife, Linda Kapral Papp. What a beautiful elegant lady—one who really cares about our service members and their families. Who is as approachable as she is caring. What a wonderful team they make.
>
> The Coast Guard needed another great leader. Bob Papp is both a warrior and a thinker—and that is needed for the multitude of missions of the Coast Guard and the challenges they face in these next few years As Admiral Papp so proudly stated: "The Coast Guard protects the people on the sea, they protect our country against threats delivered by the sea and they even protect the sea itself." Please help me welcome the 24th Commandant of the United States Coast Guard, Admiral Bob Papp.

Other commanding officers, executive officers, chiefs, and master chiefs participated. There were greetings from community members as they recognized service men and women as members of their churches and organization. The Coast Guard boss spoke at local Navy League luncheon and the base paper the *Periscope* had this article by Kelly Wirfel:

> *Community support and true Southern hospitality were on display as the Camden-Kings Bay Navy League, The Camden Partnership and nearly 200 Camden County business and community leaders welcomed Adm. Robert J. Papp, Commandant of the United States Coast Guard, to Naval Submarine Base Kings Bay, March 9.*
>
> *The visit gave Papp a first-hand look at the vital role that the both the Maritime Force Protection Unit and the Maritime Safety and Security Team play for the security of Kings Bay and allowed him to see how strongly the community supports the Coast Guard.*
>
> *Prior to Papp speaking to the audience, a proclamation was signed by the cities of Kingsland, St. Marys and Woodbine, as well as Camden County, declaring March 9 as Adm. Robert Papp Day. Papp began by lunch addressing before base guests and community members, thanking all for the support he has received. "I am completely overwhelmed with the response I have received from the Camden County community," Papp said. "In fact, with the powers invested in me as the Commandant of the Coast Guard, I declare Camden County a Coast Guard County."*
>
> *Papp continued by outlining the basic mission of the Coast Guard. "To make it very simple, our mission is to make sure bad things don't happened from the sea, bad things don't happen to people on the sea and bad things don't happen to the sea," he said. He continued by addressing the budget cuts and the "uncertain and stormy seas" that face the Coast Guard, but quickly followed up by saying he is confident that the service will be able to face these challenges head on.*
>
> *"I am confident we are ready to face those uncertain and stormy seas, because we have great patriots that are stepping up to serve this great county," Papp said. "Regardless of how bad the weather is, it is going to get better. Our Coast Guard men and women give me great confidence." The visit was the result of an invitation by and the persistence of Sheila McNeill, the president of The Camden Partnership and former national Navy League president.*
>
> *"Once we received confirmation he was coming the community, support was absolutely overwhelming," McNeill said. "There was a lot of working parts to this visit, and we could not have pulled it off without the support of this community."*

The statement he made gave us the approval we needed from the Coast Guard. (Note: We were working then to obtain letters from our mayors and community leaders for Admiral Papp to reinforce this declaration with an official application to present to the two authorizing congressional committees that approves this designation.) Admiral Papp came with the knowledge of what we had done to help restore the 2010 Coast Guard budget. Later he told me he would forward our package to the Senate committees with his approval.

We later received the word that it was approved! There is a separate story on Coast Guard community.

It was October 2012 and Adm. John Richardson had just taken over nuclear reactors coming from Submarine Force Atlantic Fleet. I was talking with Dana, his wife, and the conversation went to her new home. I was very familiar with the house since Adm. Kirk Donald and his wife, Diane, were also friends and I stayed over many times. It was being renovated so Dana and John were staying at Bollinger Air Force Base. I asked the address and it was right down from Admiral Papp and Linda. I suggested they get together and Dana was pleased to get acquainted with some of her neighbors. I e-mailed Bob and Linda Papp and CC'd Dana and John and they proceeded to match available dates. I felt good about them getting together. They were both special and I knew they would enjoy the evening. *But* once the date was set Bob told me I had to join them. It didn't take too much pushing to take them up on that. It was a great evening and I enjoyed touring the new commandant's quarters. I suggested that Bob might want to talk to nuclear reactors about some of the ships he was going to build.

At Sea Air Space (SAS) in 2014, Admiral Robert Papp was the main speaker. As the seating goes at SAS it is all about putting the right folks together. Navy League members (and professional staff) are not the sought-after dinner guests. I never believed this about some of the professional staff. I had wished during my term I had merged the staffer in charge of SAS, the editor of *Seapower*, and the legislative director in with the guests. Each could certainly hold their own and their contribution to our defense is incredible. At any rate, we were all sitting in the very back when Admiral Papp was speaking. He said, "One day a woman walked into my office when I was in Legislative Affairs and said, 'My name is Sheila McNeill and I'm here to help.' I didn't know what to expect at that time, but she really did help and that is when I first became involved with the Navy League. Sheila and I are still friends." Everyone at the table was grinning.

What a thrill to have him tell the story to 1,200 or so guests.

When he retired, he continued his service as a member of the State Department. I love the personal touch to Secretary Kerry's announcement:

Retired Admiral Robert Papp to Serve as U.S. Special Representative for the Arctic
Press Statement
John Kerry, Secretary of State
Washington, D.C.
July 16, 2014

> *Earlier this year we decided to appoint a Special Representative for the Arctic for a simple reason: President Obama and I are committed to elevating these issues in America's foreign policy and national security strategy because the United States is an Arctic nation, and Arctic policy has never been more important, particularly as we prepare to Chair the Arctic Council in 2015.*
>
> *We set out to find the right American official for this assignment, a distinguished and senior, high-level public servant with broad foreign policy experience and a passion for the Arctic.*
>
> *I could not be more pleased to announce that Admiral Robert J. Papp, Jr. will lead our efforts to advance U.S. interests in the Arctic Region as the State Department's Special Representative.*
>
> *Admiral Papp served with great distinction as Commandant of the Coast Guard, retiring this May after a stellar thirty-nine-year career. As Commandant, Papp navigated a difficult budget environment to recapitalize the Coast Guard's fleet, working with Congress to secure funding to complete five of eight National Security Cutters and to refurbish and restore the Polar Star heavy icebreaker to service. I could not be happier that he agreed to postpone his well-deserved retirement and join our effort in a cause about which he is both passionate and wise.*
>
> *I am also extraordinarily grateful that in our efforts, I will be able to rely on senior advice from a remarkable Alaskan, former Lieutenant Governor Fran Ulmer who, as President Obama's Chair of the U.S. Arctic Research Commission, will provide invaluable counsel as a Special Advisor on Arctic Science and Policy. We have a great deal of work to do, and that work starts right away. Admiral Papp will soon travel to Alaska to consult with policy-makers on the front lines of America's Arctic state. As we have throughout this process, we will rely on the close consultation of Senators Begich and Murkowski. The Arctic region is the last global frontier and a region with enormous and growing geostrategic, economic, climate, environment, and national security implications for the United States and the world. With the team, we're building at the State Department, we will make sure that the United States is in the strongest possible position to meet these challenges and seize these opportunities.*

Linda was the sponsor for the USCG *Hamilton*, WMSL (733). December 6, 2014, was the commissioning date. Arlie and I were both in attendance. She did a wonderful job in her remarks in front of a full crowd. Linda is wonderful. Beautiful as well as gracious and that is evidenced by the fact that she was a former Miss

Connecticut. The ceremony was in Charleston, so our friends Malcolm and Shirley Fages also attended. What a great relaxing evening we had after the ceremony. There was some angst. Everywhere I turned there were Coast Guard—men and women that I had met over the past twenty to thirty years from different commands and different eras. All here tonight as friends and me trying to remember where I had met each of them. In all my years of being married to Arlie, he has never mentioned any piece of women's clothing that he like, but he still tells me he wants me to find a green suit like Linda had on that day!

When Bob retired, there was an opportunity to post a note on the Coast Guard's webpage:

PAPP, ADMIRAL BOB AND LINDA

Message: Time passes too quickly. Who would have thought when I first met you that we would become such good friends? Your tour has been incredible. With all you have to do you have managed to make our entire community feel special with your visit and your words. Our designation as the First Coast Guard Community will always be linked with you and Linda. We will continue to do everything we can to support your shipmates. You know I will! And since Arlie has been on the Coast Guard Committee with the Navy League since 1966 you are assured of his continued support. This cannot end with your retirement so please stay in touch and when you find yourself driving south on I-95 plan to stop at our house and spend some time.

You continue to be one of the top ten speakers in the thousands of speeches I have heard over my 40 years of support. And Linda, what a fantastic advocate you have been for our Coast Guard families. As with Bob, you have been accessible, caring, and effective. This country owes a debt of gratitude to you both.

In 2017, our mutual friend Lieutenant Commander Dan Hurd retired and Bob, Linda and Arlie, and I were all there! Linda and Bob Papp will always be the ones I can pick up a phone, and even if it's been months, we catch up like we had talked yesterday.

SECRETARY OF DEFENSE BILL PERRY

When I was serving on the Defense Advisory Committee on Women in the Services, Bill Perry was secretary of defense. He was such a gentleman and very well regarded. He made it clear that he considered what we were doing important. Our opening statement at every focus group was "If you had five minutes with the secretary of defense, what would you say?" No more was said—if we had offered suggestions we would be creating the outcome, so we waited. As vice chairman, my responsibility was to train the committee on visits, to read each of the reports from the members' visit and compile a report for the secretary. This was sent to the secretary with a summary of the top issues. One year, in spite of our committee name, was insufficient pay for junior enlisted and maintenance issues. My first focus group with those issues is remembered in another chapter.

One day we were all waiting for Secretary Perry to arrive—there were thirty-five to forty of us. When he walked in the room, someone started singing "You Are My Sunshine." An unusual reaction but indicative of our respect and affection for him. I asked Secretary Perry to visit and speak to our Navy League and the community. I was amazed when he accepted and even more amazed by the number of phone calls days out from his visit. The day before I was getting very nervous that he would have to cancel and worried more with each call. When I did mention the possibility that he would cancel… well, maybe what I said to his staff was "Don't you cancel on me!" They assured me that the secretary was making a real effort and did not want to cancel.

The day finally arrived and Rear Admiral Chuck Beers, Captain Jim Alley, and I were at the small helicopter pad on base as two black hawk helicopters landed. I was very surprised when the first to step out was Major General Paul Kern whom I had known when he commanded Fort Stewart. Melody Somers CSG-10 Protocol Officer was there to make things go well—that always gave me comfort. As Secretary Perry landed, General Kern said, "I'm sorry we're going to have to cut this short. President Clinton has called a meeting at the White House at three o'clock, so we will only have fifty-five minutes on the ground."

"Sheila is in charge of this so talk to her," Chuck said. It was obviously better for someone out of uniform to "manage" this meeting.

We immediately went to the club at Kings Bay walking as fast as we could with about ten other people including Major General Kern and Pentagon spokesman Ken Bacon. I walked to the podium as Secretary Perry and his staff took their seats. There was no time to eat, no time for small talk but he was here! As Secretary Perry came to the end of his Q and A, I received a note from one of the staff telling me that the winds had changed and the flight back to DC would take another five minutes, so I was to get the secretary to finish up.

I gently put my hand on his back. "There is time for one more question," I told him. After the last question, he thanked everyone, and we then quickly left the building. I had already told Secretary Perry and Mr. Bacon that they didn't have to worry about press. We were a small town and I didn't expect many to attend. Imagine my surprise when we opened the door and several television stations and various print reporters were waiting for us. As we walked through the virtual gauntlet, I held my hands up and shielded Perry and gave "statements" as we walked through:

"Sorry, he is in a hurry."

"I'm sorry, he has a meeting in DC."

"So sorry."

"Yes, a meeting with the president."

There was a barrage of questions from the press. When they asked if they could get a picture, I had to say, "Only if you can walk backward and faster." I even smiled today as I picture it.

When we got in the van, Secretary Perry turned his head to the back of the van and mimicked me. Repeating each of my remarks, he concluded, "Mr. Bacon, General Kern, you two are wimps compared to Sheila!" Everyone had a good laugh and I was amazed and delighted that the very distinguished and reserved Perry would tease me like that. We arrived back at the helo pad, and Secretary Perry gave me a big hug!

As they were flying back to DC, they received word that our beloved chief of Naval operations Adm. Mike Boorda had died. A very sad end to a very wonderful day.

REAR ADMIRAL STEPHEN PIETROPAOLI

CHIEF OF INFORMATION, UNITED STATES NAVY
EXECUTIVE DIRECTOR, NAVY LEAGUE OF THE UNITED STATES

When Rear Admiral Steve was the special assistant to the chairman of the Joint Chiefs of Staff, General Shalikasvili, they had one of their meetings on Sea Island. I was one of the local organizers helping Woody Woodside and the Brunswick Golden Isles Chamber of Commerce. Stephen was with the General. It was a pleasure for me to introduce him to the local community.

We saw each other fairly often and it was always interesting and fun to talk with him. When I national president of the Navy League, we needed a new executive director. This is a position that runs the fifty or so staff and matters from legislative affairs to publishing our magazine. Steve agreed to meet with me to discuss possible candidates for a new national executive director of the Navy League. I had known him a long time—even before he was chief of information for the Navy. Wow, I thought. Wouldn't he make an incredible executive director for the Navy League and a great person to help me during my two years.

We met at the Ritz-Carlton, Pentagon City. I had about a dozen names, but I was really only interested in Stephen. We discussed all the options and I then asked him what I wanted to ask from the beginning. "Would you be willing to consider the position?"

"No, thank you, Sheila, I have other options I want to pursue. I just want to help you."

He gave a dozen reasons as I tried to convince him to come help me with the Navy League. We continued to talk. I pointed out that he had not committed to anyone and that he would take the job, and if it didn't work out, he could help me find someone. Finally, he relented. He wanted to talk to Dawn before it was announced.

When he got home that evening, Dawn asked, "Was Sheila very disappointed?"

He answered, "Not so much since I told her I'd take it."

Ramona Joyce, Navy League public affairs officer, sent the following press release out on November 6, 2003:

> *Sheila McNeill announced the appointment of a new executive director. "We are very fortunate to have someone of Stephen Pietropaoli's caliber as our new executive director," McNeill said. "Stephen is committed to helping the Navy League promote public understanding of the sea services and the critical role they play in the security of the nation, building on the efforts from his predecessor Charles Robinson."*
>
> *A retired rear admiral Pietropaoli previously served as the Navy's chief of information where he was charged with overseeing all aspects of the Navy's public affairs program. Before that, he served as special assistant public affairs to Army General Hugh Shelton, then chairman of the Joint Chiefs of Staff. Pietropaoli, a 1977 Cornell University graduate, began his naval career as a surface warfare officer in the Atlantic Fleet, in 1984. He applied for and received re-designation as a public affairs specialist. He has served in a variety of assignments including head of the Navy's national news desk in the Pentagon and as the media relations officer for the commander of the Atlantic Fleet and the U.S. Atlantic Command.*
>
> *In addition to his studies at Cornell University, Pietropaoli completed his master's degree in Broadcast Journalism at American University and graduated from the National War College in 1997 where he was awarded the Master of Science in National Security Strategy. Pietropaoli, his wife Dawn, and their sons Daniel and Matthew reside in Arlington, Va.*

The Navy League of the United States was founded in 1902 with the encouragement of President Theodore Roosevelt. The league is a civilian organization with nearly seventy-two thousand members, who for more than one hundred years have supported the sea services, which includes the Navy, Marine Corps, Coast Guard, and the US Flag Merchant Marine. The League is dedicated to educating American citizens and elected officials about the importance of sea power to the United States since we are a maritime nation.

Steve gave me a copy of the speech he gave to Falls Church Rotary Club on 27 May 2004 and this is part of that speech:

> Like many retiring military officers… I really hadn't decided what I wanted to be when I "grew up" and left the Navy. So, there I was… on what the military calls "terminal leave"… hanging around the house making my kids spoiled and my wife crazy! When I get a call from the Navy League President… Sheila McNeill… first woman president of our 100-year-old organization… and she asked me if I'd consider taking the position of Executive Director. Well… since I knew Sheila… and had enormous respect for her… and for the organization… I said I'd be happy to talk to her about ANYTHING. But that it probably wouldn't be a good fit for me.
>
> As you can see… Sheila's a pretty persuasive leader. The jury's still out on how good a fit it will ultimately be as I've only been on board for six months. So, When the Navy League offered me a chance to continue to be a "voice" for these great young American's well, it seemed like more than a coincidence… and I'm sure glad I gave it a shot!

And an excerpt of the *Florida Times Union* article, June 26, 2005, by Gordon Jackson:

> *ST. MARYS—Retired Rear Adm. Stephen Pietropaoli never intended to accept an offer to become executive director of the Navy League two years ago. Of course, he had never met Sheila McNeill. Pietropaoli agreed to meet with McNeill, who had just been elected president of the 70,000-member Navy League, and planned to tactfully reject the job offer. When Pietropaoli got home from the meeting, his wife asked how McNeill reacted to his refusal to take the job. She didn't get the answer she expected. "Sheila's a very persuasive woman," he said. "She was right and I was wrong. Her passion for what she was doing is infective!*

Steve arranged for me to present an award from the USS *Stennis* to the Daughters of the American Revolution at their annual meeting in DC. It was an amazing evening that is covered in another story.

July 2004: An e-mail he wrote one of his old friends, Vice Admiral Scott Redd, who also served with me on Governor Perdue's GMACC (Georgia Military Affairs Committee) after he retired and had assumed the position of executive director and Commission on Intelligence Capabilities of the US regarding weapons of mass destruction.

> *As for me… I too am an Executive Director for the Navy League. The president, Sheila McNeill (first woman to be president in a 103-year-old organization) caught up with me during that awkward time AFTER you've left the military but BEFORE you've really decided what you want to be when you grow up! She's a persuasive woman who's trying to shake things up in the great but hidebound association… and that's been nice to participate in. It's also a nice 'halfway house' for a guy like me that really loved being a spokesman for those who were the uniform. This at least lets me remain a voice for Sailors, Marines, Coasties and Merchant Mariners.*

On October 22, Steve sent Arlie and me a thank you for our donation to the building committee. He began, "You know, it seems more than a little strange for me to be sending you two a letter about *anything* having to do with Navy League. I've very fortunate to have such close and frequent personal contact that letter-writing is seldom necessary. But some things cry out for recognition more formal than a 'thank you' in the hallway." That man sure had a way with words.

We had a wonderful two years. I loved his work and his charm and his work ethic. I loved the conversations and debates we had. Of course, in a debate he actually had concrete information stored in various parts of his brain but I did all I could to debate my side. The last year of my presidency, he and John Alexander, with the Navy-Marine Corps Relief Society, worked with the Navy and the office of the secretary of the Navy to produce a remarkable book: "Defending Freedom."

The book jacket read, "The Navy League of the United States is pleased to publish this tribute to America's heroic Sailors and Marines in partnership with the Navy-Marine Corps Relief Society. Both organizations are entering their second century of service in support of our Navy and Marine Corps personnel and their families." Secretary of the Navy, Gordon England, did the foreword.

The book jacket also told of the work of the Navy-Marine Relief Society and the Navy League.

The last section of the book cover was "About Military Photographers."

Historically, Navy photography took root in 1914, when the Navy's first "official" photographer Walter L. Richardson, a cook aboard the battleship USS *Mississippi*, documented the training and aircraft tests being conducted at a naval station, later to be known as the Cradle of Naval Aviation in Pensacola, Florida.

In the early 1900s, photographers used 4 × 5 press cameras and worked out of crude, makeshift photo labs set up in storage rooms and closets. Now twenty-first century military photographers are respected professionals armed with advanced digital camera systems and laptops. They are deployed throughout the world, assigned to combat camera teams, ships at sea, aircraft squadrons, and combat teams, ships at sea, aircraft squadrons, and combat units on the ground. Today's photography "visual information" requires no film and is often acquired, captioned, released, and transmitted within minutes of an event.

This book serves to showcase the extraordinary dedication and capability of the US military, with attention to the Navy and Marine Corps team. These ordinary but highly motivated, highly trained men and women defend our democracy, while freeing the people of Iraq from the misery and tyranny suffered at the hands of the Saddam Hussein regime. Each image presented in this book displays the very best photojournalist captured by military photographers, journalists, and service members who placed themselves in harm's way in an effort to fully document the events leading up to and then through the first days of Operation Iraqi Freedom.

Christopher J. Madden
Director Naval Visual News Service
Navy Office of Information

T. L. McCreary
Rear Admiral U.S. Navy
Chief of Information

As Navy League president, my name was on many documents of other's work. That is especially true of this book. Steve Pietropaoli was the force and the talent working with the chief of information for the Navy (CHINFO) and John Alexander for this wonderful capture of history. I was pleased to have Defending Freedom come out during the last few months of my presidency. The cover forward has the following: "The Navy League of the United States is pleased to publish this tribute to America's heroic Sailors and Marines in partnership with the Navy-Marine Corps Relief Society. Both organizations are entering their second century of service in support of our Navy and Marine Corps personnel and their families." Secretary of the Navy, Gordon England, did the foreword.

The book jacket told of the Navy-Marine Relief Society and the Navy League the last section was:

Navy Office of Information

Chief of Information

We had a great reception on Capitol Hill. Many of the photographers were in attendance and signed books for the guests.

We had an issue with the American Shipbuilding Association during that time, and I think he realized the issues at an early stage and guided the Navy League through the turmoil of keeping our reputation and mission intact. The position as national president of the Navy League of the United States is a big job. You deal with legislation, military issues, individual issues for our military members, a magazine, millions of dollars in a budget, renting a two-hundred-square-foot building and keeping the current occupants happy. Steve had a staff of about fifty. He managed it all beautifully and I was able to do what Navy League presidents are supposed to do—get the message out!

Thank you, Steve, for all you did for me during my tour as president. I think we made a great team and I couldn't have done it without you.

SENIOR CHIEF KEITH POST, US NAVY

DIRECTOR, ST. MARYS SUBMARINE MUSEUM

Keith Post is intricately connected with almost every event I've sponsored. He is an incredible patriot and works harder than anyone I know. He left the submarine force when he as a senior chief. He could have stayed and made master chief, but he had a conflict. He was gay and could not bear the thought of working to remove someone from the service because they were gay. I was at Keith's home when the chairman of the Joint Chiefs, Admiral Michael Mullen, first spoke on gays in the military and how they would now be accepted. He immediately wrote an e-mail to Admiral Mullen and asked me to forward it. I forwarded it that evening and immediately had this response: "Sheila, I am on Capitol Hill tomorrow—please thank your friend for the letter."

I fuss at him a lot. He takes on too much and doesn't take care of himself. I've talked to his partner, Bradley, many times and we both agree. But what makes Keith someone we love also makes Keith someone we try to change! He is an intricate part of most of the events I have sponsored. None of them would have been as successful without Keith. In 2016, Keith was awarded the Ben Bastura Historical Achievement Award.

He sent me this e-mail: "It was an amazing night last night at the banquet. If it was not your time zone when I got back to my room I would have called you last night. USSVI honored me with the BEN BASTURA Heritage Award last night at the Banquet. It was an unbelievable evening. I am so humbled and honored. Keith."

It was just one of the many he has received—and I think he is surprised at all of them!

Gordon Jackson with the *Brunswick News* runs a column on veterans every week. One week he honored Keith.

> Sailor serves three times at Kings Bay by Gordon Jackson, the *Brunswick News*, October 1, 2013:
> Today's veteran: Keith Forrest Post, 53
> Born: Bayshore, NY
> Residence: St. Marys
> Service: Navy 1981–2003
> Highest rank: senior chief petty officer
> Recognitions: Enlisted Submarine Dolphins, Ballistic Missile Submarine Patrol Pin (16 Patrols), Meritorious Service Medal, Navy Commendation Medal (3 Awards), Navy Achievement Medal (5 Awards), Naval Submarine Base Pearl Harbor Sailor of the Year 1990, Navy League Honolulu Council Outstanding Military Service Award 1990. Main duties: Submarine sonar technician, Navy career counselor Duty stations: USS Nathan Hale; USS Casimir Pulaski; Naval Submarine Base Pearl Harbor; Trident Training Facility (Kings Bay); USS Nebraska (Groton, Conn., and Kings Bay); SP-205 Team, Strategic Systems Programs (Arlington, Va., and Cape Canaveral); Force Career Counselor, Strategic Systems Programs Headquarters (Washington, D.C.).
> His story: Keith Post's family has a history of sea service, but he had no plans to make the Navy a career when he enlisted for six years in 1981.
>
> *"My dad, Oakley (Post), who is a retired master chief and my biggest inspiration for joining the military, served in the Coast Guard for 29 years from New York to Hawaii and many places in between," he said. An uncle, Allan Stock, was the person who influenced him to choose the Navy. Stock's service included the landing at Normandy in 1944 when he was 17 years old.*
>
> *"He taught me a lot about honor, courage and commitment, as well as selfless devotion and dedication to those serving with you," Post said. During a tour of duty on the USS Nathan Hale—where he made lifelong friends—Post said he decided to make the Navy a career. His 22-year Navy career took him to many duty stations, but one of the most gratifying was at Pearl Harbor, where he served as the base career counselor. After he retired, Post said he visited family on the East Coast and ran the New York and Marine Corps marathons,*

before returning to Camden County, where he lived three different times while serving at Naval Submarine Base Kings Bay.

"It was close to home in Florida, not far from Jacksonville, where my Navy career began in 1981, and because of the people here," he said about settling in St. Marys. "I fell in love with Southeast Georgia. Wasn't sure what I would do after I got out, but I knew where I wanted to be."

Post has remained busier than he intended since retiring from the Navy. He is currently completing his first term on the St. Marys City Council and will not seek re-election. He is on the board of directors at Orange Hall, a member of the local Navy League Council, an advisory board member for the College of Coastal Georgia and manager of the St. Marys Submarine Museum. He is also the co-owner of a computer company.

When John Crouse died, I called Keith. I asked him if he was interested in serving as the executive director of the museum. He was hesitant, so I asked if he would take over the management until we could find someone. He agreed to take the job until we found someone. We never looked! It's eight years later and he still can't get away!

We had our twentieth anniversary celebration on Saturday, March 19, 2016, and Keith did the planning and preparation. That and more about Keith is in the St. Marys Submarine Museum story.

I admit most people who know us know that I often referred to him as an "idiot," but that was always said with love and only because he takes on so much—more than he has ever been and could ever be compensated for—but we should all strive to do that! Thank you, Keith, for your dedication to the museum, to our military and to Camden County.

Note: You'll find Keith's name throughout the book.

GENERAL DENNY REIMER, CHIEF OF STAFF U.S. ARMY

I met General Reimer at the first Georgia Governor's Military Affairs Committee in Atlanta. I did not know him at the time—I believe it was around 1993 or 1994. He was commander of US Forces Command which was responsible for all Army forces in the Continental U.S.—Active, Guard and Reserve. I sat next to him, as debates were going on about the need for the committee, preparing for a future BRAC (base realignment and closure) and, if the committee was created, just what the mission would be.

I was a little uncomfortable as a Navy League member at the directions the committee might go. It all seemed to conflict with what the military needs to maintain the right size military within their budget. I agreed with much of what they were discussing but at odds with what the Navy League's responsibility is to support the services vice working against them on a BRAC.

When I mentioned this to the General, he smiled and said, "I understand—I'm in that same position you know."

General Reimer was confirmed by the Senate on May 23, 1995, to become the army chief of staff. His confirmation was reported in the *USA News* as "smooth sailing" and referred to questions by then Senator Sam Nunn on quality of life issues for junior enlisted. "We have got to take care of soldiers and their families, but there are limited resources." General Reimer replied that the moral in the Army is high now. "Soldiers enjoy being in the Army, but there is great uncertainty about the future. Retiree pay, and health benefits are eroding a bit and that adds to the uncertainty."

I sent the article from the local paper, the *Brunswick News*, to the general on his nomination. I also sent a congratulations card. He sent me a nice note dated April 25, 1995:

Sheila,

Thank you for your card and the clipping. I'm sure they are all not going to be that way so I appreciate you sending it to me. It is a humbling experience, but we'll give it our best shot—appreciate all you and GMACC are doing for the military. Denny Reimer

The next time I talked with General Reimer was when we were at a formal Defense Advisory Committee on Women in the Services dinner in Washington, DC. We had just returned from our European trip and I had given my report. Gender issues did not rise as one of the issues. The issues that did come up with the troops were increased pay for junior enlisted and the fact that they were cannibalizing their planes to be able to fly. They wanted to see the funding for maintenance.

I was seated between General Reimer and an assistant secretary of one of the services. (I'm trying to be delicate here.) The secretary was trying to convince me that we were wrong on pay for junior enlisted. He told me that I didn't understand BAH (bachelor allowance for housing) and health care. When it was all added up, they were receiving more than the average amount their civilian counterparts made.

We were debating this when General Reimer stretched his arm across me indicating he wanted me to lean back, so he could make a comment to Mr. Secretary. As I leaned back, the general said, "I have thousands of soldiers on welfare. Keep it up, Mrs. McNeill." That was the only time I have ever seen a service chief speak so freely to a senior appointed official. He has been added to my hero list.

Note: *Air Force Times* covered a hearing with the service chiefs in late September 1998. Army General Dennis Reimer, Navy Admiral Jay Johnson, Air Force General Michael Ryan, and Marine Corps General Charles Kulak testified at a budget hearing to discuss status of military forces. They will get an opportunity in late September to a make a pitch for Congress for better pay and benefits for rank-and-file services members.

I am sure General Reimer shared his concerns about pay for our junior enlisted and I'm glad he was there that night to refute the Secretary's opinion.

And in that same paper on September 14, 1998, they ran an editorial.

Just tell it like it is

> *If there was a time for straight talk, this is it.*
>
> *The military service chiefs will have a unique opportunity in late September to make the case for more money. The venue will be the Senate Armed Service Committee, which prodded by Senate Majority Leader Trent Lott, R, Miss, is holding a special hearing on military readiness, pay and morale.*
>
> *Lott and some of his fellow Republicans have seized on sagging military readiness and retention as a campaign issue in this fall's congressional elections.*
>
> *The hearing comes too late to affect the Air Force's 1999 budget. But it certainly could lay the groundwork for additions to the 2000 budget that will be sent to Congress in February. Republicans—at least some of them—are convinced that defense spending is too low given the growing and seemingly open-ended commitments to places like Saudi Arabia and Bosnia. They argue convincingly that the festering military pay gap, combined with diminished health-care benefits and a crushing operational tempo, are making it difficult to recruit and retain the high quality people need by the Air Force and the other services.*
>
> *The pro-defense group, however, is not the only voice on the Hill. Deficit hawks like House Budget Committee Chairman John Kasich, R-Ohio, continue to argue that the military need only spend the money it already received more wisely.*
>
> *So, the chiefs' testimony at the Armed Services Committee hearing will be crucial. If they parrot the tired Clinton administration line that budgets are tight, but still manageable, the wind will go out of any effort to give the services more money. It's up to the chiefs to publicly confirm what everyone privately knows—that the services are in trouble and something has to give.*

> *This is not an easy assignment for the chiefs. There's the natural military inclination to salute and say, "Yes, sir. Can do." Also, the chiefs work for the president. They have to be careful not to appear to be in revolt against their civilian leader.*
>
> *At the same time, they also are obliged to give the lawmakers who set their budget the unvarnished truth. This case, doing so might allow them to meet another sacred obligation: taking care of their troops.*

I would say that General Reimer and the Defense Advisory Committee on Women in the Services (DACOWITS) were both right

VICE ADMIRAL CHAS RICHARD AND LISA AND TAKING THE LEADERSHIP TO ATLANTA

COMMANDER SUBMARINE, GROUP 10 DEPUTY COMMANDER, US STRATEGIC COMMAND

After fourteen group commanders, you wonder with each one if you will be able to establish a relationship. That was not a problem with Chas and Lisa. In fact, I cherish the conversations I had with Chas on the issues. He made it a point to discuss them with me and make sure I understood. He seemed to respect my "predications" and analysis and he helped my efforts to learn more.

In one of our conversations we discussed the base's relationship with our state. We are a long way from Atlanta! I told the admiral, "With the distance and the mission of Kings Bay making connection with the Georgia leadership is important." We discussed the Trident Refit Facility (TRF) meeting with community leadership and VADM Tofalo's (then rear admiral) comments on visiting the governor and state leadership. Senator William Ligon had told me, "There are a number of people at the Capitol I'd like to hear that message." When I met with the group commander, RADM Joe Tofalo, he told me, "Yes, that's a good idea. I'll do it or pass the word on to RDML Richard."

Chas agreed for me to set up a meeting at the Georgia Capitol with Governor Nathan Deal and others that I thought would benefit from a visit and brief from the base.

A month later after talking with Captain Larry Hill, commanding officer of Trident Refit Facility (TRF), and Captain Harvey Guffey, commanding officer of Naval Submarine Base Kings Bay, we started making plans to go to Atlanta.

Although many of our issues are federal there still is great value in a good relationship with our Governor and others at the state capitol. Many issues that affect our sailors, marines, and coast guards at Kings Bay are state issues but that is not why I encourage the leadership to travel to Atlanta. Also, I think it's important to remind the state that there is a Naval base in South Georgia!

Of course, we couldn't meet until after the session began in January 2014, so I waited until after the change of command to discuss details with the new group commander, RDML Chas Richard. The change of command was set up for November 22 (what a day that was for me!). I did have a meeting with RDML Richard before the change of command and briefly discussed this and many other issues with him. He thought it was a good idea.

In late December, I began working on a date we could make this happen. It was not until late January that Captain Hill, Captain Guffey and RADM Richard could come up with two dates that I could give to Senator Ligon to begin setting up the date. Ligon's assistant, Marci Draper, started working on trying to coordinate these dates with the Governor, Lt. Governor and Senator Jack Hill, the head of the state budget committee. Those days while not ideal would work for me and for Senator Ligon. It was a little late in the legislative session but hey, trying to get this many to agree on a date is significant.

I had to cancel my flight from DC to Jacksonville and changed it from DC to Atlanta. I had the Submarine Industrial Base Council in DC on March 4 and 5 (another fabulous event for me) and flew into Atlanta on Thursday, March 6, 2014.

I had asked one of my board members and someone who knows everyone in Atlanta to join us. Bill Gross is one of our leadership in Camden. He owns a construction company and is the best community advocate that we have. He told me he would be there.

The day before I left I heard from the schedulers. We had three appointments and they didn't begin until 2:30 p.m.—the Navy was arriving at the airport at 10:00 a.m. and would arrive at the Capitol at 11:00 a.m. What do I do with them—who could meet with them? Of course, it was time for the JAG—could they, indeed meet with these gentlemen I had on my list? And if they could meet with them could the guests come for lunch? They were high level folks in Atlanta and we were two weeks out. It took almost a week to get an answer so now I'm supposed to ask these high-level folks—that I'm sure would be happy to have lunch with any of them to clear their calendars a week later. It couldn't happen. They had excellent reasons: they were making a speech somewhere, they were not in town, and they were attending a BOD meeting they had committed for. The Georgia Department of Economic Development was very supportive as was Rogers Lane who suggested I contact Pat Wilson with that department. I did and he agreed but it was too late to call anyone else—I was tied up for two days' prior with the Submarine Industrial Base Council sponsored by Electric Boat and it was just impossible. But hey, why don't we just ask folks as we saw them—and how about Amanda Seals who is the chairman for Georgia Leadership visit to Kings Bay—yes, she could make it.

And from the Jag—how much was the meal and who was paying? My solution: have it in the cafeteria, have the military pay their own way, and anyone could stop by. Brilliant! And the military liked it also.

The day arrives.

Bill and I had met earlier at the hotel where I was staying and had breakfast together. We both discussed what we would say—but decided it was only at the end of the brief if we thought it was necessary. We wanted to emphasize the support of our community and how important the base was to our economy—it has been determined that it is about 70 percent of the economy in Camden County at $1,142,000 annually with over five thousand jobs. We arrived at the Capitol about thirty minutes early and he went to find Nancy Stasnis, who is registering that day for state representative. I stayed on lookout for the military to arrive! What a coincidence that we are here on the same day.

The Navy arrives. Joining them was Lt. Ryan Collins, aide to RADM Richard. We'll just walk over and say hello to Nancy, I thought. But then I made a quick decision, perhaps too conservative, but most protective of our military officers and decide, no, they cannot go and meet Nancy and they cannot be seen with her. An image appeared with them shaking her hand. Everyone has a camera. Just that sort of image could have devastating effects on our purpose of the visit and any resulting fall out could mean criticism for these officers. I rushed them in the opposite direction. Nancy would understand—her husband is a retired naval officer.

We went immediately to the Galley to watch Senator William Ligon, our state representative in action. I texted William to see if he was going to recognize our military. He asked for the names. As I am texting the names, I hear him introducing everyone. *What?* Yes, I look up just as he is introducing everyone. We all stood with great applause for those uniforms. After that a state Senator came up and sat with Captain Guffey and talked for about ten minutes. We sat through most of Jack Hill's presentation—a broad overview of the 2015 state budget. We had to slip out toward the end.

We went to lunch and I was pleased by the number of folks that stopped by. Pat Wilson with the Georgia Department of Economic Development and others received informal briefs by our military officers as they joined the table in the cafeteria. Someone approached. I didn't recognize the name, but as soon as I saw him, I wondered if I had met him. He cleared that up quickly by telling me we met at a BRAC meeting in Atlanta

We then met with Governor Nathan Deal. The folks at TRF has made a replica of the USS *Georgia* submarine painted black but with the ship's bottom a University of Georgia red. It was gorgeous. The guys did great. They were very well organized with a professional brief—about three slides each. They each picked compelling issues to brief. They could in no way lobby—and any nuance or statement that happened was significant. As active-duty military, they can educate—but there could not be an "ask." Hmm, aren't those words familiar. I've only said them several times a week for over forty years in the Navy League. But this time neither Bill nor I could lobby either.

The governor's office visit went well. He was seeing us the day the House was voting on the annual budget and there were hundreds, maybe thousands of visitors in the Capitol. We were lucky to be meeting with him and he was most gracious. Captain Hill added that he would like the Governor to speak at the apprentice graduation in July. RDML Richard told him he needed to get him out on a submarine and of course, I chimed in with putting together a community luncheon when he visited. No commitment was made but he indicated his interest—which isn't surprising but obviously the pressures of the office will dictate. The amazing mission described by the admiral and the economic impact numbers and numbers of jobs briefed by Captain Guffey as the "mayor" of NSBKB with a clear description of the layout of NSBKB was impressive. I added as we left that I enjoyed serving on GMACC—although that was a stretch with what was going on. We had not had a meeting in months and no one had received any word on the status of the committee.

I had received a call from Marci at lunch that our appointment with Lt. Governor Casey Cagle was being pushed from 3:50 p.m. to 5:00 p.m.—thirty minutes after Senator Jack Hill's meeting.

As we left the governor's office I told everyone they were off duty for an hour and could work on e-mails and make contact with the offices. We all sat down to do that. Obviously, Bill Gross was "working the halls" because here he comes with Senator Ron Stephens, chairman of the state economic development and tourism committee. A few minutes after Ron left he comes up with Dr. Mark Williams the commissioner of the Department of Natural Resources from Jesup, who discussed the Weekend for Wildlife event every year at the Cloister and the group's trip to NSBKB.

After Mark leaves Bill arrives with Senator Joe Wilkinson, a retired naval officer and head of the state's Ethics Committee. Joe lives on St. Simons Island half the time. He attended the thirty-fifth anniversary of the base with then president of the College of Coastal Georgia, Valerie Hepburn. She was on the board of The Camden Partnership and is a great supporter of the base.

He insisted we go to his office where he had drinks and refreshments and we could all have a more comfortable wait. I joked about it being scotch. His office was like a museum—a full afternoon to hear all the stories behind the pictures and memorabilia would be needed. He worked with the Reagan and Clinton administration as a naval officer and knew the Reagans well. As we arrived he begin fishing through his desk for the scotch. I laughed and told him, no, it was 3:30 p.m. and I was joking about the scotch. He continued to pull a bottle out with a John Wayne glass. It had a great saying on the glass—perhaps, "sometimes there are just things a man cannot run from"—I don't remember exactly but it had to have been a manly quote and it ended with "pilgrim."

He poured a couple of fingers worth as I told him: (1) "I was just kidding." (2) "I really didn't care for any scotch at three thirty in the afternoon." And finally (3) "Hey, not so much." All in order as I considered what to do.

Here I am in the office of the chairman of the state committee on ethics, with three high-ranking military officers at three thirty in the afternoon while on important business to educate our state on Kings Bay and at the same time do nothing to embarrass the Navy. He offered it to everyone but, of course, they declined. I looked at them. Would they be jeopardized by my actions—taking a drink in the middle of the afternoon at the Capitol? Didn't I have to accept graciously? Wouldn't that be hospitable? I looked at Chas. He was smiling. He didn't seem to have that "Oh no, Sheila, don't do this" look. And just think of the stories I can tell over the years. The stories did it. I took a sip of the drink as the others smiled, laughed, or pretty much indicated with their body language that the Navy could survive being in the same office with this audacious behavior.

While we were there, Senator Alex Atwood, representing the Brunswick area, stopped by and visited for a few minutes. We stayed until the very last minutes before we left for the visit with Senator Hill. At some time between meetings I ask the Navy leadership if they would prefer that I not add my comments at the rest of the meetings. RDML Richard told me, "No, you add credibility. Some think we have to say this and it's evident that you do not. You add value to our briefing." Nice to hear and easier to comply with than keeping my mouth shut.

We were meeting Senator Ligon at Senator Jack Hill's office and the receptionist told us to go ahead and wait in the office he would be right back. Jack is Chairman of the Appropriations Committee. He served for thirty-three years in the Georgia National Guard as a unit commander and as State Inspector General. He retired in 2004 from the US Air Force Reserve as a Reserve Forces Officer assigned to the Selective Service System. His military service totaled thirty-seven years. He has been interested in Kings Bay for years—he is always attentive when I brief him on our annual visits. He came in as soon as we got settled and RADM Richard began. William arrived just a few minutes later—exactly on time—and joined us. Before we began, Senator Hill said to me, "We've got to get you a technical college. We've got to get you a technical college." Yikes, great to hear but he is talking about the community requests. I smiled and then told him something about being there to let him know the importance of the mission at Kings Bay and some of our workforce needs. *But* I will never forget that he knew what the community needed and expressed that need when he saw me.

The officers were brilliant and impressive. I think we could have stayed an hour if we had not scheduled at five with Lt. Governor Cagle. I think Jack might have been just a little relieved that he was not put on a spot with questioning about our technical college but with additional knowledge of the major workforce needs at Kings Bay.

We arrive at Lt. Governor Casey Cagle's office and waited while standing up in a crowded reception area. He greeted us in his usual gracious manner and escorted us back through the maze that is his staff's quarters. He made sure we all had seats and pulled the one next to him out. I had made sure I didn't have this seat on the other calls, but everyone recognized that I should just sit and not try to be gracious—so I did. He was engaged. They were again impressive—I'm proud of Richard, Guffey, and Hill, I'm thinking. I'm so glad we did this I add to myself. He is obviously impressed and asks several questions. At one point, he tells them, pointing to me, "You know she is one of your best supporters. Is she on your payroll?" he asks with a smile.

Casey doesn't mind making the comment from time to time: "I didn't know this." I like him more every time I meet with him. We probably could have stayed a little longer, but we've finished and we know he is busy.

There is comment about The Camden Partnership and our support of the base and Cagle adds, "And she gives you access too!" As if the senior military from Kings Bay needs someone else to provide access, but it was a flattering statement and that was his intent.

We leave, and everyone goes their own way. Captain Guffey heads back to vacation with his wife in North Carolina taking the northern door and we proceed to the opposite door with Bill who is dropping us off at the airport.

We have plenty of time to get to the airport. It's about 6:15 a.m. and our flight isn't until 9:30 a.m. Captain Hill's a little earlier. Foolishly I had taken the front seat of Bill's car, and I should have realized that would be the seat for the navigator. We got a little turned around at the airport, which resulted in a concentrated tour of the entire area, and Bill ended up in just the right location.

We had time to kill at the airport. I must admit that traveling with two nice looking military officers in uniform was a nice treat. I'm reminded of my daughter's paranoia when she was a young teenager, asking, "Why are they looking at us?" when we were in a restaurant or at an event.

"It's just people watching," I'd tell her.

Now I see the looks and smiles and know it's who I'm walking with. There was just a moment when I paused and made a small mention of the fact the Ferragamo shoe store was in the airport! Just a short pause. That's all it was. Short.

When Captain Hill had his change of command a couple of months later, he told the huge crowd that I had to go shopping in the airport—and made him carry my pink (it is red, mind you) suitcase. Not true—not any of it—but he got a good laugh from the audience and from me.

We had a couple of hours at the gate and we discussed the day. Everyone saying that we couldn't think of a thing we would change, and we think we covered everything we needed to cover. In fact, RDML Richard at one time said, "Sheila I'm trying to think of one thing about today that made me feel uncomfortable—one glitch in the day and I can't think of a thing. I think it was a perfect day."

Yes, the trip was worth everyone's time and was also an enjoyable day. I'd say, mission accomplished.

A few years earlier we had a "Triad" event where Air Force Brigadier General Garrett Harencak was one of the speakers. He was so impressive we invited him to come back to speak to our Navy League Council and to meet with Rear Admiral Richard. After that meeting the general joined me for lunch. He was quite impressed with the admiral but commented, "He is really smart and has done very well in spite of his limited education, hasn't he?" I was totally taken aback.

I did not immediately respond. I didn't know how to. "He *is* a graduate of Alabama, isn't he?"

Then I realized he was joking. When I relayed this to Chas he immediately knew what was coming up and laughed with me about the great personality of now Major General Harencak.

Lisa was very active with the Submarine Officers Spouses Club and we served together on the board of the St. Marys Submarine Museum. The special treat for me was when Lisa, Sue Jones and Katherine Jenks and I could get together for breakfast or lunch. We always had a great time!

I had managed to get all three couples to come to the house and we had a wonderful night on St. Simons Island. Dinner at Ocean Lodge, owned and greeted by Joe McDonough, a USS Georgia (729) SSGN supporter), with Michael Hulett on the sax makes for the perfect evening.

We also attended the Veterans Day event on St. Simons where RADM Richard spoke very eloquently to a huge crowd on lawn chairs in front of the ocean. It is quite an event and I was proud of him that day.

Chas finished his tour and he and Lisa went to DC where he served as director of Submarine Warfare. This is the position we call on when we visit DC for our annual fl-in. And 2016 was no exception. Chas gave us an update on the issues of the Ohio Replacement Program and he and Lisa joined us for dinner that night. Everyone had a wonderful time catching up.

He received his third star so he and Lisa moved again to Omaha where he served as deputy commander of US Strategic Command. He later relived VADM Joe Tufalo as Sublant-Commander Submarine Forces.

The community was proud to learn this. It is nice to catch up with them from time to time.

ADMIRAL JOHN RICHARDSON AND DANA

CHIEF OF NAVAL OPERATIONS

SEA AIR SPACE—I had heard several times before and during SAS the goal of partnerships that the chief of Naval Operations (CNO), Admiral John Richardson, had published. Off and on during Sea Air Space I had the opportunity to speak with Admiral Richardson. At one point when no one else was around and we were chatting—I said, "Admiral Richardson, I had a conversation with a senior military officer—I'm not saying who or what part of the country they were from—but I had what I thought was a good idea and told it to this officer ending with "and it ties right in with the CNO's goals for partnerships."

That senior officer answered, "But those goals are not yours to do, Sheila, they are the Navy's goals."

Before I could say anything about my reaction to the gentleman, he said, "*What!* Are you serious… No, no, no, someone didn't say that to you? Did he know who you were?"

"Yes, he did."

"Well, first he was wrong. Seriously did he know who he was talking with? Did he know you?"

"Yes," I said, "he knew me well."

"Then he is crazy—no one who knows you would speak that way. Who was it?"

"I'm not telling you. I just needed confirmation—"

"He was wrong!" he interrupted. "Sheila, do me a favor tell him you told me his name. He needs to worry."

And that is the kind of man CNO John Richardson is.

This comment had bothered me much more than it should have. I am grateful that Admiral Richardson immediately understood. One day I might tell that officer but at least with Admiral Richardson's comments I can be assured that I am focused in the right direction.

I had not met Admiral Richardson or his wife, Dana, until he was SUBLANT, commander of Submarine Forces; commander in chief, US Atlantic Command; and NATO Supreme Allied Command Atlantic.

As COMSUBLANT one of the 'duties' his wife Dana inherited was to take over the reins of the Dolphin Scholarship Foundation as Chairman. Rear Admiral Chuck Beers continued as president.

I am on the board of directors and try to attend as many of the meetings as possible—when I can't be there I attend by conference call. On one trip Chuck Beers had agreed to take me to Yorktown to visit the Coast Guard Cutter *Sea Horse*. I am sponsor of that cutter. I had made an appointment with the Commanding Officer, CWO Stephen Atchley, to visit with him and the crew. Chuck ran into a conflict and was talking with me about it at lunch after the meeting. Dana was with us and offered to take me. I knew she was busy and felt like we might have put her in a bad spot. But she convinced me that was not the case and that she would love to visit the ship.

I called ahead and told Stephen I was bringing a friend with me. I really didn't want them to be concerned with protocol. And to tell this crew who she really was would have put them in a difficult situation. Vice Admiral Richardson had just received orders to take over as director of naval nuclear reactors. This is an eight-year job that carries with it a promotion to admiral—a fourth star.

We arrived at the cutter and everyone was pleased to welcome us. We had a tour of the ship and Dana had everyone pumped with her questions. She and the Captain talked about the fact that Coast Guard cutters were used in Norfolk at times to guard the submarines as they transited. We found out that the crew had escorted fifty-two submarines in and out of port. At Kings Bay there is the special Coast Guard unit, Maritime Force Protection Unit, to do the same with our strategic submarines.

We had a nice lunch with the officers—and since I still had some time before my flight the captain suggested I stay in the cabin and work and he would take me to the airport later.

When Dana left, he asked how she knew so much about the Navy and I told him of Admiral. Richardson's job and his new promotion. I asked if he had ever heard of RADM Hyman Rickover. He had not but quickly started typing and turned the laptop around and asked, "Is this her husband's new job."

"Yes, that right."

"Oh! Wow… She was really nice."

I attended the submarine ball in Norfolk in April 2011 and was seated with the Richardsons. Admiral John Harvey was seated next to Vice Admiral Richardson and I made the glib remark. "There are two Johns sitting together—how can we know who everyone is referring to?" I asked them.

"Easy," said Admiral Harvey, "he is the smart John and I'm… maybe I need to rethink that one," he said with a grin. It gave us all a big laugh.

That was an evening I won't forget. I wish I'd had have some idea it was going to happen; I would have recorded it! Admiral Richardson introduced me as "the one who enlightened everyone on SSGN."

In all these years—those nine years of advocating for the SSGN that was such a good moment. I've had a few submarine officers and others ask me about it and with it a thank you but it's never been a so public and never from anyone so senior. It just took my breath away. Thank you, sir.

A few months later I attended the change of command for VADM Richardson and VADM Michael Conner. There were many attendees there—probably three thousand. It is always like old home week at a COMSUBLANT change of command. All my old submarine friends were there.

When VADM Richardson gave his last remarks, he thanked Dana for "making every night like prom night." What a wonderful comment. Admiral Richardson became the sixth director of naval reactors following in the footsteps of Admirals Hyman G. Rickover, Kinnaird R. McKee, Bruce DeMars, Frank "Skip" Bowman, and Kirkland Donald.

They had to move to Bolling AFB while their quarters were being renovated. I told him my suggestions. I had stayed with Adm. Kirk Donald and his wife, Diane, when he had the job and loved the house. I'm sure he didn't take any of my suggestions, but he was amazed that I knew so much about the quarters he was moving to. He had not had an opportunity to see them.

The quarters were a wonderful old, large house in DC. His new job was one of the most classified in the Navy and came with a security detail. I'll bet it was the first time that the architects dealing with the design changes had dealt with the fact that there were also five children that had to be taken into account with the security changes! Nathan was a Navy lieutenant I had met earlier at another ball and we had a great time! The other children were still at home.

When I found out where their temporary lodging would be, I suggested they get in touch with Admiral Bob Papp and his wife Linda. Admiral Papp was commandant of the Coast Guard and lived just down the street from their new temporary quarters. Dana told me they had not become acquainted with many of the four stars and they would love to meet them. I called the Papps and started an e-mail between them.

They decided on a date about a month out on October 9, 2012, and Admiral Papp asked me if the date would work for me. "Oh no, I had not planned to come—this was so you four could meet," I told him. He insisted and teased me with the possibility that they would not meet unless the one who put them together would attend. I went and it was a magical night. We had such fun. I'm so pleased these two couples could get together.

After only three years, Admiral Richardson received new orders. He was to be our next chief of Naval Operations, relieving Admiral Jon Greenert. How blessed we are in this country. With such responsibility, they both did it well with charm and personality.

ROBERTSON, REAR ADMIRAL TOM AND JULIE

MEAD, CAPTAIN JACK AND VICKIE

The Robertsons were the first ones to occupy Dolphin House—the admiral's quarters (home) at Kings Bay. We were already friends and I offered to help Julie plan the open house.

It sounds crazy now but we were a little crazy back then. We planned it like a Walmart Opening making the most of our small-town charm. We had clowns and gave away moon pies and RC Colas. It was a beautiful day and the house and lawn were packed with people. What a great way to celebrate a milestone with the community. Captain Jack and Vickie Mead, Captain CJ and Jennifer Ihrig and Captain Malcolm and Shirley Fages, Captain Jim and Marsha Fletcher—all were good friends and we got together often. We miss that.

The first time we were in a restaurant and people started staring at us, I couldn't understand their fascination. I had gotten so used to Julie's pipe it didn't dawn on me that others were not and many couldn't take their eyes off her. She smoked that pipe for years. We also dined in many very good restaurants and some not so good. Arlie took the funeral home limo many times with us all packed in

This was a time when the Dolphin Scholarship Auction included many unusual fun events. The officers and crews at each of the commands were generous with the offers for dinner at their quarters and their units. Yes, back then there were even parties for the Dolphin Scholarship Auction at the training facility. We bought that auction item and celebrated Arlie's sixtieth birthday at a casino night at the Trident Training Facility.

Prior to the admiral's quarters located at Kings Bay, the group commanders were based at Charleston. Our friendship with The Robertsons began during that time. Arlie was auctioneer for the Dolphin Scholarship Auction in Charleston and Tom and Julie invited us to stay with them. We stayed another weekend when we attended one of the parties bought at the auction. It was an "Italian night" with Tom the "godfather" and all of us lining up for our "blessing." Favors were asked for. Favors were received. Or that was what he wanted us to believe. I recently found the picture I had blown up into a poster for the reception at Tom's retirement. I was on my knees requesting a "favor." We spent a lot of time with the Robertsons and the Meads and that friendship continued when they retired. Jack was the executive officer on the USS *Canopus* (AS 34) when C. J. Ihrig was commanding officer so Jennifer and CJ joined us. Later after the Ihrigs moved, Jack retired on March 11, 1994. Arlie was proud that Jack asked him to sing the national anthem at his retirement ceremony. Captain C. J. Ihrig introduced the guest speaker, Rear Admiral T. J. Robertson, commander of Submarine Group 6. It was a poignant moment when he and Vickie were piped over the side. We were so pleased that he and Vickie stayed in Camden We alternated dinners at the homes of the Robertsons, Meads, and McNeills. Yes, I even cooked back then but was not on the level as Julie and Vickie. Well, just maybe Julie.

Another event was when the Navy League National President, Bill Kelley came to Camden to speak at the Navy League meeting. He and his wife, Nancy, stayed at the base "hotel" and Julie hosted dinner at their quarters (now at Kings Bay). Captain Chuck Ellis Commanding Officer of Kings Bay and his wife, Judy were there along with Chuck's relief Captain Michael O'Neill. Captain O'Neill was working the turnover with Captain Ellis and he must have thought we were crazy. The admiral was serving and we were telling him what to do.

"Are the wenches drinking in the kitchen?" I asked Tom.

Tom lifted an eyebrow and said, "No, ma'am."

I was about to remark about the cover-up when he completed his sentence, "They're drinking everywhere."

Can you imagine being a new commanding officer of the base and sitting at that table as we bossed the admiral around?

That was a time when we were very socially involved with the military leadership at Kings Bay. Every Friday night at the clubs of Kings Bay was seafood buffet night. We were all there. At change of commands every command was at every ceremony. The captains would all be on the second row and if I managed to get there early enough for the third row I had a chance to meet with any of them. They were all particularly close.

In April 1996, the Robertsons donated a party to the Dolphin Scholarship Foundation auction and Arlie and I helped with the serving that evening. Dori Brink who worked at Trident Refit Facility (TRF) and her husband Dan, were always very generous in their support of Dolphin Scholarship and other programs supporting our military. Dori was one of the first apprentices in the TRF program. They were the top bidders for this dinner that was held January 18, 1996.

We had a fun time planning it with very specific instructions for the guests. Among other instructions, they had to sing for their salads, tell clean jokes as they were cleansing their palates, and tell sweet stories about marriage and spouse over dessert That evening when they arrived the women were given hats to wear when photos were taken later. Tom was wonderful with his limericks.

Arlie was auctioning at the Dolphin Scholarship event in Charleston and they introduced him as a retired Navy captain. Arlie was in the Navy for four years and was proud to be a third-class dental technician. Later Tom gave Arlie his captain's cover (hat). When people see in on our bookshelves and ask us about it Arlie fesses up and tells the story.

When Tom spoke to the council, I sent a formal letter to Julie as the spouse offering her local entertainment as the speaker's spouse. Back then we would have said wife. I offered her the following:

1. A backstage visit to Tide Treasures Hallmark. What really goes on? How do they keep that thing running?
2. A guided tour of Edo Miller & Sons Crematorium with slides and handouts.
3. Your reputation as a gourmet cook has traveled far. Therefore, we will make arrangements to tour one of the school cafeterias and receive pointers from the head dietitian.

I attended the Hail and Farewell for the Robertsons and the Ellises on September 30, 1993, and was asked to speak. Julie and Tom will be missed in Camden County. Julie made an impression her first day in Camden when several local women took her to lunch. She fit right in and has contributed to the community in many ways including the Chamber of Commerce and the Navy League. Once we found out that she was a gourmet cook, we enlisted her services on the black-tie event for the chamber's Auction the Moon event. It was one of the finest evenings anyone could enjoy. She also served as a committee chair on our Navy League Council and both she and Rear Admiral Robertson offered their home for Navy League functions.

This was my first year as Navy League president of the Kings Bay Council and any success we had can also be credited to Rear Admiral Robertson. He hosted our initial board meetings at a luncheon and my board members were challenged by his endorsement and offer of support to the council. He approved and helped me initiate an education program for our members that is unprecedented in the Navy League. He has made it a point to attend all of our meetings and bring briefings that kept our members updated on the real story of the happenings at Kings Bay. His home and his office have always been open to our community and we thank them both for a great two years.

Vicki, a registered nurse continued to drive to the Jacksonville area to work. One of us was always trying to get free advice from Vicki on our aches and pains. She is the only wife we know who gave a brand-new car to her husband at his retirement.

After retirement, Jack agreed to help me with the Sea Cadet program when I was president. He and Dr. Jerry O'Donoghue (he was also my doctor) took our cadet program to new heights. As a retired Navy captain Jack knew just what those young cadets needed. Over seventeen years they gave guidance to hundreds of young people, just as Jack had done in his active duty years. There were a couple of times that Jack was ready for some relief on the program but we always had to depend on Jack and Jerry. They "trained" Barbara Johns who now runs the program. Jack said, "Barbara is doing a great job. She runs the cadet program which involves a lot of hard work and time and additionally is Youth Program vice president. She and her husband sacrifice a lot for the cadets."

Tom and Julie stayed close by in Fernandina Beach. We joined them and Jack and Vicki for a monthly dinner rotating in each other's home. The 'girls' even had a pajama party one night. Vicki has a great sense of humor so she and Julie with similar traits get along with everyone.

When I was appointed to DACOWITS in 1996 they came to the house for dinner and gave me a framed print entitled "Women are Always Right." It was very funny and very politically incorrect but by that time he was retired and could relax a little. I loved "The Rules" and they remain on the wall in the downstairs bathroom (of all places) for everyone to see.

The Rules

1. The Female makes the Rules.
2. The Rules are subject to change at any time without notice.
3. The Male cannot possible know all of The Rules.
4. If the Female suspects that The Male has learned The Rules, then she must immediately change some of The Rules.
5. The Female is never wrong.
6. If the Female decides she is wrong, The Male must acknowledge that is was due to a misunderstanding caused by something he said or did and he must apologize at once.
7. The Female may change her mind at any time.
8. The Male cannot change his mind without consent of The Female.
9. The Female can, at any time, be upset or angry, scream or throw things, with or without cause or reason.
10. The Male must remain calm at all times unless The Female wants him to be angry or upset.
11. The Female must, under no circumstances, let The Male know whether or not she wants him to be angry or upset.
12. If the Female has PMS the Male is hereby notified that he probably won't do anything right for the next several days.
13. The Male is expected to mind read at all times.
14. The Male must be ready for anything at any time.
15. The Female is ready when she is ready and not a moment before.
16. If two Females disagree about the rules they are both right.
17. Face reality, The Male is always wrong.

Was everything just crazier back then? Was it the extra time we had before the obsession with computers and cell phones?

I recognize that during this time I had not begun my relentless "career" in the Navy League. While I was a member, I had not served before in leadership roles. Thus, my recollections with them are those more on the social side. They both had prestigious careers and were respected by everyone, but you could also tell they knew how to have fun.

Arlie and I are grateful to call the Robertsons and Meads our friends. They represent a dozen or so couples that will always be special to us. We can run into them at any time and it's like we just saw each other a week ago. Friends that you can call if you need them even if you haven't seen them in months.

ADMIRAL GARY ROUGHEAD

CHIEF OF NAVAL OPERATIONS
SEPTEMBER 29, 2007–SEPTEMBER 23, 2011

I first met Admiral Roughead when he was the head of the Office of Legislative Affairs for the Navy. At that time, I was the Navy League's national vice president for legislative affairs. I had cut my teeth with Rear Admiral Cutler Dawson, so Admiral Roughead probably had a little warning. Whether it was a prior warning or he made a decision I don't know, but I do know what a joy it was to work with him.

We made sure he saw the Navy League's "interpretation" of what the Navy's issues were. They were very much in line. One of the big issues was encroachment. The Navy and especially the Marine Corps had installations where training programs were running into obstacles due to encroachment. Late one Friday afternoon, I had a call from Gary. There was a vote coming up in Congress on the following Tuesday that would help rectify some of these issues. It would help if certain congressional members could hear from their constituents.

I called Jeremy Miller, the Navy League's director of legislative affairs.

"Hi, Jeremy, what plans do you have for this weekend."

"I don't know of anything Sheila but I'll bet I'm about to find out."

"Yes, you and I are calling about twenty state presidents [of the Navy League] and have them get word out to their congressional members on an upcoming bill."

"Yes, ma'am. Who do you want me to call?"

Now that is what I call a great legislative affairs director! We worked the weekend calling and e-mailing everything they needed. On Tuesday that bill passed with each of these congressional members voting yes.

We had receptions, breakfasts, and lunches during those years and I think Gary and I made a fine team. When he was commander, Second Fleet, and I was national president, and he sent me the following letter:

> Commander Second Fleet
> Commander Striking Fleet Atlantic
> 18 May 2004
>
> Sheila,
>
> I would like to extend to you my personal invitation to visit Second Fleet during the execution phase of Combined Joint Task Force Exercise (CJTFEX) 04-2. Live exercises have always been the venue of choice for confirming combat capability while concurrently advancing concept and experimental development and

coalition interoperability. The significant number of participants from both U.S. and coalition nations, speaks to the continued primacy of CJTFEX's in achieving these objectives.

We have recently completed the Final Planning Conference for CJTFEX04-2, and I want to assure you that my previous invitation still stands. While training has already commenced, the majority of live exercise play will occur during the week of 14 June 2004. I would be pleased to host you if you are interested in viewing portions of the exercise. Specific events and venue details will be provided to our staff as they are confirmed. My point of contact for initial questions is my Protocol Officer, LTJG Elizabeth De Angelo, who may be reached at…

I look forward to seeing you on the waterfront.

Sincerely,
G. Roughead
Vice Admiral, U.S. Navy

My first arrested landing! My first opportunity to observe war games! I had to do it! There were some logistic issues. I had to be in San Diego for our national convention from June 9 to 13. I would be there two days early preparing for the convention and exhausted after the five days—but an arrested landing on an aircraft carrier! Observing war games up close! I had to do it.

I just made it. I went straight from San Diego to Norfolk arriving late on June 14. They took me to the Norfolk base hotel for the evening. The next morning, I flew from Norfolk to sea landing on the USS *John F. Kennedy* (CV 67) and then was transported to the *Mount Whitney* by helicopter. The USS *Mount Whitney* (LCC/JCC 20) a Blue Ridge–class command ship of the US Navy was the flagship for the Second Fleet.

It was an incredible experience. On the helicopter one of the young sailors was sitting at the open door of the helo and dangling his legs outside. "That looks like fun. Could I do it?"

Looking at each of the sailors on the helo and hearing no objections, the young sailor said, "Yes, ma'am, but we are going to have to lock you in."

I moved in quickly as they put a harness around my waist attaching it to a tether bolted to the helicopter. It was exhilarating. The day was beautiful. The weather was perfect. And here I am swinging my legs off a helicopter chatting with the crew. Thank goodness one of my shoes didn't fly off!

I arrived at the carrier and those participating in the war games let me mix with them and even made me feel like I was contributing. You've got to love that!

That night, standing on the deck with the planes landing and taking off just feet away was something you cannot describe. I had no idea I would be this close to the action.

This experience gave me such an insight on the talented dedicated young men and women who protect us. The training necessary to keep them "war ready" is essential. Years later, I'm hearing stories in the news about the need for more training for our aviators and how funding was needed for maintenance and how they are cannibalizing one aircraft to be able to fly another. It sounded like our issues when I was on DACOWITS (defense committee) a few years earlier. I am seeing first-hand the result of good training.

I sent him a note in August 2004.

Dear Gary,

> It just doesn't stop. Seems like a few months ago that we were working on legislative affairs. I'm not sure I ever expressed my deep gratitude for allowing the Navy League to take a bigger part in our (meaning the Navy) legislative affairs program.
>
> I think you will be pleased with the programs we'll be rolling out soon. Thank you for giving me the opportunity for my first tailhook landing. Everyone I know had to hear about it. The crew was great. Please give Admiral Doran my best regards. I'll be stopping by in February for my Pacific travels—hope you'll have time for a cup of coffee.

Sincerely, Sheila

He responded with a wonderful handwritten letter that gave me such encouragement during my last year as national president. When I returned from the Asian trip I stopped by to brief Admiral Bill Fallon and his deputy Vice Admiral Gary Roughead on my recent travels. Gary told Fallon "She did what we did last week but with no aides and flying commercial."

Admiral Roughead relieved Admiral Mike Mullen as CNO on September 29, 2007.

> *Roughead was relieved that same day as Commander, Fleet Forces Command by newly promoted Adm. Jonathan Greenert.*
>
> *Mullen called Roughead "exactly the right officer" to lead the Navy and praised Roughead's wife Ellen for her support and service as well. "Whenever you're in command you always worry about who you leave it to," he said. "I can assure you I don't have a single doubt*

> *today. Nobody could be better to lead the Navy in the future than Gary Roughead. And there is no better team than Gary and Ellen.*

The US Naval Institute's September 2007 edition said the admiral selected to be the next chief of Naval Operations has been recognized throughout his career for his leadership, integrity, and concern for his sailors and brings extensive experience in the Pacific at a time of increased military and economic focus on the Asia-Pacific region.

At the time, he was on active duty, Roughead was one of only two officers to have commanded the fleets in the Pacific and Atlantic, and Joint Task Force 519, as well as US Fleet Forces Command, where he was responsible for ensuring Navy forces were trained, ready, equipped, and prepared to operate around the world, where and when needed.

I didn't see the admiral for a few months after that—and only for a few minutes at his change of command. But I did see him at Rear Admiral Frank Thorp's retirement and he asked, "Which gatekeeper is keeping you out of my office?" I told him I wouldn't give a name but I was sure going to use that line when I called for lunch soon.

It was great to watch him in action as CNO at the Eleventh Annual Commemoration of the United States Victory at Midway in Jacksonville, Florida. US Representative Ander Crenshaw, a great Navy supporter, was in attendance. Rear Admiral Michael C. Vitale, commander of Navy Region Southeast, introduced Gary. Keith Post, executive director of the St. Marys Submarine Museum and former cochairman of the return to service for the USS *Georgia*, and Captain Brian McIlvaine, commanding officer of the USS *Georgia*, were there. We enjoyed seeing old friends and talking with everyone.

I went to the Pentagon and met with CNO Admiral Roughead and we discussed women on submarines. Chairman of the Joint Chiefs, Admiral Mike Mullen, had just introduced the Navy's plans to incorporate women on subs. Gary told me the submarine force was losing some of the best and the brightest. Looking at the graduates of the Naval Academy, many of the top graduates were women and the Navy was losing that great talent. They a had a workable plan to incorporate women on submarines over a period of time. It seemed the perfect plan, beginning with the SSBNs and with senior enlisted and officers, in particular the supply officers who had prior service on ships.

Gary was at the USS *George H. W. Bush* commissioning and we had time to talk. It is amazing that you could talk with the CNO with no interruptions. Of course, no one wants to interrupt him so they aren't going to break into a conversation. And at least this time, he didn't give his aide "the look" to rescue him. We talked about our work in OLA and I congratulated him on the Supreme Court decision in favor of the Navy on sonar testing—that, too, began back in about 1998 when many of my briefings and point papers were on this.

At our national Sea Air Space in DC, Gary was recognized for his leadership and for his support of the Navy League. It was great to see Ellen with him. It was a who's who at that meeting. Secretary of the Navy, Gordon England, and Admiral Vern Clark and Connie were there, as were Admiral Bob Papp and Linda, Admiral Bozeman, and former secretary of the Navy Will Ball to name a few. That was the evening I had a surprise statement from Secretary England and CNO Clark, but that is another story.

He spoke at the fairly new command—the Navy Installations Command where Vice Admiral Michael C. Vitale relieved Vice Admiral Robert Conway on January 30, 2009. I was pleased to be there and see him.

After he retired from the Navy, Gary accepted my invitation to come to Naval Submarine Base Kings Bay to attend a statewide Georgia Military Affairs Committee meeting. He was then and remains a fellow at the Hoover Institution at Stanford University and continues to remain engaged in national security, energy, and Asian policy.

Since I was the host for the event I asked Keith Post to pick him up at the airport but Gary and I had a chance to get caught up late that evening. The next day was the meeting and Gary spoke on Law of the Sea. He could have slipped out as soon as his brief was over but due to the study he decided to stay. I had an aha moment with him in the audience. The committee was discussing community and state support of our bases.

I stood up and shared with the group what Connecticut did for the Groton base after being saved from the sledgehammer of BRAC (base realignment and closure). They pledged fifty million dollars to upgrade the facilities at Groton. I added that I was surprised the Navy would agree to take funding to improve their infrastructure adding it must be the fact that the services were so strapped for funds. Right in the middle of my remarks I looked at Gary and said, "You were the one! You were CNO at the time this was accepted!"

He laughed and said, "Yes, we needed the money."

I owe so much of my success in the Navy League senior leadership to Admiral Roughead.

JACK SCHIFF

THE ANGEL OF ST. MARYS

Jack Schiff and I met at an annual meeting at the Navy League in 1996. He was a member of the national board of directors. I was involved with building the St. Marys Submarine Museum. I was telling him about the effort and asked him, as a Navy veteran, if he would like to join the museum. He cocked his head and said, "Well, I don't know. How much will it cost me?"

"Fifteen dollars, but it must be renewed every year."

"Send me the info and I'll be happy to join the submarine museum."

We talked a little more about our progress, what artifacts we had and those we were looking to receive and when we might be open. I told him we would have an update in the newsletter. A few weeks later, John Crouse stopped by the store. He said we have a contribution from Jack Schiff—it's in stock. I took the material that was sent and using my calculator said, "Wow, he has sent almost four thousand dollars! I can't believe it."

I only talked with him about a membership. I thought we could show him later what a great thing a submarine museum would be. "Check again, Sheila—move the decimal."

"Oh, my! I can't believe it."

I *was* off a decimal. It was thirty-seven thousand dollars! And such a nice note with it. "Immediately we ordered a better door, bought a conference table, finished all the construction that needed to be done. We are now able to have our grand opening with a completely finished museum. But how I wish we could have kept this stock.

Jack was not able to make the commissioning ceremony but he did visit us in December 1997. He told me it was the most publicity for the least amount of money he'd ever seen. Gordon Jackson was with us that day and wrote the following story:

> **12/31/97**
> **By** Gordon Jackson, Times-Union staff writer, ST. MARYS, Ga
> **St. Marys 'angel' made sub museum possible**
>
> During a tour of the St. Marys Submarine Museum in Georgia, businessman Jack Schiff (center) discusses one of the exhibits with Sheila McNeill of the Navy League and John Crouse, the museum's curator. Schiff donated $34,000 to the museum and saw it for the first time yesterday. Jack Schiff's first tour of the St. Marys Submarine Museum yesterday was long overdue, according to many people associated with the facility.

After all, they said, more than 21,000 people have visited the museum since it opened in March 1996.

And Schiff, museum officials said, was largely responsible for getting the project completed on schedule with his $34,000 contribution—the largest individual donation to the museum. Schiff downplayed his visit and role in opening the museum, saying he wanted to give something back to the Navy for helping him achieve success as a businessman. He was one of the founders of the Cincinnati Insurance Co. in 1950, which now has nearly $7 billion in assets, Schiff said.

"The Navy did so much for me," Schiff gave as the reason he made the contribution to a museum nearly 1,000 miles from his hometown. "I can never repay what the Navy did for me. I'd like to give the Navy half of what it has given me." Schiff first learned the museum needed contributions at a national Navy League meeting in Washington in 1995, said Sheila McNeill, regional president of the Navy League and chairwoman of the museum's commissioning ceremony. But McNeill, who had never met Schiff before, said she never anticipated a stranger would become the single largest donor. Schiff's donation nearly doubled the amount of money raised before the museum opened.

More than $75,000 in donations was raised and 6,000 volunteer-hours put in to open the museum, McNeill said. But Schiff was the key, she said. "He's been our guardian angel," McNeill said. "He's the one who made it happen." The museum was formed in response to growing public interest in Kings Bay Naval Submarine Base. It was formed by a community group with volunteer labor from the Navy, area residents and others.

The two-story museum has things like a working periscope, a World War II dive suit, replica sleeping quarters from a submarine; models and memorabilia, a library and a first-floor exhibit that concentrates on the diesel era of submarines. Schiff seemed overwhelmed as he thumbed through the many manuscripts in the library, which is named in his honor, saying the facility exceeded his expectations. "I had no idea the library was so extensive and cohesive," Schiff said.

Capt. Will Frye, an officer serving at nearby Kings Bay Naval Submarine Base, told Schiff the museum was an important way to "instill a sense of pride about the military" in youth that visit the facility. After Schiff's tour, John Crouse, museum curator, said he was confident Schiff would be pleased his money was well spent. "It was nice seeing him being impressed with everything he saw," Crouse said. "We think we did it right."

Jack died in 1998. He made a tremendous impact on many.

An article on Friday, October 16, 1998, by Phillip Pina of the *Cincinnati Enquirer* included this:

> *John J. "Jack" Schiff, who helped start what would become Cincinnati Financial Corp. and was a leader in local arts and civic groups, died Wednesday at Deaconess Hospital. He was 82. Mr. Schiff of Western Hills was an honored man in the insurance industry as well as the community. He is credited with guiding a firm that started with $200,000 in capital into a corporation with $9.5 billion in assets. And he was recognized for his community service in 1997 when the Greater Cincinnati Chamber of Commerce named him a Great Living Cincinnatian. "His business achievements and philanthropic acts left a lasting impression on everyone who knew him," said Robert B. Morgan, chief executive officer at Cincinnati Financial. The company Mr. Schiff co-founded will continue to let his vision guide it into the future, Mr. Morgan added…*

Jack and his family have continued to support the museum and at the writing of this book it has been twenty years. There were many times we wondered if we could keep afloat and then Jack's check came. He really is the angel of St. Marys.

COMMAND MASTER CHIEF JIMMY SCHUBERT AND CARRIE

I thought about what it was going to be like without Jimmy when he retired. He knew me and we understood each other—I would now have to start all over! We both talked about the time we were having a luncheon at the clubs of Kings Bay on April 1, the chief's birthday, and I asked Jimmy to get all the chiefs there early and line them up all around the room so each could be seen, and we sang "Happy Birthday" to them. Jimmy was always ready if we wanted to recognize any of his sailors or chiefs and their families.

We had many projects together including cochairing the Military Community Council for the Chamber. Jimmy and I were a lot alike. If it was something that needed to be done, we were each ready to do it! He was one of the best examples of what a master chief can do and does do and a wonderful example to his sailors and to us. He could make things happen.

He asked me to join the party to roast him October 11, 2012, the night before his retirement. He was always upbeat and reached out to the community. The crowd that night was proof of that. As I looked across the room, I saw the leadership in Camden County—but I also saw that we had the community and the active duty. It was a remarkable cross section of Camden County. There were many "roasters" that evening. Everyone was having a good time but I wondered, as the evening went on if I should cut my remarks short. I slipped the roast out and began looking at what I should leave off. *However,* as I gave the first couple of paragraphs the audience was howling.

This is how it went:

> *Everyone wonders—how in the hell did he get so far? What can we say about Jimmy? I asked him if he wanted to reconsider asking me to roast him—in front of his family no less. I told him I had the stories that would destroy him but he laughed and took it like the master chief he is. Everyone knows Jimmy Schubert. Master Chief. That brings up great attributes. Master Chiefs are calm, cool, and never get rattled… I'm sorry—another speech for next week. Jimmy has the greatest of ideas—he is a genius at solving complex issues—okay, I don't know how I got these two speeches mixed up. Give me just a minute.*
>
> *Oh yes, Schubert—I've been interviewing his family and some old friends. What I didn't know before tonight was that he was an athletic giant in high school… however his high school would not give him a letter until he could prove he could read one… and that never happened. His friends told me he always had three girlfriends at one time—it took that many to get a full set of teeth. By the way, a new law has been passed in his home state—When a couple gets divorced they're still brother and sister. After graduation, he decided to join the Navy. When they signed him up he was classified him as 4-Y… Yes 4-Y meaning in case of war he is a hostage—please, take him as a hostage. That designation gave him an advantage for getting in the submarine force—when they heard about the 4Y they thought he might come in handy, so to the good fortune of the surface fleet Jimmy went into submarines.*
>
> *The Navy believes in education and training. And there is more training in the submarine force than almost any other. Jimmy always worked with his sailors to improve themselves. He also had taken many courses himself until it was decided that he was being educated beyond his intelligence. You know that cleared up a lot of questions for a lot of people I understand that within weeks of coming to St.*

Marys he was stopped by a St. Marys City Policeman who pulled him over and asked, "Got any I.D?" Jimmy with his usual clear mind answered, "Bout what"! The police officer finally just let him go.

Everyone was hooting and yelling. I ended my idea of cutting off half the speech. The other roasters had set them up and the liquid refreshment didn't hurt either. I continued.

As base master chief, he was given many duties. But he took them head on. You couldn't ever find him to talk with him about it but you knew he had to be out there somewhere. And everyone would be paddling like crazy and at the last minute, here he comes with his team of sailors and makes everything happen.

He loves his sailors; of course, he loves himself too. He can get anything done on base—after all he is THE MASTER CHIEF—In fact, everyone knows he moves more dirt than a John Deer Tractor. They certainly know him at the Galley. I understand that Carrie has now ordered a special diet of only soft foods for him at his advanced age.

Have you ever heard anyone talk so fast? It's a shame that his brain can't keep up with him. That would be a powerful package. Have you noticed his hairline has changed? It isn't receding—it's just trying to get away from his mouth. He is my co-chairman on the Military Community Affairs committee. I can depend on him to always know what to say—not always when to say it—but he never lacks for words. Of course, we had to have a special sit down with him at the chamber. When he first started, he was so excited when he heard it was Military Affairs—that word "affairs" was going to open up a whole new ballgame for him. But we straightened him out

His lovely and patient wife Carrie is a pharmacist—imagine free drugs—of course Jimmy calls it medication. Carrie one day you will be nominated for some kind of Peace Prize for not killing him. She tells me she has been substituting his Viagra with salt peter and he doesn't know if he's coming or going which explains even more. Not only is he involved at the base but he has made an impact on the community. Chris has talked about his contribution to the chamber. He received the volunteer of the year award for the chamber—It should have been" bSer" of the year—you know he likes the sound of his own voice. And when you know who he has been listening to that explains a lot!

Now I'd like to get serious. Yes, he has contributed to the chamber, but I can add the St. Marys Submarine Museum, The Camden Partnership. The Navy League, and the cities of St. Marys, Kingsland and Woodbine—they all have benefited from Jimmy with their various annual events. They all know him and love him. With his struggling sailors, he was a wonderful mentor. He is quick to correct and quick to praise. Even in the community if he could praise someone and give them credit he would do that. My entire reputation is built on Jimmy Schubert's lies. Thank you, Jimmy. He has touched the lives of thousands of sailors. He is the driving force that made many of them want to stay in the Navy. To Jimmy it is all about leadership and taking care of his people. Yes, the sailors were lucky but we in the community have been lucky as well. We've all heard stories about his wonderful family. I know you are all dear to him and he has shared with us his stories about each of you. The most poignant and truly Jimmy story I know I read in the Periscope. Kings Bay has Special Olympics on the base each year. Jimmy is at all of them.

"They bring a lot of love and understanding. They don't know anger," Schubert said of the competitors. He encouraged each and every one of them to never give up. As he spoke, he scooped up a young boy from Altamaha Elementary School in Brunswick and plopped his dress uniform cap on the boy's head. Teaming up with a child is the key, Schubert said. "I love 'em. I love every one of them," he said. We love you too Jimmy

Captain Harvey Guffey had just relieved Captain John O'Neill as commanding officer of Kings Bay. He and his wife, Wanda, were in the audience. We had met but had not really had a chance to get acquainted. Captain Guffey said to me, "Sheila, if I ever have to put together a roast, I want to have you as one of the roasters, but if I am ever roasted, I will make sure you know nothing about it!"

One sailor came up to me and said, "I peed my pants—really—I've never laughed so hard."

The next day at his retirement ceremony Jimmy was quite out of protocol when he announced, "For those of you that were not at the roast last night Sheila sent me to *Jesus!* I had never heard the phrase before but the audience howled again. We miss Jimmy and Carrie.

And a thank-you again to my friend Jack Chancellor for all his help in finding just the right words to give Jimmy a hard time.

HORST SCHULTZE AND THE RITZ CARLTON

In 2001, when Carla Carper was president of the Camden County Chamber of Commerce she connected us with Horst Schulze who was a friend of hers. Arlie and I picked him up at the airport and became fast friends. He was the most relevant civilian speaker I have ever heard. In checking my spelling and facts I found this on the internet:

> *Meet Horst Schulze: As founding president and COO of Ritz-Carlton, Horst Schulze established a new standard of excellence in his industry. He energizes organizations to reconnect with their service commitment. Horst Schulze revolutionized the hotel industry, creating one of the most recognizable international brands, forever altering the very nature of customer service by creating a culture of "ladies and gentlemen serving ladies and gentlemen." A charismatic leader and entrepreneur with an intimate understanding of market demands, he created a legion of loyal customers by raising the bar for customer service expectations to previously unimagined levels. Schulze provides audiences with successful service-oriented strategies to build and maintain lasting customer relationships that keep them coming back for more. A man of rare ability and prophetic vision, Schulze himself was named "Corporate Hotelier of the World" by HOTELS magazine and was awarded the Ishikawa Medal for his contributions to the quality movement. Currently chairman and CEO of Capella Hotel Group, Schulze is launching the newest standard in luxury hotels creating an unmatched tier of customer service.*

Annual Banquet and Installation of Officer
July 31, 2001

Keynote Speaker
Horst Schulze

This year the officers were:

Jim Wells	Chairman of the Board
Jackie Morrissett	Vice Chairman
Nancy Stasnis	Secretary/Treasurer
David Brown	Immediate Past President
Carla Carper	President/Chief Executive Officer

Board members included: Rachel Baldwin, Alan George, Minnie Johnson, Jeanne Knight, Leon Cochran, John Minor, Bevelyn Duerr, Stan Fowler, Harvey Fry, Pat Kelley, J. C. Knoll, Tracy Mizelle, Jim Steele, and Jimmy Whiddon. Carla was quoted in the paper before the event, saying, "This is the event of the year for this chamber."

Carper said, "[Schulze] is an absolutely mesmerizing speaker. He literally puts you on the edge of your seat."

The *Tribune & Georgian* pointed out, "Due to the great relationship we have developed with or military neighbors we decided to make them feel more involved and a part of this event we will be having the dinner on base."

As at all chamber events there was a full program. With speeches from the incoming and outgoing chairs, the installation of officers, etc., the program can run a little long. It was fairly late when Horst came up to speak. Even I received an award. I was presented with the Chamber's Special Award for Continued service for all my efforts and the work I had done to help the community. "She touches just about everything that happens in Camden County," Jim Wells said as he presented the flowers.

I think my thank you to Horst tells it all:

August 6, 2001

Dear Horst, You were magnificent. I knew you must be, I'd been told, I was expecting it. So why was I so blown away? You have changed the way of thinking for a community. Some of us think we do a pretty good job of service. In fact, I think I have the Ritz-Carlton of service at Sheila's Hallmark. But, believe me we are re-thinking everything we do. I have already met with employees—as has my husband. Arlie has a funeral home in Brunswick that has 89.7% of the funeral business in the county. That's about 458 funerals a year. He is good, his people are good, and he's going to be better.

When I think about the number of businesses and services you touched Tuesday night I am excited about how much you raised the level of quality in this community. I know what an imposition it was for you to take this engagement. I know how tired you were and how valuable your time is. Please know how appreciated the service you have given Camden County is. Carla is a great asset to this community—she does a great job and not everyone appreciates her as much as they should (never me, I sing her praises all the time) but your agreeing to speak in our little town helped everyone appreciate just what she does. You have a jewel in that crazy woman Juliana—and we owe her a debt of thanks.

I met with the Commanding Office the next day and we were still marveling over your speech. I talked with the Admiral and he said, "He hit all the right notes, he was absolutely spectacular." The Chief of Staff said, "He was mesmerizing—he gave us information we can use in our work also… it has already begun." Jim Wells, our outgoing Chairman, said we have never had a better speaker. We'll all use your motto: "Ladies and gentlemen serving ladies and gentlemen"—even in the Navy League. I have made you a member of the Navy League of the United States. I've enclosed this month's magazine, mostly because you can see a picture of yours truly on page 53. And know that I will do everything I can to incorporate your advice in the Navy League operation.

Thank you, Horst. Sincerely, Sheila McNeill

The *Tribune & Georgian* headlines read:

International executive offers advice to locals
By Heather Culp

Building a successful business depends upon building a loyal army of employees and customers, according to a man who helped build an empire of hotels.

Horst Schulze, vice chairman of the Ritz-Carlton Hotel Company shared his experience and knowledge of the business world with more than 140 guests on Tuesday at the Camden/Kings Bay Area Chamber of Commerce Annual Banquet and Installation of Officers. Schulze is responsible for development, owner relations and brand strategy for the hotel company that is ranked No 1 in customer satisfaction. Since he joined the company in 1983 as vice president of operations, the Ritz-Carlton has expanded more than 75 percent from seven hotels in North America to 38 hotels in 14 countries.

"He is an icon in the business world as well as married and the father of four," Jackie Morrissette, incoming chairperson for the chamber, said as she introduced the speaker. Jim Wells, the chamber's outgoing chairperson, told guests that Schulze had traveled long and hard to make his appearance in Camden. In the past two days, Schulze had traveled from Germany to Atlanta to New York to Florida to St. Marys. The acclaimed speaker said that he had spoken for two groups on Tuesday alone, In spite of his travels, Schulze showed no sign of fatigue as he told the guests at the dinner about

> *the secret to building a successful business. The business man said the most important component is service. "Service is the key thing you have to add to everything in business," said Schulze. Even if there are faults in the product, the customer is more likely to forgive you if they receive good service, Schulze explained. "They want to feel important." Schulze said of customers. According to Schulze there are three steps to customer service: a friendly greeting, complying to the desires the customer expresses or does not express and a friendly farewell. According to Schulze, success in the business world depended on giving customers what they want. Customers want a defect-free product delivered in a timely manner with service, he said.*
>
> *"This is especially true for the small business owner, they cannot hide behind a large income.," said Schulze. The business man warned the business leaders that service alone does not build a successful business, and as business owners they constantly must work to remove defects from their products. "That is what business is all—about—no defects." Schulze said. To eliminate defects in a product, not matter what business you are in. You must have a constant process to eliminate the cause of constant mistakes.*
>
> *Schulze also advised business owners that it is essential to have employees that have e pride in their jobs. "You must create an environment where they want to do the job. You do this by including them, in decision processes," Schulze said. Employers can do this by having employees help to locate and eliminate defects in the product and listen to their ideas. The business leader also advised audience members to not just hire people, but to select their employees based on their skills, no matter what business they are in.*
>
> *Schulze filled his hour-long speech with lively examples to help local business owners understand that success in the business world depends on constantly improving the product and providing the best possible service. After completing his speech, Schulze was greeted by a standing ovation and was presented with a key to the city of St. Marys by mayor Jerry Brandon.*

Later when I was with Horst in DC, he asked why I was not staying at the Ritz-Carlton. I told him it was my favorite hotel but I could not afford it—and the Navy League budget couldn't afford it. He said he would match the cost of where I was staying and he did! For several years, the Ritz-Carlton became my home away from home. I knew the staff, the bellmen, the chefs, and the front desk. They treated me like family. If I was in the hotel and a military event was going on, they would let me know—just in case it was some friends, I might know. They gave me a Ritz-Carlton robe on my fiftieth stay. Juliana Carroll with the Ritz-Carlton Hotel even sent me an e-mail that included "P.S. I told Carla that I am sending the *Georgia Trend* magazine back down to you so I can get it signed before you get too dern famous and 'top brassy.' Hope all is well and it was fun-tastic to see you again. Let's do chocolate subs again in DC! OXOX."

BRIGADIER GENERAL ROBERT L. SCOTT, USA

I met Scotty when I visited the Museum of Aviation at Warner Robbins Air Force Base as a member of the Defense Advisory Committee. He was often found at the museum talking aviation to visitors to the museum. He worked almost every day. When I heard he was the Scotty that wrote *God Is My Co-Pilot*, I was even more impressed and asked him to come to speak to our Navy League in Camden county I also suggested he bring some books to sell. Council President Captain Jack Mead, USNI) was pleased to add him to our speakers. I introduced him that night. He had an amazing story.

At age twelve, General Scott crashed a home-built glider off a three-story house. He knew then that he wanted to fly. After failing to receive appointment to West Point, he joined the Army as a Private. In 1928, he won a presidential appointment to West Point. After graduation in 1932 he won his wings in 1933.

When President Roosevelt canceled Commercial Air Contraction in 1934, General Scott flew air mail. He then served a tour of duty in Panama then became a flying instruction where he advanced to lieutenant colonel. By "stretching the truth" (saying he had flown many mission in the BN-17 when, in fact, he had never been in one), he got out of the training command and joined the ultra-secret task force Aquila mission: to bomb Tokyo. The mission was scrubbed because the staging bases in China had fallen. General Scott ended up flying the "hump" in Gooney Birds (C-47) loaded with drums of aviation fuel. He met General Chennault and the Flying Tigers. On July 4, 1942, he was assigned the best job in the war for him—first commander of the Twenty-Third Fighter Group of China Air Task Force under General Chennault as a combat leader, General Scott flew many missions, becoming an Ace. He was awarded three silver stars, three distinguished Flying Crosses and Air Medals. He was credited with twenty-two kills-enemy aircraft shot down.

In January 1943, he was ordered back to the U.S. to make public relations speeches to war plant personnel. He wrote the best seller *God Is My Co-Pilot* and served as technical advisory to Warner Brothers in making a movie based on the book. The world premiere was at the Grand Theater, Macon, Georgia in 1944. After the war, General Scott served in the Pentagon on a task force to win autonomy for the Air Force from the Army. He commanded the First Jet Fighter School at Williams Field, Arizona from 1947 to 1949. He then moved to USAFE to Command the Thirty-Sixth Fighter Wing at Furstenfieldbruck, Germany from 1950 to 1953. In 1954, he graduated from the National War College in Washington. He was promoted to Brigadier General and assigned as director of information, USAF Undersecretary Harold Talbot.

He retired as brigadier general in 1957. General Scott walked the entire length of the Great Wall of China at age seventy-two (over two thousand miles). At age seventy-six, with special permission of General Gabriel, chief of staff, USAF. He flew over twenty miles solo in an F-16 on July 19, 1984. He became more active as speaker and author of a dozen books.

General Scott served as chairman of the Heritage Eagles Campaign to help build the Museum of Aviation at Robbins Air Force Base. When he turned eighty in 1988, he flew an F-15—a birthday gift from the Georgia National Guard. He again flew an F-15 in 1993 at eighty-five years old!

I sent him a letter after his visit:

> March 24, 1997
> Dear Scotty,
>
> You completely enthralled our Navy League members. It's not every day that we get to meet and hear from a real military hero! Everyone really enjoyed your sense of humor. It was a very fast evening and most didn't want it to end. Thanks for taking the time to autograph books. I hope they did well for the museum. P. O. Boyle (your driver) was so excited about his trip with you! In fact, I understand he is taking his wife back this weekend to tour the museum. I believe the Smiths and Stewarts will be here in April. Major General Smith is going to be our April speaker and we will have tours on Friday. I'll tell him we had one month between you two so he wouldn't have to follow you! Thank you for taking the time to visit us and share your experiences
>
> Warmest Regards, Sheila

He was one of the most charming, dynamic individuals I have ever met. General Scott died on February 27, 2006.

SEPTEMBER 11, 2001 AND COASTAL BANK

I received a call a few weeks before from Jim Wells, a retired captain in the Navy who now was the Coastal Bank manager at the Kings Bay Village Shopping Center in St. Marys. He said the board of directors of Coastal Bank wanted to thank me for what I have done for Camden County.

For that reason, I was home watching television as I was getting dressed for my meeting at the bank at eleven. Like so many others when the first plane hit I exclaimed out loud. That was unusual because I was alone. "Oh no!" then thought what a horrible accident. Then as the world watched the second plane hit. It was stunning and I quit dressing and sat down. I was so distraught I called everyone I could. I didn't know what to do about the meeting. It might be possible that they really didn't know what awful thing had just happened. I got dressed and drove to the bank.

When I arrived at the bank, I found that was true. No one was watching television, no one was upset. I asked everyone if they knew what happened and did the board know. They didn't. I told those in the bank. They were stunned. I was escorted into the board room and sat down as they finished their meeting. I didn't want to interrupt them to tell them about the attack. There was nothing anyone could do. It felt awful realizing I had to tell them. They presented me with a framed copy of my cover on *Georgia Trend.* The plaque on the bottom read,

> *Congratulations "Admiral McNeill" on your many achievements*
> *—from your friends at the Coastal Bank of Georgia*

It made me think of the wonderful support I received from the bank when I was elected national president of the Navy League. They ran a **series of ads of congratulations.**

President Keith Caudell said some wonderful things about my service to the Camden County community. I then told the board what I had seen. We were all just horrified. Afterward Keith, Jim, and I went to lunch. They took me to the new restaurant that had opened at Sea Island. We changed that to a room in the bar so we could watch television. We watched in horror as they related what had happened to so many in New York. When we heard they had hit the Pentagon, I cannot describe the feelings. I was glad that there was a submarine flag conference going on in Groton as many of my friends were safe. What I didn't know at the time was that they hit the Navy Command Center and the N77 submarine office was also destroyed as the floors caved in. Some of my friends were at the Navy Command Center—not injured but not able to go back into their offices.

Captain Joe Gradisher was a public affairs office when I was national president and gave me tremendous support. He would sit with me in my suite after the Navy League national meetings and recount the day—its successes and missteps. He told me years later about 9/11 when the Pentagon was hit—everything that wasn't destroyed was in places that were damaged and he left the Pentagon leaving everything in his office. He remembers a woman giving him the money for the metro ride home. I think everyone was kinder to each other that day.

Lt. General Timothy Maude was killed that day. He served as the army's chief of personnel and was a familiar face at the defense committee that I served on. Such a nice man and such a loss. Of course, my flight on September 13 to the region meeting in Texas was canceled. This should give increased emphasis on homeland security and may bring funds to an often-neglected Coast Guard budget.

I thought about the trip to Saudi Arabia and the terrorist attack and bombing of the Khobar Towers. This was a combination housing complex and headquarters for a Saudi air base and, at that time, home to some of our marines. This was my first realization of security and what stress our military is under every day. There were barricades in front of the Marine base and we had to go around them like a snake.

Note: I am writing this in 2016 from notes I wrote in 2001. The barricades are a known and recognized security measure at Kings Bay and other military facilities. It is commonplace now.

JEANNE AND BILL SHARKEY

There are no better Navy League supporters than these two. They pretty much bleed Navy League and the sea services and for Jeanne the for past five years, especially the Coast Guard. My experience in chairing one commissioning put me in awe of Jeanne who had chaired two Navy and two Coast Guard ship commissionings—the USCG National Security Cutter *Bertholf* (WMSL 750) and USCG National Security Cutter *Waesche* (WMSL 751). Bill is a retired naval officer and they make a great team.

During the time, I was president of the Navy League, I had unbelievable support from the field. When you look at the list of places I visited you will see the enormity of that statement. I can't talk about them all but Jeanne and Bill exemplify that support.

In January 2004, I flew to California for a region meeting at Vallejo. Jeanne was region president and had "booked" meetings for me to speak at four councils. Bill acted as chauffer and "bodyguard." He drove us everywhere! He gave me a map to have an idea of where we were traveling—all color coded! The schedule was tough—and fun.

On the twenty-first, we visited Coast Guard Station Alameda where we called on Rear Admiral Kevin Eldridge, deputy commander, Pacific Area / commander, Eleventh Coast Guard District. Kevin would later be transferred to Coast Guard headquarters in DC, and we became great friends. That evening I spoke at the Stockton Council. The next day we were at the Monterey Peninsula Council where I spoke and installed officers. I spoke at the Contra Costa Council the next night for their 50th anniversary as a council. The Pacific Central Region meeting was at the California Maritime Academy where I spoke to the entire region. The Sharkeys were most gracious hosts and opened all three of their homes as we traveled. I get cold very easily. I'll have an electric blanket on when Arlie has a sheet. This was a real problem in Southern California. I was cold most of the time.

At their home in Discovery Bay, it was so cold I turned on my hair rollers then wrapped them in a towel, and put them in the bed with me. It worked until I got up during the night for a quick trip to the head and each of those rollers fell and started hitting their beautiful wooden floor. They seemed to hit one or two at a time. I didn't think they were ever stop. They made a huge noise! The next morning, I was up early, made my coffee, and sat in the chaise lounge in the sunroom (there was no sun) reading the papers. I also had mittens on my hands and a heavy coat on and they caught me. We still laugh about that incident and years later they told me they had a new furnace and I should try to visit again!

When we received word about the WAESCHE commissioning on May 7, 2010, Arlie was able to go with me. And we decided to take Bill and Jeanne's invitation to see the Yosemite Valley. We were on the road to Yosemite Valley enjoying an interesting countryside. We were driving along and suddenly Bill said, "I think that highway patrol man is pulling me over." Sure enough, we turned around and the lights were flashing. Bill pulled over.

"Sir, you were doing seventy-two in a fifty-five-speed zone and the lady in the back is not wearing a seat belt."

"I didn't know it was against the law not to wear one in the backseat," I explain.

I did remember that the day before Jeanne had told me to put it on but still… against the law? Jeanne said to the officer, "Would it help if we tell you Bill's dad was in the highway patrol and his badge number was five?"

They talked for a while and he finally said he wouldn't give a speeding ticket but would have to give him a ticket because I wasn't wearing a seat belt! I told him I should be the one getting the ticket but that wasn't to be. I did ask.

"Could you tell me how much the ticket will be so I can reimburse them?" (He told me, and I sent the check, but I don't remember the amount! Arlie told me it was a lot!) Bill then asked him how long it would take to get to Yosemite.

"About two hours," he answered.

"How long would it take us if we slowed down?" I asked.

Thank goodness, he had a sense of humor. "In that case, it will take about three hours."

We slowed down and there were no more incidents on the way.

We arrived at Yosemite after the run in with the law and found out that due to the rain in the past few days the road to the big redwood trees was closed. To see them, we would have to walk two miles there and two miles back—much of it uphill. Needless to say, we didn't do it. We instead checked in the hotel and discovered that getting to the bathrooms was a challenge but we had a great time. The large granite mountains are beautiful as are the waterfalls and the landscape. But it turned out that Glacier Point was also closed. We learned this as we started to go for cocktails, so we turned around to return to our rooms. It turned out Bill had a little package he brought. The cocktail hour was still on.

Leave it to Bill to save the day.

SHEILA'S HALLMARK AND THE WAKE

I ran a retail store in St. Marys for twenty-eight years and for most of that time it was a Hallmark store. We expanded several times and I had great people working for me. I managed to serve on a Defense Advisory Committee and as national president of the Navy League knowing the business was being taken care of. We won national awards and at a national Hallmark conference I was asked to be one of the speakers. The Hallmark representatives continue to be friends even after they left. See Military Card and Gift Service for our special programs.

In 2008, we started going down in sales and I made the decision to close the store. We closed it when the business climate was at its worse. The hardest part was telling my staff. I had the best staff anyone could have. They were so very loyal and so gracious with our customers. We had a great reputation in town for customer service.

Jerry Samuels was my first manager. She left to finish her education and became a school teacher. We have talked thirty years later about the great time we had traveling to merchandise shows and trying new food in so many different restaurants. Dinah Ulmer who already worked at the store took over duties as the manager, years later Barb Unger took over the responsibility. Judy Marsh served as my secretary and advisor for many years. She was so lovely to work with—very levelheaded but she moved with her family back home. Amanda Gross was then hired and she was crucial in my work for the defense committee. What I didn't know about computers she knew in spades. We managed to create a great system for compiling the members' installation visit reports. This new system gave me better information to provide the report for the secretary of defense and that gave the Defense Department a much better evaluation of our installation visits.

I had employees that became friends and took care of my store as if it were their own: Emily Wise, Audrey Chaney, Charlie Mullis, Stacy Parr, Amy Ridenour, and others were all so faithful in their work. I had some wonderful Navy wives who worked for me. One was a squadron commander's wife. We had three others at the time—all married to enlisted sailors. She asked me not to mention the fact that her husband was a captain and a commanding officer. I didn't and all of them became good friends. It was interesting when her husband had his change of command and she invited everyone to the ceremony. They were pleased for her and had a great time. Kelsey Mitchell began working for me as a high school student and continued through college. She would slip in in the middle of the night and take care of my monthly reports and leave me a note on what she had done. She made it so easy. That girl was so responsible—she was older than her years! Todd Sullivan was the only male who worked for me at the store. Todd was stationed at Kings Bay Naval Air Station, and we were delighted to have a strong male to help us. Todd comes back into my life when we had the USS Georgia return to service event.

For about a year I discussed my concerns with the landlord and he did all he could to help us make it. I also put out feelers to Hallmark and others to try sell the business. But never advertised it or made much of an effort to sell it. I often wondered why in the world I ever went into the retail business. I hate shopping and will do all I can to avoid it. Even to wearing the same suits for twenty years! Of course, when I think back it was because Miriam Tollison, my good friend, was in the retail business and saved my sanity after I was fired from Concrete Products. So while I didn't like the buying and was not a shopper, I loved walking out front when my paperwork got to be too much and talk with the customers. And when I think of all the friends we made, it was amazing. But it was time to close the store.

You aren't married to a funeral director for forty years without some effect on your outlook. I decided to have a wake for our best customers prior to announcing the closing. We treated the closing like a death in the family. I suggested they might want to dress for a funeral—or casual—it didn't matter. I also suggested that they bring a covered dish as many Southerners do when they go to the home of a friend who has lost a family member. I sent a notice to all our good customers. Some of that notice was this:

WAKE FOR SHEILA'S HALLMARK

> You are invited to a wake to celebrate the 28 years of the life of Sheila's Hallmark.
>
> To work in a Hallmark store means listening to the stories of life's events. We've known many of your families and seen children from babies to all grown up. We've found just the right card for you when you were happy and celebrating and also for those times when we've cried with you on your sorrowful occasions. Some of you have shopped with us from the beginning—remember that small 1,000 sq. ft. store in the same mall? It was originally called Tide Treasures. Some of you have only shopped with us a few months—we appreciate each of you. Bring a covered dish—we'll bake a ham or a turkey and have some iced tea... and wear black—if that's not convenient and you really don't have a lot of black like Sheila does—come as you are and we'll tie on a

> black arm band! Cry with us and celebrate with us our 28 years with Camden County. And why not a wake, Sheila's husband Arlie is a funeral director and it seems appropriate. Our thanks to the Bakkar Group, Mike Akel and Linda Johnson for their support and understanding and for being great landlords for 28 years We'll close the store at 5:00 and begin the celebration
>
> Thursday, May 31 from 5:00–8:00
>
> P. S. If you've had someone help you in the store with an unusual problem and they found just the right card, write it down and share it with us. We'll have a few words midway through the evening.

And they came! We had people in every corner of the store, some wearing black and little hats and all came with a dish. Everyone received a 40 percent discount and we read a eulogy and thanked everyone.

That evening I read "Sheila's Hallmark: A Christmas Story" written my Lt. Col. Wendy Goyette and family. Wendy was the commanding officer for the Marine Corps Security Force Battalion at Kings Bay. At Christmas, we were able to find a cherished ornament that was part of their Christmas tradition and this was recognizing that service.

The next day we slowed down the sale a little but closed in a few weeks with even the fixtures being sold.

I had employees who became friends and took care of my store as it was their own. They were with me at the end and had been with me a number of years: Wenda Munoz, Terry Ford, Dinah Anderson, Hazel Crowe, Mary Jones, Twana Anderson, Dee Morgan, Ann Devine, Mary Ann Intravia, Natalie Figueroa and numerous young women who worked during the summer and came back from college during the holidays and helped in many ways. It took a few weeks to close but we sold everything. It was a poignant few weeks. Many stopped by to say goodbye and let us know how much they would miss the store. The last night the store was open I received a big surprise. Keith Post had told our friends that it was the last day of Sheila's Hallmark and he didn't want me to close it alone. He and Brad, Alyce and Hunt Thornhill, Jim Wells, Georgia and Coby Stilson, and all who came in at nine as I closed the door for the last time.

I received an e-mail from a good friend and the former commanding officer of Kings Bay, Captain Mike McKinnon when the store closing was announced. It was indicative of the reaction of my friends and customers:

> *I was so sorry to see Sheila's Hallmark close. Broke my heart, but I know you did everything physically and fiscally possible to keep her up and running. So many fond memories of your folks coming*

> *down on my ship when I was XO on WEST "by God" VIRGINIA. You certainly allowed me to keep the home fires burning by mailing cards to Rhonda while I away and my kids wondering "how did Dad get me a birthday card?" Things did change when I went on to command KENTUCKY, but your shop always had the best cards and gifts to let Rhonda know how much I missed her and had her in my thoughts. Thanks for all you did for me, but more so, what you did to not only our Navy families and community, but the Camden County community as well. I am going to miss dropping in on you at your shop when I visit St. Marys from time to time.*
>
> *Mike*

That was one negative I didn't anticipate when I closed the store. All those years when someone returned for another tour of Kings Bay or others just to visit old friends they would come by and say hello. Now they don't know where to find me

Ten years later, and I still walk into a business or restaurant that someone doesn't tell me how much they miss the store. Me too.

SHIPYARD WORKERS IN BRUNSWICK DURING WWII

> World War II Shipyard Workers Gather in Brunswick
> Honoring Dedication of Worker
>
> Nearly 300 people gathered at First Presbyterian Church Sunday afternoon to remember the dedication of the thousands of workers at the Brunswick shipyard during World War II. The shipyard was responsible for building Liberty Ships, vital war vessels necessary for delivering supplies to fighting soldiers in Europe and the Pacific realm. Sunday's reunion was attended by former shipyard workers, such as Eunice Pittman of Maryland, family members and friends. The Rev. Greg Garis, one of the organizers of the event, said he hoped to make the reunion an annual event.

I was privileged to speak that day representing the Navy League. My dad was one of those workers at J. A. Jones until he joined the Army in May 1943. His foreman, J. B. Norman Jr., sent a letter about Ken Mobley, my dad, to Captain Charles W. Blackburn, who was an engineer in the Army that said,

Dear Sir: This is to introduce Mr. K. Mobley who has worked for me with J.A. Jones Construction Company, and the Brunswick Marine Construction Company, for the past year. Mr. Mobley is one of the few men in this Yard who has really mastered ship blueprints. We can ill afford to lose him, but due to his age we have been unable to keep him out of Military Service. Mr. Mobley served, first in layout, from Blueprints, all the parts for the Cargo Ships we are building. He was promoted to Leaderman, and at present is serving as Quarterman in charge of building all the Upper Deck Assemblies for the eighty-five Ships we are to build. I am sure that, if given the chance, he will serve you as faithfully and as efficiently as he has our Company.

Sincerely yours, J. B. Norman, Jr.

The Islander had a wonderful article a few days later:

Brunswick Shipyard Celebration Deemed "Perfect"

Several hundred enthusiastic former workers, families, and friends braved severe weather on December 14 to attend the Shipyard Commemorative Celebration of 1997. "The mood was joyous, the emotion was heartwarming, and the satisfaction was obvious," said Reverend Greg Garies, who told the deeds and accomplishments of the award winning shipyard 'miracle.' Telegrams and letters from high government officials, top ranking military figures, ship captains, and 'ordinary' fighting men were narrated by Garis, interspersed with readings by church members as if they were the original correspondents. Sincere gratitude for the unselfishness and sacrifice of the Brunswick artisans was recounted. The Christmas story of 1944 was filled with emotion for this group who worked on Christmas Day, and sent their earnings to support the war effort.

A lighter note was hit by recognizing that 98-year-old Carley Zell, who was sitting on the front row, had fed Christmas dinner at no charge to over one thousand workers approximately 58 years ago. Representing the Navy League Ms. Sheila McNeill expressed sincere appreciation to this superlative group, and stressed the essential part that supply ships have always played in the road to victory.

MAJOR GENERAL RONDAL H. SMITH AND DEBBIE

COMMANDER, WARNER ROBINS AIR LOGISTICS CENTER

One of the Air Force's five logistics centers and Georgia's largest industrial complex.

I was to travel to Robbins Air Force Base as a part of my duties with the Defense Advisory Committee on Women in the Services (DACOWITS). It was when I learned one of my first lessons on the committee.

I flew in from other travels and a young airman picked me up at the airport. I had not eaten all day, and when I saw a fast food restaurant, I asked if he would run through the drive in so I could pick up a sandwich. He did that and we chatted as he drove. During the drive, he shared with me that this was the first time he had driven through a drive in with an official van. I didn't understand and questioned him. It turned out that it was a rule—no stopping by anywhere with the van, picking up meals, etc. "Why didn't you tell me? I could have gotten something out of a vending machine."

He replied, "Oh no, I was told to give you anything you wanted. That you were a three-star general and not to ask questions."

The next day I was being escorted from one building to another as they pointed out the commissary and other buildings. I see a leading pizza drive in advertising a new pizza with pineapple and ham. Making small talk, I said, "That would be an interesting pizza. I'll have to try it one day." (Remember, it's 1996 and Hawaiian pizzas were a new thing.)

I met with focus groups all afternoon. Groups were divided by rank and gender. Between one of those I had about ten minutes and in came a Hawaiian pizza. If I had not learned my lesson earlier, I did by then. I had not met yet with the commanding general. He had recently had back surgery and had not returned to work and would not be able to join me for dinner that evening. That afternoon they took me by his quarters. We had a great time, and after about twenty minutes, he said, "Where are we eating?"

"I don't know, sir, but I know you won't be able to join us. Just take care of your back."

"No, no, I said that in case I was bored. I'd love to have dinner with you.," the general answered.

I loved that he told me the truth! The two of us had dinner that evening, and it was a productive, informative dinner. I learned more about the Air Force and Warner Robbins and he learned more about DACOWITS. The rest of the visit went well. At the end of the visit, the governor's Military Affairs Committee had a meeting at Warner Robbins, so I was right where I needed to be.

That evening MG Smith was hosting the evening, and toward the end, he had a surprise. "The last few days we have hosted a guest who is a member of a Defense Advisory Committee," General Smith said. He never said the name of the committee. "It's been a great visit. I understand she's received a call from the governor's committee wanting to know how the visit went."

She told them, "They've done everything but powder my butt and put me to bed. I'd like to call Sheila up and present a gift to her on behalf of me and my staff." It was such a surprise but that wasn't the biggest surprise. When I accepted the bag, it had a box of body powder! Can you be any more politically incorrect! I just loved it. We all had the biggest laugh and Ron and his wife Debbie continued as friends.

In fact, in April 1999, I invited Ron to speak at the Camden Kings Bay Navy League—he accepted, and we decided to make it an overnight at our home. We were also able to get him a tour of a submarine, and I'm sure that the picture of him at the controls of a ballistic missile submarines is one of his favorites. At the end of his remarks someone asked if the community needed a lobbyist.

He answered, "Sheila McNeill has dinner with the CNO all the time. She has access at the Pentagon—you don't need anything else."

When he retired, he stayed in Warner Robins and joined the Twenty-First Century Partnership—the base support group.

He was a great mentor to me over the years.

THE SPIRIT OF HOPE AWARD

The award recognizes a military member, civilian or organization that epitomizes the values of Bob Hope—duty, honor, courage, loyalty, commitment, integrity, and selfless dedication. On September 5, 2004, I received a call from Lynford Norton who was public affairs/community relations officer for the United States Coast Guard. He started talking about the Spirit of Hope Award named after Bob Hope. An award that the services and the USO participate in. I didn't think too much about it knowing that he might want my opinion on someone or perhaps for the Navy League to sponsor a reception for the event. Then he said, "The US Coast Guard has selected you for this award."

I was shocked. I was speechless and sat there with tears streaming down my face. I was aware of this award but never, never considered that I might one day be the recipient. I was so honored that Commandant Thomas Collins would even consider me. Lynford said the presentation would be made at the Coast Guard Ball. I was anguished. Six months ago, I had promised Texas that I would speak at their state meeting. I told Lynford of the conflict and that I would call him back.

I called my "right-hand man," Linda Hoffman, director of executive services at Navy League headquarters. She offered to call the Navy Leaguers in Texas asked me to wait until she had talked with them. When she told them about the award, they understood even though the programs were printed with my name on them! They would expect me to come another time

In October Arlie, and I attended the Coast Guard Ball. We were seated with Assistant Secretary of Homeland Security Ms. Fran Fragos Townsend. I was taken aback when she told me she had wanted to meet me for years. She explained that she had worked for the Coast Guard for a number of years and knew of my support. Of course, I knew who she was. I would later watch her on television as a Fox News contributor. Fran later became a national security analyst for CNN and I remember that night every time I see her on television. Also attending but seated at the next table was secretary of transportation, Norm Mineta, and of course, the commandant, Admiral Collins. Admiral Collins presented the medal and the citation was read:

> To Sheila M. McNeill
>
> For a lifetime of service to the Coast Guard as a member of the Navy League of the United States, the only civilian organization dedicated to supporting the sea services. Ms. McNeill joined the Navy League in 1966 and served at every leadership level. She ascended to the position of National President of the Navy League in 2003 becoming the first woman to hold this position since the Navy League was founded in 1902. As National President Ms. McNeill is responsible for leading the Navy League's 70,000 members who are dedicated to educating American citizens and elected officials about the importance of sea power. Throughout her career, Ms. McNeill has been effective in relating to the highest echelons of the military service as well as the most junior enlisted families. Service chiefs know her well and appreciate her private counsel and junior members open up to her, expressing concerns about quality of life issues and the needs of their families. In her previous position as National Vice President of legislative affairs, Ms. McNeill was instrumental in advancing the Coast Guard's' legislative agenda in the '07th and '08th Congress, one of the most fundamentally significant legislative periods in Coast Guard history. During this period, Congress debated and enacted the Homeland Security Act, which affected the historic transfer of the Coast Guard to the Department of Homeland Security, the Maritime Transportation Security Act, one of the most sweeping maritime security legislative packages in the Nation's history, and the first Coast Guard Authorization Act in nearly half a decade. Ms. McNeill and her legislative affairs team orchestrated numerous Navy League hosted events with member of Congress, which provided forums for the comprehensive airing of Coast Guard issues during the political process. Of particular note was her

team's showcasing of the need for major Coast Guard acquisition through the Integrated Deepwater Systems project. Their efforts were key to promoting and securing Congress' $80 million Deepwater appropriation—the largest acquisition project in the Coast Guard's history. As National President, Ms. McNeill has developed a groundbreaking Legislative Affairs Grassroots project, which will increase involvement by Navy League Regions, Areas, and Councils in legislative affairs activities. She has traveled to Navy League Councils worldwide to motivate members at the local area to renew their support of the U.S. Coast Guard. She regularly attends and speaks at national level events, spreading the message of the Sea Services, and the U.S. Coast Guard. Ms. McNeill has even had the opportunity to take her message to the highest levels of power when she had a recent audience with President George W. Bush. Under Ms. McNeill's leadership the Navy League's annual Sea Air Space Exposition has grown exponentially, experiencing record attendance by both senior military officers and industry. As an example of her dedication, Ms. McNeill almost always wore her Coast Guard Distinguished Public Service Award pin at public events giving her yet another opportunity to spread the good news about the men and women of the Coast Guard. Ms. McNeill's leadership, dedication, and outstanding support of the Coast Guard, as well as her deep devotion to all of our Nation's Sea Services are most heartily commended and are in keeping with the highest traditions of the Coast Guard.

The following also appears on the commendation:

The Spirit of Hope Award is presented to outstanding entertainers and other distinguished Americans and organizations whose patriotism and service to the troops through the USO reflects that of Bob Hope, who was designated the first honorary veteran of the U.S. Armed Forces for his decades of entertaining troops, both in peacetime and in combat zones. This honor was bestowed by the U.S. Congress and signed into law by President Clinton.

About the Spirit of Hope

In 1997, the USO, Congress, and the president came together to designate Bob Hope as the first and only honorary veteran of the United States Armed Forces. At the USO Holiday Gala that same year the Spirit of Hope Award was unveiled. The award itself is a portrait bas-relief of Bob Hope, created by St. Louis sculptor Don F Wiegand and donated to the USO by Mr. Wiegand and Michael Fagin of the International Group. Each year, the award is bestowed upon Americans who, like Bob Hope, have demonstrated tireless dedication to our country and to the US troops both in times of peace and war. The USO has already presented the Spirit of Hope Award to many outstanding patriots including Walter Cronkite, one of America's most respected journalists; Senator Strom Thurmond; and former senator and astronaut John Glenn.

Entertainers who have been recipients of the award include Johnny Grant, the honorary Mayor of Hollywood and veteran of fifty USO tours; the Dallas Cowboy Cheerleaders, who have given up their holidays for almost twenty years to entertain the troops with the USO; and the Country Music Association, in recognition of many artists who have donated their time and talent to US service men and women worldwide. In addition to this prestigious award, in 1998 the USO established the Spirit of Hope Endowment" to carry the legacy of Bob Hope into the new millennium and continue the USO services he championed.

Bob Hope and the USO: A Lifelong Partnership of Good Will Six Decades of Laughter

Thanks to the USO, I have some wonderful memories—like box lunches, yellow fever shots—and I've learned to say "Kaopectate" in nine languages. Hey, the USO has given me things that will stay with me the rest of my life... so my doctor tells me.

But I'm not complaining. How else would I get to travel with Carroll Baker, Jill St. John, Lana Turner, Ann-Margaret, and Raquel Welch and have my wife wish me "bon voyage"?

The fact that it doesn't depend upon tax money for support may be the reason why the plans the USO provided were not always the greatest. The first year, I knew the plane was old when I saw the pilot sitting behind me wearing goggles and a scarf. When they rolled the steps away the plane fell over on its side." But the audiences truly appreciate the USO and the performers.

At the suggestion of the Spirit of Hope Committee, I sent a letter to Mrs. Hope letting her know how thrilled I was to receive this honor.

A few years later my friend (who was a rear admiral at that time) Bob Papp told me he had heard that a permanent display was being erected at the Pentagon for the Bob Hope Award. I almost had a fit! To have my name forever on the walls of the Pentagon! He couldn't remember where he had heard it but promised to let me know when he heard more. A short time later he told me it had been done. I called the chief of information, Admiral Denny Moynihan. I was bursting at the seams as I told him I thought there was a display that had my name on it. I asked him to check it out.

"Denny, if this is correct I have to have a picture. After all, I explained to him. No one can carry a camera in the Pentagon. Your public affairs people are the only ones I know who can have a camera."

Denny's staff e-mailed me a couple of days later with pictures. It was so exciting.

Later when we planned the Camden Washington fly-in. I called Denny again and asked if one of the public affairs officers could meet us at the Hope display and take pictures. I was so proud that day. As we approached, I looked for my name. Yes, it was still there. It was an emotional time for me. I will always be grateful to the Coast Guard. In years to come, my name will be on this display for my grandchildren to see. I hope I can get them into the Pentagon!

Press Release For immediate release
Office of Public Affairs. U.S. Coast Guard, U.S. Department of Homeland Security

Coast Guard Presents Spirit of Hope Award to Navy League President

WASHINGTON, D.C.—The Coast Guard presented the 2004 U.S. Armed Forces Spirit of Hope Award to Sheila McNeill, Navy League of the United States national president, during the annual Coast Guard Ball. Oct. 2, in Arlington, Va.

The award recognizes a lifetime of volunteer service in the Navy League, the only civilian organization dedicated to supporting the sea services. McNeill joined the organization in 1966 and served at every leadership level, becoming the first woman to be elected president since the organization was founded in 1902. McNeill and the Navy League have been instrumental in advancing the Coast Guard's legislative agenda in the 107th and 108th Congress. Her efforts were key to promoting and securing Congress' $800 million Deepwater appropriation, the largest acquisition project in the Coast Guard's history. During this period, Congress debated and enacted the Homeland Security Act, which effected the historic transfer of the Coast Guard to the Department of Homeland Security; the Maritime Transportation Security Act, one of the most sweeping maritime security legislative packages in the nation's history, and the first Guard Authorization Act in nearly half a decade.

"Sheila McNeill has been one of the Coast Guard's most consistent supporters," said Adm. Thomas H. Collins, commandant of the Coast Guard. "Her influence is felt throughout the Coast Guard at all levels, from adopting local units and taking on the quality of life issues for our sailors to providing trusted counsel to our senior leaders. I am delighted to use this award to thank her and the Navy League for using their considerable efforts and influence to help keep the Coast Guard; Semper Paratus, always ready."

The United States Armed Forces Spirit of Hope Award is presented to outstanding entertainers and other distinguished individuals whose patriotism and service to the troops reflects that of Bob Hope, who was designated the first honorary veteran of the U.S. Armed Forces for his decades of entertaining troops, both in peacetime and in combat zones. This honor was bestowed by the U.S. Congress and signed into law by President Clinton. The Spirit of Hope Award was created by St. Louis sculptor Don. F. Wiegand and Michel Fagin, president of The International Group, Inc. Wiegand has work on display in public and private collections around the world, including pieces created for Presidents Reagan and Bush.

The U.S. Coast Guard is a military, maritime, multi-mission service within the Department of Homeland Security dedicated to protecting the safety and security of America.

I will always be grateful to the Coast Guard for this honor.

See Admiral R. J. Papp's story for more on the Spirit of Hope Award

SSGN AND UNDERWAY ON THE USS GEORGIA (729)

After the end of the Cold War and the results of the Start II Treaty and the 1996 Nuclear Posture Review, it was determined that the United States only needed fourteen of its eighteen Ohio-class SSBNs. This class of nuclear powered submarines is armed with up to twenty-four Trident II missiles. They are also known as Trident submarines and provide the sea-based leg of the strategic triad of the United States. A nuclear triad refers to a nuclear arsenal which consists of three components: strategic bombers, ICBMs (land based intercontinental ballistic missile) and SLBMs. The purpose of having a three-branched nuclear capability is to significantly reduce the possibility that an enemy could destroy all a nation's nuclear forces in a first-strike attack; this, in turn, ensures a credible threat of a second strike, and thus increases a nation's nuclear deterrence. Because of the stealthy nature of submarines, the SSBNs are considered the most survivable of the triad.

One of the more interesting conversations with Rear Admiral Chuck Beers was when we discussed this new arms control treaty with Russia and the impact it would have on the submarine force and the Camden County community. Current plans called for the destruction of the four oldest boats, the USS *Ohio*, the USS *Michigan*, the USS *Florida*, and the USS *Georgia*. Each boat is built for a forty-year life span with refueling at twenty year or halfway during the life of the boat. Rather than refuel these four the treaty called for eliminating them thereby bringing the United States in compliance with the new treaty and the Nuclear Posture Review.

He then told me of an interesting concept to save these four submarines. A solution he had heard from Admiral Skip Bowman, commanding officer of naval reactors who was the person behind the concept to utilize these boats.

It was a great idea but, at that time, it looked impossible. If the country would agree to modify these four boats, they could be maintained in our country's arsenal. The proposal was to take those four boats and remove the capacity for nuclear weapons—which would make them in line with the agreed treaty. But to make the concept even better to use those same boats for convention weapons. The size of the boat is so large that and the diameter of the Trident missile tubes so large that they would have the capacity for a cluster of seven Tomahawk cruise missiles. In this configuration, the number of cruise missiles carried could be a maximum of 154. This is equivalent of what is typically deployed in some surface battle groups.

The missile tubes also had room for stowage canisters that could extend the forward deployment time for special forces. The other two Trident tubes could be converted to swimmer lockout chambers. For special operations, the boat would be able to carry sixty-six special operations forces. These special forces could be from any of the armed services. (Later, but I'm getting ahead of myself, I talked with General Eric Shinseki, who was chief of staff of the US Army about this concept. The Army was the first to provide funding for research and development of the SSGN concept.)

That was exciting news and I couldn't wait to talk to our congressional delegation about it. *Could it be possible?* I thought. It makes so much sense. To convert them from SSBN to SSGN! To save those four boats that each have a life span left of twenty years each! That's eighty years of submarine life. That sounded like good economy for our country and for Camden County who would save those jobs by keeping the crews of those two boats at Kings Bay.

It should make good sense and I was on the way to Washington. I didn't call for appointments but first went to Congressman Jack Kingston's office. He was on the floor of the House of Representatives voting. The staff gave him a call and told him I was on the way to see him. As soon as he could, he came out in the reception area to see me. I told him of the concept. He was as intrigued as I was, and that day became one of the biggest supporters we ever had. I then went to the offices of Senator Paul Coverdale. While I was not able to see Senator Coverdale I talked with his staff. He later assured me of his support and that he would also talk to other members of Congress. Paul was former military stationed in Vietnam and knew the importance of the SSGN to the seal and other special forces units in their mission.

Since I had been friends with Senator Cleland for fifteen years dating back to his days in the Georgia Senate I talked with him personally. He worked tirelessly on this funding. Georgians and citizens of Camden County owe a great debt of gratitude to these three men. They never faltered in their support of the conversation of the SSGNs.

The year 1996 began a journey for me that lasted for almost eight years. Finding the support from these congressional members and individuals I talked with in the submarine force I began this battle that in some measures was a battle against the Navy that I loved so much. Not only the Navy but the submarine force would not support this concept this time.

In 1997, I went to the Camden County Chamber president, Carla Carper and the chairman of the Military Community Council of the chamber Jack Gross who was later relieved by Tom Turner and we organized the very first Washington fly-in of the Camden County Chamber of Commerce. About forty individuals traveled to DC on February 10–11, 1998. This began our first of our annual fly-ins. We met with Senators Max Cleland and Paul Coverdale as well as Representative Jack Kingston. We discussed this concept as well as other issues that affected Camden County. Representatives from each city and county and many other entities made the commitment that we would all agree on each of the issues. We would go to DC with one voice for all the cities and the county. And that concept continues to this day.

In March 1999, our local Camden paper the *Camden County Tribune* calls for the Pentagon to "Bring Georgia Home."

In May 1999, I organized a letter writing campaign on the SSGN. We wrote key members in the house as well as governors from Georgia, Florida, Ohio, and Michigan. We included buttons in the governor's packages reading "Save the USS Ohio," "Save the USS Michigan," "Save the USS Florida," and "Bring the USS Georgia Home."

In June 1999, the Office of the Secretary of Defense released a study on an analysis of converting SSBN to SSGN and in August the Defense Authorization Act for fiscal year 2000 supported thirteen million dollars for SSGN. The US Army was an early supporter of SSGN and provided some of the initial funding for research and development.

The years 1999 and 2000 were roller coaster years. We organized a formal SSGN committee in Camden County. The Military Community Council asks for assistance from local businesses to help with funding for our mailings, and the community responded.

We thought there was serious trouble in the conversion when news came out that the twenty-four launch tubes on each Trident submarine—even without their missiles—would still be counted in the total number of launch tubes allowed the United States under the Start II treaty. This would not allow the concept to proceed. But that issue was later resolved.

Then good news, the *Washington Times* editorial supports SSGN and *Defense News* says converted submarines could bolster US power projection. Then trouble again: The Pentagon's five-year budget presented to Capitol Hill contains $1.2 billion in submarine funding that could be used *either* to advance the design for the SSGN concept *or* to refuel Los Angeles class boats. This is a real problem and reminded me of the biblical story known as the Judgment of Solomon. Two women came before King Solomon to resolve a quarrel over which was the true mother of a baby. When Solomon suggests dividing the living child in two with a sword, the true mother is revealed to him as she is willing to give up her child rather than see the baby killed. Solomon then declares the woman who shows compassion to be the true mother and gives the baby to her. There is no Solomon to decide this issue.

In February and March 2001 petitions are placed in businesses all over town for citizens to sign and for the committee to send to congressional members. MIT's Security Studies Program endorsed SSGN and the *New York Times* editorial endorsed acceleration of SSGN. The *Georgia Times Union* published a full front-page story on "Can Kings Bay subs be saved?" and gave our committee needed exposure.

In January 2001, the committee sent letters to submarine contractors in Georgia asking them to contact their congressional delegation. Then we decided it's time to return to Washington but to go with a new twist. This was our plan:

Washington Fly-In
March 7–8, 2001
SSGN issues would be the main topic.
Review any background information staffs might need.
Obstacles:
The combination of a tight technical deadline for conversion

- A defense budget on hold.
- A decision by the Bush administration to conduct a review of the nation's defense before any funding is discussed.
- Arms control issues. If the Pentagon arms-control experts determine that a more expensive renovation of the submarines hulls is required to meet Start II arms control treaty concerns, the conversion would be doomed.
- Funding.
- Educating so many US legislators on the value—we asked that Dear Colleague letters be written.

The word was out—we had talked with our legislators. It was time to visit the entire Congress. First a position paper had to be written. I again called my friend, Ted Hack, who was with Electric Boat, a division of General Dynamics. We talked so much I had him on my speed dial. That was a relationship that would be strong over the eight years and beyond. I wanted the paper to be written in layman's language. It had to convince many people with different levels of understanding of submarines. I picked and cajoled/convinced my submarine friends to read "my paper" and correct any errors. As it turned out there were very few edits.

At that time, we had about thirty-five individuals, including my husband, Arlie, who were interested in paying their own way and traveling to DC. This trip had to be done right! We had the Georgia senators and our congressman on our side but what about the other 534 members of Congress? We knew we only had to get the story of this great concept to them and they would agree to its funding. Today it sounds a little naive, but I've always said that it is amazing what individuals can do in Congress.

But we had to have something to get their attention. We found a company who agreed to produce chocolate submarines. Linda Cook with the Camden/Charlton Board of Realtors was active with the Georgia Association of Realtors and she approached them for funding. They agreed! We ordered several thousand and shipped them to the hotel in DC to hold for us. We divided all the House and Senate names into lists depending on the location of their offices. We then went to Washington! The first night was spent getting the bags ready. The Wells, Norrises, Mizelles, Mike Mahaney, Carla, Arlie, and I stuffed each with a bag of chocolate submarines and tucked the position paper in the top where it showed. The next morning everyone came by and got their bags and the list of congressional members they would visit that day.

Attendees also included; Bill Gross, Deborah Hase, Steve Berry, James Gilman, Dr. Will Hardin, Celso Gonzales, Bob Noble Jeanne Knight, and the Weisensees.

The next morning, bright and early we began our visits but not until I'd given the final instructions: "You don't ask to see the senator or congressman. You'd never get in. But you ask them to promise to pass the chocolates around to the staff and to save one for the congressional member along with the paper." It took two days, but all 435 members of Congress were visited. Observations made: Senator Hillary Clinton would begin her political career as a senator in a basement with very cramped spaces, and all congressional staff were very receptive to chocolate and a Georgian's smile.

The fly-in participants left and I stayed in DC to attend functions in my capacity as national vice president for legislative affairs for the Navy League. One of those functions was a reception on Capitol Hill sponsored by the Navy League. There was a huge turnout. Much to my amazement, I kept hearing about chocolate submarines. One senator was talking to me when she turned to her staffer and said, "I just thought about those chocolate submarines that were delivered to our office today. Did anyone save me one?" She was surprised when she found out that I was head of the committee that delivered them. And I was surprised that she happened to bring it up when she was talking to me! Others during the evening mentioned it. Four years ago, it seemed that no one had heard of SSGN. Now it seems that everyone on Capitol Hill is talking about it!

The *Tribune & Georgian* had an editorial in the March 14, 2001, paper:

58 HOURS IN WASHINGTON

Last week 30 residents of Camden County spent 58 hours in Washington, D.C. For those who choose to participate in the Washington Fly-In sponsored by the Camden/Kings Bay Area Chamber of Commerce and the Military Community Council, 58 hours was a long time. D.C. was cold and windy. It was busy. For 58 hours, residents of Camden County launched a public relations attack on Washington. They fell upon the Capitol with one thought in mind—to send an SOS to members of Congress. They walked the halls of Congress announcing to all they are friends of Kings Bay. They left behind calling cards—Save Our Submarines (SOS). They handed out pamphlets talking about the importance of Naval Submarine Base Kings Bay, the submarine force, the need for the SSGN conversion and encouraged elected leaders to remember Kings Bay. And, they sweetened the blow of the attack by passing out chocolate submarines.

For the past five years' businessmen and residents have taken to the halls of Congress, announcing the importance of the subase to our community and supporting the idea of the Trident conversion plan. We're now at a critical stage of the plan. This is the year funding will have to be allocated for this project to begin. For those who went to Washington, they left the Capitol feeling optimistic. Although we would all like to see the conversion program get under way, the chamber delegation left a strong message behind in D.C. Kings Bay is part of our community, they told representatives. They are our neighbors, our friends, our family. We couldn't have asked for more dedicated community leaders than we have at Kings Bay, delegates said. We'd like you to utilize the base to its fullest potential. We've made an investment in Kings Bay. It's your opportunity to do the same.

What was 58 hours in D.C. worth to Camden County? Priceless.

Linda Cook would later convince the Georgia State Board of Realtors to substitute their issues for the SSGN. Realtors from across the state talked with their legislators about SSGN.

On March 23, 2003, thirty-seven members of Congress led by our Georgia Delegation wrote letters to President George W. Bush with copies to the Secretary of Defense Donald Rumsfeld. Congressman Jack Kingston had been on a flight with President Bush to a US Army installation at Ft. Stewart, Georgia. The congressional delegation was told after boarding the plane that they would have five minutes to bring up anything they wanted to the president. Jack tells me he thought, *What do I say in these five minutes?* Then he thought, *What would Sheila say?* Then it dawned on him: the SSGN concept! He did just that. When his time came he told the president about SSGN. The president turned to deputy secretary of defense, Paul Wolfowitz, and asked for information on this concept. Secretary Wolfowitz replied that they would present a brief when they returned from the trip

Rumsfeld and Secretary of State Colin Powell asked for support of SSGN

Things started looking up in May, while driving to Atlanta I received a phone call from a DC newspaper asking me for comments on the president's remarks at the Naval Academy graduation. The graduation had been that morning and I had no idea on what he might have said. When the reporter told me, I was stunned! The president's speech included a remark that future submarine commanding officers may command modified Trident submarines carrying hundreds of next generation cruise missiles. I asked if I could call him back while I verified what he had to say. I called Navy League headquarters and held the phone while they checked it out. It was true. I called the reporter and acknowledged my extreme pleasure in President Bush's comments.

An excerpt from the May 20, 2001, article in the *Times Union* read,

> *Other elements of his future vision included "modified Tridents submarines carrying hundreds of next generation smart conventional cruise missiles." Reached by telephone, Sheila McNeill, a resident of St. Marys and vice president of the Navy League of the United States said she felt buoyed by Bush's mention of the use of converted Trident submarines. "The only way they will do that is to fund the construction of what we have now (proposed)" she said. Without such a program Kings Bay Naval Submarine base would likely lose two of its 10 boats and a thousand job, as a result of an arms control treaty with Russia. Under the existing proposal, modified Trident submarines, incapable of carrying nuclear weapons, could continue to be based in Southeast Georgia. Rep. Jack Kingston, R.-Ga, whose*

district covers Kings Bay spoke with the president about the possible submarine conversion during a trip Bush took to Ft. Stewart in Georgia in February

But storms arise again in July when Congressman Jack Kingston announces that the administration will reconsider their recent decision to convert only two of the four Tridents. "To pass only the two Tridents is to sentence them to death," laments a Navy official.

We decided on a new letter writing campaign and scheduled a meeting for September 11, 2001. That day was the tragic events in New York City and Washington, DC. The attacks at the World Trade Center and then the Pentagon shocked the nation. That evening we kept our meeting of the SSGN committee. I called our chaplain and we spent the evening in prayer.

Early in the new year, Congressman Kingston announces that the first funding for the trident conversion is almost final. He and Connecticut Congressman Sam Gejdenson sent a "Save Our Submarines" letter to colleagues. In part, because of the dedication and perseverance of our congressional members and the good citizens of Camden County, not to mention many other civil and government representatives, the SSGNs are not only saved, but Kings Bay is now home to the USS *Florida* and the USS *Georgia*. The USS *Ohio* and the USS *Michigan* are at Bangor, Washington. All the effort and energy and chocolate submarines were worth this splendid outcome for Naval Submarine Base Kings Bay and for our country. I am proud to have been a part of the process.

On June 28, 2002, I received this note with a fax from Congressman Kingston:

Facsimile Cover Page
To: Sheila McNeill
From: U.S. Rep. Jack Kingston
Sent: 6/28/2002
Subject: Trident
To the Awesome Sheila McNeill… Here's a copy of our release… it should have been faxed to you along with the media. Your fax # is now logged in our system.

Robyn (Ridgley) (District Rob Asbell)

News from Congressman Jack Kingston (R/Ga.1)

Washington, D.C.—Congressman Jack Kingston announces $907.8 million funding in the 2003 Defense Appropriations bill to continue the conversion process of four nuclear-powered Trident submarine from SSBN (ballistic missile system) to SSGN (guided missile system.)

"After a struggle to get initial funding in past years, and last year successfully getting the conversion increased from two to four boats, it appears we're on solid ground for this year. Though we can't take anything for granted during the long and unpredictable funding process over the next few months, we'll carefully watch it and fight to keep it in the final funding bill. It helped this year that President Bush supported the program and put enough funding in his initial budget request. Still, I am appreciative and pleased that the other Members of the House Appropriations Committee agreed with the importance of the conversion program and fully funded the President's request. This will also make it easier to get continued funding for the project in next year's FY '04 funding bill." said Kingston. "Local support has also been a tremendous help with this, through the efforts of the Chamber of Commerce, Sheila McNeill and the Navy League, and the city and county governments."

(*Note: During Kingston's first meeting with the newly sworn in President Bush—it was a brief meeting aboard Air Force One, the Trident program was the only issue Kingston brought to the President's attention.) That story is told later.

Congressman Kingston's office sent the following press release on May 28, 2002:

> As part of the FY 03 appropriations plan, there is also language in the bill requiring the Navy to submit a report to the House Appropriations Committee by February 15, 2003 on the overall acquisition strategy for the program," Kingston continued. "We want to ensure that the long-term savings of the program ae not overcome by any unnecessarily complex acquisition strategies."

* * * * *

Success! Senator Max Cleland issues a press release on the Conference Committee appropriating $825 million for procurement and research funding for the SSGN. The bill also provides an option to convert two additional Tridents in the future.

My further note: When Congressman Kingston spoke at the Return to Service for the USS *Georgia*, he told this story and said, "I'd rather aggravate the President than disappoint Sheila."

In the May 28, *Florida Times Union* was the Navy's decision to send the USS *Georgia* and the USS *Florida* to Kings Bay.

> *"Kingston said the 'unofficial' Navy plans are to station the Florida at Kings Bay after the conversion is completed in 2006. The Georgia will arrive at Kings Bay the following year, he said. Nearly $1.6 billion to fund the conversion off the Trident submarines has been authorized by the House and will be funded after the bill clears the appropriations committee," Kings said.*
>
> *Sheila McNeill, national president-elect for the Navy League said many people have been lobbying for the Georgia and Florida to be home-ported at Kings Bay since the Navy announced the boats would be stripped of their nuclear Trident missiles and converted to carry Tomahawk missiles. The boats, each with the firepower of an entire battle group will be an important tool in the war against terrorist, supporters say. Each submarine will also carry 60 special Forces troops who can be deployed in coastal areas without the boat surfacing. McNeill said the announcement has great public relations value. "we've ask for this constantly," she said. "We felt there would be a certain advantage for everyone with the two boats being right here."*

Yes, in part because of the dedication and perseverance of our congressional members and the good citizens of Camden County, not to mention many other civil and government representatives, the SSGNs are not only saved, but Kings Bay is now home to the *USS Florida* and the *USS Georgia.* The *USS Ohio* and the *USS Michigan* are at Bangor, Washington. All the effort and energy, and chocolate submarines, were worth this splendid outcome for Naval Submarine Base Kings Bay and for our country. I am proud to have been a part of the process.

When the *USS Georgia* arrived at Naval Submarine Base Kings Bay, it was quite an event and to make it even more special the commanding officer was Captain Rob Hutton, an old friend. He met with us many times as we were planning the events. He was transferred before the Return to Service ceremony. I have been referred as the "mother" of the *USS Georgia.* I am very proud of that.

Once the four boats were funded, our community lobbied to have the USS *Georgia* and the *USS Florida* home based at Kings Bay.

The remaining two guided missile submarines, the *USS Ohio* (SSGN) and the *USS Michigan* (SSGN) are stationed at Kings Bay's sister base in Bangor, Washington. With the approval to bring *Georgia* and *Florida* "home," the state of Florida did a wonderful job of welcoming that boat with the help of many in Camden County. As the second boat to come to Kings Bay, I became chairman of the return to service of the *USS Georgia*. That story is told under *USS Georgia* return to service. Lt. Commander Todd Sullivan worked with us on the planning and execution of the return to service ceremony but was transferred just days before the actual ceremony. There were three special commanding officers we worked with: Captain Rod Hutton brought the ship home to Kings Bay and worked with us on initial planning, Captain McIlvaine, relieved Rod, and was a great sport as we told him of the planning—most taking heavy lifting that he had stepped into and Captain Mike Brown relieved him before the return to service ceremony.

A few years later I was leaving a ceremony at the Kings Bay Naval Submarine Base chapel when a gentleman stopped me. He said, "Are you Sheila McNeill?"

I said with a smile never dreaming who he might be or what he might say, "Yes, I am."

He then stuck his hand out and said, "I'd like to shake your hand. My friend Pat Gray, former FBI director"—then he made a reference to Deep Throat; you know he was a submariner—"told me stories about you and the SSGN, and if I ever met you, I should shake your hand."

I was so shocked I didn't have the time to think before he was gone. But wow! A former head of the FBI.

UNDERWAY ON THE *GEORGIA*

Due to my work as chairman of the committee I was invited to go to sea and spend the night on the *Georgia*. The captain was hosting/having a Tiger Cruise. This is a rare opportunity for fathers, brothers, and sons (or could say typical male family members) to see just what their relative does when he is gone for three months. Joining me was Marty Klumpp, cochairman for development on the committee. The cochairman for logistics, Keith Post, was a retired submariner.

Cruising along the surface you might feel a little motion—but underway you'd never know you were moving—that is, until maneuvers—especially those "angles and dangles," which refers to the pitching and yawing of the ship as they perform exercises. I had been underway many times over the past twenty-five years of supporting the submarine force. But I had never had the opportunity to spend the night on a submarine. That underway was one of the most remarkable thirty-six hours anyone could ever experience.

The enormous size of the Ohio-class Trident submarines is awesome. I frequently point out to those who might not be familiar with our submarine fleet that if you turn the boat on its end it is 560 feet and five feet taller than the Washington Monument. I always think of the boats back home when I'm in DC and see that beautiful monument.

Yes, they are huge but once inside the boat visitors are shocked by the limited crew space. This is especially true in the berthing area. Junior enlisted Berthing areas are for nine sailors. They share a stateroom that consists of a bunk with maybe four feet of head room. A space of the tray and closet. All 156 crew share one industrial size washing machine.

Junior officers share a three-bunk “rack room” and that is where we were escorted as we came onboard. Another of our bunkmates was the female doc who was onboard to do physicals. Being the oldest I claimed the easiest bunk to climb into—the middle one. Later in the day when I was resting and reading a young sailor came by with his father to show him the cabin I quickly welcomed them in, stood up to show off my “stateroom,” wanting to be gracious both to the officer and to his father. As a now “seasoned sailor” (I must have had twelve hours at sea), I pointed out my brilliant decision to select the middle bunk, adding that it is the most comfortable and easiest to climb into. Yes, the young officers said, “It’s my bunk.” Oh my, here I am showing off “my” stateroom) and the real occupant has been evacuated to make room for my visit. I then looked again at the picture on the locker and sure enough it was his bunk. There was a nice picture of him and his wife. We both laughed, and he urged me to enjoy his bunk and my time on the *Georgia*.

The commanding officer and the executive officers have the private space. They share a common head. There are times when a very senior official comes aboard that the executive officer has to give up his space but never the captain. The XO, as the second in command, can take over any berthing area he wants and sometimes this domino effect results in some of the crew sleeping between the missile tubes.

And then there is the chief’s quarters. This is an area never to be entered without permission. A sign is on the entrance, “Knock before you enter,” and you knew you’d better obey those orders. While they do have a small area to work, eat, have meetings, and they too enjoy very cramped sleeping quarters.

Imagine spending ninety days underwater with no windows, no sunlight, no moon, no stars. What they do have are movies and food. Food is the best on a submarine. Meals are eagerly anticipated and offer the submariner the only measure of time. If they are eating breakfast, it must be morning. I always enjoy the ice cream machine. It was fun to pull that lever and have immediate soft-serve ice cream. However, the real treat is the hard ice cream. That takes space and once it’s gone there is no more. Midnight rations are the best. Never would I think of eating at midnight any other time. I was tired during this trip—it was during the holiday season and I’d been working none stop. It was a bad time to take off from my Hallmark store, but this was the chance of a life time. After all, this was the best Christmas present I could hope for.

I would later have the opportunity to go overnight on a fast attack, the USS *Memphis*. It wasn’t Christmastime, so I did enjoy midnight rations, or midrats as it was known, during that overnight and I can’t wait to tell you about that! But on the

Georgia, I found myself staying up late but sleeping in the next morning. I discovered first hand that all actions are known by everyone—there are no secrets, no privacy on a submarine.

As I walked from my rack to the mess hall, I was greeted by everyone I met with "Did you enjoy the long night Sheila?" and "You are late for breakfast" from another. Yet there is another: "The Captain has been wondering when you would get up." Most of the guests had been up for hours when I decided to join them. It was a great night of sleeping. One of the pictures I have shown is when Marty and I ran into the captain and executive officer at 2:00 a.m. while in our pajamas on the way to the head. There was no vanity about walking around in my pajamas with no makeup—just trying to make sure I remember how the plumbing worked! Actually, there was a little makeup, which is why I was seeking the head. I admit to being a little bit of a "wuss" when I teased the captain about no tissue to remove my makeup. He called in the supply officer and we had a little fun with that issue in the early morning hours. There was no head in the cabin and to go to the head we had to go down a corridor. The head had a sign that said women and it would flip to say men when we left.

Food is the only deterrent to the length of time you can spend at sea. When food runs out, you must return to port. Stocking the food for ninety days for 156 crew members is a brilliant logistical feat. The freezer must be loaded in the exact order you will need the food—that means that 42,126 meals are exactly planned and executed. The masters of this are called CSs—culinary specialists. This is a fairly new MOS and I frequently use the old "mess specialist" term out of habit. *Mess* is the term used for the area used for the meals and for the meals themselves. The military over the past few years has made an effort to change some of the titles to run more in line with the civilian terms. This certainly makes it easier for those retiring or leaving the service to prepare their resumes so that they are understood by their civilian employers. For instance, who looking for a chef wants to hire a *mess* specialist?

Submarines have an extended training period and if you aren't one of the elite who wear the "dolphins," then you are using every spare minute to study to obtain this qualification. The only thing I couldn't understand were the long work hours. I argued with them that everyone needs a good night's sleep—even the hardiest of sailors. A few years later I was pleased to hear that this was changed, and hours now allow for everyone to have a full night's sleep. I'm sure there are exceptions to this during certain times but at least it is addressed.

Some movie is being played every night. Years ago, I was on a short—seventeen-hour cruise on another boat and the crew was watching Das Boat—an old German submarine movie and one that shows one disaster after another. Using my "official" voice I went to the mess hall and announced, "Due to the negative actions shown in this and other war movies showing submarine action we will no longer be able to show these movies on board subs. We believe it may have a detrimental effect on your morale." They were stunned and didn't like that a bit. I gave them a couple of seconds and smiled. I got a big laugh, and they continued watching the same movie for the umpteenth time.

There is a dignity and a depth of respect paid to each other that is evident after a short time on the boat. Perhaps it is the closeness. Perhaps it is the length of time you spend with your shipmate and these are most times, the only faces you see for weeks. Perhaps it's because your life may depend on the man sitting next to you.

A certain etiquette is evident. To earn your dolphins, you must learn every job on the submarine. So if you are not on watch, eating, or sleeping, you are studying. If something happens to a crew member, you have to assure that everyone is safe so you must be able to take on another job. You will never find a closer-knit crew. They take care of each other. They protect each other. The commanding officer's designee used to review the old 'family grams' that were to be so anticipated. Now with computers and the internet this is a little harder. All messages to the crew must be monitored. No one wants a shipmate to receive bad news while underway. Each crew member is so essential and the pressure so intense that all must be focused at all times they are on station.

Signs are hanging on the bulkheads that remind everyone of the concept of stealth. The head has signs over the toilet seat that warns, "Dropping seats can send loud signals in the water." A dropped instrument, a shout, or a careless bump could alert the enemy of your presence. Try as I might, there is no way I could determine the identity of the various underwater sounds heard by the sonar man. It all sounds like white noise to me.

"Excuse me, ma'am" or "After you, ma'am" was heard constantly during those thirty-six hours I was at sea. This courtesy was likewise extended to their shipmates. Captain Mike Brown and chief of the boat, Gary Aston, smile at me as they begin maneuvers. The chief of the boat is the most senior of the enlisted ranks. Being chief of the boat is also the most sought-after position of any enlisted submarine. You often hear that the chiefs run the Navy. I've never heard this disputed by an officer. The age of the junior officers who come on board are as young as twenty-four. They depend on the "old man," the chief, to advise them and have to set them straight if they are headed in the wrong direction. Only on SSGNs do both the captain and the COB must have prior SSBN experience before being assigned to this boat. The responsibility is that awesome.

The "angles and dangles" creating havoc for anything not locked down, including me! I'm an old veteran at this, though, so I lock my knees and hold on tight. "Sheila, keep your hands by you side, don't touch anything and go stand at the ship control station next to the COB," the captain said with authority. We were in a training exercise where we were being sought after by an enemy submarine. It was tense. I'm aware that underneath all the fathoms of sea—the unclassified depth is eight hundred feet—that it is serious business. This is the time where everyone is focused—no jokes here—just making sure every precaution is taken and the "enemy" doesn't find us. I'm also aware that even in this exercise if a mistake is made we could all be dead. But at the same time, I am not concerned. I know we have the best of training in this crew and they know what must be done. I don't say a word as the COB hears the orders of the commanding officer and repeats them:

"Con sonar, receiving loud transient bearing 350," says Captain Brown as he paused to listen to the sonar report. He said in a louder voice, "Con sonar, high speed screws bearing 350." He then immediately jumped into action ordering torpedo evasion which ordered the ship to man battle stations torpedo. Then the orders flew from the captain.

As COB Gary Aston repeated Captain Brown's orders and relayed them to the driver and the helmsman he would 'tap' the shoulder of the one he was directing. Back and forth he tapped—sternly as things got more intense. As others are given orders—the navigator, the engineer, and fire control all repeat the exact order of the captain. There can be no mistakes. Zero tolerance. Silence is essential. The captain is an outgoing, friendly personality. Respected by the crew, he is almost a father figure to many. But there is no father figure now—there is no friend—there is only the commanding officer, and everyone respectfully and intently listens.

"Helm, all ahead flank cavitate."

"Helm flank cavitate," was the response from the helmsman.

"Helm, left full rudder."

"Helm, left full rudder," was the response

"Dive, make your depth torpedo evasion depth."

"Fire control, launch counter measures," orders the captain

"Launch counter measures, aye." The fire control party began plotting a solution.

"Fire control, plot a solution to target and report as soon as it is complete."

At this point, there was a considerable change in the attitude of the crew. Everyone had a very intent expression on their face. Something was going on. The ship itself pitched downward and shook as speed increased rapidly and a down angle was attained. The captain continued to bark out orders while evading the torpedo. The fire control party was intense while plotting a solution. All the riders were at awe in watching the professionalism of the crew. Never before had they seen eighteen thousand tons of submarine in such a serious light. I would go into more details of that exercise but as the old story goes, "Then I would have to shoot you."

Maneuvers complete we head back home.

What an opportunity to spend twenty-four hours at sea with our nation's best sailors! Being able to see the SSGNs from advocacy to be a part of the fleet was an amazing journey.

ST. MARYS SUBMARINE MUSEUM

We had been talking about the need for a submarine museum for several years. A small group of museum supporters got together to finally go forward with our hopes for the museum. I was on the original committee with Bill Weisensee; Art Robb, general manager of Johnson Controls (the base operating services contractor); Debbie Harper, St. Marys tourism director; and John Crouse. We met monthly. We decided downtown St. Marys would be a great place to start and we started talking with city leadership. Bill had recently retired from the Navy as commanding officer of Trident Refit Facility and taken the position of executive director of the Camden Kings Bay Chamber of Commerce. He volunteered to chair the committee to build a submarine museum. The waterfront in St. Marys seemed to be the best place.

There were no specific plans and little funding (although we had many promises) but we knew that we had to convince the St. Marys City Council to recognize the positive aspects of a submarine museum in downtown St. Marys. Discussions began with city leadership.

A former theater then used for paid parties for children was offered. It was designed for a theater so there was just a large empty building with huge ceilings. The renovation would take real experts. A second floor to accommodate the artifacts would have to be built as well as offices, storerooms, and sufficient display place. It was pretty daunting but the price (no cost) and the location was right. Denny Reasoner prepared architectural plans to renovate the building in downtown St. Marys.

It was discussed at a city council meeting and all seemed to agree on the idea. While Bill Weisensee was passionate about building the museum, and he would have liked to continue as chairman, after talking with his board of directors, and decided it would be more time consuming than his work would allow. I was self-employed and could find a way to get my work done during off hours so when the committee met again I agreed to be the chairman. As chairman, I would have the responsibility of not only raising the funds but working with the architectural drawings, find volunteers who could handle the renovations, oversee the construction to renovate the building, and furnish it with necessary furniture and artifacts.

Bill encouraged me to have the museum built by the end of the year 1995 for the ninety-fifth anniversary of the submarine force. That was a little too ambitious I told him. There were a lot of people to convince it was a good idea and to support that idea. Not only a good idea but something they would financially support. We didn't make that 1995 deadline set by Bill, but we did have it built by March 1996.

In December 1994, the council discussed providing the city-owned theater building on the waterfront in the city's historic district to the group of Chamber of Commerce and local business people. The vote was headline news for the *Southeast Georgian* newspaper. Reporter Andy Drury quoted two councilmembers who spoke enthusiastically about the project. "I enthusiastically endorse the museum," said

Councilman Billy Frank Woods. "The location of Weekends is great and will serve as a basis to expand into something else." Councilman Kyle Lewis offered his stamp of approval as well. "I'm more enthusiastic about this than anything in twenty-five years," he said. "I'm totally committed to this." There was a headline quote that read, "We've never been able to tell the story of our submarines as we can tell it now" (Sheila McNeill, Kings Bay Navy League).

Gordon Jackson with the *Georgia Times Union* reported that those supporting the museum said it would draw tourist into the county and chronicle the sacrifices of Navy submarine veterans. "I think it's a super Christmas present for all of us," said Bill Weisensee. "I've received calls and letters from a lot of people supporting this project." He reported that more than thirty people, ranging from business leaders to state Rep. Charlie Smith Jr. were in the audience at Monday's meeting to show support for their project.

With the first obstacle overcome at Monday's meeting, Weisensee said he has plans to work quickly to gather the artifacts that will be displayed at the museum in downtown St. Marys about ten minutes off Interstate 95. However, we didn't have a written agreement with the city of St. Marys and no work could be done until then.

As chairman of the committee I felt very strongly about the importance of honoring and recording the history of our submarine force. We knew we wanted an area for watching films/documentaries on submarines, a working control panel, history files on every submarine, a working periscope, a reference area, and a section dedicated to our submarine Medal of Honor recipients as well as our submariners who made it to the very top of the Navy as our chief of Naval Operations. Ship's logs from WWII, plaques and other items were quickly donated.

At the beginning, we just hoped to be able to open the museum for a few hours a day with volunteers. "The biggest thing we've got is that we've made a quantum leap from an idea to having an organized committee in place to actual production," Captain Weisensee told the *Tribune & Georgian* in February 1995.

We developed a list of potential interested local individuals and submariners across the country. We offered plank owner certificates to encourage donations and created a keepsake that would give each of them recognition for being a part of history.

There were ideas flying and everyone wanted to begin fund-raising but I told them we had to have a firm plan. "When we can tell the public how much it will cost them and what value they can get for their money, we can start asking for donations, but not before then," I told the committee. "Our best estimate is that we need $105,000 for the renovation and installation of memorabilia."

On February 15, 1995, the following article was in the *Southeast Georgian*.

> SUB MUSEUM SURFACING BY SUMMER?
> On April 18, 1995 Mayor Jerry Brandon sent the following memo:

Memo to: Council Members
From: Jerry Brandon
Re: Submarine Museum

The Submarine Museum Committee has approved plans for re-structuring the interior of the old theater building. They apparently have donations of money and materials lined up, as well as a group of volunteers who are anxious to get moving on the project. Sheila McNeill has called me regularly since our last meeting and this memo is an attempt to get the project off the starting line. Because two members of council were not present at our last meeting, we took no action on giving them the go-ahead. Terry Floyd had (and has) some serious questions about "leasing" them the building for any longer than a year, because this council cannot bind future councils.

We have discussed an alternative which should be agreeable to all parties. I have talked to Sheila McNeill, Denny Reasoner, and others about the City retaining ownership of the St. Marys Submarine Museum. The City would contract with the St. Marys Submarine Museum Committee, Inc. to operate the facility on our behalf. This would legally allow the City to provide the free use of the building, to provide utilities, maintenance and insurance on the structure, etc. Clearly, this facility is designed to help the City of St. Marys, and the Committee is having trouble understanding why we seem to be holding up the project. I've tried to explain that we are trying to make sure that whatever agreement we have with them protects them and the City, and that such an agreement needs to be in place before they begin any demolition work in the building.

I am proposing that at the next Monday's meeting, or sooner, we give them the authorization to proceed with their plans for the interior, based on our agreeing to certain stipulations to be included in a formal contract to be prepared soon. Furthermore, I propose the following stipulations be included in such contract:

1. That the Museum be a City of St. Marys facility.
2. That the Committee have the authority to modify the interior however they see fit (and the exterior, so long as the Historic Preservation Committee concurs).

3. That the Committee provide whatever coverage is necessary to protect volunteers, workers during the course of construction.
4. That the Committee provide insurance coverage for the contents of the museum.
5. That the Committee provide (at least initially) manpower to operate the facility when it becomes functional.
6. That the City provide the utilities for the facility.
7. That the City provide insurance coverage for the building
8. That the City maintain the exterior of the building, including the roof and air conditioning unit.

> We have a very well-organized and enthusiastic Committee in place. They are not asking for any funding for the demolition and construction work that needs doing, and they are anxious to see the Museum open this summer! Their understanding was that we have made the building available to them and now we won't let them get to work. We should not, in my opinion, hinder progress on this vitally important downtown project.
>
> Please give the above some thought. I will call each of you on Thursday. If I can get a majority of council members who agree with the above essential stipulations, and I have agreement by the Submarine Museum Committee, I propose to give them the go-ahead to begin work, with the understanding that a final contract with the above stipulations included will be forthcoming.

We all went to that meeting with a lot of trepidation. We had met for weeks discussing the plans. We needed final approval from the city of St. Marys and that decision was in the hands of the city council. They were all hesitant for the same reasons. "What if we give them a building that is functioning now in a limited way and it's not finished?" "If we allow them to begin dismantling some of the structure and adding a second floor who can guarantee they will finish it?" "What if they begin but can't finish it?" were said by many. We kept looking at each other concerned that it was headed toward a "no vote." And then Councilman Kyle Lewis said, "Ya'll must not know Sheila." The mayor called for a vote and it was unanimous.

The following month I wrote an article for the local paper that closed with "I have told those who have volunteered their time and energy for the submarine museum that we will have reason to be very proud of what we are doing. Those who have come and gone from Camden County always try to put their finger on just what it is about this community that makes the difference. I believe it is the esprit de corps which is evident in many of Camden's events. This spirit is once again seen in the commitment to make a submarine museum a reality."

One of the more successful fund-raising activities was "An Evening Under the Stars." It was sponsored by the Kings Bay Submarine Officers Wives Club (KBSOWC) and held in May 1995 at the old beautiful Orange Hall. It was chaired by the most effective women—Kathy Dempsey, Sue Garwood, and Rhonda McKinnon. Kathy was the coverall chairman. Her remarks:

> *Ladies and Gentlemen, may we please have you're your attention. May we please join in with Mr. Arlie McNeill and sing the National Anthem. Rep. Smith, Mr. Mayor, Captain Williams, Mr. Scheer, ladies and gentlemen. On behalf of the Kings Bay Submarine Officers Wives Club and the St. Marys Submarine Museum Committee, I would like to welcome you to our Gala event of An Evening Under the Stars. I would like to thank you, the citizens of Camden County for supporting this event. What makes this community as wonderful are people like you and that's why Camden County is so very special.*
>
> *Preparing for this event could not have happened without the members of the Kings Bay Officers Wives Club, my energetic and creative committee, the many merchants of Camden County, people who just wanted to help, and you, the community. Thank you for making this happen The St. Marys Submarine Museum Committee is comprised of many talented people. They had this dream and today is the first day of making it a reality. The community will benefit mightily from your efforts. Someone once questioned a certain submarine Board member about how this project will or can, in so many words, survive. Sheila's answer was, "You don't know me." This kind of spirit has made this event seem so effortless. Thank you. Please take this opportunity to join the Submarine Museum and help build the community. Now Ladies and Gentlemen, May I introduce Mrs. Sheila McNeill, the Director of the St. Marys Submarine Museum.*

That evening I recognized Tom Hurley with the plank owners certificate and Chief Tom Denton artist and Dori Brink, chair of the logo and art contest. Our four speakers were Mayor Brandon, WWII veteran George Shear, commanding officer; NSB Kings Bay Captain Gary Williams; and the Honorable Charlie Smith Jr. And my husband Arlie was the auctioneer.

The article in the *Southeast Georgia*:

> *"Evening Under Stars" Reaches New Heights*
> *By: Andy M. Drury, Staff writer*

When the final tallies came in last Saturday night Sheila McNeill was understandable elated. "An Evening Under the Stars touted as Camden County's social event of the year, raised $3,500 to be used toward the St. Marys submarine museum scheduled to open later this year." (note: I still couldn't convince them from saying it will be built in 1995) "We really only expected about $1,500," Mrs. McNeill said. "This is just wonderful." The event held on the grounds of Orange hall in St. Marys, provided chamber music and hors d'oeuvres to the more than 100 people in attendance.

Kathy Dempsey, a member of the Kings Bay Officers Wives' Club (and the) Submarine Museum Committee, said the fundraising event was the beginning of a dream. "Today is the first step in making the museum a reality," she said in the opening remarks. State Representative Charlie Smith, the evening's keynote speaker, said he was proud to be a part of such an historic occasion. "It's great that in Camden County we don't have an 'us' and 'them' attitude between the military and the civilians that's in so many other places," Rep Smith said. "Here in Camden County, it's just 'us.'

He briefed the audience on the history of the submarine base which culminated with the U.S. Navy choosing Kings Bay as the preferred site for the Poseidon submarine base in November 1976. "It's clear to me that the destiny of the submarine force is to have the greatest submarine museum in the world here in Camden County and St. Marys, Ga.," he said. The event was well attended by representatives from the City of St. Marys, including Mayor Jerry Brandon, Mr. and Mrs. Mike Mahaney, Tourism Director Debbie Harper, Councilman and Mrs. Ken Hase and Councilman and Mrs. Bill Frank Woods. Mr. and Mrs. John Love, Commissioner and Mrs. Artie Jones, Captain. and Mrs. Craig Root, Captain. and Mrs. Bill Weisensee, Mr. Arlie McNeill and Kings Bay Captain Gary Williams were in attendance as well as many other community leaders.

Mayor Brandon announced the museum was well underway and that he looked forward to it being a great asset to St. Marys and Camden County. "its phenomenal to be moving as fast as we are," he said. I look forward to the museum opening in the very near future." Camden County/Kings Bay Chamber of Commerce Executive Director Bill Weisensee said the museum quickly became more than a vision. "The idea has come a long way from the November 14th St. Marys City Council meeting when the idea was first introduced," he said. "It's certainly more expedient than anything I've ever seen in Camden County, and it has taken a lot of cooperation. "Even some of the naysayers have given us some notoriety," he continued. At the fundraiser, the winners of the submarine logo contest were announced. Matthew Grimes won in the first grade category; Ryan Carter won in the second grade category; and Marilyn Carter was the sixth grade winner. Lim Langevin won for the ninth grade entry; Dianne Knowles, was the adult amateur winner and Daniel Cross won in the amateur black and white category.

In the amateur color logo category, Joe Novell took top honors, and Anjela McEahern won for her professional logo entry.

What the paper didn't cover was much of the fund-raising could be attributed to Arlie's auctioneering.

* * * * *

Jill Bauter covered the event for the Camden County Tribute featuring George Sheer, a World War II submarine veteran:

World War II submarine veteran George Sheer, who served as a Navy cook, recalled his personal experiences in an emotional speech. Sheila McNeill, chairperson of the submarine museum committee, said Sheer exemplifies the museum's value to submariners and their loved ones.

Captain Gary Williams. Base commanding officer, also addressed the crowd at the event.

Evening Under the Stars attracts over two hundred supporters.

More than two hundred supporters of the St. Marys Submarine Museum gathered downtown on Saturday to raise money and awareness about the future tourist attraction, held on the grounds of Orange Hall, the "Evening Under the Starts" fund-raising event was hosted by the Kings Bay Submarine Officers Wives Club (KBSOWC). "What make this community so special is people like you. Thank you for making this happen," said organizer Kathy Dempsey of KBSOWC.

In addition to arranging for food, entertainment and door prizes, club members (attendees) also donated $3,500 for renovations to the waterfront museum building. "This benefit for the sub museum has shown to us all how much he community cares as a whole," she said. According to Dempsey, the museum will provide a meaningful link between the community and service members at Kings Bay while also honoring service aboard submarines.

"It is great that in Camden County we don't have the 'us' and 'them' attitude," said State Representatives Charlie Smith Jr. of the relationship shared by the community and the Navy. State Representative Charlie Smith gave a brief synopsis of the history of the submarine and its home at Kings Bay. "It is clear to me that the destiny of submarines

is to have the greatest submarine museum of the world right here in Camden County, Georgia," he said. "This frankly is a very historic occasion."

Prominent officials from Kings Bay Naval Submarine Base and the community including St. Marys elected officials who voted in favor of the project, were represented at the gala. "We look forward to having a submarine museum for St. Marys and the surrounding county. I think it is phenomenal we are moving this fast," said St. Marys Mayor Jerry Brandon.

Another large group to embrace the effort was the St. Marys Merchants. They had a big event in downtown St. Marys on September 9, 1995, from 9:00 a.m. to 5:00 p.m. They had live entertainment all day with the Camden County Band and the Medieval Group performing. K-Bay Radio broadcasted live all day from the waterfront. Other innovative events included:

- A car wash by USS *Pennsylvania* Blue Crew.
- A cut-a-thon by Judy Humphries and other local hairstylists.
- Face painting by Lois Rebstock for the children.
- Glamor shots at Orange Hall by David Kidd of Kidd Photography. For the more daring, Jack Mounts donated a Harley-Davidson for use in the photos.
- Betty Mounts lent her makeup talents.
- The Downtown Merchants sold live plants donated by K-Mart and carpet samples donated by Camden Carpet. They also raffled off a cabinet donated by Henry's cabinet.

And in an unbelievable offer Wal-Mart volunteered to match the amount raised from donations by the Downtown Merchants Association. They ended the press release with "This is a great opportunity to enjoy a full day of fun with the kids and support our new and exciting Submarine Museum." With this kind of support, we *have* to be successful. In December, Roger Dumont and Tom Perrine and I signed a proclamation to make our plan work:

PROCLAMATION
Kings Bay Chief Petty Officers' Association
Hereby Agrees to Adopt the St. Marys Submarine Museum
The parties signed below ascertain that they will work
together to further the efforts of the
St. Marys Submarine Museum
The parties signed below ascertain that they will work
together to further the efforts of the
St. Marys Submarine Museum in Commemorating the

Proud history and traditions of the UNITED STATES SUBMARINE FORCE
By our hands on this day in December 1995

Roger Dumont	Sheila McNeill	Tom Perrine
MMCM(SS), USN	President	MMCM(SS), USN
COMMAND MASTER CHIEF		ST. MARYS COMMAND MASTER CHIEF
COMSUBGRU TEN	SUBMARINE MUSEUM	SUBBASE KINGS BAY

Talk about help! Tony Cobb. The name demands respect. I will always be grateful to Tony Cobb. Tony was in charge of the building. He was remarkable. Not a day went by that I wasn't at the museum for the eleven months it took to build. Tony knew how to build, if he wasn't already, he became an expert in masonry, carpentry, plumbing, air conditioning, fixtures—you name it. I didn't realize how little his background was in building. His sole experience had been a small project at home. When he was interviewed by the newspaper after the museum was finished he emphasized this and I almost jumped out of my chair. "You didn't know any more than that?" The beauty of it was if he couldn't do it he knew someone who could!

Volunteers would report to Tony who assigned the day's work. The response was incredible. He kept a log of all volunteer hours and formed the fifty-hour club and a one-hundred-hour club. As the hours grew he formed a five-hundred-hour club. I would bring possible donors by the museum where Tony and all of his volunteers were working. It was amazing to see—and hard to believe that all of these experts were not charging anything! Tony and I would discuss the progress and decide on what might be needed for the next day's work. He kept track of all the hours and formed a fifty-hour club and a one-hundred-hour club. He later had to add another club with even more hours donated. One volunteer was in the area on vacation and spent almost every day working on the museum.

Every week or so we had a picture in the paper with a new large donor to try to encourage others. We considered one thousand dollars a large donation! Our levels were as follows: fifteen dollars for an individual member, twenty-five dollars for a family, one hundred dollars for the chief, five hundred dollars for the commodore, one thousand dollars for the captain, and five thousand dollars for the admiral.

In November 1995, the base held their annual WWII Submarine Veterans event with approximately one thousand attendees from twenty-five states. Although we were behind and far from completion we invited them to attend a reception at the museum. That evening I told the submarine veterans, "I am pleased to have reached the stage in the building of the museum to have the reception for the World

War II veterans. You veterans are one of the reasons for the museum. Your history is the history we want to preserve. You are what it is all about. John Crouse, artifacts chairman, had done a great job listing the items needed and describing the position of the anticipated artifacts on the wall, so you really have an idea of the layout. In each museum room, we have signs that indicate what type of memorabilia will be placed there and what items are still needed." I was honored to interview many of these veterans who shared their memories and that tape is in the museum. I was so pleased with their candid answers.

It was January 1996, and we had set the opening date for March. There were a few sleepless nights. We needed more funding and by this time we had volunteers who had to cut some of their hours. Then good news. But first a little background.

At a Navy League meeting in DC weeks earlier I had approached a very successful Navy League member and friend, Jack Schiff, president of Cincinnati Financial Corporation and a retired Navy lieutenant commander. I told him all about the museum and the efforts we were making to build the structure. He seemed interested—and then I asked if he might want to join our membership. He asked how much and when I said, "Fifteen dollars." He laughed that it was the least amount he had ever had requested. He told me he might be able to find a few extra dollars. One day John Crouse came hurrying into my office. He said, "Look at this letter. Someone by the name of Jack Schiff has sent us stock in his company." Read more about Jack in his story.

I told Tony we would replace the cheap front door with a nice one, order the conference table we needed for the upstairs library area, buy the floor covering, buy the paint we needed, and get me a list of other things we needed before opening and let's tell the press we will have an opening date of March 31! I called everyone, and they were ecstatic. Admiral Chiles wrote me back with congratulations and a note that he was looking for a periscope for us.

I was quoted in the *Georgia Times Union*: "We went from wondering how we were going to finish this project to going over the top. I used to wake up every morning praying, 'Please God, let us finish this museum.'" That same week I received word that I had been selected as a member of the Defense Advisory Committee on Women in the Services. It was quite a week.

Jack not over came through for our opening but as of 2018 has continued to support the museum for over twenty years. The museum might well have not made it were it not for Jack Schiff's generosity. The *Tribune* had my picture with a different story on each side of the picture: McNeill ready to serve on advisory committee and on the other side; opening date for new museum set for March. I was able to take deep breaths and breath again. The opening date would be March 13, 1996, and my first defense advisory meeting was the next month. There would not be much time to relax and enjoy the completion of the museum.

The following year It was time to make a decision on our insurance for the museum and we had no trouble putting it all with Cincinnati Insurance Companies. A few weeks later I received this letter from Jack Schiff:

> March 27, 1997
> Dear Sheila,
>
> Many, many thanks to you for arranging to have Arthur Pittman write Cincinnati Insurance policies for St. Marys Submarine Museum. You are a wonderful, loving, charming young doll. Cincinnati Insurance Company loves you.
>
> Best wishes, Jack

We again, asked him to come visit the museum and he promises to try.

By that time construction cost was about $130,000 and only about 85% complete. We were two weeks out from the opening. Tony called me and said he needed at least one Seabee to complete what needed to be done. He told me that we might have to open with construction incomplete. Although the submarine base's Chief Petty Officers Association adopted the museum months before they still needed help that only the Seabees could do. Construction Battalion 412 was just the answer.

The only problem was it was a Friday and Captain Gary Williams, the commanding officer of Kings Bay, had to give approval and he was on travel. Could I please call him? I called his office and found out that he was at the base in Hawaii. I was concerned, what are the chances I could make contact. The opening is a little more than two weeks away. But, he answered his cell and agreed to send a Seabee to help us complete the work. That Monday the entire battalion came. They had a program called CAP—Civic Action Program—which allowed the Seabees to take time away from work to volunteer their time for a nonprofit cause. Gerald Cooms, the Seabee crew leader, said there were plumbers, electricians, carpenters, and other professionals so tell them what was needed, and they would begin work!

In an article that appeared in the *Camden County Tribune* on March 13, Tony was quoted saying, "Having the Seabees has made the difference. They supplied a large amount of labor. We wouldn't have made the deadline without them, and we would have had to pay several thousand dollars doing what we as volunteers didn't have the expertise to do, such as laying the carpet and tile, texturing the ceiling and other jobs." The Seabees and Chief Petty Officers Association volunteers are working side by side to make the museum a reality.

The next two weeks the papers were full of the good news and announcement of our Submarine Museum "Commissioning" (*Southeast Georgian*, Wednesday, March 27).

SUBMARINE MUSEUM COMMISSIONING SATURDAY

The Grand Commissioning of the St. Marys Submarine Museum will be held on Saturday, March 30—turning the dream of some into a reality for all. It has taken over a year, but the Grand Commissioning, slated to begin at 10 a.m. will mark the culmination of thousands of hours of labor by dedicated volunteers who believe that submarine lore must be preserved. In an almost military-like ceremony, Rear Admiral Eugene B. Fluckey, USN (Retired) will be the keynote speaker. RADM Fluckey, a Medal of Honor recipient and holder of four Navy Crosses is the author of *Thunder Below,* a book of wartime adventures taken from his World War II naval career.

Mistress of ceremonies for this history-making event will be Sheila McNeill, president of the board of the St. Marys Submarine Museum and a leader in the establishment of the museum in St. Marys. We've never been able to tell the story of our submariners as we can tell it now," said Ms. McNeill. The Camden County High School Band will set the pace prior to the ceremony, with patriotic musical selections performed throughout by "Cumberland Sound." The Sea Cadets and Navy Junior ROTC of Camden County High will also perform the parading of the colors and rifle demonstrations.

Special acknowledgements will be made of sponsors, volunteers and plank owners of the museum. Also speaking will be RADM Charles J. Beers, Jr. Commander Submarine Group 10, Naval Submarine Base, Kings Bay. Jack Schiff of the Cincinnati Companies will be recognized for his substantial contribution to the museum by the dedication of the "Jack Schiff Library."

A specially-designed museum pennant will be broken and flown signifying the official opening. The museum will be open for tours following the ceremony with free admission all day. RADM Fluckey will hold a book-signing from 11: a.m. to 1 p.m. outside the museum with all profits to be donated to the museum. A small reception will be held in the pavilion across the street from the museum with Kings Bay Submarine Officers' Wives Club members serving as hostesses.

Cakes by Claudia has donated a specially-designed cake to mark the event. Southern Cross Gardens will decorate the stage and pavilion area with trees, shrubs and flowering plants.

Members of the Rotary Club of Kings Bay, who adopted the Grand Commissioning as a club project, will serve as commission guides. "We encourage everyone to come and be a part of history in the making," said Sue Garwood, commission chairman."

Sue did a wonderful job with planning, organizing and implementing the commissioning. I knew I'd not only be busy but enjoying the moment and wanted someone in charge! From the planning of the order of the commissioning to designing the program Sue was a true professional.

The *Times Union* also had a front page story on the museum:

March 29, 1996
SUBMARINE MUSEUM OPENING
St. Marys stages ceremony tomorrow
By Gordon Jackson, staff writer

Bill Weisensee estimated it would take about six months to open a submarine museum when he first asked St. Marys city officials to donate a vacant building in November 1994. Weisensee and other organizers visualized a demand for a submarine museum after they learned that at Kings Bay Naval Submarine Base—home of the Navy's Atlantic Trident submarine fleet, tours are not given because of security reasons. Weisensee, executive director of the Camden County Chamber of Commerce, thought the museum project was simply a matter of gathering a few artifacts, purchasing some display cases and renting a few billboards to publicized the museum.

After 15 months, $75,000 in donations and more than 6,000 volunteer hours, the St. Marys Submarine Museum is set to open tomorrow at 10 a.m. with all the pomp and circumstances of a ship's commissioning. Retired Rear Adm. Eugene B. Fluckey, a Medal of Honor recipient, will be the keynote speaker during the one-hour ceremony. Rear Adm. Charles Beers commander of Submarine Group 10 Kings Bay Naval Submarine base will also speak at the grand opening. "It's an extraordinary effort the volunteers put into this," Weisensee said. "The museum is the 21st in the nation chronicling the history of submarines but the closest one to Kings Bay is in Groton, Conn." said Sue Garwood, the ceremony's chairwoman.

After the ceremony, the museum will open for guided tours by World War II submarine veterans and retired Navy chiefs with free admission all day. Regular museum hours are Monday through Saturday from 10 a.m. to 5 p.m. but hours may be adjusted depending on demand museum officials said. Admission will be $2.00 for adults and $1.00 for children and students. Museum board members gave special credit to Sheila McNeill, museum president, for raising funds, gathering memorabilia and keeping the project on schedule for the past year. McNeill will step down as president tomorrow to devote more time to her St. Marys gift shop, the Georgia Navy League where she serves as the States' first woman president and as a member of the Defense Advisory Committee on women in the services.

"I'm going to owe people the rest of my life for this museum," McNeill said. "it's amazing how much money has been spent and how much has been accomplished." Volunteers renovated an old movie theater, added a second floor, rewired electrical systems, laid carpeting, painted the building's interior and are in the process of getting up displays for tomorrow's opening. The first floor will include hands-on displays of a working periscope, a World War II dive suit, sleeping quarters, submarine models and memorabilia focusing mostly on the diesel era of submarines. Visitors will also be able to purchase T-shirts, coffee cups, hats and other memorabilia from the gift shop. Other gifts specific to the nearby Trident base may be added if there is a public demand for them, organizers said. "The second floor will house a library that eventually will include about 1,000 topic reports chronicling the history of every submarine squadron and group in the world, as well as displays of the nuclear submarine—including the Tridents at Kings Bay" said John Crouse, a retired Navy chief and museum director After tomorrow's ceremony, guided tours by submarine veterans will only be offered to groups who contact the museum in advance.

The museum is designed so people can visit it without a tour guide. And Art Robb, who will replace McNeill as museum president, said he plans to change the displays on a regular basis as a way to encourage return visits. "A museum should be dynamic, constantly changing," said Robb, a manager at Johnson Controls. "We want to keep public interest in the museum. We want to make the museum an interesting, learning tool," Robb said.

> St. Marys city officials don't know how many people will attend the grand opening, but they hope it will rival the annual Fourth of July celebration when as many as 10,000 people crowd into the city's historic district. Mayor Jerry Brandon said most people should be able to park within a few blocks of the museum, located across from the Cumberland Island boat ramp in downtown St. Marys, about 10 minutes off interstate 95. Brandon said the timing of the museum's opening, combined with a recent Monday magazine report naming St. Marys the best small city in the country, has officials excited about the city's future.
>
> "The museum is everything I hoped it would be." Brandon said. "I'm sure this will benefit all the businesses in Camden County." State rep Charlie Smith, Jr D-St. Marys credited the volunteers who donated their time and efforts to complete the project some said couldn't be done and said the museum would be an important, not just to the area, but to Georgia. "St. Marys has a rich and important heritage, and in recent years the Navy has become a part of that heritage," Smith said. "I'm hoping this becomes a real important fixture that gives recognition to sacrifices these men and women make for our nation's security,"

Just in time! The day before the commissioning the periscope arrived. Workers from Trident Refit Facility's periscope shop delivered and installed a working periscope. It was a wonder to watch the installation. The base paper had a great picture showing the installation. It was quite a feat. I still cannot believe we were able to have Rear Admiral Gene Fluckey as the commissioning speaker. I also can't believe the vast amount of energy he had. I stayed with him throughout the day. He met with the museum board of directors and autographed books and then we went to the base exchange where he sat for a couple of hours and talked to sailors and marines and signed books. We had a short lunch and headed back for the three o'clock ceremony. Everything was just superb. Gene did a wonderful job and had everyone laughing and then wiping their eyes.

Shirley Fages came for the weekend and worked frantically with us to get the museum ready to open. Most of the board of directors were there and working. It was a high for each of us—we all felt that building the museum was a most rewarding experience. The community spirit and hundreds of volunteer hours donated were unbelievable.

RADM Fluckey was incredible. He knew I felt like the crowning touch for the museum was our active area with a "real" submarine control center so that visitors could push a button and hear a sound. To be able to sit at the chairs, the submariners sit at and get a feel for all the buttons and gauges they needed to learn to use was planned. We even talked about having a system that picked up the sounds from the St. Marys River across from the museum, so children could hear the fish swimming by with the sonar. The equipment from the USS *Polk* was giving to the museum but refurbishing it and wiring it to give children some "bells and whistles" has proven to be more of a task than we expected.

After the ceremony RADM Chuck Beers and his wife, Susan, hosted a dinner party for the Fluckeys. By about eight o'clock we were all fading. I don't think I've ever been so tired. Yet Gene acted as if he'd just gotten up. He was telling wonderful stories and we all sat enthralled. But his wife, Margaret, told Gene she was tired and all the table was tired and it was time to go home. I will never forget that wonderful evening.

Wednesday, April 3, Mark Jicha had a great article on the event.

SUBMARINE MUSEUM COMMISSIONED

> The St Marys Submarine Museum was officially commissioned Saturday morning when the museum pennant was unfurled on to flagpole, but the dream which produced the museum began nearly four years ago.
>
> And even though hundreds of men and women invested thousands of hours in the project local businesswoman Sheila McNeill, outgoing president of the Camden County Navy league spear-headed the project from start to finish. "This is typical of a Sheila undertaking," said Bill Weisensee, executive director of the Camden/Kings Bay Chamber of Commerce. "She accepts every challenge with great enthusiasm and brought this museum from a dream to a reality." The March 30 Grand Commissioning was attended by hundreds of active duty and retired military personnel, who joined with local citizens and visitors to welcome the new facility on the St. Marys Waterfront.
>
> But of all those assembled, one man stood out as one of America's most respected submariners: RADM Eugene B. Fluckey, USN (retired) and proud recipient of the nation's highest military honor, the Congressional Medal of Honor. He was introduced as "one of America's greatest combat submariners" by RADM Charles Beers, Jr. during the ceremony, a commander who was credited with sinking 16 Japanese ships during World War II including an aircraft carrier.
>
> But RADM Fluckey down-played his own role in these accomplishments and compared his experiences with that of the museum. "The only thing I ever won on my own was a freckle

contest at age 6," RADM Fluckey told the audience. "Everything else is teamwork. It is so appropriate to be here today and feel this magic involved in making dreams become reality." "This," he said gesturing toward the museum behind the dais, "is what dedication is all about and it is appropriate to be here close to our largest submarine base. "They're the ones that won the Cold War," he said about the active duty and retired submarine servicemen assembled at the ceremony. "It took persistence and dedication just as this submarine museum."

RADM Fluckey chronicled the submariner's role in World War II and the Cold War that followed, and said it was that silent but deadly undersea force which made Russian Premier Nikita Khrushchev back down from the brink of nuclear war. "You've got to realize that the Russians knew every one of our missile holes and expected to kill 125 million Americans with a first strike," RADM Fluckey recounted. "But even if they eliminated all of our land-based missiles, the location of our boomers remained unknown. "That forced the Russians into a spending war and they ran out of money first." He continued. The $3 Trillion national debt we have today is cheap, and I thank God, we made the sacrifice and won it. "It was a cheap price for victory."

RADM Fluckey recounted the first 5 successful submarine engagement with a surface ship in the Civil War in the Cooper River in Charleston, S.C. reiterating his theme of persistence and dedication. But his exploits during World War II and his visionary use of rockets near the end of that war allowed him to quip about government and bureaucracies

"Toward the end of Work War II, I knew the day of the torpedo was passing and rockets would become the weapons of the future." He said, recalling how he had his submarine fitted to accept 5-inch rockets in 1945. "We came in very close to a large city and hit the largest paper factor in Japan setting off a huge fire. If I would have been able, I would have called General Eisenhower and told him to hold off sending the Enola Gay (with the atomic bomb which was dropped on Hiroshima.)" he said. "Everyone knows that a government without paper shuts down in five days."

Museum sponsors were recognized by Art Robb, museum vice president and Master Chief John Crouse (USN retired) who is the museum treasurer Chief Tony Cobb, who supervised

> construction recognized volunteers noting that 129 volunteers invested 6,344 hours in the project.
>
> Then Mrs. McNeill made a special presentation to Ohio businessman Jack Schiff, who donated $33,825 worth of stock to put the museum's fund-raising drive over the top. The museum library will be named in his honor and Mr. Schiff, who was unable to attend the ceremony will visit later this year. "As my last official duty I want to thank everyone in the community and the scores of volunteers who made this possible," she said. "This is a tribute to submariners, American heroes from World War II to present. Our nation's security depends on the submarine force because it remains the greatest deterrent to war we've ever had."
>
> Following a rifle demonstration by the Navy Junior ROTC from Camden County High School and a musical selection by Cumberland Sound, the museum banner was unfurled and the museum was officially commissioned

I turned over the presidency to Art Robb and wrote a memo to the board of directors. They were Art Robb, Jim Wells, Marcie Price, John Crouse, Janet Brinko, Tony Cobb, Loretta Conner, Sue Garwood, Charlotte Glover, Tom Hurley, John Minor Tilden Norris, Bill Weisensee, and Billy Frank Woods. The honorary board was Adm. H. G. Chiles, USN; RADM Charles J. Beers, USN; RADM Al Konetzni, USN; RADM Thomas Robertson, USN (retired); Captain Gary Williams; Mayor Jerry Brandon; and Jack Schiff.

Capt. Gary Williams, commanding officer of Naval Submarine Base Kings Bay, included the submarine museum in his Skippers Viewpoint Column on April 5. While recognizing the recent designation of St. Marys as the one of the top fifty "boom towns" in *Money Magazine*, he talked about the commissioning:

> *"The grand commissioning of the St. Marys Submarine museum this past Saturday is right in step with the spirit of this booming community. If you have not had a chance to visit the museum, you are in for a treat. Currently the museum operating hours are 10 a.m.–4 p.m. Monday through Saturday. It is full of artifacts commemorating the history of the U.S. Navy submarine service, memorabilia donated by submarine veterans, and plaques contributed by past and present submarine commands. My thanks also go out to all the Navy and civilian volunteers who helped make the museum's grand commissioning possible. More than 6,000 volunteer hours have gone into construction labor and support."*

Margaret Fluckey sent a letter dated April 4, 1996

Dear Sheila and Arlie,

We hope you have a "Happy Easter" and a well earned rest after your extra valiant efforts in making "The Museum" possible. Thank you both very much for ferrying us about and also for a delicious dinner on Friday night amidst fun company. Our return home was uneventful and spot on time! No luggage dramas either. Gene is now sitting over his taxes and I'm casting my eyes to the garden and all than means.

Again a "Big Thank You,
Affectionately yours, Margaret

The letter from Gene came a few days later:

12 April 1996
Dearest Arlie and Sheila,

We do appreciate so very much all these precious, historic St. Marys events and your very kind letter plus publications. Yet, somehow, your wish list was missing. I know some of the museum people re submarines. Particularly, I have been impressed with the USS COD museum in Cleveland where I gave the rechristening speech. Two civilians John Bakar, President and Paul Sarac, his cohort does seem to have the best knowledge of submarine parts in the U.S. So, I await your "wish" list.

Your publicity was fantastic as is the museum. At the Annual Submarine Veterans of WWII in Milwaukee, August—Sept. '96 I am the Memorial and Banquet speaker—so I can see what they have. Also, I can check the Naval Academy Museum and Nautilus Museum at Groton, Ct. We had so much fun with you. Thanks a heap in which Margaret joins. She dropped you a line via Sue Garwood.

Good luck. God Bless
Gene Fluckey

Note: Years later the building that houses the commanding officer of the base and the submarine group commander was named Fluckey Hall for RADM Fluckey. I was very disappointed that I was traveling and could not attend.

In April 1996, our first big visitor after the ceremony was master chief petty officer of the Navy, John Hagan, and his wife, Cathy, who had been on a quality of life tour of the base. The base paper the *Periscope* showed MCPON Hagen looking through the periscope at the museum. Art and I were both on hand to greet and welcome the Hagans. We felt very honored to have him visit our new museum

In August, I received another card from Margaret:

> Annapolis August 9, 1996
>
> Many thanks for the pictures. Sorry you couldn't make the dedication in Japan—a unique (group of) expatriates with 22 Japanese admirals attending. The Hall cost $27 million to build minus contents.
>
> Al and Missy were in great form and made us most welcome. Gene was showered with memorabilia!! The return flight took 34 flying hours due to delays!
>
> Margaret

*Twenty-seven million and we had such a time with $111,000!

The 1996 Newsletter went out in September and included this news:

> From the President Art Robb CWO2 USN Retired
>
> The St Marys Museum is off and running. The Grand Opening was outstanding. The guest speaker was EUGENE FLUCKEY, RADM, USN—RET, Subvet of WWII CONGRESSIONAL MEDAL OF HONOR recipient. Over 500 people attended the event and then toured the museum. All were amazed at what a group of volunteers could do with so little Sue Garwood was our event coordinator and did a great job. At the Annual Meeting, we selected a new Board of Directors (1/3) and I replaced Sheila McNeill as the President. Sheila was the backbone for this successful opening of the museum. When everyone said no way, Sheila continued on and found the correct answer. She raised more funds with new sponsors and new memberships than any other board member. She is now involved with

> giving direction to the Department of Defense, they will never be the same.
>
> As the general manager of Johnson Controls Kings Bay and change in the contract I will be moving on to another area of the state with my company. As of 9 October 1996, Jim Wells will be assuming the position of President. I'm glad to have been a part of the creation of the submarine museum. I wish to thank the Board of Directors and all of the volunteers who keep the museum open.
>
> If you haven't visited the museum, you have missed something. The majority of our visitors are tourists from out of the area. Some are relatives of the local sailors, but many are here because they heard of the #1 Boom Town in the USA St. Marys or heard specifically of the Museum. So, keep passing the word. The museum Vice President Jim Wells sent a notice out in the September 1996 newsletter: As the sponsor chairman, I wish to report a very outstanding fiscal year for the museum. I wish to thank our sponsor who made the commission of the museum possible. Total contributions, FY 1995 and FY 1996 to Sept totaled $111,103. And we can't forget our local contractors and suppliers who donated material and workmanship or material at reduced costs. Well done to all who helped raise the funds and who donated the funds. Without this support, as well as, support from our membership dues, we could not have made it. But the fun is not over! We still need to raise $12,000 to complete the museum set up this fiscal year, as budgeted. But what we must note with pleasure is the fact that we raised almost 90% of our projected budget. Most organizations that have started a museum will take 2-6 years to get where we are.

Remaining work items will be covered in other sections of the newsletter. The sponsor program will continue to be the main source of our operational funds, followed by membership and museum entrance fees. As noted above to Sheila McNeill, who raised most of the funds.

And from John Crouse, artifact manager:

> *The artifacts just keep coming through the front doors. We started with 1400 + items at the commissioning. We now have over 2,300 items logged into the museum artifacts data base. Some very interesting items are here. The most notable is the Type 8B periscope. This scope is operational. Most all other museum periscopes are an*

older Type 2 periscope. This provides an outstanding view of NE Florida and SE Georgia. The majority of other items are photos, plaques of submarines and various support commands. If anyone know the location of a spare periscope camera attachment plate, please contact me.

P.S. Don't take the one off your boat, unless the CO says it's OK.

Our 6' scale model of the USS ASPRO SS-309 has been an outstanding display. Our visitors are impressed when they find out the model building was an ex-crew member during WWII, thank you, Joe. Another gentleman came in one day and said he had a few plaques. Went to Yulee, FL and picked up 80 + plaques, none of which are a repeat of any currently in the museum. He said we can have the rest later; thank you, Bill. Just as I was finishing this newsletter a box showed up on our front door, a 600 + pound box. Came from someplace called West Pac. Thank you RADM Konetzni, Honorary Board member. Some of the plaques were my past boats, Christmas in September. We are still looking for things from Mid-Pac, NE Atlantic coast and various other submarine base locations.

PS And just about everything about the diesel boats.

We have collected about 200 books concerning submarines and various wars. We have provided information for CNN twice. Several individuals who didn't know what happened to a Subvet relative or friend, on Eternal Patrol, have now found the answer. Anybody who wants to know where is the satisfaction by working here, they only need to provide the answers to one family. I'm averaging two per month, some who just saw our I-95 museum signs. The artifacts manager is looking for items from the USS FLASHER SS-249 & SSN 613 (Sorry, Frank. Helo Roger, picked up any ensigns at the airport lately)

The next two computer systems will be for visitors, researchers and the museum Honor Roll of Subvets. More about the computers next Newsletter. You won't believe who came to visit the museum Sept. 27.

BUILDING RESTORATION/MAINTENACE STATUS

The major restoration is complete, now we just have to do all the normal building and display case maintenance. We are still installing some hand rails, doing some painting and finish wood work type projects. Our first dynamic display is going to be built around our periscope. As we obtain the boat parts, a long-term process from various sources, we plan to have a generic control room.

> *Received a positive phone call from the people we hope to provide the hydro phones for our St. Marys River Operational Sonar system.*
>
> *But what must be said is 'THANK YOU' to all of the individuals (civilian, military and contractor) volunteers who made it possible to open. Whether you worked 1000 hours (General Contractor Tony) or one hour you are the ones to whom the entire Submarine Force and the local community must say "Thank You." One thing the volunteers said they will miss was the support from the local restaurants that provided some nice lunches. And a special Thanks to Jack of Britt's Plumbing, for emergency plumbing repairs last month, with an assist by the city plumbers.*

The new board of directors was named and Captain Jim Alley relieved Captain Gary Williams and RADM Jerry Ellis, USN (retired), was added to the honorary board of directors. In November 1996 the board of directors determined that funding needed to be raised for operating expenses, procuring museum items and maintenance. An appeal went out for membership and for volunteers. The attendance at the museum is more than we had planned and we continue to receive artifacts and information to add to our records.

We were off and running with the museum but needed funds to keep it going. In August, my husband Arlie, agreed to auction and, working with fund-raising chairman Sue Garwood, we planned another party. The *Periscope*, *Tribune*, and the *Southeast Georgian* all helped us get the word out. It was to be a casual event held at the museum. Arlie has auctioned for the Dolphin Scholarship Foundation for over thirty years and has done the Coastal Symphony's auction at Sea Island for a number of years. He estimates over the past forty years he has auctioned at hundreds of events and raised millions of dollars for charity. There is no one better. The auction items were very good ones and included a weekend getaway to St. Simons Island at the Kings and Prince Hotel and a gourmet dinner for eight at the Submarine Group commanders home. We estimated we could raise a net $4,000 but it netted $5,435. That would go a long way toward the museum's goals.

It is December 1997. We've had about twenty-one thousand visitors to the museum and we get the word from Jack Schiff that he is coming to visit on December 30. That story is covered in the Jack Schiff section.

Jack told me before he left that that was the most publicity he had receive for the least amount of donation. God bless him. After his death, his sons continue to support the museum and have every year for over twenty years.

Article in the *Submarine Review*, July 2007:

THE ST. MARYS SUBMARINE MUSEUM WHERE THE LEGACY LIVES ON

BY Ms. Sheila McNeill
Commissioning President
St. Marys Submarine Museum

The St. Marys Submarine Museum located in St. Marys, Georgia celebrated i[ts] 10th anniversary last year. For those readers not already familiar with our museum, here are a few interesting facts for you. The Museum is:

- *The fifth largest submarine museum in the U.S.*
- *The largest in the southeastern United States*
- *Located in historic St. Marys, just 10 miles east of I-95, close to the Kings Bay Submarine Base—the recipient of the 2007 Commander-in-Chief's Award for Installation Excellence.*
- *Houses over 20,000 artifacts, photos and written history items and the displays include a working type 8 periscope*
- *Is host to the annual WWII Subvets Memorial Service held at Kings Bay Sub Base each year.*

In a very trying period for the military generally and submarines in particular, this museum serves a particular need and does it very well. That is educating the public about this vital segment of our military. The Silent Service need this voice more than ever before. And there is that fascination with submarines that exists for most of us.

Additionally, the submarine force needs the visibility that is not generally available to the public. A very few people are privileged to visit submarine bases and our submarine museum is the alternative source for supplying submarine history as well as needed data for the media when required. We have the largest collection of printed copies of WWII patrol reports outside of the Naval Archives. Our Jack Schiff Research Library has been used by CNN, National Geographic and many other media outlets, historians, authors and individuals. Major shipboard components from submarines on display include the Type 8 periscope, ship control panel, ballast control panel, torpedo tube breach door, watertight door and several other shipboard items. In 2003, we were bequeathed the Ben Bastura Submarine Library and Museum. An Army veteran, Ben started in the 1950s collecting WWII submarine history and artifacts. We are very proud of this collection.

The St. Marys Submarine Museum contains a vast treasure of submarine history that links the past with the present. Members of the Naval Submarine League know how important it is for the visual thrills of actually seeing these splendid artifacts of their service in the continuing effort to educate the public on the many contributions to our national defense. I believe it immensely helps the well-being of our Submarine Force.

Our museum's over 1,700 WWII patrol reports, as well as the many artifacts: photos; boat histories, books etc. make our museum a primary research source. Since our opening, well over 100,000 people have visited this museum. While many have had previous experience regarding submarines, the majority of visitors have not. Our museum, along with the others in the U.S. has provided a widening acquaintance with the submarine service. We had visitors from Poland, China, Canada, and Germany as well as from a dozen different states. What a mission in education this shows! In this little town in southeast Georgia, we are ensuring that our story is known by people around the globe.

It is a bit difficult to believe that this fine museum was conceived; built; and supported almost entirely by the residents of the small towns of St. Marys, Kingsland, and Woodbine. But we must not forget those submariners at Kings Bay and around the world who answered our call and made the difference in our opening. I called on many of my submarine friends—you know who you are. Thank you. And Jack Schiff our museum angel has been our constant contributor and has truly kept the doors open.

I told those who volunteered their time and energy and who contributed to the building fund for the museum that they would have reason to be very proud of what they were doing. I believe that is true today. Our museum has become a major part of downtown St. Marys. Visitors enjoy the laid back Southern hospitality they find when visiting this historic area and our unique museum.

With the increasing costs associated with operations we have been hard-pressed to do the preservation work required to properly display the many artifacts donated to our museum with the funds we have had. To continue to do this we need help from subvets, individuals and corporations across the country.

If the readers of this article believe in the preservation of our submarine history and the need to educate the public on the importance of our submarine service—we ask you to think about our museum! Any help would be appreciated. Finally, if you intend to be one of the many thousands visiting Florida each year, look for the St. Marys exit 3 on I-95. We are in the building with the periscope sticking out of our roof. This stop will be the highlight of your trip. We look forward to seeing you.

The submarine museum was the first of many events I chaired in Camden County. None of this could have been done without John Crouse. See recollections on John in his section.

MY REMARKS AT TWENTIETH ANNIVERSARY, MARCH 19, 2016

We had been talking about building a submarine museum for years. Finally, we had enough interest! Our first meeting was at Seagull's bar in mid-1994. Bill Weisensee was then president of the Chamber of Commerce. He had been researching possible locations in Camden County. Later in December 1994 about thirty dedicated individuals attended the St. Marys Council meeting to urge approval for the city to 'work out all the details' of leasing the building to the museum. Bill was excited about being chair of this project and I was to be his cochairman. Due to a business conflict, he was unable to chair the project. Guess who was then chair?

I went through the scrapbook as I was preparing my remarks and read a letter to the editor from a gentleman who was against putting the museum in a city building, which said, "This building they are considering was designed for a theater. It is essentially a large open space inside. How they plan to make it into a functional museum is beyond me. That couldn't have asked for a worse floor plan."

But that gentleman didn't know Tony Cobb. Or Denny Reasoner who drafter the architectural and engineering plans—no charge of course.

John Crouse
Master Chief Roger Dumont
Gull and Royal Weaver
Craig and Mary Root
Dori Brink
Sue Garwood
Marci Price
Trish McMillian
Tilden Norris
Tom Stafford
Mayor Jerry Brandon
The Downtown Merchants
The St. Marys City Council

And many others sitting in this audience today. We didn't get approval right away but began our fund-raising and design of the building as if we already had approval. Sometimes you must be aggressive no matter how much that is against your nature. There were so many ups and downs during that time. We estimated we needed $105,000—that is a lot of money today, but it was more money in 1995. For the next year, Tony supervised the crew and as he will quickly tell you I supervised Tony. Actually, we were a great team. We had so many volunteers! Tony created the 100-hour club and later the 250-hour club. We even had a tourist stop by to see what was going on and ended up working for four days.

Members were as follows:

Bill Danley 700*
Mark Blow
Scott Harris
Bobby Ferrell
Ron Rein
Tom Felder
Dennis Swanson
Steve Wolsley
Jim Collins
Dan Rayley
Tom Hurley

That's about three months! There were 6,344 volunteer hours—that is not counting those who just donated a few hours and did not enter them. That's 793 days—66 weeks, 16 months of volunteer hours. We had 129 volunteers and over 500 Plank owners (536). All our fixtures were donated: Britt Plumbing—Sam Pickren, JE Howard Electric, Wright and Evans—we would order, then we'd ask if they would donate and they did! As Tony was quoted, "We were using top quality materials and products that will be there forever." He and the crew worked around me as I brought people—almost every day to show them the progress and try to convince them to donate. I could never control the music Tony played—it was always blaring! Kathy Dempsey who, as chair of the Submarine Officers Wives Club had our first fund-raiser "Evening under the Stars" with Arlie auctioning that remains today one of the most profitable and classier events we've had in these twenty years. Alyce Thornhill, Charlotte Glover, Sue Garwood, and Cindy Hagemann were instrumental in making that so successful. Charlie Smith was state representative at the time and he and Trish were our honored guests that evening. Another couple who have done so much for this community.

Ben Bastura, a gentleman I didn't know, called my office one day and told me he had an entire house full of submarine memorabilia. He told me he was an Army veteran. The Navy museums had expressed interest in his artifacts, but if I would come to Connecticut, he would give it all to the St. Marys Submarine Museum. I checked it out—sure enough other museums valued his collection, so I called friends Malcolm and Shirley Fages who were stationed in Groton and went to Connecticut. Shirley went with me to look at his collection. It was amazing. It took a tractor trailer to get it here, but it was worth it. Imagine an Army veteran that interested in our submarine force.

That last week we were in a crunch to get finished. Tony was pressing me. Everyone was in an organized panic. Tony told me of the Seabees Civic Action Program and that he was to get a Seabee to help him finish in time for the opening a week later. He had heard nothing and couldn't get in touch with anyone. So, who did Sheila think to call but the Commanding Officer of the base who turned out be on the golf course in Hawaii. (It was late on a Friday afternoon.) But God love him he answered the phone. The March 13 edition of the *CCT* newspaper headlines: "Seabees make museum opening date possible." As Tony told it he asked the help of one Seabee and got an entire battalion. You should have been there when they all walked in! Each an expert in welding, electrical, plumbing, carpentry—an expert to finish the last details—what a glorious day.

Our principal speaker was Admiral Gene Fluckey a recipient of the Congressional Medal of Honor. He was credited with sinking sixteen Japanese ships during WWII including an aircraft carrier. He wrote of his experiences on the USS *Barb* in *Thunder Below*. The building that Admiral Crites and Captain Jenks's offices are in are named after him—look for Fluckey Hall. He was one of the humblest sweetest and most personable people I've ever known. He was eighty-six when he spoke at our ceremony. He never ran out of energy that day. He signed books on the base and at the museum—toured the base, talked with everyone. After the ceremony at the end of the evening we had dinner at Admiral Chuck and Susan Beers quarters. He and Susan had only been in town just a few weeks—what a way to get to know each other! About ten I was worn-out. Margaret, his wife, was also worn-out and she told me I had to make him go to bed. I finally said, "Gene, is it time to go, I'm exhausted!" and we departed. We corresponded several times over the years and those cards and letters are some of my prized possessions.

John Crouse and I were inseparable during those years. He was determined to make the museum a success. He was our first manager. One day he was preparing to leave for a submarine veterans meeting—but not before I fussed at him that he must have information on everything that we would need if he were to die. I gave him a really hard time. And he did die that trip. Thinking back if he had to go there is no one he had rather be with then our submarine veterans. it was a shock me—it was a shock to the community. But God love him, before he wrote twenty-nine pages of instructions on everything we needed to know about the museum and he included his funeral plans. Royal was to be his executor. He wanted everything Hawaiian, he wanted me to do the eulogy because "she taught me how to be a civilian and was a lady, so she wouldn't use bad names to describe me."

As a disclaimer, I was never able to get him to wear anything but flip flops and a Hawaiian shirt. Boy, would he have loved today. John died on September 4, 2010, and we asked Keith Post to fill in for a few weeks until we could find a relief. Then we talked him into staying just six months. He did that without pay. I'm sorry, Keith, how long ago has that been? Six years this year. Keith is the most dedicated executive director we could have—as a senior chief he knows the submarine business and has the greatest heart for what needs to be done to ensure that we capture the history of our submarine force.

Note: Sr. Chief Tony Cobb retired from the Navy he asked me to speak at his retirement along with his commanding officer, Commander Brad Gehrke. He continues to be there for the museum when we need him.

We had our twentieth anniversary celebration on Saturday, March 10, 2016. Keith designed a wonderful coin that commemorates this twenty years.

Our speakers were Congressman Buddy Carter, Rear Admiral Randy Crites (the first officer at Kings Bay to return as an admiral and a great leader), and Rear Admiral Chuck Beers, USN (retired).

Keith shared with the audience:

> I want to mention for a minute, the top one percenters in or country. Anyway, back to my thoughts, you hear this term top one percenters tossed around a lot. In secret recorded conversations of politicians, in presidential debates, on the nightly news or in some economic statistics. But I think CNN, ABC, NBS, CBS and FOX have it all wrong. You see some of the Top One Percenters are right here around you. They were Blue, Red, Green and Orange. They are our Army, Navy, Marine Corps, Air Force, and Coast Guard who in my mind are the TRUE TOP ONE percenters of our nation, who defend liberty and preserve freedom around the globe every day in places you and I can't even imagine, under condition we would not believe, and they do it for what some of the other 99 percent would not accept for a paycheck. We owe them more than we can ever give… I still have faith in our future… I know we will continue to strive to be that great American shining city on the hill. I know in my heart that so long as we have young men willing to serve like Brian Lemmo, Erick Clourteau, and Ebin Assis we are in good hands.

The base paper, the *Periscope*, had the following story on March 23, 2016:

Museum milestone
20 years of documenting sub history celebrated in St. Marys
By EM1 Mark Treen
Naval Submarine Base Kings Bay Public Affairs

The 20th Anniversary Celebration of the St. Marys Submarine Museum was March 19 on the waterfront in downtown St. Marys waterfront in downtown St. Marys.

The celebration chronicled the museum's role in preserving the history of the submarine force for the future. The early years of the museum foreshadowed its role in town, in the Navy and in the lives of residents. Sheila McNeill, museum founding president, talked about the construction of the museum. From early on it was evident volunteers would be a vital aspect of the museum. Volunteers came in from all around the country, some donating more than 700 hours. Near opening, Naval Submarine Base Kings Bay sent a Seabee Battalion, prompting an article for the opening to be headlined, "Seabees make museum opening date possible." From its beginning, it was a project of the community and the base. The celebration included history as well. A bell was tolled remembering lost submariners.

Guest speaker Rear Adm. Chuck Beers (Ret.), former commander of Submarine Group Ten, remarked how he values the work being done by museum volunteers to conserve the World War II submarine war patrol reports. The reports include accounts of a submarine close to Beers, his father, as well as those known to all submariners, such as Adm. John McCain and Rear Adm. Eugene Fluckey. Rear Adm. Randy Crites talked about how the museum is used today to impact the community and the Navy. "It's jammed packed full of amazing artifacts," Crites said. Crites went on to highlight the Naval history of Fluckey, retelling his famous surface transit to shoot all torpedo tubes inside a Japanese naval harbor, making eight hits on six fleet targets. He also spoke of Fluckey's raiding party that landed on the Japanese mainland to destroy a train loaded with war supplies. "His history is something we can't let fade into the past," Crites said. U.S. Rep. Buddy Carter (Georgia, Dist. 1) summed up the museum's history and future by saying, "The mission is to preserve the legacy of submarines. We always need to be reminded just how important Kings Bay plays in our national security."

It is so important that we capture the legacy of our submarine force. Our submarine veterans—some of whom were very young men who gave up or were willing to give up their chance to be fathers and grandfathers. They gave up everything for our country, for us and we should never forget—remembering is what this museum is all about. We had big plans in 1995 and we have big plans today. We accomplished some things we were told couldn't be done. Thank you, Camden County.

Coming together is a beginning. Keeping together is progress. Working together is success. (Henry Ford)

ST. MARYS MAGAZINE—SUPPORT OF OUR SEA SERVICES

Protecting our Country, Cultivating our Community
A Salute to The Men & Women of Kings Bay.
By Barbara Ryan

I grew up in a military town. My family hails from Fayetteville, NC, home to Fort Bragg and Pope Air Force Base. In Fayetteville, there was the military. And there were the civilians. Such is life in hundreds of military towns throughout the United States where transient service personnel come and go, and the community knows little and feels little of their impact. Not so in Camden County, Georgia. The men and women of Kings Bay Naval Submarine Base not only play a major role in community leadership, they are an integral part of our success as a community. Assimilation means involvement, and clearly the men and women of Kings Bay are involved in the community on a day to day basis—fostering our charities, our schools, our churches, and our friendships.

"I've always marveled on the amount of time our military personnel donate to the community," said Sheila McNeill, President ofThe Camden Partnership and Past National President of the Navy League of the United States. "Many spend half their time at sea and still volunteer when they are home." Kelly Wirfel, Community Relations Manager for the Navy Base agrees. From food distribution to the Special Olympics, Wirfel said that every command on the base has volunteers who eagerly contribute toward making their adopted hometown a great place to live. "Kings Bay is definitely more immersed in the community than is typical for a military town," Wirfel said. "And a lot of that is because they feel the community really embraces and appreciates the military. They feel that they are definitely an integral part of the community."

Wirfel said that service members often stay here as long as nine years making Kings Bay one of the leading Navy bases when it comes to retention. Kings Bay is also at the top of the list for places that Navy personnel choose to retire. While the great quality of life and low cost of living are contributing factors toward the desirability of Camden County as a place to re-enlist or retire, Wirfel believes a lot of the satisfaction service people have with the area comes from their connection to the community. One of the community events in which the men and women of Kings Bay enjoy participating the most is the annual Special Olympics. This year, 890 volunteers from Kings Bay helped dozens of children achieve the thrill of victory. "It's one of our favorite days," Wirfel said.

Kings Bay Navy Command Master Chief Jim Schubert said it's easy to find volunteers for the Special Olympics. "There is just so much satisfaction from both sides," he said. "The kids provide more to us than we do for them. Every one of these kids deserves a perfect day." Personnel from the Coast Guard, Navy, and Marines recently worked on a major project for the community as part of Oprah Winfrey's Lovetown USA series.

The Tribune & Georgian donated a building downtown to be used as a Live United Center where the United Way and other charitable groups can reach out to the community. In just two days, Wirfel was able to assemble military volunteers to help totally rebuild the interior, repair and refresh the exterior, and put on a new roof. "It was done in 18 days," Wirfel said. "Thanks to the generosity of spirit shown by the men and women of Kings Bay along with other community volunteers." "Spirit" is something that our service people seem to exude. On any given week, they may be coordinating the distribution of food to 550 needy families; washing cars to raise money for a good cause; cleaning up the river or the roadsides, or doing a major build for Habitat for Humanity. And always, they are in our schools, taking special care to help groom today's youth into tomorrow's good citizens and great leaders.

"About 30% of our school children are from military families," Wirfel said. "So, it's only natural that our service men and women have a stake in our educational system." But they go far beyond the call of duty, giving up their free time to make a difference in a child's life, according to Wirfel—tutoring, coaching, mentoring, and sometimes simply reading to the students.

> Every school in Camden County has been adopted by a Kings Bay command through their "Personal Excellence Partnership."
>
> In addition to the school partnerships, the men and women of Kings Bay have a partnership with White Oak Conservation Center. White Oak Conservation Center's mission is to conserve and sustain some of the earth's rarest wild animals through training, research, education, and breeding. White Oak is located less than 30 minutes from Kings Bay and is known as one of the world's premiere wildlife breeding and research centers. Kings Bay service men and women have performed numerous tasks there including moving a Cheetah pen and other maintenance and feeding duties. "The community is much better for their support," McNeill said. "There is most likely not a civic, community, or charitable organization that hasn't benefitted from their help." "Our service people are so good about supporting the community because the community has been so good to them," Wirfel said.

The Camden County Chamber of Commerce reaches out and recognizes a Service Member of the Month. The Camden Partnership and the Navy League are all about fostering and promoting the welfare of our military personnel. And even the smallest of businesses recognize and appreciate how much they contribute to the community both in volunteerism and economically.

"EDICCIMAD" is a sign you may have seen in the window of virtually every business in Camden County. It stands for "Every day in Camden County Is Military Appreciation Day."

CAPTAIN FRANK STAGL AND MARY

COMMANDING OFFICER, NAVAL SUBMARINE BASE KINGS BAY

When Frank came to Kings Bay in 1988 he was newly married to Mary and she was expecting. Being a Navy wife was a new thing to her and being the wife of the base commander would not be easy for a seasoned Navy wife. I took her under my wing and I think made life a little easier for her. Later I found out she was pregnant and we all watched her "grow" over the next few months. I encouraged her not to participate in the pie eating contest at the Dolphin Scholarship Auction a week or so before the baby was born. Their daughter Katerina Marie was born March 23, 1999.

As she tells the story, we were with a large group of Navy Leaguers and were having a spirited discussion. At some point in the conversations, I said, "Mary, what do you think?" She was great with her answer and was pulled into the conversation. She told me I did that again with another group and after that she was always included. They were very gracious to me and invited me to stay at their home in St. Marys when I stayed in town which was about once a month. I became very comfortable in their home and treated it like my own! Mary even roomed with me and Arlie on one of our DC fly-ins. We had great times—they gave several dinner parties while I was staying over so there was never a dull moment.

Frank always shared with me insights that would help my support of the base. I stayed at their home the night before the Bancroft Sail commissioning. At dinner, I had a call from Senator Cleland that there was a good chance he would not be able to make it the next day. There was an important vote on the armed services committee. Planning for the USS *Bancroft* sail exhibit was all done during his tour.

I remember my first meeting with Captain Stagl. I went to the office to meet him joined by Karla Carper and Jack Gross who represented the chamber. He was very welcoming and we all felt like friends. One thing that made me warm to him was his very charming story he told us that day about meeting with our legislators and how he shared that story. He also related that story is in his remarks when we commissioned the USS *Bancroft* Sail Memorial.

Captain Frank Stagl's introduction:

April 7, 2000 at dedication of Bancroft

It is now my pleasure to introduce the spark plug behind the fund-raising for this magnificent exhibit. I first met Sheila McNeill many years ago, at a change of command party at Admiral Robertson's house, just after he was relieved as Commander Sub Group Ten by Admiral Ellis. Well, just two years ago, while attending a training course in Washington D.C. to prepare me for this command, I visited Senator Cleland, Senator Coverdell and Congressman Kingston to introduce myself. After introducing myself to Senator Cleland he asked me: "Do you know Sheila McNeill?" I said, "Why yes I do." He said, "Great! She's a friend so I would appreciate it if you would keep her cut in on what's going on at the base." I said, "Yes, Sir," and I thought "How about that! A mutual friend!" We continued to talk about base issues and I left. Well, my next stop was to Senator Coverdell. I introduced myself and he said, "do you know Sheila McNeill:" I said, "Why yes, I do" And then he said, "Great, please keep her informed on the happenings on the base." And I thought, "Isn't that interesting." Well, my final stop was to visit Congressman Kingston. After I introduced myself, he said, "Do you know Sheila McNeill?" And I said, "Yes, sir, and I will make sure she knows what is happening on the base!"

As many of you know Sheila has a long history of service to the community and our country. She serves as Chairman of The Friends of Kings Bay. She was the commissioning President of the St. Marys Submarine Museum. She served from 1996 through 1998 on the Defense Advisory Committee on Women in the Service. She has been a member of the Navy League for 30 years (she obviously joined as a teenager) and in July of 1999 was elected as a National Vice President of that 69,000-member organization. I think that when God created Sheila somewhere in the recipe there is sure to be one tablespoon of Southern charm and a half cup of persistence. Please join me in giving a great big Kings Bay welcome to Sheila McNeill."

When Frank completed his tour he and his relief, Captain Walt Yourstone asked me to speak at their change of command. That was stunning. I agreed and these are my remarks. The change of command was held at the USS *Bancroft* Memorial.

Remarks by Sheila McNeill
Change of Command SUBASE Kings Bay
23 June 2000

Distinguished visitors, men and women of SUBASE Kings Bay, ladies and gentlemen.

I am so pleased to be invited to speak at this most honored of Navy traditions, the change of command ceremony. I'll try to keep my remarks short today, but anyone who knows me knows I cannot miss the opportunity to talk about the Navy League and the mission we have. The men and women serving in today's military are the finest ever to wear their country's uniform. They are the best trained, best motivated, and best led in our nation's history. Nonetheless, and it is becoming more and more evident every year, America's services need the Navy League's help now more than ever before.

Last Saturday the Navy League approved the Navy League's Maritime Policy Statement at our convention in Philadelphia. This statement recommended force numbers for our services. We state strongly that our country needs 72—not 50 but 72 submarines. In this dangerous world, the value of America's submarine fleet cannot be over-estimated. As the Navy League's official voice on the hill for legislative issues, rest assured that this is the message I will take to our representatives in Congress. As America's premiere educational organization dedicated to the support of the nation's sea services, the Navy

League is in a unique position to provide that help—primarily, as we have been doing for almost a century, by educating the American people, the media, Congress, and the Executive Branch of the importance of sea power. In 2002, we will celebrate the 100th anniversary of our Navy League. I don't know of a better time to refocus our vision and give the support that is so badly needed for our sea services.

Now let me talk to you about the change of command tradition. The tradition of calling the crew to quarters to witness the change of command dates back to the days of the ancient ships. This was so there could be no question in the minds of the crew who bore the awesome, the overwhelming, the totally absolute, responsibility for their well-being. Today, changes of command still accomplish the same purpose… they show who is responsible.

Responsible… that term carries tremendous significance. For the last two years at SUBASE Kings Bay, we've known who is responsible… Captain Frank Stagl. Being commanding officer of the Navy's east coast strategic submarine homeport is like being the mayor of a small city. He's got seven hundred million dollars in facilities; he's got electrical utilities, water, sewer, phone, fiber optic systems. He owns two thousand bachelor quarters, three galleys, six hundred and sixty-five family housing units, the gym, the exchange and commissary, fire department and police department, Family Service Center, Child Development Centers, Youth Center, clubs, Navy Campus and base chapel. What else is there? If it involves the mental, social, physical, moral, spiritual or material well-being of the people living and working here on base, Frank has been responsible for it.

I recently had dinner at the Stagl's beautiful home. Inside his house, you see all this magnificent furniture which Frank has crafted with his own hands. You can see right away this is way above the caliber of furniture you would find in the finest showrooms or auction houses. In the basement of Frank and Mary's house is the most incredible array of tools you have ever seen.

If you've ever watched "This Old House" or the "New Yankee Workshop" on PBS, you've probably heard of master carpenter Norm Abrams. He's the guy on "This Old House" who is actually doing all the work. I understand that Norm Abrams is Frank's hero. What kind of man has a tool man as his hero? Anyway, Norm, and the "This Old House" cast, and their producer, Russ Morash, visited the base recently and they were all treated to dinner at the Stagl's home. You can imagine what a treat this was for Frank, who was proudly displaying all his toys to Norm. As Frank showed off more and more of his tools, it became quite evident that his toys were better than Norm's toys. Norm started lifting his eyebrow to his producer, Russ Morash. It seems that Norm told his producer that he wanted new toys like Franks.' I guess now Frank is Norm Abram's hero, because the producer had to buy all new tools for Norm after visiting Frank's workshop. I hear the producer said Frank and Norm can't play together anymore—it cost him too much money!!!

What I want to talk about today is Captain Frank Stagl's commitment to this community. Frank never has believed that his responsibility as base CO ends when he drives out the gate. For that, we are all lucky. In fact, we are quite blessed with a genuinely warm relationship between the base and the communities of Camden County. Not all Navy towns have it this good. We've got low crime, excellent schools, great jobs, good cost of living, little traffic and lots of natural beauty.

Twenty-two years ago, only twelve thousand people lived here. The Navy brought twenty-eight thousand <u>more</u> people here and made us the fasting growing county in Georgia. It is thanks to the efforts of the Navy people living here that this community's phenomenal growth has been so well-managed. Service to one's country translates to service to one's community, and that has made life better for all of us. These people, people like Frank Stagl, have been role models in the community. They are good neighbors. They have built in this community a network of mutual support and respect, a tradition of excellence, of service and of honor. In fact, just this week Frank was presented the 3rd consecutive Environmental Award. This is unprecedented! They have made this little corner of Georgia a better place to live.

Last month, as part of Senator Coverdell's Military Advisory Committee, I visited Army installations in Georgia. Some of the issues they covered were the optempo and perstempo of their troops. They also discussed the tremendous amount of volunteer work done by service members in their limited off-duty time. I thought of Kings Bay and the quality of life we all enjoy thanks to our Sailors and Marines stationed here. I thought of the schools whose students have higher grades because of our volunteers who tutor every week. Think what this community would do if our military were to decide that we were asking too much of them and they gave the communities less of their off-duty time. Ask the underprivileged children who get Christmas presents from a sailor Santa. Ask the patient whose life is saved by blood or bone marrow donated by a Sailor or Marine.

As I said, few Navy towns have it this good. That can be attributed to the long line of base commanding officers who have done so much to enhance the relationship between the base and the community. Few, if any, have thrown themselves into that aspect of their job as enthusiastically and exuberantly as Captain Frank Stagl. Nowhere is there a more enduring monument to the great relationship between Kings Bay and Camden County, than this site where we stand right now. This magnificent Bancroft Memorial was truly a joint effort of the community and the base. It was Frank's enthusiasm and boundless energy that were instrumental in ensuring this memorial was completed in time for the Submarine Centennial weekend. We are all very proud of it.

By virtue of his position as Commanding Officer of the Submarine Base, Frank has served these past two years as co-chairman of the Chamber of Commerce Military-Community Council. But he did not just show up once a quarter to sit at the head table. He was actively involved, always seeking ways to make the base-community bond stronger, always looking out for his Sailors and Marines. If he saw things in the community that he thought could harm his troops, believe me, he did not hesitate to let the MCC—or anybody else—know of it. And every month Frank and Mary have been a team at Navy League. Frank has made it a point to keep our Navy League current on what is happening at Kings Bay. This commitment to good relations between our base and the community is evident in everything Frank does.

He was also an honorary member of the St. Marys Submarine Museum Board. Again, he did not take the position lightly, bringing his expertise and his deeply ingrained pride and knowledge of the submarine force to board meetings. His energy and enthusiasm have helped the Submarine Museum Board immeasurably. The same holds for the St. Marys Rotary Club, of which Frank is a member.

Frank and Mary have given freely of their time to support the annual Soberfest Celebration, as well as the Navy League, Friends of Kings Bay, Camden-Kings Bay Chamber of Commerce, the USO and the Navy Submarine League. Frank's honesty and integrity have earned him the respect and affectionate admiration of this community. And Mary, what a challenge she had when she arrived at Kings Bay. A new wife, new to the Navy, new to the community, and your husband is commanding officer of the base! But did she ever meet this challenge! With her warm, caring personality we all knew that Mary had the right heart. She has blessed this base with her common-sense approach to challenges and her uncommon concern for the well-being of our Sailors and Marines.

She instantly became involved with the SOWC and as the Navy League's liaison officer for SUBASE. And—like all good wives—she didn't give her husband any slack. If it was something she wanted to make happen for the Navy League, and it was the right thing, and it took moving Frank, she moved him.

We all know Frank and Mary have the right Navy spirit. Their baby Katarina's very first outing was to a Navy League meeting. She was only a few weeks old and the Navy League welcomed her as our youngest guest ever. Their daughter Vickie is such a delight... and Michael I am sure you are proud of your father, and I'm sure Jennifer is as well, though she couldn't be with us today. Frank and Mary have both just always been there. They give, and give, and give... and keep on giving. They are special friends, not just to Arlie and me, but to so many others in the area.

Frank, it has been a profoundly rewarding experience to be able to work and socialize with you. And I'm especially happy that you are moving just across the breezeway to the Group 10 Chief of Staff job. You don't have to worry about giving me your new phone number, I already have it.

Finally, I want to congratulate Captain Walt Yourstone and Dee... you're not strangers to Kings Bay, so I don't have to tell you how great it is! And Walt let me thank you from this community for taking part in the recent Camden Leadership class. This took a great deal of time and commitment and it can only result in dividends for this community. I wish you all the best as you take command of the finest submarine base in the world.

Thank you. God Bless You; Gold Bless our Military Past, Present, and Future; God Bless America.

Captain will you join me at the podium. (I know that was a surprise for Captain Stagl. It is quite unusual for a civilian to present a medal, but this was a special medal for his volunteer work in the community.) The XO will now read the citation.

The Georgia Times Union
June 24, 2000

A change of command
Submarine Base gets a new boss
By Gordon Jackson

The audience at yesterday's change of command certainly perked up as Capt. Frank Stagl announced he had a confession. With a somber expression, Stagl commanding officer at Kings Bay Naval Submarine Base, admitted he accepted money for a job he would have done for free. But he also said he had no plans to return the money for the job, he had performed the past two years because it was already spent. "This job has been an absolute blast," Stagl said as many in the audience chuckled.

During the hour-long ceremony Stagl's service was recognized by speakers and the unexpected presentation of two medals to the outgoing base commander. The first medal was presented by an unexpected source, keynote speaker Sheila McNeill, national vice president of the Navy League. It's unusual for a civilian to present a medal to someone serving in the military, Stagl said. McNeill presented the Military Outstanding Volunteer Service Medal to Stagl, who received it for his active role in community service. "I have rarely seen anyone so in tune with the community as Frank Stagl," McNeill said. "Frank never has believed his responsibility as base C.O. ends when he drives off the base." Later in the ceremony, Stagl was also awarded the Legion of Merit medal for his performance running Kings Bay the past two years. Stagl credited his staff and the sailors and civilian workers.

It was certainly a successful tour and Captain Walt Yourstone was just awesome in the next two years as the base commanding officer. He has also remained as a good friend.

STATE OF THE UNION PRESIDENT BILL CLINTON

THURSDAY, JANUARY 27, 2000

Senator Max Cleland, Congressman Jack Kingston, and RADM Rich Terpstra

It was an honor to attend President Clinton's State of the Union address. I was invited to attend by Congressman Jack Kingston. I had already planned to be in Washington the week of the twenty-fourth, which is why Congressman Kingston extended the invitation. He had been in Camden County a few weeks prior on a visit to meet the new admiral at Kings Bay, Rear Admiral Rich Terpstra. We were touring the St. Marys Submarine Museum and I told him I would be meeting with his staff in a few weeks. I had a box of chocolate submarines bagged together with a label saying, "Friends of Kings Bay" that I planned to deliver to our US legislators. In addition, I had an appointment at Navy League headquarters in DC.

To have this opportunity to attend the State of the Union was a chance of a lifetime and I was excited to be a part of history. No matter what your politics are you would have to be in awe of being present in this chamber together with almost all our national leaders and their guests.

I arrived in Washington on Monday evening just in time to be snowbound for the next thirty-six hours. Fortunately, at the same hotel the Navy was hosting an all flag (admirals) conference, so it gave me an opportunity to visit with many old friends and to make a few more contacts! The hotel was the Ritz-Carlton where they were so good to me both with price and making me feel so welcome. They sent a letter to all guests that included this message: "Due to extreme weather conditions in the metropolitan area, we are experiencing limited staffing levels. In this unfortunate situation, we will be unable to provide you with room service as a dining option this evening or tomorrow morning.

Please be advised that the Lobby Lounge will be serving a "Blizzard Box" until close this evening, which includes a deli sandwich, chips, fruit, and dessert. The Grill, our fine dining restaurant, is open for dinner on first come first served basis." I sat around the fire with several of the admirals at the conference and had a wonderful time. On Wednesday, the snow had stopped but the federal government and schools were still closed. I received a call from the Navy League's executive director, Charlie Robinson, and National Navy League president, Jack Fisher, who told me they were at headquarters and asked if I wanted to join them. Of course, I did. This gave me an opportunity to make up a little of the time I had lost on Tuesday. I never was able to officially visit our legislators but did get a couple of the offices including Congressman Jack Kingston where his staff was busy preparing a mailing. We had a nice visit and chatted while they worked.

On Thursday, I received a call from a member of Senator Max Cleland's staff asking if I would like to join the senator for dinner. Traditionally the senate has a dinner for families at the Capitol the evening of the State of the Union. Of course, I was pleased to go. And I thought the evening could not be any more exciting! I arrived at Senator Cleland's office in the Dirksen Building and went to the Capitol via the underground subway for members of Congress and their guests. On the way, we met several senators and their wives, and everyone was in a festive mood. We toured the Capitol and had a buffet dinner in the Capitol Reception Room. What an evening. The buffet was beautiful and delicious—you'd think I would be too excited to eat—not a chance! The room was full of familiar faces. Funny how you can see someone constantly on C-SPAN and the news shows and meet them and feel like you know them. I thought about Jennifer Ihrig, one of my friends who is a Navy wife who watches C-SPAN all the time and can name any senator or congressman she sees. Amazing woman. It was a very relaxed evening for the senators and they seemed to have a good time with the informal atmosphere. We sat at a round table for eight and people came and went and visited from table to table. At our table at different times were Wayne Allard from Colorado, who was on the Armed Service Committee Senator Bob Kerrey, the senator from Wyoming (of course we discussed the USS *Wyoming* stationed at Kings Bay). I met Senator Bob Graham, Trent Lott, and dozens of others.

You could feel an excitement in the air. Even the Capitol guards and police were smiling and pleasant. Of course, with just the senators and their families there they were not worried as much about security. I read the next morning that the evening was prom night for workaholics and that was an apt description. I wore a black suit but counted fourteen red suits worn by the female legislators. I guess red was the power female color for the event.

Everyone had assigned seats and we were requested to be in our seats at eight thirty for the nine o'clock address. I didn't like being seated so early—I'm not known for my patience. However, when the military chiefs almost immediately entered the chamber, I realized I was none too early. The commandant of the Coast Guard, Admiral Loy's chief of governmental affairs, Rear Admiral Patrick Stillman, was seated next to me and he had just escorted Mrs. Loy to the gallery. When Mrs. Clinton and her party arrived, I had a clear view of them. Chelsea absolutely looked beautiful. I thought, good for her, she come into her own and become a beautiful woman in spite of the cruel statements made about her as she was growing up. It turned out the Supreme Court did not attend, and this put the service chiefs on the front row. Yay for our military. I was pleased to see Secretary Bill Cohen. I served on a Defense Advisory Committee, first under defense secretary William Perry and later Cohen. Secretary Cohen's wife, who has been very supportive of the military and had accompanied him on many base visits, was seated in Mrs. Clinton's section and received special recognition.

President Clinton was a masterful speaker. I knew there were prompts and was sure he must have used them, along with his script but it was very smoothly done. Again, politics aside, you must admire President Clinton's ability to captivate an audience for over one and a half hours in what appeared to be an effortless and completely confident manner. Of course, what do you expect of the President of the United States! The press was directed above and behind him and in my direct view. It was interesting to watch one hundred press members simultaneously turning pages as he talked. It was like a giant wave at a football game, but much more subdued! Senator Cleland had told me that the president's speech was going to be eighty-two minutes and with applause it could last over ninety minutes. I knew once I was seated I couldn't leave and that made me more nervous about having to make a pit stop. I also knew there would be a long line at the restrooms at the end of the speech.

The address itself contained references to numerous programs—sort of a strategic plan for the future—that are difficult to argue with on their face value. However, the politics that come into play regarding the funding involved, national versus states right, Democrats versus Republicans, and so on become clear when you watch to see who applauds and who rises—and who remains seated. We all relate other situations to our own and I found myself thinking about my work for the Navy League and how I too want to add items that I would like to see accomplished as we reach our one hundredth anniversary. As vice president of strategic planning and development for the Navy League. (I later became the legislative affairs vice president, which suited me better.) I am looking at the way we do business in the Navy League, the way we meet and communicate, and how we fulfill our mission. I had just talked with several members of the staff and asked that they give me goals they would like to see accomplished both those that are funded and achievable within the budget we have and those they would like to see added if additional funding was possible.

My work with the military and more specifically the Navy League has always been a nonpartisan effort. Certainly, the military has to remain nonpartisan and as Navy Leaguers we constantly stress what is best for the nation and the nation's defense. This effort enables us to work with both democrats and republicans on issues that affect our military. We are fortunate to have our Georgia US legislators who have worked so diligently for our military. So the evening sponsored by our Democratic Senator Max Cleland and Republican Congressman Jack Kingston was made even more special by this relationship.

I was pleased the president voiced support of the military, pay and benefit increases, and funding for some of the equipment needed. There were many wonderful items on his "wish list" as there are on mine, but perhaps harder to find the funding for. I understand that his suggested initiates equaled $4B a minute. That makes our Navy League budget very small indeed! It would be good sometimes if politics did not play such a part in our national process, but it is a fact of life and evident that evening. The president even mentioned how much would be based on who stood and who applauded that evening and how much fun the commentators would have. Standing or not standing it was obvious there was enthusiasm and it appeared almost like an electric current was flowing through the room.

Debbie Jans, an aide to Senator Cleland, who also works as a disability expert for the Capitol, knew every policeman in the Capitol. She introduced me to one of her friends who turned out to be deputy sergeant at arms. I didn't see him until I watched the tape Arlie has recorded and saw him introduce the attendees including the vice president. I could see some things better on the tape, but nothing could take the place of being there. I was back in my hotel room by eleven thirty and called Arlie. He said he would wait up until he heard from me and I was anxious to tell him about it. Looking back on this event, I am pleased to have witnessed a piece of history. I was moved by the opening of the address when the president said, "We are fortunate to be alive at this moment in history." Most newspapers had coverage, and it was interesting reading. The USA reporter had an article entitled:

> *"Shorter on drama, still plenty long"*
>
> *Even without bizarre subplot, speech is a big deal, Clinton enjoys it while it lasts. And lasts.*
>
> *It's hard to imagine a State of the Union address more momentous than the first one, which George Washington presented in 1790 to a brand-new congress assembled to represent a fledging nation. Yet the father of our country summed up his thoughts in a page and a half. As the nation has gotten older, its chief executives have gotten wordier. President Clinton's 89 minutes State of the Union address Thursday gave new meaning to the term 'Clinton Fatigue." As the president lapped the one-hour mark, lawmakers began slipping out the back door. By the time he finished more than a quarter of the seats on the Republican side had been vacated. So had a few of the Democratic side.*

I, on the other hand, enjoyed every minute. I did get a little tired of standing up so much! Later in the article he called it prom night for workaholics.

The local paper the *Tribune & Georgian* had the following article:

> ***McNeill attends Clinton's State of the Union address***
>
> *By Amelia A. Hart*
>
> *Last Thursday's State of the Union address was a little bit of history, a little long and, says a Camden County businesswoman who was there, a lot of fun. It was incredible, said Sheila McNeill, "It's like the Academy Awards for politicians." McNeill received the opportunity to sit in the gallery of the House of Representatives and hear President Bill Clinton's final State of the Union address on Jan 27 courtesy of U.S. Congressman Jack Kingston of Savannah.*
>
> *McNeill, who is also a national vice president of the Navy League, has mentioned to Kingston that she was going to be in Washington, D.C. the week of Jan. 24. McNeill said she speaks with Kingston regularly regarding concerns of the military and when he offered her a ticket to the president's annual address she jumped. "To have the opportunity to attend the State of the Union was the chance of a lifetime and I was excited to be a part of history," said McNeill. "No matter what your politics are, you have to be in awe of being present in this chamber together with almost all of our national leaders."*

Dinner at the Capitol

Arriving in Washington on Monday, McNeill had the unfortunate opportunity to be a part of another history-making event—one of the worse storms to hit the East Coast in years. "I arrived in Washington on Monday just in time to be snowbound for the next 36 hours," McNeill said. Even before the actual State of the Union, McNeill had another unique opportunity, this one provided by U.S. Senator Max Cleland. Traditionally, McNeill explained, the Senate has a dinner for the families at the Capitol the evening of the State of the Union and she happily accepted when Cleland invited her to attend.

McNeill rode the congressional subway from the Dirksen Building, where the senator from Georgia has his office to the U.S. Capitol, where the buffet dinner was held in a reception room. "The room was full of familiar faces. Funny, how you can see someone constantly on C-Span and the news shows and then you meet them and feel almost like you know them," McNeill said.

Among the senators, she met that night were Strom Thurmond of South Carolina, Wayne Allard of Colorado (who is on the Senate Armed Services Committee), Bob Graham of Florida and Senate Majority Leader Trent Lott of Mississippi. She also had a chance to talk about the USS Wyoming, one of the 10 Tridents homeported at Naval Submarine Base Kings Bay with Senator Craig Thomas, the senator from the boat's namesake state.

McNeill said that although it was a very relaxed atmosphere, she also could feel the excitement in the air. "I read the next morning the evening was described as prom night for workaholics and that was an apt description," she said.

A gallery view

McNeill had to be in her assigned seat at 8:30 for the 9 p.m. address. She recalled she was not happy to be there so much ahead of time, "however, when the military chiefs almost immediately entered the chamber, I realized I was none too early." When Hillary Rodham Clinton and her party, including daughter Chelsea, arrived, McNeill realized that from her seat in the last row of the House gallery, she had a clear view of where the first lady was seated as well as of where the president would be speaking.

"Chelsea looked absolutely beautiful." McNeill said. "I thought "Good for her."" She's come into her own and become a beautiful woman in spite of the cruel statements made about her as she was

growing up." One thing that McNeill said she noticed being in gallery was that she had never thought about during all the other State of the Union addresses she had seen on television, was how the House of Representatives' chamber accommodated the addition of 100 senators and dozens of cabinet members, chiefs of staff and other dignitaries' who attend the event. "They used some kind of benches, like old-fashioned church benches, and they sat in those instead of the regular desks and chairs." "McNeill said. She also noticed and counted fourteen red suits worn by female legislators. "I guess red was the female power color for the evening," McNeill said.

McNeill described Clinton as a 'masterful speaker' as he delivered his final State of the Union. "I knew there were prompters and I was sure he must have used them, along with his notes, but it was very smoothly done." McNeill said. "Politics aside, you have to admire President Clinton's ability to captivate an audience for over one and a half hours in what appeared to be a effortless and completely confident manner."

A new perspective

Clinton did make one notable mistake last Thursday when he said Vice President Al Gore had been working to make American cities more 'liberal" instead of "livable." "Everybody there couldn't stop laughing," McNeill recalled with a chuckle. "And it broke everyone up when he did it again."

One thing she saw that television viewers did not see were the member of the press corps in the House chamber who were comparing Clinton's speech with the printed version released earlier that day "It was interesting to watch 100 press corps members simultaneously turning the pages as he talked. It was like a giant wave at a football game, but more subdued," McNeill said. The Navy League vice president said she also was pleased with the courtesy shown to the first lady by the audience when she was introduced by President Clinton. "I was so pleased that no matter what has happened that the proper respect was shown Mrs. Clinton when she was introduced," McNeill said. "There are times that the office of the president demands respect and it was given to both the office and the first lady that night and I thought it was very appropriate."

Even though Clinton was well received at the Capitol, McNeill said it was very easy to see by the applause how the numerous projects proposed by the president during the speech would do when Congress got down to business. "It would be good sometimes if politics did not

> *play such a part in our national process, but it is a fact of life and evident that evening." She said. "The president even mentioned in his speech how much would be based on who stood and who applauded that evening and how much fun the commentators would have. "Standing or not standing, it was obvious there was enthusiasm and it appeared almost like an electric current was flowing through the room." The departure of guests from the gallery was delayed a little after the president concluded his speech because of how long he spent outside the House chamber speaking with people," McNeill said. "He was feeling so good from the evening, I guess he didn't want to give his prom night up." She said. McNeill said she is grateful to Kingston and Cleland for giving her an opportunity to witness the State of the Union.*
>
> *"I will always look at these speeches a little bit differently now that I've been there," she said. "It was a glorious night.*

My friend Jennifer Ihrig sent an e-mail: "Hi, we will miss you." (It was her —— birthday party she was referring to.) "Watching for your lovely face at the State of the Union. How the hell did you wing that one? Love, C. J. and Jennifer."

When Rear Admiral Rich Terpstra presented a 16 × 20 poster with my picture and the following article I loved it and knew he was making fun but until I was writing this book in 2016 and typing the newspaper article I didn't realize just how much I gushed. He caught it right away! Look for that in the individual stories section.

I am grateful to Congressman Kingston and Senator Cleland for a night I will never forget.

CAPTAIN WES STEVENS AND JANE

COMMANDING OFFICER, NAVAL SUBMARINE BASE KINGS BAY

Captain Wes Stevens came to Kings Bay in July 2007. He was a pleasure to work with and well respected by his staff and the community. I would always try to keep him from referring to me as ma'am. He would call me Sheila but always answered me with a Ma'am.

Arlie and I invited Wes and his wife Jane to spend a weekend with us. Jane was a former Navy pilot and we always enjoyed our talks. The week before the visit to our home I went to his office. "Wes, when you are at my home you'll be in your shorts, sitting in our recliner drinking a cup of coffee barefooted. Do you think then you might be able to drop the *ma'am*?"

"No, ma'am," he answered. I gave up on that one!

He took the time when I was recognized for the Emory Dawson Humanitarian Award to come to Brunswick for the ceremony. That meant a lot to me and to my family. The city doesn't see the Navy uniform that often! Captain Stevens was one of the speakers at our Military Community Forum in February 2010 and was always open to whatever was needed to reach out to the community. The local paper covered the event with the article quoting me saying, "It certainly proved to be a forum for news and information when Capt. Stevens gave us an update about the letter sent to the St. Marys Airport jump school on airspace violations."

Stevens noted that two parachutes landed inside the security fence at the base recently. One had equipment problems and had to land and a second person landed beside her to make sure she was all right.

He was relieved in August 2010 by an old friend, Captain John O'Neill. During this ceremony, the *Times Union* had the following story on that change of command:

"O'Neill takes reins at Kings Bay"

By Gordon Jackson

ST. MARYS—Early in his Navy career, Capt. John O'Neill served as a flag aide to the commander of Submarine Group 10 at Kings Bay Naval Submarine Base. His second tour at Kings Bay officially began Friday, with many more responsibilities. O'Neill assumed command of Kings Bay, replacing Capt. Ward "Wes" Stevens, who is retiring after a 27-year career.

Rear Adm. Townsend "Tim" Alexander, commander of Navy Region Southeast, praised Stevens for leading the base in energy conservation programs that have earned Kings Bay national recognition. "He set the standard in energy conservation," Alexander said. Stevens received praise for helping initiate an ongoing series of meetings to help the public understand the Navy's role at Kings Bay and surrounding communities. "He has done a tremendous job representing the Navy in this close-knit community," he said. "It takes vision to lead." Alexander presented Stevens with the Legion of Merit medal for his accomplishments as base commander the past three years. Stevens said he was overwhelmed with the praise and admitted it is emotional to leave the Navy. He predicted O'Neill will have his best tour of duty serving as commanding officer at Kings Bay. "We have the highest retention rate and are the most requested duty assignment of any submarine base in the Navy," he said.

He credited sailors and civilian workers for his success. "I cannot put into words the enormous admiration that I have for each and every one of you," he said. "Your professionalism and willingness to accomplish the mission no matter the sacrifice has been inspiring." He also shared a recent conversation with his wife, Jane, that drew roaring laughter and applause from his audience. "Just the other night we were looking back, and I said to her, 'Did you in your wildest dreams ever think that I would be CO of a sub base?'" he said. "And in true Jane fashion she said, 'Darling, I hate to break it to you, but you have never been in any of my wildest dreams.'" After his speech, Stevens and O'Neill faced each other as Stevens read the final orders of his Navy career.

"Regard yourself relieved of all active duty," the last line of the orders said. O'Neill replied, "You stand relieved." After they saluted and shook hands, O'Neill also followed Navy tradition by making a brief speech." You have made a lasting impact on Kings Bay and the community," he said. "I'm honored to lead such a fine group of professionals."

The *Tribune & Georgian* added some of the lighter and more personal remarks

O'Neill takes reins at Kings Bay
By Johna Strickland

As Capt. Ward "Wes" Stevens left the post of commanding officer for Kings Bay Naval Submarine Base on Friday, he passed down three words of advice to successor Capt. John O'Neill.

These three words came from Capt. Michael McKinnon who offered them to Stevens when he came to Kings Bay to Stephens when he came in 2007. Stephens told O'Neill he would have three bosses, Rear Admiral Townsend "Tim" Alexander who commands the Navy Southeast Command, the Navy Southern Region Submarine Group 10 commander Rear Adm. Barry Bruner "Who thinks he's your boss" and Camden County resident Sheila McNeill, a military advocate and former national preside of the Navy League. "So, John to help you sort through that I will pass on three words of advice my predecessor Mike McKinnon gave me "Keep Sheila happy," Stevens said.

What a wonderful and humorous thing to say. It particularly touched my heart because it came from these two highly professional

and highly respected officers. Wes is a straight shooter, a charming military officers but doesn't use humor—usually. He had everyone laughing at his change of command. For him to take that way to recognize my work was indeed special. To make those comments even more memorable was that my mother and my friend Lynn Warwick attended that change of command. It was a first change of command for both.

I am so grateful to Wes and people like him who make this sometimes tough job a pleasure.

STRATEGIC DETERGENT COLLATION

The column that I never submitted shows my pride in being a member of the Coalition.

There is a new organization in the country, the Strategic Detergent Collation. Its purpose is to connect the policy community of DC and around the country with the people who man the missiles, bombers, and submarines. A defense contractor recommended me to become a part of the coalition, and I attended my first meeting as a member on April 15, 2013. There were six speakers addressing the thirty-three-member attendees representing fourteen states. All other members had Air Force connections and one of those was a former astronaut. We were appreciative to Alliant Techsystems (ATK) for hosting the meeting at their headquarters in DC and the Boeing Company for hosting the reception that evening.

Captain Johnny Wolfe, technical director for Strategic Systems Programs (SSP), reviewed the organizational relationships and structure, strategic deterrence, and the Air Force/Navy commonality. The D5 missile used on the Ohio class of submarines is the newest and most capable missile having 142 successful test fights and twice the service life of its predecessor C4. SSP is working to increase the missile life to match the projected design of the new SSBN (X) with a life of fifty years. (Current SSBNs have a life of forty to forty-two years and are all currently in the last half of that life.) "Our strategic submarines will support 70% of the Nuclear Triad under the New Start Treaty," said Captain Wolfe. Wolfe also discussed the value of the Nuclear Triad in regard to deterrence:

- ICBMs provide prompt response and hard target defeat capability.
- SSBNs prove second strike capability through survivability (at sea platforms are assumed survivable).
- Bombers prove visible increase or decrease in posture and additional strike capability.

Regarding the third comment above on visible increase or decrease in posture for the bombers, I was reminded of one of the values of our eighty thousand tons of diplomacy—our aircraft carriers. There is no doubt our carriers make a huge impression simply by their arrival and the same can be said of our bombers flying over a rogue group in another country. We should remember the full meaning of deterrent: to keep others from using nuclear weapons against the US or our allies. Over thirty-one American allies have joined with us and have depended on the US for the past fifty years to protect them and their citizens. America's strength allows small countries to survive under our nuclear umbrella. Yes, our allies depend on the United States. With the closure of many of our overseas military installations, the US likewise will depend on the support of our allies. If the US were to reduce its nuclear deterrent to a point where it could not be extended to its allies or even to a point where it was perceived to be unable to protect the vital interest of our allies, it could create instability.

Peter Huessy, president of Geostrategic Analysis, spoke at a recent event held in Minot, North Dakota where participants toured the B-52 and Minuteman III facilities at Minot Air Force Base. Mr. Huessy, organizer of the event said the symposiums will be held as a community of people working together to promote, sustain, and try to modernize the triad, and to make a connection between the thousands of people who work on the base, who sustain the base and who are critical to our deterrent, and let them know that we remember them because they are there.

President Obama is predicted to announce in the near future a new round of strategic nuclear warhead reductions as part of a disarmament agenda that could reduce US strategic warheads to as few as one thousand. The 2010 START Treaty created a balance in America's strategic deterrent structure sufficient to deter our adversaries and assure our allies. The treaty promised to maintain a modern, safe, secure, reliable, and stabilizing Nuclear Triad deterrent. America must not unilaterally reduce our strategic deterrent to less than agreed in our 2010 START Treaty.

I was always a fan of the Squadron 16 motto: "War ready to preserve peace." I have no doubt our nuclear deterrents have deterred incidents with some of the major powers. Admiral Richard Mies, USN (retired), a submariner and former commander, US Strategic Command, very clearly pointed out that "even with the horrifically huge numbers of loss of life of our military members we saw in WWI with fifteen million dead and twenty million wounded this loss was not a deterrent and was insufficient to prevent World War II. "Nuclear power has moderated the behavior of the great powers toward one another."

Our current nuclear force consists of fourteen submarines (reducing to twelve as the current ones retire), more than four hundred ICBMSs, and sixty strategic bombers. Our warheads are scheduled to reach 1,550 by the end of this decade compared to over 12,000 at the height of the Cold War and 2,200 under the 2002 Moscow Treaty between the US and Russia.

Mr. Hussey's response to those who say they don't believe in nuclear weapons is "We could ask North Korea, we could ask Pakistan, we could ask China to get rid of their nuclear weapons, and they've already given us their answer." He said Kim Jong-il, the former leader of North Korea, when asked, "Are you going to give up your nuclear weapons?" He replied, "You first."

The defense sequesters and budget cuts mean that more and more citizens will have to speak up and ask that our deterrents are maintained. Franklin Mill in his paper "The Need for Strong U.S. Nuclear Deterrent in the 21st Century" summed it up by saying, "One of the classic questions confronting defense analysts and military planners is 'How large is a nuclear stockpile required to be for an effect deterrent?'… Given the world we live in, US deterrence requirements are driven primarily by the need to deter a future Russian leadership, should it develop hostile intent toward us or our allies, and secondarily by the need to deter a future Chinese leadership in the same circumstances. While other deterrent requirements exist, from a force structure and force sizing standpoint, these can be treated as lesser included cases."

Citizens of Camden County have a powerful voice in the future of our nuclear deterrents. Many of you have already traveled to DC to speak to our legislators about the funding for the replacement of our Ohio-class submarines—the Ohio Replacement Program (ORP) also known as SSBN(X). This program has already been delayed by two years. We must not fail to ensure the peace. We must maintain a modern nuclear deterrent. We must stay engaged with not only our Georgia legislators but with other congressional legislators who are on committees dealing with these critical issues and issues of support for those installations.

*Five years later and as I work to finish this book the following individuals are board members of the Strategic Deterrent Coalition:

- Joe Sherman McCorkle
- Bruce Christianson
- David Weissman
- Lamberth Blalock
- Mark Jantzer
- Lamberth Blalock
- Murray Viser
- Sheila McNeill
- Stuart Purviance
- Joe Scallorns

I am proud to serve with these gentlemen

REAR ADMIRAL RICH TERPSTRA AND SUE

COMMANDER SUBMARINE GROUP TEN

Rear Admiral Rich Terpstra was a great group commander. I never heard a negative word from his staff or from anyone for that matter. I'm only sharing the fun issues because they are so rare, as is he. I had a meeting with RDML Terpstra. I was a frequent visitor to Group 10. This visit was no exception. I arrived and immediately saw the picture. The flag office is right next door to the large conference room. On the narrow wall between them was always a picture of the President of the United States. Not today. Today my official Navy League picture was on the wall. It was disconcerting at first. It didn't take me but a minute but I knew it was a colossal joke. Was RADM Terpstra up to this? Who else could have done it? It was his office so no one else would have the nerve.

It was there every time I visited. One day it dawned on me. I went to the picture and turned it over. Sure enough. the president was on the other side. RADM Terpstra had it turned every time I came to his office. Now what kind of a man goes to the trouble to have a picture blown up and add such humor to a situation! It's not often that I get 'taken' but he had me on that one.

We attended the Navy Ball on April 8, 2000. When we arrived the first person, I saw was Melody Somers, protocol officer for Kings Bay, and she was with the Rear Admiral Terpstra's aide, Lieutenant Chris Williams. They both look troubled. In fact, so many of them had such a troubled look that I was afraid that something had happened to one of the sailors. My mind is very active and I wondered if someone had been hurt or killed that day. I asked, "What's wrong?" They hesitated, and I pushed. "Something terrible has happened, tell me."

"The admiral is wearing the wrong uniform," they answered.

I couldn't help but laugh. Of course, I realized that for the admiral to have one uniform on and the guest, Adm. Vern Clark, to have another was a big deal. But compared to what I was thinking it didn't compare. We were still in the reception and someone was called to bring the correct uniform from their home at Kings Bay to Jekyll Island.

Rich's parents were seated with us at dinner as Rich waited for his uniform to arrive. So was Admiral Ed Giambastini. When I smiled about the situation, his father urged me to talk with Rich and tell him he would laugh about this one day. Rich redeemed himself when it came time for his talk. He spoke eloquently about Admiral Clark and what a momentous occasion this was. But not before he built the room up like it was an upcoming championship football game.

"Let's have a cheer for those in attendance tonight."

The room cheered.

"Let's have a cheer for the submarine force."

The room cheered louder.

"Let's have a cheer for the surface force."

Knowing who our guests were, they made it a little louder.

"Let's have a cheer for the Navy."

They r*eally* got with it.

And let's have a cheer for an admiral who doesn't know what uniform to wear!"

And the room went wild!

It was so like Rich to be able to turn it into a great evening.

My story on the opportunity to go to President Clinton's State of the Union is in my stories section. Obviously when I met with RADM Terpstra and told him about it I gushed a lot. One day I walked into my office and there was a big poster with my picture and the following story.

Poster:

> *McNeill attends Clinton's State of the Union Address*
> *By: B S. Err*
> *Terp Chronicles Staff Writer*
>
> *Last Thursday's State of the Union address was a little bit of history, a little long and, says Camden County's favorite and vivacious businesswoman who was there, a lot of fun.*
>
> *"It was incredible," said Sheila McNeill, owner of Sheila's Hallmark in St. Marys. "It's like the Academy Awards for politicians, "There was Max, and Jack, and Paul, and Strom, and Tillie and Arlen, and Charles, and Pat, and Jesse, and Steny, and Van. I ran into Newt, and Sam, and Barney, and Chet, and Vernon, and Duke, and Saxby, and Sonny, and Herbert and Spencer, and Dick, and Olympia and we just had the best time chatting."*
>
> *How McNeill received the opportunity to attend the State of the Union was a chance of a lifetime and I was sooo excited to be a part of history," said McNeill. "No matter what your politics are, you have to be in awe of being present in the oval office, oops, I mean in this chamber together with almost all of our national leaders."*
>
> *"But the trip wasn't just all about fun. Through personal exchanges I was able to obtain commitments from the Congressman and President Clinton for the SSGN's. They should be here very soon.*

You have got to love a man with this sense of humor.

He and Sue came over to the house and we visited the island a couple of times. We always had a great time.

Rich had assumed command relieving Rear Admiral Joe Henry. The Florida Times Union quoted him in the September 11, 1999, edition:

> *I believe that this is the most important military base performing the most important mission for our nation and for freedom. I am honored to join all of you who work so hard to keep our country's insurance policy rock solid. The people—the sailors and civilians—of this complex have already impressed me greatly with their skill and dedication. My first job will be the continued orchestration of their team efforts set in a community that gives outstanding support.*

The staff gave a wonderful "Hail and Farewell" for Rich and Sue and his relief Rear Admiral Jerry and Judye Talbot on June 28, 2001. RADM Talbot and I had worked on the breakfast for new legislators in DC with the three sea service chiefs when I was national vice president so that made the introduction a little easier!

Rich's tour was a great period for Kings Bay. Group 10 had the highest retention rate in the Navy and during his tour the USS *Bancroft* Sail Exhibit was built as was the RV Park and campground on base.

We continued to get together when I was national president and he was stationed at the Pentagon. I invited him to join me for a drink at the Ritz-Carlton—just a metro stop away—and we always enjoyed catching up.

THE CAMDEN PARTNERSHIP

I was national president when the Base Realignment and Closure Committee came (BRAC) came up. The community formed a Community Action Group (CAG) in August 2003. Jim Wells and Walt Natzic were instrumental in creating both the CAG and in April 2004, The Camden Partnership.

Captain Walt Yourstone who was the former commanding officer of Naval Submarine Base Kings Bay (June 2000 to July 2002) was hired in October 2004 as the executive director. The partnership received a grant of $144,500 from OEA for Camden County Diversification Study and Marty Klumpp was hired as director of fund-raising in June 2005 and her title was changed to executive director in 2006. When Walt left to take a position with VT Group, Captain Mike McKinnon was just turning over his position as commanding officer of Kings Bay (August 2004–July 2007) and agreed to continue the partnership's mission of support to Kings Bay as the next president in March 2004. When I returned home after serving as Navy League national president, I was invited to join the board of directors. I later was asked to serve as president.

These three articles help give the expanse of The Camden Partnership.

2009—Camden Partnership names McNeill as its next president.
By Staff *Tribune & Georgian*

Sheila McNeill, a St. Marys businesswoman, has been elected president of The Camden Partnership, a lobbying group that works to support and strengthen military missions at Kings Bay Navy Submarine Basie. McNeill, former national president of the Navy League of the United States and owner/manager of Sheila's Hallmark, has been involved with the organization from the beginning. The Camden Partnership, a 501C4 organization, grew out of the community Action Group that was formed to address community issues relating to the Base Realignment and Closure Committee.

"Because of Ms. McNeill's extensive knowledge and experience with the Department of Defense and the Sea Services, plus the acquaintances she has made and continues to foster throughout the military establishment and on Capitol Hill, The Camden Partnership has the ideal individual to represent them in its primary mission to support and strengthen military missions at Naval Submarine Base Kings Bay" said director Marty Klumpp in a new release from the organization. McNeill replaces the previous president, Mike McKinnon, who resigned to take a position with a firm in Tennessee. "Ms. McNeill brings a wealth of experiences to the presidency, as well as an extensive net-work within DOD and in Congress. She has been active in the Navy League of the United States (NLUS) for 43 years," stated the release.

During those 43 years, she served at every leadership level, culminating as national President from 2003-2005, the first female to hold that position since the league was founded in 1902. McNeill served as national vice president for the organization's legislative affairs activities, aggressively seeking support on Capitol Hill. Other positions within NLUS at the Nationals level include vice president for strategic planning and development, national director of the US Navy Sea Cadets Corps and on the National Maritime Policy Committee. She is currently serving on the Navy League's national advisory committee and is a board member of the Dolphin Scholarship Foundations.

"Because of McNeill's long history of active involvement with the Sea Services, she served as a member of the executive committee of the Defense Advisory Committee on women in the service (DACOWITS), an influential advisory committee to the Secretary of Defense and other DOD officials. During her three year DACOWITS tour, she visited 45 U.S. military installations throughout the world. Many of the commanding officers she met during these visits are now flag offices in strategic locations, further expanding her extensive network,"

In Georgia, McNeill serves as a member of the executive board of the Governor's state wide Military Affairs Coordinating Committee.

Camden Partnership Tours NSB Kings Bay
Group accompanies by teachers during June 9 training
From The Camden Partnership, July 11, 2012

The Camden Partnership recently sponsored one of the favorite Naval Submarine Base Kings Bay tours, Guns, Bombs Bullets and Dogs. This year the partnership working with Rachael Baldwin, chairman of the chamber's Workforce Development Committee, encouraged local teachers to participate. Teachers from Brantley, Camden, Charlton, Glynn, McIntosh and Wayne counties earned professional development units for participating in the Trident Coast Georgia Work Ready Science, Technology, Engineering and Math Institute Grant initiative. STEM is a growing initiative in education to promote and encourage more students to consider pursuit of careers that require performance and rigor in those content areas. Teachers in the institute were exposed to more than 20 hours of the application of STEM concepts to related careers and work sites. The Guns, Bombs, Bullets and Dogs Tour was an optional component which allowed teachers to see the connection between robotics and the defense industry. A shooting simulation incorporated math related applications, and the training required of the dogs related to applications in animal and behavioral science.

On June 7, Trident Refit Facility instructed teachers about math formulas used in non-destructive weapons testing and multiple applications for electronics. Baldwin said the opportunity for teachers to link their curriculum to real-world applications is important in creating relevance. "Students always ask, 'Why do I have to learn this?', she said. "When a teacher can authoritatively respond about their experience last summer at Kings Bay... 'when I blew up 24 pounds of C-4'... and relate it to an instructional objective they have likely increased the attention and engagement of the student in learning the concept.

"One of the lessons a teacher produced from this activity incorporated teaching the properties of circles to solve problems involving the length of an arc and the area of a sector. Sharing real-world experience can support a simulated scenario to examine circular debris patterns that could result at a bomb detonation site." Baldwin said the final project will glean more than 90 STEM-related exposures or activities for linking STEM to curriculum standards. "It is always exciting when anyone has the opportunity to get a better understanding of the mission of our base here at Kings Bay," he said. "But it is most important that teachers not only understand the mission but also the skill sets, and expectations required of entry level military and civilian workers. Teachers are the strongest link to creating tomorrow's workforce. The next partnership event will be Aug. 9, regarding family advocacy Fleet and Family Support Services will provide a briefing on its services specifically focused on family advocacy.

Law enforcement partners, including Camden County Sheriff Tommy Gregory, St. Marys Police Chief Tim Hatch, Kingsland Police Chief Darryl Griffin and invited Naval Criminal Investigative Service representatives will be joining the forum, said Marty Klumpp, chairman of the Forums and Tours committee. The purpose of the partnership is to continue to nurture the partnership between the base and Camden County. Partnership programs include tours of various commands and forums to educate the community and bring together community and military projects and expertise.

In October 2012, we had a leadership forum. Commanding officer of Naval Submarine Base Kings Bay, Captain Harvey Guffey, Lt. Cmdr. Matt Baer, commanding officer of the Coast Guard's Maritime Safety and Security Team 91104, Cmdr. Steve Love, commanding officer of the Coast Guard's Maritime Force Protection Unit, and Lt. Col Kevin Moody, commanding officer of the Marine Corps Security Force all presented.

The *Tribune & Georgian* made a great group picture with the following story:

Leadership forum follow up

This month the community had an opportunity to hear from the top military leadership in Camden County. The Navy, Marines,

> *and Coast Guard had some heavy hitters at this continuing series of forums to broaden the connection the military and county residents. In this third year of forums/tours sponsored by Kings Bay Naval Submarine Base and The Camden Partnership, the community response was superb, according to organizers.*
>
> *The purpose of the forums and tours is to strengthen and enhance the relationship between the military and civilian communities in the Camden area and to educate and promote their collective interest in Camden County. At the October 13 (2012) forum, the audience of more than 60 civilians and military personnel heard briefings on each of their respective service… after their briefings they answered questions from the audience.*

I am grateful to serve this organization in supporting our military and I am proud to serve with our board of directors:

President: Howard Sepp
Secretary: Alecia Webb
James Coughlin
W. H. (Bill) Gross
Joel Hanner
Marty Klumpp
Al Konetzni, VADM, USN, R
J. C. Knoll, USN, R
Post, Keith, Sr. Chief, USN, R
Roberts, Lonnie
Allison Shore
Jim Wells, Captain, USN, R
Walt Yourstone, Captain, USN, R
C. B. Yadav

THE KINDNESS OF STRANGERS

Edward Nielson

I had not had time to read the papers. I was answering e-mails when I received word from my friends congratulating me on the nice letter to the editor. I quickly found the paper and read it. I didn't know Edward Nielsen. Who would be that kind about someone they didn't know! I sent him flowers with the note: "I cannot tell you how stunned I was when I read today's paper. Thank you for the kindest gesture

I've ever seen." I later found a telephone number for him and called. He had been in town for twelve years and works on base in cryptology. He had read stories about me and thought someone should thank me! Hopefully, those were the first flowers he had ever received! Thank you, still, Edward Nielson.

His letter to the editor below:

> McNeill has done much for Camden County
> Published: Wednesday, July 1, 2009 10:18 AM EDT
>
> Dear Editor, after reading Sheila McNeill's article in Friday's Tribune & Georgian (June 26), you can't help but wonder just how much positive impact this lady has had on our community. Her accomplishments no doubt would fill this newspaper, but two of them, for me anyway, stand out. She was the first woman to be president of the Navy League of the United States—an achievement only a few can testify to, and, probably the most significant, it tirelessly promoted the idea of the Trident SSGN to congressional leaders and Navy brass.
>
> To take a plan that was only on paper and using influence, panache, and dogged determination to see it all the way to fruition is a daunting task for even a most seasoned politician, let alone a civic-minded citizen. Along with The Camden Partnership, Sheila McNeill has played a pivotal role in supporting and expanding the Navy/Marine Corps mission at Kings Bay, and more recently, the additional roles of the Coast Guard. The entire Camden County community owes a huge debt of gratitude to Mrs. McNeill; if it hasn't been done already, the citizens of the county need to prompt our elected and civic leadership into setting aside a proclamation that recognizes the superb contributions Sheila McNeill has given to not only Kings Bay, but to the wellbeing of all in Camden. Truly, a small gesture for such a deserving recipient.
>
> Edward A. Nielsen, Kingsland, Geogia.

Thank you, Mr. Nielsen.

THEY WILL BE HOME SOON

THE PACIFIC NORTHWEST AND THE HAINAN ISLAND INCIDENT

March/April 2001

I was invited to speak at our Northwest area councils. Marilyn Crist, the region president, met my plane and I stayed the first night with her. She had a very nice apartment with a panoramic view of Seattle from the space needle to the waterfront. Boy, is she dynamic and energetic at seventy-nine years old. She prepared a nice meal and we had a leisurely evening with her giving me much information about the region and their accomplishments.

The next day we caught the ferry over to Bangor and were met by Carol Metney, the council president. Carol Metney was one of the best Navy Leaguers we had and there were two occasions when she took me in. She took me to about four Navy League councils to install officers at each. It reminded me of DACOWITS—going as fast as we could and taking in as much information as we could. That same evening, she had a cocktail party at her home for about fifty to give me an opportunity to meet as many from the region as I could. By the time we caught the ferry to Seattle, then on the cab home, we were bushed—or I was bushed.

The following day we went to Whidbey Island and I stayed with Ann and Bruce Van Tassle. They were a very nice couple who made us feel right at home. That evening we had a welcome aboard. Don Boyton, a Navy League Hall of Fame recipient, came over and shook my hand and encouraged me to run for national president with some wonderful supportive words.

The next day I spoke on what's happening at headquarters and RADM Vinson E. Smith, commander of Navy Region Northwest, was the keynote speaker. That evening at a Navy League meeting at Whidbey Island I spoke with the admiral in the audience along with several captains including the commanding officer of the base. I knew most of what I was saying had been said by the admiral earlier. However, this was not a problem. I know that he appreciated that the Navy League message was one he supported!

As I was speaking, two sailors came in the door and went to the captain's table, and whispered something. He left, and they went to the admiral and he left. The admiral came back after a while and sat down at his table. I continued to speak as if nothing had happened. But try as I might, I could not find out why the room kept emptying while I was talking. Later I was told to watch CNN the next morning, it would probably all be there.

It was, and the news channels gave variations of the story:

> *April 1, 2001 one of the Navy EP-3E ARIES II was operating about 70 miles away from the People's Republic of China island province of Hainan when it was intercepted by two Chinese J-8 fighters. A collision between the EP-3 and one of the J-8s caused the crew to have an emergency landing in Hainan. Over two dozen of their men and women! It was a terrifying situation. The news showed that the crew destroyed sensitive items and data on board*

the aircraft, as was protocol. They were kept under guard and were interrogated at all hours.

No wonder there was such secrecy at the meeting. Those men and women were stationed at this base! I won't go into detail because it was all over the papers. But everyone waited on pins and needles for the outcome.

Navy Times had the pictures of each of some of those sailors and all the names.

A Lot of waiting, praying in Oak Harbor, Washington
By Darlene Himmelspach

The international standoff centered in southern China struck a raw nerve in the small community of Oak Harbor, Wash. Oak Harbor, close by Whidbey Island Naval Air Station, is home to 14 of the 22 Navy people detained by the Chinese. It's a close-knit community of 22,000 people—roughly 75% of them with ties to the air station.

"They are either active duty, retired or they work on base," said Priscilla Heidecker, executive director of the Oak Harbor Chamber of Commerce. So, when the Chinese fighter jet knocked an EP-3E plane based at Whidbey Island from the sky April 1, the town took it hard, Heidecker said. "There is a lot of waiting and praying." At the Oak Harbor Pub and Brewery, a Navy sonar technician, who declined to give his name said in an April 5 telephone interview, "They should send our guys back—right now! They have no reason to hold them." "One huge side effect of the incident is the swarm of local, national and international news media," said Jeff Chew, editor of the twice-weekly *Whidbey News-Times*. Whatever nuisance some might find the onslaught to be, their influx, Chew said, has been good for business in the normally pastoral island in the San Juan Island chain.

He said locals have "rallied around the families" of the captive crew to protect them from reporters and photographers.

Ten days later, on April 11th, I was at the Navy League's Sea Air Space Expo.

I saw Jim Hessman, editor of Seapower magazine coming down the stairs and, he gave me a 'look' so I went over to him and met him at the foot of the stairs. As I did I saw the Taiwanese delegation right behind him. I was thrilled to have a chance to see them and spent a few minutes shaking hands and welcoming them. He told me later that his 'look' was a signal to me to meet them as they came down the stairs. The Taiwanese delegation were happy as they were greeted properly.

As there is every year, there was an International Reception for foreign attaches with many countries' attaches represented. I was standing, watching everyone for a quiet moment when a Chinese military officer approached me. We talked for a few minutes but as I am trying to talk with him there was just one thing in my mind. I wondered about the irony of our men and women being held by the Chinese and here I am talking with a military officer from China.

In the middle of our conversation he said, "I know you are worried about your men"

"Yes, I am."

"They will be home soon"

"How soon"

"Very, very soon.

"Would you just whisper in my ear when that will be?"

He threw his head back and laughed and said, "I get it, joke, right?"

And then he turned and left.

I didn't know what to think and if I should believe him.

But later Admiral Vern Clark made the announcement that our crew had been released.

I didn't know how much credence to give my encounter with the Chinese officer but, obviously, it was true What is the chance that I would be at Whidbey Island when it happened and was blessed to be at the announcement when they were released?

JOHN THRONE PAO USCG

US COAST GUARD PUBLIC AFFAIR

John was "the voice" at the Navy League conventions. For years he was the hidden voice who read the citations for the service awards. The United States Coast Guard recognizes two levels of extraordinary work by a Navy League member. The levels are Meritorious and Distinguished. The Department of the Navy has three levels: Meritorious, Superior, and Distinguished. They are presented annually at a Navy League national meeting by the service. Presentation of these medals is a special event at Navy League and John sets the stage with his deep, melodious voice that is always a perfect read and a perfect pitch.

We worked together for a couple of years before I had a specific job that really "justified" his help. I just loved running things past him. I finally convinced Jack to assign me as vice president of legislative affairs. I sent the following letter to John Thorn to tell him of my new appointment.

April 29, 2001
Dear John,

ON WHY I'VE ALWAYS FELT PASSIONATE ABOUT MY SUPPORT OF THE COAST GUARD

I began 25 years ago, when Arlie became a member of the Navy League's national Coast Guard Affairs Committee. My first 20 years of Navy League work was primarily as a supportive wife (our local council did not have women serving in leadership positions) so as Arlie supported the Coast Guard—I supported the Coast Guard.

We visited small units as we traveled along the coast—just to stop by and say hello and thanks. We supported the first reserve unit established in Glynn County—many of the original members are still active. We made sure that any recruiting support and recognition always included the Coast Guard and have always been there for the annual picnics and special events for our local unit.

We became friends with the local commanders and worked with them after retirement to find employment—I even hired the commander's wife as a manager at one of my shops—one of my smartest moves and the chiefs** are still in their positions at the Federal Law Enforcement Training Center. When I became a member of the Defense Advisory Committee on Women in the Services (DACOWITS) I used every opportunity to keep focus on the parity of Coast Guard members—and kept in mind to make all issues inclusive of the Coast Guard. My committee was Quality of Life, so all work was for both the men and women of the services. My later appointment to Vice Chair and Installation Visit Coordinator gave me an opportunity to review every visit made by every member and prepare committee reports and recommendations from these visits. I strived for fair and honest assessments of all installation visits and kept an awareness of the Coast Guard's needs.*

When a situation at the training base at Aberdeen (an Army installation) required we visit all services training bases, I requested the Coast Guard training base at Cape May. This enhanced my commitment. Several "off the record" conversations with the Captain and my conversations with the new Coasties have given me an insight that has enabled me to support the Coast Guard with more understanding.

In my work with the Navy League, the Defense Department, and in my contacts both social and business, I have used every opportunity to educate and enlighten those I meet on the mission and needs of the Coast Guard. My Georgia legislators have all heard my "pitches." My election and assignment as national vice president, legislative affairs, has finally given me a means by which I might act on this passion. You tell me, what can I do to be more responsive and supportive? How can I improve our communications and my knowledge of the great needs we have?

Sheila

**Gail Blanda ** Chief Tony Blanda and Chief Baynes*

John retired from the Coast Guard in 2002 as chief of community relations in the Office of Public Affairs. When he was with the Coast Guard, he was the liaison with the Navy League. We convinced him to become active in the Navy League when he retired and assume the responsibilities as chairman of the Coast Guard Affairs Committee. One of the perks of that job was that he would continue to work with Rear Admiral Joel Whitehead, chief of government and public affairs, and his relief, Lynford Morton.

He was always looking for ways we could build on the wonderful relationship the Navy League had with our Coast Guard leadership. Arlie and I will never forget how gracious he was to take our sixteen-year-old grandson under his wing at the National Navy League meeting in New York. John, Arlie, Ryan, and I went to the Broadway show *Tony n' Tina's Wedding*. We had a wonderful time that evening.

John was essential to my success as legislative vice president. He was up for the job! He knows the needs of the Coast Guard and is the best writer you could find. We worked together the three years I had that job. He encouraged me to run for president. When I decided to run, he was behind me in every way. Planning the strategy and giving me encouraging words.

I am proud to call John my friend.

REAR ADMIRAL FRANK THORPE IV

CHANGE OF COMMAND THORPE'S RETIREMENT

August 7–8, 2009

Frank had so many friends in his public relations community, the flag officers he worked with, family, defense companies, and friends who all liked and admired him. I was amazed and honored to receive an invitation. I was pleased that the party was being held at the foyer of the Navy League building. Steve Petropolis must have had something to do with that! Kudos for both.

Franks remarks at the reception included the comment that everyone there had touched his life in a positive fashion. I was pleased to have been national president when he was Public Affairs Officer for the chief of Naval Operations (CNO) Admiral Vern Clark. I suppose that time in our lives was why I received the invitation. There was a special circumstance that cemented the respect we had for each other but that won't be revealed here.

There must have been fifty flag officers at the ceremony. This included the current chief of Naval Operations, Admiral Roughead, and Admiral Vern Clark and Connie, former chairman of the Joint Chiefs Dick Myers, many public relations experts, media types, and a spattering of neighbor and lots of family. There were several civilians there who were on television, so it was a lot of "Where do I know him/her from?"

I talked with a couple of those folks that night at the party. People I thought I knew very well but just couldn't remember where I knew them from so I faked it. I went up to them and began talking. After a while I'd realize, I knew them only from the news, but I wasn't about to let them know that. I just talked and eased off.

His speakers for the event were the Honorable Robert Work, undersecretary of the Navy, Admiral Gary Roughead, and Rear Admiral Dennis Moynihan. Frank and I had many conversations with many visits when Admiral Clark was CNO. I could call him anytime I had questions or needed advice when I was national president. It was an honor to know and work with him.

He was relieved by Rear Admiral Dennis Moynihan on Friday, August 7, 2009. The fact that the transition was so seamless and the relationship with Denny was so great is a testament to the quality of both men.

VICE ADMIRAL JOSEPH TOFALO AND SUZANNE

COMMANDER SUBMARINE FORCE

Time passed very quickly when the Tofalos were at Kings Bay. It was a busy time. From the beginning, Joe and Suzanne Tofalo got it! Suzanne worked hard to ensure the Dolphin Scholarship auction continued to be successful and was active in the Submarine Officers' Wives Club (SOWC) later changed to Submarine Officers Spouse's Association (SOSA). She participated fully in the spouse issues and still maintained her career.

A couple of times when Suzanne was on travel Joe and I would have dinner and catch up—not only on the military issues but on their friends in Fernandina and their love for boating.

At that time, they would have no idea that Joe would become commander of Submarine Forces and with that usually the spouse would serve as chair of Dolphin Scholarship Foundation along with many other expectations.

Joe understood why organizations like The Camden Partnership exist and so much appreciated the community involvement. Looking back to his time at Kings Bay and reading his letter below makes me even more indebted to Vice Admiral Tofalo. His appreciation made my job so easy.

18 September 2013
Dear Sheila,

I wanted to personally thank you for your extensive efforts in putting together today's impressive collection of over 30 local/state government officials and education professionals for briefs, as well as a tour of Trident Refit Facility (TRF). Our ability to educate this extremely broad group, to include a State Senator, all three local college presidents, economic development representatives from all four local municipalities, and even the Camden County High School career counselor, was invaluable in spreading our message.

With one quarter of the TRF work force eligible for retirement, getting the word out on the apprenticeship program and other hiring opportunities at TRF is extremely important, and this would not have been possible without your support. As I said in my remarks to the group, the scenario we have here is a win-win-win, for individuals, the local economy, and TRF.

I understand that Senator Ligon is interested in going to the state capitol to carry this message to a high level, and I'll ensure Rear Admiral Richard is fully briefed on what we are trying to accomplish here.

Thanks again for all you do.
J. E. Tofalo, Rear Admiral, U.S. Navy

And he did just that. Our visit to the state capitol with Rear Admiral Richard; Captain Harvey Guffey, commanding officer of Naval Submarine Base Kings Bay; Captain Larry Hill, commanding officer of Trident Refit Facility; and Bill Gross are in Rear Admiral Richard's stories. I believe this letter went a long way in giving a comfort level to everyone.

A couple of weeks before his transfer to his new position we held the Triad Conference. He and Captain Harvey Guffey, commanding officer of Naval Submarine Base Kings Bay, put a lot of trust in me as I worked with Peter Hussey and for that I am grateful. We had a packed house with top-level speakers. It took months to implement. I am grateful for their support. That story is told in the Triad Conference section.

Vice Admiral Michael Connor was the speaker at the Tofalo/Richard change of command on November 22, 2013, and he described the mission of submarines at Kings Bay as the "most important work in the entire United States government."

Rear Admiral Tofalo acknowledged the fiftieth anniversary of the assassination of President John F. Kennedy and described the tumultuous times when an arms race and the threat of nuclear war were concerns for most Americans. As the local paper reported, he spent much of his time recognizing the work of the different commands on base that support the submarines and their crews in their mission as well as the officers in command of the boats. "For the submarine commanding officers, you have the most important job in the Navy," he said.

I am rarely surprised but Rear Admiral Joseph Tofalo simple stunned me at that change of command.

Toward the close of his remarks I heard my name. Those comments were an article in the *Periscope*, Naval Submarine Base Kings Bay's newspaper:

During the Submarine Group 10 Change of Command ceremony Nov. 22, Sheila McNeill received a huge surprise from outgoing commander Rear Adm. Joseph Tofalo. McNeill, a former national Navy League president and current president of The Camden Partnership, was appointed the title of honorary Submarine Group 10 Commander for her tireless efforts in supporting the Kings Bay military community.

In his remarks, Tofalo expressed gratitude to the civilian community surrounding the Kings Bay base. "There are few civilian communities that are as supportive as ours, and it's one of those things that just makes you feel great about being an American and living here in Southeast Georgia and Northeast Florida," Tofalo said. "From the Navy League to The Camden Partnership, to our congressman, mayors, county officials, school districts and first responders, we are so blessed to have the outstanding community support that we have." Tofalo pressed on the theme of community support, specifically recognizing McNeill's dedication to local military initiatives.

"Whether it's Camden Partnership activities, Georgia Military Affairs Council advocacy, pulling together state and local leaders and educators to help me address our aging TRF demographic, or flawlessly executing the extremely successful recent Triad Council, Sheila gives her heart and soul to the advancement of Kings Bay," he said. McNeill was presented with a specially monogramed hat and certificate as a token of appreciation in addition to her honorary title.

I had a hard time holding my tears. I was pleased when *Seapower* magazine sent a press release with this story as well as posting it on their website.

I went to the change of command when then Rear Admiral Tofalo relieved Vice Admiral Connor as commander of Submarine Forces. After the ceremony, I went the Joe and Suzanne's quarters (home) for a smaller reception with family and friends. I smile when I think about this. First, let me make it clear: I understand that commanding the US submarine force is a very senior position. I understand that his position, as do others in the Navy, command respect. But we were with friends and sometimes I can't help myself. There was a discussion and I responded to Vice Admiral Tofalo with something like, "That was a dumb thing to do" or something equally inappropriate. Those who were standing there were taken aback to say the least. Joe laughed and said, "Only you, Sheila could get away with that."

I will never be able to express to Joe Tofalo what this meant to me. He and Suzanne were a great team and at the writing of this book continue to serve. I have that monogramed hat proudly displayed on my book shelves. One day I want to put it in my car, so people can see it and park in the group commander's reserved spot on the base.

If I could just get the nerve...

TRIAD CONFERENCE

NOVEMBER 2013

Peter Hussey called and asked me to help him bring the Triad Conference to Kings Bay and Camden County. A similar conference was at Bangor and brought in a half dozen nuclear deterrent experts-both active duty and civilian. He wanted to do the same thing in our area. Peter is president of his own defense consulting firm, Geostrategic Analysis founded in 1981 and was the senior defense consultant at the National Defense University Foundation for twenty-two years. He is a defense analyst specializing in congressional budget and policy developments on nuclear deterrent policy, strategic nuclear modernization, and terrorism. He is familiar with the nuclear and missile defense issues reflected by think tanks, nongovernmental organizations and the US government.

I met with Captain Harvey Guffey, commanding officer of Naval Submarine Base Kings Bay and his staff. They could not do anything until approval was given for the conference, but he told me he wouldn't try to stop me; they just could not help. I was busy the next two months. I reserved hotel rooms and conference rooms, enlisted caterers, and responded to Peter's daily requests. We had about 180 coming. These attendees were defense contractors, experts in the field of nuclear deterrents as well as tentative responses from senior active duty Navy and Air Force.

Plans were made to have the event in early November. Since the same thing was held in Bangor I *assumed* that approval would be given. Most of this reassurance came from Peter who had hosted these conferences for years with senior flag (admirals) speaking. Peter had utmost confidence.

While still waiting for approval Keith Post and I attended the Naval Submarine League symposium in October—just a month out from our Triad Conference. At the opening reception, I was told by Rear Admiral Rick Breckenridge that the conference was not approved by the Secretary of the Navy. I could not believe it. How could you look at the list of speakers and not know the importance of the subject and approve this conference? The Air Force had just completed a similar conference. The Air Force can host it but the Navy cannot? What do we tell those speakers? The Navy just isn't that interested? (Today the replacement of our Navy deterrents is the number one issue of the Navy and the Defense Department. This fact was well known by all but the Navy and Defense Departments were not as vocal about it until recently.)

But now it is official. The replacement of our sea based nuclear deterrents is the number one issue of the Navy and the Defense Department, but they would not allow the Navy to reciprocate on a forum the Air Force had already sponsored! What kind of "cluster" would this action create? I went up to my room and vented by writing the following:

If I could talk to SECNAV… is ORP really that important

1. Cost to Navy is miniscule—yet ORP is the # 1 for CNO and Navy. At public expense Navy gets to advertise top priority.
2. Minot was to educate on AF. (Air Force) KB (Kings Bay) event is to educate on Navy subs. Having AF flags (should have been general officers but I was mad and was writing fast) on SSBN is good. Could all those speakers be wrong!
3. Educators, elected officials, state officials, community leaders are committed to attending event.
4. Again, minimal cost to Navy—Yet excellent opportunity.
5. There is little urgency with ORP. The general public—even our own community (NSBKB) considers it a long way off. We desperately need to educate.
6. Sponsored by chamber, Navy League, The Camden Partnership in association with NDIA, ROA, AFA.
7. Paid for by defense contractors and supporters.
8. Much to gain for conference and much to lose if canceled.
9. People involved have been working on this outreach for a year.

I was so angry and that rarely happens. I had it written in five minutes—had I taken a little longer it might have made more sense, but everyone should get the message. It needed some editing, but I didn't take time. Anyway, it was handwritten, and editing would have meant starting all over.

When I was in my room writing the reasons the conference should happen, I had a call from Captain Kevin Brenton who said VADM Benedict was looking for me and did I have time to come down and say Hi. Wow—I did! Kevin was a former Squadron Commander at Kings Bay and we had become good friends.

After we met I went back to my room and picked up the list from my yellow pad. I took it to the check in desk and asked for twelve copies. I don't think they even charged me. I arrived at the reception and gave copies to every flag officer (PACFLT, N97, SSP, PEO Subs, Sublant, Budget, etc.) in attendance and to Electric Boat's Mike Cortese. I kept one for the chief of Naval Operations Admiral John Greenert. Everyone was around him and I hated to interrupt him, so I asked his wife Darlene to give the list to him. She said, "No, he'll want to talk with you—just wait a minute." How nice. So I did. I told him the Triad Conference at Kings Bay had been canceled and I had a list of reasons why this was not a good decision and gave him the paper suggesting he read it later.

I made a few more connections that night but that will have to wait until I'm dead for someone to share.

The next morning RADM Rick Breckenridge (now Vice Admiral Breckenridge) told me that he and a few other flag officers were meeting with the CNO earlier that morning. After the meeting Greenert asked Breckenridge to stay and said, "Have you seen Sheila's list?" as he picked it up from his desk. RADM Breckenridge said yes, he had seen it and they were working to get it turned around. Admiral Greenert offered his help if needed. The next day we received a phone call while driving home saying the conference was approved.

TRIAD EVENT AT NAVAL SUBMARINE BASE KINGS BAY

The Camden Partnership hosted the Triad Conference at Naval Kings Bay. This event is sponsored by Peter Hussey, President of Geostrategic Analysis and the senior defense consultant at the Air Force Association and National Security Fellow at the American Foreign Policy Council. I had no idea what I was getting into. It was the most significant conference that I have had a part of in the 30 years of support for Kings Bay.

A nuclear triad refers to a nuclear arsenal which consists of three components, traditionally strategic bombers, intercontinental ballistic missiles (ICBMs), and submarine-launched ballistic missiles (SLBMs). These are located at Kings Bay and Bangor, Washington. The purpose of having a three-branched nuclear capability is to significantly reduce the possibility that an enemy could destroy all of a nation's nuclear forces in a first-strike attack; this, in turn, ensures a credible threat of a second strike, and thus increases a nation's nuclear deterrence. Submarines are considered the most survivable leg of the triad. There was an incredible level of expertise in the speakers. It was interesting to see so many Air Force uniforms in town (all featured speakers):

- General Robert Kehler, Commander, US Strategic Command
- Major General Garrett Harencak, Assistant Chief, Staff for Strategic Deterrence and Nuclear Integration
- Major General Scott Vander Hamm, Commander, Eighth Air Force

They joined a "who's who" in the submarine world:

- Vice Admiral Michael Connor, Commander, Submarine Forces
- Vice Admiral Terry Benedict, Director, Strategic Systems Programs
- Rear Admiral Richard Breckenridge, Director, Undersea Warfare Division
- Rear Admiral Dave Johnson, Program Executive Officer for Submarines

From the UK, Rear Admiral Mark Beverstock, Royal Navy, chief strategic systems executive, UK Ministry of Defense was in an attendance.

These active duty members were joined by an elite group of submarine and nuclear issues:

- The Honorable Franklin Miller, Principal, the Scrowcroft Group
- Ambassador Linton Brooks, Center for Strategic and International Studies
- Amy Woolf, Library of Congress/Congressional Research Service
- Professor Matthew Kroenig, Georgetown University
- Mark Schneider, National Institute for Public Policy
- Peter Hussey, Geostrategic Analysis

None of the issues facing us today can be done without the help of Congress and Representative Joe Courtney (D, CT) attended and spoke about the necessity of the conference because these are very big commitments that the country must make. "They're important commitments and they're important to our national security and defense."

At the conference, the next morning when VADM Connor spoke he started with "I happened to be with Sheila McNeill when the word first came down that said that this conference was disapproved. And for any of you who think that no is the final answer on this sort of thing, take a lesson from her. No simply means it's time to get your cell phone out, apparently, and get to work. So we appreciate all the people very much that had a role in making this conference happen."

It was a great success and worth all the angst to bring it to fruition. I am now working on Triad 2018. It has been approved!

UNDERWAY ON THE USS MEMPHIS (SSN 691)

COMMANDING OFFICER CHARLIE MAHER

I had the rare opportunity to go overnight on the USS *Memphis*. As a supporter of Naval Submarine Base Kings Bay, I had been to sea on an SSBN many times although overnight only once on the USS *Georgia* (that story is told elsewhere!) but had never had this opportunity on a fast attack. My thanks to Vice Admiral Jay Donnelly and RADM Barry Bruner for making this happen.

The submarine picked up the group at Jacksonville. Friends from St. Marys included Hunt Thornhill, Dave Reilly, Mayor Kenneth Smith, Katherine Zell, councilwoman and from Jacksonville Bill Dudley. I didn't know the other guests, but we became good friends over our twenty-four hours at sea.

Hunt and I enjoy telling our story of the continuous contact in our head. The men and women shared a common bathroom—we just knocked to make sure no one was there. It seemed that every time I went Hunt was there. Even at three in the morning! I knocked on the door after waking up and making the huge effort to leave the warmth of the rack and knocked but no one answered, so I went in. I immediately heard Hunt say, "I'm taking a shower." Who takes a shower at 3:00 a.m.? I either couldn't or didn't want to wait so I just told him to keep showering—just not to come out until I was done! He likes to tell tales that I scrubbed his back and I like to protest.

We would all be a little embarrassed by our devotion to the movie that was shown while we were enjoying midrats. I'm glad the captain was so gracious. I sent the commanding officer the following e-mail:

> August 2, 2010
> Dear Captain Maher,
>
> What a wonderful experience we all had aboard the MEMPHIS. Your officers and crew are very impressive. We were all amazed at the quality and professionalism of even the most junior of sailors. I know we were taking over their living spaces and requiring them to not only perform their jobs but be gracious to a group of civilians. And gracious they were and so knowledge-

able. It is a mark of a good leader to see all the officers and crew with such good morale and with and pride in what they do.

With all of us experiencing one of the most amazing 24 hours in our lives I found it amusing (in retrospect) that when we were in the wardroom watching the final 4 minutes of Inglorious Bastards, we wanted to see the end before we went to the control room to observe the process of surfacing the boat. We all laughed later and hope you found it slightly amusing that we finished the movie before we joined you. Obviously, the movie was a good pick as was the food, beverages, racks, briefs, etc. Everyone was very aware that this was serious business and we were fortunate to have the opportunity to observe. We were spellbound as you gave orders and your officers responded. In my remarks around the world for the Navy League I used the submarine squadron 16's old motto, "War ready to preserve peace." Your officers and crew epitomize this. I continue to be one of the submarine forces biggest supporters. My awe of you all continues.

Sheila

And his very gracious reply:

Sheila,

So happy you enjoyed your time with us on MEMPHIS! It was great to have you and the Navy Leaguers from FL and GA underway with us. We all had lots of fun!

I'm very proud of the crew—it is the crew that makes MEMPHIS the great warship that she is. They make my job easy! I should say that I learned quite a lot about the good work you and the Navy League do to support our sailors and our mission. During our discussion, I was very impressed by the interest, knowledge and passion the group had about keeping our Navy strong. Thanks for your amazing support! We'd love to have you on board again anytime!

CDR Charlie Maher CO, USS MEMPHIS (SSN 691)

What a wonderful opportunity this was.

UNITED STATES COAST GUARD:

MARITIME SAFETY AND SECURITY TEAM 91108 COMES TO CAMDEN MARITIME FORCE PROTECTION UNIT THE COAST GUARD BUDGET CUTS, 2010 AND FINALLY, THE TENTH ANNIVERSARY OF MSST 91108

When Admiral Allan was commandant of the United States Coast Guard he established the Maritime Safety and Security Teams. I was with him and a group of his officers when I first heard about them. It was intriguing. After the enormous evacuation of New York after 9/11 the Coast Guard made the decision to create unique highly trained teams in strategic locations throughout the United States. A Maritime Safety and Security Team, or MSST, is a United States Coast Guard anti-terrorism team established to protect local maritime assets. It is a harbor and inshore patrol and security team that includes detecting and if necessary stopping or arresting submerged divers using the Underwater Port Security System. They are a quick response team table of rapid deployments anywhere in the county via air, ground, or sea transport.

MSSTs were created under the Maritime Transportation Security Act of 2002 (MTSA) that Navy League worked so hard to support. It was in direct response to the terrorist's attacks on September 11, 2001, and are a part of the Department of Homeland Security. I asked and was given permission to have *Seapower* magazine cover this new mission for the Coast Guard. As I learned more, I knew it would be the perfect unit for Camden County, so I went back to Admiral Allan and made my case. Weeks went by. I went to a big event on Capitol Hill that we were sponsoring, and several Coast Guard officers had special smiles and told me I was going to be happy with some decision the Coast Guard had made. We always had several decisions in the hopper, so I wasn't sure which one they were talking about and they were tightlipped except for their cryptic remarks. The next day I had a call from Admiral Allen. The Maritime Safety and Security Team 91108 was coming to Camden County. We had the commissioning ceremony on October 6, 2003, at Orange Hall. I was national president at the time so changes in schedule was hard, but I wasn't going to miss this one.

These were my remarks:

> I cannot tell you how pleased I am to have the privilege to speak at this great occasion. A couple of years ago, I had the opportunity to tell Secretary of Transportation Norman Mineta just what the Navy League is all about. At that time, the Coast

Guard had not been moved from Transportation to Homeland Security. After a moment, he said, you know the Coast Guard needs a League. I said, "Mr. Secretary you do have a league and it's call the Navy League. I told him that he would have a hard time finding a Coast guard unit that did not know of the Navy League and had not received the direct support of our members.

We in Camden County now have just that opportunity—to add the Coast Guard unit that did not know of the Navy League and have not received the direct support of our members. We now in Camden County have just that opportunity—to add the Coast Guard to our family and to support this elite team who have so much to offer our country in this Global War on Terrorism and in the security of our country.

I assured the then District Commander, Vice Admiral Jay Carmichael, Coast Guard headquarters staff and Commandant Admiral Tom Collins that Camden County loved its sailors and we would love our Coasties just as much.

July at our convention in Hawaii, the Coast Guard presented Navy league with a framed copy of the Coast Guard Authorization Act passed in the last Congress. The Navy League has lobbied vigorously for the Maritime Transportation Act passed in the last Congress—one of the most sweeping maritime security legislative packages in the Nation's history and the first Coast Guard Authorization Act in nearly half a century.

The Navy League also received a Coast Guard Proclamation signed by Secretary of Homeland Security Tom Ridge, praising the Navy League for playing an 'instrumental' roll in educating Congress and the American people about Coast Guard "Missions and Issues" and for its help in promoting the "largest major acquisition in the Coast Guard's history, the Integrated Deepwater System Project." Our commitment to the Coast Guard is constant and it is unwavering. Our support of MSST 91108 will be constant and unwavering.

I was on Capitol Hill when Congress approved the largest ever budget for the Coast Guard. The Coast Guard also received $670 million for Deepwater—$170 million over the president's budget. This project will completely recapitalize the Coast Guard fleet of ships, aircraft and all the associated sensors over the next 20 years. While homeland security remains the Coast Guard's top priority along with Search and Rescue they do not lose their focus on their other 14 legislatively mandated services. On the

Saturday night of the convention, Vice Admiral Tom Barrett reported to an audience in Washington that drug interdiction had exceeded the amount seized last year and gave numerous examples of incidents of great work by our Coast Guard units in preventing oil spills with proper inspection and quick actions. The Coast Guard continues to do more with less.

When I speak to groups across the country I always point out that out of 41 countries in the world who have Coast Guards our Coast Guard is 38 in the age of the fleet. They also perform their many duties with less active duty than the New York City Police Department. In addition to all the safety law enforcement, buoy tender and aids to navigation service the United States often utilized the Coast Guard as a 'non-threatening" representative of the United States. By sending in a Coast Guard cutter the United States has a presence in the county that is not considered adversarial—they are considered by all seaman as a friend.

Every dollar directed to Coast Guard will contribute to a careful balance between safety and security mission, both of which must be properly funded for effective mission accomplishment. We as citizens must make every effort to let our legislators know how important the essential services of the Coast Guard are to America. Admiral Collins recently said in a *Seapower* article "Even before we were in the department of Homeland Security, we were developing a more forward maritime strategy, and part of it was the idea of a layers of defense and pushing the borders out.

This Maritime Safety and Security Team is one of 12 units created after 9/11. With homeland security as their primary mission MSST sets up and defends a security zone around high value asset. Without fanfare or publicity, they just do their jobs. Most Americans aren't even aware of the behind the scenes work that MSST teams perform to help secure 75,000 miles of coastline and 25,000 miles of navigable seas. They are 100-person teams and will be used to provide force protection and port security around the nation. I've met many of them and they are also the best of the best... The Coast Guard's elite capable of protecting our shores and responding to crisis anywhere in the county.

I am impressed with the commanding office of the unit LCDR Billy Mitchell, his executive officer and the highly skilled team that has been assigned to MSST 91108. I was also impressed with the welcome and briefings given by Kings Bay.

> Great job Captain Cahoon and your excellent staff. I hope we all have conveyed to you in many ways how fortunate we are as citizens of Camden County to have you here and to know that this nation's young capable sons and daughters are willing to devote their careers to insure our safety.
>
> I thank the Coast Guard for making the decision to have St. Marys, Georgia as the strategic location of their newest elite force and I welcome the opportunity to work with them in the future. Thank you to the crew for your commitment to training and education to ensure that as America sleeps we do so with the assurance that you remain vigilant. Welcome MSST 91108 and your families. God Bless you, God Bless the Coast Guard, God Bless the U.S. Military and God Bless America.

We were honored that day to have Vice Admiral Jim Hull as the keynote speaker. He would later be one of the two Coast Guard admirals I called for help when the budget was cut.

MARITIME FORCE PROTECTION UNIT

In 2007, another Coast Guard unit was added. Navy News on 7/25/17 had the following press release:

> *KINGS BAY GA. (NNS) The U.S. Coast Guard commissioned the Maritime Force Protection Unit (MFPU) July 24 at Naval Submarine Base Kings Bay.*
>
> *The unit, the first of its kind, was officially activated during formal commissioning ceremony presided over by Vice Adm. D. Brian Peterman, commander of the Coast Guard's Atlantic Area*
>
> *"This is a new and unique mission," Peterman said during his commissioning remarks. He also praised the Navy for helping develop training techniques and specialized equipment for the new mission from scratch. "It shows a great relationship with the Navy and Coast Guard."*
>
> *The Coast Guard unit will provide enhanced security for the Trident submarines (SSBN) with their homeland transit area. Tridents generally operate on the surface during transit and the MFPU will provide additional measures while performing under these conditions.*

Commanding Officer of the new unit Cmd. Alan Reagan, said the first 87-foot Coast Guard Cutter Sea Dragon will arrive in November. An additional cutter, smaller patrol craft, and around 200 additional Coastguardsmen are scheduled to arrive at the strategic, coastal Georgia submarine base within the next two to three years, he said.

MFPU Kings Bay is a single-mission unit that has specially trained and equipped Coast Guard personnel to man and operate escort vessels procured by the Navy specifically for that use. The unit will have broad law enforcement authority, including the authority to establish patrol and security zones supporting Naval Operations.

"Maritime Force Protection Unit Kings Bay provides an invaluable service to the Navy and our nation through its unique ability to exercise the Coast Guard's law enforcement authorities while enforcing a naval vessel protection zone," said Peterman. "Maritime force protection is critical if our nation's strategic naval assets are to safely operate in close proximity to vessel traffic in confined bodies of water."

A second unit is scheduled for commissioning in Bangor, Wash., July 26.

The ceremony was held at the base chapel. We are so pleased to have two very unique Coast Guard units in our County.

THE COAST GUARD'S BUDGET CUT

MARITIME SAFETY AND SECURITY TEAM TO BE ELIMINATED

Keith Post and I were invited to attend an awards ceremony by Commander Doug Stark, commanding officer at the Maritime Safety Security Team in St. Marys in early 2010. We had never met the admiral who was presenting the awards. We were pleased to be invited. After the awards were over the admiral told those present that he had an announcement. He told the crew that the Coast Guard would be closing the St. Marys unit and several others. That was a stunning announcement. We waited to talk with Commander Stark and the admiral. We talked for a while, me with more questions than there were answers. It was also a surprise to Commander Stark.

Shortly afterward, I went to DC to talk with the commandant. I asked plainly, "Is this budget driven or have you determined that the five units you are decommissioning are not needed?" I asked.

"No, they have performed well and are needed. We had to make some decisions when we had a three hundred million dollars cut to the budget." Admiral Thad Allen told me.

I went back to Camden to make plans. First, we had to get the community involved—which was easy. The economic impact of that unit was significant, and the community loved having the Coast Guard in St. Marys. We made a massive plan. I called Dan Branch, current national president of the Navy League and shared with him what had happened. I asked him if I could visit congressional offices in the name of the national Navy League. This was not only about Camden County it was about the entire country. To bring up a county or state would ensure that I would not be listened to outside my state. He agreed and offered any help from him or the staff that I needed. It was going to be costly. To visit the congressional members and the committee staffers would take many trips to DC. I talked with the board of directors of The Camden Partnership and they were on board. I went to John Morrissey, Mayor of St. Marys and he was appreciative of the help and was pleased to support.

The rest is laid out in my guest column on restoring the three hundred million dollars to the USCG.

The Tribune & Georgian March 24, 2010
Plan to close Coast Guard unit will cost millions locally.

Camden County recently received some startling news. As a result of the Obama Administration's decision to reduce the fiscal year 2011 budget, the Coast Guard will have to make drastic cuts.

There are Coast Guards all over the world. Yet our fleet is in the bottom 10 percent when it comes to the age of our fleet. With cutters as much as 50 years old, the Coast Guard has begun a robust program to recapitalize their fleet. Yet one proposal will be to reduce the acquisition, construction and improvements account (AC&I), which will delay this critical recapitalization program. While there is documented evidence that the 50-year-old, 378-foot cutter fleet is in need of replacement, and scheduled to go out of commission in 2014, this proposal has them taken out of service three years early without adequate replacement.

With the Coast Guard's critical mission of safety and search and rescue, the program to support maritime domain awareness—knowing where ships are at sea in real time—is now being jeopardized. The Coast Guard has seen its missions dramatically increase since the tragedies of Sept. 11, 2001. The previous administration and the congress, in recognition of this fact, have steadily increased the end strength (number of personnel) for the past few years.

> *This proposed budget will decrease our active-duty Coast Guardsmen by 1,112 people. Cutting jobs is the easy way to save money, but it makes no sense in this case, because at the same time the federal government is considering appropriating unthinkable amounts of tax dollars in jobs bills. Compared to the jobs bill this is a very small investment in not only jobs but jobs for defense. Jobs where our military are on call 24/7. This jobs bill investment reaps enormous benefits for our country. While no less startling but more significant to Camden County, another proposed cut will be decommissioning the Maritime Safety and Security Team (MSST) in St. Marys. Decommissioning our local unit would result in a loss of over $8 million annually in our community. In addition to our unit the proposal is to also close the MSST units in New York, New Orleans, San Francisco and in Anchorage.*
>
> *These critical units were established after the terrorist attacks on Sept. 11. The current threat level is high, if not higher, than when the teams were commissioned. Now is the wrong time to be reducing any anti-terror units.*
>
> *President Obama has proposed a freeze in federal spending, with the exception of the Department of Defense (DOD) due to the nation being engaged in two wars. While the Coast Guard is not a part of DOD and is under the Department of Homeland Security (DHS), they are one of the five arms of the military and with the homeland security challenges that we face their mission to protect our ports and our coastline has never been more essential.*

So what do we as a community do about this? Everything we can. With The Camden Partnership taking the lead we have partnered with all local governments, the Chamber of Commerce, the Joint Development Authority, and the Navy League to begin a rigorous campaign to have Congress restore the Coast Guard's budget. Marty Klumpp, Keith Post, and I made plans—the first was sending a letter to everyone! Everyone we approached for help was ready to do whatever they could.

On Friday, March 12, we mailed out 150 packages. These packages were sent to President Obama, the secretary of Homeland Security Janet Napolitano, and members of Congress who have oversight of the Coast Guard. Copies were also sent to the Coast Guard itself as well as the chairman of the Joint Chiefs. These packages included a cover letter, position papers on maintaining the current level of funding for the US Coast Guard, retaining the MSST (91108), a letter from Gov. Sonny Perdue, and a joint resolution from the cities of Kingsland, St. Marys and Woodbine, the Camden County Board of Commissioners, and Dr. Will Hardin, superintendent and Camden County Board of Education.

It also included a letter from the City of St. Marys, a joint letter from the JDA and the Chamber pointing out the fact that in comparison to the East Coast (MSST) missions not slated for decommissioning; the economic impact is 9,000% greater than Boston and 8,000% greater than Miami (the location of the MSST units that would remain on the East Coast). The economic impact will be far more detrimental to our community than any other MSST based community. Also included is a letter from the Camden–Kings Bay Council of the Navy League pointing out the quality of life attributes of Camden County and the benefits our military friendly community offers.

We've made some progress. Senators Isakson and Chambliss and Congressman Kingston have jointly sent a letter to Secretary Napolitano in strong opposition to the budget cuts to MSST. Senators Isakson and Chambliss also sent a letter, along with Senators Joe Lieberman, Susan Collins, George LeMieux, and Scott Brown to the chairman and ranking member of the Senate Committee on Appropriations requesting that the two hundred million dollars set aside to cover security expenses of the terrorist trials in NY be reallocated within the DHS budget to prevent reductions in the Coast Guard's budget. We've been able to get our letter into the hands of Secretary Napolitano. We've had valuable advice from DC firms who understand our need and our pocketbook.

We are asking that the current level of services of the Coast Guard be maintained in the 2011 budget, adjusted for inflation, and that we retain all twelve MSSTs. We are asking for a true augmentation of funds and that no reapportionment of the already scarce funds is made. In the true nature of this community—this community who never complained when the security requirements our nation determined the need to transfer two of our submarines to the west coast—we understand national security. We also understand budget cuts and when it comes to the need for preserving national security we will fight.

The Camden Partnership will be in DC several times over the next few months. Our friends are helping us meet with key legislators. While the budget vote in Congress may not come until late summer, we can't take any chances. Please consider writing your friends now in other states to help us in this effort, asking them to contact their representatives in congress. It won't hurt for our representatives to hear from you as well, to let them know we appreciate their efforts to win this fight. We respectfully request that the country does not lose this battle to save our Coast Guard.

(Sheila McNeill is president of The Camden Partnership and a guest columnist in the Tribune & Georgian.)

This was the letter that was sent:

The Honorable Barack Obama

President of the United States of America
The White House
1600 Pennsylvania Avenue
Washington, D.C. 20500
RE: MAINTAIN THE CURRENT LEVEL OF FUNDING FOR THE U.S. COAST GUARD
Included:

(1) Maintain the Current Level of Funding for the U.S. Coast Guard
(2) Retain MSST (91108) St. Marys, GA
(3) Letter from the Honorable Sonny Perdue, Governor State of Georgia
(4) Joint Letter from Senator Johnny Isakson, Senator Saxby Chambliss and Congressman Jack Kingston
(5) Resolution from the Georgia House of Representatives
(6) Joint Resolution from the Cities of St. Marys, Kingsland, and Woodbine, Camden County Board of Commissioners and Camden County Board of Education
(7) Letter from St. Marys City Council
(8) Joint Letter from Camden County Joint Development Authority and Camden County Chamber of Commerce
(9) Letter from Camden Kings Bay Council Navy League of the U.S.
(10) Distribution List—Attachment I

Dear President Obama,

On February 2, 2010, the Coast Guard, in response to a budget reduction for FY11, stated they would decommission five of the 12 Maritime Safety and Security Teams (MSSTs). The MSSTs were established after the 9/11 terrorist attacks in response to heightened security levels. The current threat assessment is as high, if not higher, than when the teams were commissioned after the 9/11 attacks. Now is the wrong time to be reducing any anti-terror units. The number of MSSTs should remain at twelve.

As you well know, before the 9/11 terror attacks, 38% of the Coast Guard's operational hours were devoted to homeland and maritime security missions. Today, because of the 9/11 terror attacks, it spends more than 57% of its operational hours on homeland security missions. The facts on their face are startling: The Coast Guard is being driven well below what is needed, especially in this post-9/11 world. It should be obvious how critical funding is for the Coast Guard. We urge and request that the current level of services of the United States Coast Guard be maintained in the 2011 budget, adjusted for inflation, and we retain all twelve (12) MSSTs. We ask for a true augmentation of funds and that no reapportionment of the already scarce funds be made. A decrement of funds is not warranted.

We respectfully request, as citizens of America, that the country does not lose this battle to save our Coast Guard. However, if any MSSTs are to be decommissioned, we, as concerned citizens from Camden County, request reconsideration of the extensive attributes MSST 91108 offers.

Respectfully,
Sheila M. McNeill, President
Past National President
Navy League of the United States

This was the original plan:

USCG—MSST 91108

Community Action Plan—**Draft***

A. Solicit support from:

a. National Elected Officials:
   1. Senator Isakson
   2. Senator Chambliss
   3. Congressman Kingston

b. State Elected Officials:
   1. Governor Perdue
   2. General Browning (GMACC)
   3. State Senator Chapman
   4. State Representative Hill

c. Local Elected Officials:
   1. County, Cities, School Board Joint Resolution/Letter
   2. Specific Letter from St Marys Mayor and City Council

d. Local Community Entities:
   1. Chamber of Commerce
   2. Joint Development Authority
   3. Local Navy League Council

    4. The Camden Partnership
    5. Local Coast Guard Auxiliary
    6. Superintendent and Board of Education
e. Other Individual/Groups
    1. Navy League Councils in the other 12 MSST Homeport Cities
    2. AIFBY Chamber of Commerce
    3. Golden Isles Chamber of Commerce
    4. Chambers of Commerce in other MSST Homeports
    5. Local Maritime Community (Pilots Association, Savannah, Jacksonville)

B. Game Plan:

Develop main 1 or 2-page point paper focusing on the need to keep <u>all 12 MSST's</u>

a. Make presentations to all 5 Camden County Government bodies on the impact of closing our MSST
b. Educate our local, regional and state leadership on the issue, with continual updates
c. Develop, submit, get signed a resolution of support for St Marys MSST from all 3 Camden Cities, the County and the school board
d. Continue outreach to available retired Coast Guard personnel knowledgeable on the MSST concept and missions
e. Reach out to other Navy League Leadership in all 12 homeport cities to exchange ideas, develop joint strategies
f. Monitor congressional websites of MSST, locate Representatives and Senators for information/press release/speeches/etc. on MSST issue
g. Monitor Navy Times/USCG Website/Homeland Security website and publications for MSST information/updates
h. Prepare package (Point Paper/Letters/Etc.) to mail/deliver to:
    1. Homeland Security Secretary Napolitano
    2. Under Secretary focused on Coast Guard
    3. Chairman of House and Senate Homeland Security Committees with copies to each committee member
i. Select/Prepare individuals for possible testimony to congressional committees

C. MSST Kings Bay compared to other MSST's: (*If one or more must close*):

a. Duty station of choice for USCG personnel assigned to MSSTs
b. Cost of living in Camden County vs other areas MSSTs are located
c. Proximity to NSB Kings Bay—advantages to CG personnel (exchange, medical, commissary, MWR, etc., Quality of Life issues)
d. Immediate back-up to MFPU mission if needed at NSB Kings Bay

e. Strategic location—not in major port, easily deployable, I-95 North-South corridor, I-10 East-West corridor, between 3 major Tier 1 Ports, Charleston, Savannah, Jacksonville and also close to Port of Brunswick
f. Modern facilities at St Marys—building, joint training opportunities with St Marys Police/Fire Departments
g. Closing New York and Kings Bay puts MSST's at extreme ends on East Coast—Miami and Boston
h. Training opportunities—Trident Training Facility, FLETC, local river systems, joint training with Navy and Marine Corps personnel, weapons ranges on base and at FLETC
i. Weather—no major direct hit from Hurricane in over 100 years.

On February 9, 2010, I went to DC to meet at Navy League Headquarters with Liz Drummond to prepare our agenda and discuss our upcoming legislative agenda with the Editor of *Seapower*, Amy Wittman and with Dale Lumme, the new executive director. In January 2011, Dale told me that the legislative affairs admiral asked that I be in attendance when the budget is released, and they give a report to Navy League on agenda items. He told Dale that our visits to Capitol Hill were the single most successful grassroots effort in the history of the Coast Guard. This meeting will probably be around the first of March; hopefully Dale will be able to arrange the briefing from the Navy and Marine Corps at the same time.

I knew it was necessary to put the entire "ask" for Congress on one sheet of paper. As I visited congressional offices, I didn't want to take a chance that it would be lost in a sea of papers. And short. It had to be short. It was simply. Facts only. Then I put it in a plastic sleeve. This way they couldn't misplace it. It would slide to the top every time! Of course, this was my hope.

I worked with former Commandant of the Coast Guard Admiral Jim Loy and former Atlantic Fleet Commander VADM Jim Hull. I wanted them to make sure I had no errors.

This was the result of the paper I took to DC. It was one sheet front and back:

Maintain the Current Level of Funding for the United States Coast Guard
By the Numbers

Military Personnel Reduced	*Cutters decommissioned without replacements*	*Where U.S. stands in the ranking of world-wide Coast Guards in the age of the fleet*
1,112	**3**	**Bottom 10%**

Number of military Services being reduced	*Age of some cutters in fleet*	*Percentage proposed*
1	**50 Years**	**2%**
		Percentage needed
		+4% to 6%

WHO DO WE CALL?

When the country needs federal agencies the most—the Coast Guard is the one we call. With the record responsiveness, our Coast Guard has provided our nation, why aren't we increasing rather than decreasing its budget?

Do we remember what happened on 9/11? The Coast Guard evacuated half a million people that day. Look at the agencies involved with Katrina. The Coast Guard arrived and restored order to the tragedy and saved 33,000 lives. This is equal to the number of lives usually saved in 6 years by the Coast Guard and it was accomplished in about 6 days. Of 12 major cutters assigned to Haitian relief efforts over January/February 2010 time frame, 10 suffered mission altering breakdowns and three were forced to return to port or dry dock with propeller or propeller-shaft problems. This is one-fourth of the Coast Guard's fleet of vessels of that size. The Ethos and Leadership of the Coast Guard allows them to stand up and be counted no matter the limits that have been placed on them by far too small budgets for far too many years. We are in the midst of a great national responsibility to support the military service that we call on in our darkest hours. That is why we appeal to you today.

The points we would like to emphasize are as follows:

1. Equitable consideration of all military services:

- The administration has proposed a federal spending freeze that does not include the Department of Defense (DoD). We believe this should apply to the United States Coast Guard as well, since as one of the five military services of the United States (by statue Title 14—Part 1—Military Service) its core mission is the protection and defense of our homeland.
- In May 2008, the Coast Guard ensured its integration with its fellow armed services by updates to the "1995 Memorandum of Understanding (MOU) on the Use

of Coast Guard Forces to Support the National Military Strategy." The Department of Defense (DoD), the Department of Homeland Security (DHS). The Chairman of the Joint Chiefs of Staff and the Commandant of the Coast Guard signed this updated MOU that identifies eight mission areas where the Coast Guard supports the Department of Defense.

- Coast Guard stations and MSSTs provide crews and small boats for security and escort missions including military outload operations that support DoD operations throughout the United States.
- The Coast Guard has multiple units that deploy globally to support combatant commander's military operations.

2. Recapitalization of critical Coast Guard Assets:

- The proposed budget will require a 1% reduction in operating expenses. However, a 4-6% increase is required simply to maintain current services.
- It will reduce acquisition, construction, and improvements (AC&I), the capitalization account, by 10%, thus delaying or effectively canceling the critical recapitalization program.
- The Coast Guard has just acquired its first new major cutters since the 1980's. The most capable cutters, the high endurance cutters, are almost 50 years old, 20 years beyond their design service life. Yet, the President's FY2011 budget proposal includes a 10% cut in the Coast Guard's recapitalization funds from FY2010.
- In order to keep the recapitalization of these ships on track, the President's Budget proposes to recover funds by decommissioning some of the high endurance cutters up to three years before their scheduled decommissioning dates. This will create an operational gap and reduce the security of the United States and our allies.
- The choice between operations and recapitalization is not well conceived. In fact, the Coast Guard must operate <u>and</u> recapitalize its assets to ensure our national security. One cannot be used to offset the other.

3. Maritime Safety and Security Teams:

- On February 2, 2010, the Coast Guard, in response to a budget reduction for FY11, stated they would decommission five of the 12 Maritime Safety and Security Teams (MSSTs). The MSSTs were established after the 9/11 terrorist attacks in response to heightened security levels. The current threat assessment is as high, if not higher, than when the teams were commissioned after the 9/11 attacks. Now is the wrong time to be reducing any anti-terrorism units. The number of MSSTs should remain at 12.

4. Jobs Bills:

- A net reduction of 1112 full-time military positions will be required. We believe this is the reason for the decommissioning of 5 MSSTs and 4 Hamilton Class WHECs, our 378' high endurance cutters, as well as taking 5 HH-65Cs out of service. The units are sorely needed to meet operational requirements but we all know the only way to get quick funding cuts is to cut people. So, the operational and support capability will suffer.
- There is an increase of 338 civilian full-time positions, but this still yields a net reduction of 774 military and civilian full-time positions. This reverses the current plan to increase end-strength.
- Military positions offer the best return on investment in personnel that this country has. Our military personnel are, by definition, on duty 24 hours a day 7 days a week. This is how they can rapidly respond to natural and man-made disasters. Yet, under this budget proposal, the Coast Guard will lose over 2% of its military workforce in one year... in addition to the corresponding much-needed operational capability.
- These are JOBS THAT MATTER.
- The Coast Guard is being cut at the same time the federal government is appropriating unthinkable amounts in jobs bills. Compared to the Jobs Bill this is a very small investment in not only jobs but JOBS for DEFENSE.

SUMMARY AND ACTION REQUIRED OF CONGRESS:

We request that the current level of services of the Coast Guard be maintained in the 2011 budget, adjusted for inflation. We also request there be a true augmentation of funds and no reapportionment of the already scarce funds are made. The Coast Guard cannot move forward without the planned command reorganization and that cannot be achieved without the statutory authority request in S.1194—the Senate Coast Guard authorization bill for fiscal 2010 and 2011 and the reconciliation with H.R. 3619. The future of our Coast Guard and the security of our nation depend on it.

Sheila M. McNeill
President, The Camden Partnership
Past National President
Navy League of the United States
With my phone number and email address
Source: Coast Guard Outlook 2010. Revised July 7, 2010

* * * * *

With The Camden Partnership taking the lead, we partnered with all local governments, the Chamber of Commerce, the Joint Development Authority, and the Navy League to begin a rigorous campaign. We mailed out 150 packages. These packages were to President Obama, the Secretary of Homeland Security Janet Napolitano and members of Congress in the House and Senate who have oversight of the Coast Guard. Copies were also sent to the Coast Guard as well as the Chairman of the Joint Chiefs.

These packages included a cover letter, position papers on maintaining the current level of funding for the U.S. Coast Guard, retaining the MSSTs and a letter from Governor Sonny Perdue, a joint resolution from the cities of Kingsland, St. Marys and Woodbine, the Camden County Board of Commissioners, and the Camden County Board of Education.

It also included a letter from the City of St. Marys, a joint letter from the Joint Development Authority and Chamber pointing out the fact that in comparison to the East Coast MSST missions not slated for decommissioning the economic impact is 9,000 percent greater than Boston and 8,000 percent greater than Miami—the location of the MSST units that would remain on the East Coast. We left no argument unturned! The Camden Kings Bay Navy League also had a letter pointing out the quality of life attributes of Camden County and the benefits our military friendly community offers. (Note: see the Coast Guard Community designation we received in 2015.)

We were able to get our letter into the hands of Secretary Napolitano. I was at a ceremony at the Federal Law Enforcement Training Center when Director Connie Patrick made sure Secretary Napolitano had her copy. It was amazing to watch as Secretary Napolitano sat next to Director Patrick on the stage she leaned over to Napolitano and pointed me out in the audience. I knew then she had delivered the letter!

On April 20, 2010, I had eight appointments in the first five hours of arriving. The paper covered all twelve units, Camden County and Georgia were never mentioned. I had a variety of reaction from my visits and brief but all of them were positive. They were all experts on the issue but found at least one item that I discussed to be a different slant on the issue: appropriations, transportation, Senate Committee on Commerce, science and transportation, Homeland Security, and others. I made sure I called on Rear Admiral Chuck Michel, a Coast Guard admiral who was the military advisor for the Secretary of Homeland Security. They all agreed it would be a fight but were impressed that someone would be passionate enough to make a visit to DC. I told them that "someone" was fifty thousand Navy League members. Each discussed various members and their likely response indicating there is still a big fight.

In late May through early June 2010, I was back in DC for two days on Capitol Hill, the Navy League meeting and a meeting with the Legislative Affairs Advisory Board that I chaired.

Admiral Bob Papp spoke at the final event of the National Navy League's Board meeting, a dinner on Friday night. After discussing the oil spill, he then said he wanted to speak on the budget. He stopped, turned to the near left toward me, bowed, and said, "Thank you Sheila and The Camden Partnership for all of your trips to Capitol Hill." I was so shocked at the mention of The Camden Partnership I almost missed the next couple of sentences, but he said if the funds are restored he would reinstate all budget items from the original submitted FY2011 budget.

Now at the beginning: The Navy League Maritime Policies were ready to be delivered to Capitol Hill, so I agreed to take the Rayburn Building for our congressmen and the Hart building for the Senators.

The Navy League had made the decision to only take the maritime policy to key legislators, but I stopped by all the offices. I tried to get in with the person who handles Coast Guard issues. Since Congress was in recess most key staffers were in the district and MLAs on CODELs on fact finding trips to military installations. I visited sixty-three offices in two full days and explained my purpose. Maritime policies went to about forty offices. There were a few who remembered me from my capitol hill days.

I attended a sea service panel luncheon where I escorted RADM Karl Schultz. Also present were RADM Miller, Navy OLA, a major general from the Marine Corps, and the acting administrator from the maritime administration.

I was present at the well-attended Coast Guard meeting where we had both a budget brief and an oil spill brief. I also briefed on our efforts to restore funding to the Coast Guard budget. I attended board meetings, legislative affairs meetings, a brief on the war, and the need to recapitalize the Marine Corps. It was a busy, satisfying week. This was the report to my board of directors at The Camden Partnership.

It is cheaper to retain than to recruit.

Report on efforts to restore Coast Guard budget:

1. **April 8:** My first visit to Capitol Hill where I saw staffers from the House Appropriations Committee as well as the House Homeland Security Committee and sat down with legislative Coast Guard officers.
2. **April 20:** I met with staffers from House Appropriations, Homeland Security, Senate Committee on Commerce, Science and Transportation and Senate Homeland Security, Appropriations. I also met with Senator Nelson's Chief of Staff and Secretary Napolitano's Military Advisory at his office at DHS, RADM. Michel
3. **April 20–25:** Chamber FLY IN where thirty-five to forty will take the message to DC.
4. Have a conference call with eighteen regions and another with all leadership of NL to plan the support of the NL. NP agreed for me to represent the national at all visits and correspondence.
5. **May 1–3:** SAS where I talked with about 40 defense companies and the GAO staffer who handles Coast Guard issues
6. **May 5:** The commissioning of the USCGC Waesche where I talked with contractors and Californian's eliciting their efforts with their congressmen and senators. I made arrangements for one couple to meet me at Feinstein's office. And another to meet me at the two NY senators' offices.
7. **May 17:** I met with project managers with VT Group across the country representing one hundred locations and asked them to e-mail their legislators.
8. Attended change of command for CG commandant and talked with them both and met with the two retired CG flags who are working with me as well as Admiral Loy.
9. Attended national NL meeting and spoke at length with many members. Met with members from NY and CA with their senate offices. Spent two days on Capitol Hill.
10. Eight trips since April 8 where I covered:

    All committees who have oversight
    General accounting office/Coast Guard
    Thirty to forty defense companies

Seventy-five to eighty Congressional offices
Constituents in CA, NY, LA
Our senators have sent three joint letters
Press release and op-ed from NL
Regular meetings with Coast Guard OLA
Former and current commandants
National Advisory Board

* * * * *

I was so appreciative of the national Navy League and the public affairs director Daisy Khalifa who worked with me and sent out the following press release:

OPINION

Coast Guard Is an Investment in Our Safety, Security

By Sheila M. McNeill

Advocates for the nation's sea services are sending out an "SOS" to save the U.S. Coast Guard—the nation's perennial first-responders to catastrophic events, including military, environmental and criminal activities on the high seas. The Coast Guard, a fifth branch of our U.S. military forces, is the only service that resides outside the Defense Department and the only federal agency with law enforcement authority in U.S. waters.

At issue is the proposed budget for fiscal 2011, which will result in an overall funding decrease of nearly 3 percent, a reduction of approximately 1,112 military personnel (in an agency of just more than 41,000 active-duty personnel) and retirement of five cutters, nine aircraft and five of the 12 90-person Marine Safety and Security Teams (MSSTs). The Homeland Security budget, in which the Administration has requested $43.6 billion for the Department of Homeland Security (DHS), is in mark-up for review and debate by members of Congress.

As of the end of June, a House panel approved a $44 billion fiscal 2011 spending bill for DHS, which, among other things, restores the proposed fiscal 2011 budget cuts to Coast Guard personnel and operations, providing $10.2 billion for the Coast Guard compared with the $9.9 billion sought by the Administration. Nonetheless, the debate continues, and regardless of the outcome, clearly more needs to be done to give the Coast Guard the tools it needs to execute its ever-increasing mission portfolio. The time is now for sea service advocates to rigorously canvass Capitol Hill and local districts, and implore lawmakers not to allow any proposed reductions to stand.

"Who do we call in our darkest hour?" Daniel B. Branch Jr., national president of the Arlington, Va.-based Navy League of the United States, said in a recent message to the organization's members. "Reductions such as these will likely result in reduced safety and security for the nation. For over two centuries, the U.S. Coast Guard has safeguarded the nation's maritime interests at home and around the globe. The failure of Congress to adequately fund replacement cutters has threatened the Coast Guard's vital mission of coastal protection and emergency response. Is our country providing the most they can to the Coast Guard?"

The United States has one of the most antiquated Coast Guard fleets in the world. The average age of the cutter fleet is 40 years. New Coast Guard Commandant Robert J. Papp Jr. told Navy League members at a dinner June 4 that the need for new ships is paramount. "I cannot emphasize enough we desperately the ships to replace 40-year-old ships that are literally falling apart," he said.

The Coast Guard is self-effacingly known within defense and military circles as something of a marvel for doing so much with so little—a valiant, if superhuman, agency that, time and again, delivers a lot of manpower and strategic skill on a shoestring. The public has simply come to expect the Coast Guard to be the agency first on the scene in the face of a major disaster, as was the case April 20 when Mobile Offshore Drilling Unit Deepwater Horizon exploded and caught fire 40 miles off the Coast of Venice, La.

Indeed, in less than 24 hours, it was the Coast Guard in charge, as Coast Guard Rear Admiral Mary Landry was named Federal On-Scene Coordinator. Within two days, the Coast Guard helped ensure the 15-agency emergency body known as the National Response Team was activated, and by May 1, Janet Napolitano, Secretary of the Department of Homeland Security, named newly-retired U.S. Coast Guard Commandant Thad Allen as National Incident Commander.

In July 2010, I was on Capitol Hill and visited with Senator McCain's military legislative fellow and had an hour with him. He called two of his colleagues to make sure they gave me sufficient time to discuss the issues. A couple were on the Homeland Security Committee.

I met with Congressman Jack Kingston, Jeff, his MLA fellow, and Norah Jones his senior policy advisor. Language on the house committee bill is still embargoed but they believe four of the five MSSTs will be restored and expect the report to come out any day. I asked Jack to be ready to add an amendment if full funding is not restored and got his commitment that this did not create an awkward position for him. He said it did not. I suggested he talk now with others who might support him since he thinks there will be a little time between the report on the subcommittee markup and the full committee report. Imagine! Me advising this very seasoned congressman. But he took it well, as usual!

These are frequent responses to my briefings: "Really?" I heard it every time I gave a new fact to staffers; "I guarantee the congressman/congresswoman/senator will support this!" "I wish we'd known this sooner—we didn't realize we were losing an MSST."

In total, I visited 210 congressional offices and every committee that had oversight over the Coast Guard. Marty Klumpp, who was a member of the board of directors, helped me by making appointments for the first visits. However, I found this was not going to work. Either I needed more time and had to leave for another appointment or finished the visit and had to waste valuable time waiting.

The Navy League had an intern in the office, Becca Ball. The Navy League gave permission for her to help me a couple of days. That made a big difference. On one visit, I kept getting comments from staffers who indicated a report from the appropriations homeland security subcommittee was going to come out later in the days. But that didn't happen.

Of the 210 visits, I was able to talk with *someone* in every office but five although I did have to go back a couple of times with a few of them. "May I talk with someone about our Coast Guard?" I asked. The Coast Guard had the respect of everyone and no one questioned why I wanted to meet or what the subject was they found me someone! I never asked for a specific staffer although before it was over many times others would join us. I have a few favorite stories: I waited in a filled reception area. After about ten minutes a woman came out of the door. It was obvious she was not an intern or a junior employee.

"First, I appreciate the Coast Guard, but you don't have an appointment. Look at those who have appointments that are waiting," she told me. "What if I could tell you in three minutes?" No answer but a look that told me no. "What if I could tell you in ninety seconds?" I asked. That got an answer: "If you can tell me in ninety seconds go for it right here." She answered as a dozen men watched as they sat and waited. I did it with the highlights and gave her the paper in the plastic sleeve. Simple compared to most of what she received. She paused, then said, "I'll read the paper. If what you are saying is true, I will recommend to the Senator that we work to eliminate this cut" (not sure if it was House or Senate). She smiled at those waiting in the reception area and went back to her office. They looked at each other and then to me as one said, "Lady, you have made our jobs so hard."

At one of the committees I briefed there was a nice looking young man who had many questions. He asked about each of the issues I was bringing to him but also had more questions. I enjoyed the talk with him and marveled at the different questions he had. He then said, "I'm sorry Ms. McNeill. I have to tell you I am active duty Coast Guard. I was just curious about how much you knew about the Coast Guard and how passionate you are. Thank you for that." Another committee staffer told me he had been with the committee for several years and that I was the first person to brief him that was not a government employee.

Only one in the 205 I talked with asked about my background. He recognized the accent. He was from Georgia but not working in a Georgia office. He had been to Kings Bay. He told me he was amazed by our community effort. But for the most part they were all busy but courteous and only having a no from five offices was remarkable. It is a testament to the respect that this country has for the Coast Guard.

A couple of weeks later Admiral Bob Papp was chosen to be the next commandant of the Coast Guard and was on Capitol Hill visiting members of the committees who had oversight over the Coast Guard before his confirmation hearing. "Sheila, everyone I have visited mentioned your visit and their determination to reinstate the three hundred million dollars. They didn't know your name or who you were with but they all had your paper and assured me of their support." That was remarkable.

We found on the February 15, 2011, that our efforts were successful. The president's FY2013 budget includes full funding of the Coast Guard, restoration of that three hundred million dollars, and scraped plans for closing the MSST, not only in St. Marys but in New York, New Orleans, and San Francisco. Anchorage was the only one not spared and was not in the original plans for the location of the MSSTs. This was the work of hundreds of hours of volunteer effort from many citizens in Camden County who truly care about our United States Coast Guard. Yes, the three hundred million dollars was restored and our Coast Guard Maritime Safety and Security Team is still home.

Coast Guard Lobbying Efforts Paid off

February 18, 2011

By Johna Strickland Rush

Tribune & Georgian Staff

A yearlong battle to maintain U.S. Coast Guard funding—and keep an 85 member in Camden County—ended with success this week. In his version of the Budget, President Barack Obama agreed to hold the Coast Guard at its 2020 allotment. Last year, the Coast Guard recommended disbanding five of the Safety and Security Teams, which were established at strategic locations after September 11, 2001. Threatened were teams stationed in St. Marys, San Francisco, New Orleans, New York and Anchorage, Alaska.

The Kings Bay team performs port security, harbor defense missions, maritime law enforcement while supporting the military and detecting weapons of mass destruction and explosives. In February, Camden County leaders and military advocates began lobbying to retain the security team. Letters were sent to President Obama and secretary of Homeland Security Janet Napolitano, Georgia U.S. Senators Johnny Isakson and Saxby Chambliss and U.S. Rep Jack Kingston dispatched the missives to the leaders of the Senate Appropriations Committee.

"We start fighting. This is a national security issue that really impacts our community," Sheila McNeill, a past national president of the Navy League and president of the community-military group The Camden Partnership, said in July. McNeill, who made nine trips to Washington, D.C., to visit 194 congressional offices and meet with senior staff on each committee with oversight on the Coast Guard, heard the news on Tuesday, her birthday. "That's the best birthday present I've ever had," she said. "It was just such a good day… You do feel good that this county had an impact on the entire Coast Guard Budget." The Camden Partnership spent about $14,000 on the effort and the City of St. Marys paid $1,500 for one trip. The investment ensures the community will continue to benefit from the unit's $8.6 million economic impact and St. Marys will receive more than $200,000 annually from the Coast Guard to rent a portion of its police department building. St. Marys Mayor Bill DeLoughy did not return a call seeking comment by press time.

While leaders wanted to keep the unit at Kings Bay (Camden), they advocated for the "whole picture" of the Coast Guard missions, McNeill said. "As a community that made a decision a long time ago to support our military and to always support what is best for our country and for our national security, we went with the message that the entire Coast Guard budget be reinstated and with that our own MSST," McNeill wrote in an e-email this week.

Navy League members from New York and California met McNeill in Washington sometimes and they talked to congressmen together. "It wasn't just this one woman from Georgia doing this, McNeill said, adding Marty Klumpp and Keith Post helped the cause by organizing the visit schedule and writing letters. "I cannot believe it is over."

With the culmination of a yearlong petition, members of The Camden Partnership are preparing for the Washington Fly-In and other fights.

"There will be something else that we need," McNeill said. "Camden County will need to increase the missions for Kings Bay. There will be enough to keep us fighting the fight."

Federal funding restored for St. Marys Coast Guard unit
St. Marys Coast Guard escapes axe
Obama's budget proposal puts money back in for security base
By Teresa Stepzinski, The Florida Times Union
February 16, 2011

The Coast Guard's Maritime Safety and Security Team in St. Marys will remain afloat with the restoration of federal funding for the specialized 85-member unit in President Barack Obama's budget. In addition to St. Marys, funding also has been restored to the maritime safety and security teams in New York, New Orleans and San Francisco, said Sheila McNeill, president of The Camden Partnership, a nonprofit military and community advocacy group. Camden County community groups and elected officials welcomed the funding restoration, which U.S. Sen. Saxby Chambliss, R-Ga., announced Tuesday. McNeill, with the support of individuals, businesses and community groups, had visited 194 congressional offices with the mission of saving the Coast Guard's budget from the axe. Restoration of the maritime safety units is a major victory for the entire community, said McNeill, a former national Navy League president. "Besides an annual economic impact of $8.6 million to Camden County, this means 85 members of the MSST team and their families can stay in Camden County where we appreciate them," McNeill told The Times-Union.

Tuesday was her birthday, and McNeill said the news that the teams won't be decommissioned was the best present she could have received. "I'm so excited... so proud for the Coast Guard, for the country, for St. Marys and for Camden County," McNeill said. St. Marys Mayor Bill DeLoughy echoed McNeill's sentiments. The Coast Guard pays more than $231,000 a year in rent to the city to share a large building with the St. Marys Police Department. The team plays a vital role in national security, and the protection of Kings Bay

Naval Submarine Base. In addition, Coast Guard personnel and their families are also good neighbors, active in many community and civic organizations, DeLoughy said. "They are good folks to have around... They are important to us and important to Kings Bay," DeLoughy said.

Formed in response to the Sept. 11, 2001, terrorist attacks, each unit has three teams trained as demolition experts, marksmen and canine teams. Each unit has six boats capable of deployment anywhere in the country within 12 hours.

In 2006, the team in St. Marys received the Coast Guard Unit Commendation for providing security at the 2004 G-8 Summit at Sea Island, the Republican National Convention later that year and the presidential inauguration in Washington in 2005. Over the past several months, Chambliss and fellow Georgia Republicans U.S. Sen. Johnny Isakson and U.S. Rep. Jack Kingston have registered with Secretary Janet Napolitano of the U.S. Department of Homeland Security and former U.S. Coast Guard Commandant Adm. Thad Allen their "strong opposition" to proposed budget cuts targeting the St. Marys team and four others nationwide.

The lawmakers also called for the restoration of the funding. Their efforts and those of Camden County community leaders paid off. "Given the critical nature of the team's missions and the capabilities it provides for the Department of Homeland Security, its decommissioning would have been imprudent," Chambliss said in a statement announcing the funding restoration. Decommissioning the teams would have dealt a serious blow to national security, Kingston said. "From Kings Bay to Mayport and the ports from Charleston to Jacksonville, they cover a region of growing economic and strategic importance to our nation," Kingston said. "I appreciate the administration's recognition that these teams are critically important to the safety and security of our region... That said, no state and no district can be immune to cuts necessary to face our fiscal reality and I look forward to working with the administration to find common sense savings elsewhere," Kingston said.

The *Tribune & Georgian* had an editorial on Friday February 18, 2001:

MSST will stay in Camden

The recovery of federal funding for the Maritime Safety and Security Team (MSST) located in Camden County is a great success story for our community. One Coast Guard official said it was one of the most successful grassroots campaigns in their history. It not only saves our team, but similar ones in California, Louisiana, Alaska and New York. Which had been slated to be decommissioned. The team in Camden County protects our coast and gives us an added layer of protection from those who would target Kings Bay, Mayport and critical ports all along the Atlantic seaboard. Fighting the tide of federal budget cutbacks is near to impossible for small communities like ours and victories such as this are indeed rare. The effort was spearheaded by Sheila McNeill, a St. Marys businesswoman who has built deep friendships and alliances in federal and military circles. She is past national president of the Navy League and a founder of a local military-community advocacy group, The Camden Partnership.

Although she does not live in Camden County she has done far more than the average citizen in promoting our community as well as the entire South Georgia and North Florida region. We owe a debt of gratitude for the price she and her Navy League brethren have paid on our behalf. We should also applaud our local government officials who adopted resolutions on saving the MSST and supported efforts to make our case with key decision makers. Voices from our community enlisted the help of our governor and congressmen, who also wrote letters of support.

Much can be accomplished with all oars rowing in the same direction.

So we survived the budget and later celebrated our tenth anniversary.

MSST91108 10TH ANNIVERSARY CELEBRATION

FRIDAY, OCTOBER 4, 2013

Keith Post, St. Marys City Councilman, was Master of Ceremonies and remarks were made by Mayor William Deloughy, City of St. Marys, David Burch, President, Camden-Kings Bay Navy League, LCDR Matt Baer, USCG Commanding Officer, MSST and me! Volume One from Camden County High School sang the National Anthem and later Semper Paratus and Lt. Len Driskell, Sector Charleston Chaplain gave the benediction. The Executive Officer was LCDR Ron Nakamoto, Operations Officer, Lt. Sal Shelton and Command Senior Chief was MKCS Curt Urani. They were a great team to work with!

My remarks:

Captain Allen, Commander Baer, Lt. Commander Nakamoto, Sr. Chief Urani, thanks for having us today! CDR Steve Love and his Executive Officer Tom Evans from the Maritime Force Protection Unit. Thank you to our submarine base Executive Officer Ed Callahan and his very talented wife Krista. Chairman Chip Keene Mayor Bill Deloughy, Mayor Kenneth Smith, Mayor Steve Parrott, Mayor Pro Tem St. Marys John Morrissey, Councilwoman Nancy Stasnis, Sidney Howell and Keith Post, Superintendent of Schools Dr. Will Hardin, Leslie Hamrick, executive director of the Chamber of Commerce, Director College of Coastal Georgia Holly Christensen, Dave Reilly, National VP, NLUS Some of you were present in 2003 and heard these words:

"The Maritime Safety and Security Teams were established to bolster the Coast Guard's ability to protect this country's shores from any threats and to respond to specific episodic events requiring an increased security posture for a limited duration. They are capable of deploying personnel and equipment on short notice via air or ground. 91108 will also exercise security contingency plans in major ports and augment Coast Guard and Captain of the Port capabilities in Georgia and Florida. Today promises to be a memorable day."

These words were spoken by VADM Jim Hull on September 2, 2003. Camden County heard those words with a great deal of pride. That pride has increased. For those of you who may not know 911 is for the day the world trade center was attacked and 08 is the 8th unit commissioned. The Coast Guard evacuated over 2,000 people that day and the Maritime Safety and Security Teams were created as a result of that horrific terrorist attack. Several years ago, when these units were announced we asked, advocated for a unit in Camden County. We wanted the MSST in Camden County. We were thrilled when we received the call that MSST 01108 would be located in St. Marys, we were thrilled when the announcement came out that brought to our community a great group of 85 professionally trained men and women. And today as we celebrate a decade and hundreds of our Coast Guardsmen and women and their families who have lived in our community, taken their children to our schools, attended our churches and have made such an impact in our community.

We have worked and made friends with tremendous commanding officers: Bill Mitchell, Paul Murphy, Doug Stark and now Matt Baer and former Executive Officer Dan Deptula and LT CK Moore—each contributing to this community in various ways. The Coast Guard will always supply our Homeland Security. And these men and women bring a spirit of professionalism, pride and community involvement that enriches our lives.

On February 2, 2010, we had quite a shock when we were told that this unit would be decommissioned. Keith Post and I were invited to sit in on an announcement from an admiral from headquarters. It was a stunning announcement. MSST 91108 was being decommissioned. We quickly went to D.C. to find out why this was happening. We found that the Coast Guard in response to a budget reduction for FY11 stated they would decommission five of the 12 Maritime Safety and Security teams. Teams that were established after the 9/11 terrorist attacks in response to heightened security levels.

The current threat assessment is a constant concern. This was the wrong time to be reducing five of these anti-terror units. The number of MSSTs should remain at 12 we said. And that was not all. A new reduction of 1112 full time Coast Guard position would be eliminated, the Coast Guard's operating expenses would be reduced, 3 cutters would be decommissioned without replacement. We went to work writing everyone from President Obama, the Secretary of Homeland Security, our legislators and everyone in between. Our state House and Senate as well as all of our cities and counties entire bodies voted in proclamations in support of the entire Coast Guard Budget—not just our MSST 91108.

We went to Washington and called on every committee that had oversight over the Coast Guard and 210 congressional offices. We found that there is a deep respect for our Coast Guard. 205 of the 210 offices sat down with us when they were told that we were there to talk about the United State Coast Guard. We told them what was happening. We also told them that in addition to the operational and support capability that would suffer, the reduction in Coast Guard positions were a mistake. These military positions offer the best return on investment in personnel that this country has. Our military personnel are, by definition, on duty 24 hours a day 7 day a week. This is how they can rapidly respond to national and man-made disasters. These are jobs that matter. We requested the same level of service of the Coast Guard be maintained in the 2011 budget, and that there be a true augmentation of funds and no reapportionment of the already scarce funds be made. The future of our Coast Guard and the security of our nation depend on it. And it worked!

The entire Coast Guard budget was reinstated. I know exactly when that happened. There were lots of phone calls from D.C. The current commandant, Admiral Bob Papp, had called the week before as he was visiting congressional office prior to his confirmation. He said that EVERY office he visited mentioned the visit they had had. They didn't remember who visited or who they represented but the senators and congressmen had the paper and assured the incoming commandant that they were supportive of the request to reinstate the $300 Million to the Coast Guard and they did. I once ran into an older woman (probably my age) after the announcement that this unit would be saved, and she told me all about her encounters with the Coast Guard personnel. "They are so well behaved—such nice ladies and gentlemen. We really should give them a party." Well it took us a few months—that was in 2012—and that makes it even sweeter. We are having our party and we are doing it to celebrate 10 years of relationship with this fine unit.

In closing I will quote the beginning of an editorial that appeared in the Tribune & Georgian the week of the commissioning of this unit*: Camden County will create a warm and supportive environment for the Coast Guard to flourish as they set out to fulfill their mission.*

We hope we have been able to do that.

UNITED STATES COAST GUARD CUTTER *SEA DOG* (WPB 87373)

The *Sea Dog* was commissioned on July 2, 2009. This was one of the ships required due to the new Maritime Force Protection Unit at Kings Bay. Keith Post worked with the local and national Coast Guard on the ceremony. We were all excited that our own Julianne Chambliss, wife of Senator Saxby Chambliss, would be the sponsor of the ship and Senator Chambliss the keynote speaker. I was pleased to give her a little advice on being a Coast Guard ship sponsor. Commander Joe Raymond, commanding officer of the Maritime Force Protection Unit introduced Rear Admiral

Steve Branham, Commander, Seventh Coast Guard District. And the commanding officer of the *Sea Dog*, Chief Warrant Officer Tyrone Tillette spoke at the ceremony. My contribution was to enlist Jack Davis, famed illustrator to work with the Coast Guard on a "Coast Guard bulldog" atop the *Sea Dragon*. It was beautiful!

The *Tribune & Georgian* reported the upcoming event:

Sea Dog arrives at Kings Bay

By Susan Respess

The U.S. Coast Guard's Maritime Force Protection Unit at Kings Bay Naval Submarine Base gained its second cutter Monday with the arrival of the Sea Dog. The 87-ft coastal patrol boat has a crew of 10 and is commanded by Chief Warrant Officer Tyrone Tillette, The Sea Dog and its sister ship, the USCGC Sea Dragan, which was commissioned in January 2008, provide security for Kings Bay's submarine fleet as it transits in and out of the base.

Keith Post, a Kings Bay Navy veteran who grew up at Coast Guard stations and bases throughout the nation as the son of a Coast Guard master chief, said he's personally thrilled to see Coast Guard men and women join with Navy and Marine Corps personnel in the Kings Bay area. "They are now an integral part of the missions at Kings Bay, supporting and protecting our nation's deterrent force, as well as other missions they are called on to perform," said Post who also is president of the Camden-Kings Bay Navy League.

"The Navy League is looking forward to joining with the entire community in welcoming the crew of the newest cutter to call Kings Bay home," Post said. The cutter will be commissioned in a ceremony July 2 at the base, and the Navy League is sponsoring a reception after the ceremony. "We love having them here," Christine Daniel said of the new cutter and crew. Daniel is president and chief executive officer of the Camden County Chamber of Commerce. "When we met with the Coast Guard in Washington, D.C., during our annual Fly-in, one of the Coastguardsmen told us "Kings Bay is one of the choice places to go, everyone loves it down there."

Sheila McNeill, past national president of the Navy League of the United States said she feel a special connection to the Coast Guard personnel and was the sponsor of the USCGC Sea Horse, which she visited last week in Norfolk, Va. "It is just great to see our Coast Guard grow in Camden County," McNeill said.

"For years, we in the Navy League have supported the sea services and have talked of the 14 legislatively mandated missions of the Coast Guard. Now with the Coast Guard's transfer from the Department of Transportation to the Department of Homeland Security; and with the nation's emphasis on antiterrorism and the security of homeland, the Coast Guard has further increased their mission by two and both are in Camden County. In addition to Trident submarine escort protection, the Coast Guard also operates a Maritime Safety and Security Team at Kings Bay. "They are a very elite unit, like the SEALS of the Navy and are deployed much of the time," McNeill said.

The protection unit, led by Cmdr. Joe Raymond, quickly became a part of the fabric of the base attending Navy League meetings, the annual submarine ball and changes of command events, McNeill said. During the Sea Dog's commissioning ceremony, everyone will be in for a treat when they see the design St. Simons artist Jack Davis has done for the new cutter, McNeill said. Though a sea dog is a marine mammal, the cutter Sea Dog art by Davis likely will have a University of Bulldog flavor.

U.S. Senator Saxby Chambliss (R-Ga) and his wife, Julianne Chambliss, the Sea Dog's sponsor, are expected to speak at the commissioning. Rear Admiral Steve Branham, Commander of the Seventh Coast Guard District will preside over the event that marks the formal establishment of the new cutter.

Susan Respess's report after the event:

Veterans' sponsor welcome Sea Dog

This Georgia Bulldog's spiked collar is U.S. Coast Guard orange, but nobody's complaining about the logo, for Kings Bay's newest cutter, the USCG Sea Dog, commissioned into the fleet yesterday. St. Simons Island artist Jack Davis designed a ferocious dog wielding a shield and a trident to protect submarine as part of the Coast Guard's Maritime Force Protection Unit at Kings Bay Naval Submarine Base. The cutter's sponsor, Julianne Chambliss, and her husband U.S. Senator Saxby Chambliss (R-Moultrie) are both University of Georgia graduates and avowed Bulldogs. "When I saw the log, I knew the Bulldogs would lead on and we were bound to have a good relationship," Saxby Chambliss said of the new cutter. "As you will learn, there is always room in Georgia for another bulldog." Even Rear Admiral. Steve Branham, commander of the Seventh Coast Guard District and the guest speaker, got into the bulldog spirit.

UNITED STATES COAST GUARD NATIONAL SECURITY CUTTER STRATTON (WMSL 752)

I left early Wednesday, March 28, 2012, for California for the USCG National Security Cutter Dorothy Stratton commissioning. I had e-mailed my friends Jeanne and Bill Sharkey to find out if I could stay with them as I had done the past two commissionings. I had attended the commissionings for the USGC Cutter Bertolf (WMSL 750) and the USCG Cutter Waesche (WMSL 751) and I didn't want to miss this one. They agreed. I arrived at four thirty and was on board the Stratton by five thirty for a reception.

Compared to the Hamilton-class 378s they are replacing, the 418-foot NSC design provides higher sustained transit speeds, greater endurance and range, an improved ability to launch and recover small boats, helicopters and drones, and advanced secure command, control, communications, computers, intelligence, surveillance, and reconnaissance systems (C4ISR) and ability to handle sensitive information. They are an awesome ship. The Navy League had been advocating funding for this new ship.

Barbara Price, the chairman of the commissioning introduced me that first evening and that gave me a wonderful opportunity to have small meetings and discussions with a number of people. One of the best discussions was with Phillip. I believe I spent more time with him than anyone I've ever met at a reception. Usually I'm concerned with mingling and meeting and talking with as many as I can. Since I had been with many of the attendees over several days I felt less responsibility to work the room so I talked with him a long time about the Coast Guard recapitalization, the future of ship building, and our mutual support and respect for all things Coast Guard.

After we had talked a while he told me he was the chief designer for the Hamilton class. Imagine my surprise. He told me they had done it right and there were "almost no flaws." I asked him a lot of questions and we discussed the challenges of the Coast Guard. He stopped as we were talking and said, "You are a smart lady-how do you know all this? I told him a little about my background but continued to encourage his comments. Later I was talking with Rear Admiral Chris Colvin and told him how impressed I was with my new friend and chief designer, Phillip. I never did get his last name. He agreed with me but also told me to ask him about the expansion joints in the hull house. "During the first sea trials, the hull house completely blew off the ship due to the lack of expansion joints." He told me. (There may have been a little exaggeration here to enhance the story.)

I had seen Phillip leaving the ship, so I hurried over, looked down, and saw him departing on the gangplank. I yelled, "Hey, Phillip, what about those expansion joints?"

"Yes, that was the one problem we had!" he called back with a big smile.

The namesake of the ship was Dorothy Stratton, who was the first chief of the SPARS, the first woman to join the Coast Guard. It was a wonderful celebration with about twenty women who ranged in age from forty to eighty-five. Retired VADM Jody Breckenridge was chair of that great group and the Coast Guard did them proud with several events including a very nice afternoon tea. I enjoyed hearing the stories and meeting the women who broke that ceiling in service to our country. Vice Admiral Manson K. Brown was serving his last few weeks as Pacific area commander to return to headquarters to serve as deputy commandant. All of them were very nice to me and after three days of events all were treating me like family

When Vice Admiral (VADM) Sally Brice O'Hara came, it was a big hug and her aide Commander Weaver gave me heads up on the admiral's upcoming retirement and said I was on the list and would receive the invite shortly. I have known Sally for a number of years. She was the district commander in DC when I was national president of the Navy League. In a rare opportunity, Arlie joined me the day we met with her for a briefing. She arranged for us both to ride one of the small boats for a nice ride on the Potomac. She did an amazing job with the remarks honoring the SPARS that evening. Her remarks were both interesting and informative. I had known Sally for years and always seemed to be visiting a unit she owned. She was a very savvy woman who had the ear of the past three commandants. She and Vice Admiral Vivien Crea are the only female three stars ever in the Coast Guard.

The biggest event—other than the commissioning was the Friday night event. I was standing alone for a moment and Linda Papp came up, hugging me and saying in thirty years of military they had never had anything like what Camden County did for them. (I'm sure she has to give similar compliments to everyone but that just made my day!) If you want to know what Linda was referring to, you'll find them in the stories section under Admiral and Mrs. Papp.

President of the Navy League, Phil Dunmire, introduced me that night as the person who almost single handedly restored the Coast Guard budget. I'm glad that Rear Admiral Karl Schultz was not there that evening—although he said almost the same thing. The day of the commissioning it was storming. I was seated with Jeanne and Bill in the VVIP section. We were in the second row, which gave the sheets of rain plenty of room to hit us. While we could have stayed indoors and watched it by remote we did not want to appear rude by not sitting in the audience before the first lady, Michele Obama who was the sponsor. Every time we stood the rain filled our seats. We were all wearing plastic raincoats, but they didn't do much good.

Mrs. Obama had another event, so she asked that the ceremony be a shorter so others on the platform were not able to speak and the soloist was not able to sing. How sad after all the months of preparation. The weather was so bad that as the command master chief escorted the First Lady off the ship the umbrella reversed itself and she was hit with rain until they could repair it. It was an interesting time. Thank goodness for a ball cap as we left that event and went to one last reception honoring our national president, Phil Dunmire, and given at the home of Sam Sause with the local council of the Navy League.

UNITED STATES NAVAL SHIP BRUNSWICK

JOINT HIGH-SPEED VESSEL (JHSV)

We were all surprised to learn of a new ship that was named after our city. I was especially pleased when I realized it was a class of ships that I advocated for when I was vice president of the Navy League for legislative affairs—a joint high-speed vessel.

The sponsor of the ship was Secretary of the Navy Ray Mabus's scheduler, Mrs. Alma Bootebaugh. I contacted Woody Woodside, executive director of the Brunswick—Golden Isles Chamber of Commerce to discuss with him the possibility of the chamber heading up activities we might have for the USNS *Brunswick*. He liked the idea and assured me the chamber would execute any events but asked me to take the chair. Knowing I live in Brunswick and work in Camden he understood that my time in Brunswick would be limited. I shouldn't have worried, they did a wonderful job.

I found the Military Sealift Command's contact information and we sent the following request:

> October 31, 2014
> Dear RADM Shannon,
>
> We are honored to have one of the country's new Joint High-Speed Vessels named after the City of Brunswick! Brunswick Georgia has a strong history of support for our defense as we built 99 Liberty Ship in Brunswick during WWII and are now home to the USCG Station Brunswick. Our community leadership is excited to welcome our namesake ship and would like to extend an invitation to the ship to visit our city on the way to her new homeport on the East Coast.
>
> We would like to suggest the following schedule:

- A two day visit by the USNS *Brunswick*—preferable on a weekend.
- A welcome celebration with a formal ceremony and reception, our own version of a small commissioning! We would have a formal program and perhaps a coin for our supporters.
- Events and opportunities for the officers, crew and families.
- Depending on the number of crew who will be off duty we could have a night's stay on our beautiful island for many of them as well as golf at one of our many golf courses and meals around Glynn County.

Several of our leadership would like to attend the christening in Mobile, Alabama. Please let us know if this is possible and a tentative date for that event. Once our visit is accepted—and we do hope it is—we will make detailed plans and send them to your designee for approval.

We look forward to working with you on this exciting project.

Sincerely,
Sheila McNeill
Chairman

M.H. "Woody" Woodside
President, Brunswick Golden Isles Chamber of Commerce
Cornell Harvey, Mayor—City of Brunswick
Mike Browning, Chairman Glynn County Commission
Britt Elrod President, Golden Isles Council, Navy League of the US
Bill Dawson General Manager, Georgia Port Authority
Dave Olender Chairman, Veterans Council of the Golden Isles

I was pleased to receive the following e-mail:

From: Aadnesen, Alicia L CIV NAVSEA TEAM SHIPS
Sent: Thursday, November 13, 2014 7:25
To: The Camden Partnership
Subject: Keel Laying of the Future USNS BRUNSWICK (JHSV 6)

Dear Mrs. McNeill, I hope this e-mail reaches you! My name is Alicia Aadnesen and I work for the Navy's Program Executive Office for Ships, the organization responsible for the design and con-

struction of the future United States Naval Ship BRUNSWICK, our nation's sixth Joint High-Speed Vessel. The ship is being built for the Navy by Austal USA in Mobile, Alabama.

I understand from Rear Admiral Reilly that, in addition to your longstanding (and selfless) service to the sea services through the Navy League, you also have a very special connection with the city of Brunswick and I wanted to reach out to make you aware of an upcoming milestone in the life of the ship, the keel laying. This event marks the joining together of the first major modules of the ship—signifying the point where the ship begins to take true form. The milestone will be celebrated with a modest ceremony in Mobile, Alabama on the 2nd of December. This is a very small and informal event, which will be followed next spring by a much larger and more significant ceremony, the christening.

We would certainly like to invite you and any other individuals that you deem appropriate to attend the keel laying on 2 December. Invitations will be going out electronically within the next few days, so if you could please provide the best e-mail address for yourself and any others you would like me to include, I would appreciate it. Thank you so much for your time and please don't hesitate to let me know if you have any questions at all.

Very sincerely, Alicia Aadnesen, Ship Introduction Specialist, Program Executive Office Ships

And a few days later:

From: Aadnesen, Alicia L CIV NAVSEA TEAM SHIPS
To: Sheila McNeill
Sent: Tuesday, November 25, 2014 11:20 AM
Subject: RE: BRUNSWICK (JHSV 6) Keel Laying Ceremony, 2 December 2014

Ms. McNeill, Austal has also asked for me to check with you to see if you would be interested in making brief remarks (3-5 minutes) at the keel laying ceremony. This is 100 percent optional, but they would love to hear from you if you would like to. We are looking forward to meeting you in the very near future.

Very sincerely, Alicia

Of course I agreed to speak.

Arlie and I were excited to be able to attend the Keel Laying. We met the commanding officer of the ship, Master (Captain) Jason Ivey as well as Charles Gray the chief engineer and Victor Martino the chief mate. Within one afternoon, we felt like I had known them forever. They made our visit memorable. These were my remarks at the ceremony of the USNS *Brunswick* Keel Laying:

> *Who could have imagined back in 2001 when I had the responsibility for our national legislative affairs programs in the Navy League and was advocating on Capitol Hill for our military to have its own JHSV (not a leased one—but owned by the military) that I would be here today?*
>
> *Who would have imagined when my husband was committee chair to build a replica of the ninety-nine Liberty ships build in Brunswick during WWII that I would be here today? This monument is the only one of its kind on the East Coast. Now Brunswick will have a traveling monument called USNS Brunswick.*
>
> *By 1942, German U-boats had already destroyed more than five hundred million tons of Allied shipping. Later that year in reacting to the critical shortage of cargo ships needed to keep the Allied war effort going, the US Maritime Commission chose sixteen sites, including Brunswick, Georgia, to build the aptly named Liberty ships. Ninety-nine ships were built at the Brunswick shipyard between 1943 and 1945.*

During this time, our small town of Brunswick was only fourteen thousand citizens and within less than a year's time it jumped to seventy thousand due to work in the shipyard. You can imagine the impact that this made on Brunswick and their sense of pride and patriotism for the war effort. One of those workers was my father who later joined the Army. Brunswick was also the home of Naval Air Station Brunswick until its closure in 1974.

We are pleased and excited to have a ship named after Brunswick. These ships are incredible assets to our Army, Navy, and Marine Corps. They will enhance our forward presence and our global security by quickly transporting a huge array of supplies and equipment throughout the world. What flexibility these ships will give our services.

Thank you to the men and women who have built this wonderful ship. Thank you for your excellent workmanship. The lives of our mariners depend on your work. A productive and economic industrial base is essential to the safety and defense of our country.

This is indeed a special day for Brunswick, Georgia, and for our county. Brunswick and its surrounding communities look forward to having Captain James Ivey and his crew for a visit. We understand the responsibility of the connection between a ship and its namesake. We look forward to many, many years of support. The mayor and city of

Brunswick, the county of Glynn, our Chamber of Commerce, our Navy League, our port authority, our Coast Guard station, the veterans' council, and more plan quite an event in Brunswick for our officers and crew so everyone please join us. And thank you for giving this native Brunswick girl a chance to express our pride in the USNS Brunswick and the US Flagged Merchant Marine.

On December 15, the Keel Laying was covered by the *Islander Newspaper*:

Future USNS Brunswick authenticated

Mobile, Ala. (NNS)—the keel of the future USNS Brunswick (JHSV 6) was authenticated at the Austal U.S.A. shipyard in Mobile Alabama, Dec. 2. Longtime civil servant and ship sponsor Alma B. Bootebaugh served as the keel authenticator, etching her initials into the keel plate to verify that the ship's keel was "truly and fairly" laid.

"The Navy is excited about the capabilities this ship will provide to the Navy. The program is benefitting greatly from serial productions and we look forward to delivering this ship less than a year from now" said Capt. Henry Stevens, Strategic and Theater Sealift program manager.

Joint High-Speed Vessels are versatile, non-combatant vessels designed to operate in shallow-draft ports and waterways, increasing operational flexibility for a wide range of activities including maneuver and sustainment, relief operations in small or damaged ports, flexible logistics support, or as the key enabler for rapid transport. They will be capable of interfacing with roll-on/roll off discharge facilities, as well as on/off loading a combat-loaded Abrams Main Battle Tank (MIA2).

JHSV 6 was named for Brunswick, Georgia in April 2013 by Secretary of the Navy Ray Mabus to honor the values and men and women of the city as well as the state. Brunswick is one of the three JHSVs currently under construction at Austal and is scheduled to deliver in late 2015.

It was a busy few days with the Ceremonial Mast Stepping on Friday, May 8. The christening was on May 9. Friday evening was the sponsor's dinner and Captain Ivey used one of my coins in the ceremony. There was a distinguished visitors' assembly and platform briefings at eight thirty with the ceremony at ten and a reception after the ceremony. Several from Brunswick attended:

Glynn County Commissioner, Bob Coleman, and his wife, Sherry

David Boland with the Golden Isles Council of the Navy League
Arlie McNeill with the Golden Isles Council of the Navy League
I representing USNS *Brunswick* Committee and The Camden Partnership

Mayor Harvey and I presented the newly minted USNS *Brunswick* coins to each of the officials as well as the ship's crew. The program had the following dignitaries:

Mr. Craig Perciavalle, President, Austal USA
Mr. Michael Eagan, Vice President and General Manager
Rear Admiral Thomas K. Shannon, USN, Commander, Military Sealift Command
Vice Admiral Robin R. Braun, USN, Chief of Navy Reserve
The Honorable Cornell Harvey, Mayor of Brunswick, Georgia
Principal Address, the Honorable Ray Mabus, Secretary of the Navy
Sponsor's Address, Mrs. Alma B. Booterbaugh
Invocation, Lieutenant Joseph Johnson, CHC, USN, Naval Construction Training Center Gulfport
Christening, Mrs. Alma B. Booterbaugh

Platform participants were as follows:

Mr. Frederick J. Stefany III, executive director, Amphibious and Auxiliary Sealift Office, Program Executive Office, Ships
Captain Henry W. Stevens III, USN, Strategic Theater and Sealift Program Manager (PMS 385), Program Executive office, Ships
Captain Jason Ivey, USMM, Ship's Master, BRUNSWICK (JHSV 6)
Mr. Chuck Batten, Deputy Supervisor of Shipbuilding Gulf Coast
Mr. Dave Growden, Director of JHSV Programs, Austal USA
Lieutenant Joseph Johnson, CHC, USN, Chaplain, Naval Construction Training Center Gulfport
Flower Girl, Miss Devon Rae Bauer, Daughter of Matt Bauer, Austal USA Associate General Counsel
Color Guard: Navy Junior ROTC, Pascagoula High School, Pascagoula, Mississippi
Band: Murphy High School Band, Mobile, Alabama

After the Program Master Captain Susan Orsini, Commanding Officer USNS *Trenton* JHSV gave us a tour of her ship.
The news article:

Austal christens USNS Brunswick

Posted: May 09, 2015 4:04 PM EDT Updated: May 09, 2015 4:08 PM EDT

AUSTAL—Austal celebrated the christening of *USNS Brunswick* (JHSV 6) with a ceremony this morning at its state-of-the-art shipyard in Mobile, Ala. *USNS Brunswick* is the sixth of ten Joint High-Speed Vessels (JHSV) that Austal has under contract with the U.S. Navy as part of an overall 10-ship block-buy contract worth over $1.6 billion.

JHSV 6, a 338-foot shallow draft aluminium catamaran, is a multi-mission, non-combatant transport vessel characterized by its high volume, high speed, and flexibility. It is the fourth ship to be named *Brunswick* after the seaport city located on the southeast coast of Georgia. The city of Brunswick played an important role during World War II as the site of a 435-acre shipyard that employed up to 16,000 workers at its peak. The yard produced 99 Liberty ships by the end of the war. "Brunswick displays American values of community, hospitality and resourcefulness at their very best," said Secretary of the Navy Ray Mabus. "I chose to name the Joint High-Speed Vessel after Brunswick to honour those values and the men and women of the city, as well as the state of Georgia. "Brunswick is the result of the successful industry/DOD partnership that has developed between Austal USA, Military Sealift Command, and the Navy," said Craig Perciavalle, president of Austal USA. "We're very excited about how stable and mature the JHSV program has become as we prepare JHSV 6 for trials and delivery in the fall." *Brunswick* will soon join her sister JHSV's that have been delivered over the last two-and-a-half years including *USNS Spearhead* (JHSV 1) which is deep into her second deployment since she was delivered in 2012.

"The fast-growing JHSV fleet has proven to be flexible in ways we didn't even consider when this program first started," said Perciavalle, "Without the dedication and pride of the hard-working individuals that make up Austal's awesome shipbuilding team, this program wouldn't be experiencing the success we're celebrating today." The ship's sponsor, Alma Booterbaugh, joined the immediate office of the Secretary of the Navy in 1999 and she is currently the Office Manager and Scheduler for the Secretary of the Navy. Booterbaugh has been a civil servant for over 30 years with the Federal Government and is the recipient of the Navy Meritorious Civilian Service Award and three Navy

Superior Civilian Service Awards. Booterbaugh was joined on stage today by her daughter, *USNS Brunswick's* Maid of Honor, Brittany Booterbaugh. More than 300 naval guests, civic leaders, community members and Austal employees attended the ceremony held beneath the hull of *Brunswick* in the Austal final assembly bay.

Three JHSVs and seven Littoral Combat Ships (LCS) are currently under construction in Austal's Mobile, Ala. Shipyard. The company is scheduled to launch JHSV 6 before the end of the month, while the future *USS Jackson* (LCS 6) prepares for its acceptance sea trials later this summer.

For the LCS and JHSV programs, Austal, as prime contractor, is teamed with General Dynamics Mission Systems, a business unit of General Dynamics. For the JHSV program, General Dynamics is responsible for the design, integration and testing of the navigation and communication systems, C4I and aviation systems.

On April 27, 2015 Captain Jason Ivey, Commanding Officer of USNS Brunswick and his wife welcomed a baby boy: Halen Hawk Ivey.

The *Brunswick News*, Ga. | Nov 13, 2015 | by Gordon Jackson

USNS Brunswick Passes Sea Trials

The future joint high-speed vessel USNS Brunswick (JHSV 6) was launched from the Austal USA shipyard, May 18, 2015.

The USNS Brunswick has successfully completed sea trials in the Gulf of Mexico. The testing for the Brunswick, an expeditionary fast transport, was recently conducted by the shipbuilder Austal in Mobile, AL. The company conducted intensive comprehensive tests to show the ship's major systems and equipment meet Navy standards. The required tests are considered the last significant hurdle before the ship is delivered to the Navy later this year.

Camden Partnership President Sheila McNeill, past national president of the Navy League, said the ship will undergo several more months of testing by the Navy before it goes into service. "I'm excited it's passed sea trials," she said. The Brunswick is named in honor of the Southeast Georgia city for its role in building Liberty ships for the Navy during World War II. It is the sixth expeditionary fast transport built for the Navy.

The 338-foot ship is a versatile, non-combatant vessel designed to operate in shallow ports and waterways. It will be used in a wide range of assignments, including maneuver and sustainment, relief operations in small or damaged ports, humanitarian missions, logistics support, and for rapid transport of troops, military vehicles and equipment. The ship is capable of transporting 600 short tons of cargo as far as 1,200 miles at an average speed of 40 mph. It will include a flight deck to support day and night aircraft launch and recovery operations. Its top speed is 49 mph.

"We're proud to have successfully completed acceptance trials for USNS Brunswick, and excited to see the continued improvement ship to ship on this mature program," said Craig Perciavalle, Austal USA's president in a prepared statement. "Austal's EPF team continues to do a tremendous job constructing incredible ships and preparing them to enter the fleet." The Brunswick was originally classified as a joint high-speed vessel until several months ago when Navy Secretary Ray Mabus decided some ship classes were given long or unusual names. He designated three classes of ships E-class, similar to L-class amphibious ships, S-class submarines and A-class auxiliaries.

The change will create a better understanding of the purpose of the ships, Navy officials said. McNeill said she has talked with the ship's captain and the vessel will make a visit to its namesake city some time next spring. She said the Brunswick will likely make more than one visit to town in coming years because it will be home ported in Norfolk, Va. This coin had been minted in support of the new Joint High-Speed Vessel USNS Brunswick JHSV 6. It was beautiful on our program. "If you are fortunate enough to have a 1971 Bicentennial coin that was auctioned off at Lanier Field you can make a pair! Both represent a part of history."

The USNS coin considers the city of Brunswick's defense background with the building of 99 Liberty Ships during WWII. These Liberty ships were built for troop and equipment transportation—or carrier. The same is true of the USNS Brunswick. On one side of the coin the WWII liberty ship is shown as well as the city and county seals. The other side of the coin has a picture of the USNS Brunswick with the Navy and Merchant Marine seals. They can only be purchased at Main Street Frame Shop on

Newcastle Street or from various committee members. The cost is $10.00.

The coin is a fundraiser for activities to support the ship and crew when they come to Brunswick. When the ship visits the committee and officers and crew will host visits aboard the ship and will have a special ceremony with all of Glynn and surrounding counties invited to attend.

The keel laying was held in Mobile, Alabama on December 2, 2014 at the shipyard of Austal, USA. Sheila McNeill, former national president of the Navy League spoke at the ceremony: "We are pleased and excited to have a ship named after Brunswick. These ships are incredible assets to our Army, Navy and Marine Corps. They will enhance our forward presence and our global security by quickly transporting a huge array of supplies and equipment throughout the world. What flexibility these ships will give our services. This is indeed a special day for Brunswick, Georgia and for our county. Brunswick and its surrounding communities look forward to having the Captain Jason Ivey and his crew for a visit. We understand the responsibility of the connection between a ship and its namesake. We look forward to many, many years of support."

The mayor and city of Brunswick, The Chairman of the Glynn County Commission and the county, our chamber of commerce, the Golden Isles Council of the Navy League, the port authority, our Coast Guard station, the veterans' council, The Propeller Club and more plan quite an event in Brunswick for "our" officers and crew so everyone please join us. And thank you for giving this native Brunswick girl a chance to express our pride in the USNS Brunswick and the US Flagged Merchant Marine." Mrs. McNeill said at the keel laying ceremony.

The joint high-speed vessels were originally designed for fast transportation of soldiers and any supplies the military needed but the roles are expanding as the Navy is considering putting a rail gun to test in the future as well as utilizing as a hospital ship. The 338 Foot shallow draft vessel is the fourth ship to be named Brunswick.

Several Glynn county residents attended the christening on May 9, in Mobile Alabama: Mayor Cornell Harvey, Commission Bob Coleman and his wife Sherry, David Bolen representing the Golden Isles Council of the Navy league, Arlie McNeill, who was chairman of the committee to build the replica of the liberty ship now located at the waterfront and Sheila McNeill, Chairman of the USNS Brunswick JHS 6 Committee. Mayor Harvey was asked to speak at the event and all were given special seating as the representatives of Brunswick and Glynn County.

The committee enjoyed meeting the officers and crew of the USNS Brunswick. The officers and crew are Merchant Mariners and operate under the Military Sealift Command. The Commanding Officer, Captain Jason Ivey has been corresponding with the committee for months and this gave the committee a chance to meet and get acquainted.

The community will be advised when the visit for the ship is scheduled."

Austal USA launches USNS *Brunswick*, the US Navy's sixth joint high-speed vessel in ten-ship contract.

Austal launched Tuesday, May 19, 2015, the recently christened USNS *Brunswick*, the Australian shipbuilder's sixth joint high-speed vessel in a $1.6 billion, ten-ship contract.

By Kelli Dugan, May 19, 2015

Austal launched Tuesday the recently christened USNS Brunswick, the Australian shipbuilder's sixth joint high-speed vessel in a $1.6 billion, 10-ship contract. The milestone also marked the second U.S. Navy ship launched at Austal USA's Mobile shipyard in less than three months. The 338-foot Brunswick will now undergo final outfitting and testing before sea trials and delivery to the U.S. Navy before the close of 2015. Austal's customer in the 10-ship contract is actually the Navy's Military Sealift Command, the transportation provider for the U.S. Department of Defense.

Austal USA President Craig Perciavalle said Tuesday's successful launch "further supports the level of maturity this program has reached." "The credit for accomplishing this major milestone belongs to Austal's team of talented shipbuilders in cooperation with the support provided by the other members of the Austal launch team including BAE Systems, Berard Transportation and our U.S. Navy client," Perciavalle said in a prepared statement.

Four joint high-speed vessels—Spearhead, Choctaw County, Fall River and Millinocket—have already been delivered, with Spearhead and Choctaw County completing overseas deployments to Europe, West Africa and the Caribbean. The aluminum catamarans are designed to transport as many as 600 short-tons of cargo at an average speed of 35 knots. The non-combat ships operate with 22-member crews and are capable of supporting rapid intra-theater deployment of personnel, equipment and supplies. Three joint high-speed vessels and seven littoral combat ships are currently under construction in Austal's Mobile shipyard with the future USS Jackson, or LCS 6, preparing for acceptance sea trials later this summer.

Austal USA, a business unit of Henderson, Australia-based Austal, employs roughly 4,200 at its Mobile shipyard.

On September 15, 2015, Stars and Stripes had an article on the reclassification of the USNS *Brunswick* Joint High-Speed Vessel to an Expeditionary Fast Transport. Of course, too late for us to make changes to the coin and the printed items—so it's still a JHSV to us!

The *Brunswick News*, Ga. | Jan 21, 2016 | by Gordon Jackson
The USNS Brunswick is officially part of the U.S. Navy.

The sixth Expeditionary Fast Transport vessel has been delivered to the Navy by its builder, Austal USA. "We're proud to deliver yet another great ship to the U.S. Navy fleet," Austal USA President Craig Perciavalle said. "The five Expeditionary Fast Transport vessels in service today have already proven to be a valuable resource for our nation and we're excited to deliver another ship that will add to that global capability."

The Brunswick is a 338-foot shallow draft aluminum catamaran capable of transporting 600 tons 1,200 nautical miles at an average speed of 35 knots, or 40 mph. The ship's deck can support flight operations for a wide variety of aircraft, including a CH-53 Super Stallion, the largest and heaviest helicopter in the military. It is described as a "multi-mission, non-combatant transport vessel characterized by its high volume, high speed, and flexibility."

The ship is named after the Coastal Georgia city which played an important role during World War II as the site of a 435-acre shipyard that produced 99 Liberty ships. "Brunswick displays American values of community, hospitality and resourcefulness at their very best," said Secretary of the Navy Ray Mabus during the ship's commissioning ceremony. "I chose to name the Joint High-Speed Vessel after Brunswick to honor those values and the men and women of the city, as well as the state of Georgia. Sheila McNeill, former national Navy League president and an organizer of an upcoming ceremony to welcome the ship to its namesake city, said it was a significant

> *milestone for the ship to pass all its tests and become an official part of the Navy. "To the crew, it's a big deal," she said.*
>
> *The crew is aware of the plans for the ship's first visit, tentatively scheduled for the weekend of May 8 during the Blessing of the Fleet. "They are excited how Brunswick is receiving them," McNeill said. The first vessel in the class, USNS Spearhead, was delivered in 2012 and has already logged more than 100,000 nautical miles supporting combat and humanitarian operations in Africa, South America and the Pacific.*
>
> *"The EPF program is very mature thanks to the hard work and dedication to excellence of the amazing shipbuilders here at Austal USA," Perciavalle said. "The Austal team is delivering incredible ships for our nation's defense while further establishing Austal USA as a major defense contractor."*

We were working hard and meeting weekly as we approached the date of the ceremony on May 7, 2016. We had buttons made for our businesses to wear that said, "Ask me about USNS *Brunswick* JHSV 6" with flyers that told about the ceremony and "did you know" information on the ship.

USNS *BRUNSWICK*

A new ship has been named *Brunswick* and is coming our way Mother's Day weekend. Mark your calendar to attend the welcoming ceremony on Saturday, May 7, at Mary Ross Park in downtown Brunswick. We'll have a tour schedule the week before the event.

1. Did you know: The US Navy Military Sealift Command operates USNS *Brunswick* with a crew of only twenty-two civil service mariners who navigate and maintain the platform.
2. Did you know: USNS *Brunswick* is capable of transporting six hundred tons, 1,200 nautical miles at an average of thirty-five knots.
3. Did you know: USNS *Brunswick* is one of four US Navy ships named after Brunswick.
4. Did you know: USNS *Brunswick* is a 338-foot-long aluminum catamaran ship, complete with a twenty-thousand-square-foot mission bay that reconfigures quickly with adaptive force packages.
5. Did you know: USNS *Brunswick* functions as a delivery vehicle for cargo, personnel, and modular tailored forces in response to a wide range of mission demands.

6. Did you know: USNS *Brunswick* provides high-speed, agile-lift capability to deliver operationally ready units to small, austere ports and flexibly support a wide range of missions including maneuver and sustainment, humanitarian assistance and special operations support.
7. Did you know: USNS *Brunswick* has an embarked force seating of 312.
8. Did you know: USNS *Brunswick* was built in Mobile, Alabama by Austal USA and delivered to the U.S. Navy on January 14, 2016.
9. Did you know: The concept of a cargo catamaran was first validated by the Royal Australian Navy, when its high-speed experimental vessel, the Jarvis Bay, was used to ferry more than twenty thousand peacekeepers to East Timor starting in 1999.
   The Navy leased a similar catamaran, the Swift, for nearly a decade ending in 2013, using it as transport for Marines and for US trainers going to Africa and South America. With the Spearhead-class of ship, the Navy is preparing a wider role for catamarans across theaters. Brunswick is sixth of eleven Expeditionary Fast Transport Vessels purchased by the Navy.
10. Did you know: Expeditionary Fast Transport Vessels, like USNS *Brunswick*, represent a departure for US Navy Military Sealift Command, whose vessels are typically mission-specific and include oil tankers and hospital ships.
11. Did you know: There have been three other ships named *Brunswick*.
12. Did you know that the Navy changed the designation of the ship from Joint High-Speed Vessel.
13. Did you know that the city and county have named May 7, 2016 as USNS *Brunswick* Day.

And she arrives!

USNS Brunswick arrives at Mary Ross Park for three-day visit
By Terry Dixon
338-foot catamaran will be open for public tours Saturday and Sunday

BRUNSWICK | Those who went to the St. Simons Island pier Friday morning to watch the arrival of the USNS Brunswick for a three-day visit at its namesake city got more than they expected; in fact, a lot more. The ones who arrived at the island pier by 7:30 a.m. to watch the ship pass had to wait about a half hour longer in a cold wind. When it passed, however, they marveled at the speed of the 338-foot Expeditionary Fast Transport Vessel as it "jetted" past, but a short distance after it should have turned to sail past Jekyll Island, it stopped. Then it pivoted with its side thrusters throwing up spray and came back and put on a ballet right in front of the pier. Capt. Jason

A. Ivey, the master of the ship since the Navy accepted it in January, said he did it at a request from the Brunswick harbor pilots

The pilots wanted me to show off. I said somebody wanted me to do loop the loops," he said. "So I stopped and spun it around. I walked the ship sideways when I was facing the pier." As 2nd Mate Ray Burnett put the ship through its paces, the crews of four highly maneuverable pilot boats watched. The USNS Brunswick can do about anything the pilot boats can do only bigger.

The ship wasn't designed for water shows, but it has the capabilities. "The main mission is the fast transport of troops and ammunition intra-theater," Ivey said. As situations arise, however, the ships' missions are expanding. The USNS Spearhead, the first of 11 of the ships, was loading Friday to deliver relief supplies to South America and it has provided assistance in Africa, he said. "They're supposed to be the Swiss Army knives of ships," he said.

For most of the crew, the weekend trip to Brunswick was a chance to see the city for which the vessel is named for the first time. For Melissa Gooch, it's a homecoming. The 34-year-old Gooch is the ship's third assistant engineer. She grew up in Brunswick and graduated from Glynn Academy a few blocks southeast of where the USNS Brunswick was moored. She decided to become a civil service mariner at the urging of her sister, whom she calls "my true seafaring sister." But it didn't work out as they planned.

"A year into training, she got pregnant," Gooch said of her sister. Gooch continued without her and graduated from the Great Lakes Maritime Academy with a degree in marine engineering. Sitting at an array of screens and controls, Gooch said the engineers "do a little bit of everything" in monitoring and operating the ship's systems. Among them are the power management systems, the four 12,000-horsepower diesel motors, compressed air systems, 34 bilge pumps, the air conditioning, a ride control system and many others.

Ride control is used to keep the ship comparatively level for passengers, she said. She has only been aboard since Monday. She had trained on a number of other ships and was on the Brunswick at Little Creek, a Navy base in Virginia, doing "type rating," a sort of proficiency test Coast Guard requires for specific maritime skills. Speaking with Ivey, she asked, "Are you going to dock at Mary Ross Park?" "Are you from Brunswick, 'Ivey said. Told she was, Ivey said, "I'll be right back."

It took him five minutes to get Gooch into the 3rd assistant engineer's slot, and she sailed south on the Brunswick. She planned to visit family and, while in town, to use some of her time off to visit her favorite hair dresser. Leaving the bridge, Ivey stopped in what is called "the 312," named for the number of seats. "This is where we carry troops up to 72 hours, then we dump them off somewhere," he said.

There are sleeping accommodations, but many troops just find a place on the floor, Ivey said. The ship also has a flight deck that can accommodate a landing H-53, a long-range search and rescue helicopter known as a Jolly Green Giant, or a hovering V-22 Osprey, he said. A deck below "the 312" is the 20,000-square-foot mission bay capable of handling 60 Humvees. The ship can move 600 tons 12,000 nautical miles at an average speed of 35 knots. Navy Reserves Cmdr. Lori Cumbie, who lives at Virginia Beach, was aboard for the trip from Little Creek and called it a good ride. The Navy puts personnel like her aboard the Military Sealift Command boats when requested or needed, she said. The fast transport ships could be very useful in a crisis to evacuate a lot of people quickly, but she stressed that the ships missions are not simple. "Logistics missions are extremely complex," Cumbie said.

The Brunswick will be open for tours over the weekend, but it's already had plenty of admirers and not just at the pier. When it went under the Sidney Lanier Bridge, a large crowd watched, and as it eased along the East River to its mooring at the city docks at Mary Ross Park, a third crowd took videos and pictures. It is the sixth of the 11 Spearhead-class transport vessels the Navy bought and it's operated by a crew of 22 civil service mariners.

After a welcome ceremony at Mary Ross at 11 a.m. Saturday, the ship will be open for public tours from noon until 5 p.m. with the last tour starting at 4:30 p.m. and Sunday from 9:30 a.m. until 2 p.m. and from 3:30 until 6 p.m. Sheila McNeill, a past national president of the Navy League, will emcee the ceremony and was one of the first aboard the Brunswick when it was secured at the dock. As soon as she learned there would be a USNS Brunswick, McNeill began working to arrange the visit. When told by text message Friday, the Brunswick had come over the horizon, McNeill replied with a simple, "Hallelujah."

We had a beautiful program:

USNS *BRUNSWICK* (EPF)

Program for Welcome Ceremony
May 7, 2016, Mary Ross Park
BRUNSWICK, GEORGIA

PROGRAM

WELCOME MASTER OF CEREMONIES	SHEILA MCNEILL
PARADING OF THE COLORS	NJROTC
NATIONAL ANTHEM	STAN MORAN
INVOCATION	
INTRODUCTIONS AND COMMENTS	SHEILA MCNEILL CHAIRMAN
CHAIRMAN, BRUNSWICK-GOLDEN ISLES	
CHAMBER OF COMMERCE	DONNA POE, PRESIDENT
REMARKS	SHEILA MCNEILL
PRESENTATION OF PROCLAMATION	MAYOR HARVEY CORNELL
	CHAIRMAN RICHARD STRICKLAND
REMARKS	CAPTAIN JASON IVEY
	COMMANDING OFFICER
REMARKS	NAVY COMMANDER
INTRODUCTION	
REMARKS	CONGRESSMAN CARTER
REMARKS	STATE SENATOR WILLIAM LIGON
	STATE REPRESENTATIVE ALEX ATWOOD
	STATE REPRESENTATIVE JEFF JONES
CLOSING REMARKS	

OFFICIAL PARTY DEPARTS

THE AUDIENCE IS REQUESTED TO REMAIN IN PLACE UNTIL THE PLATFORM GUESTS HAVE LEFT THE PODIUM

It also included our committee members and supporters:

A SPECIAL THANK YOU TO OUR COMMITTEE MEMBERS

Chairman Donna Gowen Poe, and the Brunswick Golden Isles Chamber of Commerce

Committee Chairman Sheila McNeill President, The Camden Partnership
Millard Allen—Glynn County Board of Education
Mel Baxter, Brunswick and Glynn County Development Authority
Bill Dawson, Georgia Ports Authority
David Boland, Navy League
Jim Drumm Brunswick City Manager
Wayne Johnson Coastal Bank of Georgia
Britt Elrod, Navy League
Bruce Fendig, Brunswick Pilots
Golden Isles Maritime Club
Moon Warwick, Marshside Grill
Cornell Harvey, Mayor, City of Brunswick
Jonathan Havens, H2o
Mathew Hill, Downtown Development Authority
Mike Hodges, Ameris Bank
David Proctor Logistec USA
Bob Miller International Auto Processing
Ben Jones, BeSeen Outdoors, Inc.
Lea Badyna Keep Brunswick Golden Isles Beautiful
R. H. "Buff" Leavy IV, The Brunswick News
Scott McQuade, Golden Isles Convention & Visitors Bureau
Mike Maloy, McGinty Gordon & Associates
Arlie McNeill, Edo Miller & Sons
Danny Maddox, Prime South Bank
Dave Olender, Veterans Council of the Golden Isles
Alan Ours Glynn County Administrator
Matt Permar, Islander
Sr. Chief Rudy Radakovich, USCG Station Brunswick
Bill Redford, Nalley of Brunswick
Drummond Spence, Grandy's
Richard Strickland, Chairman, Glynn County Board of Commissioners
Jerry Rhyne, Navy League, MOAA
Mary and Manuel Rocha, Blessing of the Fleet
Bob Thompson, Creative Printing
R. H. Tostensen III, Poteet Seafood
Phil Viviani, Korean War Veteran
Lynn Warwick, Main Street Frame Shop
Mason Waters, United Community Bank
Michelle Harrison WGIG RADIO iHeartMedia
Beachview Tent Rental

Special thanks to the Brunswick Police Department, Glynn County Police Department, Sheriff's office, Department of Natural Resources (DNR), Coast Guard Station Brunswick and all our friends at Military Sealift Command

I concluded my remarks with "This is indeed a special day for Brunswick, Georgia and for Glynn county. Thank you all for being a part of it."

We finished in sixty minutes!

We had ship's tours after the ceremony on that Saturday and again on Sunday. We couldn't believe the crowd. The lines were all the way from the ship and wrapped around the park—there were always about two hundred in line. The Navy League council did a wonderful job of managing the crowd, talking to people, and answering questions and having water for everyone. And we added many new friends as we talked to Raymond Barnett the navigator and Douglas Carter the operations officer. They all enjoyed the tours and talking with the community as they toured their ship.

I've kept up with the USNS *Brunswick* with calls and e-mails from Captain Ivey and from news clipping like the one below: The *Brunswick* chamber was a great partner in bringing USNS *Brunswick* to Glynn County and worked hard to make them feel welcome and give local citizens a chance to enjoy their namesake ship. They planned and executed the reception for our community dignitaries, the committee, and our sponsors.

It was a wonderful evening—not without a little angst—but with help from a senior admiral everything ran smoothly, and the evening finished without a glitch. It was great watching the crew mingle with the community leadership. Captain Ivey was the star for the evening and everyone wanted to talk with him. In January 2015, he had told me he and the crew were naming various rooms after businesses in Brunswick. One of those selected was Tipsy McSway's owned by Susan Bates. Susan was thrilled with the idea. At the reception after the program he asked me to come with him. One of the rooms had my name on it. Oh my, what a thrill for me too!

USNS Brunswick leaves namesake city and puts on a show on the way out

By Terry Dixon, *Georgia Times Union*

338-foot catamaran drew 3,600 for tours Saturday and Sunday during annual Blessing of the Fleet

The USNS Brunswick left its namesake port Monday after a weekend visit, but on the way to open seas the crew did an encore of an early show.

As he did on the way into port Friday morning, Capt. Jason Ivey sped past the St. Simons Island pier, brought the 338-foot cat-

> *amaran to a stop then "spun it around," as he says in non-nautical terms, and showed off its maneuverability.*
>
> *Sheila McNeill, the past national president of the Navy League and chairman of the visit, said she had asked Ivey Sunday night if there would be another demonstration. She had missed Friday's water show because she had been downtown at Mary Ross to greet the ship on arrival. "He said it depended on the size of the crowd," she said. It turned out to be hundreds lining the T-shaped pier and along the walkways bordering St. Simons Sound all waving as the ship's horn sounded.*
>
> *And Ivey didn't disappoint. He turned the Brunswick to face the pier as he did Friday to give spectators a view between the twin hulls of the Expeditionary Fast Transport Vessel, which can carry and seat 312 combat equipped soldiers and 600 Humvees in its spacious mission bay. The ship's crew conducted guided tours Saturday and Sunday that were so successful, the hours were expanded. After turning away hundreds Saturday, McNeill said the crew decided to change the open time of the Sunday tours from 9:30 a.m. to 7 p.m. "We just told the people who couldn't get on Saturday," but word spread, McNeill said. "From 7 to 9, we had 250." About 3,600 people toured the ship, and lines were so long Saturday that organizers ran out of water for those standing in the heat and had to get more, she said. "The crew were excellent guides," McNeill said. "They were all exhausted."*
>
> *As the ship pulled away from the dock Monday at 10 a.m., Mariners and some crew members waved from the upper deck. Ken and Cindy Miller held two small signs that, held together, read, "Thank you!" The Millers said it had been a good weekend and, like many local boaters, marveled at the ship's agility.*
>
> *"We've got a 44-foot boat and can't maneuver like this guy," Cindy Miller said.*

We had hundreds lined up after the ceremony. The crew and the volunteers were so gracious. They wanted everyone who stood in line to have a tour so everyone stayed late.

Donna Gowen Poe, Chamber Chair and I sent all supporters the following letter:

> On behalf of the Chamber's USNS Brunswick Committee, we wish to express our deepest appreciation to you for your commitment and dedications for the past year in preparation

for and ultimately hosting the visit to the Port of Brunswick and Dedication of the USNS Brunswick, May 6–9, 2016 The USNS Brunswick Captain, Jason Ivey and his entire crew were overwhelmed by the reception given them at the ship's official Dedication Ceremony Saturday morning, May 7th at Mary Ross Park in downtown Brunswick. Certainly, highlights for them were the VIP reception honoring the crew aboard USNS Brunswick Saturday evening; plus, approximately 4,000 residents who had the opportunity Saturday and Sunday to tour the magnificent ship named after our historic port of the City of Brunswick.

Indeed, from the time of the arrival of the USNS Brunswick in the City of Brunswick on Friday morning May 6th until its departure Monday, May 9th, your generous giving of time and resources insured the ship's crew received our warmest welcome and most memorable experience, made the entire community and its citizens most proud.

Again, we ae most grateful for your support.

The hospitality Donna showed to the officers and crew was extraordinary. In the day of preparation of the event she was everywhere. When she found out the women's head didn't have a full-length mirror she purchased one for each of the four heads!

USNS Brunswick and its crew left on its first deployment on January 30, 2017.
Staff, WVEC 8:02 PM. EST January 30, 2017
NORFOLK, Va. (WVEC)—USNS Brunswick (T-EPF 6) departed on its maiden voyage Monday.

The Navy's Expeditionary Fast Transport vessel and its crew of nearly 50 sailors and civil service mariners left from Joint Expeditionary Base Little Creek-Fort Story.

Captain Jason Ivey told 13 News Now, "It's relieving, and it gives a sense of closure and accomplishment to what we've been doing. We've been working so hard to get here that to finally see it done and to, you know, we're leaving our home away from home here in Little Creek, but we're heading out West and San Diego and then farther west and it should be fun. Everybody's ready to go. That's for sure."

The ship first will travel to Naval Forces Pacific Command, U.S. Third Fleet, where the Brunswick will remain for three months. After that, the ship will transit to its home port in

Saipan, U.S. Naval Forces Far East Command and be deployed to support the Seventh Fleet.

We are so proud of the USNS *Brunswick*, Captain Master Jason Ivey, and his crew, who were wonderful to work with. USNS *Brunswick* was transferred to the Pacific Fleet but we'll do all we can to keep up with our ship and its crew.

USS *BANCROFT* SAIL MEMORIAL/ DEDICATION ON JULY 7, 2000

RADM Chuck Beers wanted a monument at the entrance of the base and not only found the sail from the USS *George Bancroft* SSBN (643)* but had it "dropped off" from a barge on its way from California to Virginia. The one hundredth anniversary of the Submarine Force was coming up and he thought it would make an excellent exhibit. The 180-foot exhibit would be constructed so that members of the public who otherwise are not able to visit the submarines at Kings Bay could see a realistic impression of a submarine's size. The exhibit would also honor those who have served in the submarine force.

The exhibit would be a life-size model of the front end of a Poseidon-class submarine jutting from the ground at a ten-degree angle like it was surfacing on the water. The model would be topped with a forty-five-foot sail—the tower on a submarine that crew members use to enter and exit from the vessel. I told the reporter from the *Tribune*, "For those who don't have an idea of the magnitude of these vessels, this will give them a good idea." Of course, building the exhibit would take funding and the Navy didn't have a way to provide that. So I volunteered or as many say was "voluntold" to find the funding.

My good friend Admiral Hank Childes who was national chairman of the one hundredth anniversary of the Submarine Force sent an encouraging letter on the importance of this anniversary. Serving on the committee were LCDR Ciesielski, Lt. Maysonnet, CWO4 Pummell, BUC (SCW) Slattery as advisors and reporting on the progress of the building project, Royal Weaver, Bob Hurley, Bridget Wenum, Linda Johnson, Alice Hurley, Gary Gallagher, Bill Hunter, Bill Weisensee, and Tilden Norris.

On June 29, 1999, we received word that Seabee labor had been approved.

I called John Crouse who was the manager of the St. Marys Submarine Museum and we began work. We wrote every active duty military who had previously been stationed at Kings Bay that I had maintained contact with. The committee began the fund-raising and the result was amazing.

On the same day, I wrote President Jimmy Carter inviting him to be our principal speaker. As a former submariner and a native and resident of Georgia it seemed the thing to do. However, I closed the letter with "Sir, with your busy schedule, we really do not expect you to be able to accept this. However, you are our first choice, so we wait to hear from you before we retreat to second choice!" We received regrets shortly after and I received word from a friend who was going to see him and offered to give him the letter that he said. "I wish I could tell her I could do this."

John and I wrote requests to everyone that included the following:

25 July 1999

"Kings Bay Submarine Base has acquired the sail from the decommissioned submarine USS George Bancroft SSBN (643). Of the 600+ submarines in the U.S. Navy since 1900, only 59 were designated "Ballistic Missile Submarine." The original "Forty-One for Freedom" and today's 18 Ohio Class Submarines. With the present-day cutback in government funding for the military, if it's not being used it is scrap material. We have a chance to preserve a piece of history.

The plan is to install the Sail as it would be as it surfaces in the ocean. Estimated funds required are $50,000. The majority will go for site preparation, sail installation and hull construction. A large portion will be for memorial and sponsor signage. The submarine base will perform tasks to support the installation, but by law is limited to what it can pay for. The museum has volunteered to help support his project to raise the funds required. We need to raise the funds priory to the groundbreaking. We hope to complete the project in time for the Submarine Force Centennial Celebration schedule for April 2000."

Signed: Sheila McNeill and John Crouse

We had response from both locally and across the county. Major contributor's names can be found on the plaque in front of the Bancroft. That plaque reads as follows:

USS GEORGE BANCROFT SSBN 643 SAIL EXHIBIT
Forty-One for Freedom Cold War Warrior
Peace through Deterrence
Sponsor Plaque as of 11 January 2000
Dedicated 7 April 2000

For their support in the sail preparation, installation and exhibit site construction. COMSUBGRP TEN: RADM Richard Terpstra, USN and exhibit coordinators: CAPT. Frank Stagle, USN and LCDR Don Ciesielski, USN)
SPECIAL ACKNOWLEDGEMENTS TO THE ST. MARYS SUBMARINE MUSEUEM our local non-profit organization who raised the funds needed for this exhibit.
(Fund-raising co-chairmen: Sheila McNeill and John Crouse MMCM-SS USN-RET)
Please complete your visit of the USS GEORGE BANCROFT sail exhibit by visiting the
ST MARYS SUBMARINE MUSEUM Located in downtown historic St. Marys.
Directions to the museum: take Spur 40 to route 40; turn left at the light and continue straight until the road ends at the St. Marys River. Turn right at the St. Marys River. We are the second building on the right. Look for the building with the periscope.

* * * * *

At the same time Captain Frank Stagle, Naval Submarine Base Kings Bay's commanding officer's staff began their work of designing and preparing for the exhibit.

There was a great picture in the *Periscope* with the St. Marys Submarine Museum, Naval Submarine Base Kings Bay representatives and Seabees from Construction Battalion Unit 412 in front of the site where the sail would be on exhibit.

* * * * *

FUNDS STILL BEING ACCEPTED FOR BANCROFT EXHIBIT
BY JO1 Victor Brabble
CENTENNIAL CELEBRATION of the UNITED STATES SUBMARINE FORCE

The following made this exhibit possible:
PLATINUM $5,000
City of St. Marys Tourism SUBASE Kings Bay Construction Battalion Unit 412
Trident Refit Facility Strategic Weapons Facility
J.A. Jones Management Service, Inc.
BAE Systems

GOLD ($3,000)
Georgia Power Company Wal-Mart (St. Marys)

SILVER ($1,000)
Arlie and Sheila McNeill St. Marys Submarine Museum
USS MARYLAND SSBN 738 (Blue & Gold)
Kings Bay Village Merchants Assoc. Reese James (*) Cumberland Inn and Suites
Donald & Marquita Miller Navy Federal Credit Union USPA and IRA
J. E. Howard Electrical Contractor Fort James Corporation

Generous donations of $500 are on the display but are not printed here.
Collective Individual donations less than $500 each (Total $2, 816.50)
(*) Indicates former USS Bancroft crew members

SPECIAL THANKS to COMSUBGRP Ten and the NAVAL SUBMARINE BASE KINGS BAY for obtaining the sail and having this exhibit open to the public. An additional thanks goes out to the NAVAL SUBMARINE BASE CONSTRUCTION BATALLION 412, TRIDENT REFIT FACILITY, STRATEGIC WEAPONS FACILITY AND J.A. JONES MANAGEMENT SERVICES, INC.

USS BANCROFT
Tribune and Georgia

On September 29, a groundbreaking ceremony was held dedicating an area to display the USS George Bancroft (SSBN 643) Sail Exhibit outside of the Naval Submarine Base Kings Bay Franklin gate. As of now the site is 90 percent excavated. For the project to be completed, sixty thousand dollars needs to be raised. The St. Marys Submarine Museum and the local Subvets Kings Bay Trident Inc. / WWII took on the project of raising funds.

The goal is to have the exhibition completed in time for the Submarine Force Centennial Celebration scheduled for April 7 and 8, 2000. The sail, which is forty-two feet wide by nine feet high and weighs sixty-five tons, will be part of exhibition that will be 180 feet long, simulating a submarine surfacing. In addition, the site will have a touch-computer display telling the "Forty-One for Freedom" story. (Note: we were never able to do this.)

Since 1900, more than six hundred submarines have served in the United States Navy. Out of them, fifty-nine were designated ballistic missile submarines, including today's eighteen Ohio-class submarines and the first SSBNs known as the "Forty-one for Freedom." USS Bancroft was one of the original "Forty-One for Freedom" boats that served during the Cold War era.

Four exhibit sponsor levels will be recognized on the Exhibit Sponsor Plaque, which will be on display at the site. The four levels are platinum for at least five-thousand-dollar donors, gold for three-thousand-dollar donors, silver for one-thousand-dollar donors, and bronze for five-hundred-dollar donations. The exhibit sponsor plaque deadline is

January 31, 2000. However, donations will be accepted continuously for exhibit upkeep and additions.

According to project cochairman and St. Marys Submarine Museum board of directors' member, Sheila McNeill, 75 percent of the fund-raising goal has been reached so far and 100 percent is expected. Also, she said she is pleased with the fund-raising progress. "I am proud of the fact that we raised money as quickly as we have," she said. "Our goal was to keep the fund-raising local, from people in the area and people who visit the area." Retired Navy captain and Cold War era submariner veteran, Bill Weisensee said the exhibit is needed to educate people. "For many reasons, we should appreciate Cold War era veterans, especially the ones who served on the 'Forty-One for Freedom,'" he said. "This exhibit will tell the stories of those who stood the watch during the 1960s, '70s, '80s, and '90s. It will help to relate to families what they do."

The USS *Maryland* called me and asked me to come down to the waterfront. I was thrilled to do so and especially proud when they presented a check for one thousand dollars.

Representing the blue crew were as follows:

Commander Keith Bowman, Commanding Officer
STSCM(SS) Herbert Runnels,

Representing the gold crew were as follows:

Commander Christopher Haynes, Commanding Officer
Lt Commander Randall Sykoro, Executive Officer
ETCM (SS) Lawrence Keen, Chief of the Boat
Captain Will Hansen Jr., Squadron 20 Commodore

Earl Braddock, from the Maryland Eastern Shore Navy League joined us that day.

That picture was in *Seapower* magazine and is on the wall at my office today.

Prior to the groundbreaking, Captain Frank Stagle and I placed some items in the ground at the ground breaking, beginning with each of us placing our respective coins in the bag.

Joe Norrell, the official artist for the George Bancroft Sail Exhibit completed a beautiful work of art in February 2000. Two hundred limited edition prints were produced and went on sale during the Submarine Force Centennial Weekend on April 7 and 8. The cost was fifty dollars each. The first twenty sold went toward the George Bancroft Exhibit Fund for a one-thousand-dollar donation from Norrell.

The Seabee construction battalion Unit 412 began building the exhibit. The hull of the submarine was formed in dirt and Playtime Pools covered the dirt hull with gunite cement on March 14.

We only had six weeks to raise funds, so we began a big campaign that included as much advertising as we could get telling everyone "the sub exhibit needs cash to surface." We had the help of the *Tribune & Georgian*. The headlines said, "I should have done that." I knew there would be many active duty and retired sailors who would look back years from then and wish they had been a part of this great exhibit. There were so many supporting the exhibit

Now to plan a big ceremony—it was time to celebrate. April 7, 2000, at three was decided on with a rehearsal the night before. When that day arrived, it was a beautiful glorious day. The pictures and news clipping captured much of it but there was nothing like seeing it in person.

We stood in formation waiting for the proper time to walk to the dais. And here I am, part of the official party—I knew it was worth all the worrying and the work. The Fages, Robertsons, and Meads, my husband, Arlie, sister, Debbie, and mother, Nora, were all there. At the last minute, we had managed to get enough funding to put sodding down and with the new green grass, the sunny day, the white carpeted walkway, the black submarine, and those uniforms it was magnificent.

Opening the program was a nineteen-gun salute for RADM Richard Terpstra, commander, Submarine Group 10. The National Anthem was played by Camden County High School with the invocation by Captain Robert Malene, command chaplain.

Mike Swain, St. Marys Postmaster announced the new Submarine Centennial Stamps and LCDR Donald Ciesielski, executive officer of NSB Kings Bay introduced Captain Stagl for remarks and introduction of RADM. Richard Terpstra. The Edward Waters Concert Choir of Jacksonville did a wonderful rendition of "Georgia on My Mind" and "The Battle Hymn of the Republic."

Captain Frank Stagle introduced me. I'll never have a better introduction or a funnier one! I was pleased that he gave me a copy of it: "It is now my pleasure to introduce the spark plug behind the fund-raising for this magnificent exhibit. As many of you know Sheila has a long history of service to the community and our country. Please join me in giving a great big Kings Bay welcome to Sheila McNeill." (The full introduction is in my remembrances of Captain Stagle.)

My remarks went well as I gave my words and read a letter from Senator Max Cleland. The day before the ceremony there was a big vote on the Armed Services Committee and he could not leave DC. I read a letter from him

The Camden County High School Choir finished with "The Lord Bless You and Keep You, the Animals Are Coming," "America the Beautiful," and "God Bless America." Captain Stagle unveiled the exhibit, YNC (SS) Alan Huppman sang "God Bless the USA." We closed with the Navy Jacksonville Band playing Anchors Aweigh. LCDR Ciesielski had closing remarks and an invitation to the reception.

The ceremony was at three, the reception at four thirty, and Arlie and I stayed at the reception for three hours! No one wanted to leave. The executive officer of NSB

Kings Bay, CDR Dan Ciesielski surprised me with a framed picture of the Bancroft with the one hundredth anniversary coins that now has a place of prominence in my home. The Bancroft has become such a fixture at Kings Bay that this entrance of the base is known by many as the gate with the submarine.

Attending the ceremony that day was George Frances Bancroft III and I had him sign my program!

The following is a part of the article in the *Tribune & Georgian* on April 12, 2000:

Hunnicutt recalls Bancroft patrols

By Fred Hill (Tribune & Georgian Staff)

> *Capt. Thomas G. Hunnicutt, deputy commander of Submarine Squadron 16 at Kings Bay, was the commanding officer of the blue crew of the USS Bancroft when that submarine was decommissioned in 1993. "The boat itself was in great condition, but I understood why it was decommissioned. The Cold War was over and the Navy reduced the size of its fleet and it was going to the Trident submarine," Hunnicutt said in an interview on Sunday, April 9, two days after the sail of the Bancroft was exhibited as a permanent memorial to both the men of the Bancroft and to submariners everywhere, past and present.*
>
> *"I felt terrible when the boat was decommissioned but only because it would break up such a great crew as we had on the Bancroft. We had a fantastic attitude and camaraderie," Hunnicutt said. "We thought we were the hardest-working crew ever, but of course all submarine crews may feel that way. That's what separates sailors from others in the service. We go deep and we are isolated and we depend on each other so much," the captain said. Hunnicutt served two tours on the Bancroft, one as navigator of the gold crew from 1982 to 1986, the second as its commanding officer of the blue crew in 1992-1993 or until its decommissioning. "The boat," the captain said, "becomes almost a part of yourself. You tend to serve the boat first. Even families may have to come second." "The nuclear submarine force can convince rogue nations that attacks on us will not be worth the risk," Hunnicutt said.*

*George Bancroft was born in 1800. He was a secretary of the Navy, the founder of the US Naval Academy and was referred to as the "father of American History." The Thirty-Third Fleet Ballistic Missile submarine was named in his honor. She was commissioned January 22, 1966. They completed nineteen Polaris patrols, twenty-seven Poseidon patrols, and twenty-four Trident patrols for a total of seventy deterrent patrols. After decommissioning it was our turn to protect and preserve the George Bancroft Sail in honor of all submarine veterans who have gone to sea in the nation's defense.

* * * * *

In July 2016 Cadets from the Navy Junior Reserve Officers Training Corps program at North Port High School in North Port, Florida, assisted in the painting of the memorial. The renovation project was a joint effort between multiple tenant commands at NSB Kings Bay, Submarine Group 10, St. Marys Submarine Museum, and the USS *George Bancroft* Association.

Thank you, RADM Beers, for having the vision and thank you RADM Rich Terpstra, Captain Stagle, LCDR Ciesielski and the staff for having the determination to see it through.

USS *GEORGE H. W. BUSH* COMMISSIONING

JANUARY 10, 2009

The aircraft carrier named after the first President Bush was commissioned in Norfolk. The Hampton Roads Council of the Navy League and its executive director, Mary Ellen Baldwin, chaired the commissioning committee. I thought it was tough raising a couple of hundred thousand—they had to raise over four million! This is something the Navy League does and they do it well. Especially the Hampton Roads Navy League Council! This spectacular reception was made possible by sponsors enlisted by Mary Ellen and her committees. This is not paid with taxpayers' dollars! I was pleased to be able to attend. Pleased nothing—I was honored.

The events started with a luncheon. Past president Bush (forty-one) gave some very eloquent and emotional words. He called his wife, Barbara, to the podium with the words "tell everyone about our commander in chief." She looked up to him and said, "George you'll always be my commander in chief." And this began an unforgettable two days. She then introduced herself as Barbara Bush, the only Bush that doesn't cry!

The Gala the evening before the commissioning was in a huge tent at the waterfront. Chandeliers, hardwood floors, groupings of white leather couches with exotic flowers and at the end of the tent was the bow of the *USS Georgia H. W. Bush*. It was spectacular. That night George Bush gave casual remarks to the crowd. He happened to say that he was pleased that his only daughter was the sponsor. At that time, Mrs. Bush stood up and went to the podium and reminded everyone that she would change that sentence to "our" daughter. Everyone laughed! Then he shared with the audience that they were celebrating their sixty-fourth wedding anniversary and it only seemed like sixty-three years. Everyone I met with the Bush family was just delightful.

I was staying that weekend with Chuck and Susan Beers. Their only other "guest" each evening was the President's aide, Lieutenant Commander Clay Beers—also known as the Beer's son. He was an F-18 pilot. I grilled him nightly to learn about the life of a presidential aide but he gave me none of the juicy details! Clay has the duty on the twenty-first when President Obama is sworn in as the new President of the United States. Wouldn't you want to be a witness on that historical day! Clay will have had a year with each of the Presidents, both Bush and Obama.

The day of the ceremony was supposed to rain but it was beautiful. We started out at a breakfast and then to the ceremony. It was on C-SPAN and a few other stations. Bush talked about his father and how he was admired by his children. He also said, "What do you get for someone who has everything? An aircraft carrier!" He told the audience he was reading some of his father's old letters in preparation for this event and ran across one written many years ago, to a friend. "It said," Bush continues, "Little Georgie is doing well. He is starting to talk and he uses words we don't understand… but it is hilarious." The president paused and then said, "Some things never change." It brought the house down!

President George H. W. Bush, in his remarks, talked about wishing he could be where he was sixty-five years ago, preparing to serve aboard a new ship. "As you prepare to man this ship, I do know that you take with you the hopes and dreams of every American who cherishes freedom and peace and you take with you the undying respect and admiration of the entire Bush family." After the ceremony, I spent a lot of time answering Keith Post's calls trying to hook up. He and Jon Hageman were seated in another section and Keith kept calling me on my cell phone. As I was walking to the reception, a male voice called, "Sheila!" I turned around and it was Camden County's old friend the chairman of the Joint Chiefs Admiral Mike Mullen. I finally answered Keith's calls and told him I was talking to Admiral Mullen and he was taller so Keith could find me that way.

Admiral Mullen and I had almost ten minutes to talk as he told me of the upcoming sixty-minute interview, what he was doing in his spare time (there is none) and all about his new grandbaby. Deborah was with him and they kept getting pulled away—someone wanted their picture at the bow of the Bush and they invited me to join them in one of the pictures. They are both wonderful patriots and I don't know how they keep up the pace. (I sent him a long e-mail Sunday night planning to critique his time on sixty minutes but could not find any fault—and I told him so.)

When Keith and CDR. John Hagemann caught up with me I introduced them both and we proceed to walk to the reception. Rear Admiral Kirk Donald's stories to learn more about this encounter! The reception had about one thousand folks and lasted over an hour. Keith, Jon, and I found ourselves with the top military. I have never seen so many "loops." In one place! I even had a long talk with the chief of Naval Operations, Gary Roughead, and we had time to catch up.

Admiral Jon Greenert and I had a chance to talk. He was now Atlantic Fleet Forces Command and he revealed the "real" background of my visit with Admiral Walt Doran when he was his administrative assistant. That is found in the stories under Admiral Greenert's name as is the conversation with Admiral Gary Roughead.

I ran into Beci Brenton which is always a pleasure. I've known Beci for years. She always has a level head and over the years I would get her sage opinion on some of my plans. She was in the Public Affairs Office of the Navy when I met her and went on to become the special assistant to the secretary of the Navy. When she retired, she went to Huntington Ingalls Industry as the corporate director for public affairs. She told me her husband, Kevin was coming to Naval Submarine Base Kings Bay as Squadron 20 commodore. I told her I'd take care of him! He had the same temperament as Becky, so it didn't take long for our friendship to develop. When Kevin left Kings Bay, he went to strategic systems programs to serve as deputy. When he retired, he was hired by Huntington Ingalls as corporate director for customer affairs for submarine programs.

But I digress. Some of the aides were whispering to me to help them get some of the bosses to leave—they all were behind schedule. But I knew the opportunity for these officers to have this much time to visit with each other on a strictly social basis was rare.

I was privileged to be there.

USS *GEORGIA* (SSGN 729) RETURN TO SERVICE

- Keel laid April 7, 1979
- Launched November 5, 1982
- Commissioned as SSBN, February 11, 1984
- Converted to SSGN and returned to service, March 28, 2008

In June 2007, the Camden Kings Bay Council of the Navy League, The Camden Partnership and The Camden County Chamber of Commerce partnered to develop, plan, and implement the homecoming and "return to service" events for the USS *Georgia* (729). I accepted responsibilities as Chairman with Keith Post as vice chairman for logistics and Marty Klumpp, vice chairman for finance.

Having the USS *Georgia* in Georgia was significant. I wanted to have every one of Georgia's governors, senators, and congressmen as honorary chairman of the committee. Governor Sonny Perdue agreed to be honorary chairman and I started contacting the others. It didn't take very long once I found a way to reach them and everyone agreed to have their names on the letterhead and wanted to attend the event. Several of the congressional members worked hard to support the strategic missile boats as well as the ballistic missile USS *Georgia*.

The names of honorary committee and working committees are listed below.

HONORARY CHAIRMAN
The Honorable Sonny Perdue
Governor, State of Georgia

HONORARY COMMITTEE
Senator Saxby Chambliss
Senator Johnny Isakson
Congressman Jack Kingston

FORMER GOVERNORS
President Jimmy Carter
Governor Roy Barnes
Senator Zell Miller
Governor Joe Frank Harris
Governor Carl Sanders

FORMER SENATORS
Senator Sam Nunn
Senator Max Cleland
Senator Mack Mattingly
Senator Wyche Fowler
Mrs. (Paul) Nancy Coverdell

FORMER CONGRESSMAN
Congressman Lindsay Thomas

RETURN TO SERVICE COMMITTEE

CHAIRMAN
Sheila M. McNeill, Past National President. Navy League of the United States
Co-CHAIR FOR LOGISTICS
Keith F. Post, President, Camden-Kings Bay Council.
Navy League of the United States
Co-CHAIR FOR DEVELOPMENT
Marty Klumpp, CFRE. Executive Director. The Camden Partnership, Inc.

Dave Reilly, Coordinator, Georgia Navy League
Councils. Navy League of the United States
Christine M. Daniel. President/CEO
Camden County Chamber of Commerce
Walt Natzic, Camden-Kings Bay Council, Navy League of the United States
Harley Jones, Atlanta Metropolitan Council, Navy League of the United States
Gary Johnson, Savannah Council, Navy League of the United States
Bob Morrison, Golden Isles Council, Navy League of the United States
Bill Weisensee, Naval Submarine League

History of USS Georgia

USS GEORGIA (SSGN 729) is the fourth TRIDENT Class Nuclear Powered Fleet Ballistic Missile Submarine, and the third ship to bear the name of this great state (see below for additional history on earlier ships to carry the name USS GEORGIA) The keel for USS GEORGIA (SSGN 729) was laid on 7 April 1979 and was presided over by First Lady Rosalyn Carter, wife of President Jimmy Carter, both Georgia natives. Mrs. Carter's initials can still be seen on the ship's keel.

In October 2004, USS GEORGIA was re-designated to SSGN after the successful completion of exercise "Silent Hammer," the SSGN proof-of-concept operation. In February 2005, USS GEORGIA entered Norfolk Naval Shipyard for a scheduled Engineered Refueling Overhaul and conversion to SSGN. In December 2007, USS GEORGIA departed Norfolk, Virginia for her new home in Kings Bay, Georgia.

We began the website, Welcome to the USS GEORGIA (SSGN 729) a Return to Service website sponsored by the Camden-Kings Bay Council of the Navy League of the U.S., The Camden Partnership, the Camden County (GA) Chamber of Commerce and the Naval Submarine League—Atlantic Southeast Chapter. A ceremony to welcome the USS GEORGIA Return to Service as a Guided Missile Submarine (SSGN), following her conversion from a Ballistic Missile Submarine (SSBN), was held aboard Naval Submarine Base Kings Bay on Friday, March 28, 2008. Several thousand people—including national, state and local dignitaries—were on hand for this unique and memorable ceremony welcoming the USS GEORGIA and her crew to her new home in Camden County, Georgia. We never wanted the USS GEORGIA to leave Georgia.

Keep the USS GEORGIA in Georgia
An Online Petition to Support Permanent Berthing of USS GEORGIA in Camden County, GA

The planned useful life of the original Ohio Class submarines was originally set at 30 years, later extended to 42 years, meaning that the first Ohio Class submarine retirement would take place in 2024. At some point, the USS GEORGIA will reach the end of her useful life and be decommissioned, and the Navy will have to decide what to do with her. After removing sensitive material and equipment, the options for disposal include sinking, scrapping or saving. This petition is meant to encourage early discussion among all stakeholders about the future of USS GEORGIA (SSGN 729), and show support for the transfer of ship and title to Camden County, Georgia, upon decommissioning, and permanent berthing of USS GEORGIA at a suitable site in the County.

USS GEORGIA should remain in Georgia as a monument to the men and women who have served aboard the ship, and as a reminder to all citizens of the sacrifices made to keep our country safe. With a permanent home in Camden County, GA, the USS GEORGIA will be guaranteed an honored and revered future, and the community will benefit from a unique, one of a kind, tourist attraction, and an educational asset for all citizens.

Please sign the petition below and help prepare for the future of USS GEORGIA (SSGN 729).

Yes, I encourage and support permanent berthing of the USS GEORGIA (SSGN 729) at a suitable site in Camden County, Georgia, following her decommissioning.

* * * * *

I wanted the entire state to have an opportunity to participate in the return of the USS *Georgia*. We also wanted to involve the Governor and the state. That part was easy. We'll get the governor to fly the Georgia Flag over the Capitol and then present it to the ship. That covered the ceremony with the Governor. We also had Dean Slusser promoting an art contest for schools across the state. What if we took the flag flown over the Capitol by the governor and, working with the state patrol, have every county in Georgia have a flag ceremony. I called my friend, Don Giles, a retired Navy captain whom I had worked with in the Navy League for years. He liked the idea but recognized the enormity of it. He wanted to think about it. He called me back a few days later and declined. It was just too big a project. I agreed and told him we would just have the governor fly it over the Capitol.

"You mean you aren't going to do it?" Don asked with surprise.

"No, Don. You are right this is a big commitment. You are the only one I would trust to do it. If you can't there is no one else."

"Okay, I'll do it." And he did.

Georgia State Flag Project

On January 14, 2008, Governor Sonny Perdue and the USS *Georgia* Return to Service Committee announced the USS *Georgia* Flag Project, an ambitious effort to take a Georgia state flag across the entire state and into all 159 Georgia counties for recognition by local officials and the signing of a log book. The flag and log book traveled the state, visiting every one of Georgia's counties so that all Georgians could participate in welcoming the USS *Georgia* home.

On March 27, 2008, the flag and log book, along with countless proclamations and other official documents, were presented to the captain and crew of the USS *Georgia* during the final flag ceremony held in Camden Country, home of Naval Submarine Base Kings Bay, the proud new home base of the USS *Georgia*. The flag will be displayed onboard the ship as a testament to the support of her namesake State for the crew of the USS *Georgia* now and into the future.

The Flag Project was headed by Navy League member and RTS Committee Flag Project Coordinator Capt. Don Giles, USN (ret.) who worked with the sixteen Georgia Regional Development Centers in planning and carrying out this unprecedented project. This is the first time such a project has ever been attempted anywhere in the US. There were articles from sixty-five different newspapers across the state of Georgia all picked up by Dave Burch an important part of the committee.

Steve Howard, county administrator for Camden County, had the final leg of the journey with the ceremony at the Bancroft Memorial in front of Naval Submarine Base Kings Bay. Captain Wes Stevens arranged for his staff to set up the area in front of the memorial.

Student Art Competition

Involving the children across Georgia was another big undertaking. And for this there is also just one person who could pull it off. I called Dean Slusser. We met and discussed how best to involve students. Dean was an art teacher at the Camden County High school and had a background of success in directing major events. We decided on the theme "Brining Georgia Home: Georgia's Ambassador for Peace." This statewide art contest was held in all 160 school districts across the state including elementary, middle, and high school students. Over one thousand children participated in this incredible project. The twenty-one-finalist began a three-city tour in Camden County before being shipped back to their school districts.

The three evenings before the ceremony we had chefs from three different restaurants/organizations prepared for various groups in Georgia and Florida. Parties were from: The Cloister at Sea Island, The culinary students from both the College of Coastal Georgia and Florida Coast Technical College. Our last evening with the crew was a wonderful ending of a week we won't forget. The committee hosted a dinner for five hundred crew and family members who were able to celebrate the day's event and accept the love and thanks of the community. It was truly special to have the families get together and to be able to thank them for the service of their sons, fathers, and husbands. It turned out to be an emotional, eye watering event. We are sure there was not a family member in attendance who did not have renewed appreciation of the role they played in support of their family member. Each family received a red duffel bag with the Georgia Bulldog/Sailor insignia and gifts from many, many merchants.

The Return to Service Committee were sponsors of "Bringing the USS *Georgia* Home: Celebrating Georgia's Ambassador for Peace"—a statewide student art competition for Georgia art students of every age. Camden County High School student Nicole Wasson's entry was chosen as the "Captain's Choice" grand prize winner. I might note that the names and schools of the students were not known by the judges. It was amazing that the winner was from Camden County. Nicole's color pencil drawing incorporates the submarine, state seal, state bird, state flower, and a Georgia peach.

Here are winners in all categories:

CAPTAIN'S CHOICE

Nicole Wasson, 10th Grade
Camden County School System

CATEGORY WINNERS

Elementary School

Anthony Williams, 4th Grade, DeKalb County School System
Molly Caitlin McCord, 5th Grade, Coweta County School System
Christiana Herron, 3rd Grade, Houston County School System
Telvin Martin, 5th Grade, Dublin City School System
Luis Gutierrez, 5th Grade, Clark County School System
Christo Hickey, Pre-K, Brunswick ~ Savannah Diocese School
Sebastian Wilson, 1st Grade, Muscogee County School System

Middle School

Brooke Smith, 8th Grade, Troup County School System
Rachel Hawk, 7th Grade, Muscogee County School System
Edwin Vazquez, 8th Grade, Hall County School System

Alex Cortez, 7th Grade, White County School System
Erin Lynch, 7th Grade, Peach County School System
Cody Woodle, 7th Grade, Coweta County School System
Javontae Koonce, 7th Grade, Atlanta Public School System

High School
Tiffany Housey, 12th Grade, Dekalb County School System
Garrison Muelhausen, 9th Grade, Thomas County School System
Brey Littleton, 12th Grade, Lanier County School System
Whitney McDaniel, 9th Grade, Carroll County School System
Wynton Redmond, 11th Grade, Cobb County School System
JoAnna Heath, 11th Grade, Barton County School System
Nicole Wasson, 10th Grade, Camden County School System

USS GEORGIA (SSGN 729)
Return to Service Committee
Post Office Box 5096
St. Marys, Georgia 31558

BECOME A PART OF HISTORY!

The USS GEORGIA (SSGN 729) will be coming to Camden County very soon where she will call Naval Submarine Base Kings Bay home. The submarine has gone through an extensive refueling overhaul, modernization and conversion from a BALLISTIC MISSILE SUBMARINE (SSBN) to a GUIDED MISSILE SUBMARINE (SSGN) during this process.

For those of you not familiar with naval terminology, a 'plank owner' is typically an individual who was a member of the crew of a ship when that ship was placed in commission. In earlier years this applied to a first commissioning, since then it has often been applied to one who was part of a re-commissioning crew as well. While 'Plank Owner' is not an 'official' Navy term, tradition has it recorded that way.

A Return to Service (RTS) ceremony to commemorate this milestone will be held on the base in March 2008. You have the opportunity to participate in this historic event in our area by becoming an *HONORARY PLANKOWNER* of SSGN 729. For a minimum of $100.00 you will receive a Plank Certificate similar to the one displayed below. Additional sponsorships are available. PLEASE return this sponsorship form along with your check by *January 10th, 2008* to ensure that you will be listed in the Commemorative Program.

USS GEORGIA (SSGN 729) Return to Service Sponsors

The USS GEORGIA Return to Service Committee wishes to thank all of our generous sponsors for their contributions to help defray the costs of the many events and activities surrounding the March 28, 2008, gala Return to Service ceremony. Our special thanks go to the following organizations and individuals:

GOLD SPONSORS—$10,000

The Coca-Cola Company
Lockheed Martin Maritime Systems and Sensors
Tribune & Georgian

SILVER SPONSORS—$5,000

BAE Systems
First Coast Technical College—Culinary Arts
General Dynamics Electric Boat
Georgia Pacific St. Marys Extrusion Operations
Georgia Ports Authority
Georgia Power Company
Northrop Grumman Corp.—Electronic Systems—Marine Systems
VT Griffin Services
W.H. Gross Construction Company

BRONZE SPONSORS—$2,500

Ameris Bank
Mr. and Mrs. Frank Barron Jr.
Brunswick—Golden Isles Council, Navy League
Camden—Kings Bay Council, Navy League
Coastal Bank of Georgia
ComSouth Corporation
Freedom Self Storage
Georgia Department of Economic Development
Gilbert, Harrell, Summerford & Martin
Kings Bay Village Shopping Center
Mayport Council, Navy League
Northrop Grumman Space and Mission Systems, Corp.
Raytheon Missile Systems
Southeast Georgia Health System

ADMIRAL SPONSORS—$1,000

Dr. and Mrs. Rob Baird
Brian Signs of Atlanta
Bulldawg Illustrated
Camden/Charlton County Board of Realtors
Dr. Mary Faye Craft
Mary and Jack Dinos
Pete and Rachel Harper
City of Kingsland
Privett-Bennett & Associates, Inc.
City of St. Marys
Satilla Community Bank
Satilla Temps
Vista Outdoor Advertising

CAPTAIN SPONSORS—$500

Atlantic Auto Brokers
Barco Federal Systems
Bayer Crop Science
Tad and Norm Berkowitz
Camden County Chamber of Commerce—Military Community Council
Camden Printing
First Atlantic Bank
Debbie and Stu Graham
Harbor Pines Apartments
Col. & Mrs. Franklin A. Hart Jr. USMC (Ret)
Capt. And Mrs. Hollis Holden USN (Ret)
John and Marianne Innes
Jacksonville Florida Council Navy League
CAPT & Mrs. Harley T. Jones, USN (Ret)
Jim and Debbie Keller
Mr. & Mrs. John Lindgren, Capt. USNR (Ret)
Captain Bob Morrison USNR-R and Dr. Leslie Morrison
Navy Federal Credit Union
P & A Engineering, Inc.
S & S Pools/Spa
St. Marys Kiwanis Club
St. Marys Psychiatry—Ruxandra Mares, MD
Mayor Kenneth E. Smith
Soncel at The Lakes

CHIEF SPONSORS—$250

AGL Resources
MTCM (SS) Gary and Cheryl L. Aston
Mr. and Mrs. Richard A. Butler
Mike and Anne Campbell
William Carreira Jr.
Coastal GA. Regional Development Center
Coastal Nurse Care
The Cumberland Financial Group LLC

NCCM William David and Kelly Gibbs
CPO Taylor J. Dean, USN (Ret)
Casper P. DeFino, TMC USN (Ret)
Britt and JoAnn Elrod
Express Scripts, Inc.
FED Consulting
Gas South
The Heritage Bank
State Representative Cecily Hill
George and Lorie Holmes

Kings Bay CPOA
Kings Bay Mail and More, Inc.
Marty and Charley Klumpp
Louis Lambremont
Terry and Darlene Landreth
Pat and Don Lang
Clifford and Karen Lindholm
Brenda McAlister—Ross
CAPT & Mrs. Charles McCluskey, USN(Ret)
Tracy and Barbara Mizelle
Robert C. Paulk—C-21 Tri City Realty
Keith F. Post
Mr. and Mrs. William T. Schwendler Jr.
Spencer House Inn
CRD William H. Sidner, USN (Ret)
Uncle Bob's Self Storage
Jack and Laura Williams

CREW SPONSORS— Plank Owners—$100

Steve Adams
Albany Chamber of Commerce, Military Affairs Committee
John and Sharon Aston
Mary Lou and Richard Austin
Cle Baker
Wilbur and Mary Becker
RADM Charles J. Beers Jr.
Barry and Amy Beeson
Clinton and Andrea Behringer
Lee and Margaret Bernasek
David W. Bird
Greg and JoBeth Bird
Alex Bishop and Zach Goldwire
The Blatz Family
Chris and Valarie Bonner
CDR Matthew Braatz, USNR (Ret)
Lt. Col. Charles Breslauer USAF (Ret)
John and Annette Briggs
Patrick Brown
Michael and Bonnie Browning
Mr. and Mrs. William Boydston
David and Marci Burch
Eugene H. Buttle
Camden County Joint Development Authority
Danny Camp
Donnell M. Camp
LCDR Frank Campbell, USN (Ret)
Lenore H. Campbell
Leon W. Campbell
Robert and Mary Rose Cannistraro
Cantrell Properties, Inc.
John and Jeanne Capozzi
Bob and Verna Carlisle
Carla C. Carper
Chris and Lori Chalmers
Mr. and Mrs. James Steven Chambless
The Camden Partnership
Charter Bank Mortgage
Holly A. Christensen
Joan and Donald Civitanova

MMCM Doug & Joy Cooper, USN ®
Country Inn and Suites
Harry Crossley
Culligan Water Services
Cumberland Insurance Agency
Dalton Signs, Inc.
Kevin and Christine Daniel
William B. Dawson
Ken Day
CPO Taylor J. Dean, USN (Ret)
Bill and Candy DeLoughy
Democrats of Camden County
Robert J. Demsey
William W. Dohn
End Time Gospel Church
Joshua Ehrhardt
Logan Ehrhardt
Patti Ehrhardt
Mr. and Mrs. Rick Faber
Robert A. Fell
In Honor of Fleet and Family Support
Mrs. Joan P. Forrestel
Stan Fowler
Irene Franklin
Betsy Friedman
Mark Friedman
Jim and Robbie Frye
Luke Gaston
CAPT and Mrs. David Geer, USN (Ret)
Georgia Military Officers Association, Inc.
Robert J. Gephart
Dorothy Glisson and Ward Hernandez
Joost A. Gompels
Hilton Head Island Council, Navy League of the United States
Pedro and Ivonne Gonzalez
Bobby L. Green, LCDR USN (Ret)
Tommy and Jodi Gregory
Allene and Bob Groote
Len and Mary Gullickson
Edward and Lily Gushen
Royce and Faye Hall
Kathleen Haller
Lee Haller
CAPT & Mrs. Larry D. Hamilton, USN (Ret)
Hampton Inn
George L. Hannaford
John and Jan Harper
Gregg and Tanya Harrell
Mr. Wayne R. Harrigan Sr.
Penny Harris
Bob Hightower
Michael W. Hodson
Steve L. Howard
Howe Construction, Inc.
Elizabeth Howe
Michael and Arlene Huber
James F. Hunter, LCDR
Gary A. Johnson
Mark and Barbara Kevan
Jim and Linda Kimpel
Barrett and Elizabeth King
Robbi and Katrina King
Wiley B. King
William Robert and Marian C. Kuhn
Mr. and Mrs. Hubert W. Lang III
Chuck and OJ Lanham
Jinny Latham
Thomas H. Latham
Lockhart and Associates Realty
Dr. Dorothy L. Lord
Dave and Ginny Lovett
Patrick J. Lynch
Dr. Arnetia S. Maasha
Main Street Frame Shop, Inc.

Marianne's Sterlings Southern Café
Vernon and Kanda Martin
Bud McCleskey
James R. McCollum
Jeanne & Jack McConnell
Ed and Diane McCoy
John W. McDill
Melinda McGrath
J. Michel and Gloria McGrath
Sarah Kate McKinney
Captain Michael & Rhonda McKinnon, USN (Ret)
Sheila and Arlie McNeill
City of McRae, Georgia
Jack and Vickie Mead
Capt. and Mrs. Richard C. Miller, USN (Ret)
Louise V. Mitchell
Patricia and Keith Moore
Paul R. Morrow
Walt and Donna Natzic
Nautilus Models
Katherine Nisi-Zell
Arlene C. Norris
Oak Grove Island Yacht Club
Devin and Emily O'Brien
Thomas C. O'Connor
Mr. and Mrs. Warren R. Onken
R. Michael Patrick
Peds and Parents Family Care, LLC
Paul H. Ploeger
CDR Arthur R. Porcelli Jr. USN (Ret)
In Memory of Alice Post
Robert and Ann Prescott
Jerry Quigley
David and Yvonne Rainer
Richard Radcliffe, CDR, R.C.N. (Ret)
David and Betty Reilly
Preston Rhodes
Edwin D. Robb
Lesley and Pargen Robertson
Mary M. Rocha
Ricky Rodriguez
Mary Root
Ross Irrigation & Consulting
J. Ronald Ross
Patty C. Ross
Rotary Club of Camden County
The Rotary Club of Kings Bay
James and Linda Rothwell
Royal—Skies Realty
Allan and Sandra Ryysylainen
Dr. William & Mrs. Sally Rush
St. Marys Submarine Museum
Brian and Andrea Schultz
The Robert William Scott Jr. Family
Charlene Sears
Howard and Judy Sepp
Robert L. Shad and Family
Willard G. and Susan W. Shafer
Sheila's Hallmark
Dean and Susan Slusser
Charlie Smith Jr.
Diana Smith
Tricia Smith
John C. Snedeker
Space Coast Council Navy League of the U.S.
Captain Frank and Mary Stagl
Blair C. Stain
Johnny Y. Stanfield
Richard A. Steele
Stein & Guy, P.C.
CAPT Mrs. Charles A. Stevenson, USN (Ret)
Colby and Georgia Stilson
Summit Sports Medicine & Orthopedic Surgery
Kenneth L. Surber Jr.
Max Tinsley

John and Pat Toler
Charles Trader Family
Jimmy Turner
Thomas E. Turner
United Community Bank
A.J. Velez
VetJobs
Bernard and Patricia Viellenave
Kenny and Deborah Warden
Mark and Rita Warren
The Weathers Family
Royal and Gull Weaver
LeRoy and Bobbie Weggenman
Capt. Bill and Nancy Weisensee, USN (Ret)
James Wells
James A. Wheeler QM-2 (SS)
David Whidby
Gary Willis
Christopher M. Wilson
Christopher M. Wilson Jr.
Maury and Jo Wishnoff
WKBX-FM * K-BAY 106
City of Woodbine
Wrens Better Hometown, Inc.
Lynn & Tom Wright
Justin and Cory Wyatt
Debbie and Larry Younger
Capt. Walt and Dee Yourstone

* * * * *

Senator William Ligon Jr. and Senator Harbison sponsored the following resolution

Senate Resolution 65 By: Senators Ligon Jr. of the 3rd and Harbison of the 15th

A RESOLUTION

Recognizing January 30, 2013, as USS *Georgia* Day; and for other purposes.

WHEREAS, the USS *Georgia*, named after our great state, was first launched in 1982 and has since played an important role in protecting our nation; and

WHEREAS, the submarine's return to service was celebrated in Kings Bay, Georgia, in

March 2008 after being converted from a Submersible Ship, Ballistic missile, Nuclear powered (SSBN) submarine to a Submersible Ship, Guided missile, Nuclear powered (SSGN) submarine; and

WHEREAS, the USS *Georgia*'s relocation was the result of the tireless efforts of dedicated citizens in Camden County and throughout our state; and

WHEREAS, this great submarine is operated and cared for by the extraordinarily brave men and women of the United States Navy who have chosen a life of service to their nation, and to whom we are forever grateful; and

WHEREAS, the USS *Georgia* will soon depart her home in Kings Bay for a tour of service beneath deep waters, fulfilling her mission of protecting peace and fighting for freedom; and WHEREAS, all Georgians will anxiously await the safe return of the USS *Georgia* and those who travel with her.

NOW, THEREFORE, BE IT RESOLVED BY THE SENATE that the members of this body commend the USS *Georgia* and recognize January 30, 2013, as USS *Georgia* Day.

BE IT FURTHER RESOLVED that the Secretary of the Senate is authorized and directed to transmit an appropriate copy of this resolution to the USS *Georgia*.

And then the ceremony:

USS GEORGIA (SSGN 729) RETURN TO SERVICE CEREMONY

A ceremony to welcome the USS *Georgia* Return to Service as a Guided Missile Submarine (SSGN), following her conversion from a Ballistic Missile Submarine (SSBN), was held aboard Naval Submarine Base Kings Bay on Friday, March 28, 2008. Several thousand people—including national, state, and local dignitaries—were on hand for this unique and memorable ceremony welcoming the USS *Georgia* and her crew to her new home in Camden County, Georgia.

LCDR Todd Sullivan, the young man who worked for me at the Hallmark store on his off hours was also the officer who worked with me on the planning for the return to service. He was transferred just days before the ceremony. Later I had an e-mail from him:

> *Hello, Sheila, Well, I am settled in to a dull routine in Iraq. I am working all of the requirements for the base here that goes to our US civilian contractors; everything from maintenance on vehicles to a $14M project revamping our aviation fueling for the airfield. I live in a 20' x 12' trailer on my own. I have internet (that I pay for) A/C, TV (8 channels of Armed Forces Network), a fridge, microwave and a coffee pot. A good friend lives next door and we share a porch that was made from wood with some camouflage netting around it.*
>
> *The base is pretty safe, with some amenities. We have a coffee shop, theater and a place where we can play pool. There is a nice gym and in indoor pool. There is an outdoor pool but it is not operational. This base used to house three Iraqi fighter squadrons and was home to their Olympic training grounds. We have had a few sandstorms so far, but they have all been pretty small. All in all, it isn't the worse thing in the world, but I could be happier! Hope all is well back home and that you are enjoying some shorter days!*
>
> *Todd*

I continue to keep up with the *USS Georgia* as much as I can. It's easier when I can meet the commanding officers early on. And even easier when I knew the commanding officers when he was a lieutenant and aide, when I first met Rhett and Dinah. This was the case when Jaehn and I first met.

I was introducing him to Dr. Valerie Hepburn, the president of the College of Coastal Georgia as the commanding officer of the *USS Georgia*. Rhett told Valerie, "Sheila introduced me as a captain but in her eyes, I'll always be a lieutenant."

I wondered, "How did he know that?" It's true. But the reason is more of a loving, protective way. I'm always so proud to see them get promoted but don't forget what it was like when they were young and just starting their careers.

Everyone who worked on the Return to Service has reason to be proud.

USS *NEW YORK* (LPD 21)

DR. PHILLIP DURR, RADM

I received an invitation to attend the ceremony at the foundry for the USS *New York*. On September 9, 2003.

Dr. Philip A. Dur
Requests the honor of your presence at a
Laying of the Keep Ceremony for the
Amphibious Transport Dock Ship New York (LPD 21)
Authenticating the keel will be
Mrs. Dotty England, Ships' Sponsor
Friday, September 10, 2004 at 11:30 a.m.
Northrop Grumman Ship Systems Avondale Operations

USS *New York* is number five of eight of the Navy's newest and most advanced amphibious ships. They were designed to deliver Marines and their equipment where they are needed to support a variety of missions ranging from amphibious assaults to humanitarian relief efforts. They are longer than two football fields at 684 feet. It will carry a crew of 360 sailors and 700 combat-ready marines to be delivered ashore by helicopters and assault craft. These ships will be homeported in Mayport—just an hour away from my hometown. But this ship was special. Steel from the World Trade Center was to be melted down in this Northrup Grumman foundry in Amite, Louisiana to cast the ship's bow section. A total of seven short tons of scrap steel will be used.

Dotty England, wife of Gordon England, who was deputy defense secretary at that time was the sponsor. She smashed the traditional bottle of champagne at the

Christening on March 1, 2008, and the commissioning was November 7, 2009. In August 2005, Northrop Grumman finished construction of the bow stem. Hoisting and welding the 7.5-metric-ton bow stem to the ship was completed in August 2006.

The USS *New York* website gave me great information on how this came about.

> *"It's a tremendous feeling," said Capt. Bill Galinis, Navy program manager for LPD 21. "It's a tie that will forever bind the Sailors and Marines who sail this ship with the citizens of New York."*
>
> *The idea for using steel from the WTC as part of the ship's frame could not be attributed to any one individual or organization. However, New York Gov. George Pataki worked to acquire the steel and deliver it to the Amite Foundry and Machine, Inc., Amite, La., as a gift from the citizens of New York to the Navy. The steel was treated and smelted for use as the ship's bow stem (Unit 1120) during construction. The bow stem is the foremost portion of the ship where it cuts through the water and offers hull integrity.*
>
> *"The significance of where the WTC steel is located on the 684-foot-long ship symbolizes the strength and resiliency of the citizens of New York as it sails forward around the world," said Cmdr. Quentin King, Navy program manager representative on site. "It sends a message of America becoming stronger as a result, coming together as a country and ready to move forward as we make our way through the world." The design of New York and its sister ships directly reflects considerations given to the day-to-day activities of the Sailors and Marines who will serve aboard.*

Arrangements were made to travel by bus to the foundry—I joined about a dozen others. When the bus arrived in Amite, Louisiana we were greeted by Dr. Phil Durr, president of Northrop Grumman Ship Systems. He held out his hand as I stepped down from the bus. He introduced himself and I introduced myself as president of the Navy League. He smiled and commented, "I didn't realize we had the local Navy League council president attending."

"No, I am the national president."

He held out his hand and said, "Let me show you in."

Dr. Dur was most gracious and escorted me into the building where the pre-reception was being held. He told me to stay close that in a moment the secretary of the Navy would be arriving. As I saw the SECNAV approach I stood behind him. As soon as Secretary H. T. Johnson arrived and reached out to shake hands with Dr. Durr, H.T. held his arms up in the air and turned around and around, "Sheila, what do you think?"

I told him, "Looks like the diet is working, sir."

He gave me a hug and then spoke to Dr. Durr and we all went back to join the group. A few minutes later Dr. Dur told me, "The deputy Homeland Security is arriving with his wife, Dotty, who is sponsor of the ship."

Again, I waited slightly behind Dr. Durr. As soon as Secretary England arrived, he started to shake hands with Dr. Durr and saw me and said, "How is my favorite Navy League president?"

They talked as I rejoined the group. Phil, as I now called Dr. Durr said, "That is the last time I try to introduce you to anyone!" He then asked me to join the party on the dais. What an honor!

The ceremony was incredibly moving. There were New York city firemen and police officers who were at the towers on 9/11. There were those there who lost family members on 9/11. Someone was quoted in a news article later that "those big rough steelworkers treated it with total reverence."

Kevin Wensing, Public Affairs for the Secretary of the Navy said it best: "It was a spiritual moment for everybody there." He was right.

USS *RONALD REAGAN* (CVN 76) COMMISSIONING

The Navy League is well known for its ship's commissionings. If you talk with anyone who has ever been in charge of one, they will tell you it is a magnificent occasion. Mary Ellen Baldwin, Executive Director of the Hampton Roads Council of the Navy League is the Guru of ship's commissionings. She was chairman of the *Reagan* commissioning with the assistance of Connie O'Shaughnessy-Los, president of the Santa Barbara Navy League. She had super special events in Santa Barbara, but I was not able to attend. I was within the first couple of months after my election and the time had been full of briefings and learning about the job. It was strange to see my name in the letter in the program welcoming everyone.

Veronica Brandon, our person in charge of "Giving," and I were escorted to a table at the front of the room. When we sat down I realized, I didn't know anyone there. I had expected to be seated with some of the military and had not questioned who that might be. I had such trust in Linda Hoffman, Katy Doud, and Mary Ellen Baldwin, but this time I wondered. Those at the table, all seemed to know each other and were in the middle of conversations. We sat down quietly and listened, all the time wishing I'd ask who I was going to be seated with. And I must admit, a little disappointed that I would not be with someone I could talk to about the Navy League.

The very nice lady next to me said hello and someone immediately asked her something. She started talking about education. My confusion continued. I did smile at a gentleman across from me who did look a little familiar. In the meantime, Veronica and I talked to the gentleman who was between us. He was AC Lyle, of Paramount Pictures. AC had introduced the Reagans and remained friends this entire time. In fact, he still had an office at Paramount. Someone called the gentleman across the table Edwin. Something clicked. Edwin Meese! It dawned on me the gentleman across from the was Edwin Meese Attorney General under President Reagan. I was sitting with the Reagan cabinet! What a treat and what a surprise!

Michael Reagan spoke on the family's behalf. I had several conversations with Michael over the two days of activities. The reception was a "who's who" in the Navy, but there were a couple of celebrities that didn't wear uniforms: Bo Derek who was just as beautiful as when she had that famous picture taken. Karri Turner who was currently starring on JAG was also a beautiful lady and both were so gracious to all the crew and guest. Karrie and I exchanged e-mails and I received a very nice e-mail from her later.

Arlie and I were part of the platform, so we waited and then were escorted to the ship. When we were seated, I realized that we were not going to be able to hear the ceremony. The loud speakers were all directed to the huge audience and we only caught a word or two. I'm sure the powerful guests on the front row could hear: Vice President Richard Cheney, Nancy Reagan, Michael Reagan, Governor Mark Warner. Senator Allen and his wife, Acting Secretary of the Navy H. T. Johnson, Chief of Naval Operations Admiral Vern Clark and Connie, Director of Naval Nuclear Propulsion, Admiral Frank (Skip) Bowman and Linda, Fleet Forces Command Admiral Bob Natter and Mrs. Natter, Assistant SECNAV John Young and Mrs. Young and the Mayor of Norfolk Paul Fraim and my friend Mary Ellen Baldwin—but I never asked them. Arlie and I were just pleased to be there. There was a small problem. Since we couldn't hear anything we didn't know who was speaking or what they said. I turned to Arlie and whispered something, and it turned out that my whispering was in the middle of the prayer. My mother saw it on CSPAN as did many of my friends. It took a lot of explaining! I didn't know the camera was catching me almost the entire ship's commissioning. Mother told me she was going to go back and tell all her friends I couldn't hear anything, so they wouldn't think I was rude!

Michael Reagan, President Reagan's son was at all the activities. At that time, I had my Hallmark Store and "beanie babies" were selling like crazy. One of the popular ones was the USS *Ronald Reagan*. After the ceremony, we were talking to Michael on the gangplank. I told him about the customer's delight with the bear. He called "Ty" the owner of the Beanie Babies company and let me talk to him. All proceeds went to the crew and I was able to thank him for his generosity and share with him the delight of those in a Navy community. Captain J. W. (Bill) Goodwin, Commanding Officer, was most gracious and handled the task of so many VIPs with great finesse. It was two days of events that I won't soon forget.

We received e-mails from all over. My good friends Tom and Lisa Prusinowski sent a nice note as did Bill and Ann Nisbet who watched it all on C-SPAN. The friends in town just gave me a hard time for whispering to Mac. I'll say again, "You couldn't hear a thing that was being said. All of the speakers were directed off the carrier!"

It was two days of events that I won't soon forget. Most of my friends and family continued to give me a hard time about whispering to Arlie.

VICE PRESIDENT AND PLAYING WITH THE BIG BOYS

(Another of those "What are you doing here?" moments)

At Sea Air Space in April 2001 I was assigned to escort Admiral Jim Loy, the commandant of the Coast Guard. It was a great assignment! I left Admiral Loy to go to the ladies' room before we entered the ballroom for the banquet. When I returned, I saw Admiral Loy talking with CNO Vern Clark and several others. When I saw a former Navy League president, who was very much against me I decided to wait to go over. He had previously told someone that every time he talked with someone important I came over. Really? Rubbish. I stood and waited. Although it was my responsible to escort Adm. Loy I was trying not to offend the former president by interrupting them. But as Admiral Clark saw me waiting he raised his eyebrows, made eye contact, and kept contact as I walked over. Arlie said evidently the former president was in the middle of one of his long stories because when the CNO turned to greet me with a big "Sheila!" *and* a big kiss the past president turned away and said, "I can't compete with that."

Later at the banquet we were all lead in for the head tables and I was seated next to him. Everyone in the room—1,200 people were all standing and talking. He said to me, "Let me seat you."

"I'll wait just a minute," I said with a smile.

"You've won, why don't you just be gracious and sit down!"

(I suppose his reference is the fact that I was the first woman to serve as vice president of legislative affairs. But the word was out that I was running for president.)

"What do you mean?"

"You women, you win everything, why don't you sit down and be gracious when it's appropriate!"

It literally took everything I had not to respond. I sat down like a good little girl, the other ladies then had to sit and we remained—the women seated with no one next to them to talk to because the good ole boys stood and talked for another five to ten minutes. Ironically his wife told Arlie, "Sheila is going to make a wonderful president."

And went on to extol my virtues. God bless her for standing up for herself against his opinion, although I'll bet she never shared her opinion with him again. She is a great lady.

After Sea Air Space, we joined our old friends. There is nothing like sitting down with friends after the up and downs of life.

It was the usual suspects: Chuck and Greer Meyer, C. J. and Jennifer Ihrig and Mal and Shirley Fages. The next evening Mal and Shirley picked us up to have dinner at their quarters at the Navy yard. We were next door to the Tingy House where Admiral Clark and Connie lived but I managed to keep my impulses in check and not ring the doorbell.

WARWICK, LYNN AND PAUL

I've known Lynn since high school. I enjoy teasing about her being so much older. A year makes a big difference when you are in high school. It's hard to write about someone who has been a friend for fifty years. Lynn is smart as hell and stays up to date with national and local politics, who married who, who divorced who, who is whose mother. No one can touch Lynn on the history of Glynn County and its citizens.

The 80's were a marvelous time with dancing during the evening and the beach almost every weekend. That was a time people really knew how to dance—that romantic kind and that great jitterbug. Paul and Arlie were always super reserved with the drinking yet didn't try to deter others. There wasn't that much drinking, but everyone knew there were two men who could always be the designated drivers: Paul and Arlie. Lynn was very popular in high school and came from a prominent family. She was raised by her grandparents and her grandfather was the well-known county medical examiner.

As popular as she was we were still friends. Not as close as we are now but she didn't shun me. We had a gang of us when we started. Lynn was not so much a beach bum as many of us were. I paid for some of that excessive sun bathing years later with skin cancer, but you couldn't have stopped me then. Lynn got cutest in high school and she still is. She has her own style and she carries it off well. I, on the other hand, am still wearing clothes from sixteen years ago. I hate shopping—she loves it. I like to read novels—Lynn doesn't. I like movies—Lynn doesn't. I used to like just hanging out—Lynn never did. She must be going somewhere and doing something all the time.

Lynn is a great business woman. She has been in business for about twenty years managing to continue in the worst of times.

My mother and aunt were very close. Every Friday or Saturday for about ten years Lynn played cards with my mother, her sister and me. We all became closer than ever. I loved seeing my mother and aunt as friendly rivals in a game of cards. Lynn would do most anything to make them happy. One weekend she talked us into coming to her house for the weekend. It was a long drive—about fifteen minutes—and she waited on them all weekend. They had a great time and talked about it frequently. My mother and her sister both died within six months of each other. Thank you, Lynn.

Arlie uses her as his computer. She remembers everyone and everything. (She can tell you who married who and how many first cousins they have.) There was only one person who knew Glynn County residents as well, and he is deceased.

She has wonderful children who are as different and as complex as my siblings are. As did Paul. Since we've known her children since they were born we are supposed to be 'Sheila' and 'Arlie' but it's been "Mrs. McNeill" from Jeff from day one. I remember Jeff being out with Lynn and me for lunch, when he was in his late teens saying, "Mrs. McNeill, if you weren't married to Mr. McNeill, I'd ask you to marry me. At his and Kelly's wedding reception at the Marina Village he came up to me and said, 'Mrs. McNeill it's now or never. Do you want to take one of the yachts and go away somewhere?'" When I agreed, he wanted to know how much money I had. When I told him five dollars, our lifetime plans vanished. Their entire family is fun to be with!

Years later when I was Paul's campaign manager for mayor of Brunswick. We would have to leave Lynn at home for some meetings. She thought it was morally wrong not to express her opinion. But to her credit she took it in stride and was a wonderful first lady of Brunswick.

Lynn's birthday party for him January 20, 1996, was a roast. It was easy, not because he did a lot of funny or unusual things but because he was so proper with no improper tendencies so we all just made stuff up.

It was 1998. Paul was diagnosed with pancreatic cancer. He and Lynn tried many different treatments and they did prolong his life. One evening about four months into his illness he felt well enough to have dinner at Spankys now known as Marshside. Lynn, Paul, Arlie, and I had a fun evening, and everything was looking up. That night he became sick and was admitted to the hospital and went into a coma. Lynn let me stay with him for a couple of hours one day. I don't know what he heard but I talked for a long while about the fun we'd had.

During this time, I was running for the first time for national vice president. The meeting was in Seattle, Washington. The week of the meeting he died. Of course, we canceled our trip. Lynn asked me to give one of the eulogies. The funeral was held at St. Mark's Episcopal Church with Father Liam Collins and Rev. James Crandall officiating. Ellie Weeks, a longtime friend of Paul and Lynn's sang.

These were my words:

> *I was Paul's campaign manager when he ran for Mayor. The right choices in polities as well as in life are seldom easy ones, but Paul never compromised his principles or settled for less than what was absolutely right. He held himself to a higher standard than most.*

He was a man of integrity and honor. A friend told Lynn that the fact that Paul could be the Mayor of Brunswick and an insurance salesman and still have no enemies tell of his true nature. He always seemed to do the right thing for all the right reasons. The flags at half-mast all over the city are a poignant reminder of what Paul meant to this community.

Those of you who attended the roast of Paul Warwick will remember Joe Sousa imitating Paul's "positive attitude." This attitude helped him through his bout with cancer and subsequent treatments. He never gave up.

To Paul it wasn't the reward that mattered or the recognition he might receive. It was the depth of his commitment, the quality of the service he gave his clients—those were the things that counted in his business. One of his insurance colleagues and friends was telling us this week that no one really wanted to bid against Paul. He was just too nice. If they did happen to win the bid they felt so bad about it that the next time they just decided, when they heard they were bidding against Paul, not to even try for the business. This week on one of the morning radio talk shows, I was told that a woman calling in said, "I sometimes didn't agree with Paul Warwick, but in our dealings, he was always such a gentleman. I still felt good after our business was done, even when I lost." Paul made both men and women feel special.

His soft spoken, steady demeanor was respected by men and women, but I have been told by many men that they considered Paul a "man's man." One friend told me, "I have the most profound respect for Paul, but I have always felt somewhat inadequate around him. He was good looking, charming and always seemed to know just what to say. He is what I would have liked to be."

Paul loved God, his community, his country his friends and he did so love his family. Lynn and Paul have been married for 22 years and someone told her this week that they seem to be still having a love affair. Have you ever seen two people more meant for each other or better suited? If you went out with Lynn and Paul, you prepared yourself. They didn't see friends and simply say hello, they took time out to really talk to people, to ask about their families and their lives. They cared and people knew this. Of course, this didn't help when you were the friend waiting so long to eat. Paul truly loved Lynn and it was evident in everything he did. They had a special kind of love we all strive for and few will ever know.

Paul was a wonderful father. Jeff says, "Imagine if we hadn't had Paul and we had to go straight to Mom on everything." Paul was always the one who wanted to wait and hear you out and understand the situation. He always prepared Mom for our crisis." Mikes talks about Paul as his mentor and best friend as well as his father. He said that once Paul "set you straight" on something you never forgot."

He talked about his organized methods and meticulous nature. Yes, Paul loved his family and they had great times as a family. You can see the love Janet and the boys have for each other. And there are no stepbrothers and stepsisters in this family—they love one another and tease each other as siblings who obviously have special ties. Paul's death is tragic, and we can't understand the whys. We've all asked why Paul? Paul who cared and treated everyone with respect.

We will not understand the 'why' but we can be grateful for the time we had to say our goodbyes. The children were discussing this at the hospital and said if we tell him what he means to us, to tell him of our love. As friends, we are all also grateful we had this opportunity. I am sure Paul was not plagued by the 'what if's' or regrets. He didn't have to say, "If I had only tried." He always did what he said he was going to do and set the benchmark for others to follow. Quitting was not an option and he gathered strength from distress. I'm sure if he were not the humble man he was he would have discovered that he had exceeded his own expectations.

Every meal Paul said the same prayer:

Give us grateful hearts O Father for these and all our blessings—And make us mindful of the needs of others.

Paul lived by this creed. He was a good husband, father, brother and friend. He has left a legacy for this community that will be remembered. We are all better people for having known Paul Warwick.

* * * * *

Two years later the portion of Highway 17 as you approach the Sidney Lanier Bridge was named in his honor. The ceremony was in July 2000. Amy Horton, a reporter for the *Brunswick News*, and Lynn's niece covered the event:

CEREMONY SET FOR RESPECTED EX-MAYOR

BY Amy Horton
News staff writer
7-24-2000

Friends and relatives of former Brunswick Mayor Paul Warwick, Jr. are touched and tickled at the thought of an upcoming ceremony dedicating one of the busiest sections of U.S. Highway 17 to his memory. They know Warwick would be honored by the gesture, but they also know what his blushing response to it would be.

"With his lips kind of puckered up and his head half-cocked to one side, he'd say, "Well, for gosh sakes!" said Brunswick Golden Isles Chamber of Commerce President Woody Woodside, who enjoyed a healthy belly laugh at the thought. That was Warwick's signature line, delivered in a style many imitate but none can quite match.

An autoreactive but gentle man who invited praise and admiration for his work as mayor and a longtime community activist, Warwick always shielded from the limelight with his modest, "Aw shucks" response and sheepish grin. He's no longer able to dodge that acclaim, but Warwick's memory is still alive and well and inspiring praise, more than two years after his death.

The latest honor bestowed In his name will be unveiled at 4:30 p.m. Friday when the 2 ½ mile stretch of U.S. 17 between the F.J. Torras Causeway and the new Sidney Lanier Bridge will be christened the "Paul Warwick Jr Memorial Highway."

The chamber, the Georgia Department of Transportation and the city of Brunswick will host a ceremony in the shade underneath the ramp of the new bridge on the north bank of the Brunswick River. Woodside said that particular segment of U.S. 17 is symbolic of all that Warwick knew and loved during the 40 plus years he called Brunswick and the Golden Isles home It links his favorite barrier island with the mainland he loved, passing the historic Victorian style home that Warwick worked to see converted for use as the chamber's headquarters. It is also the gateway to historic downtown Brunswick, where Warwick lived amid centuries old beauty he also labored to preserve. It even passes Spanky's a business partly-owned by his son George "Moon" Warwick, who inherited his father's love of politics and proves it by holding court there regularly with the movers and shakers today—never missing a beat of work while he's at it.

But the most lasting monument to Warwick's memory stands just a few more miles down the road: the new Lanier Bridge. "It's very appropriate that the city of Brunswick and the state of Georgia name that section of highway after Paul as it is adjacent to a project which he, as mayor initiated by gathering the leadership—and acting as the catalyst which ultimately led to a unified local state and federal effort to replace the Sidney Lanier Bridge," Woodside said.

"That bridge will ensure Glynn County's future prosperity as an international seaport and forever provide a safe crossing over the Brunswick River.

Mayor Brad Brown said, "A lot of people travel that stretch of 17 and will see his name up there and remember his name. "When they come off the Lanier Bridge they'll see, and it will keep his honor out there because he did such great things during his term as mayor… and as a citizen after his term as mayor."

It was a full program:

Tom Triplett, Chairman of the State Transportation Board was the master of ceremonies.

Father Liam Collins, from Paul and Lynn's church—St. Mark's Episcopal Church gave the invocation and Stanley Moran sang the national anthem.

Brad Brown gave the welcome and the introduction of guests. The speakers were:

Lindsay Thomas, former Congressman from this district now President and CEO of the Georgia chamber of Commerce

Rene Kemp, State Senator

Friends: Sheila McNeill, Wiley Virden and George Morris

Ken Tollison, for Brunswick City Commissioner

Tom Coleman, Georgia DOT Commissioner

Stephen Scarlett, State Representative District 174 presented the resolution

Mike Maloy, Paul's son and Lynn, his wife gave response

The benediction was given by Richard Varnell, Pastor, First United Methodist Church

These were my remarks:

Paul would be so pleased and honored to be recognized in his way. Those who knew him are constantly stuck by our memories of him. He was a powerful presence in many lives. Paul always seemed to do the right thing and for the right reasons. I was Paul's campaign manager when he ran for Mayor. The right choices in politics as well as in life are seldom easy ones, but Paul never compromised his

> *principles or settled for less than what was absolutely right. He held himself to a high standard. He was a man of integrity and honor.*
>
> *How appropriate that this highway passes in front of the chamber where Paul was instrumental in the location, the purchase and the restoration of the building. It also leads to the connection of the island he so dearly loved to the mainland he so honorable served. As one of the Board of Directors and part of the original group that flew to Atlanta to meet with DOT on the proposal for the bridge, I remember Paul's vision for the magnificent bridge and the opportunities it will bring to the Golden Isles.*
>
> *This stretch of highway to the bridge that he envisioned will be a reminder to all of us of the legacy he left.*

COMMAND MASTER CHIEF ROYAL WEAVER AND GULL

Royal remembers this as the first time he ever saw me speechless.

"Has Royal talked with you yet?" Gull asked me as we were serving ourselves at a buffet reception.

"No, I haven't seen him yet," I answered.

"He wants you to speak at his retirement."

"Oh, no! He doesn't want to do that. Tell him to keep trying to get someone. His retirement speaker is too important. But tell him if he doesn't find anyone I'll be happy to but he can let me know later," I was quick to tell her.

"He doesn't want anyone else. You are his first choice. He wants you to speak," was Gull's surprising answer.

Royal approached us, his plate already loaded, and he was ready to sit down. "Did you ask her?" he said with a big grin.

"Yes, but she didn't believe me. She wants you to try to get someone else."

They finally convinced me that they really wanted me to speak. These were my remarks:

> *Royal Weaver was Command Master Chief of the Strategic Weapons Facility Atlantic (SWFLANT), a highly secure area where the missiles for the Trident submarines are assembled. This was one of the major commands at Kings Bay Naval Submarine Base. I had known he and Gull during the time they had been in Camden County. They were both very involved in the community. Gull would later be elected to the St. Marys City Council and Royal's dedication to the St. Marys Submarine Museum would never falter.*

Weeks later as I am working on the remarks and talking to everyone I could who had worked with Royal, he told me he had invited several of his old friends but made sure he never let them know of my gender. He told me he wanted to surprise his old submarine buddies, so he just said "McNeill" was speaking.

It was August 7, 1998 and a beautiful day. The ceremony was held at the Submarine Veterans of WWII Pavilion. It was a big crowd. This was the first time I had ever spoken at a retirement or change of command, so it was very special. It was also interesting for me to be able to stand to the side on the podium as the other members of the official party are introduced. All of them were military and the uniforms looked awesome.

Master Chief Weaver, Gull, Admiral (Joe) Henry, Admiral (Tom) Robertson, Captain (Dave) Reilly, Captain Digan, Captain (Will) Frye, Judge Proctor, family and friends of Royal and Gull, welcome. Our purpose today is both solemn and nostalgic. We are here to say goodbye to a friend and in so doing to recognize his years of outstanding service. I would like to thank all of you for being here to share this special occasion.

Master Chief Royal Weaver is a man who has dedicated most of his life to the service of his country and to the support of the United States Navy and the Submarine Force. He is a man of uncommon ability and diplomacy, a keen observer of people, a man of foresight who seeks and loves a challenge. He is also a gentleman of integrity and old-fashioned honesty. Many of you have known Royal longer and better than I. I have known he and Gull far too short a time, but I recognize a friendship that will endure. I consider it a high honor to have been asked to speak at the retirement of one of the Navy's finest. Master Chief Weaver has amassed a record of service and achievement that any man would be proud to claim, and of which most could only dream. Sir Winston Churchill was fond of saying that there are three kinds of people: Those who make things happen, those who watch, and those that wonder what happened. I've never seen Master Chief Weaver watching and wondering what happened!

I am neither a sailor nor a submariner, yet know of the stories of chiefs and their power and their responsibility. I use the word "power" rather than "authority" because I always sense a special kind of awe when you hear the word "Chief." Admiral Mike Boorda said, "The work "leadership" and the title "Chief Petty Officer" go together. You cannot say one without thinking of the other… The chief petty officers provide the technical expertise and experience, they know how to get the job done, and they know how to make all the right things happen."

We had Admiral Boorda speak to our Navy League right after he became CNO. This is one of my favorite stories so, since I have the podium, I guess I can tell it! We proceeded the dinner with a small reception at Admiral Ellis's quarters. Arlie was driving and Admiral Boorda and I were in the back seat. On the way to the clubs, he noted the red lights that had been turned to caution, the police at every light ushering him past, and the Marine guards on station. Expressing his humility, he said, "Sheila don't you think this is somewhat ridiculous?" I answered, "I know Sir, but they do it for me every time I come on base!" I'm glad he had a sense of humor. Admiral Boorda's respect for the rank of Chief Petty Officer is well known. From my earliest days of the Navy League, some 30 years ago, I was made aware of the contributions of "the Goat Locker." Even before that, my father's youngest brother was a Navy chief, and was and is a man I love and admire. Of course, I recognize that some of his tales of power and persuasion may have been somewhat exaggerated.

One thing I have seen is that when the chief says something people jump. This is the "old man" and when the "old man" talks, you listen. It is also impressive the way a chief trains and grooms young officers, and is able to do so without the young officer even knowing it. The Chief says "Aye, aye, Sir," but somehow manages to convince the young officer that what he really wanted to do is what the chief suggested in the first place. The officer learns and grows in confidence and experience, and in most cases, doesn't recognize until much later just how much he was gently guided by the Chief. I have attended many retirement ceremonies of officers and most times there is a reference to a Chief who influenced a turning point in their careers.

I have learned the sincerity and the traditions of the Chief's role. I have also met with chiefs from all five services in my role with The Defense Advisory Committee on Women in the Services, and have always been impressed with the responsibility, sense of pride and duty and the caring for their juniors These traits are evident in everything Master Chief Weaver does. Perhaps because Royal spent the earlier part of his career as a single man he has always gone out of his way to make every decision a good decision for every sailor—married or single. He has never been conventional and doesn't always go with the traditional answer. Perhaps this is why his career has progressed steadily. Another reason is surely because once he teamed up with Gull, it was a classic "winning combination." For years I heard the saying that has been used so much I think it sometimes loses its significance, that the hardest job in the Navy is being a Navy wife. Running a household, raising the children, and being supportive of your husband is a career in itself. Being a mother, wife, and handling a career is not exactly easy in the best of circumstances, but it is magnified many times when you husband is at sea.

Of course, I have also heard from many wives that the separation isn't always so bad… and then they come home and want to start making decisions!! Gull told me when I tried to say that her life had been just a little more challenging than most, that she didn't consider herself any stronger than other women. "Navy wives are not necessarily any stronger when they get married, "she said, "but the Navy makes them stronger. You have to decide what you want done, and you have to do it yourself. This helps you to learn and makes you stronger." In other words, as Nike says, "Just Do It."

The Weavers have truly undertaken the Navy adventure together. It seems that every time Royal and Gull learn of a promotion, they have also gotten other momentous news. The year he became chief Royal turned 30 and got married, when he became Senior Chief he and Gull had their first child. In fact, they learned of the child and the promotion at about the same time. When Gull became pregnant with Cera, they looked for notice of a promotion—and sure enough it arrived. Gull jokes that while she would have loved for Royal to be Master Chief of the Navy, she didn't know if she wanted a third child!

Gull and Royal speak fondly of all of the places they had lived and visited. Gull told me both she and Royal knew right away that Camden County was their home. She spoke of the way the community opened their arms and accepted them and made them feel like family. When Royal asked me to participate today, the first thing I thought of was their community involvement. They have both represented the Navy at many, many functions throughout the county. Royal was Past President of the Fleet Reserve Association, Treasurer of the Submarine Veterans, and Associate Member of the Submarine Veterans of Work War II. I have seen Royal at the annual World War II Sub Vets reunions and he has a wonderful time with our veterans. He truly respects the history these heroes represent and listens for hours on end to their "sea stories." His father was on the Yorktown and the pride he has for his dad combined with his love for history has made him a favorite with our veterans. He has continued to be a staunch supporter of the annual reunions. Royal is also a member of the Navy Submarine League, the American Legion, supports Gull who is a member of the Navy League and he is Vice President of the Submarine Museum.

Admiral Beers told me that he always appreciated that when he put out a call for a CPO he could always depend on Royal. He told me of the chief's initiations, the Dolphin Scholarship Fund, and anything that called for CPO leadership… Royal was always there. He spoke with appreciation of both Royal and Gull and their support of Navy projects in the community and professionally. Of course, Admiral Beers continued to call Royal long after the Dolphin Scholarship Auction to lick his wounds because I outbid him on Dolphin pins. Thank goodness Royal could find what the Admiral wanted, or he would still be after me for those dolphins! When you join a community and make contributions like this is it any wonder you feel at home and the community embraces you? And likewise, Master Chief Weaver has embraced the Navy which he and Gull so dearly love. He has balanced the demanding operational needs of the Navy with the professional development and welfare of his enlisted people. He has ensured that today's sailors are given the opportunity to grow and achieve as professionals so that they one day will be ready to take their place among the Navy's leaders—the Chief Petty Officers.

I asked Captain Reilly if he had any comments he would like to make on Master Chief and I would like to share with you the letter he sent me: "Royal has been an exceptional asset to SWFLANT over his tour of duty. He is SWFLANT's link with the local communities including Kings Bay, St. Marys, Kingsland, Woodbine and Camden County

As SWFLANT's link he represented the command on several committees including the Military Community Council, the Submarine Museum, Dolphin Scholarship and the various on base committees. He was always at the forefront of the quality of life initiatives and all the sailors at Kings Bay have benefitted from his personal drive and desire to make life for the sailor better. His superb insight and innate sense of the needs of the people have made him the expert and one that is most often sought after for advice and counseling. Captain Reilly said, "His dedication and loyalty to the Navy and SWFLANT is ever present. He is an extraordinary sailor who wears his uniform with a sense of pride second to none.

Honor, Courage, and commitment are his guiding principles. Whether it be leading his sailors in cleaning up SWFLANT's section of the highway or heading up one of our start treaty teams during the grueling inspections of our buildings and magazines, or meeting with the sailors to resolve issues, he stands out as the epitome of leadership. His diplomacy and ability to communicate have made him most effective in all of his interactions.

An example of this dedication, Captain Reilly volunteered to escort a team of Russian inspectors for an additional four hours beyond the completion of a start treaty inspection, after only two hours sleep over a period of almost 40 hours. This is the norm for Master Chief. And let us not forget the quiet and gracious manner in which Gull has contributed so much to this command the Kings Bay team. An active member of the Navy League, she has supported our sailors well. As a co-chairperson for the Dolphin Scholarship Fund drive, she has been responsible for the tremendous success in the last two auctions. She has truly been the consummate "Navy Wife" always there and always ready to help Royal and the Navy he so dearly loves." What person wouldn't feel honored to have their boss express such praise!

There is an old Chinese proverb about the difference between knowledge and wisdom, "Knowledge is proud that he learned so much. Wisdom is humble that he knows no more." Royal is a man who took advantage of every opportunity the Navy provided him to learn. Royal is also the type of man who will always continue to add to his knowledge and wisdom. He is a man who has fully dedicated himself to the highest principles of service and achievement to which only the finest may aspire.

I then shared with them highlights of Royal's career.

Master Chief Weaver was born and raised in Des Moines, Iowa, a fertile ground of budding sailors. While his training was on the West Coast, most of his career has been spent on the East Coast. In October, 1975 he reported aboard USS Lafayette (Gold),. Home ported in Groton, Connecticut. He completed eight strategic deterrent patrols in Lafayette. He completed six patrols on the USS Sam Rayburn (Blue). He served as Technical Assistant to the Deputy Chief of Staff for Strategic Warfare Systems at the office of Submarine Force Atlantic Fleet.

During his tour on the USS Francis Scott Key (Blue) he completed his 20th strategic patrol as the Missile Division Leading Chief Petty Officer. In March 1992, Master Chief Weaver reported as Chief of the Boat USS Trepang. During this tour, he completed a six-month Mediterranean deployment. I would like to point out here that Chief John Bradley had some stories to tell of this particular Med tour which included a certain British Rugby team in Gibraltar. To prove to each of you that I can use discretion when it is needed, I will only say it was a heck of a way to get acquainted with the Brits! Back to Royal's tour as Chief of the Boat… Master Chief Racquer, a longtime friend of the Weavers said that in submarines the COB plays a key role as the molder of junior officers, confidante, disciplinarian, and most importantly, leader of countless sailors who, time and time again, set their sights to be just like them. Being at your best has always included recognizing and developing the potential in others. This type of leadership—the foundation of the submarine service and our Navy—is personified in Royal Weaver.

Master Chief Weaver reported to Strategic Weapons Facility, Atlantic (SWFLANT) as the Command Master Chief on May 17, 1995. This was a red letter day for Camden County—we just didn't know it yet. Royal and Gull have learned to love this community as I have and plan to retire here.

The Navy's loss is the Submarine Museum's gain. Royal already has served on the Board of Directors and is presently the Vice President. His keen insight, energy and contributions have meant a great deal to me and to other who so faithfully work for our beloved museum. Royal tells me a good bit of his retirement time will be spent volunteering at the museum and we are going to hold him to that! Master Chief, this Navy, our submarine force and all of us are the better for having known you. On behalf of a grateful Nation and all your friends and admiring shipmates you leave behind, Thank You.

At the reception, I received wonderful comments from the chief who were present. I was really honored when a chief from the Groton, Connecticut, base asked me if I would send my comments for them to use as their chief's initiation. And a really cool comment was made by a gentleman who had retired a few years prior to Royal. He said, "We didn't know who was speaking at Royal's retirement. I have to admit when you walked out I thought, *What was Royal thinking about? When you sat down I thought, that Royal always did have class.*"

This was one of my "What are you doing here?" moments that will always be one of the happier ones! Yes, the Weavers always did have class.

WOMEN ON SUBMARINES—THE ISSUE

My interest in women on submarines dates by to 1996 when I was a brand-new member of the Defense Advisory Committee on Women in the Services (DACOWITS).

After all committees had met, we had a joint assembly to vote on recommendations from the committees. The recommendation from the Forces Development Committee (one-third of our members) was (a) to commend Adm. Kelso for his support of women in the military and (b) to allow women on submarines.

I was very nervous about ruffling any feathers at my first meeting, but I had to ask that these two issues be separate issues. I told the room full of members, military and press that "Now I really know how members of Congress feels. I had a great deal of respect for Admiral Kelso and want to vote yes. But I do not think that women on submarines is a good idea right now."

I believe it was unusual to have this type of pull back. The issues were taken back to committee and the two issues split. As best I remember most—or maybe even none of the committee had been on a submarine. We really needed to better understand what we were asking for.

The issue of women on submarines was not brought up again at that meeting. It did result in several visits on submarines over the next couple of years but the issues changed the following year.

The second year I was asked to take the installation visits coordinator position. It turned out on our overseas visits that the top issues were pay for junior enlisted and maintenance issues.

After leaving DACOWITS I wrote a letter to the editor of *Washington Times*:

> Years later, I recently attended a meeting of the Defense Advisory Committee on Women in the Services (DACOWITS). As a former member and vice chairman of the committee I previously participated in committee discussions on the issue of women on submarines. After hearing the recent Navy briefings and listening to the DACOWITS discussions I was surprised and disappointed that the committee made the recommendation to the Secretary of Defense that submarines be open to women.
>
> This is not a gender issue. Women are capable of performing every job on a submarine; this has never been in question. The question is: What is best for our national defense and for our men and women in uniform. We should not be spending limited defense dollars to retrofit submarines to accommodate women. This is simply not the best use of our tax dollars.

When our submariners' habitability conditions fail to meet minimum standards issued by the Chief of Naval Operations, we are not looking after our sailors to suggest that their standard be further eroded. Using more of the limited space would take from the mission and the benefits that make submarines the assets they are to our national defense.

I have deep respect for DACOWITS and for the hard work of the men and women who serve on the committee. However, the issues of privacy, career progression, unit cohesiveness and ultimately, cost should have far outweighed the effort toward gender equality.

Perhaps as more and more DACOWITS members tour submarines, they will change their stand.

Sheila McNeill
Brunswick, Ga.
Sheila McNeill is national vice president of the Navy League of the United States and former vice chairman of DACOWITS

The issue of women on submarines came back again in 2007. It has never been an issue of capability. The type of technical expertise that is required on a submarine can be done by a woman. Perhaps a limited number of jobs might be more physically challenging—torpedo loading and a few others—but being assigned those jobs would be based on the ability to handle the physical as well as the mental. The issue for me has always been quality of life for our submariners.

My grandson, who is thirty-two, just doesn't understand why this concern for privacy would be an issue—and others his age feel the same. Back in 1996 I talked about the ten items on the quality of life checklist that the CNO had for every sailor—except for submarine sailors—they were already diluted. I couldn't see them further diluted for what I considered political reasons.

When I was national vice president of the Navy League, I traveled to San Diego for Navy League and a DACOWITS meeting. I wasn't sure how happy they would be to have to 'put up' with a former member. However, they treated me well and, in fact, put me at a table with assistant secretary of the Navy Fred Pang and Admiral Don Pilling, Vice Chief of Naval Operation. That day at the committee meetings VADM Ed Giambastiani had briefed the committee. I had sat in on that briefing. Admiral Pilling asked,

"How do you think we did today, Sheila?"

Admiral Pilling has a PhD in mathematics from the University of Cambridge. He is very smart but also very personable. A wonderful combination but I still went on with the answer: "I'm sorry sir but I'm not sure how to tell you that without using a profanity."

Arching an eyebrow and with a nod he told me to continue.

"Sir, there was no bullshit. Many times, when DACOWITS asks for information we get just what we asked for. Sometimes that really wasn't what we meant. And sometimes when we get the information we really needed more to make a decision.

Vice Admiral Ed Giambastiani and his briefers not only gave DACOWITS the information, when questions were asked they had briefs on those issues also. There was no question asked that the submarine force did not answer and answer fully. This was one time that DACOWITS did not have to wait months to get more information on a briefing. He pushed back pretty hard on women on submarines at that time. His points were realistic and well thought out.

Ed reviewed the history of submariners who had made the rank of admiral. At that point thirty-three admirals had served on both classes of ships the smaller fast attacks the Los Angeles Class—and the much larger Ohio class of ballistic missile submarines. Of the thirty-one admirals still serving all but two or three had served on both classes of submarines. While our aviators serve on one class of airplanes their entire career it was different for the submarine force. Not taking this into account would be disadvantaging males who had been in the submarine force their entire career.

"Until we can provide adequate spacing we will not add women to submarines," Ed told the members of DACOWITS.

At that time, they were still operating the 688, Los Angeles class but future plans for the Virginia class would provide a larger submarine.

That Virginia class of submarines began the build in 2000 and was put in service in 2004. The larger submarine was a reality! Recognizing that women represented a large portion of the top graduates from the Naval Academy and the submarine force was losing some of the best and brightest Ed spoke with Admiral Kirk Donald who was then head of nuclear reactors. The plan was to work with both Submarine Forces Atlantic Fleet, VADM Grossenbacher and Submarine Forces Pacific, VADM Al Konetzni to begin the process of accepting women in submarines with these new, larger submarines.

Acknowledging there were still concerns as they moved forward. Women had been in the nuclear field on aircraft carriers. While they performed equally as well the retention rate was a concern. Women had one-third the retention rate as men. Based on that it would take more women to receive the same end results as the men. So much had to be considered and evaluated.

Submarine commanders began to work on integration. It was during that time that chief of Naval Operations Mullen became chairman of the Joints Chiefs of Staff.

In 2007, Admiral Mullen submitted the proposal to put women on subs. It had come a long way for Admiral Giambastini from 1999 to 2007 but his forecast and planning became a reality. Now chief of Naval Operations Gary Roughead and Chairman Mullen systematically and logically began integrating women.

They insured that seasoned female sailors, members of the supply corps, would be assigned as the senior officers and mentors of women on submarines.

On February 19, 2010, The Department of the Navy announced a policy change that would allow women to serve on submarines.

"Our" group commander at Kings Bay, RADM Barry L. Bruner, Commander, Submarine Group 10 led the Women in Submarines Task Force.

And interestingly the submarines that were chosen to be the first to add women to the crew were the SSGNs (see the story on SSGN)

The turning point for me was my meeting with then CNO Admiral Gary Roughead when I met with him at his office in the Pentagon and we discussed this issue of women on submarines. He said that the submarine force always recruited the brightest and the best. That top graduates from the Naval Academy and other schools that have many graduates join the services are women. The submarine services need these women to continue to recruit the very best.

The submarine force went about it in the best way—no expensive refits—no mass assignments. It was a very deliberate process. They started with a few officers on a few of the larger submarines. They included supply officers who while they have not had underway time on a submarine they did have at sea time on a ship. They understand deployments, discipline, and duty. They added to that three to five really, smart women. And it has been successful.

I thought about my past reservations a couple of years ago when I had the opportunity to go underway on a fast attack sub. The guests included maybe four women and a dozen men. All women slept in one compartment and all—men and women—shared a common head. I had to go to the head very late that night—one of my male associates, Hunt Thornhill, was there in the shower. I just yelled at that time "It's me—don't come out until I'm done" and that worked well. Although this probably isn't a good example since the male and female heads are separate.

Another time a few years later on an overnight on the USS *Georgia* we just turned the sign over on the head from male to female and it worked out just fine.

And of course, I realize in both cases I was only out for one night!

Later Captain Steve Hall who was commanding officer of Trident Training Facility at Naval Submarine Base Kings Bay would be assigned to lead the way on bringing in enlisted women.

I have enough confidence in the submarine force that they will do and are doing this the right way. And I am proud for the women who want to serve as submariners that they now have the opportunity.

WWII SUBMARINE VETERANS, SOUTHERN REGION

It was May 15, 2009. This was the speech that started the idea of this book. This was the time when I was asked, "What are you doing here?" and I realized how many time that question had been asked. John Crouse, the manager of the museum, introduced me and I began:

> Thank you, John. We are pleased tonight to recognize: Bob Brady—the Southern Region Director, Bill Castleberry—the Georgia State Commander Jim McConnel—the Past National President. And the wives' organizations: Evelyn Delaney—Southern region Director and Past National President and Ruth McConnel—Past National President
>
> I was honored to be the commissioning president of the St. Marys Submarine Museum. We want a way to honor you, to maintain your legacy and to tell your story. What wonderful cooperation we had during that time. Electricians, plumbers, painters and carpenters, all donating their services. And what would we have done without those last few days of help from the Seebees? John Crouse was with us from the beginning and continues to do an excellent job as our museum manager—he corrects me when I call him our curator. I told everyone that one day they would be proud of being a part of such a special project. And that certainly holds true.
>
> I remember when Ben Bastura called us and said he had some items he wanted to donate to our museum. The Nautilus had promised him a room named for him if he donates to them but for some reason he wanted us to have his items. And one condition of that was one of us come to look at his collection. I flew to Connecticut and went to his home. Wow, what a collection from a man who was in the Army. A soldier who was so impressed and so enamored with our Submarine Veterans of WWII that his entire two story home was chocked full of submarine history. When Ben died, it was a tractor trailer load and cost $10,000. It was well worth the costs and we are grateful that he trusted us with his lifelog collection. Others of you have shared your historic items with us. John has been working on a project to have volunteers type all the patrol reports from WWII. We are grateful to VADM Bacon for his generosity in scanning them all and giving them to all of the submarine museums, but some are

> hard to read and once our project is done everyone will be able to access and read all of the patrol reports.
>
> I think the best way I can sum up the objective of the museum is by sharing with you one of the verses of the song The Last Full Measure of Devotion: "The last full measure of devotion: And though they cannot hear our applause. We honor them forever and keep alive their story. Pay tribute to their lives and give them all the glory."

This next couple of years will be an interesting time for the submarine force. With President Obama saying he would like to have a country free of nuclear weapons yet acknowledging that as long as the world has countries with nuclear weapons we should have them. With the upcoming QDR, NRP, and START II treaty expiration we won't be lacking for studies on our submarine force levels. The last NPR determined that the US didn't need four of the eighteen SSBNs. Some smart submarine came up with the idea of removing the capacity for nuclear weapons and adding a platform for conventional weapons and special operations forces. This community spent eight years campaigning for that idea beginning in 1996. On my third trip to DC on this issue and the community's first visit we were told by the senior submarine we met with that we were wasting our time—that there was "no way in hell it was going to get approved." We didn't give up. The next time we had chocolate submarines made and position papers written and visited every member of Congress.

Now I'm not here to tell you that we are responsible for getting the funding for the SSGN, but I will tell you that it didn't hurt! Should the NPR determine that future cuts are to be made in our strategic force it will be a lot easier sale this time. With Electric Boat bringing the Ohio in under budget and early—absolutely unheard of and now the demand for SSGN funding, if there is a reduction of SSBNs, more SSGNs will be applauded.

With the amazing work that has been done by the Ohio, Michigan, the Florida, and the Georgia, carrier and strike group commanders are requesting those capabilities. Our CNO has been quoted as requesting more briefings from our submarine than with his carrier and strike group commanders. A wonderful acknowledgement of the true value of our submarine force. They truly are, as the old Squadron 16 motto said, "War Ready to Preserve Peace."

The contributions of you submariners from WWII cannot be stressed enough. A force of 2% was responsible for 55% of the tonnage sank. Incredible. We lost fifty-two submarines in WWII and the submarine force sustained the highest mortality rate with one out of every five submariners killed—3,505 submariners made the ultimate sacrifice. And the enemy's numbers were devastating. Germany lost seven hundred to eight hundred and Japan lost 128. Not a bad record, Gentlemen. Our submariners sank 1,284 ships for 5,146,307 tons! What heroes each of you are to our country!

Now if you wonder where I am coming from with all of this emphasis on our military let me tell you. I have been a member of the Navy League for 40 years. The Navy League is a civilian organization that supports the sea services—the Navy, Coast Guard, Marine Corps, and the US Flagged Merchant Marine.

I was nominated by RADM Jerry Ellis, Senator Sam Nunn, Army General Ed Burba and others and appointed to a Defense Advisory Committee and served from 1996 to 1998 as vice chairman. I served undersecretary of defense Bill Perry and later Bill Cohen traveling around the world meeting military members in focus groups divided by rank and gender. In the three years with this committee, I saw firsthand the needs of the military and the work that the Navy League could do on their behalf. I wanted to do something with this newfound knowledge and made the decision to run for national office in the Navy League.

I was elected in 1997 as one of ten national vice presidents and served in that job for five years. For the last three I was vice president of legislative affairs. In this position, I was the Navy league's representative on Capitol Hill. Out of the many organizations in DC the Navy League is the only organization that supports the Navy, Marine Corps, and the Coast Guard.

We advocate for ships, planes, and weapons systems they need. Our maritime industry must remain strong and vibrant if we are to safeguard our nation's security. I knew that we should empower our seventy thousand Navy League members. When seventy thousand individuals speak in unison that sends a powerful message and Congress listens. The admiral in charge of legislative affairs for the navy told me that during those three years we put the Navy on the front burner on Capitol Hill. It was an exciting and rewarding time. After these five years and especially my three years on Capitol Hill, I decided to run for National President. There was some angst with electing a woman—the first ever in the one hundred plus years—and the first person without a military background.

But once I was elected I never had a bad moment. And Navy League's across the country and indeed around the world could not have been more supportive. I had access at the highest levels and was readily accepted. As national president, I visited council in all areas of the world. I then told of my travels. The strongest opinion I came away with—after visiting both Europe and the Far East and meeting with foreign military officials, defense ministers, ambassadors, and governors—all of whom spoke of the need to nourish and cultivate our partnerships with other countries—is that our military throughout the world and in particular our sea services are the strength of our economy and the face of our diplomacy—they are America's ambassadors for peace.

I will never forget that evening.

EPILOGUE

I've had such an incredible life with so many diverse friends and the opportunity to travel all over the world. I have met people that I might not have ever seen other than on the news. My goals in life changed as I grew older. There are regrets, but I wonder if those circumstances had changed would I have had the unbelievable opportunities I had?

I am reminded of the time when I was national president and Arlie was traveling and for once I was at home alone.

When he called, I said, "It's so quiet here. I wish you were home."

I immediately realized what I had done and was horrified. I said, "Mac, I am so sorry. You never say things like that to me when I'm traveling."

"Sheila, when you say it to me I feel loved, when I say it to you, you feel guilty. That's why I never tell you I miss you. But keep saying it to me."

What a perceptive husband. Based on that thought, I've tried to feel less guilty. During my travels with the Navy League and DACOWITS, I missed everyone's birthday and our anniversary, but I wouldn't have given anything for the trips that took me away. Destiny has taken me in a totally different direction, but that direction could not have been more fulfilling.

My frequent wish is that I could remember all those special moments. In writing this book and researching my files and scrapbooks, those events were brought back. I read years ago, that if there were only an invention that could bottle up memory like scent. It would never get faded or become stale. Anytime you wanted, you could open it up and relive that moment. Now with this book, we'll be able to do just that.

Oh, I'm not finished yet.

INDEX

Bauter, Jill
Baynes, Chief
Beach, Capt. Ned and Ingrid
Bearley, Rev. Bob
Beck, CDR Michael
Bedinger, Jim
Beers, RDML Chuck and Susan
Beers, LCDR Clay
Bell, Griffin
Bell, Rob
Benedict, VADM Terry
Bennett, Warren
Betancourt, RADM Jose
Berry, Steve
Berry, Walter
Bernard, Al
Beverstock, RADM Mark
Bew, Dr. David
Bilby, Elizabeth
Bishop, Henry
Bishop, Katie
Black, Bryant and Ashley
Blackburn, Capt. Charles
Blackwell, James
Blalock, Lamberth
Bland, Major General Bill
Blanda, Chief Tony
Blanda, Gail
Bledsoe, Bob
Blow, Mark
Bluestein, David
Boland, David
Boler, Wendy
Bollinger, Dick
Bonner, Jim and Jewell
Boone, Pat
Boorda, CNO Michael
Bootebaugh, Alma
Borgnine, Ernest
Bowman, CDR Keith
Bowman, RADM Michael
Bowman VADM Frank (Skip)
Boyce, Capt. Bob
Boyton, Don
Bozin, RADM Stan D.
Brabble, JO1 Victor
Bradlee, Ben
Bradley, MMCM
Bradley, GEN Omar
Brady, MG Patrick H.
Brandon, Mayor Jerry and Gaila
Brandon, Veronica
Branham, RADM Steve
Branch, President Dan
Branch, Kathleen
Braun, VADM Robin
Breckenridge, VADM Jody
Breckinridge, VADM Richard
Brehm, Captain Barbara
Brenton, Captain Kevin
Brenton, Beci
Brenton, Captain Kevin
Breslauer, Lt. Col. Chuck
Brewer, VADM Dave
Brink, Dori
Brinko, Janet
Brinson, Janet
Brooks, Ambassador Linton
Brooks, 1st Class Cody
Brown, Bob Dart
Brown, Mayor Brad
Brown, CAPT Michael and Kathy
Brown, Cindy
Brown, David
Brown, LGen Jeffery E.
Brown, RADM Mason
Brown, Senator Scott
Browning, Mike
Browning, Major General Phil
Brownlee, Ed
Bruce, Dan
Bruner, RADM Barry and Elizabeth

Cobb, Sr. Chief Tony
Cochran, Leon
Cockey, CAPT Michael
Cofer, Sam
Cohen, SECDEF William
Cohen, RADM Jay and Nancy
Cohoon, Capt. John E., Jr.
Cole, Bruce
Cole, William
Coleman, Bob and Sherry
Coleman, Jim
Coleman, Commissioner Tom
Collins, Jim
Collins, Father Liam
Collins, Lt. Ryan
Collins, Senator Susan
Collins, Admiral Tom
Coltrane, Karen
Colvin, RADM Chris
Conlin, Carter
Condit, LCDR Richard
Conner, Loretta
Connor, VADM Michael
Connor, Preston
Coogan, MSCM
Cook, Linda
Cooms, Gerald
Cooper, VADM Dan and Betty
Cooper, Joy and Doug
Cortese, Michael
Corwin, Major General Tony
Costello, VADM Barry
Cotton, VADM John
Coughlin, James
Couturier, Bill, Producer
Coutour, RADM. Raymond and June
Coverdell, Senator Paul and Nancy
Cozzone, Deborah
Crea, VADM Vivien and Ron
Creary, RADM Terry L.
Crenshaw, Congressman Ander
Crenshaw, VADM Lewis
Cricsek, MS1 Charles
Crist, Marilyn
Crites, RADM Randy and Cheryl
Crouse, CMC John
Cross, VADM Terry
Crowe, Hazel
Cumbie, CDR Lori
Cummings, Jim
Dalton, SecNav John
Daniel, Chris
Danley, Bill
Danzig, SECNAV Richard
Davis, Archie II
Davis, Edwin
Davis, Jack
Davis, James G.
Davis, Senator Susan
Dawson, Bill and Wanda
Dawson, RADM Cutler
Dawson, Emory
Deal, Governor Nathan
Debbink, RADM Dirk and Terry
Dees, Doug
Deloughy, Mayor Bill
DeMars, Adm. Bruce
Demery, Edward and Elmo
Demery, Granny
Demery, Vergil and Angie
Dempsey, Kathy
Denny, Executive Chef Cloister
Derek, Bo
Dessie
Devine, Ann
Dicks, Congressman Norm
Dickson, Terry
DiRita, Lawrence
Docking, Jill
Dodson, James
Donald, Adm. Kirk & Dianne
Doran, Adm. Walt

Donnelly, VADM Jay & Mimi
Dooley, Barbara
Doran, Admiral Walt
Doubleday, Charles W.
Doud, Katie
Douglas, John
Downs, Jared
Draper, Marci
Drennan, RDML Frank
Driskell, Lt. Len
Drumm, Jim
Drury, CPL Andy M.
Dryden, Jim
Dudley, Bill
Duerr, Beverly
Dumont, Bonnie
Dumont, CMC Roger
Dugan, Kelli
Dunham, Deb and Don
Dunham, Corporal Jason L.
Dunmire, President Bill
Ebright, LT Sonya
Edenfield, Alma and Robert
Edwards, RADM Mark
Eischen, Joan
Eisenhower, David & Julie
Eisenhower, President Ike
Eldridge, RADM Kevin
Ellis, Captain Chuck and Judy
Ellis, RADM Jerry & Rosemary
Ellis, Roz
Elphick, Anita V.
Elrod, Britt
Emory, VADM George
England, Dottie
England, Secretary Gordon
Enright, Lt. Sonya
Erlinger, Jim
Ervin, MSSA
Estes, Harold and Doris
Etnyre, RADM Terrance
Evans, LCDR Tom
Evanzia, Bill
Ewing, J.R.
Ezelle, LT
Fagen, Michael
Fages, VADM Malcolm and Shirley
Fages, Meredith
Faharenwald, Richard
Fallon, Susan
Fallon, VADM William T.
Fanning, Tim
Farland, LTJG., Eric
Farrington, Fletcher
Felder, Tom
Fendig, Bruce
Fernandini, St. H. Gonzales
Ferrell, Bobby
Figueroa, Natalie
Fisher, RADM l/President Jack and Kit
Fitch, President Morgan
Fitz, Amando (NASCAR)
Fitzgerald, VADM Mark
Fleming, Capt. Dave
Fletcher, Capt. Jim and Marsha
Flenniken, Mike
Fluckey, RADM Eugene & Margaret
Forbes, Congressman Randy
Forbes, Steve
Fowler, Stan
Fowler, Congressman Wyche
Fraim, Mayor Paul
Franklin, Irene
Frasca, Frank
Fratz, MS2
Fredrick, President Al
French, VADM Bill and Monika
Fresca, Frank
Froman, RADM Ronnie
Fry, Harvey
Frye, Captain Will
Fuentes, Sara

Fullman, Jennifer
Gainor, Vic
Galinis, Captain Bill
Gallagher, Gary
Garcia-Reyes, Dr. J.
Gardina, RADM Tim and Missy
Garis, Rev. Greg
Garren, CDR Bill
Garwood, Sue
Gaston, RADM Mack
Gates, SECDEF Robert M.
Gaudio, RADM Jan
Gehrke, CDR Brad
Gejdenson, Congressman Sam
George, Alan
Giambastini, Admiral Edwin
Giardina, RADM Tim and Missy
Gilbert, James B., Jr.
Gilchrest, Congressman Wayne
Giles, Captain Don
Gilman, James
Glitz-Kane Avery
Glover, Capt. Ron and Charlotte
Golden, Darlene
Golden, LTJG William
Goldstein, Richard
Gonzales, Celso
Gooch, Melissa
Goodman, MGen John E.
Goodwin, CDR Deborah R.
Goodwin, Captain J. W.
Gosser, MSC Timothy
Goyette, Lt. Col. Wendy
Gradishik, Captain Gary
Gradisher, Capt. Joe
Graham, John and Giovanna
Graham, Senator Bob
Grantham, Albert D.
Graves, Shannon
Gray, Captain Gene
Gray, Captain Scott
Gray, Chief Engineer Charles
Green, Captain Johnny L.
Green W. Parker
Greenert, Admiral Jon and Darlene
Gregory, Sheriff Tommy
Griffin, Chief Darryl
Griffin, Vice Admiral Henry III
Grimes, Matthew
Gross, Amanda
Gross, William (Bill)
Gross, Jack
Grossenbacher, VADM John
Growden, Dave
Guevarra. CDR Mark B.
Guffey, Captain Harvey and Wanda
Gunter-Schlesinger, Dr. Sue
Guthrie, General Sir Robert
Guy, Judge Bert
Haas, Mayor Deborah
Hackley, Carol Ann
Haddad, Ben
Hagamann, Captain Jon and Cindy
Hagan, MCPON John
Hagee, Commander USMC Michael & Silke
Hagel, SECDEF Chuck
Hagman, Larry
Hahnfelt, Captain Don
Hall, Alice Joy
Hall, Royce and Faye
Hallas, Sheila
Hart, Amelia
Hamilton, Robert (Bob)
Hamrick, Leslie
Hancock, Scott
Hanner, Joel
Hardin, Dr. Will
Harencak, Major General Garrett
Harper, Debbie
Harrell, MSC Gregg
Harris, Fred and Kaz

Harrison, Clyde, Jr.
Harrison, Judge Tony
Harrison, Lt. Holly
Hart, Amelia
Hart, Nick and Emily
Harter, Claire
Harvey, Mayor Cornell
Hase, Mayor Deborah
Haskins, Captain
Hassert, Congressman Dennis
Haven, Jonathan
Hedgecock, Roger
Heidecker, Priscilla
Helton, Jill
Hendrickson Capt. Bill and Sherry
Hendrickson, Captain Dean M.
Henry, RDML Joseph
Hepburn Dr. Valarie
Herberger, VADM Albert
Hereth, RADM Larry
Hernandez, CAPT Danny PAO
Hessman, Editor James
Hill, St. Senator Cecily
Hill, St. Senator Jack
Hill, CAPT Lawrence
Hill, Matthew
Himmelspach, Darlene
Hodges Mike
Hoewing, VADM Gerald
Hoffman, Jim
Hoffman, Linda
Holder, CDR Brenda
Holgrath, William T.
Holland, Richard
Hollstein, Randy
Holmgard, Pat
Holmes, Denny
Hope, Bob
Horton, Amy
Houston, MSCS
Howard, Captain Tracy
Howard, J. E.
Howard, Steve
Howell, Sidney
Houck, RADM Richard
Hoyer, Congressman Steny
Hubert, Glen
Hudson, Lynn
Hughey, Lt. Gen. Gary
Hulett, Michael
Hull, VADM Jim
Huls, Kelly
Huly, Lt. Gen. Jan C.
Humphries, Judy
Hunnicut, Capt. Thomas
Hunter, Bill
Hunter, Congressman Duncan
Hunter, Dr. Lori
Hupperman, YNC Alan
Hurd, CDR Dan and Erin
Hurley, Alice
Hurley. Bob
Hurley, CMC Tom
Hussey, Peter
Ihrig, Captain C. J. and Jennifer
Intravia, Mary Ann
Isakson, Senator Johnny
Issa, Congressman Daryll
Ivey, Captain Jason
Ivey, Halen Hawk
Jacha, Mark
Jackson, Gordon
Jackson, Lt. Gen Tony
Jacobs, Captain JoDee
Jaehn, CAPT Rhett
James, CAPT Michael
Jans, Debbie
Jantzer, Mark
Jarvis, Carolyn
Jenks, Captain James
Jenks, Katherine
Jicha, Mark

Johns, Barbara
Johns, Phyllis
Johnson, RADM Arthur
Johnson, Bill
Johnson, RADM Dave
Johnson, Adm. Gregory G.
Johnson, SECNAV H.T.
Johnson. Joseph
Johnson, Katie
Johnson, Linda
Johnson, LT. Lawton
Johnson, Minnie
Johnson, SKCM
Johnson, RADM Steve
Johnson, Wayne
Jones, Artie
Jones, Ben
Joo, RADM Choi Ki
Jones, General James L.
Jones, J. A.
Jones, LCDR Mark
Jones, Bill Alfred W, III
Jones, Howard
Jones, Harley
Jones, General James L.
Jones, Joan
Jones, Mary
Jones, Norah
Jones, Sue
Jordan, Herb
Jordan, Michael
Joyce, Ramona
Juarez, MS1
Jurand, Captain George
Katsutoshi, RADM. Kawano
Kaufman, Robert
Kay, Stephen
Keen, ETCM (SS) Lawrence
Keene, Commissioner Chip
Keeter, Hunter
Kehler, General Robert
Keith, RADM Steve
Keller, Bill
Keller, Colonel Uli and Sandy
Kelley, BG John F.
Kellner, Evan
Kelley, Bill and Nancy
Kelley, Pat
Kelly, RADM Jamie
Kelly, CMC Mark
Kelso, Adm. Frank
Kemp, State Senator Rene
Kempton, JO2
Kennedy, President Jack and Pam
Kennedy, Kraig
Kennedy, Richard
Kenny, RDML Mark
Kent, Peter
Kern, Colonel Paul (Lt-Gen)
Kerry, John SEC STATE
Kevan, Captain Mark andBarbara
Keith, RADM Steve
Kidd, David
Kilbourne, Rex
Kilcline, RADM Thomas J.
Kingston, Congressman Jack
Kirby, RADM John
Kiss, James
Kitches, BMCS Michael
Kloner, Rabbi Bill
Klumpp, Marty
Konetzni, VADM Albert
Knee, Seymore
Knight, Dick
Knight, Jeanne
Knoll, J. C.
Konetzni, Kyle and Lori
Koppel, RADM Dan
Kopper, Bill
Kroenig, Professor Matthew
Krusa-Dossin, BGen Mary
Kruz, Colonel John

Kylie
LaFleur, VADM Timothy
Lane, Rogers
Lang, Hubert W. III
Lang, Linda Kay
Lavin, Ambassador Frank
Lawlor, MCCF Peter
Lawson, Glen and Talaxe
Lawson, Keith
Learson, Harold
Leavy, C. H. "Buff"
Leftwich, ASECDEF Bill
Legel, Allen
Leland, RADM Ted
LeMieux, Senator George
Lemmo, Brian
Lentz, Douglas A.
Lewey, Dale
Lewis, Kyle
Lewis, Lt. Col. Sandy
Libutti, Under SEC (LTGEN)Frank
Lieberman, Senator Joe
Ligon, State Senator William
Lingle, Governor Linda
Link, James L.
Lippert, RADM Keith
Livingston, Asst. SECNAV Susan
Lobiondo, Senator Frank
Lodmell, CDR Joseph
Logan, Bert
Loganzino, Rich
Lord, Dr. Dorothy
Lott, Senator Trent
Love, Mr. and Mrs. John
Love, CDR Steve
Loy, Adm. Jim & Kay
Lumme, Captain Dale
Lyle, A. C.
Maas, Peter
Maas, RADM Stephen and Barbara
Mabus, SecNav Ray
Macke, Admiral Dick
MacMaster, Ron
Madden, Christopher
Magnus, General Robert
Maher, CDR Charlie
Mair, CDR Mike
Malene, Chaplain Capt. Robert
Mallard, Josephine (Wishnoff)
Malley, RADM Kenneth C.
Maloy, Jeff
Maloy, Mike
"Mamer"
Manoukian, Leslie
Marciello, Lou
Marina, Petty Officer Joe
Marks, Captain N. A.
Marsh, Judy
Martin, Robert
Marsha
Martineau, LTCDR Glen
Martino, Chief Mate Victor
Mathieu, Captain Ben
Mathis, Evan
Mattingly, Senator Mack
Mattis, Lt. Gen James N.
Maude, LTGEN Timothy
Maxwell, CPO Myra U.
May, Keri
Mayberry, Hugh
Maysonnet, Lt.
McAllister, Suzanne
McAnery, RADM Douglas Jr.
McCain, Captain John
McCain, Senator John
McCarthy, Greg
McCarthy, Kenneth
McCaslin, John
McClain, Captain John
McClelland, Mac
McCollough, RADM Barry
McCreary, RADM Terry

McCullough, Amy
McDill, John
McDonough, Joe
McGrath, President Michael
McIlvaine, Captain Brian and Shirley
McInerny, General Thomas
McKee, Adm. Kinnaird R.
McKinney, RADM Henry C.
McKinnon, Captain Mike and Rhonda
McKissock, Lt. Gen. Gary
McLendon, LT Michajah T.
McMichael, Alford, SSgt Major of USMC
McMillan, Trish
McNeill, Arlie
McNeill, Blaire
McNeill, Ryan
McPherson, Joyce
McQuade, Scott
Mead, Captain Jack and Vickie
Meese, Attorney General Edwin
Meinicke, RADM Tom and Alice
Meltons
Metney, Carol
Metzger, VADM James
Meyer, Captain Chuck and Greer
Michel, Adm. Chuck
Mies, VADM Rich
Miffing, Honorable Fredo and Gwyneth
Mikulski, Senator Barbara
Miller, Cindy
Miller, The Honorable Franklin
Miller, Jack
Miller, Jeremy
Miller, Governor/Senator Zell
Mineta, Secretary Norm
"Minnie"
Minor, John
Mitchell, LCDR Billy
Mitchell, Kelsey
Mizell, Tracy
Mobley, Brian
Mobley, Kenneth Darryl
Mobley, Kenneth Lewis
Mobley, Lewis Monroe and Cora
Mobley, Nora
Mobley, Ricky
Moffit, David
Moody, Lt. Col Kevin
Moore, Major Brian
Moore VADM Charles
Moore, Patrick
Moore, Peggy Ann
Moorer, VADM Joseph
Morash, Russ
Moran, Stan
Morgan, Dee
Moronta, SGT Jimmy
Morris, George
Morrison, President Bob
Morrissette, Jackie
Morrissey, Mayor John
Morton, Lynford
Mossally, Fred
Mota, Al
Mounts, Jack and Betty
Moynihan, RADM Dennis
Mullen, Admiral Mike and Deborah
Mullis, Charlie
Mulloy, Captain Joe
Munns, VADM Charles
Munoz, Wenda
Mumms, VADM & Mrs. Charles
Murph, Katherine
Murkowski, Senator
Murphy, LCR Paul
Murray, LT. COL Andrew J.
Murray, MS3
Muszynski, Amy
Muth, CDR Seth and Stephanie
Myers, Don
Myers, Richard, JCOS

Nakamoto, LCDR Ron
Nakao, VADM Seizo
Nall, Jim
Napolitano, SEC HLS Janet
Nathman, VCNO John and Sue
Natter, Admiral Bob
Natzic, President Walt
Navy League local officers
Naughton, RADM Richard J.
Neller, Gen. Robert
Nemeth, Brad
Nettles, Shannon
Ney, Captain Edward F.
Nielson, Edwaard
Nix, James
Noble, Bob
"Norah"
Norman, J. B. Jr.
Norrel, Joe
Norris, Tilden
Norton, Lyford PAO
Nunn, Senator Sam and Colleen
Nunn, Michelle
Nuremberger, Capt. John and Sue
Nyland, General William
Obama, President Barack
Obama, Michelle
O'Donough, Dr. Gerald
Offutt, President Jim
Ogden, ENS Michael
O'Hara, VADM Sally Brice
Olender, Dave
Oliver, David
Oliver, Tim
Olness, Major Michael
O'Neill, Captain John and Shelly
Orrel, Wally
Orsini, Captain Susan
Orton, Fred
Overstreet, Cindy
Padgett, RADM John B.
Pafford, CDR Jeff
Pang, ASDEF Fred
Panneton, President John and Alice
Papp, Admiral Robert J. (Bob)
Papp, Linda
Park, Hee
Parks Family
Parr, Stacy
Parrott, Mayor Steve
Patrick, Connie and John
Patton, Vince MCPOCG
Paul, 2nd Class Don
Pawlanty, First Lady
Payne, Gary
Pease, RADM Kendall
Percialle, Craig
Perdue, Governor Sonny
Perdue, Senator David
Perkins, VADM James
Perrett, Dr. Greg
Perrine, CMC Tom
Perron, Colonel Robert
Perry, CDR Ken (RADM)
Perry, SEC DEF William
Peske, Lt. Tom
Peterson, Gordon
Peterson, Dr. G. P. "Bud"
Peterman, VADM Brian D.
Petters, Michael
Pharr, Sandy
"Phillip"
Pickard, Bill
Pickren, Sam
Pickett, Congressman Joe
Piedfort, Chief Brian and Susan
Pietropaoli, RADM Stephen and Dawn
Pilling, Adm. Donald L.
Pittman, Eunice
Poe, Donna Gowen
Poisson, VADM Maurice
Pollard, SK2

Porter, Tim and Sharon
Porterfield, RADM Richard
Post, Keith, Sr. Chief
Post, Oakley
Powell, Gen Colin and Alma
Prevatt, Captain Carolyn V.
Price, Barbara
Price, Marci
Proctor, Dr. Ann
Proctor, David
Proctor, Gene
Prusinowski, LCDR Tom and Lisa
Puller, Chesty
Pummell, CWO4
Purcell, Ann
Purviance, Stuart
Puzon, Captain Ike
Quigley, RADM Craig
Quinn, RADM Kevin
Rabarich, Rebecca
Racquer, CMC Buddy
Raine, LCDR Robert
Rainer, Dr. David
Rameriz, MS1 Patrick
Ramsey, St. Senator Virginia
Rapkin, Jerome
Raulerson, Louise
Ravitz, Bob
Rayley, Dan
Raymond, Captain Joe
"Rayne"
Readinger, Jeffrey
Reagan, Michael
Reason, Admiral Paul
Reasoner, Denny
Reagan, CDR Alan
Reagan, Michael
Rebstock, Lois
Redmond, John
Reese, Betty
Reidenour, Amy
Reilly, Captain Dave
Reimer, GEN. Dennis Army COS
Rein, Ron
Rendon, CDR Jim
Respess, Susan
Reu, President John M.
Reynolds, Wayne
Rhyne, Jerry
Richard, VADM Chas and Lisa
Richardson, CNO Adm. John and Dana
Richardson, Nathan LT
Ridge, Secretary Tom
Rieger, MCBM Mark
Rinderin, SKCS
Rinkovich, Charlie & Sara
Ritter, Diane
Ritter, Paul
Rivera, MSSN Angel
Robb, Art
Roberts, CAPT A. Renee
Roberts, Lonnie
Robertson, RADM. Tom and Julie
Robinson, Charlie
Robinson, Ellen
Roegge, RADM Frederick J.
Roland, Herb
Rondeau, RADM Ann
Roosevelt, President Theodore
Root, Craig and Mary
Rosado, Tonya
Rose, Gail
Rose, CMC Richard
Rosen, Mark
Rossier, Sally
Roughead, Admiral Gary
Rumsfeld, SECDEF Donald
Runnells, STSCM (SS) Herbert
Ruppersberger, Congressman Dutch
Rush, ASECDEF Frank
Russell, Captain D. J.
Russell, LCDR Tony

Ryan, Barbara
Ryan, Michael, COS Air Force
Ryan, VADM Norb
Rylie, Major General Jim and Linda
Sacarob, Don
Sacks, Joe
Sainz, Stephen
Saiz, Sgt. James
Saliterman, Richard
Samuels, Evan
Samuels, Jerry
Sanchez, Congressman Loretta
Sanders, Governor Carl
Sang, Cathy
Sarac, Paul
Sarbenes, Senator Paul
Sarro, Paul
Sawyer, RADM Phillip G.
Scarlett, Judge Stephen
Scallorns, Joe
Schechinger, Master Sgt. Robert
Scheer, George
Schiff, Jack
Schiff, Jack, Jr.
Schneider, Mark
Scholosser, Sherry
Schoolcraft, Lisa R.
Schrock, Congressman Ed
Schubert, Administer William
Schubert, CMC Jimmy and Carrie
Schultz, Chef
Schultz, RADM Karl
Schulze, Horst
Schmeiser, CAPT
Scorby, RADM John C.
Scott, Doreen
Scott, VADM Redd
Scott, Brig. Gen. Robert
Scott, Terry MCPON
Scotty, Mr. and Mrs. Rob
Seals, Amanda
Sedden, Scott
Seki, CAPT James T.
Seo, Cheol-Jae
Sepp, Howard
Sesman, David
Sesman, Sam
Setser, Mary & Joe
Shackelford MS3
Shalikashvilli, General John M.
Shanahan, Ward
Shanks, Sam
Shannon, RADM Thomas
Sharkey, CDR Bill and Jeanne
Sheer, George
Shelton, Lt. Sal
Sherock, Congressman Ed
Shinseki, General Eric
Siegel, Howard
Simpson, Ginger L.
Sinclair, Sandy
Skorus, Staff SGT James
Skotty, Rob
Stanfield, Jackie
Skelton, Senator Ike
Skelton, Dr. Lana
Slattery, BUC (SCW)
Slusser, Dean
Smith, Barbara Jacobs
Smith, Sheriff Bill
Smith, State Representative Charlie
Smith, Dr. Harold P.
Smith, Jackie
Smith, Mayor Kenneth
Smith, Marcia
Smith, Maj Gen. Ron and Debbie
Smythers, Mr.
Somers, Melody, Protocol
Spell, Freda
Spittler, President Jack
Spratlin, Commander Dean
Spence, Congressman Floyd

Sprouse, Barbara
Stagl, Captain Frank and Mary
Stanfield, Jackie
Stark, CDR Doug
Starling, RADM
Stasnis, Nancy
Steel, Jim
Stefany, Frederick
Steilen, Scott
Stephens, St. Senator Ron
Stepzinski. Teresa
Stevens, Captain Henry
Stevens, Jackson
Stevens, MCPON Mike
Stevens, Captain Wes
Stillman, RADM Patrick
Stiller, Honorable Allison
Stilson, Georgia and Colby
Stoke, Allan
Stokes, Rev. David and Felecia
Stosz, VADM Sandra L.
Straughn, Sue
Street, CAPT George L.
Strickland, Johna
Sublett, Tom
Sullivan, RADM Paul F.
Sullivan, CDR Todd
Swain, Mike
Swanson, Dennis
Sweeney, John
Swick, Julie
Sykoro, LCDR Randall
Szenbroski, VADM Stanley
Taggart, MS3 Brian
Takeshisa, RADM Kawano
Talbot, RADM Jerry and Judye
Temple, Phil
Teneyck, Don
Terpstra, RDML Rich & Sue
Terry, Hampton
Thomas, Doug
Thomas, Congressman Lindsey
Thompson, Mayor Brian
Thompson, Freddie
Thompson, Chief Freddie
Thorn, John
Thornhill, Alyce
Thornhill, Hunt
Thorp, RADM Frank
Tilleate, CWO Tyrone
Tjoflic, Gerald B.
Tofalo, VADM Joseph and Suzanne
Tollison, Ken
Tollison, Miriam
Tosi, Gloria C.
Toti, Captain William
Tottenham, Captain John
Townsend, Honorable Fran Fragos
Tracy, VADM Michael
Tracy, VADM Patricia
Traub, Carol Ann
Traub, Pat
Treen, EM1 Mark
Tribia, Lt. Jeffrey
Triplett, Chairman Tom
Thorn, John
Trost, CNO Carl
Troutt, Lt. Col. Kay
Trump, Linda
Tumu, David
Tul, Paston
Turcott, RADM Steve
Turner, Kari
Turner, Peter and Marica
Turner, RADM Stanford (CIA)
Turner, Tom
Tuten, Judge James
Ulmer, Dinah
Ung, Minister Nat Defense, Yoon Kwang
Ung.
Uprichard-Kontezni Dr. Kristen
Urani, MKCS Curt

USNS Brunswick Donors and Dignitaries
USS Georgia Return to Service Donors and Dignitaries
USS Bancroft Sail Exhibit Donors and Dignitaries
Utley, RADM Ralph
Valley, MG Paul E.
Vanderhamm, MGen Scott
Van Echo, LTJR Kara
Vanlandingham, Andy
Van Tassle, Bruce
Varnadoe, Jeanne Earle
Varnell, Pastor Richard
Vergara, Iturriga de
Victory, Linda
Villablobos, Adm. Migel
Virden, Wiley
Virden, Wiley
Viser, Murray
Vitale, RADM Michael
Voekler, Rand
Volonio, Capt. Dave and Naoko
Unknown Chinese Officer
Wagner, Lt. Gen Robert
Walling, Alton
Walling, Brannon
Walling, Clevie
Walling, Julie Benton
Walling, Laurie
Walling, Raymond
Walling, Virgie Demery
Walsh, RADM Joseph A.
Wamsley, Mary J.
Ward, Jim
Warner, Governor Mark
Warner, Senator John W.
Warren, Gun. SGT Brenda L.
Warwick, "Moon"
Warwick, Paul and Lynn
Watkins, Sheila and VADM James
Waylett, Bill
Weaver, CMC Royal and Gull
Webb, Alecia
Webber, Lee
Weeks, Ron
Wehman, Bridgett
Weisensee, Capt Bill & Nancy
Wells, Captain Jim
Wensing, Kevin Harley PAO
Wenum, Bridgett
Werner, LTCDR Dave
Wessinger, Tim
Whelch, CDR Tala
Wheeler, Commissioner Pete
White, Robert
Whitehead, RADM Joel
Whiteside, Lt. Col. Duane & Verna
Whitlock, Craig
Whittenberger, Cynthia
Wiegand, Don F.
Wilkinson, State Representative Joe
Wilkerson, Major General Tom
Williams, Judge Amanda
Williams. Lt. Chris
Williams, Captain Gary and Linda
Williams, Jacqueline A.
Williams, Commissioner Mark
Williams, VADM Mel
Williams, Susie
Wilson, BMC Joseph
Wilson, Pat
Winslow, MKC Kenneth
Winter, SECNAV Donald
Wirfel, Kelly
Wise, Emily
Wiseman, LGEN Davis
Witham, SA
Witunski, Skip
Wittman, Amy
Wolfe, CAPT Johnny
Wolfowitz, Dep SECDEV Paul
Woods, Billy Frank

Woodside, Woody
Woolf, Amy
Work, Honorable Robert
Wright, Barbara
Yadav, C. B.
Yates, State Representative John
Yuen, Jon
Young, Candace Richey
Young, VADM Charles & Karen
Young, Asst. SECNAV John J.
Young, Neely
Youngman, Dr. Judith
Youngner, Debbie
Youngner, Kristy
Youngner, Larry, Sr.
Youngner, Larry Jr.
Yourstone, Captain Walt
Yun-Hee, RADM Choi, Superintendent
Zami, Chow, Nora
Zegers, UrendaZell, Carley
Zell, Katherine
Zeller, Captain Randy and Debbie
Zukunft, Admiral Paul and Fran

1993- Sheila as president of the Camden Kings Bay Councils and all past presidents (page 225)

BGEN Robert L. Scott, Scotty in his book, *God is my Co-Pilot* speaking at the council with Capt. Jack Mead USN (R) council president page 532

Sheila and the National Steering Committee before the presidency

Everyone who went to DC to educate Congress on the SSGN conversion. (page 548)

2001 as Legislative Affairs VP with MG Tony Corwin VADM Gary Roughead, Senator Warner, SECNAV Gordon England and me as VP Legislator Affairs

With Ned Beach at dinner in 2000 when he received the Navy League's Alfred Thayer Award for Literary Excellence from President Fisher. Page 204

Marine Corp Commandant Jon Hagee, Coast Guard Commandant Tom Collins, me as President, SECNAV England, CNO Vern Clark and VP Legislative Affairs Randy Hollstein.

Ambassador of Spain, George Argyros, on my visit to Spain. Page 479

Michael Reagan at the Reagan Commissioning aboard the USS Ronald Reagan with a beanie baby! Page 714

Captain Bill Goodwin, Commanding Officer of the USS Ronald Reagan with his wife and comedian Jerry Lewis's son and Sheila and Arlie. Page 714

At the reception – A.C. Lyle, who introduced the Reagans and Griffin Bell who was on the Reagan Cabinet and whose son was the opposing lawyer in my lawsuit – small world. Page 714

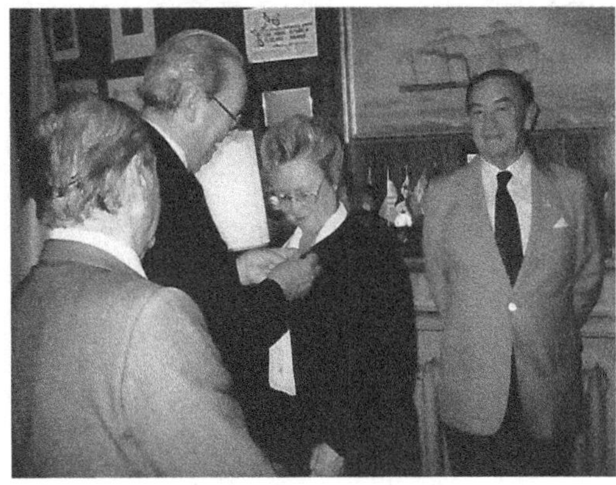

Sheila receiving medal from Spanish Navy League. Page 337

Speaking to the sailors.

My speaker at my Navy League meeting when I turned over the presidency, Admiral Ed Giambastini. Page 348

Enjoying a talk with Judge Tony Alaimo. Page 181

Captain McIvaine CO of USS GEORGIA. Page 421

About the Author

SHEILA M. MCNEILL
President, The Camden Partnership
Past National President,
Navy League of the United States

Sheila M. McNeill was the national president of the Navy League of the United States from 2003 to 2005. The Navy League is the only civilian organization dedicated to supporting the sea services—US Navy, US Marine Corps, US Coast Guard, and US Flag Merchant Marine.

As national president, McNeill was responsible for leading the Navy League's seventy thousand members who are dedicated to educating American citizens and elected officials about the importance of sea power. The Georgia native is the first woman to hold this position since the league was founded in 1902. McNeill served as a national vice president responsible for the organization's legislative affairs activities. While serving in that position, she aggressively sought support on Capitol Hill and made educating congressional members about the sea services her top priority.

She is a region leader for the Submarine Industrial Base Conference and on the board of directors for the Dolphin Scholarship Foundation. She is a member of the board of directors for the National Strategic Deterrent Coalition.

Because of McNeill's long history of active involvement with the sea services; she served as vice chairman of the executive committee for the Defense Advisory Committee on Women in the Services (DACOWITS), an influential advisory committee to the secretary of defense and other DOD and DOT officials. During her three-year DACOWITS tour, McNeill visited forty-five US military installations throughout the world.

In her home state of Georgia, McNeill serves as president of The Camden Partnership. McNeill was commissioning president of the St. Marys Submarine

Museum and charter chairman of the Military Community Council. She continues to serve in both organizations. She serves on the College of Coastal Georgia Advisory Board and was co-chairman of the USS *Bancroft* Sail Exhibit at Kings Bay Submarine Base to celebrate the one hundredth anniversary of the submarine force. She has been on the board of directors of the Chambers of Commerce in Glynn and Camden Counties. McNeill was named one of the "100 Most Influential Georgians" in *Georgia Trend* magazine. She is the sponsor of the USCGC *Sea Horse* (WPB 87361) and served as chairman of the USS *Georgia* (SSGN 729) Return to Service Committee. She was chairman of the USNS *Brunswick* (Spearhead-class expeditionary fast transport—Military Sealift Command) Committee.

For eighteen years, a Fortune 500 company employed McNeill where she was responsible for industrial relations and labor negotiations.

McNeill has received numerous awards including the secretary of the Navy's Distinguished, Superior and Meritorious Public Service medals; the United States Coast Guard's Distinguished and Meritorious Public Service medals; the 2004 US Armed Forces Spirit of Hope Award; and the International Federation of Maritime Associations Service Medal, and she was the first female recipient of the Spanish Navy League's highest honor, the Golden Anchor Award, the Navy League's Distinguished Service Award in 2011, and the Georgia Chapter of the National Defense Industry Association (NDIA) selected McNeill for their Citizen Soldier Award.

McNeill is married to Arlie McNeill, a Navy veteran and long-time Navy League member and national director emeritus. They have one daughter, Leslie, and four grandchildren, Ryan, Norah, Rayne, and Kylie.

CPSIA information can be obtained
at www.ICGtesting.com
Printed in the USA
BVHW081258240519
549181BV00010B/14/P

9 781644 249567